Women's International and Comparative Human Rights

Women's International and Comparative Human Rights

Susan W. Tiefenbrun

PROFESSOR OF LAW
DIRECTOR OF CENTER FOR GLOBAL LEGAL STUDIES
THOMAS JEFFERSON SCHOOL OF LAW

CAROLINA ACADEMIC PRESS
Durham, North Carolina

Library of Congress Cataloging-in-Publication Data

Tiefenbrun, Susan W.
Women's international and comparative human rights / Susan Tiefenbrun.
   p. cm.
Includes bibliographical references and index.
ISBN 978-1-59460-703-5 (alk. paper)
1. Women (International law) 2. Women's rights. I. Title.

K644.T54 2011
341.4'858--dc23

2011042162

Carolina Academic Press
700 Kent Street
Durham, North Carolina 27701
Telephone (919) 489-7486
Fax (919) 493-5668
www.cap-press.com

Printed in the United States of America

To Jonathan, my loving husband and
to Michele, Gregory, and Jeremy, my loving children, and
to Julian, Max, Levi, Isadora, and Otis, my loving grandchildren
and the new generation of human rights advocates.

Contents

Preface

This book is a collection of excerpted cases, statutes, treaties, newspaper articles, law review articles, books, and UN committee reports that provide insight into the complex issue of women's international and comparative human rights, as protected and provided by laws in countries all over the world. The international law of human rights is defined as the laws dealing with the protection of individuals and groups against violations of their internationally guaranteed rights. International human rights include civil, political, economic, social, and cultural rights. Since women in society are regarded as child bearers and a primary source of child care and child rearing, women's human rights are intricately related to children's human rights.

This book looks into the history of the global human rights movement and how international and comparative human rights laws,[1] instruments, and institutions respond to women's human rights violations. Since World War II, there has been a significant development of international human rights institutions and conventions emanating from the UN Charter and the international bill of human rights. These institutions and treaties have influenced the protection and provision of women's human rights all over the world.

Human rights are not found exclusively in laws. They are reflected in political policies, moral ideas, customs, international relations, and in foreign policies. In this book we adopt an interdisciplinary approach that takes into account the multiple sources of women's rights and their diverse representations in international human rights laws, international legal instruments, UN treaty organs and reports, the jurisprudence of regional and international tribunals, and the work of non-governmental organizations (NGOs) in the human rights movement to protect and provide women's rights. Rules and standards of contemporary human rights are expressed in states' constitutions, laws, practices, international treaties, customs, court decisions, investigative reports, and recommendations of international institutions and of governmental and non-governmental actors. These sources help to understand the ongoing development of women's human rights in the world.

In the comparative vein, we focus on women's rights reflected in particular legal instruments and practices of other countries like Chinese criminal law, the Chinese Constitution, Iranian family laws, French case law, European human rights laws, Guatemalan human rights practices, African practices regarding the use of girl children as soldiers, and US statutes as well as the US Constitution protecting women. Moreover, we analyze and com-

---

1. *See* A. MARK WEISBURD, COMPARATIVE HUMAN RIGHTS LAW, vols. 1 and 2 (Carolina Academic Press 2008), a short casebook featuring variations in approaches to human rights in several legal systems of the world including Japan, Europe, India, and the United States.

pare state and international policies, practices, and attitudes in many countries in order to understand the causes and consequences of discrimination and abuse perpetrated on women.

Gender justice and the empowerment of women to facilitate the full enjoyment of their human rights, accountability, and enforcement is a central theme of this book. We pay special attention to the international crimes of sex slavery, human trafficking, child soldiering, and rape as a weapon of war in the development of massive human rights violations in which women and girls are particularly vulnerable.

In this book we look at both international law and international human rights law because human rights are an integral part of international law. International law has traditionally been defined as the law of nations or the law governing relations exclusively between nation-states. Therefore, only states have been the subjects of, and have legal rights under, international law. After World War II, this definition was expanded to include newly created intergovernmental organizations having some limited rights under international law. However, even according to this expanded definition of international law, individual human beings have had no international legal rights as such and are said to be objects rather than subjects of international law. Because international law does not apply to human rights violations committed by a state against its own citizens, the jurisdiction of a human rights case falls exclusively within the domestic jurisdiction of each state. According to the sacred rule of non-intervention and the importance of the doctrine of state sovereignty, other states are barred from intervening on behalf of the nationals of one state who have been mistreated by their own government officials. There are, of course, exceptions to the rule of non-intervention and the threat or use of force against the territorial integrity or political independence of any state; however, generally the principles of non-intervention, as articulated in Article 2(4) of the UN Charter, and the doctrine of state sovereignty are sacred in international law and can deter or even prevent a humanitarian intervention that might otherwise avoid the denial of human rights to individuals and especially to the most vulnerable who are the women and children.

Another branch of international law that has a human rights component is known as "humanitarian law" or the law of armed conflict, one of whose basic tenets is the principle of respect for "humanity" during war. Therefore, in the spirit of interdisciplinary analysis, we will refer to women's human rights as reflected in international law, international human rights law, and international humanitarian law.

The purpose of this book is to investigate international as well as comparative women's human rights. Comparative law is the study of differences and similarities among the laws and legal systems of other countries. Different legal systems that are relevant to women's human rights in the world include the common law, the civil law, socialist law, Islamic law, Hindu law, and Chinese law. The importance of comparative law has increased in the present age of internationalism, economic globalization, and democratization. The human rights laws and practices of other countries are greatly influenced by international law. If a country is a signatory to an international treaty which is not self-executing, that country must enact domestic laws enabling the provisions of the international treaty, and then it must implement the treaty's norms in its own state. Even if a country is not a signatory to a particular international treaty, the country may be bound to the laws of that convention by "customary international law."

Women's international and comparative human rights law is a vast subject that cannot be covered in one relatively short book. Therefore, we have chosen some of the most important and controversial women's rights issues, knowing that we will not be able to touch upon many other serious problems that women face all over the world. This book examines women's civil, political, social, economic, and cultural rights; women's human rights in armed conflict; women's fundamental right to manifest their religion; their right to be free from slavery and sex trafficking; the rights of women with disabilities; and the right of women to be free of institutionalized female infanticide, sex-selection abortion, child soldiering, sexual violence, and torture.

The major human rights treaties and other international instruments discussed are provided in the Appendix to this book.

I would like to give special thanks to Thomas Jefferson School of Law and its wonderful library research staff for enabling me to do the research and writing of this book. I would also like to thank my research assistants, Christie Edwards, Oksana Golovina, John G. McCreary, and Brian J. Link for their patience, determination, and invaluable assistance with the production of this book.

Acknowledgments

The author is grateful for permission to use material from the following sources:

Abdullahi Ahmed An-Na'im, *Human Rights in the Muslim World*, 3 HARV. HUM. RTS . J. 13, (1990) (Copyright Clearance Center).

HILARY CHARLESWORTH AND CHRISTINE CHINKIN, THE BOUNDARIES OF INTERNATIONAL LAW: A FEMINIST ANALYSIS 1–19, 201 (Juris Publishing Incorporated 2000). Reprinted excerpts with permission from both authors.

Tracy Higgins, *Anti-Essentialism, Relativism, and Human Rights*, 19 HARV. WOMEN'S L.J. 89 (1996).

Donna Hughes, *The Demand for Victims of Sex Trafficking*, June 2005, *available at* http://www.uri.edu/artsci/wms/hughes/demand_for_victims.pdf.

Susan Jones, *Obama Directs US to Sign "First New Human Rights Treaty of the 21st Century,"* CNSNews.com, July 27, 2009.

Laura Lederer, *In Modern Bondage: An International Perspective on Human Trafficking in the 21st Century*, remarks at the Federal Acquisition Regulation Compliance Training for Government Contractors, July 17, 2007.

Mohammed Mattar, *Human Security or State Security? The Overriding Threat in Trafficking in Persons*, 1 INTERCULTURAL HUM. RTS. L. REV. 249 (2006).

Kenneth Roth, *The Court the US Doesn't Want, in* NEW YORK REVIEW OF BOOKS, vol. 45, No. 18 (Nov. 19, 1998).

Patricia Viseur Sellers, *Individual(s') Liability for Collective Sexual Violence in* GENDER HUMAN RIGHTS 153–94 (Karen Knop ed., Oxford University Press 2004).

Barbara Stark, *The "Other" Half of the International Bill of Rights as a Postmodern Feminist Text, in* RECONCEIVING REALITY: WOMEN AND INTERNATIONAL LAW 19–33, 38 (Dorinda Dallmeyer ed., Washington DC, American Society of International Law 1993, Copyright Clearance Center).

Susan Tiefenbrun, *Sex Sells but Drugs Don't Talk: Trafficking of Women Sex Workers and an Economic Solution* 24, 2 T. JEFFERSON SCHOOL L. REV. 161 (Spring 2002), Symposium Issue, First Annual Women in the Law Conference.

Susan Tiefenbrun, *The Semiotics of Women's Human Rights in Iran, in* DECODING INTERNATIONAL LAW: SEMIOTICS AND THE HUMANITIES 263 (Oxford University Press 2010).

Women's International and
Comparative Human Rights

Chapter 1

Women, International Human Rights Law, and Feminist Theory

A. International Law and International Human Rights Law

What is "international law"[1] and what role do women play in the development of rights under international law? International law has traditionally been defined as the "law of nations" or the laws governing relations exclusively between nation-states. The traditional definition of international law as the "law of nations" has changed.[2] Historically, international law was a separate legal system with the emergence of the modern nation-state in the sixteenth and seventeenth centuries. At that time and until recently, international law referred to rules and norms regulating exclusively the conduct of nation-states. International law was typically concerned with regulating interstate relations, diplomatic relations, and the conduct of war. States, not people, were the only subjects of international law. But since 1945 the scope of international law has changed and expanded with regard to its subjects and content. Contemporary international law is still considered to be principally the law governing relations between states, but it is no longer exclusively limited to those relations. The more modern definition of international law is the law that deals "with the conduct of states and of international organizations and with their relations *inter se*, as well as with some of their relations with persons, whether natural or juridical."[3]

1. International Law and International Institutions Involving Individuals

After World War II and the establishment of the United Nations, international law changed and developed; many new public and private international organizations were created; and states began to handle internal issues of international concern collectively. Public or intergovernmental international institutions are distinguishable from private

---

1. *See generally*, 1 Oppenheim's International Law: A Treatise 118–19 (H. Lauterpacht, 8th ed. 1955). *See also* Malcolm N. Shaw, International Law (Cambridge Univ. Press, 5th ed. 2003); Jack Goldsmith, The Limits of International Law (2005); Louis Henkin, How Nations Behave: Law and Foreign Policy (2nd ed. 1979); Mary Ellen O'Connell, The Power and Purpose of International Law (Oxford U. Press 2009); Rebecca M. Wallace, International Law (London, Sweet & Maxwell, 5th ed. 2005).
2. A.L.I. Restatement of the Foreign Relations Law of the United States (Third), Section 101 (1987).
3. *Id.*

or non-governmental international organizations (*e.g.*, Amnesty International, the International Law Association, and the International Committee of the Red Cross), which are dedicated to the protection of individual's rights. Public intergovernmental organizations are established by treaty and governed by international law. They have an international legal personality and are subjects of international law. For example, the League of Nations and the International Labor Organization are public international organizations created after World War I. The United Nations and many of its international organizations[4] were established after World War II. Presently, intergovernmental international organizations and even individuals can be the subjects of rights and duties under international law. For example, the direct responsibility of individuals for war crimes established under the Nuremberg Charter in 1945 and the subsequent development of the international law on human rights reflect that individuals now have rights under international law that did not exist earlier.

2. Spurious Claims That International Law Does Not Exist

Despite the overwhelming evidence of a proliferation of international laws, treaties, charters, optional protocols, and covenants, signed by many if not most of the countries of the world, some skeptics continue to believe that international law does not work and may not even exist at all.[5] International law is definitely law, and some states actually refer to international law in their constitutions. In fact, the rights and obligations which a state has under international law are superior to any rights or duties it may have under its domestic law. International law requires enforcement mechanisms in order to be effective; however, states obey laws even in the absence of coercion,[6] and enforcement and implementation are admittedly the weakest links in the international legal system. Nevertheless, international law is law, and we know it is law because we can identify its sources.

3. Sources of International Law

The primary and most authoritative source of international law is found in Article 38(1) of the Statute of the International Court of Justice, which identifies international law in international conventions, international custom, and general principles of law. Rules originate in treaties, custom, decisions of tribunals, *opinio juris,* state conduct, and resolutions of international organizations. "Judicial decisions" and the "teachings" of the publicists are subsidiary or secondary sources of international law. (*See* the *Paquete Habana* case, 175 US 677 (1900)). Customary international law is law that develops from the practice of states, consented to and followed widely and for a long period of time, and deemed by states to be obligatory as a matter of law. International law also includes hu-

---

4. *See generally,* Frank Newman & David Weissbrodt, International Human Rights; Law, Policy, and Process (Anderson Publishing Co., 2nd ed. 1996), providing an in-depth analysis of the United Nations human rights system, a list of United Nations human rights bodies, a discussion of UN procedures for violations of human rights (*e.g.,* ECOSOC Resolutions 1235 and 1503), and the obligation of States Parties to report under international human rights treaties.

5. *See* Jack Goldsmith, *supra* note 1. *See* Jordan J. Paust, *Customary International Law and Human Rights Treaties Are Law of the United States,* 20 Mich. J. Int'l L. 301 (1999).

6. Thomas M. Franck, *Legitimacy in the International System,* 82 Am. J. Int'l L. 705 (1988).

manitarian law or the laws of war[7] that constitute the rules of engagement during an internal or international conflict.

4. International Law and State Sovereignty

International law protects the sovereignty of a state and denies a foreign state the right to interfere in that state's internal affairs, even if the state is depriving its citizens of their inalienable human rights. State sovereignty is the quality and power of having supreme, independent authority over a geographic area or territory. The idea of sovereignty dates back from Socrates to Thomas Hobbes[8] and has always required a moral imperative on the entity exercising sovereign power. Therefore, it is generally understood that if a state does not act in the best interests of its own citizens, it should not be thought of as a "sovereign" state.

Sovereignty involves the notion of territorial integrity, border inviolability, the supremacy of the state (and not the Church), and a sovereign who is the supreme lawmaking authority within its jurisdiction. The United Nations requires that a sovereign state have an effective and independent government within a defined territory. The Treaty of Westphalia in 1648 established the notion of territorial sovereignty as a norm of noninterference in the affairs of other nations ("Westphalian sovereignty"). In international law, sovereignty means that a government possesses full control over its own affairs within its own territorial or geographic area. Foreign governments use various criteria and politics when they decide whether to recognize the sovereignty of a state over a territory.

5. International Law, State Sovereignty, and Humanitarian Intervention

Adherence to the doctrine of state sovereignty can result in the refusal of humanitarian intervention. This is why many internationalists believe that sovereignty is outdated and an unnecessary obstacle to achieving peace. They argue that because we live and work in a global community, intervention may be justified to protect the rights of individuals that are being violated by the abusive acts of a state. Moreover, human beings are not always protected by a state which may abuse its power, such as Hitler's Germany, Stalin's Soviet Union, or Khaddafi in Libya.

Kofi Annan, the former Secretary General of the United Nations, frequently expressed the need to rethink the notion of state sovereignty and non-intervention codified in Article 2(4) of the United Nations Charter, especially after the Rwandan genocide and the massacre of more than 800,000 people in the course of 90 days. This genocide was partially a consequence of the failure by the international community to intervene, which if it had done so without Security Council approval, would have violated the state sovereignty doctrine.

A state may limit its sovereignty by treaty. If one state concludes a treaty with another state agreeing to treat the citizens of both states humanely by providing them with cer-

---

7. "The Laws of War" are also referred to as "The Laws of Armed Conflict" or "Humanitarian Law." *See* Antonio Cassese, New Humanitarian Law of Armed Conflict (1979); M. Cherif Bassiouni, Crimes Against Humanity in International Law 192–234 (1992). *See also* Jordan J. Paust *et al.* Human Rights Module: On Crimes Against Humanity, Genocide, Other Crimes Against Human Rights, and War Crimes (Carolina Academic Press 2001).

8. Thomas Hobbes, On the Citizen 30 (Richard Tuck & Michael Silverthorne eds., 1998).

tain inalienable human rights, then these states can disregard the "sovereignty" rule and intervene on behalf of a citizen of the other state whose rights have been denied. This process is known as the "internationalization" of human rights, and it occurs every time a human rights treaty enters into force.

6. International Humanitarian Law

Another branch of international law that has a human rights component is known as "humanitarian law" or the law of armed conflict. Humanitarian law began very early and developed in the 19th century. Certain humanitarian rules applicable in the conduct of war are memorialized in the Geneva Convention of 1864, which was designed to protect medical personnel and hospital installations. The Geneva Convention of 1864 also provided that "wounded and sick combatants, to whatever nation they may belong, shall be collected and cared for." (Article 6(1)). Thus, humanitarian law, which is a branch of international law, reflects human rights principles.

Even the very basic humanitarian law tenets—humanity, necessity, distinction, and proportionality—focus on the need to protect civilians at all times and to act humanely. The Lieber Code of l863, an important manual of the rules of engagement during the American Civil War, defined "military necessity" in Articles 14, 15, and 16:

> "Military necessity, as understood by modern civilized nations, consists in the necessity of those measures which are indispensable for securing the ends of the war, and which are lawful according to the modern law and usages of war." (Article 14). "Military necessity does not admit of cruelty—that is the infliction of suffering for the sake of suffering or for revenge, nor of maiming or wounding except in fight, nor of torture to extort confessions ..." (Article 16).

The Hague Convention No. III of 1899 established humanitarian rules applicable to naval warfare. The Hague Convention No. IV Respecting the Laws and Customs of War on Land, and its Annex[9] was adopted on October 18, 1907, and in the Preamble the drafters expressed the "desire to serve, even in this extreme case, the interests of *humanity* and the ever progressive needs of civilization."

"Inhumanity" is defined as the quality of being inhuman or inhumane, being "destitute of compassion for suffering," acting with "barbarous cruelty," and not "having the qualities proper or natural to a human being"; being "especially destitute of natural kindness or pity, brutal, unfeeling."[10] Much of the vast body of law dealing with modern armed conflict is codified today in the four Geneva Conventions of 1949 and the two 1977 Protocols Additional to these Conventions. Common article 3 of the Geneva Conventions of 1949 prohibits violations of the most basic human rights principles:

> "(1) Persons taking no active part in the hostilities, including members of armed forces who have laid down their arms and those placed *hors de combat* by sickness, wounds, detention, or any other cause, shall in all circumstances be treated humanely, without any adverse distinction founded on race, color, religion or faith, sex, birth or wealth, or any other similar criteria.

---

9. Hague Convention (No. IV) Respecting the Laws and Customs of War on Land, and Annex, 36 Stat. 2277, T.S. No. 539, 1 Bevans 631 (1907).

10. R. v. Imre Finta [1994] 28 C.R. (4th) 265 (S.C.) (Canada), comments by the trial judge on Section 7 (3.71), *cited in* PAUST, *supra* note 7, at 43.

To this end, the following acts are and shall remain prohibited at any time and in any place whatsoever with respect to the above-mentioned persons:

a) violence to life and person, murder of all kinds, mutilation, cruel treatment and torture;

b) taking of hostages;

c) outrages upon personal dignity, in particular, humiliating and degrading treatment;

d) the passing of sentences and the carrying out of executions without previous judgment pronounced by a regularly constituted court, affording all the judicial guarantees which are recognized as indispensable by civilized peoples.

(2) The wounded and sick shall be collected and cared for ..."

7. Customary International Law

Article 38 of the Statute of the International Court of Justice includes customary international law as one of the sources of international law.[11] Customary international law results from a general and consistent practice of states which is followed by them out of a sense of legal obligation (*opinio juris*). The practice of states is found in official governmental conduct reflected in a variety of acts, including official statements at international conferences and in diplomatic exchanges, formal instructions to diplomatic agents, national court decisions, and legislative actions taken by governments in order to deal with an international issue. A practice does not become a rule of customary international law merely because it is widely accepted by many states and has been followed over a long period of time. It must also be deemed by states to be an "obligatory" rule.

Even though the United States has not signed many international human rights treaties, it may be bound to the provisions of these treaties by international customary law. In the famous *Paquete Habana* case (175 US 677, 700 (1900)), the US Supreme Court made it clear that international law is part of US law, and international customary law is a source of international law:

"International law is part of our law, and must be ascertained and administered by the courts of justice of appropriate jurisdiction, as often as questions of right depending upon it are duly presented for their determination. For this purpose, where there is no treaty, and no controlling executive or legislative act of judicial decision, resort must be had to the customs and usages of civilized nations ..." *Id.* at 700.

The *Paquete Habana* case acknowledged and applied international customary law in the US Courts. Customary law is one of the sources of international law. Custom is conduct that becomes international law by consent of parties in time and consists of four elements. The conduct must be practiced by (1) a number of states, (2) over a long period of time; (3) and the conduct must be consistent with international law, and (4) consented to by other states. Thus, customary international law is a general practice, consented to

---

11. *See* MARK W. JANIS, AN INTRODUCTION TO INTERNATIONAL LAW 41–48 (Aspen, 4th ed. 2003), discussing the history of custom as a source of legal rules. *See also* Michael P. Scharf, *Seizing the "Grotian Moment": Accelerated Formation of Customary International Law in Times of Fundamental Change,* 43 CORNELL INT'L L.J. 439 (Fall 2010).

by parties, and in use over a long period of time and not inconsistent with international law. Customary law may be found in the actual practice of states, from newspapers reports, from statements made by government spokesmen to the press or at international conferences or at meetings of international organizations, or from states' laws and judicial decisions, in writings of international lawyers, in judgments of national and international tribunals, and in treaties.

Customary international law can bind non-signatories of a treaty to the provisions of that treaty, if it is signed by many nations. The United States has not signed the International Covenant on Social, Economic, and Cultural Rights, and yet the United States protects its citizens against unfair deprivation of social and cultural rights and offers unemployment benefits when its citizens are deprived of employment. Similarly, the United States has not signed the Convention on the Elimination of All Forms of Discrimination against Women, and yet the United States has made enormous strides in advancing and protecting women's rights and especially in preventing and protecting women from the scourge of sex trafficking, which is an international crime perpetrated all over the world including the United States. Similarly, the United States has not signed the Convention on the Rights of the Child, even though the very basis of American family law is identical to the philosophical underpinnings of the Child's Convention which is to protect the best interests of the child. These three United Nations human rights conventions have been signed by overwhelming numbers of nations all over the world, but the United States has put forth many reasons why it refuses to sign and ratify these and other international treaties. Nevertheless, customary international law arguably binds the United States to the provisions of the ICESCR, CEDAW, and the Child's Convention.

8. Relationship between International Law and International Human Rights Law

There is no doubt that international human rights law and international law (including customary international law and humanitarian law) are intricately related. International human rights law has its historical antecedents in a number of international law doctrines and institutions. For example, humanitarian intervention,[12] state responsibility for injuries to aliens, and the protection of minorities are all examples of connections that exist between international law and international human rights law. International law has created various institutions and doctrines to protect certain groups of individuals like slaves, minorities, indigenous peoples, foreign nationals, combatants, and victims of massive human rights violations. The body of international law protecting certain groups of individuals provides the underpinnings for the development of what is known today as human rights law. Thus, modern international human rights law has been influenced by international law.

9. Relation of International Law to Domestic Law

If an international law is not self-executing, national law must be enacted to implement the international law. In this way, international law has a direct impact on national laws. An example of the impact of international law on domestic law is the adoption of many

---

12. *See generally,* Theodor Meron, The Humanization of International Law (2006).

new trade-related as well as human rights laws in foreign countries, reflecting their need and desire to become part of the global trade arena. For example, in order for China to become a member of the World Trade Organization, it had to enact new domestic laws that would be in conformity with international treaties underlying the General Agreement on Tariffs and Trade and the World Trade Organization. As a member of the WTO, China necessarily became a party to the fifteen multilateral treaties, including TRIPS (Trade-Related Aspects of Intellectual Property), which prohibits the piracy of intellectual property. Since human rights violations are directly linked to trade, by virtue of the Jackson Vanik Amendment, countries wanting to engage in international trade must have adequate domestic human rights laws and practices. Despite a proliferation of new laws in China that are in compliance with the laws of the WTO and with the UN human rights conventions, China's failure to enforce its domestic laws results in the continued piracy of intellectual property and in the continued violation of basic human rights, especially with regard to women and girl children.

10. Reservations to International Laws

In order to understand the laws of other countries and how they protect against violations of women's human rights, it is essential to examine the relevant international treaties that these countries have signed and the reservations they may have made to certain provisions of these treaties. The international law of treaties has been codified in the Vienna Convention on the Law of Treaties (1969) (see Appendix), which entered into force in 1980 and has been ratified by many countries. The Vienna Convention on the Law of Treaties is generally accepted to be declaratory of the customary international law of treaties. The US is not a party to the Vienna Convention on the Law of Treaties, but the US recognizes that the substantive provisions of this convention state the international law on treaties. (*See* US Restatement (Third), Part III, Introductory Note.) Article 2(d) of the Vienna Convention on the Law of Treaties defines a "reservation" as follows:

> "... a unilateral statement, however phrased or named, made by a State, when signing, ratifying, accepting, approving or acceding to a treaty, whereby it purports to exclude or to modify the legal effect of certain provisions of the treaty in their application to that State." A "reservation" might otherwise be referred to as a "declaration," an "understanding," or a "clarification," which have slightly different meanings from a "reservation." States are free to adhere to a treaty with reservations, unless the treaty permits only certain types of reservations and the one being made is of a different type or, if the reservation is incompatible with the object and purpose of the treaty." (Vienna Convention on the Law of Treaties, Art. 19). "In those cases where the reservation is either acceptable as a matter of law or has been accepted, the treaty is in force between the reserving state and the other parties, but their obligations are modified by the reservations." (Vienna Convention on the Law of Treaties, Art. 21(1)(a)).

If many states sign a treaty, but each state makes some or many reservations to the treaty, like CEDAW, that treaty becomes a weakened legal instrument. The fact that many parties have made reservations to CEDAW is a sign of the delicate nature of the subject matter of the treaty itself, the human rights of women, which is the very subject of this book. Because women's rights are considered "private" issues that individuals often prefer not to discuss, statistics relating to women's rights are often unreliable. This is particularly true of statistics on rape, sexual violence, and sex trafficking of women.

11. International Human Rights Law

Modern human rights law developed primarily after World War II, as a result of the massive human rights violations that went unchecked throughout the war. "There is no question that the international human rights movement has done a great deal of good, freeing individuals from great harm, providing an emancipator vocabulary and institutional machinery for people across the globe, raising the standards by which governments judge one another, and by which they are judged, both by their own people and by the elites we refer to collectively as the 'international community.'"[13]

Unlike international law, modern human rights law recognizes that individual human beings have internationally guaranteed rights. With the birth of the United Nations, certain international institutions and international human rights conventions, having their own respective implementing institutions or organs, were created to protect individuals against human rights violations committed by their own states or by other states. In today's political climate, the protection of human rights is one of the most important but sensitive issues involving the relationship among governments. Human rights violations committed by one government against its own people are often handled with great diplomacy by other governments. In the interests of maintaining peace and security, this well-intended diplomacy by the international community can result in an inordinate delay of human rights protection. We have witnessed such delays many times in the past and most recently in the genocide committed in Darfur. Progress in the field of global human rights has been slowed down not only for political reasons but also because of poverty, illiteracy, discrimination, and cultural traditions that prevent certain segments of society (women in particular) from enjoying their internationally recognized human rights.

The field of international human rights has received a great deal of attention and criticism. Some argue that the human rights movement "increases the incidence of descriptions of women as mothers-on-pedestals or victimized caregivers...."[14] Others claim that enforcing human rights is hegemony or simply an example of the abuse of power of the developed world over the developing world. Some argue that the human rights movement takes too narrow a view of violations against individuals by the state, failing to address indirect harms committed by governments or by private parties. The human rights movement speaks in terms of "universal" rights, "universal" goods, and "universal" evils which may be too general, too abstract, a "one-size-fits-all" approach that disregards the validity of cultural differences. Moreover, by focusing on individuals, the human rights movement may be blurring the need to think of people more generally living in a community.[15] The human rights movement has been criticized for expressing "the ideology, ethics, aesthetic sensibility and political practice of a particular Western eighteenth- through twentieth-century liberalism."[16] Moreover, as far as positive rights are concerned, many claim that human rights laws promise more than they can deliver (which is one of the questionable reasons why the United States has refused to sign and ratify many of the human rights treaties). Another serious criticism of the

---

13. David Kennedy, *The International Human Rights Movement: Part of the Problem?*, 15 Harv. Hum. Rts. J. 101 (2002).

14. *Id. See also,* Elizabeth Defeis, *"The United Nations and Women—A Critique,"* 17 William & Mary J. Women & Law 395 (2011), discussing the role of the United Nations and the protection of women.

15. Kennedy, *supra* note 13, at 112.

16. *Id.*

human rights movement is its inability to get things done because of its deeply embedded bureaucracy. Some even argue that the legal regime does more to produce and excuse violations than to prevent them or cure them. For example, humanitarian laws may do more to legitimate violence than to restrain it because of "vague standards, broad justifications, lax enforcement, or prohibitions"[17] In addition, the human rights movement has been criticized for strengthening bad international governance by focusing too much on rules and institutions rather than standards and cultural enforcement. Finally, the promotion of human rights can result in bad politics and bad consequences. It may even strengthen repressive regimes.[18] These are some of the problems that legal scholars and politicians have identified with regard to the human rights movement. These problems deserve serious consideration in order to reach the well-intended aims of the human rights movement which is respect for human dignity and recognition of the legitimacy of individual differences.

12. Regional Human Rights Laws

Despite the generally slow progress of the human rights movement, rapid developments in the establishment of national human rights laws have been made in some regional systems. For example, in addition to the American Convention of Human Rights,[19] which is modeled closely on the International Covenant for Civil and Political Rights, the Additional Protocol to the American Convention on Human Rights in the Area of Economic, Social and Cultural Rights[20] was added to further define the rights of individuals to economic, social and political rights in Latin America. Finally, the Inter-American Convention on the Prevention, Punishment and Eradication of Violence against Women[21] was enacted in 1994 to give greater protection and rights specifically to women in that region.

13. Cultural Relativism and Human Rights Laws

Women's human rights is a complex phenomenon that is deeply rooted in cultural traditions that sometimes fly in the face of human rights laws. Tradition and culture may in fact deprive women of human rights. Respecting different cultures is a value that cultural relativists rightly defend; however, when certain traditions like female genital mutilation and male child preference rise to the level of torture or blatant gender discrimination,

---

17. *Id.*

18. *Id.*

19. *See generally,* Dinah Shelton, *"Self-determination in Regional Human Rights Laws: From Kosovo to Cameroon,"* 105 Am. J. Int'l L. 60 (2011). *See also* Elizabeth F. Defeis, *"The Treaty of Lisbon and Human Rights,"* 16 Ilsa. J. Int'l & Comp. L. 413 (2010); American Convention on Human Rights (Pact of San Jose), signed 22 Nov. 1969, entered into force 18 July 1978, 1144 U.N.T.S. 123, OASTS 36, O.A.S. Off. Rec. OEA/Ser.L/V/11/23, doc. 21, rev. 6 (1979), *reprinted in* 9 I.L.M. 673 (1970), *available at* http://www.oas.org/juridico/english/treaties/b-32.html (24 states parties).

20. Additional Protocol to the American Convention on Human Rights in the Area of Economic, Social and Cultural Rights (Protocol of San Salvador), adopted 17 Nov. 1988, entered into force 16 Nov. 1999, OASTS 69, *reprinted in* 28 I.L.M. 156 (l989), corrections at 28 I.L.M. 573 and 1341 (1989), *available at* http://www.oas.org/juridico/english/treaties/a-52.html (14 states parties).

21. Inter-American Convention on the Prevention, Punishment and Eradication of Violence against Women, (Convention of Belem do Para), signed 9 June 1994, entered into force 3 March 1995, *reprinted in* 33 I.L.M. 1534 (1994), *available at* http://www.oas.org/juridico/english/treaties/a-61.html (32 states parties).

then universalists will cry out against these practices. Cultural relativism cannot be used as a defense of practices that devalue women and put them in harm's way.

14. The Headscarf Cases and the *Burkha* Ban

Most democratic countries would agree that freedom to manifest one's religion is a basic human right. However, in certain countries like France and Turkey, the threat of fundamentalist Islamic forces is prevalent, and secularism is treasured as an important democratic value. Muslim women in these and other countries have been denied the right to wear the headscarf in public places. Moreover, the wearing of the *burkha* anywhere in public has been banned for security reasons in France, Belgium, and in a city in Spain. Unlike the headscarf, which merely covers the head, the *burkha* is a total body cover that women may choose to wear or be forced to wear by their husband or father, according to Islamic tradition. The French government objected to the wearing of the total body cover because it hides the face, makes it possible to hide a weapon, and denies women their freedom of movement and association. Women wearing a *burkha* are naturally forced into submission and segregated from society. In Italy a recent draft law banning women from wearing veils that cover their face in public was passed by the Constitutional Affairs Commission in August 2011. This draft law expands an older Italian law that prohibits people from wearing face-covering items such as masks in public places for security reasons. Women in Italy who violate the ban will face fines of 100 to 300 Euros, while third parties who force women to cover their face in public will be fined 30,000 Euros and face up to 12 months in jail.

The arguments in favor of a headscarf ban in public institutions is a harder case than the *burkha* ban which is arguably justified for reasons of national security. Nevertheless, the European Court of Human Rights (see Statute of European Court of Human Rights in Appendix) actually voted 16 to 1 to deny women the right to wear the headscarf in public institutions because of the political and symbolic significance of the headscarf. The European Court of Human Rights decision has been enacted in the national laws of France and Turkey, to name but a few countries engaged in the denial of the right to manifest one's religion. This decision, emanating from the highest court of human rights in Europe, is unthinkable in the courts of the United States where freedom of speech and expression is one of the most treasured and basic human right reflected in the US Constitution (see US Constitution in Appendix).

15. History of the Development of United Nations Human Rights Conventions

The international law of human rights[22] developed because international law did not adequately protect individuals. International human rights law evolved over the last four decades beginning with the adoption of the United Nations Charter (see Appendix) in 1945 and with the establishment of the Universal Declaration of Human Rights (see Appendix) in 1948, resulting in the enactment of two separate UN treaties (the ICCPR and the ICESCR) (see Appendix for both treaties) to implement the aspirations contained in

---

22. *See* THEODOR MERON, HUMAN RIGHTS LAW-MAKING IN THE UNITED NATIONS (Oxford University Press 1986).

the Universal Declaration of Human Rights. Before 1945, there was no comprehensive body of law protecting individuals as human beings.

International law enacted before the UN Charter era did develop certain rules and did create certain institutions that are an integral part of the international law of human rights today.[23] For example, the doctrine of humanitarian intervention, which flies in the face of the UN Charter's state sovereignty principle and its rule of non-intervention espoused in Article 2(4) of the Charter, recognizes the need to protect individuals from human rights violations imposed upon them by their own state.

Humanitarian intervention is the right of states and international organizations to assist individuals in another state, if that state subjects them to treatment that "shocks the conscience of mankind."

Early international agreements condemning the slave trade of the 19th century also reflect human rights protection in international law. Similarly, the international treaties underlying the Peace of Westphalia (1648), the Treaty of Paris (1856) and the Treaty of Berlin (1878) all covered religious freedom of individuals. The Covenant of the League of Nations (the Mandate System), established after World War I, administered a formal system for the protection of national, religious and linguistic minorities and the promotion of the welfare of native populations. The law applicable to the responsibility of states for the injuries to aliens is another source of international human rights law found in international law.

After the end of World War II, the establishment of the United Nations by its Charter and the enactment of a series of declarations and treaties outlined the beginning of a legal system protecting universal human rights. A treaty (also called a covenant, a convention, a protocol, or a charter) is binding only if a certain number of states ratify it. Every treaty in force is binding upon the parties to it and must be performed by them in good faith. (Vienna Convention on the Law of Treaties, Art. 26). (See Appendix.) A declaration is not legally binding but is rather hortatory or aspirational. Nevertheless, a UN declaration does carry moral weight in the international community.

16. United Nations Charter and the International Bill of Human Rights

The United Nations was established after six long years of a world war that raged from 1939–1945. The UN was created in order to maintain international peace and security (UN Charter, Article 1(1)); to achieve international cooperation in solving international problems of an economic, social, cultural, or humanitarian character; and to promote and encourage respect for human rights (UN Charter, Article 1(3)). There are currently 192 member states in the United Nations, and each state has one vote in the General Assembly.

The United Nations established what is commonly referred to as the International Bill of Human Rights, which originally was composed of three international instruments: The Universal Declaration of Human Rights (1948) [UDHR], the International Covenant on Civil and Political Rights (1966) [ICCPR], and the International Covenant on Economic,

---

23. *See* THEODOR MERON, HUMAN RIGHTS IN INTERNATIONAL LAW (Oxford University Press 1984); THEODOR MERON, INTERNATIONAL LAW IN THE AGE OF HUMAN RIGHTS (Martinus Nijhoff 2004).

Social and Cultural Rights (1966) [ICESCR]. Actually, the International Bill of Human Rights also includes the Optional Protocol to the ICCPR and the Optional Protocol to the ICESCR.

The United Nations General Assembly adopted the UDHR in 1948, setting forth a comprehensive statement of inalienable human rights. Even though the UDHR is not legally binding, it has had an enormous influence on the development of human rights laws. It is arguably binding on all states by customary international law because it has been in existence for the past 50 years.

17. The ICCPR and the ICESCR and Their Optional Protocols

In order to give legal effect to the aspirations of the UDHR, the United Nations General Assembly asked its Commission on Human Rights to draft a convention that could become a binding treaty. The ICCPR and the ICESCR were both opened for signature in 1966 and entered into force ten years later in 1976. The ICCPR includes civil and political rights such as the right to freedom of conscience and religion, the right to be free from torture, and the right to a fair trial with due process of the law. These are negative rights that the government has a duty to protect if they are denied to individuals. The ICESCR includes economic, social, and cultural rights that are considered positive rights because the government has a duty to provide these rights.

Two Optional Protocols to ICCPR

The ICCPR has two Optional Protocols. The First Optional Protocol to the International Covenant on Civil and Political Rights establishes the right of the United Nations Human Rights Committee to hear individual complaints from people alleging that the state has violated their individual human rights under the ICCPR. The findings of the ICCPR Human Rights Committee are not enforceable. The Second Optional Protocol to the ICCPR binds states to eliminate the death penalty. While the United States has signed the ICCPR, it has not signed the Second Optional Protocol because of the existence of the death penalty in the United States.

The ICESCR

The ICESCR includes the right to an adequate standard of living, the right to education, the right to fair wages, and the right to safe working conditions. The rights in the ICESCR are referred to as positive rights because a State party to the convention must take steps, including legislative measures, to achieve the progressive realization of ICESCR rights. A United Nations Committee on Economic, Social, and Cultural Rights (the CESCR Committee) monitors compliance with the ICESCR and provides guidance on the interpretation of the convention. The United States signed but did not ratify the ICESCR.

The Optional Protocol to the ICESCR

The ICESCR has an Optional Protocol which was adopted by the General Assembly on December 10, 2008 and opened for signature on September 24, 2009. The Optional Protocol to the ICESCR establishes complaint and inquiry mechanisms for the ICESCR.

18. Other Major UN Human Rights Conventions

After the enactment of the International Bill of Human Rights, several international United Nations human rights conventions were adopted and entered into force. Some of these include the Genocide Convention (1948) (see Appendix), The Convention on the Political Rights of Women (1953), The International Convention on the Elimination of All Forms of Racial Discrimination (1965) [CERD], The International Convention on the Suppression and Punishment of the Crime of Apartheid (1973), The International Convention on the Elimination of All Forms of Discrimination against Women (1979) [CEDAW] and its Optional Protocol (see Appendix), The Convention against Torture (1985) [CAT] and its Optional Protocol (see Appendix), The Convention on the Rights of the Child (1989) [Child's Convention] and its Two Protocols (see Appendix), and The Convention on the Rights of People with Disabilities (2006) [Disabilities Convention] and its Optional Protocol (see Appendix). This book will deal primarily with those international human rights conventions that specifically affect women and their human rights. We will discuss each of the relevant treaties and declarations in more detail in the next chapter.

19. Fundamental Human Rights: Civil, Political, Social, Economic, and Cultural Rights

What exactly are "human rights"? Human rights are first, second, and third generation rights otherwise referred to as negative, positive, and collective rights. Human rights are a basket of fundamental rights including civil, political, social, economic, and cultural rights that are provided to individuals and protected by the state. "First generation human rights" (civil and political human rights) are also referred to as "negative rights" because the state must not deny these rights to individuals, and the state must protect individuals against abuse of these first generation rights. The state is not obligated to "provide" first generation rights, just protect against their denial. The United States and other democratic nations typically support and defend first generation human rights characterized by protection, rather than provision. "Second generation" rights (social, economic, and cultural human rights) are also referred to as "positive rights." The state has to actively provide second generation rights such as affordable housing, health care, education, and cultural activities. Socialist nations have typically excelled at providing second generation rights. The United States has traditionally shunned their obligation to provide positive second generation rights because of a firm belief that the government should not interfere in such private matters as children's rights, women's rights, and obligations of a husband to his wife. The recent adoption of health care legislation by President Barack Obama, and the contentious debates that grew out of that controversy, reflect the general reluctance by the United States to provide second generation positive rights. The United States does not like to sign aspirational treaties guaranteeing every US citizen positive rights that the US knows or believes it may not be able to provide. "Third generation rights" (collective rights) are the rights of a group of people or the right of the people of a country to self-determination.

International law protects states from violations by other states. Human rights law protects individuals from violations of their fundamental rights committed by the state. **Civil rights** include the individual right to life, liberty, and the pursuit of happiness, as provided by the US Declaration of Independence. Other civil rights include the right to work, the right to freely associate with a group of choice, the right to free speech, the right to religion, and the right to manifest one's own religion, the right to be free from torture, the right to due process of the law, the right to a fair and speedy trial, the right to equal protection under the law, etc. **Political rights** include the right to vote and the right to run for office and hold a government position. **Social rights** include the right to privacy, the right to associate, and the right to belong to a particular group or religion. **Economic rights** include the right to earn a living and the right to make and save money in a bank. **Cultural rights** include the right to marry the person of your own choice, the right to religion, the right to manifest your religion, the right to freedom of choice, etc. These rights are interdependent and interrelated.

Existing human rights laws are encoded in declarations, charters, and conventions such as the UN Charter (1945) (Arts. I, 55, 56), the UDHR (1948), the Genocide Convention (1948), the ICCPR (1966–1976), the ICESCR (1966–1976), the Convention against Racial Discrimination (1965), the Apartheid Convention (1973), CEDAW (1979), The Convention against Torture (1985), the Convention on the Rights of the Child (1989), and most recently the Convention on the Rights of Persons with Disabilities (2006).

20. Adequacy of Human Rights Laws for Women: Feminist Theories

Are these human rights laws adequately protective of women's rights? We have shown that women's rights are not protected by international law *per se* because international law applies primarily to states and not to individuals. Feminist scholars like Hilary Charlesworth and Christine Chinkin, Karen Engle, and Catherine MacKinnon demonstrate that international law has been written by men, for men, in a male world. Women's rights are protected intermittently by the human rights legislation listed above. Women's rights are protected more specifically in CEDAW and in ICESCR. These two UN conventions protect women in the private sector where women's work and women's social, economic, and cultural rights are often denied. It is interesting to note that the United States has refused to sign both CEDAW and the ICESCR, which reflects poorly on its political position regarding women and actually misrepresents its otherwise humanitarian views on women's rights.

21. Hilary Charlesworth and Christine Chinkin

Where do women fit into the international legal system and the international human rights legal system? Hilary Charlesworth and Christine Chinkin wrote a seminal book in 2000: THE BOUNDARIES OF INTERNATIONAL LAW: A FEMINIST ANALYSIS. In it they declared that "the absence of women in the development of international law has produced a narrow and inadequate jurisprudence that has, among other things, legitimated the unequal position of women around the world rather than challenged it."[24] The unequal position of women around the world is also reflected in comparative law and in the laws of many countries. Women worldwide are "economically, socially, politically, legally, and

---

24. HILARY CHARLESWORTH & CHRISTINE CHINKIN, THE BOUNDARIES OF INTERNATIONAL LAW: A FEMINIST ANALYSIS 4 (Juris Publ'g Inc. 2000) [hereinafter CHARLESWORTH & CHINKIN].

culturally disadvantaged compared with similarly situated men,"[25] and the laws of these countries reflect that reality.

Violence against women within the family, community, and by the State perpetuates the marginalization of women and the continuation of their subordinate position in societies throughout the world. In many countries women are closely and oftentimes brutally controlled by male family members, as well as religious and political authorities in local and national governments. The male-dominated micro-management of women reinforces their dependency and powerlessness in society. Certain customary or traditional practices that might shock the conscience of people in developed countries are sometimes tolerated and even justified in developing countries. Government officials and officers of the law may turn a blind eye to cultural practices such as female infanticide, sex-selective abortions, rape, torture, female genital mutilation, wife beating, and other more disguised forms of violence against women which are tolerated in the name of "cultural relativism" and even sanctioned by government authorities as a form of justifiable population control.

Despite the existence of equality of men and women under the law, women's actual status in society is unequal because they are linked primarily to their undervalued role as child bearers. Women are viewed in some societies purely as child breeders rather than as individuals endowed with certain inalienable human rights. Moreover, the significance of cultural practices and customs are often defined or interpreted by men. Thus, culture and custom can actually prevent or hinder women from entering public life rather than protect them. Tradition and culture may cause women to be excluded from the public world and be relegated solely to the private sphere of domestic family life. Culture and religion may prevent women from making choices about their husband and about their own reproduction.[26] The UN Development Programme summed up women's condition globally: "[W]hat unites countries across many cultural, religious, ideological, political and economic divides is their common cause *against* the equality of women—in their right to travel, marry, divorce, acquire nationality, manage property, seek employment and inherit property."[27]

The first chapter of this book sheds light on the inadequacy of international law to respond to the deplorable condition of women in the world. Charlesworth and Chinkin explain persuasively that international and national laws are designed to protect women within a male-dominated society, but these laws are drafted according to male-centered norms. This is true of international human rights laws as well. Many human rights treaties still use only the masculine pronoun, reinforcing a historical deference to men. International laws place value on what has been referred to as "male" traits: objectivity rather than subjectivity, logic rather than emotion, the protector rather than the protected. These gendered values reflect and reinforce general stereotypes of women and men.

22. Karen Engle

Professor Karen Engle reinforces the view that women are not adequately represented in international law. She also claims that women are not adequately represented in human

---

25. *Id. See* Susan Deller Ross, Women's Human Rights: The International and Comparative Law Casebook (2008), an important text on the topic of women's human rights.

26. *See* Arati Rao, *The Politics of Gender and Culture in International Human Rights Discourse, in* Women's Rights, Human Rights 172 (J.S. Peters & Andrea Wolper eds., 1995).

27. UN, The World's Women 1970–90: Trends and Statistics 72 (New York, UN 1991).

rights laws either because these laws do not take into account violations that occur in the "private" sphere. She argues that women are generally secluded in the private sphere whereas men dominate the public sphere. In her ground breaking article "After the Collapse of the Public/Private Distinction: Strategizing Women's Rights,"[28] Professor Engle explains what she means by the public/private distinction:

> "... Central to the critiques of international law have been analyses of the public/private distinction. They generally take one of two forms. Either women's rights advocates argue that public international law, and particularly human rights theory, is flawed because it is not really universal [that is, because international law excluded from its scope the private, or domestic sphere—presumably the space in which women operate—it cannot include them], or advocates argue that international law does not really exclude the private, but rather uses the public/private divide as a convenient screen to avoid addressing women's issues."

"Those who take the first approach, then take for granted that public international law in its present form cannot enter what they see as the private sphere. For women to be included, they maintain, international law must be re-conceptualized to include the private.

Those who take the second approach, on the other hand, assume that doctrinal tools are present in international law—particularly in human rights law—to accommodate women. The public/private dichotomy, they assert, is both irrational and inconsistently applied. According to this second approach, the human rights regime and states are disingenuous in their claim that they do not enter the private sphere. The private sphere is entered all the time, for example, through regulation of the family, or the ability to impute to states the acts of non-state actors in disappearance cases. Moreover, these critics argue, a state's failure to protect rights in the private sphere is not distinguishable from direct state action. Finally, they point out that the human rights regime applies a double standard when talking about women. The international legal regime would never argue, for example, that it could not intervene to ensure that states end certain forms of 'private' violence, such as cannibalism or slavery.

... Concentrating too much on the public/private distinction excludes important parts of women's experiences. Not only does such a focus often omit those parts of women's private lives that figure into the 'public', however that gets defined, it also assumes that 'private' is bad for women. It fails to recognize that the 'private' is a place where many have tried to be (such as those involved in the market), and that it might ultimately afford protection to (at least) women.

... The critiques of the private-public distinction make us think of the unregulated private as something that is necessarily bad for women. We rarely look at the ways in which privacy (even if only because it seems the best available paradigm) is seen by at least some women to offer them protection. A number of examples immediately come to mind, each of which centers on women's bodies and, not surprisingly, on women's sexuality. The language of privacy, and sketching out zones of privacy, many would argue, is our best shot at legally theorizing women's sexuality. In United States legal jurisprudence, the First Amendment has been used to a similar end as often seen in the debates about pornography.

Examples of where 'the private' is sometimes seen to have liberating potential for women are abortion (which is most obvious to us in the United States); battering; the

---

28. Karen Engle, *After the Collapse of the Public/Private Distinction: Strategizing Women's Rights, in* RECONCEIVING REALITY: WOMEN AND INTERNATIONAL LAW 143, 148–49 (Dorinda G. Dallmeyer ed., Washington DC, Am. Soc'y of Int'l Law 1993) [hereinafter RECONCEIVING REALITY].

protection of 'alternative' sexual lifestyles; prostitution; the right to wear the veil as protection from sexual harassment; and the right to participate in *or be free of* clitoridectomies, *sati*, breast implants, the wearing of spike-heeled shoes. Failure to focus on these issues affecting women's relationships to their bodies obscures the ways that many women see their lives.

... [T]he critiques often prevent us from taking seriously women who claim not to want the regulation or protection of international law. Arguments about 'culture,' particularly those that attempt to use claims of cultural integrity or community to maintain practices that some women might find abhorrent, get transformed into arguments about the private. That is, women's rights advocates often treat these arguments as though they are yet another manifestation of the mainstream legal regime's exclusion of the private or women (or both) at all costs. As a result, advocates either ignore those women who defend practices they see as an important part of their culture, or assume that such women are replete with false consciousness.

... [T]he critiques often lead us to conspiracy theories. Our exclusion indicates that they're all out to get us. We point out that *they* don't include *us* in the mainstream, that *they* give *us* our own marginal institutions and then ensure that the institutions lack enforcement mechanisms, that *they* don't really care about *us* or take us seriously. We rarely ask, though, who *they* are, who *we* are, and why they're out to get us. We also fail to notice that others are singing a similar tune to our own. Those who argue for economic and social rights, for example, seem to feel just as isolated and outside as women's advocates do. In fact, sometimes it seems that international law, particularly human rights law, has been built by its own criticism. That is, every time some group or cause feels outside the law, it pushes for inclusion, generally through a new official document. The vast proliferation of human rights documents, then, is as much a testament to exclusion as it is to inclusion." [End of citation from Karen Engle's article.]

23. Catherine MacKinnon

Catherine MacKinnon, one of the great women's rights advocates of the twentieth and twenty-first centuries, argues that we must actually *change* the laws if women are to be adequately protected. Right now women are marginalized, excluded, subordinated, and even raped systematically as a weapon of war. MacKinnon exposes the flaws in the doctrine of state sovereignty which can work to deny women their inalienable and fundamental human rights. In her article "Comment: Theory Is Not a Luxury,"[29] Professor MacKinnon explains how and why in the Second Circuit US Federal Court and under the Alien Tort Claims Act she successfully defended *pro bono* three groups of Croatian and Muslim Bosnian girls and women who were raped in Serbian-run concentration camps. She expresses the following views on the state of women's human rights in the current international legal system:

"... To accept reality as men see and define it ultimately means accepting reality as men make and live it. Women can no more afford this in the international legal order than we can anywhere else. We need to analyze critically and systematically create new approaches together...."

"The hand of men as such is seen behind the international legal order, with consequences for the status and treatment of women as such. Women's position under inter-

---

29. Catharine A. MacKinnon, *Comment: Theory Is Not a Luxury, in* RECONCEIVING REALITY, *supra* note 28, at 83–92.

national law is like women's position in domestic legal regimes: marginalized, excluded, subordinated. It is quite a trick to keep a people on the edge, out, and down all at the same time, but men have figured out how to do it to women.

A final theme, both too obvious to state and incapable of being repeated too often, is the need for change.... [T]he state is patriarchal, militarized, and hierarchical ... more fundamentally, it is sovereign. Sovereignty as a definition of the state as such, within an international order defined as an order of sovereign states, can work to deny women's human rights. States bond with each other internationally to permit men to violate women—just as men bond with each other for this end within states....[30]

In October, 1992, a piece of reality came over my fax machine. It eventually resulted in my being retained *pro bono* by now five women's groups, three in Croatia and two in Bosnia-Herzegovina, to help them get international legal justice for mass sexual atrocities. It stated:

> Serbian forces have exterminated over 200,000 Croatians and Muslims thus far in an operation they've coined "ethnic cleansing." In this genocide, in Bosnia-Herzegovina alone, over 30,000 Muslims and Croatian girls and women are pregnant from mass rape. Of the hundreds of Serbian-run concentration camps, about twenty are solely rape/death camps for Muslim and Croatian women and children. There are news reports and pictures here of Serbian tanks plastered with pornography and reports that those who catch the eye of the men looking at the pornography are killed. Some massacres in villages as well as rapes and executions in camps are being videotaped as they're happening. One Croatian woman described being tortured by electric shocks and gang raped in a camp by Serbian men dressed in Croatian uniforms and filmed the rapes and forced her to "confess" on film that Croatians raped her. In the stress of Zagreb, UN troops often ask local women how much they cost. There are reports of refugee women being forced to sexually service the UN troops to receive aid. Tomorrow I talk to two survivors of mass rape—thirty men per day for over three months. We've heard the UN passed a resolution to collect evidence as the first step for a war crimes trial, but it is said here that there is no precedent for trying sexual atrocities.

These are familiar events: rape, forced motherhood, prostitution, pornography, sexual murder, all on the basis of sex and ethnicity together. Whether formally illegal or not, these practices of sexual and reproductive abuse and murder—it is clear from the newspapers—occur on a daily basis in one form or another in every country in the world as well as in war. The international legal order is not predicated on the need to address them, but many are formally prohibited under international law, all of them in armed conflicts. Whether or not they are prohibited on their face, however, these practices are nonetheless widely permitted as the liberties of their perpetrators, or excesses of passion, or spoils of victory, or products of war. Virtually nothing is done about them, within any nation or among nations. They tend to be legally rationalized, officially winked at, or in some instances even formally condoned. They are ignored.

This particular war exemplifies how existing human rights institutions ... can work to cover up and confuse who is doing what to whom and thus effectively condone atroc-

---

30. I should also mention Barbara Stark's distinction between the Civil Covenant's replication of hierarchies and the Economic Covenant's inversion of them. I am not persuaded that the concept of equality embodied in the Economic Covenant inverts those categories; in many ways it seems to replicate them.

ities. The atrocities in this war, and the parties to it, are covered by international humanitarian law and the laws of war.[31] Yet nothing so far has been invoked to stop the abuses or to hold the perpetrators accountable. Understand that the fact of Serbian aggression is beyond question, just as the fact of male aggression against it is beyond question, both here in this war and every day. "Ethnic cleansing" is a Serbian policy of extermination of non-Serbs with the goal of creating a "Greater Serbia." It is a euphemism for genocide. Yet this war of aggression has repeatedly been construed as bilateral, as a civil war, or an ethnic conflict, to the accompaniment of much international wonderment that people cannot get along, and pious clucking at the behavior of "all sides." This reminds me of the way women are blamed for getting ourselves raped by men that we know and then chastised for not killing them very well afterwards.

One result is that these rapes are not grasped either as a strategy in genocide or as a practice of misogyny, far less as both at once. What is happening to Bosnian and Croatian women at the hands of the Serbian forces is continuous both with this ethnic war of aggression and with the gendered war of aggression of everyday life. For most women, this war is to every day rape what the Holocaust was to every day anti-Semitism: without the every day, you could not have the conflagration, but do not mistake one for the other.[32]

In this war, Muslim and Croatian women and girls are raped then murdered; sometimes their corpses are raped as well. When this is noticed, it is called *either* genocide *or* rape, rather than rape as a form of genocide directed specifically against women. It is seen either as part of a campaign of Serbia against non-Serbia, or an onslaught by combatants against civilians, but not as an attack by men against women. Or, it is just another instance of aggression by all men against all women all the time, especially in all wars, rather than what it actually is, which is rape by some men against certain women in this genocide, which is being carried on through war.

The point of much of this theorizing appears to be to obscure by any means available exactly who is doing what to whom and why and to define the problem so that no one can or need do anything about it. When the women survive, the rapes tend to be regarded as an inevitability of armed conflict—the war of all against all—or as a continuation of the hostilities of civil life, of all men against all women. So why intervene, and on what side? Rape does occur in war, among and between all sides. Rape is also a daily act by men against women and is always an act of domination by men over women. This has been consistently recognized in the literature. But the fact that *these* rapes are part of an ethnic war of aggression being misrepresented as a civil war among equal aggressors means that Muslim and Croatian women are facing twice as many rapists with twice as many excuses—two layers of men on top of them rather than one, one layer attempting to exterminate the other layer, with two layers of impunity serving to justify the rapes, the "just war" level and the "just life" level. And nothing is being done about either of them.

Like all rapes, these rapes are particular as well as generic, and the particularity matters. This is ethnic rape by official military policy. It is not only a policy of male pleasure and male power unleashed, not only a policy to defile, torture, humiliate, degrade, and demoralize the other side, and not only a policy of posturing to gain advantage and ground over other men. What this is—and this particularly invokes the international

---

31. Documentation and discussion are provided in Catharine A. MacKinnon, *Crimes of War, Crimes of Peace*, in OF HUMAN RIGHTS (Stephen Shute & John Gardner eds., 1993) and Theodor Meron, *Rape as a Crime under International Humanitarian Law*, 87 AM. J. INT'L L. 424 (1993).

32. The lives of prostituted women are probably changed the least by the conflagration, as they are forced to have sex with scores of men on an everyday basis, war or no war.

legal context—is rape under orders. It is not rape out of control. It is rape under control. It is also rape unto death, rape as massacre, rape to kill and to make victims wish they were dead. It is rape as an instrument of forced exile, to make you leave your home and never want to come back. It is also rape to be seen and heard by others: rape orchestrated as spectacle. It is rape to shatter a people and to drive a wedge through a community. It is the rape of misogyny liberated by xenophobia and unleashed by official command. It is rape as genocide....

... To say that the international system is gendered is no exaggeration, and its gendered dynamics do revolve around state sovereignty. Bosnian and Croatian women are not a state; they do not control a state; no state represented them until Bosnia sued Serbia for genocide in the International Court of Justice.[33] With a few exceptions (those exceptions either not applying here or having no teeth), human rights instruments empower states to act against states, not individuals or groups to act on their own behalf, whether against states or individuals. Given that only state violations of human rights are recognized as violations, this is particularly odd—especially after 1945, when it might have been learned that states can violate the human rights of those who are not states and who have no state to act for them. Under international law, for the most part, only states can violate human rights, and only states can act to redress them.

... [W]hy has no state—those with the power (and most of them the legal obligation) to do something about all these atrocities—moved to act on behalf of these women under the vast panoply of available human rights instruments? Perhaps it is this: no state effectively guarantees women's human rights within its borders, so internationally, men's states protect each other from women's rights within states. Sovereignty means that men respect this for themselves and for each other. At least this is one explanation ... for the failure of international human rights law to empower individuals or groups to enforce their own human rights effectively against individuals and states alike. Which state is in a position to challenge another on women's human rights? Which state ever will?

As to men's so-called private acts against women, wartime is largely exceptional. Atrocities by soldiers against civilians are always seen as state acts. But men do in war what they do in peace, only more so. When it comes to women, or at least to civilian casualties, the complacency that surrounds peacetime extends to war, however the laws read.... The more a conflict can be framed as within a state, as a civil war, as social, as domestic, the less human rights are recognized to be violated. The closer a fight comes to home, the more feminized the victims become, no matter what their gender, and the less likely international human rights will be found to be violated, no matter what was done." [End of citation from Catherine MacKinnon's article.]

Thus, in the face of a clear public/private dichotomy in international law, Professor Karen Engle shows that some attempts have been made to give women greater freedom and equality in both spheres. However, Professor Catharine A. MacKinnon argues that unless international law as well as human rights law are taken out of their inherently gendered or sexualized context and changed, there can never be true equality between men and women. Both of these scholars, as well as Hilary Charlesworth and Christine Chinkin

---

33. *See* Application of the Convention on the Prevention and Punishment of the Crime of Genocide (*Bosnia and Herzegovina v. Yugoslavia (Serbia and Montenegro)*) (filed Mar. 20, 1993) 46–57, 45–68F (detailing rapes and sexual torture); Order of Provisional Measures, Application of the Convention on the Prevention and Punishment of the Crime of Genocide (*Bosnia and Herzegovina v. Yugoslavia (Serbia and Montenegro)*), No. 93/9 I.C.J. (April 8, 1993).

point out the serious weaknesses of the international legal system and the international human rights legal system designed to protect women's rights.

24. Conclusion

Women are often excluded from the international legal arena, and their human rights are sometimes denied and remain unprotected because of the force of the doctrines of state sovereignty and non-intervention. Nevertheless, women's participation in government, in schools, and in the debate about women's rights is key to the establishment of comprehensive international laws protecting and implementing women's human rights. However, it is important to note that issues specific to women are not the same in all countries. This is why we must consider the substance and context of comparative laws when discussing women's human rights. While subtle gender and class differences can oppress women in developed countries, women in developing countries have to contend with crushing poverty, as well as omnipresent religious and racial barriers to equality. That is why women in developing countries prefer to focus attention on their economic marginalization, starvation, and the violence perpetrated on them during and after war.

B. International Law Is Gendered and Male Dominated

1. Hilary Charlesworth and Christine Chinkin,
The Boundaries of International Law: A Feminist Analysis[34]
Women and the International Legal System[35]

Introduction[36]

This book is about why issues of sex and gender matter in international law. Its central argument is that the absence of women in the development of international law has produced a narrow and inadequate jurisprudence that has, among other things, legitimated the unequal position of women around the world rather than challenged it. In this case, the absence of women in international law is a critical feature of the traditional canon—its boundaries depend upon it. Our aim is to encourage a rethinking of the discipline of international law so that it can offer a more useful framework for international and national justice.

The scope of international law increased significantly throughout the twentieth century. It now pervades international relations and national political and legal systems. International law is a mechanism for distributing power and resources in the international and national communities. It offers a wide range of normative prescriptions: from regulating coercive behavior between states, and between states and non-state actors, to the allocation and control of space and territory from Antarctica to the high seas to outer space; from the protection of human rights, the global environment and endangered

---

34. Charlesworth & Chinkin, *supra* note 24, at 1–19.
35. *Id.* at 1–19.
36. *Id.* at 1–3.

species to the management of the international system of trade and finance. However, while the international legal system may be broadening in scope, it remains narrow in perspective. Its constraints could be analyzed in many different ways, for example from the perspectives of those states that have played a little role in its development, or of non-governmental organizations (NGOs), or of individuals that seek access to it. This book examines the boundaries and limits of international law from a critical and feminist perspective. Women form over half the world's population, but their voices, in all their variety, have been thoroughly obscured by and within the international legal order. This book attempts to give expression to some of those voices....

Gender and Sex[37]

Feminist investigations of different areas of knowledge frequently concentrate upon gender as a category of analysis. The notion of gender captures the ascribed, social nature of distinctions between women and men — the excess cultural baggage associated with biological sex. 'Gender' draws attention to aspects of social relations that are culturally contingent and without foundation in biological necessity. The term also has the advantage of particularly emphasizing relationality, that is the connection between definitions of masculinity and femininity,[38] thereby avoiding the implication that only women should be involved in an investigation of gender. Sex, on the other hand, is typically used to refer to biological difference between women and men.

Much theoretical writing about gender assumes that sex is a fixed, immutable characteristic and that it is a given, rather than a contestable category. Indeed, it has been argued that terms such as 'sex' or 'sexual difference' carry with them the resonance of biological determinism and thus should be avoided.[39] ... The major difference between the notions of 'gender' and 'sex' is in their focus on different elements of dichotomies such as body/mind and nature/culture. Sexing draws attention to body and nature while gendering emphasizes mind and culture.... Particular understandings of both gender and sexual differences help construct the 'realities' of international law.

The Global Position of Women[40]

Although its forms differ significantly across societies and cultures, the phenomenon of women's subordination is found worldwide. Throughout the world women are economically, socially, politically, legally and culturally disadvantaged compared with similarly situated men. These disadvantages operate on a number of levels, international, regional, national, local, communal and familial. While these areas can be usefully separated out for the purpose of analysis, they are interconnected and mutually reinforcing. Indeed, as is discussed in chapter 2, the very categories used — 'economics,' 'society,' 'politics,' 'law,' 'culture' — are defined by reference to male lives and male experiences.... On internationally recognized socio-economic indicators, men's quality of life regularly rates better than that of women, whether they live within the industrialized or developing world. Although women tend to live longer than men, the quality of life for most women is considerably worse, and in many areas there is little sign of improvement over time....

---

37. Charlesworth & Chinkin, *supra* note 24, at 3–4.

38. Joan W. Scott, *Gender: A Useful Category of Analysis*, 91 THE AMERICAN HISTORICAL REVIEW 1053, 1054 (1986). *See also* Ann Oakley, *A Brief History of Gender, in* WHO'S AFRAID OF FEMINISM?: SEEING THROUGH THE BACKLASH 29 (A. Oakley & J. Mitchell eds., New York, The New Press 1997).

39. Scott, *supra* note 38, at 1054.

40. Charlesworth & Chinkin, *supra* note 24, at 4–14.

Women's average wage rates are consistently lower than men's. Although there is incomplete data, especially on rural and agricultural wages, the average wage for women globally, outside agriculture, is approximately three-quarters of the average male wage....[41]

What causes this significant difference between women and men's access to income? Part of the problem lies in the fact that the majority of women continue to work in so-called 'female' occupations resulting in the *de facto* segregation and the undervaluation of 'female' work. Occupational evaluations and classifications often depend on gender stereotypes: a typically 'female' job is almost always less well remunerated than a comparable male one.[42] Added to this is women's relative lack of bargaining power through trade union action, cultural and social norms that assign primary parenting duties to women, together with the unavailability of adequate maternity leave and unfounded assumptions about the absenteeism of women workers.[43] Women are also particularly at risk in workplace restructuring in times of economic deterioration....

The UNDP has observed that when paid and unpaid work are combined, women typically work longer hours than men.... In rural areas, the total work time of both women and men is much longer than in urban areas. The weight of this work falls disproportionately on women who spend an average of 20 per cent more time than men working in rural areas.[44] Further, worldwide the greatest proportion of the work that women do is unpaid, unrecognized as economically productive and largely invisible in national accounts....[45]

Of the 1.3 billion people estimated by the UNDP to live in poverty in 1995, 70 per cent are female,[46] largely as a result of women's unequal access to paid economic activity and their absence of status and influence within the family and community. Poverty is increasing in both the developing and the developed world,[47] and the proportion of women in poverty is on the rise.[48] Moreover, in many societies women face significant cultural and social disadvantages. Women's cultural and social status are typically linked to their roles as childbearers and child carers rather than their individual capacities. Culture and custom, invariably defined by reference to male perspectives,[49] become vehicles for keeping women out of the male-dominated spheres of public life such as the economy and politics....

In developing countries the largest single cause of death among women of childbearing age is complications from pregnancy and childbirth.[50] Indeed, an African woman is

---

41. UNDP, Human Development Report 36–37 (New York, Oxford University Press 1995) [hereinafter UNDP 1995].

42. Richard Anker, *Theories of Occupational Segregation by Sex: An Overview*, 136 International Labour Review 315, 316 (1997).

43. Sara Charlesworth, *Stretching Flexibility: Enterprise Bargaining, Women Workers and Changes to Working Hours* (Sydney, Human Rights and Equal Opportunity Commission 1996).

44. UNDP 1995, *supra* note 41, at 92; UNDP, Human Development Report 53 (New York, Oxford University Press 1998).

45. Marilyn Waring, Three Masquerades: Essays on Equality, Work and Human Rights 58 (Sydney, Allen & Unwin 1996).

46. UNDP 1995, *supra* note 41, at 36; Beijing Platform for Action, Critical Area of Concern, Women and Poverty.

47. UNDP, Human Development Report 3 (New York, Oxford University Press 1997) [hereinafter UNDP 1997].

48. UNDP 1995, *supra* note 41, at 36.

49. Arati Rao, *The Politics of Gender and Culture in International Human Rights Discourse*, in Women's Rights, Human Rights 167 (J.S. Peters & Andrea Wolper eds., New York, Routledge 1995).

50. Gigi Santow, *Social Roles and Physical Health: The Case of Female Disadvantage in Poor Countries*, 40 Social Sciences and Medicine 141 (1995). *See also* UNDP 1997, *supra* note 47, at 3.

180 times more likely to die from pregnancy and childbirth than a woman in Western Europe.[51] Amartya Sen has argued that women's inferior social status is a direct cause of the fact that there are a hundred million women 'missing' in the world's population.[52] Sen has pointed out that, in conditions of equal nutrition and health care, on average women live slightly longer than men. Using the female: male ratio found in sub-Saharan Africa of 102.2:100,[53] he has calculated that there should be over a hundred million more women alive: 4.4 million in Latin America, 2.4 million in North Africa, 1.4 million in Iran, 4.3 million in West Asia, 44 million in China, 36.7 million in India, 5.2 million in Pakistan, 3.7 million in Bangladesh and 2.4 million in South East Asia.[54] Sen has contended that these dramatic figures are the result of a web of social customs and practices that discriminate against girls and women. Prominent among them is the societal preference in many communities for male children, which encourages female infanticide and abortion of foetuses because they are female, and accords priority to the health and nutrition of boys. Other practices that affect women's survival include access to education, the ability to do paid work outside the home thus earning both income and social status, and subjection to violence in the family and community.

Women in many countries are discriminated against by the national legal system. They are disadvantaged in areas such as nationality laws, property rights, including ownership and management of, access to and enjoyment of matrimonial and commercial property, inheritance, marriage, divorce and custody of children, enjoyment of fundamental civil and political rights, lack of participation in and access to law and policy-making, courts and legal remedies, and access to certain types of employment and governmental benefits.[55] The UNDP has noted that: 'Ironically, what unites countries across many cultural, religious, ideological, political and economic divides is their common cause against the equality of women—in their right to travel, marry, divorce, acquire nationality, manage property, seek employment and inherit property.'[56]

Even where 'formal' equality is legally guaranteed in national constitutions or legislation, discrimination exists in both the process and principles of legal systems....

In no country do women have equal political power to men. Political disadvantage ranges from denial of women's right to vote, through to the under-representation and low participation of women in international and national law and decision-making bodies....

Many women are treated as economic commodities. Modern forms of slavery include trafficking, forced detention and prostitution and forms of servile marriage.... Sexual slavery is generated by a complex array of factors. Kathleen Barry has argued that 'the conditions of poverty combine with female role socialization to create vulnerability that makes young girls and women susceptible to procurers. Social attitudes that tolerate the abuse and enslavement of women are reinforced by governmental neglect, toleration or even sanction.'[57]

---

51. UNDP 1995, *supra* note 41, at 36.

52. Amartya Sen, *More Than 100 Million Women Are Missing, in* New York Review of Books 61 (1990).

53. *Id.* Sen observed that in the sub-Saharan region of Africa there is great poverty but little evidence of discrimination between women and men with respect to basic health care. He noted that in 1986 the female: male ratio in Western Europe was 105:100 and in North America, 104.7:100.

54. UN, The World's Women 1995: Trends and Statistics 1–3 (New York, UN 1995).

55. UN, The World's Women 1970–90: Trends and Statistics 72 (New York, UN 1991).

56. UNDP 1995, *supra* note 41, at 43 (emphasis in original).

57. Kathleen Barry, Female Sexual Slavery 67 (New York, New York University Press 1984).

In times of armed conflict, women are particularly vulnerable to slavery.... As has been the case throughout history,[58] women are regularly forced into prostitution, raped, and subjected to other forms of sexual abuse in armed conflict. For example, early in the conflict in the former Yugoslavia in 1993 estimates of the number of rapes that had occurred ranged from 12,000 to 20,000....[59]

The prolonged fighting in Afghanistan from the mid-1980s produced, in 1997, an uneasy victory for an Islamic fundamentalist group, the Taliban. Strict clothing restriction on females, removal of female students and teachers from schools and universities, and the confinement of women and girls to the activities of working in the home and shopping have accompanied the Taliban assertion of control.[60]

The most consistent manifestation of the subordinate position of women worldwide is the prevalence of women-specific violence that is either tolerated or even sanctioned by state and community leaders. This violence takes many forms and includes such acts as abortion of foetuses because they are female, female infanticide, sterilization and compulsory childbearing, inadequate nutrition, wife-murder, assault and rape, 'dowry deaths', practices such as *sati* (where a widow is burned on her husband's funeral pyre) and genital mutilation. The most pervasive type of violence against women reported in all regions of the world is abuse by a husband or partner.[61] Figures on women's violence against their partners indicate that the assaults are less serious and less frequent, and that they are generally in self-defense.[62]

Common to all these expressions of violence is the fact that the victims suffer because of their sex and gender. Womanhood means a particular and universal vulnerability to diverse forms of physical and psychological violence....

Radhika Coomaraswamy has proposed four major reasons for this violence. First, men's view of female sexuality and its role in the social hierarchy make women susceptible to sex-related crimes.[63] Women in particular positions of powerlessness, such as refugees, migrant workers and girl children, are especially vulnerable to sexual violence.[64] Second, a woman's familial relationship to a man or to a group of men makes her vulnerable to types of violence that are 'animated by society's concept of a woman as the property and dependent of a male protector.'[65] Third, violence against women may be directed towards the social group of which she is a member. For example, 'to rape a woman is to humiliate her community....'[66]

---

58. *See* SUSAN BROWN MILLER, AGAINST OUR WILL: MEN, WOMEN, AND RAPE (London, Secker & Warburg 1975).

59. UN, The World's Women 1995, *supra* note 54, at 164. *See also* UNDP 1997, *supra* note 47, at 182–83.

60. *Afghan Females Vanish Under Barrage of Mullah Edicts*, THE WEEKEND AUSTRALIAN, 5–6 April 1997, at 14. *See also* SC Res. 1214, 8 December 1998 and the report by Dr. Kamal Hassain, Special Rapporteur on Afghanistan to the UN Commission on Human Rights, UN Doc. E/CN.4/1999/40, 24 March 1999.

61. UN, The World's Women 1995, *supra* note 54, at 160 (chart 6.13). *See also* UNDP 1997, *supra* note 46, at 11.

62. UN, The World's Women 1995, *supra* note 54, at 158.

63. Radhika Coomaraswamy, *Of Kali Born: Women, Violence and the Law in Sri Lanka, in* FREEDOM FROM VIOLENCE: WOMEN'S STRATEGIES FROM AROUND THE WORLD 50 (M. Schuler ed., New York, UNIFEM 1992).

64. *See* Deeana Jang *et al., Domestic Violence in Immigrant and Refugee Communities: Responding to the Needs of Immigrant Women*, 13 *Response* (no. 4, 1990), at 2; Executive Committee of the High Commissioner's Programme, *Note on Certain Aspects of Sexual Violence against Refugee Women*, UN Doc. EC/1993/SCP/CPR 2, April, 29, 1993.

65. Coomaraswamy, *supra* note 63, at 50.

66. *Id.*

Using Feminist Theories in International Law

... Although a specialized area of 'women's human rights law' is evolving,[67] and occasionally women are acknowledged in 'mainstream' international law, by and large, whenever women come into focus at all in international law, they are viewed in a very limited way, chiefly as victims, particularly as mothers, or potential mothers, and accordingly in need of protection....[68]

Feminist analysis rests on a commitment to challenge male dominance of women. What, then, are the most appropriate feminist tools and theories in examining international law? As we noted in chapter 1, feminist inquiry into international law can be compared to an archaeological dig. One obvious sign of power differentials between women and men is the absence of women in international legal institutions. Beneath this is the vocabulary of international law. It is striking that most international documents continue to use the generic male pronoun when referring to individuals generally, reinforcing the exclusion of women.[69] Digging further down, many apparently 'neutral' principles and rules of international law can be seen to operate differently with respect to women and men. Another, deeper, layer of the excavation reveals the gendered and sexed nature of the basic concepts of international law, for example, 'states,' 'security,' 'order,' and 'conflict.' Permeating all stages of the dig is a silence from and exclusion of women. This phenomenon does emerge as a simple gap or vacuum that weakens the edifice of international law and that might be remedied by some rapid construction work. It is rather an integral part of the structure of the international legal order, a critical element of its stability. The silences of the discipline are as important as its positive rules and theoretical structures.

One technique for identifying and decoding the silences in international law is paying attention to the way that dichotomies are used in its structure. International legal discourse rests on a series of distinctions: for example, object/nature, action/passivity, public/private, protector/protected, independence/dependence, binding/non-binding, international/domestic, intervention/non-intervention, sovereign/non-self-governing. Feminist scholars have drawn attention to the gendered coding of these systems of binary oppositions with the first term signifying 'male' characteristics and the second 'female.'...[70]

The silence of international law with respect to women needs to be challenged on every level, and different techniques will be appropriate at different levels of excavation. For this reason we adopt the method described by Margaret Radin as 'situated judgment'—using a variety of analytic strategies rather than a single feminist theory.[71] In some contexts, we rely on 'liberal' feminist techniques to point out that modern international law has failed to deliver on its promises of neutrality and equality and to challenge its illusory universality. Women have been almost completely excluded from international law-making arenas, and it is important to document this and then to argue for the need of proper representation and participation of women. Simply 'adding women and mixing' is by itself inadequate because the international legal system is itself gendered. Its rules have developed as a response to the experiences of a male elite. Feminist analysis must thus

---

67. *See* Charlesworth & Chinkin, *supra* note 24, at Chapter 7.

68. *See* Judith G. Gardam, *An Alien's Encounter with the Law of Armed Conflict, in* Sexing the Subject of the Law 233 (Naffine & Owens eds., Sydney, Law Book Co. Ltd. 1996).

69. Dale Spender, Man Made Language 147–48 (London/Boston, Routledge & Kegan Paul 1980).

70. Carol Cohn, *War, Wimps and Women: Talking Gender and Thinking War, in* Gendering War Talk 231 (Cooke & Woollacott eds., Princeton, Princeton University Press 1993).

71. *See* Margaret Jane Radin, *The Pragmatist and the Feminist*, 63 S. Cal. L. Rev. 1699, 1718–19 (1990) and accompanying text.

explore the unspoken commitments of apparently neutral principles of international law and the ways that male perspectives are institutionalized in it. This involves some of the techniques and concepts suggested by 'cultural,' 'radical,' 'post-modern,' and 'third world' feminisms. All these approaches are useful in examining the sex and gender of the building blocks of the international legal order, although such an eclectic method may also attract charges of theoretical incoherence....[72]

Essentialism

Feminist analysis of international law raises the issue of essentialism in an acute form. Essentialism, or the notion that women have a fixed 'essence' or set of characteristics, has sparked a major debate within feminist theory. The problem of an essentialist approach is that it limits the possibilities of restructuring social and political life: '[Essentialist theories] rationalize and neutralize the prevailing sexual division of social roles by assuming that these are the only, or the best, possibilities, given the confines of the nature, essence, or biology of the two sexes.'[73] Thus essentialism confuses social relations with immutable attributes.

From an international perspective, essentialism does not account for the historical and social differences between women of different cultures.[74] It allows the use of monolithic categories such as 'third-world-women' which carry a baggage of poverty, oppressive traditions, illiteracy and overpopulation.[75] In reality, as Chandra Mohanty has pointed out, 'Women are constituted as women through the complex interaction between class, culture, religion and other ideological institutions and frameworks. They are not "women" — a coherent group — solely on the basis of a particular economic system or policy.'[76] For all these reasons, the term 'essentialism' (or its cognates, biologism, naturalism and universalism) have become, in Elizabeth Grosz's words, 'labels for danger zones or theoretical pitfalls' in feminist theory, both from an intellectual and a political perspective.[77]

Exploring Public/Private Distinction in International Law

... Beneath the various private/public dichotomies in international law lie divisions based on sex and gender. Historically, the formation of the European nation state depended on a sexual division of labor and the relegation of women to a private, domestic, devalued sphere.[78] Men dominated in the public sphere of citizenship and political and economic life. The state institutionalized the patriarchal family both as the qualification for citizenship and public life and as the basic socio-economic unit.[79] Then functions of the state are still identified with men, while at the same time the state depends on the work of the 'private' sphere to sustain its operations....

---

72. *E.g.*, Fernando R. Teson, *Feminism and International Law: A Reply*, 33 Va. J. Int'l L. 647, 648 (1994).

73. Elizabeth Grosz, *A Note on Essentialism and Difference*, in Feminist Knowledge: Critique and Construct 332, 342–43 (Gunew ed., London, Routledge 1990).

74. *Id.* at 335.

75. Chandra Talpade Mohanty, *Under Western Eye: Feminist Scholarship and Colonial Discourses*, 30 Feminist Review 61 (1988); Maria Lugones & Elizabeth V. Spelman, *Have We Got a Theory For You*, 6 Hypatia 578 (1983).

76. Mohanty , *supra* note 75, at 74.

77. Grosz, *supra* note 73, at 335.

78. Rebecca Grant, *The Sources of Gender Bias in International Relations Theory*, in Gender and International Relations 8, 11–12 (Rebecca Grant & Kathleen Newland eds., Bloomington, Indiana University Press 1991).

79. V. Spike Peterson & Anne Sisson Runyan, Global Gender Issues 93 (Boudler, Westview Press 1993).

International law operates in the public, male world. While it formally removes 'private' concerns from its sphere, the international legal system nevertheless strongly influences them. One form of influence is the fact that 'private' issues are left to national, rather than international, regulation.[80] This means that laws concerning 'private' matters, such as the family, can quite properly (from an international perspective) take account of cultural and religious traditions that may allow the domination of women by men. Another aspect of the assignment of particular issues to the 'private,' national, realm is that the state can devolve some of its powers to centers of authority in the private sphere that may have no concern with the unequal position of women or indeed may have an interest in maintaining it, such as the family, religious institutions, the education system, business, finance and the media.…[81]

Concern with public/private dichotomies in explaining the sexed and gendered nature of international law has been criticized by feminist scholars, for example, the American international lawyer, Karen Engle.…[82] In any event, our argument is not that there is a monolithic public/private dichotomy that can be mapped on to international legal doctrine to explain the oppression of women. It is rather that a variety of distinctions, ostensibly between 'public' and 'private,' shape international law and that many of them have gendered consequences that need to be evaluated.…

Human Rights[83]

The Evolution of Human Rights Law[84]

… Human rights law is largely a product of the post-World War II international legal order.[85] It poses a profound challenge to the notion of state sovereignty because it asserts an international interest in the way states treat their populations. The UN Charter recognized in principle the importance of the protection of human rights by states,[86] and a series of both general and particular international instruments have since given definition and texture to this commitment.[87] The three major general instruments, the Universal Declaration of Human Rights (UDHR),[88] the International Covenant on Economic, Social, and Cultural Rights (ICESCR)[89] and the International Covenant on Civil and Political Rights (ICCPR)[90] have become known as the 'international bill of rights.' Other instruments cover specific violations of rights (for example, genocide,[91] racial discrimi-

---

80. *See* Kristen Walker, *An Exploration of Article 2(7) of the United Nations Charter as an Embodiment of the Public/Private Distinction in International Law*, 26 N.Y.U. J. Int'l L. & Pol. 173 (1994).

81. Shelley Wright, *Economic Rights, Social Justice and the State: A Feminist Reappraisal*, in Reconceiving Reality, *supra* note 28, at 117, 121.

82. Karen Engle, *After the Collapse of the Public/Private Distinction: Strategizing Women's Rights*, *in* Reconceiving Reality, *supra* note 28, at 143.

83. Charlesworth & Chinkin, *supra* note 24, at 201.

84. *Id.* at 202–08.

85. *See* H. Steiner and P. Alston, International Human Rights in Context 59–116 (Oxford, Clarendon Press 1996), providing an excellent survey of the antecedents of the UN human rights system.

86. Charter of the UN, 28 June 1945, articles 1, 55, and 56.

87. A useful guide to the development of international human rights law is Human Rights in International Law (Theodor Meron ed., New York, Oxford University Press 1984). *See also* The United Nations and Human Rights 1945–1995 (New York, UN 1995).

88. G.A. Res. 217A (III), 10 December 1948.

89. 16 December 1966, 993 U.N.T.S. 3, *reprinted in* 6 I.L.M 360 (1967).

90. 16 December 1966, 993 U.N.T.S. 171, *reprinted in* 6 I.L.M. 368 (1967).

91. Convention on the Prevention and Punishment of the Crime of Genocide, 9 December 1948, 78 U.N.T.S. 277.

nation,[92] apartheid[93] and torture[94]) and specific protected groups (for example, women,[95] children[96] and migrant workers[97]). There is also a series of general regional human rights treaties that offer various forms of protection to human rights within the specified region,[98] and specialized regional treaties.[99] International human rights law is one of the most developed branches of international law. It has not only generated a considerable number of treaties and 'soft' law instruments, but has also developed relatively sophisticated monitoring regimes and institutions. The regional treaties can be invoked under specified circumstances by individuals claiming violations in specific courts and commissions, and most of the UN treaties establish expert monitoring committees that oversee compliance in a number of ways. It is often argued that many international human rights standards meet the conditions for the creation of customary international law.[100]

The development of human rights law through the UN is often, if controversially, described in terms of 'generations.'[101] The first generation of rights consist of civil and political rights. First generation of rights are typically characterized as rights that can be claimed by individuals against governments. Such rights protect against arbitrary interference by the state. Civil and political rights may be described as 'negative' in that they require abstention by the state from particular acts, such as torture, arbitrary deprivation of life, liberty, and security. They focus on 'domesticating, restraining the state, making the state obey due process of law in principle created and upheld by the state.'[102] The core of first generation rights is the preservation of the autonomy of the individual. The major general document of the first generation of rights is the ICCPR.

The second generation of rights comprises economic, social, and cultural rights. These are rights, such as those relating to health, housing, and education, that require positive activity by the state to ensure their protection. They assume an active, interventionist role for governments and can be claimed by individuals and groups to secure their subsistence, with dignity, as human beings. The most detailed definition of second generation

---

92. International Convention on the Elimination of All Forms of Racial Discrimination, 21 December 1965, 660 U.N.T.S. 195, *reprinted in* 5 I.L.M. 352 (1966).

93. International Convention on the Suppression and Punishment of the Crime of Apartheid, 30 November 1973, 1015 U.N.T.S. 243.

94. Convention against Torture and Other Cruel, Inhuman or Degrading Treatment or Punishment, 10 December 1984, UN Doc. A/39/51, *reprinted in* 23 I.L.M. 1027 (1984) 1027, substantive changes noted in 24 I.L.M. 535 (1985).

95. Convention on the Elimination of All Forms of Discrimination against Women, 18 December 1979, 1249 U.N.T.S. 13, *reprinted in* 19 I.L.M. 33 (1980).

96. Convention on the Rights of the Child, 20 November 1989, G.A. Res. 44/25, *reprinted in* 28 I.L.M. 1448 (1989).

97. International Convention on the Protection of the Rights of All Migrant Workers and Members of Their Families, 18 December 1990, G.A. Res. 45/158, *reprinted in* 30 I.L.M. 1517 (1991).

98. European Convention for the Protection of Human Rights and Fundamental Freedoms, 4 November 1950, 213 U.N.T.S. 221; American Convention on Human Rights, 22 November 1969, 1114 U.N.T.S. 123, *reprinted in* 9 I.L.M. 673 (1970); African Charter on Human and People's Rights, 26 June 1981, *reprinted in* 21 I.L.M. 59 (1982).

99. *E.g.,* The European Convention for the Prevention of Torture and Inhuman or Degrading Treatment, 26 November 1987, *reprinted in* 27 I.L.M. 1152 (1988); Inter-American Convention to Prevent and Punish Torture, 9 December 1985, *reprinted in* 25 I.L.M. 519 (1986); Convention Governing the Specific Aspects of the Refugee Problems in Africa, 10 September 1969, 1001 U.N.T.S. 45.

100. *E.g.,* Filartiga v. Pena-Irala 630 F. 2d 876 (1980); THE UNITED NATIONS AND HUMAN RIGHTS, *supra* note 87, at 7.

101. Philip Alston, *A Third Generation of Solidarity Rights: Progressive Development or Obfuscation of International Human Rights Law?,* 29 NETH. INT'L L. REV. 307 (1982).

102. JOHAN GALTUNG, HUMAN RIGHTS IN ANOTHER KEY 8 (Oxford, Polity Press 1994).

rights is in the ICESCR.[103] The comparative justiciability of the first and second generation rights is often raised in debates about the implementation of human rights.[104] Can governments be held accountable for violations of economic, social, and cultural rights in the same way as they can for violations of civil and political rights? How can causal links be established between alleged violations of economic and social rights and state actions, or inaction? What standard of compliance is required — is it a general standard, or does it depend on the level of economic development of the state concerned?[105]

The third generation of rights encompasses peoples', or collective, rights, such as the rights to self-determination, development, and peace, that can only be claimed by groups, rather than by individuals.[106] Claims of peoples' rights can be made against the international community, as well as particular nation states. The guarantee of collective rights assumes both that the benefits will flow to individuals within the group and that the interests of all members of the group will coincide. Many of the third generation rights are contained in 'soft' law instruments, such as UN General Assembly declarations and resolutions.[107] Their most complete translation into 'hard,' treaty, norms is in the African Charter of Human and Peoples' Rights . . .[108]

Human rights law is under constant challenge. Most states formally accept the international regime,[109] but undermine their legal commitment by use of extensive reservations,[110] claw-back, and derogation provisions[111] that allow states to assert imperatives of national law, public safety and security[112] or inadequate national implementation.[113] Many states are responsible for widespread human rights violations. Another form of challenge focuses on the Western origins of human rights law allowing claims of cultural relativity. For example, at the Vienna Conference on Human Rights in 1993, a number of Asian states claimed that human rights as interpreted in the West were based on a commitment to individualism and were at odds with the Asian tradition of concern with the community.[114] The vulnerability of human rights law to non-observance is exacerbated when the law touches women's lives.

---

103. *See also* European Social Charter, 18 October 1961, 529 U.N.T.S. 89; Protocol Amending the Charter, 21 October 1991, *reprinted in* 31 I.L.M. 155 (1992).

104. *See* Committee on Economic, Social, and Cultural Rights, General Comment no. 3, UN Doc. E/1991/23, 1990 Annex III.

105. *See generally* THE RIGHTS TO COMPLAIN ABOUT ECONOMIC, SOCIAL, AND CULTURAL RIGHTS (Coomans & Van Hoof eds., Utrecht, Netherlands Institute of Human Rights 1995).

106. Lake Lubicon Band v. Canada Communication , no. 167/1984 (Human Rights Committee).

107. *E.g.,* Declaration on the Right of Peoples to Peace, G.A. Res. 39/11, 12 November 1984.

108. African Charter of Human and Peoples' Rights, arts. 19 to 24.

109. As of December 1999 the ICCPR had 144 parties; the ICESCR, 142; the International Convention on the Elimination of All Forms of Racial Discrimination, 155; the Convention on the Elimination of All Forms Discrimination against Women, 165; the Convention against Torture, 118; and the Convention on the Rights of the Child, 191.

110. *E.g.,* the United States' ratification of the ICCPR in 1992. *See* Steiner & Alston, *supra* note 85, at 766–71.

111. Rosalyn Higgins, *Derogations under Human Rights Treaties, in* 48 BRITISH YEARBOOK OF INTERNATIONAL LAW 281 (1976–77).

112. *E.g.,* ICCPR, arts. 18(3), 19(3), 21 and 22.

113. *E.g.,* Hilary Charlesworth, *Australia's Split Personality: Implementation of Human Rights Treaty Obligations in Australia, in* TREATY-MAKING AND AUSTRALIA 129 (Philip Alston & Madelaine Chiam eds., Annandale, Federation Press 1995).

114. Yash Ghai, *Human Rights and Governance: The Asia Debate,* 15 AUSTL. Y.B. INT'L L. 1, 5–6 (1994). However, this governmental view should be compared with the Bangkok NGO Declaration on Human Rights, 27 March 1993, *Report of the Regional Meeting for Asia on the World Conference on Human Rights,* UN Doc. A/CONF.157/ASRM/8-/CONF.157/PC/59, 1993.

Feminist Critiques of Rights[115]

An initial issue in any discussion of women and international human rights law is whether international formulations of rights are useful for women. Some feminist scholars have suggested in the context of national laws, that campaigns for women's legal rights are at best a waste of energy and at worst positively detrimental to women. They have argued that, while the formulation of equality rights may be useful as a first step towards the improvement of the position of women, a continuing focus on the acquisition of rights may not be beneficial:[116] women's experiences and concerns are not easily translated into the narrow, individualistic, language of rights;[117] rights discourse overly simplifies complex power relations and their promise is constantly thwarted by structural inequalities of power;[118] the balancing of 'competing' rights by decision-making bodies often reduces women's power;[119] and particular rights, such as the right to freedom of religion or to the protection of the family, can in fact justify the oppression of women.[120] Talk of rights is said to make contingent social structures seem permanent and to undermine the possibility of their radical transformation. Indeed it has been claimed that the only consistent function of rights has been to protect the most privileged groups in society....[121]

While the acquisition and assertion of rights is by no means the only solution for the domination of women by men, it is an important tactic in the international arena. Human rights offer a framework for debate over basic values and conceptions of a good society....

Patricia Williams has pointed out that for African-Americans, talk of rights has been a constant source of hope:

> 'Rights' feel so new in the mouths of most black people. It is still so deliciously empowering to say. It is a sign for and a gift of selfhood that is very hard to contemplate restructuring ... at this point in history. It is the magic wand of visibility and invisibility, of inclusion and exclusion, of power and no power ...[122]

The empowering function of rights discourse for women, particularly in the international sphere where women are still almost completely invisible, is a crucial aspect of its value. As has been observed in the context of South Africa, rights talk can often seem naïve and unpragmatic, but its power relies on a deep faith in justice and rightness....[123]

---

115. Charlesworth & Chinkin, *supra* note 24, at 208–12.

116. *E.g.*, Elizabeth Kingdom, What's Wrong With Rights? Problems for Feminist Politics of Law (Edinburg, Edinburg University Press 1991).

117. Robin West, *Feminism, Critical Social Theory and Law*, 1989 U. Chi. Legal F. 59 (1989).

118. Elizabeth Gross, *What is Feminist Theory?*, in Feminist Challenges: Social and Political Theory 192 (Carole Paterman & Elizabeth Gross eds., Sydney, Allen & Unwin 1986); Carol Smart, Feminism and the Power of Law 138–44 (London, Routledge 1989).

119. Smart, *supra* note 118, at 138–44.

120. Hilary Charlesworth *et al.*, *Feminist Approaches to International Law*, 85 Am. J. Int'l L. 613, 635–38 (1991); Donna E. Arzt, *The Application of International Human Rights Law in Islamic States*, 12 Hum. Rts. Q. 202, 203 (1990); Helen Bequaert Holmes, *A Feminist Analysis of the Universal Declaration of Human Rights*, in Beyond Domination: New Perspectives on Women and Philosophy 250, 252–5 (Carol C. Gould ed., Totowa, Rowman & Allanheld 1983).

121. David Kairys, *Freedom of Speech*, in The Politics of the Law 140, 141 (David Kairys ed., New York, Pantheon Books 1982).

122. Patricia J. Williams, *Alchemical Notes: Reconstructing Ideals from Deconstructed Rights*, 22 Harv. C.R.-C.L. L. Rev. 401, 431 (1987).

123. Albie Sachs, *quoted in Economic and Social Rights and the Right to Health* 42 (Cambridge, Harvard Law School Human Rights Program 1995).

The significance of rights discourse outweighs its disadvantages. Human rights provides an alternative and additional language and framework to the welfare and protection approach to the global situation of women, which presents women as victims or dependents.[124] It allows women to claim specific entitlements from a specified obligation-holder. Because human rights discourse is the dominant progressive moral philosophy and a potent social movement operating at the global level,[125] it is important for women to engage with, and contest, its parameters.

Women's Rights in International Law[126]

At first sight, the international law of human rights offers considerable protection to women. The concerned activity of women's groups at the international level from early in the twentieth century is reflected in the range of instruments dealing with women.[127] Provisions in treaties dealing with women have been categorized as falling into three categories: protective, corrective, and non-discriminatory.[128] Some treaties contain elements of all three categories. 'Protective' treaties assume that women should be treated differently from men in particular circumstances because they are physically different from and more vulnerable than men. Examples include the ILO's Convention Concerning Night Work of Women Employed in Industry,[129] which limits the amount of night work women can undertake, and provisions of the Third Geneva Convention that require particular treatment for women prisoners of war.[130] While specific provisions for women acknowledge the differences in women's and men's lives, 'protective' laws also tend to stereotype women as weak and helpless.... Corrective' treaties attempt to improve women's treatment without making overt comparison to the situation of men. Conventions dealing with trafficking in women[131] or with the requirement for women to marry only with their full and free consent[132] are examples of 'corrective' treaties.

The major focus of the protection of women's rights has been the right to equal treatment and non-discrimination on the basis of sex.[133] The UN Charter was the first international agreement to establish non-discrimination on the basis of sex as a basic right. It refers in its Preamble to 'the equal rights of men and women' and includes as a purpose

---

124. Christine Ainetter Brautigam, *Mainstreaming a Gender Perspective in the Work of the United Nations Human Rights Treaty Bodies*, in Proceedings of the 91st Annual Meeting of the American Society of International Law 389, 390 (Washington DC, Am. Soc'y of Int'l Law 1997).

125. V. Spike Peterson, *Whose Rights? A Critique of the "Givens" in Human Rights Discourse*, 15 Alternatives 303, 303–04. For an investigation of the way moral philosophies have been generated in the international sphere *see* Anne Orford, *Locating the International: Military and Monetary Interventions after the Cold War*, 38 Harv. Int'l L.J. 443 (1997).

126. Charlesworth & Chinkin, *supra* note 24, at 212–18.

127. *See further* Jane Connors, *NGOs and the Human Rights of Women at the United Nations*, in The Conscience of the World: The Influence of Non-Governmental Organisations in the UN System 147 (Peter Willetts ed., Washington DC, Brookings Inst. 1996).

128. Natalie Kaufman Hevener, *An Analysis of Gender Based Treaty Law: Contemporary Developments in Historical Perspective*, 8 Hum. Rts. Q. 70, 71 (1986).

129. Revised 9 July 1948, 81 U.N.T.S. 285.

130. Geneva Convention Relative to the Treatment of Prisoners of War, 12 August 1949, 75 U.N.T.S. 135, arts. 14, 16, and 49.

131. *E.g.*, Convention for the Suppression of the Traffic in Women and Children, 24 April 1950, 53 U.N.T.S. 39.

132. *E.g.*, Convention on the Nationality of Married Women, 29 January 1957, 309 U.N.T.S. 65.

133. A useful guide to the literature on women's rights is Rebecca J. Cook & Valerie L. Oosterveld, *A Select Bibliography of Women's Human Rights*, 44 Am. U. L. Rev. 1429 (1995).

of the UN the promotion and encouragement of respect for human rights and fundamental freedoms for all without distinction based on sex....[134]

GENERAL INSTRUMENTS

The right of women to equal treatment and non-discrimination on the basis of sex is
part of the international canon of human rights. General human rights treaties at both
the global and regional levels contain rights of non-discrimination on a number of bases
that include sex and prohibit distinctions based on sex with respect to the enjoyment of
rights.[135] For example, article 3 of the ICCPR provides that 'States Parties ... undertake
to ensure the equal right of men and women to the enjoyment of all civil and political rights
set forth in the present Covenant.' More generally, article 26 provides:

> All persons are equal before the law and are entitled without any discrimination
> to the equal protection of the law. In this respect, the law shall prohibit any dis-
> crimination and guarantee to all persons equal and effective protection against
> discrimination on any ground such as race, color, sex, language, religion, polit-
> ical or other opinion, national or social origin, property, birth or other status....

WOMEN-SPECIFIC INSTRUMENTS

A number of international instruments focus entirely or in part on discrimination
against women.[136] These include the Convention on the Political Rights of Women,[137] the
Convention on the Nationality of Married Women, and the Convention on Consent to
Marriage, Minimum Age of Marriage and Registration of Marriages.[138] The most wide-
ranging of the international human rights treaties devoted to women is the Women's Convention, adopted by the UN General Assembly in 1979.[139] The Convention contains a
broader definition of discrimination than that contained in the earlier treaties, covering
both equality of opportunity (formal equality) and equality of outcome (*de facto* equality). It states that discrimination against women means: any distinction, exclusion or restriction made on the basis of sex which has the effect or purpose of impairing or nullifying
the recognition, enjoyment or exercise by women, irrespectively of their marital status,
on a basis of equality of men and women, of human rights and fundamental freedoms
in the political, economic, social, cultural, civil or any other field.[140] The Women's Convention also covers discrimination in the civil, political, social, economic, and cultural
fields....[141]

---

134. Charter of the UN, 26 June 1945, article 1(3). Other references in the Charter to non-discrimination on the basis of sex are in arts. 13, 55(c) and 76(c).

135. *E.g.,* ICCPR, articles 2, 3, and 26; ICESCR, articles 3 and 7; American Convention on Human
Rights, art. 1; African Charter of Human and Peoples' Rights, arts. 2 and 18(3); European Convention on Human Rights, art. 14.

136. For a useful overview of these Instruments *see* Rebecca J. Cook, *Women, in* THE UNITED NA-
TIONS LEGAL ORDER 433 (Oscar Schachter & Christopher C. Joyner eds.,Cambridge, Cambridge University Press 1995). *See also* MALVINA HALBERSTAM & ELIZABETH F. DE FEIS, WOMEN'S LEGAL RIGHTS:
INTERNATIONAL COVENANTS AS AN ALTERNATIVE TO ERA? 18–33 (Dobbs Ferry, Transnational Pub-
lishers 1987).

137. 20 December 1952, 193 U.N.T.S. 135.

138. 7 November 1962, 521 U.N.T.S. 231.

139. *See generally,* LARS ADAM REHOF, GUIDE TO THE TRAVAUX PREPARATOIRES OF THE UNITED
NATIONS CONVENTION ON THE ELIMINATION OF ALL FORMS OF DISCRIMINATION AGAINST WOMEN
(Dordrecht, Martinus Nijhoff 1993).

140. Convention on the Elimination of All Forms of Discrimination against Women, Art. I.

141. *Id.* at art. 3.

Inadequacies of Human Rights Law for Women[142]

By its nature, human rights law is vulnerable to non-observance. As we noted above, the basis of human rights principles is that a government's power over its people is limited in a variety of ways. This claim poses a direct challenge to the idea of state sovereignty, and states have identified many avenues of resistance to it. Despite problems of implementation and enforcement, human rights law has an important role in the international community as a statement, in Johan Galtung's phrase, of the 'elements of humanity.'[143] It sets out a particular understanding of the basic conditions necessary for a good life. Our argument is that, in this important symbolic function, human rights law privileges one category of persons, men, over another, women....

Marginalization of Women's Rights

In many ways, the creation of a specialized 'women's' branch of human rights law, of which the Women's Convention is the flagship, has allowed its marginalization. 'Mainstream' human rights institutions have tended to ignore the application of human rights norms to women....

In 1994, the UN on Human Rights appointed the Sri Lankan jurist, Radhika Coomaraswamy, as Special Rapporteur on Violence against Women.[144] This was the first gender-specific mandate of a Special Rapporteur. In her reports, Ms. Coomaraswamy has drawn attention to the phenomenon of violence against women in a systematic manner and made valuable proposals for change. But the very nature of the mandate may be viewed as an ambivalent advance for women in the international legal order because it can be read as implying that violence against women does not constitute torture, nor is it within the mandates of 'general' Special Rapporteurs, such as those on the right to life, disappearances and religious intolerance....[145]

Inadequate Enforcement and Implementation

Ineffective implementation of existing provisions relating to women's right to equality have reduced the force of international legal regulation. Implementation of the Women's Convention is affected by its relatively weak language, by the reservations states parties have made to its terms, and by the limited monitoring methods provided for in the Convention itself. The operative language of the Convention is much weaker, compared, for example, with the Race Convention. Most of the obligations imposed on states parties to the Women's Convention involve taking 'all appropriate measures,' a term that leaves considerable discretion to individual states. The Race Convention contains more immediate binding obligations....

The only method provided for monitoring the Women's Convention is that of states parties making periodic reports to the CEDAW Committee, established by article 18 of the Convention. The reporting system under human rights treaties generally has been strongly criticized as being inefficient and inefficacious....[146]

---

142. Charlesworth & Chinkin, *supra* note 24, at 218–44.

143. Johan Galtung, Human Rights in Another Key 2 (Oxford, Polity Press 1994).

144. CHR Res. 1994/45, UN Doc. ESCOR, 1994, Supp. no. 4, 11 March 1994. The mandate was renewed in 1997, CHR Res. 1997/44.

145. The Special Rapporteur on Religious Intolerance has noted that the Commission on Human Rights has emphasized the need for a gender perspective and has stated that he intends to pay particular attention in future to the status of women. UN Doc. A/52/477, 16 October 1997.

146. Anne F. Bayefsky, *Making the Human Rights Treaties Work, in* Human Rights: An Agenda for the Next Century 229, 233–36 (Louis Henkin & John Lawrence Hargrove eds., Washington DC, Am. Soc'y of Int'l Law 1994).

The Influence of Cultural Relativism

One strong response to the creation of a universal system of human rights protection has been assertions of the philosophy of cultural relativism. Indeed it has been argued that 'cultural relativism dominates social, political, and academic thought today.'[147] The claim is that if international human rights norms conflict with particular cultural standards, the particularity of culture must take precedence over universalizing trends....[148]

... Claims of cultural relativism are rejected by many proponents of human rights because they challenge the validity and retard the development of universal standards.[149] Such proponents have pointed out that subordinating human rights to cultural traditions provides no objective yardstick against which state behavior may be assessed; that it allows human rights to be traded as negotiable commodities; that it reconstructs the 'domestic jurisdiction' screen behind which authoritarian governments can shelter; and that it is based on the assumption that human rights standards are good for people in some parts of the world, but irrelevant elsewhere....

The issue of female genital surgeries has been raised in international fora under the umbrella term 'traditional practices.'... Generally, the issue of female genital mutilation has been discussed as implicating women's and girls' right to health.[150] This has proved to be the most acceptable context for international focus on the issue because it does not challenge its cultural or gender dimensions.[151] However, such an analysis may lead to the problematic conclusion that the surgeries are appropriate if medically supervised.[152] In 1993, the UN General Assembly's Declaration on the Elimination of Violence against Women defined violence as including female genital mutilation 'and other traditional practices harmful to women.'...[153]

The Vienna Declaration of 1993 expressed 'respect' for cultural and religious diversity, but reaffirmed the universality of human rights. It considered cultural and religious practices in the context of violence against women, but did not offer any resolution of the tension between rights to culture and religion and women's rights. It called only for the eradication of conflict between women's rights and 'the harmful effects of certain traditional or religious practices, cultural prejudices, and religious extremism,' without stipulating that such eradication should promote women's rights.[154]

---

147. Kathleen Barry, Female Sexual Slavery 163 (New York, New York University Press 1984).

148. *See generally*, Alison Dundes Renteln, *The Unanswered Challenge of Relativism and the Consequences of Human Rights*, 7 Hum. Rts. Q. 514 (1985); Abdullahi A. An-Na'im, *Religious Minorities under Islamic Law and the Limits of Cultural Relativism*, 9 Hum. Rts. Q. 1 (1987).

149. *E.g.*, Fernando R. Teson, *International Human Rights and Cultural Relativism*, 25 Va. J. Int'l L. 869 (1985); Nancy Kim, *Towards a Feminist Theory of Human Rights: Straddling the Fence between Western Imperialism and Uncritical Absolutism*, 25 Colum. Hum. Rts. L.J. 47 (1993).

150. *E.g.*, Fourth World Conference on Women, Declaration and Platform for Action, UN Doc A/CONF.177/20, 15 September 1995, *reprinted in* 35 I.L.M. 401 (1996). Beijing Platform for Action, para. 281 (I). The Convention on the Rights of the Child, article 24(3) requires states parties to take all effective and appropriate measures with a view to abolishing traditional practices prejudicial to the health of children.

151. For an argument in favor of what she terms 'clinicalization' *see* Leslye Amende Obiora, *Bridges and Barricades: Rethinking Polemics and Intransigence in the Campaign against Female Circumcision*, 47 Case W. Res. L. Rev. 275 (1997) and the rejection of this view by Dawit in a letter to the symposium on the topic: Beijing Platform for Action, para. 268.

152. Isabelle R. Gunning, *Arrogant Perception, World Travelling and Multicultural Feminism: The Case of Female Genital Surgeries*, 23 Colum. Hum. Rts. L. Rev. 189, 237 (1992).

153. G.A. Res. 48/104, 20 December 1993. *See also* Beijing Platform for Action, para. 113.

154. Vienna Declaration and Programme of Action, II, para. 38.

THE LIMITED UNDERSTANDING OF 'EQUALITY' IN INTERNATIONAL LAW

A major reason for the circumscribed protection of women in international human rights law is that the existing law identifies sexual equality with equal treatment. This 'liberal' feminist approach explains the centrality of the norm of non-discrimination, rather than a fuller set of rights, in the international law on women's rights....[155]

In 1995, the Beijing Declaration and Platform for Action elaborated in detail the international understanding of women's equality. Equality is generally presented as women being treated in the same way as men, or at least having the same opportunity to be so treated, with little consideration of whether the existing male standards are appropriate. The Platform calls for women's equal participation in a wide range of areas — from the economy[156] and politics[157] to environmental management.[158] The assumption appears to be that women's inequality is removed once women participate equally in decision-making fora.[159] This account of equality ignores the underlying structures and power relations that contribute to the oppression of women. While increasing the presence of women is certainly important, it does not of itself transform these structures. We also need to understand and address the gendered aspects of fundamental concepts such as 'the economy,' 'work,' 'democracy,' 'politics,' and 'sustainable development.'[160]

'HUMAN' RIGHTS AS MEN'S RIGHTS

The international law of human rights is inadequate as a response to the global position of women because it has been developed in a gendered way. Here we attempt to justify this claim, using examples from each 'generation' of rights. Despite their apparently different philosophical bases, the three generations are remarkably similar in their exclusion of women's perspectives.

With the exception of the Children's Convention and the International Convention on the Protection of the Rights of All Migrant Workers and Members of Their Families, all the 'general' human rights instruments use only the masculine pronoun.

Another feature of the human rights treaties is the attention they pay to the idea of the family. The family is presented as 'the natural and fundamental group unit of society' and is thus 'entitled to protection by society and the State.'...[161]

FIRST GENERATION RIGHTS

... The operation of a public/private distinction at a gendered level is most clear in the definition of civil and political rights, particularly those concerned with protection of the individual from violence. The construction of these norms obscures the most pervasive harms done to women. One example of this is often considered the most important

---

155. Compare the Convention on the Rights of the Child which contains a catalogue of children's rights.

156. *E.g.,* Beijing Platform for Action, paras. 58 to 66.

157. *Id.* at paras. 190 to 195.

158. *Id.* at paras. 253 to 255.

159. Dianne Otto, *Holding Up Half the Sky, but for Whose Benefit? A Critical Analysis of the Fourth World Conference on Women,* 6 AUSTRALIAN FEMINIST LAW JOURNAL 7, 13 (1996). *See also* Yumi Lee, *Violence against Women: Reflections on the Past and Strategies for the Future — An NGO Perspective,* 19 ADELAIDE LAW REVIEW 45 (1997).

160. Otto, *supra* note 159, at 14, 20–22.

161. *E.g.,* Universal Declaration of Human Rights (UDHR), art. 16(3).

of all human rights,[162] the right to life contained in article 6 of the ICCPR[163] and in regional human rights treaties.[164] The right is primarily concerned with the arbitrary deprivation of life through public action. Protection from arbitrary deprivation of life or liberty through public action, important as it is, does not, however, address the ways in which being a women is in itself life-threatening and the special ways in which women need legal protection to be able to enjoy their right to life....

The international prohibition on torture is similarly limited.[165] A central feature of the international legal definition of torture is that it takes place in the public realm: it must be 'inflicted by or at the instigation of or with the consent or acquiescence of a public official or other person acting in an 'official capacity.'[166] Although many women are victims of torture in this 'public sense,' by far the greatest violence against women occurs in the 'private' non-governmental sphere....

If violence against women is understood not just as aberrant behavior but as part of the structure of the universal subordination of women, it cannot be considered a purely 'private' issue....

In 1993, the UN General Assembly adopted the Declaration on the Elimination of Violence against Women which supports this approach.[167] The Declaration is a valuable development in women's international human rights law because it affirms that violence against women is an international issue and because it defines gender-based violence in a broad manner. Violence against women is analyzed as 'a manifestation of historically unequal power relationships between men and women'....

Apart from the rights to life and freedom from torture, other rights in the traditional civil and political catalogue have been interpreted in ways that offer very little freedom or protection to women. The right to liberty and security of the person set out in article 9 of the ICCPR, for example, has been considered to operate only in the context of di-

---

162. Yoram Dinstein, *The Right to Life, Physical Integrity, and Liberty*, in THE INTERNATIONAL BILL OF RIGHTS: THE COVENANT ON CIVIL AND POLITICAL RIGHTS 114 (Louis Henkin ed., New York, Columbia University Press 1981).

163. *See also* UDHR, art. 3.

164. There is debate among various commentators as to how narrowly the right should be construed. Fawcett has suggested that the right to life entails protection only from the acts of government agents: J.E.S. Fawcett, *The Application of the European Convention on Human Rights*, in TRANSNATIONAL LAW IN A CHANGING SOCIETY; ESSAYS IN HONOUR OF PHILIP C. JESSUP 228, 238–39 (Wolfgang Friedmann *et al.* eds., New York, Columbia University Press 1972). Dinstein noted that it may be argued under article 6 that 'the state must at least exercise due diligence to prevent the international deprivation of the life of one individual by another.' He seemed, however, to confine the obligation to take active precautions against loss of life only in cases of riots, mob action or incitement against minority groups: Dinstein, *supra* note 161, at 119. Ramcharan has argued for a still wider interpretation of the right to life, 'plac[ing] a duty on the part of each government to pursue policies which are designed to ensure access to the means of survival for every individual within its country.' B. G. Ramcharan, *The Concept and Dimensions of the Right to Life*, in THE RIGHTS TO LIFE IN INTERNATIONAL LAW 1, 6–8 (Dordrecht/Boston, Martinus Nijhoff 1985). The examples of major modern threats to the right to life offered by Ramcharan, however, do not encompass violence outside the 'public' sphere.

165. *See* Charlesworth *et al., supra* note 120, at 628–29. *See also* Christine Chinkin, *Torture of the Girl Child*, in CHILDHOOD ABUSED: PROTECTION OF CHILDREN AGAINST TORTURE, CRUEL, INHUMAN AND DEGRADING TREATMENT AND PUNISHMENT 81 (Geraldine Van Bueren ed., Aldershot, Dartmouth Publishing Co./Ashgate Publishing Co. 1998).

166. UN Convention against Torture, article 1(1).

167. *See* Charlesworth & Chinkin, *supra* note 24, chapter 3 for a discussion of its normative status in international law.

rect action by the state. It has only recently been understood to address the fear of sexual violence, which is a significant aspect of many women's lives.[168] The right to free movement within a territory and to have the free choice of residence have not been interpreted to cover situations where women are forbidden by husbands or other male relatives to leave their homes.[169] The right to freedom of expression has been defined in some national contexts as including the right to make, distribute, and use pornography, which contributes directly to the level of violence against women.[170] And although the right to privacy has been valuable for women in some national contexts,[171] it can also be interpreted as protecting from scrutiny the major sites for the oppression of women—home, family, religion, and culture....

SECOND GENERATION RIGHTS

Second generation rights—economic, social, and cultural rights—might be thought to apply in both public and private spheres and thus offer more to women's lives.[172] Certainly, the fact that these rights do not neatly fit the 'individual v. state' paradigm has contributed to their more controversial status, the weaker language of obligation and weaker methods of implementation at international law. The definition of these rights as set out in the ICESCR, however, indicates the tenacity of a gendered public/private distinction in human rights law. The ICESCR creates a public sphere by assuming that all effective power rests with the state. But, as Shelley Wright has pointed out, 'For most women, most of the time, indirect subjection to the State will always be mediated through direct subjection to individual men or groups of men.'[173] The ICESCR, then, does not touch on the economic, social, and cultural context in which most women live....

THIRD GENERATION RIGHTS

... The theoretical and practical development of third generation rights has, however, delivered very little to women. For example, as chapter 5 explains, the right to self-determination, allowing 'all peoples' to 'freely determine their political status and freely pursue their economic, social, and cultural development' has been invoked, and supported, recently in a number of contexts that allow the oppression of women....

The failure to value 'private' women's work is one basis for the observation that overall, the process of development exacerbates the problems of women in the South.[174] The differential valuation of the work of women to that of men often means that, within the family, women will not have an equal claim to food and other necessities....

---

168. West, *supra* note 117, at 67.

169. WOMEN OF THE ARAB WORLD: THE COMING CHALLENGE (Nahid Toubia ed., New York, St. Martin's Press 1988).

170. *See* CATHERINE A. MACKINNON, FEMINISM UNMODIFIED: DISCLOSURES ON LIFE AND LAW 163–97 (Cambridge, Harvard University Press 1987).

171. Karen Engle, *After the Collapse of the Public/Private Distinction: Strategizing Women's Rights, in* RECONCEIVING REALITY, *supra* note 28, at 148.

172. Compare Stark, *The "Other" Half of the International Bill of Rights as a Postmodern Feminist Text, in* RECONCEIVING REALITY, *supra* note 28, at 19.

173. Shelley Wright, *Economic Rights and Social Justice: A Feminist Analysis of Some International Human Rights Conventions*, 12 AUSTL. Y.B. INT'L L. 241, 249 (1992).

174. JANET MOMSEN & JANET TOWNSEND, GEOGRAPHY OF GENDER IN THE THIRD WORLD (Albany, State University of New York Press 1987). *See further* HILKKA PIETILA & JEANNE VICKERS, MAKING WOMEN MATTER: THE ROLE OF THE UNITED NATIONS (London, Zed Books 1994).

Women and Human Rights Law[175]

... Although the Optional Protocol to the Women's Convention is not significantly stronger than existing treaty complaints mechanisms, the availability of the procedure will strengthen the force of the Convention. It will allow women in states that accept the Optional Protocol to invoke international standards and scrutiny when national laws are inadequate. It will also generate a body of jurisprudence interpreting the Women's Convention. The linking of the complaints mechanism of the Inter-American Convention on Violence against Women with that of the Inter-American Convention on Human Rights[176] offers a similar prospect.

Conclusion[177]

Women's international human rights must be developed on a number of fronts. First, it is important to document the relevance of the traditional canon of human rights to women. Second, the instruments and institutions of international law with respect to women must be supported and strengthened. Third, the boundaries of the traditional human rights canon must be redefined to accommodate women's lives. At the same time, rights that focus on harms sustained by women in particular need to be identified and developed, challenging the public/private distinction by bringing rights discourse into the private sphere. This has been described by Radhika Coomaraswamy as a fourth generation of women's rights.[178] The definition of specifically women's rights is one way of moving beyond the limitations of the non-discrimination focus of women's international human rights law. These rights may include those associated with reproductive choice and childbirth.[179] Other potential women's rights include the right to a minimum wage for work within the home or in subsistence farming, and the right to literacy.

Human rights are, in essence, what we want to take out of the agenda of short-term politics.[180] They create 'a protective sphere for vital interests, and people need to persuade them that they may accept vulnerability, run risks, undertake adventures in the world, and operate as citizens and as people.'[181] The two major challenges to all human rights, and especially to those of women, in the twenty-first century will be the forces of religious extremism and of economic globalization.

---

175. Charlesworth & Chinkin, *supra* note 24, at 244–47.

176. Inter-American Convention on the Prevention, Punishment, and Eradication of Violence against Women, 9 June 1994, *reprinted* in 33 I.L.M. 1534 (1994), arts. 11 and 12.

177. Charlesworth & Chinkin, *supra* note 24, at 247–49.

178. Radhika Coomaraswamy, *Reinventing International Law*, *in* Debating Human Rights 167, 181–2 (Peter Van Ness ed., London/New York, Routledge 1999).

179. Noreen Burrows, *International Law and Human Rights: The Case of Women's Rights*, *in* Human Rights: From Rhetoric to Reality 8, 85 (Tom Campbell *et al.* eds., New York, Basil Blackwell 1986).

180. Roberto Mangabeira Unger, *quoted in Economic and Social Rights and the Right to Health*, *supra* note 123, at 13.

181. *Id.*

Chapter 2

The United Nations and Women's Human Rights Treaties

A. Introduction to the United Nations, Its Structure and Human Rights System Establishing Women's Human Rights Treaties

This chapter delves into more detail concerning the human rights provisions of the Charter of the United Nations and the laws and institutions effecting women's rights within the UN framework.

The laws and institutions protecting women's human rights derive either from the UN Charter itself or from the human rights conventions adopted by the United Nations. The Charter of the United Nations,[1] The Universal Declaration of Human Rights,[2] The International Covenant on Civil and Political Rights,[3] The International Covenant on Economic, Social, and Cultural Rights,[4] The Convention on the Elimination of All Forms of Discrimination against Women,[5] and The Convention on the Rights of Persons with Disabilities[6] are some of the treaties that most directly affect women's rights. All the human rights treaties discussed in this chapter affect women's human rights intermittently or indirectly, but these treaties deal more specifically with the civil, political, social, economic,

---

1. Charter of the United Nations, adopted June 26, 1945, 557 U.N.T.S. 143 (entered into force 24 October 1945), as amended by G.A. Res. 1991 (XVIII) Dec. 17, 1963 (entered into force Aug. 31 1965), *available at* www.un.org/en/documents/charter/index.html (192 Member States) [hereinafter UN Charter].

2. Universal Declaration of Human Rights, adopted 10 Dec.1948, G.A. Res. 217A (III), 3 UN GAOR, UN Doc. A/810, at 71 (1948), *available at* http://www.un.org/en/documents/udhr.htm [hereinafter UDHR].

3. International Covenant on Civil and Political Rights, adopted Dec. 16, 1966, 999 U.N.T.S. 171 (entered into force Mar. 23, 1976), *reprinted in* 6 I.L.M. 368 (l967), *available at* http://www2.ohchr. org/english/law/ccpr.htm (160 states parties) [hereinafter ICCPR].

4. International Covenant on Economic, Social, and Cultural Rights, adopted 16 Dec. 1966, 993 U.N.T.S. 3 (entered into force Jan. 3, 1976), *reprinted in* 6 I.L.M. 360 (1967), *available at* http://www2. ohchr.org/english/law/cescr.htm (156 states parties) [hereinafter ICESCR].

5. Convention on the Elimination of All Forms of Discrimination against Women, adopted 18 Dec. 1979, entered into force 3 Sept. 1981, 1249 U.N.T.S. 13, *reprinted in* 19 I.L.M. 33 (1980), *available at* http://www.un.org/womenwatch/daw/cedaw/text/econvention.htm (185 states parties) [hereinafter CEDAW].

6. Convention on the Rights of Persons with Disabilities, adopted 13 Dec. 2006, G.A. Res. 61/106, 61 UN GAOR, Supp. (No. 49), UN Doc. A/RES/61/106/Annex I, at 65 (2006), *available at* http://www2.ohchr.org/english/law/disabilties-convention.htm (140 states parties) [hereinafter CRPD].

and cultural rights of women. Before examining the major UN human rights laws themselves, which can be found in the Appendix to this book, let us first look at the United Nations human rights structure and system.

1.   The Structure of the United Nations

The United Nations structure is outlined in the UN Charter establishing the General Assembly (Chapter IV, Articles 9–22); the Security Council (Chapter V, Articles 23–32, Chapter VI, and Chapter VII), giving the Security Council the duty to determine the existence of any threat to the peace and to make recommendations or decide measures to maintain or restore international peace and security; the International Economic and Social Council (Chapter X); the International Trusteeship System (Chapter XII); the International Court of Justice (Chapter XIV); and the Secretariat (Chapter XV).

The UN human rights system consists of a two-track approach to achieve its goal of protecting human rights through either UN charter-based organs or through UN treaty-based organs. Charter-based organs are directly mandated by the UN Charter such as the General Assembly and the Human Rights Council (the successor to the former Commission on Human Rights). The Human Rights Council now plays the role originally played by the Economic and Social Council known as ECOSOC. Charter-based UN organs are also indirectly authorized by one of those bodies, such as the Sub-Commission on the Promotion and Protection of Human Rights and the Commission on the Status of Women. Treaty-based organs or committees are created by the many human rights conventions established by the United Nations. For example, the Human Rights Committee is formed under the ICCPR; the CESCR Committee is formed under the ICESCR, and the CEDAW Committee is formed under CEDAW. These treaty-based organs monitor compliance by states with their obligations under the respective treaties.

The principle organs created by the UN Charter in 1945 are the Security Council, the General Assembly, the Economic and Social Council, the Trusteeship Council, the Secretariat, and the International Court of Justice. The Trusteeship Council became defunct in 1994 because of the success of the post-war decolonization process. ECOSOC, mandated by Article 61 of the UN Charter, consists of 54 members of the UN elected by the General Assembly. ECOSOC used to be the intermediary between the General Assembly and the former UN Commission on Human Rights, but since 1970 ECOSOC's role as coordinator of the disparate UN system has diminished. The Human Rights Council, created in 2006 to replace the Human Rights Commission, bypasses the role of ECOSOC so that the Human Rights Council can report directly to the General Assembly. The main role today of ECOSOC is to grant "consultative status" with the UN to nongovernmental organizations.

The Security Council and the International Court of Justice have both become more involved in human rights matters since the 1990s. The Secretariat is led by the Secretary-General, who is appointed for five years by the General Assembly on the recommendation of the Security Council. The Security Council has 15 members, 5 of which are permanent members (US, France, England, Russia, and China) each with veto power. Article 24 of the UN Charter confers on the Security Council the primary responsibility for the maintenance of international peace and security, and the UN agrees to accept and carry out the decisions of the Security Council (Article 25). Article 27 of the UN Charter states that decisions on procedural matters must be made through an affirmative vote of nine members of the Security Council. Decisions on all other matters shall be made by an affirmative vote of nine members including the concurring votes of the permanent members. Thus, the appointment of the Secretary-General may be vetoed by any one member of the five permanent members of the Security Council.

The Secretary-General is typically reluctant to intercede actively in human rights issues because the Secretary-General does not want to offend any one nation and thereby jeopardize his overriding goal of promoting international peace and security. For example, in 1993 the proposal leading to the creation of the important post of High Commissioner for Human Rights was opposed by Secretary-General Boutros Boutros-Ghali of Egypt. But Kofi Annan, of Ghana, who became Secretary General in 1997, viewed human rights more favorably than any of his predecessors. He appointed a series of strong High Commissioners for Human Rights. Kofi Annan actually mainstreamed human rights throughout the UN so UN bodies dealing with development, peacekeeping or environment were encouraged to consider human rights issues relating to their particular work.

The High Commissioner for Human Rights (HCHR) is the UN official with principal responsibility for human rights. She or he is subject to the direction and authority of the Secretary-General. The Office of the High Commission for Human Rights is one of the key organs affecting the implementation of human rights. The High Commission is appointed by the Secretary-General with approval of the General Assembly, for four years and one possible renewal term.

The General Assembly is composed of all UN Member States each having one vote regardless of population, wealth or any other factor. Most issues (except peace and security, admission of new Members, and budgetary matters requiring two-thirds majority vote) are decided in the General Assembly by a simple majority vote. Its resolutions are not legally binding *per se*, but they reflect the will of the world community. The General Assembly has six Main Committees, three of which relate to human rights in particular: The Social, Humanitarian, and Cultural Committee, the Budgetary Committee, and the Legal Committee.

The UN Human Rights Council replaced the UN Commission on Human Rights which was established in 1946 but was later discredited and viewed by many as a politically-charged body. The UN Council now consists of 47 member governments, one-third elected every year by an absolute majority of the UN General Assembly. States may have two consecutive three-year terms. The Council meets three times each year for a total minimum of ten weeks, and it can meet in Special Sessions.

The Commission on the Status of Women was established in 1946 and reports to ECOSOC on policies designed to promote women's rights in the political, economic, civil, social, and education areas. The Commission on the Status of Women has 45 governmental representatives who meet for only 10 days each year. Nevertheless, this Commission drafted the key treaties dealing with women's rights including the 1953 Convention on the Political Rights of Women and the 1979 CEDAW Convention. It followed up events that occurred in the four UN Women's Conferences held since 1975, including the influential Beijing Conference of 1995.

2.   Human Rights and the Laws of the United Nations

a.   The Charter of the United Nations (UN Charter) (1945)[7]

The Charter of the United Nations was signed on June 26, 1945, in San Francisco at the San Francisco Conference which led to the founding of the United Nations. Article 1(3) of the United Nations Charter sets the goal of international cooperation to promote respect for human rights and fundamental freedoms for all as to race, sex, language, or religion. In Article 55, the UN sets out to encourage respect for the principle of equal rights and self-determination of peoples, in order to promote (a) higher standards of living, full employment, and conditions of economic and social progress and development; (b) solutions of international economic, social, health, and related problems; international cultural and educational cooperation; and (c) universal respect for, and observance of, human rights and fundamental freedoms for all without distinction as to race, sex, language, or religion. Article 56 of the UN Charter requires all members to pledge themselves to take joint and separate action in cooperation with the UN for the achievement of the purposes set forth in Article 55. To facilitate cooperation, Article 13(1) of the UN Charter provides that the General Assembly "shall initiate studies and make recommendations for the purpose of: ... (b) ... assisting in the realization of human rights and fundamental freedoms for all ..."

b.   The Universal Declaration of Human Rights (1948)[8]

The Universal Declaration is a declaration adopted by the United Nations General Assembly on December 10, 1948. It proclaims two broad categories of rights: civil and political as well as economic, social, and cultural rights. Civil and political rights include the right to life, liberty, and security of person; the prohibition of slavery, of torture, and cruel, inhuman or degrading treatment; the right not to be subjected to arbitrary arrest, detention or exile, the right to a fair trial in civil and criminal matters, the presumption of innocence, and the prohibition against the application of *ex post facto* laws and penalties. The right to privacy and the right to own property are also civil rights, as well as the right to the freedom of speech, religion, assembly, and freedom of movement, including the right to leave any country, including one's own, and to return to one's own country. The right to seek asylum from persecution and the right to a nationality (commonly denied to women who marry a man of a different nationality in certain Middle Eastern countries) are additional civil rights.

Article 21 of the Universal Declaration proclaims an individual's right to "take part in the government of his country, directly or through freely chosen representatives." The will of the people shall be the basis of the authority of government requiring periodic and genuine elections by universal suffrage.

Economic, social, and cultural rights, which are "indispensable for [a person's] dignity and the free development of *his* personality" are declared in Article 22. Examples are the right to social security, to work, and to "protection against unemployment," to "equal pay for equal work," and to "just and favorable remuneration ensuring for *himself* and *his* family an existence worthy of human dignity and supplemented, if necessary, by other means of social protection." It is interesting to note that while these last two rights are particu-

---

7. UN Charter, *supra* note 1. *See* Bertrand G. Ramcharan, The Fundamentals of International Human Rights Treaty Law (Martinus Nijhoff 2011).
8. UDHR, *supra* note 2.

larly applicable to women who are often denied equal pay for equal work and just remuneration for their work, the masculine pronouns "his" and "himself" are used here in the
Declaration and throughout the UN human rights treaties. The Declaration goes on to
enumerate other social, economic, and cultural rights such as the right "to rest and leisure,
including reasonable limitation of working hours and periodic holidays with pay (Art.
24); the right to "a standard of living adequate for the health and well-being of *himself* and
of *his* family." (Art. 25). An individual has the right to "security in the event of unemployment, sickness, disability, widowhood, old age or other lack of livelihood in circumstances beyond *his* control." (Art. 25). Article 26 states that education shall be free "at
least in the elementary and fundamental stages." Education shall be directed to the "strengthening of respect for human rights and fundamental freedoms." Article 27 provides cultural rights such as the "right freely to participate in the cultural life of the community,
to enjoy the arts and to share in scientific advancement and its benefits."

How can these human rights goals set forth in the United Nations Charter and the
Universal Declaration (which is not a treaty but merely a non-binding recommendation having no force of law) be accomplished? Today the international community attributes a moral and normative status to the Universal Declaration. Most international
lawyers believe that the Declaration is a normative instrument that reflects legal obligations for the Member States of the United Nations. But a debate still rages as to
whether all the rights proclaimed in the Declaration are binding. Does the obligatory
character of these rights derive from the Declaration's status as an authoritative interpretation of the rights contained in the UN Charter, or do the obligations derive from
customary international law? What transformed the Universal Declaration from a non-
binding recommendation to a quasi legal instrument is the attempt made by the international community for two long decades to adopt two international treaties, the
ICCPR and the ICESCR, each of which has its own enforcement mechanism and measures of implementation which are amplified by the Optional Protocol in the case of
the ICCPR.

c. The International Covenant on Civil and Political Rights (1966–1976)[9]

The International Covenant on Civil and Political rights is a multilateral treaty adopted
by the United Nations General Assembly on December 16, 1966, and entered into force
on March 23, 1976. The ICCPR commits its State Parties to respect the civil and political rights of individuals, including the right to life, freedom of religion, freedom of speech,
freedom of assembly, electoral rights, and rights to due process and a fair trial. As of December 2010, the ICCPR had 72 signatories and 167 parties. The United States signed
and ratified the ICCPR.

The civil and political rights enumerated in the ICCPR are more specific and more
numerous than those listed in the Universal Declaration. For example, the ICCPR
obliges states not to deny members of ethnic, religious or linguistic minorities the
right ... "to enjoy their own culture, to profess and practice their own religion, or to
use their own language." (Art. 27). Another right not proclaimed in the Universal Declaration is the right to be free from imprisonment for debt, the "right of all persons
deprived of their liberty to be treated with humanity and with respect for the inher-

---

9. ICCPR, *supra* note 3.

ent dignity of the human person," and the right of every child "to acquire a nationality" and to be accorded "such measures of protection as are required by his status as a minor."

The ICCPR contains a derogation clause permitting the States Parties "in time of public emergency that threatens the life of the nation" to suspend all but seven of the most fundamental rights (Art. 4). The ICCPR also permits States Parties to limit and restrict the exercise of some of its rights. For example, Article 18, which guarantees freedom of religion, also declares that the "freedom to manifest one's religion or beliefs may be subject only to such limitations as are prescribed by law and are necessary to protect public safety, order, health, or morals or the fundamental rights and freedoms of others." This restriction will be very important in the cases involving the ban on the wearing of the headscarf in public institutions in the European Court of Human Rights.

The ICCPR established the Human Rights Committee (HRC) to monitor compliance by the States Parties with the provisions of the treaty. The HRC administers a reporting system and the inter-State complaint mechanism which is provided for in the treaty. The First Optional Protocol to the ICPPR established the important right of individual petition to the HRC. The 18 members of the HRC examine the reports that all States Parties are required to submit "on the measures they have adopted which give effect to the rights" recognized by the treaty. The HRC can rely on information provided to them by nongovernmental organizations in examining state reports. The HRC has established guidelines to influence the States Parties to comply with their treaty obligations. The HRC has adopted a number of "General Comments" which it addresses to the State Parties in order to guide them in fulfilling their reporting duties under the treaty. These General Comments have become authoritative sources for the interpretation and application of the treaty.

d.   The First Optional Protocol to the ICCPR (1966–1976)[10]

This First Optional Protocol to the ICCPR was adopted as a separate instrument in 1966 and entered into force on March 23, 1976. It enhances the implementation of the ICCPR by enabling private individuals, claiming to be victims of civil and/or political rights violations, to file "individual" complaints or communications with the HRC. A complaint may only be filed against a State Party to the ICCPR that has also ratified the Protocol. There are more than 140 states that are parties to the ICCPR, and nearly 100 have ratified the Optional Protocol.

The individual petition system is a quasi-judicial system available only to those who have exhausted all available domestic remedies. Therefore, women who have been deprived of their basic civil or political rights in their own country, have the right to file a complaint before the HRC, only if they have been denied their rights to a trial in accordance with all the due process guarantees of a fair and speedy trial.

Since the Protocol entered into force in 1976, the HRC has had to deal with an increasing number of individual complaints of violations of civil and political rights. In dealing with these complaints, the HRC has developed an important body of case law interpreting the ICCPR and its application.

---

10. First Optional Protocol to the International Covenant on Civil and Political Rights, *adopted on* Dec. 16, 1966, 999 U.N.T.S. 302 (entered into force Mar. 23, 1976), *available at* www.umn.edu/humanrts/instree/b4ccprp1.htm.

e.   The Second Optional Protocol to the International Covenant on Civil and Political Rights (1989–1991)[11]

The Second Optional Protocol to the ICCPR was entered into force on July 11, 1991, after being opened for signature on December 15, 1989. This Protocol virtually abolishes the death penalty in Article 1. Notwithstanding this abolition, the death penalty may be applied in time of war pursuant to a conviction for a most serious crime of a military nature committed during wartime (Art. 2).

f.   The International Covenant on Economic, Social, and Cultural Rights (1966–1976)[12]

The International Covenant on Economic, Social, and Cultural Rights was adopted by the General Assembly of the United Nations on December 16, 1966, and entered into force on January 3, 1976. The ICESCR commits its State Parties to try to grant economic, social, and cultural rights to individuals, including labor rights and the right to health, the right to education, and the right to an adequate standard of living. As of July 2011, the ICESCR had 160 parties. Six countries had signed but not yet ratified the treaty. The United States has signed but not ratified the ICESCR.

The ICESCR contains many more economic, social, and cultural rights than those proclaimed in the Universal Declaration. The following rights are recognized: the right to work; the right to the enjoyment of just and favorable conditions of work; the right to form and join trade unions; the right to social security, including social insurance; the right to the protection of the family; the right to an adequate standard of living; the right to the enjoyment of the highest attainable standard of physical and mental health; the right of everyone to receive an education; and the right to take part in cultural life. Many of these rights fly in the face of cultural traditions that strictly prohibit women from working, receiving an education, or enjoying cultural events.

The ICESCR describes and defines these rights in detail and sets forth steps that should be taken to provide them. A State Party undertakes the obligation to take steps to achieve full realization of the rights recognized in the treaty by all appropriate means including the adoption of legislative measures. The ICESCR establishes the ESCR Committee, which does not have an individual complaints system like the HRC. The ESCR Committee requires the States Parties to submit "reports on the measures which they have adopted and the progress made in achieving the observance of the rights recognized herein." (Art. 16(1)). The reports are submitted to the UN ECOSOC, and the ESCR Committee does not review them or comment on them.

g.   The Optional Protocol to the ICESCR (2008)

The Optional Protocol to the International Covenant on Economic, Social, and Cultural Rights establishes complaint and inquiry mechanisms for the ICESCR. It was adopted by the UN General Assembly on December 10, 2008, and was opened for signature on September 24, 2008. It establishes an individual complaints mechanism similar to the First

---

11. Second Optional Protocol to the International Covenant on Civil and Political Rights, adopted Dec. 15, 1989, 1642 U.N.T.S. 414, (entered into force 11 July 1991), *available at* www.2ohchr.org/english/law/ccpr-death.htm.

12. ICESCR, *supra* note 4.

Optional Protocol to the ICCPR. As of October 2011, the Protocol has 30 signatories and 4 parties, and it will not enter into force until 10 parties have ratified it.

h.   The Convention on the Prevention and Punishment of the Crime of Genocide (1948–1951)[13]

The Genocide Convention was adopted by the UN General Assembly on December 9, 1948, and entered into force on January 12, 1951. The Genocide Convention is a major legal instrument in the development of international humanitarian rules as well as international human rights laws. It condemns genocide, committed in peacetime or wartime, and provides a definition of genocide. The Convention states that there shall be no immunity, and all persons committing this crime shall be punished, "whether they are constitutionally responsible rulers, public officials or private individuals." (Art. 4). However, the Genocide Convention does not establish a specific monitoring body or expert committee.

The Genocide Convention states that genocide, whether committed in time of peace or war, is a crime under international law, for which the individual perpetrator is punishable. (Art.1). Genocide is defined in Article 2 of the Convention as the commission of certain enumerated acts "with intent to destroy, in whole or in part, a national, ethnical, racial or religious group, as such: (a) killing members of the group; (b) causing serious bodily or mental harm to members of the group; (c) deliberately inflicting on the group conditions of life calculated to bring about its physical destruction in whole or in part; (d) imposing measures intended to prevent births within the group; (3) forcibly transferring children of the group to another group."

It is interesting to note the comparison between genocide and crimes against humanity. To be guilty of the crime of genocide under the Genocide Convention, an individual must have committed one of the acts above with the *specific intent* to destroy, in whole or in part, a national, ethnic, racial or religious group. Under the Nuremberg Charter, Article 6(c) defines crimes against humanity as "murder, extermination, enslavement, deportation and other inhumane acts committed against any civilian population before or during the war." Thus, perpetrators of crimes against humanity have a similar goal as perpetrators of genocide which is to destroy a specific group. However, unlike genocide, crimes against humanity do not require "intent." Neither genocide[14] nor crimes against humanity require a war for the acts to be considered criminal.

By systematically using the rape of women as a weapon of war in the Bosnia-Herzegovina war and in many of the wars in Africa, the *ad hoc* tribunals for the former Yugoslavia (ICTY) and Rwanda (ICTR) held that rape is a form of genocide because the perpetrators had the intention of destroying an entire population of women and children of a certain ethnic group, and ultimately that entire ethnic group. The Statutes of the UN *ad hoc* tribunals of the ICTY and the ICTR as well as the permanent International Criminal Court adopted the definition of genocide contained in the Genocide Convention as a basis for conferring jurisdiction over genocide on these tribunals. While the Genocide Convention is not typically considered a women's human rights treaty, we consider it to be critical to the understanding of the significance of the widespread rapes of women in war and the use of rape as a weapon of war. The Genocide Convention does protect

---

13. United Nations Convention on the Prevention and Punishment of the Crime of Genocide, Dec. 9, 1948, 78 U.N.T.S. 277, *available at* www.hrweb.org/legal/genocide/html.

14. *See* Samanatha Power, A Problem from Hell: America and the Age of Genocide (2003).

women when rape is used as method to eliminate an entire gender and ultimately an entire population. Thus, we are including the Genocide Convention as a treaty that indirectly provides and protects women's fundamental human rights.

i. The International Convention on the Elimination of All Forms of Racial Discrimination (1965–1969)[15]

The International Convention on the Elimination of All Forms of Racial Discrimination [CERD] is a United Nations Convention that was adopted by the United Nations General Assembly on December 21, 1965, and entered into force on January 4, 1969. As of February 2011, it has 85 signatories and 174 parties. The United States has signed it but does not accept any obligation to enact measures under Article 4 of the Convention, which bans hate speech, and which the US views as incompatible with the constitutional right of free speech.

CERD seeks to provide second generation rights. It commits its State Parties to the elimination of racial discrimination and the promotion of understanding among all races. The Convention also requires its State Parties to outlaw hate speech and criminalize membership in racist organizations. It has an individual complaints mechanism and is monitored by the CERD Committee.

CERD codifies the equality of the races and prohibits "racial discrimination, "which it defines as "any distinction, exclusion, restriction or preference based on race, color, descent, or national or ethnic origin" have the purpose or effect of "nullifying or impairing the recognition, enjoyment or exercise, on an equal footing, of human rights and fundamental freedoms in the political, economic, social, cultural, or any other field of public life." (Art. 1(l)). Since this Convention does not specifically affect women's human rights based on gender discrimination, we will not enter into details on the specific treaty obligations.

j. The International Convention on the Suppression and the Punishment of the Crime of Apartheid (1973–1976)[16]

The International Convention on the Suppression and the Punishment of the Crime of Apartheid [Apartheid Convention] was adopted and opened for signature by the UN General Assembly on November 30, 1973, and entered into force on July 18, 1976. It was ratified by more than 100 States. The Convention defines the crime of apartheid as "inhuman acts committed for the purpose of establishing and maintaining domination by one racial group of persons over any other racial group of persons and systematically oppressing them." The purpose of this treaty is to suppress and punish apartheid which is a crime against humanity in violation of the principles of international law. (Art. I). Apartheid is not only limited to the policies of racial segregation and discrimination in South Africa but covers similar policies in other regions of the world. (Art. II.) Since this Convention does not specifically affect women's human rights based on gender discrimination, we will not enter into details on the specific treaty obligations.

---

15. The International Convention on the Elimination of All Forms of Racial Discrimination, adopted Dec. 21, 1965, 660 U.N.T.S. 195 (entered into force Jan. 4, 1969), *available at* www2.ohchr.org/English/law/cerd.htm.

16. International Convention on the Suppression and the Punishment of the Crime of Apartheid, Nov. 30, 1973, G.A. Res. 3068, 28 UN GAOR (No. 50), UN Doc. A/9233/Add.1 (1973), *available at* www1.umn.edu/humanrts/instree/apartheid-supp.html.

k.   The Convention on the Elimination of All Forms of Discrimination against Women (1979–1981)[17]

The International Bill of Rights and other international human rights treaties do enumerate women's fundamental human rights; however, in 1963 the United Nations General Assembly recognized that their approach to women's rights was only fragmentary because the human rights treaties were poorly implemented and, therefore, failed to protect and promote women's rights or eliminate discrimination against women in a comprehensive manner. The UN Commission on the Status of Women was then asked to draft a comprehensive legal instrument articulating international standards for equal rights of men and women. The result of that request was the creation of the Convention on the Elimination of All Forms of Discrimination against Women [CEDAW] which was adopted by the UN General Assembly in 1979 and entered into force in 1981. President Carter did sign CEDAW on July 17, 1980, but the treaty was never ratified by the United States. In fact, the US is currently the only developed nation that has not ratified CEDAW; the six other UN member states that have not signed or ratified CEDAW are Iran, Nauru, Palau, Somalia, Sudan, and Tonga.

CEDAW requires all States Parties to the UN to submit periodic reports on any and all legislative, judicial, or administrative measures they have adopted to implement CEDAW. Following review and deliberation of each State Party's report, the CEDAW Committee then formulates concluding comments that identify underlying factors causing the State Party's difficulty to implement the Convention or to make positive changes toward that aim. The CEDAW Committee also identifies primary areas of its concern and makes suggestions and recommendations to enhance implementation of the Convention.

The UN General Assembly adopted CEDAW on December 18, 1979, and it entered into force on September 3, 1981. CEDAW specifically seeks to prohibit discrimination against women. Discrimination is defined as "any distinction, exclusion, or restriction made on the basis of sex" that impairs the enjoyment by women of "human rights and fundamental freedoms in the political, economic, social, cultural, civil or any other field." (Art. 1). States Parties must adopt laws prohibiting all forms of discrimination against women and administer sanctions against those violating these laws. (Art. 2). The goal of CEDAW is to advance the enjoyment of equal rights by women in all walks of life including the political, social, economic, and cultural fields. Article 5 specifies a challenging goal which is to "modify the social and cultural patterns of conduct of men and women" in order to eliminate prejudices and customary practices based on the inferiority or the superiority of one of the sexes or on stereotyped roles for men and women.

CEDAW is the key convention for women's human rights that has been described as the International Bill of Rights for Women. 186 countries have signed and ratified CEDAW. The United States has not ratified CEDAW basically because it believes CEDAW is in conflict with its constitutional rights of privacy, free speech and expression, and freedom of association. Moreover, the United States on principle does not usually approve of heavy government regulation of what some consider to be "private matters."

Several countries have signed and ratified the Convention subject to certain declarations, reservations, and objections. A "reservation" is defined in Article 2(1)(d) of the Vienna Convention on the Law of Treaties as a "unilateral statement made by a state when ratifying a treaty whereby it purports to exclude or modify the legal effect of certain provisions of the treaty in their application to that State." CEDAW has been subject to more reservations

---

17. CEDAW, *supra* note 5.

than any other international human rights treaty. In fact, of the 165 States Parties that signed on to CEDAW as of 2000, more than 67 made reservations to the treaty. However, Article 19 of the Vienna Convention on the Law of Treaties, and CEDAW itself stipulates in Article 28(2), that a state may not make a reservation that would "be incompatible with the object and purpose of the treaty." Several States Parties have violated that principle by making reservations to articles that represent the object and purpose of the treaty.

Specific reasons behind making a reservation may vary. States filing a reservation may believe that a particular form of protection against gender discrimination is irreconcilable with the customs and religion practiced in that state or with the country's legislation. For example, Turkey made reservations to articles regarding family relations which they held were incompatible with the Turkish Civil Code. Egypt made similar reservations regarding marital equality because this equality was in conflict with *Shari'a* law.

The effectiveness of CEDAW to promote the elimination of discrimination against women has been undermined by the number of reservations made by several ratifying States Parties to the treaty. The abundance of reservations signifies at least two important policies. States that sign and ratify the treaty with reservations indicate their belief in the over-arching principle of women's equality, but these states are not totally willing to give up their own customs, practices, and sovereignty regarding what they conceive of as "private" issues relating to women and the family. The abundance of reservations also dilutes the effectiveness of the treaty which is designed to eradicate these underlying notions of inequality inherent in certain cultural practices and beliefs. Nevertheless, some states believe that it is better to sign and ratify the treaty with reservations than not to sign it at all. The dilution of CEDAW by its large number of reservations signifies that the international community continues to place greater value on individual state sovereignty than on the protection of women's human rights.

The CEDAW Committee has attempted to convince States Parties to withdraw those reservations that are contrary to the object and purpose of the Convention or which are otherwise incompatible with international treaty law. More than two dozen states have, in fact, withdrawn their reservations.

CEDAW's provisions are implemented by periodic reports by States Parties to the CEDAW Committee that reviews the reports pursuant to Article 17 of the convention. The 23 experts of the CEDAW Committee then compile a report on its activities to the States Parties, the UN Commission on the Status of Women, and the General Assembly. The CEDAW Committee meets only two weeks per year according to Article 20(1), which is an insufficient time to comply with its obligations under the Convention.

l.   The Optional Protocol to CEDAW[18]

In the Optional Protocol to CEDAW, powers of the CEDAW Committee have been expanded to include consideration of individual complaints. The Optional Protocol to CEDAW was adopted by the UN General Assembly on October 6, 1999, and entered into force on December 22, 2000. The individual petitioner must not be anonymous and must first exhaust all available domestic remedies. The petitioner must show that she has not been examined under another procedure of international investigation or settlement and that the current Complaint has not been previously examined by the CEDAW Committee. The CEDAW Committee may request that urgent measures be taken by the State Party to prevent irreparable harm to the petitioner. The State Party has six months to

---

18. The full text of the Optional Protocol to CEDAW, October 15, 1999, 2121 U.N.T.S. 83, *is available at* www.un.org/womenwatch/daw/cedaw/protocol/text.htm.

consider the views of the CEDAW Committee and to provide a written response. Article 8 of the Optional Protocol establishes an inquiry procedure allowing the Committee to initiate a confidential investigation by one or more of its members, when it has received reliable information of grave or systematic violations by a State Party of rights established under CEDAW.

m. The Convention against Torture and Other Cruel, Inhuman or Degrading Treatment (1984–1987)[19]

The Convention against Torture and Other Cruel, Inhuman or Degrading Treatment [Torture Convention] or [CAT] was adopted by the UN General Assembly on December 10, 1984, and entered into force on June 26, 1987. The purpose of this convention is to prevent and punish torture committed "by or at the instigation of or with the consent or acquiescence of a public official or other person acting in an official capacity." (Art. 1(1)). CAT requires states to take effective measures to prevent torture within their borders and forbids states to return people to their home country if there is reason to believe they will be tortured. As of September 20, 2010, there are 77 signatories and 147 Parties to CAT. The United States signed CAT on April 18, 1968, and ratified it on October 21, 1994. To implement this law, the United States enacted the US Torture Victims Protection Act.[20]

States frequently torture women in order to identify, locate, or force information from them about men. Since torture is an integral part of the trafficking of women who are deprived of their liberty, severely punished, treated cruelly, and frequently sent home when and if they manage to escape from their captors, it is clear that the Torture Convention is directly relevant to women's human rights.

CAT covers torture inflicted by government officials as well as private groups or individuals whose conduct is tolerated or encouraged by government officials. Torture is defined as "any act by which severe pain or suffering, whether physical or mental, is intentionally inflicted on a person" for the purpose, *inter alia,* of "obtaining from him or a third person information or a confession. (Art. 1(1)). States Parties must adopt "effective legislation, administrative, judicial or other measures to prevent" torture in any territory under their jurisdiction (Art. 2(1)). It is interesting to note that the United States is a signatory to CAT and has enacted the US Victims of Torture Prevention Statute, but it has also been accused of engaging in "renditions" where an accused is tortured by another country's officials.[21] States Parties are required to treat torture as an extraditable offense (Art. 8) and not to extradite a person to a country where she "would be in danger of being subjected to torture." (Art. 3(1)). Victims of torture must have an enforceable right to compensation (Art. 14). Evidence produced by the use of torture must be

---

19. Convention against Torture and Other Cruel, Inhuman or Degrading Treatment, Dec. 10, 1984, G.A. Res. 39/46, annex, 39 UN GAOR Supp. (No. 51) at 197, UN Doc. A/39/51, *available at* www.hrweb.org/legal/cat.html.

20. United States Torture Victims Protection Act of 1991, Pub. L. 102-256, Mar. 12, 1992, 106. Stat. 73, 28 U.S.C.A. Section 1350 Notes, *available at* www.law.cornell.edu/... /usc_sec_28_00001350-000-notes.html.

21. M. Cherif Bassiouni, The Institutionalization of Torture by the Bush Administration: Is Anyone Responsible? (Intersentia 2010): "Between September 11, 2001 and April 2, 2002, it is believed that nearly 800 persons had been detained at Guantanamo Bay ... Most were tortured or subjected to cruel, inhuman or degrading treatment or punishment in violation of international law, the US Constitution, and US laws ..." *See also* The United States and Torture: Interrogation, Incarceration, and Abuse (Marjorie Cohn ed., N.Y.U. Press 2011); Jordan J. Paust, *The Absolute Prohibition of Torture and Necessary and Appropriate Sanctions,* 43 Val. U. L. Rev. 1535 (2009).

banned (Art. 15). Parties are banned from deporting, extraditing or refouling people where there are substantial grounds for believing they will be tortured (Art. 3).

The Torture Convention declares that there are "no exceptional circumstances whatsoever" to justify torture and that no orders from superior officers or a public authority may be validly invoked as a justification (Arts. 2(2) and 2(3)). Prohibition cannot be justified as a means to protect public safety or prevent emergencies. Since the Torture Convention's entry into force, this absolute prohibition has become accepted as a principle of customary international law.

Implementation of the Torture Convention is administered by the CAT Committee. The CAT Committee is composed of only 10 independent experts elected by the States Parties to the Convention. Article 19 sets forth an obligatory reporting system as well as optional inter-state (Art. 21) and individual complaint procedures (Art. 22), similar to the ICCPR and its Optional Protocol. The CAT Committee can initiate a confidential inquiry when it receives "reliable information" suggesting "well-founded indications that torture is being systematically practiced in the territory of a State Party."

n.   The Optional Protocol to CAT (2001–2006)[22]

The Optional Protocol to the Convention against Torture and Other Cruel, Inhuman or Degrading Treatment or Punishment was adopted on December 18, 2002, by the General Assembly of the United Nations and entered into force on June 22, 2006. As of August 2011, there are 66 signatories and 55 parties to this Protocol. It establishes an international inspection system for places of detention similar to the system that has existed in Europe since 1987. The objective of the Protocol is to "establish a system of regular visits undertaken by independent international and national bodies to places where people are deprived of their liberty, in order to prevent torture and other cruel, inhuman or degrading treatment or punishment." (Art. 1). "Deprivation of liberty" is defined in the Protocol as "any form of detention or imprisonment or the placement of a person in a public or private custodial setting which that person is not permitted to leave at will by order of any judicial, administrative or other authority." (Art. 4(2)). A Subcommittee on Prevention of Torture and Other Cruel, Inhuman or Degrading Treatment is established to implement the purposes of the Protocol. (Art. 2). No reservations are permitted to be made to the Protocol (Art. 30).

o.   The Convention on the Rights of the Child (1989–1990)[23]

The Convention on the Rights of the Child [Children's Rights Convention] or [CRC] was adopted by the UN General Assembly on November 20, 1989, and entered into force on September 2, 1990. By 2001, 191 states had ratified the CRC, and it is the most widely accepted of all human rights treaties. Prior to the adoption of the CRC, children's rights were enumerated in the 1924 resolution adopted by the League of Nations. Later they were enumerated in the expanded UN Declaration of the Rights of the Child in 1959.

Rather than categorizing children's human rights simply as civil political, economic, social or cultural, they may be viewed in terms of protection, provision of services and material benefits, and participation. Children's rights are based on the concept of "the

---

22. Optional Protocol to the Convention against Torture and Other Cruel, Inhuman or Degrading Treatment or Punishment, Dec. 19, 2002, *available at* www.2ohchr.org/english/law/cat-one.htm.

23. United Nations Convention on the Rights of the Child, adopted Nov. 20, 1989, 1577 U.N.T.S. 3, *available at* www.2ohchr.org/english/law/crc.htm.

best interests of the child" (CRC, Art. 3). Given the large number of child "disappearances," Article 8 of the CRC seeks to preserve the identity of the child.

Children must be accorded a long list of civil, political, economic, social, and cultural rights "irrespective of the child's or his or her parent's or legal guardian's race, color, sex, language, religion, political or other opinion, national, ethnic or social origin, property, disability, birth or other status." (Art. 2(1)). The CRC defines a child as every human being "below the age of eighteen ..." (Art. 1). Article 3(1) contains the main principles of the Convention: "... in all actions concerning children, whether undertaken by public or private social welfare institutions, courts of law, administrative authorities or legislative bodies, the best interests of the child shall be a primary consideration." Despite general agreement by US family lawmakers with the philosophical principle of the CRC which is the need to consider and protect the best interests of the child, the US is one of the few nations in the world that has refused to sign the CRC.

The CRC provides specific rights and duties such as the duty of the State to "prevent intra-familial abuse and neglect" (Article 19). Article 21 places emphasis on safeguards for adoption, while Article 24 mentions a state obligation to work towards the abolition of female genital mutilation and the preference of male children. Article 37 declares that imprisonment of children must be a last resort and limited to the shortest possible period of time. Article 40 upgrades international norms in the treatment of criminal matters involving children. Article 42 recognizes that children need to receive information about their rights. Other examples of specific children's rights include the right to free and compulsory elementary education, the right to protection from trafficking, and the prohibition from employment of children before they have attained a minimum age.

Thus, the CRC seeks to protect children against economic exploitation, abuse, illicit use of drugs, sexual exploitation, and trafficking. The CRC provides a basis for children to realize their potential, free from poverty and ill health, inequality, discrimination, and violence. The CRC bars the recruitment of children under the age of fifteen into the armed forces of the States. (The Optional Protocol to the CRC will fortunately change this age to eighteen.)

The CRC Committee has only 10 members to implement the rights given to children under the convention and to monitor compliance by States Parties. The CRC Committee reviews the reports which the State Parties are required to submit reflecting the measures they have implemented pursuant to the Convention. The CRC Committee examines "the progress made by the States Parties in achieving the realization of the obligations undertaken in the present Convention." (Art. 43(1)). The CRC Committee has no power to receive individual or inter-state complaints.

Why has the United States failed to ratify the CRC? Some believe that the United States generally distrusts the United Nations which is the underlying reason why it has refused to sign many international treaties. The US is opposed to the CRC because some claim it poses a threat to national sovereignty and to states' rights. For example, the CRC prohibits all corporal punishment (including punishment administered in the home). (Art. 19). This provision arguably violates the US constitutional right of privacy. The CRC also requires that a "values curriculum" be taught in both public and private elementary schools (Art. 29), which is arguably a violation of the First Amendment of the US Constitution. Article 16 and Article 24(f) of the CRC could be interpreted to establish abortion rights for children without the consent of their parents. Article 37(a) prohibits capital punishment and life sentences without possibility of parole for juvenile offenders, which the US objects to vigorously. Conservative groups fear that ratifying the CRC will result in a loss of parental control and an unhealthy empowerment of children. Ratification, they argue, will allow children to worship the occult, change their religion at a young age, join gangs, view pornography on the Internet, fornicate using birth control measures without the permission of their parents, or engage in homosexual conduct. Conservatives worry that an outside group of experts could prosecute parents for violating their children's rights as set forth in this treaty. Many of these interpretations of the CRC are inaccurate or at best questionable. The ratification of the CRC will depend largely on the political climate in the United States.

p. The First Optional Protocol on the Sale of Children, Child Prostitution, and Child Pornography (2000–2002)

The two Optional Protocols to the CRC were both adopted by the General Assembly on May 25, 2000. They are designed to strengthen children's protections under the CRC. The First Optional Protocol on the Sale of Children, Child Prostitution, and Child Pornography[24] entered into force on January 18, 2002. The United States signed it on July 5, 2000, and ratified it on December 23, 2002, subject to certain reservations, understandings, and declarations. The enactment of this Protocol reflects the serious concerns by the United States and by the international community at large of the spread of forced prostitution of children and child trafficking. The Optional Protocol provides that children must be protected from sexual abuse and exploitation, that perpetrators must be punished, and that victims must be adequately supported. Each State Party must criminalize the acts and activities specified in the Protocol, whether the offenses are committed within their territory or outside, on an individual or on an organized basis.

q. The Second Optional Protocol on the Involvement of Children in Armed Conflict (2000–2002)[25]

The Second Optional Protocol on the Involvement of Children in Armed Conflict was entered into force on February 13, 2002. This is the main international legal instrument that specifically addresses the use of children as soldiers, the minimum age for compulsory recruitment, voluntary recruitment, and direct participation of children in hostilities. The United States signed it on July 5, 2000, and ratified it on December 23, 2002, subject to some reservations, understandings, and declarations. The enactment of this Optional Protocol is a reflection of the seriousness of the crime of child soldiering committed all over the world and involving both girl and boy soldiers. The First Optional Protocol raises the minimum age of persons participating in armed conflicts to 18 years of age. States Parties' laws on voluntary recruitment must include special measures to protect those children under the age of 18 who shall not be permitted to take a direct part in hostilities.

---

24. Optional Protocol to the Convention on the Rights of the Child on the Sale of Children, Child Prostitution, and Child Pornography, May 25, 2000, 2171 U.N.T.S. 227, UN Doc. No. A/RES/54/263 (entered into force Jan. 18, 2002), *available at* www.2ohchr.org/English/law/crc-sale.htm.

25. Second Optional Protocol to the Convention on the Rights of The Child on the Involvement of Children in Armed Conflict, May 25, 2000, 2173 U.N.T.S. 222, UN Doc. No. A/RES/54/263 (entered into force Feb. 12, 2002), *available at* www.2ohchr.org/english/law/crc-conflict.htm.

r. The Convention on the Rights of Persons with Disabilities (2006–2008)[26]

The Convention on the Rights of Persons with Disabilities [CRPD] was adopted by the UN General Assembly in December 13, 2006, and entered into force on May 3, 2008. The CRPD seeks to "promote, protect, and ensure the full and equal enjoyment of all human rights and fundamental freedoms by all persons with disabilities and to promote respect for their inherent dignity."(Art. 1). The Preamble to the Convention, which follows the civil law tradition, states that "all human rights are universal, indivisible, interdependent, and interrelated." In the Preamble women and girls are singled out as a group requiring special care: "Recognizing that women and girls with disabilities are often at greater risk, both within and outside the home, of violence, injury or abuse, neglect or negligent treatment, maltreatment or exploitation."[27] Article 6 of the Convention specifically applies to women and girls with disabilities: "States Parties recognize that women and girls with disabilities are subject to multiple discrimination, and in this regard shall take measures to ensure the full and equal enjoyment by them of all human rights and fundamental freedoms (Art. 6(1)). "States Parties shall take all appropriate measures to ensure the full development, advancement, and empowerment of women, for the purpose of guaranteeing them the exercise and enjoyment of the human rights and fundamental freedoms set out in the present Convention." (Art. 6(2)). Article 28 recognizes the right of persons with disabilities to an adequate standard of living and social protection, especially to "women and girls with disabilities." (Art. 28 (b)).

The human rights for persons with disabilities are enumerated in the 50 articles of the Convention and include the right to equality of men and women under the law (one of the 8 guiding principles), the right to "full and effective participation and inclusion in society" (Art. 3), "the right to equality of opportunity, the right to accessibility to the physical environment, to transportation, to information and communications, to information technology"(Art. 9), the right to live independently and be included in the community (Art. 19), the right to personal mobility (Art. 20), the right to habilitation and rehabilitation (Art. 26), the right to inclusive education at all levels (Art. 24), the right to "the enjoyment of the highest attainable standard of health without discrimination on the basis of disability," the right to work and employment (Art. 27), the right to "participate in political and public life" (Art. 29), and the right to participate in "cultural life, recreation, leisure and sport" (Art. 30). Article 28 requires that State Parties recognize the right of persons with disabilities to an "adequate standard of living," and to "social protection." States Parties must also raise awareness of the human rights of persons with disabilities (Art. 8).

The guiding principles of the CRPD are to prohibit discrimination against the disabled and to promote respect for the inherent dignity, individual autonomy including the freedom to make choices, and the independence of persons with disabilities. Persons with disabilities are defined as those with "long-term physical, mental, intellectual or sensory impairments which in interaction with various barriers may hinder their full and effective participation in society on an equal basis with others." (Art. 1).

Article 10 of CRPD affords all persons with disabilities the right to life: "States Parties reaffirm that every human being has the inherent right to life and shall take all necessary measures to ensure its effective enjoyment by persons with disabilities on an equal basis with others." It is interesting to note that the United States, which signed and ratified this

---

26. CRPD, *supra* note 6.
27. *Id.* at Preamble (q).

Convention under the Obama administration, has continuously refused to sign the Child's Convention [CRC] for many reasons including the "right to life" provision. Some have misconstrued this provision to mean that abortion should be prohibited. Others object to the provision because it is in conflict with our death penalty laws.

Persons with disabilities have the right to receive "reasonable accommodations" which is defined as "necessary and appropriate modification and adjustments not imposing a disproportionate or undue burden ..." (Arts. 2–3).

Article 34 outlines the duties of the CRPD Committee which monitors compliance. This Committee, consisting of only 12 experts at the time of the entry into force of the Convention, receives a compliance Report by each State Party "at least every four years" or more often, upon demand by the CRPD Committees. The CRPD Committee will review the Report and provide general recommendations. One hundred and forty-nine nations have signed the treaty as of July 2011. This UN treaty was inspired by the Americans with Disabilities Act, and the United States has signed and ratified the treaty.

s.   The Optional Protocol to CRPD (2006–2007)[28]

The Optional Protocol to CRPD entered into force with the Convention on May 3, 2008. It is a side agreement to the Convention allowing the CRPD Committee to hear individual complaints. This Optional Protocol is similar in content and style to the Optional Protocol to CEDAW. As of July 2011, the CRPD Optional Protocol has 90 signatories and 62 parties.

t.   Conclusion

In conclusion, the above UN instruments and conventions, with their respective optional protocols, are the major human rights treaties constituting an international human rights system. Most of these treaties protect and provide for women's rights either intermittently or specifically. The United States has not signed many of these human rights treaties for reasons that will be discussed later in the book. The decision by the United States not to sign and ratify the treaties that specifically protect women's rights, notably the ICESCR, CEDAW, and the CRC, delivers a great blow to the protection of women's rights and sends a clear message of exceptionalism[29] to the international community.

In this chapter Professor Barbara Stark examines in depth, and from the point of view of women's rights in particular, the relationship between The Universal Declaration of Human Rights (UDHR), The International Covenant on Civil and Political Rights (ICCPR) and The International Covenant on Economic, Social, and Cultural Rights (ICESCR) (together referred to as the "International Bill of Rights"). Stark argues that the positive rights enumerated in the ICESCR invert the traditional male-dominated hierarchy of legal doctrine, providing women with privileges and protections not found in other legal instruments. Therefore, she makes a strong argument that the United States should sign and ratify this treaty to provide women with their fundamental human rights.

At the end of this chapter, we provide selections from the CEDAW Committee Remarks for China and Guatemala which illustrate the complex issues of CEDAW imple-

---

28. The Optional Protocol to the Convention on the Rights of Persons with Disabilities, Dec. 13, 2006, G.A. Res. 61/106, UN Doc. A/Res/61/106, *available at* www2.ohchr.org/English/law/disabilities-op.htm..

29. *See* MICHAEL IGNATIEFF, AMERICAN EXCEPTIONALISM AND HUMAN RIGHTS (2006).

mentation and the concerns of the CEDAW Committee regarding the status of women's rights in these two respective countries.

Even though the United States has not signed and ratified the ICESCR or CEDAW, President Barack Obama has shown an effort to make major strides in protecting women's rights and in providing concrete economic, social, and cultural rights to its citizens by agreeing to sign the United Nations Convention on the Rights of Persons with Disabilities (CRPD).[30]

Susan Jones, in her article from CNS News, describes how President Obama directed the United States to sign CRPD, which she calls the "First New Human Rights Treaty of the 21st Century." The CRPD, like the ICESCR and CEDAW, requires countries to provide all disabled people, and especially women, with free or affordable health care, nearby health services, health and life insurance, the right to be free from discrimination, torture or cruel, inhuman or degrading treatment or punishment, the right to marry and found a family, to decide on the number and spacing of their children, the right to assistance with child-rearing responsibilities, the right to clean water service, social protection, and poverty reduction programs, the right to participate in the cultural life, recreation, leisure, and sports, and the right for disabled children to participate in play, leisure, and sporting activities. These rights are implemented by a Committee on the Rights of Persons with Disabilities. Disabled women or women with disabled children have a right to file an individual human rights complaint with the CRPD Committee. The fact that the US is now willing to sign a treaty that requires proactive measures to provide social and economic as well as cultural rights is a serious indication that the US may be moving closer to signing and ratifying if not the ICESCR then certainly CEDAW.

B. Why the US Should Sign and Ratify the Covenant on Economic, Social, and Cultural Rights

1. Barbara Stark,[31] *The "Other" Half of the International Bill of Rights as a Postmodern Feminist Text*[32]

Introduction[33]

The International Bill of Rights is globally recognized as the definitive statement of international human rights law. It consists of two instruments the International Covenant

---

30. CPRD, *supra* note 6.

31. I am grateful to Fran Ansley, Hilary Charlesworth, Judy Cornett, Rosalind Hackett, Catharine MacKinnon, Nadine Taub, Shelley Wright, and the students in my Spring 1993 International Human Rights Seminar for their helpful comments. I also acknowledge the generous support of the American Council of Learned Societies, the American Philosophical Society, the Faculty Development Programs of the University of Tennessee and the College of Law, and the Academic Council on the United Nations and the American Society of International Law, sponsors of the 1992 Dartmouth Summer Workshop on International Organization. Rene Voigtlander, Mart Cizek, and Lori Davis provided able research assistance.

32. Barbara Stark, *The "Other" Half of the International Bill of Rights as a Postmodern Feminist Text*, *in* RECONCEIVING REALITY: WOMEN AND INTERNATIONAL LAW 19, 19–33, 38 (Dorinda Dallmeyer ed., Washington DC, Am. Soc'y of Int'l Law 1993).

33. *Id.* at 19–23.

on Civil and Political Rights[34] (the "Civil Covenant" or "ICCPR") and the International Covenant on Economic, Social, and Cultural Rights[35] (the "Economic Covenant" or "ICESCR"). The Civil Covenant, very much like the US Bill of Rights, addresses familiar "negative" rights such as freedom of religion and expression, and freedom from arbitrary arrest or detention. The United States ratified the Civil Covenant in April 1992.[36]

The Economic Covenant, the "other" half of the International Bill of Rights,[37] addresses "positive" rights. By ratifying the Covenant, a government "commits itself to its best efforts to secure for its citizens the basic standards of material existence.[38] Although some commentators claim American[39] origins for ICESCR, tracing it to the "freedom from want" described by President Franklin Roosevelt in his "Four Freedoms" speech,[40] and it has been before the Senate since 1978, the United States is the only major industrialized democracy that has not yet ratified the Covenant.[41] It is also the only State which

---

34. Mar. 23, 1976, 999 U.N.T.S. 171. *See also* G.A. Res. 2200, UN GAOR, 21st Sess., Supp. No. 16, at 52, UN Doc. A/6316 (1966) (UN Resolution adopting the Covenant); *see generally* THE INTERNATIONAL BILL OF RIGHTS: THE COVENANT ON CIVIL AND POLITICAL RIGHTS (Louis Henkin ed., 1981) (essays on civil and political rights).

35. ICESCR, *supra* note 4. *See also* G.A. Res. 2200, UN GAOR, 21st Sess., Supp. No. 16, at 49, UN Doc. A/6316 (1966) (UN Resolution adopting the Covenant).

36. *Text of Resolution of Ratification*, 3 I.L.M. 658 (1992). For a discussion of the background, *see* 31 I.L.M. 648, 649 (1992).

37. *See* The Limburg Principles on the Implementation of the International Covenant on Economic, Social, and Cultural Rights, UN Doc. E/CN.4/1987/17, Annex (1987), *reprinted in Symposium: The Implementation of the International Covenant on Economic, Social, and Cultural Rights*, 9 HUM. RTS. Q. 121, 123 (1987) [hereinafter Limburg Principles]; Louis Henkin, *The Internalization of Human Rights, reprinted in* LOUIS HENKIN ET AL., INTERNATIONAL LAW: CASES AND MATERIALS 981, 983 (2d ed. 1987) [hereinafter HENKIN, INTERNATIONAL LAW].

38. *President Carter Signs Covenants on Human Rights*, DEP'T. ST. BULL, Oct. 31, 1977, 586, 587.

39. "[O]ur common usurpation for the inhabitants of the United States." LOUIS HENKIN, THE AGE OF RIGHTS x (1990).

40. *Eighth Annual Message to Congress (Jan. 6, 1941), in* 3 THE STATE OF THE UNION MESSAGE OF THE PRESIDENTS, 1790–1966, 2855, 2860, 2875, 2881 (Fred L. Israel ed., 1966). In his 1944 State of the Union message, Roosevelt elaborated on the substance of "freedom from want:" "[t]he right to a useful and remunerative job ... [t]he right of every family to a decent home ... [t]he right to adequate medical care ... [t]he right to adequate protection from the economic fears of old age, sickness, accident, and unemployment; the right to a good education." *Eleventh Annual Message to Congress* (Jan. 11, 1944), *in* 3 THE STATE OF THE UNION MESSAGE OF THE PRESIDENTS, 2875, 2881 (Fred L. Israel ed., 1966).

41. 104 states have ratified or acceded to the Covenant as of Dec. 13, 1991. Committee on Economic, Social & Cultural Rights, *Report on the Sixth Session*, UN ESCOR, Supp. No. 8, at 2, 103–12, UN Doc. E/1992/23, E/C.12/1991/4 (1992). *But see* Morris B. Abram, *Human Rights and the United Nations: Past as Prologue*, 4 HARV. HUM. RTS. J. 69, 71 (1991), (deploring ratification by countries with "neither the intention nor the desire to abide by them.").

The US has already signed the Universal Declaration of Human Rights (G.A. Res. 217, UN GAOR, 3d Sess., pt. 1 at 71, UN Doc. A/810 (1948)), the Vienna Declaration of 1989 (Philip Alston, *US Ratification of the Covenant on Economic, Social, and Cultural Rights: The Need for an Entirely New Strategy*, 84 AM. J. INT'L L. 365 (1990) [hereinafter Need for an Entirely New Strategy]), and the Charter of Paris for a New Europe (Nov. 21, 1990) *in* 30 I.L.M. 190 (1991). These international texts affirm that everyone "has the right to enjoy his economic, social, and cultural rights." 30 I.L.M. 194. More importantly, they explicitly require the state to help its people realize these rights. The United States also participated in the Copenhagen Conference on the Human Dimension. *Document of Copenhagen Meeting of the Conference on the Human Dimension of the Conference on Security and Cooperation in Europe* (CSCE) 29 I.L.M. 1350 (1990).

These instruments are generally considered "political" rather than "legal" undertakings. Lori Fisler Damrosch, *International Human Rights Law in Soviet and American Courts*, 100 YALE L.J. 2315, 2319 (1991). The United States assumes no enforceable legal obligation by adhering to these texts. *But see*

has ratified the Civil Covenant but *not* it's other half. The end of the Cold War,[42] the growing domestic concern with economic rights,[43] and the election of a new President more receptive to these rights[44] have made ratification more of a realistic possibility than ever before.[45] American women could make it happen.[46]

The Economic Covenant is the marginalized half of international human rights law.[47] The privileged half, the Civil Covenant, replicates familiar hierarchies like "male over female" and "abstract theory over concrete practice." This essay will explain how the Economic Covenant inverts, or at least destabilizes, these hierarchies. As J.M. Balkin has pointed out, "Legal doctrines are based upon a group of fundamental concepts and principles.... Using Derrida's methods, we discover that each legal concept is actually a privileging, in disguise, of one concept over another. By revealing the opposition, indeed constructing it, we are brought to an entirely different vision of moral and legal obligation."[48] I am not suggesting that the two Covenants comprehensively

---

Oscar Schachter, *International Law in Theory and Practice*, 178 Rec. Des Cours 123–32 (1982) ("[A] State assuming an international political commitment may (under the requirement of good faith) be considered to have given up its prior right under international law to declare the matter in question as purely domestic."). The explicit recognition of economic rights nevertheless represents a rhetorical milestone.

42. The end of the Cold War provides an unprecedented opportunity to rethink priorities and to reallocate resources from defense to domestic social programs, although it is increasingly clear that it will be some time before we realize any "peace dividend."

43. *See* Theodore R. Marmor et al., America's Misunderstood Welfare State: Persistent Myths, Enduring Realities 47, 48 (1990) (noting widespread public support for the Medicare, Food Stamp, and Social Security programs); Kevin Phillips, The Politics of Rich and Poor: Wealth and the American Electorate in the Reagan Aftermath (1990) (arguing that the widening gap between rich and poor, along with greater concentration of wealth, is likely to lead, as it did in the 1930s, to a resurgence of populism). International economic rights law is not widely known in the United States for a plethora of interrelated reasons. Our ignorance may be attributed to our isolationism, our geography, our unique history, our economic hegemony and, more specifically, to our failure to require international law as a course in our law schools, unlike law schools throughout Europe, China, Japan, Canada, and Australia.

US scholarship on the Economic Covenant is "meager at best," and there is only one book on the subject in English. *Need for an Entirely New Strategy*, *supra* note 9, at 388. That book is A. Glenn Mower Jr., International Cooperation for Social Justice: Global and Regional Protection of Economic/Social Rights (1985). For a discussion of the extent to which the rhetoric of the Covenant is compatible with our own, *see* Barbara Stark, *Economic Rights in the United States and International Human Rights: Toward an Entirely New Strategy*, 44 Hastings L.J. 79 (1992) [hereinafter Toward an Entirely New Strategy].

44. President Clinton promises a renewed commitment to economic rights. Bill Clinton & Al Gore, Putting People First 84–88, 107–15, 164–68 (1992); David E. Rosenbaum, *Take a Number: What Can Clinton Change, and When?*, N.Y. Times, Nov. 8, 1992, Wk. in Rev., at 1, col. 1. *See generally* Robert B. Reich, The Work of Nations: Preparing Ourselves for 21st Century Capitalism (1991).

45. *See generally* Natalie Kaufman, Human Rights Treaties and the Senate: A History of Opposition (1990).

46. After all, they elected a President. Voter Research & Surveys, an association of ABC News, CNN, CBS News, and NBC News, "Exit Poll Result 1992" in Newsweek (November/December 1992) (54% of all voters were women, and 46% of all women voted for Clinton).

47. *See* Andrew Byrnes, *Women, Feminism, and International Human Rights Law—Methodological Myopia, Fundamental Flaws or Meaningful Marginalization?*, 12 Austl. Y.B. Int'l L. 205, 213 (1992) (noting frequent feminist criticism that, "the prevailing preoccupation of civil and political rights at the expense of economic and social rights averts resources away from areas in which they could more effectively be used to promote the advancement of women.").

48. J.M. Balkin, *Deconstructive Practice and Legal Theory*, 96 Yale L.J. 743, 754 (1987). This may also be seen as a way of inverting the "core" and the "periphery," rather than continuing to permit

or precisely invert each other. They reinforce each other, for example, in that both affirm human rights, inverting the historical hierarchy privileging a State over its people. Nor are these hierarchies the only ones inverted.[49] This paper focuses on hierarchies of gender and abstraction because they are as central to domestic jurisprudence as their inversions are to the Covenant. Moreover, in both forms these hierarchies have direct and immediate significance for American women. I will explain how the Covenant privileges women oven men — textually, by prohibiting *de facto* as well as *de jure* discrimination, as well as contextually, by focusing on substantive problems traditionally left to women. In addition, the Covenant privileges a postmodern proliferation of contextualized options over a modern quest for universal, abstract solutions. This focus on context itself privileges women, as described below, especially in conjunction with ICESCR's insistence on nondiscrimination and the protection of the most vulnerable in every context. These two inversions make the Covenant a postmodern feminist text for American women, which would enable them to generate new approaches to their diverse concerns, approaches increasingly removed from their present subordination.

An Overview of ICESCR[50]

This essay does not consider all of the provisions of the Covenant, focusing only on Articles 2.2, 3, 10, and 11. Articles 2.2 and 3 require States "to guarantee that the rights enunciated in the present Covenant will be exercised without discrimination of any kind as to ... sex" and "to insure the equal rights of men and women to the enjoyment of all economic, social, and cultural rights."

Article 10 provides in pertinent part:

1. The widest possible protection and assistance should be accorded to the family, which is the natural and fundamental group unit of society, particularly for its establishment and while it is responsible for the care and education of dependent children. Marriage must be entered into with the free consent of the intending spouses.

2. Special protection should be accorded to mothers during a reasonable period before and after childbirth. During such period, working mothers should be accorded paid leave or leave with adequate social security benefits.

Article 11.1 provides:

The States Parties to the present Covenant recognize the right of everyone to an adequate standard of living for himself and his family, including adequate food, clothing, and housing, and to the continuous improvement of living conditions.[51]

The Covenant also requires States to recognize rights to physical and mental health,[52] education,[53] work,[54] and cultural life. The focus here is on Articles 2, 3, 10, and 11 because

---

"core," privileged concepts to define "peripheral," subordinate ones. For a thoughtful and provocative argument for doing so in this context, *see* Karen Engle, *International Human Rights and Feminism: When Discourses Meet*, 13 Mich. J. Int'l L. 517 (1992).

49. It could similarly be argued that the Civil Covenant also privileges wealth over poverty and the developed North over the "developing" South, for example, but it is beyond the scope of this essay to do so.

50. Stark, *supra* note 32, at 21–26.

51. ICESCR, *supra* note 4, art. 11, para. 1.

52. *Id.* at art. 12.1.

53. *Id.* at art. 13.

54. *Id.* at art. 6.

they are probably the most important for American women, and, not coincidentally, the most contentious.[55]

The Covenant requires each party to submit a self-monitoring Report within two years of ratification and at five-year intervals thereafter.[56] In order to assure public involvement in the preparation of the Report, recently promulgated Guidelines[57] require the parties to describe "the manner and extent of public dissemination" of ICESCR and to state whether "its content has been the subject of public debate."[58]

There are no sanctions for failure to comply with these or any other ICESCR requirements. Rather than the kinds of "enforcement" relied on in the American legal system, with notably problematic results in the context of economic rights, the Covenant scheme seeks to "enable" parties to develop normative consensus and practical plans reflecting that consensus. In ratifying ICESCR, a State assumes an obligation to comply with its requirements. This becomes a legal obligation where the Covenant is enforceable in domestic courts, as it would be here upon ratification.[59]

---

55. *But see* Marilyn Waring, *Gender and International Law: Women and the Right to Development*, 12 AUSTL. Y.B. INT'L L. 177, 182–86 (1992) (arguing that Art. 7, regarding the right of "everyone to the enjoyment of just favorable conditions of work" is critical to women because it ignores the work which they do).

The question raised by domestic recognition of other clusters of ICESCR rights — "cultural rights," for example — may well require a different analytic framework. *See, e.g.*, Stephen Marks, *UNESCO and Human Rights: The Implementation of Rights Relating to Education, Science, Culture, and Communication*, 13 TEX. INT'L L.J. 35 (1977).

56. Philip Alston, *The International Covenant on Economic, Social, and Cultural Rights*, in MANUAL ON HUMAN RIGHTS REPORTING UNDER SIX MAJOR INTERNATIONAL HUMAN RIGHTS INSTRUMENTS, 71 UN Doc. HR/PUB/91/1, UN Sales No. E.91.XIV.1 at 39, 40 (1992) [hereinafter MANUAL ON HUMAN RIGHTS].

57. The precise legal significance of the Committee's Report, including its Commentary, is an open question. To the extent that Committee Reports purport to set forth customary law, their pronouncements would probably be accepted as authoritative. As Alston and Quinn have noted, the jurisprudence of economic rights is not as developed on the municipal level as the jurisprudence of civil and political rights. Philip Alston & Gerard Quinn, *The Nature and Scope of the State Parties' Obligations Under the International Covenant on Economic, Social, and Cultural Rights*, 9 HUM. RTS. Q. 156, 183–84 (1987). There is, accordingly, considerably less of a consensus on which to build.

Domestic courts are already bound by the Vienna Convention on the Law of Treaties, however. May 23, 1969, 1155 U.N.T.S. 331 (1969). Although the US is not a party, the State Department recognizes the Vienna Convention as customary, and therefore binding, international law. BARRY CARTER & PHILLIP TRIMBLE, INTERNATIONAL LAW 78 (1991). Art. 31 of the Convention provides that "[a] treaty shall be interpreted in good faith in accordance with the ordinary meaning to be given the terms of the treaty in their context and in the light of its object and purpose." The Committee's Reports should arguably be accepted as authoritative clarification of the Covenant's "object and purpose." Our courts are also, of course, bound by international law. *The Paquete Habana*, 175 US 677, 700 (1900).

58. Fifth Session Report Committee on Economic, Social, and Cultural Rights, *Report on the Fifth Session*, UN ESCOR, 1991, Supp. No. 3, UN Doc. E/1991/23, E/C.12/1990/8 (1991) 89. ICESCR resonates with recent American calls for a "republican revival." *See, e.g.,* "Limburg Principles," *supra* note 5, at 124, 11 ("Popular participation is required at all stages, including the formulation, application and review of national policies."). As Paul Brest has noted, "minimum protections' for the necessities of life ... are preconditions of civic republican citizenship." Paul Brest, *Further Beyond the Republican Revival: Toward Radical Republicanism*, 97 YALE L.J. 1623, 1628 (1988); Akhil Reed Amar, *Forty Acres and a Mule: A Republican Theory of Minimal Entitlement*, 13 HARV. J.L. & PUB. POL'Y 37 (1990).

59. This assumes that ICESCR, unlike the Civil Covenant, would be considered self-executing. *See* Louis Henkin, *Lexical Propriety or "Political Question": A Response*, 101 HARV. L. REV. 524–33 (1988). (Treaties should be considered "self-executing whenever the character of the undertaking permits."); Oscar Schachter, *The Charter and the Constitution: The Human Rights Provisions in American Law*, 4 VAND. L. REV. 643, 644–46 (1951) (A treaty should be considered self-executing unless it explicitly provides otherwise or "the power to deal with [its subject matter] is vested solely in legislature.").

The Reports are submitted to the Committee on Economic, Social, and Cultural Rights (hereafter the "Committee"),[60] which meets with the country representatives after its review. During this meeting, which is open to the public, the Committee typically asks for further information or clarification. The meeting usually ends with comments by Committee members.[61]

In its six years of reviewing reports, the Committee has developed considerable expertise in dealing with the substantive issues as well as the government parties appearing before it. Recognizing that the projection of a positive image, at home as well as abroad, remains a major inducement for adherence, the Committee tries to avoid embarrassing the reporting State while providing constructive criticism. It also focuses firmly on the need for domestic implementation. A request for further information, for example, can be an effective way of pointing out problems to domestic constituencies as well as to the states parties themselves. The Committee may also recommend further action.

American State Criticism of ICESCR

Two basic reasons are usually given for US non-adherence. First, it has been suggested that the rights set forth in the Covenant are "foreign" to the American notion of rights. It has been argued that the Covenant represents aspirations, as distinguished from "real," enforceable civil or political rights.[62] During the Cold War, the US Department of State viewed ICESCR as a socialist manifesto transparently veiled in the language of rights.[63] It is settled that economic rights are not protected under the US Constitution.[64]

But see Alfred de Zayas, *The Potential for the United States Joining the Covenant Family*, 20 Ga. J. Int'l & Comp. L. 299, 304 (1990) ("[I]t is intrinsic in a covenant that is to be implemented progressively that it is *not* 'self-executing' in the domestic legal system."). *See generally* Jordan J. Paust, *Self-Executing Treaties*, 82 Am. J. Int'l L. 760 (1988) (examining the history of the judicial distinction between "self-executing" and "non-self-executing" treaties and analyzing its continuing implications).

It should be noted that American courts have held human rights provisions of the UN Charter non-self-executing. *See, e.g.,* Frolova v. USSR, 761 F.2d 370, 374 n. 5 (7th Cir. 1985); Sei Fujii v. State, 242 P.2d 617 (Cal. 1952); Charles W. Stotter, *Self-Executing Treaties and the Human Rights Provisions of the United Nations Charter: A Separation of Powers Problem*, 25 Buff. L. Rev. 773, 773 (1976).

Although some parties, such as Portugal, have incorporated the Covenant into their national law, Alston and Quinn have observed that "an obligation to incorporate cannot be deduced from the text of Article 2, and no such proposal was even considered during the drafting of the Covenant." Alston & Quinn, *supra* note 57, at 166.

60. The Committee consists of eighteen recognized experts in the field of human rights, chosen for a term of four years by the Economic and Social Council, from a list of persons nominated by the parties. Economic and Social Council Resolution 1985/17 of 28 May 1985 (*reprinted in* Manual on Human Rights, *supra* note 56, at 71).

61. Fausto Pocar & Cecil Bernard, *National Reports: Their Submission to Expert Bodies and Follow-up*, in Manual on Human Rights Reporting, *supra* note 56, at 25, 26.

62. *See* Oscar Schachter, International Law in Theory and Practice 352 (1991). *See generally* Theodor Meron, *Norm Making and Supervision in International Human Rights: Reflections on Institutional Order*, 76 Am. J. Int'l L. 754, 756–57 (1982).

63. Paula Dobriansky, *US Human Rights Policy: An Overview*, US Dep't of State, Current Pol'y No. 1091, at 2–3 (1988); Richard Schifler, *US-Soviet Quality of Life: A Comparison*, US Dep't of State, Current Pol'y No. 713, at 1 (1985), *reprinted in* Frank Newman & David Weissbrodt, International Human Rights 388 (1990). As Diane Orentlicher has noted, "By the 1950s, US reservations about adherence to human rights treaties ripened into outright hostility." Diane F. Orentlicher, *The Power of an Idea: The Impact of United States Human Rights Policy*, 1 Transnat'l L. & Contemp. Probs. 43, 46–47 (1991).

64. *See* Harris v. McRae, 448 US 297, 318, 323, 326–27 (1980) (finding that indigent women have no constitutional right to federal or state funding for medically necessary abortions); Lindsey v. Normet, 405 US 56, 73–74 (1972) (finding no constitutional guarantee to adequate housing); Dan-

Second, political leaders have maintained that the concerns addressed by ICESCR are within the exclusive authority of the states, and that national adoption would infringe on state sovereignty. The Supreme Court and most scholars reject the notion that the federal government must defer to the states on social welfare issues as a matter of law, pointing to the New Deal, Medicaid, Social Security, and voluminous legislation enacted under the Commerce Clause. Politically, however, neither the federal government nor the states want the federal government to assume responsibility for—or authority over—social welfare issues.[65]

AMERICAN FEMINIST[66] CRITICISM

The parallels between these arguments and those used against feminists in this country are striking. To the extent American women have sought something other than "equality"—that is, other than being treated like men—their claims are by definition "alien," marginalized beyond the boundaries of accepted "human" (male) rights.[67] The degree to

---

dridge v. Williams, 397 US 471, 484–86 (1970) (finding that maximum grant regulation, creating a cap on welfare benefits to large families, did not violate the Fourteenth Amendment). *See also* Lynn A. Baker, *The Myth of the American Welfare State*, 9 YALE L. & POL'Y REV. 110 (1991) (reviewing THEODORE R. MARMOR ET AL., AMERICA'S MISUNDERSTOOD WELFARE STATE: PRESIDENT MYTHS, ENDURING REALITIES (1990)); Robert H. Bork, *The Impossibility of Finding Welfare Rights in the Constitution*, 1979 WASH. U. L.Q. 695; William H. Clune III, *The Supreme Court's Treatment of Wealth Discriminations Under the Fourteenth Amendment*, 1975 SUP. CT. REV. 289. *But see* Frank I. Michelman, *The Supreme Court, 1968 Term-Foreword: On Protecting the Poor Through the Fourteenth Amendment*, 83 HARV. L. REV. 7 (1969); Charles L. Black, *Further Reflections on the Constitutional Justice of Livelihood*, 86 COLUM. L. REV. 1103, 1105 (1986) (discussing "the derivation of a constitutional right to a decent material basis for life").

65. *Cf.* Jonathan R. Macey, *Federal Deference to Local Regulators and the Economic Theory of Regulation: Toward a Public-Choice Explanation of Federalism*, 76 VA. L. REV. 265 (1990) (Congress delegates to the states when—and only when—it receives more political support for doing so than it would were it to retain the regulatory authority delegated.).

66. By "feminist" I refer to many, sometimes inconsistent, definitions and descriptions, which vary according to context and purpose. The following may be particularly apt here: "Although varied accounts of the problem exist, animated by different factors and dynamics as determinants, feminism is distinguishable by the view that gender *is* a problem: that what exists now is not equality between the sexes.... Feminism sees women as a group and seeks to define and pursue women's interests. Feminists believe that women share a reality, and search for it, even as they criticize the leveling effects of the social enforcement of its commonalities. Women's commonalities include, they do not transcend, individual uniqueness, profound diversity (such as race and class), time and place. Feminism's search for a ground is the search for the truth of all women's collectivity in the face of the enforced lie that all women are the same." CATHARINE A. MACKINNON, TOWARD A FEMINIST THEORY OF THE STATE 38 (1989). *See also* Deborah L. Rhode, *Feminist Critical Theories*, 42 STAN. L. REV. 617 (1990) (describing three "central commitments" of feminist critical theories: "On a political level, they seek to promote equality between women and men. On a substantive level, [these] frameworks make gender a focus of analysis ... to reconstitute legal practices that have excluded, devalued, or undermined women's concerns. On a methodological level, these frameworks aspire to describe the world in ways that correspond to women's experience and that identify the fundamental social transformations necessary for full equality between the sexes."); Joan Williams, *Gender Wars: Selfless Women in the Republic of Choice*, 66 N.Y.U. L. REV. 1559, 1572 n. 64 (1991) ("Our goal as feminists is to reformulate ideas of 'real' man and womanhood in less stunted ways that do not track and reinforce current power inequities and stunted notions of human potential."). For a nuanced and insightful discussion of the difficulties presented by the use of "feminist" as a descriptive label, *see* Katharine T. Bartlett, *Feminist Legal Methods*, 103 HARV. L. REV. 829, 833–36 (1990).

67. *Cf.* Waring, *supra* note 55, at 188–89 (summarizing the argument of the Women's Legal Education and Action Fund in *Andrews v. The Law Society of British Columbia* that equality "should be understood as a matter of socially created systematic historical and cumulative advantage and disadvantage").

which such rights are perceived as "foreign" reflects women's ongoing historical exclusion from lawmaking, just as the "foreignness" of economic rights reflects the historical exclusion of the poor from the legislative process.[68]

Feminists should be even more familiar with the second objection to the Covenant; that is, that its subject matter is more appropriately addressed on a local, more "private" level. The argument that women's issues should be dealt with privately, in the home or in the community, has been used to avoid State action on problems from childcare to street harassment.[69]

The State's objections are as specious in the context of economic rights as they are in the context of women's concerns. In both cases, the objections emphasize the "claimants" distance from the core, the "foreignness" of the claim, and contend that because of that distance, such claims are better addressed "locally," in the home, elsewhere—anywhere but at the core. The State's objections to ICESCR should not deter feminist advocacy on its behalf. Indeed, the degree to which ICESCR elicits the same State response as "women's issues" is a reflection of the real overlap between women's issues and the issues addressed in the Covenant.

While American "State" criticism may be readily dismissed by most American feminists, they should carefully consider international feminist criticism of ICESCR.[70] Feminist critics of international economic rights have focused on some of the same provisions discussed here to show how international law fails women. They have pointed out that the international regime fails to take women's work into account and that its protection of "the family" leaves patriarchal norms intact. They note that the Committee responsible for international implementation of the Covenant, like almost all UN machinery, is male-dominated.[71] While the Covenant insists on gender equality and the Guidelines encourage women's participation in its implementation, moreover, there is little in the Reports filed by States to suggest that this is taken very seriously. These Reports occasionally mention women's unpaid labor, for example, and the Committee seems genuinely concerned with supporting it,[72] but it usually remains invisible.[73]

---

68. *See generally* Mary Becker, *Politics, Differences, and Economic Rights,* 1989 U. CHI. LEGAL F. 169 (discussing women's differences and the political problems of non-dominant groups).

69. *See* Cynthia Grant Bowman, *Street Harassment and the Informal Ghettoization of Women,* 106 HARV. L. REV. 517, 519 (1993).

70. *See, e.g.,* Shelley Wright, *Economic Rights and Social Justice: A Feminist Analysis of Some International Human Rights Conventions,* 12 AUSTL. Y.B. INT'L 241, 243 (1992) (calling for a redefinition of "economic rights" in order to make human rights "truly human" and take into account the issues of "reproductive control and the transmission of traditional and other cultural values through the family"). For a perceptive and thought-provoking analysis of the literature on international women's human rights, *see* Engle, *supra* note 48 (identifying three approaches, the first two criticizing existing doctrine and institutions and the latter developing an "external" critique). For a comprehensive scholarly bibliography, *see* Rebecca J. Cook, *Women's International Human Rights: A Bibliography,* 24 N.Y.U. J. INT'L L. & POL. 857 (1992).

71. Only two of the eighteen Committee members are women. Hilary Charlesworth *et al., Feminist Approaches to International Law,* 85 AM. J. INT'L L. 613, 624 n. 67 (1991). For a feminist critique of the Commission on Human Rights and the Human Rights Committee, *see* Laura Reanda, *Human Rights and Women's Rights: The United Nations Approach,* 3 HUM. RTS. Q. 11 (Spring 1981).

72. Byrnes, *supra* note 47, at 219 (noting that, "there have been some indications in recent years that some of the human rights bodies are becoming more aware of the issue of gender and are attempting to respond to it" and proceeding to describe the Committee's "Comment No. 4" on the right to adequate housing).

73. Women's work is still not considered "productive work" for purposes of international development aid, for example. *See, e.g.,* Hilary Charlesworth, *The Public/Private Distinction and the Right*

While American feminists should be aware of this criticism, they should recognize that it has different implications in an international context than it does in a domestic, American one. First, ICESCR neither generates binding precedent nor establishes binding norms, except for the normative "floor" set out in the Guidelines and described below.[74] While I agree with commentators that this presents grave problems for women globally (and I also agree that global problems of women matter to American women), this is not my focus here. The United States is not bound by pinched international constructions of "women's work" or "patriarchal international notions of the family."[75] As explained below, once the United States recognizes economic rights, it has reasons for recognizing "women's work" that most other States do not. Moreover, notions of a patriarchal family have already been forcefully challenged by American feminists, and those seeking to implement the Covenant could build on their work. Finally, while the officials responsible for implementing ICESCR are mostly male on the international level, they would not necessarily be male on the domestic level, where the real work takes place. For purposes of the purely domestic application considered here, in short, ratification of ICESCR remains crucial for American women, and American feminists should support it.

Women Over Men[76]

TEXTUAL INVERSION

The Covenant's mandate goes beyond rule-neutral "gender equality" and even beyond affirmative action, the recognition that extraordinary efforts must be made to bring women up to the starting line.[77] It requires reassessment of the starting line itself,[78] replacing a male norm with a female one in the obvious context of childbirth and leaving open the possibility of effectively challenging other male norms where they result in *de facto* discrimination.[79]

Article 2.2 provides that "the States Parties to the present Covenant undertake to guarantee that the rights enunciated in the present Covenant will be exercised without discrimination of any kind as to race, color, sex, language, religion, political or other opinion, national or social origin, property, birth or other status." Article 3 explicitly reiterates, "The States Parties to the present Covenant undertake to ensure the equal rights of men and women to the enjoyment of all economic, social, and cultural rights." While some of

---

to Development in International Law, 12 AUSTL. Y.B. INT'L 190 (1992); Waring, *supra* note 55. This may not seem as immediately critical for women in the industrialized countries, which do not depend on ICESCR to facilitate development programs and grants. What it really means, however, is that Western women can expect even less support from their States in obtaining recognition for their unpaid work, since there is no direct benefit to the State for doing so.

74. *See infra* text accompanying notes 113–14.

75. Waring, *supra* note 55.

76. Stark, *supra* note 32, at 26–33.

77. *See* Nadine Taub & Wendy Williams, *Will Equality Require More Than Assimilation, Accommodation, or Separation from the Existing Social Structure?*, 37 RUTGERS L. REV./CIV. RTS. DEVELOPMENTS 825 (1985).

78. *See* Wright, *supra* note 70, at 248 ("The problem is not just 'equality,' but the standard by which it is measured and the separation of political and economic rights into separate fields in which equality provides an uneasy and very fragile bridge.").

79. *Cf.* Rebecca Cook, *Accountability in International Law for Violations of Women's Rights by Non-State Actors*, this volume at 105 ("In contrast to previous human rights treaties, the Women's Convention ... develops the legal norm from a sex neutrality norm that requires equal treatment of men and women, usually measured by how men are treated, to recognize that the distinctive characteristics of women and their vulnerabilities to discrimination merit a specific legal response.").

the drafters considered Article 3 redundant, it was nevertheless adopted unanimously,[80] more for "psychological than legal reasons," according to one representative.[81] Although international consensus on gender discrimination is notably problematic,[82] this standard is both more muscular and more far-reaching than current US law.[83]

This prohibition applies to *de facto*[84] as well as *de jure* discrimination and recognizes the need for a full range of measures to address both.[85] These measures could include, for example, State-supported programs (run for and by women) for job training, childcare, and escort services. The State is required to ensure women's ongoing participation in planning and implementing such programs under ICESCR.[86]

Finally, and significantly, Article 10.2 recognizes a right to paid leave before and after childbirth. This does not resolve the dilemma of special treatment presented by the Cal-Fed case.[87] States are still free to give fathers paid leave during the same period, and they may arguably be required to do so under some State law. Article 10 rejects the assumption of a male norm under which childbirth is squeezed into a category like "disability" previously established to accommodate men's experience. Instead, the fact that childbirth is biologically unique to women is the starting point. While this difference is recognized under the Covenant, it cannot be used to justify disparate treatment which will disadvantage women.

Contextual Inversion[88]

By ratifying the Covenant, the State recognizes the rights of every human being to be nurtured: to be cared for, housed, fed, clothed, healed, educated, and made to feel part

---

80. Yvonne Klerk, *Working Paper on Article 2(2) and Article 3 of the International Covenant on Economic, Social, and Cultural Rights*, 9 Hum. Rts. Q. 250, 259 (1987).

81. *Id.* at 258.

82. For a comprehensive and insightful analysis, *see* Charlesworth, Chinkin & Wright, *supra* note 71. *See generally* Rebecca Cook, *International Human Rights Law Concerning Women: Case Notes and Comments*, 23 Vand. J. Tran. L. 779 (1990); Rebecca Cook, *Reservations to the Convention on the Elimination of All Forms of Discrimination against Women*, 30 Va. J. Int'l L. 643 (1990); Brinda Clark, *The Vienna Convention Reservations Regime and the Convention on Discrimination against Women*, 85 Am. J. Int'l L. 281 (1991). Prohibitions against racial discrimination, in contrast, are generally recognized as customary international law, even peremptory norms. *See, e.g.* Richard Bilder, *An Overview of International Human Rights Law*, in Guide to International Human Rights Practices 15–17 (H. Hannum ed., 1989).

83. *See* Craig v. Boren, 429 US 190 (1976) (establishing intermediate scrutiny standard for sex discrimination claims). *Cf.* Frontiero v. Richardson, 411 US 677 (1973) (sex discrimination claims entitled to same scrutiny standard as race discrimination claims).

84. The failure of international law to address discrimination in fact has been a focus of feminist criticism. *See, e.g.*, Reanda, *supra* note 71, at 15 (criticizing the Human Rights Committee for emphasizing legal rather than actual discrimination).

85. As the Guidelines observe, the "positive measures needed in order to give effect to Article 3 require more than the enactment of legislation."

86. *See infra* text accompanying notes 128.

87. California Federal Savings & Loan v. Guerra, 479 US 272 (1987) (Pregnancy Discrimination Act held not to prohibit California statute requiring employers to provide leave and reinstatement to pregnant employees). *See generally* Joan Williams, *Deconstructing Gender*, 87 Mich. L. Rev. 797 (1989).

88. Much of what is discussed in this section may evoke for some readers the infamous public/private distinction. I prefer the deliberately loose concept of "women's contexts" in part because, as Frances Olsen and others have suggested, the public/private distinction is incoherent (Frances Olsen, AALS Proc., Jan. 1993; Ruth Gavison, *Feminism and the Public/Private Distinction*, 45 Stan. L. Rev. 1 (1992)); and in part because it privileges "men's contexts"—describing what women do in terms of what men do not, defining women's "peripheral" concerns in terms of men's "core" ones. In some contexts, of course, discussion (or deconstruction) of the public/private distinction is necessary. *See, e.g.*, Charlesworth, *supra* note 73. This becomes, in part, a question of strategy.

of a community. These "nurturing rights" are inverted descriptions of "women's work" —what American women in the 1990s actually do.[89] I am not suggesting complete congruence, a perfect fit. Women obviously do not—and could not—assume sole responsibility for assuring all of the rights set forth in ICESCR. Nor does all "women's work" necessarily promote the objectives of the Covenant. Much that it [women's work] does, moreover, is consistently ignored under international law.[90] The amount and kind of nurturing work done by individual women varies as a function of age, class, family status and other factors.[91] Nevertheless, the overlap where "women's work" satisfies obligations imposed by the Covenant is substantial.

FEMINIST RECOGNITION AND AMBIVALENCE

American feminists, insisting that the "personal is political,"[92] have already made "private" concerns matters of urgent public debate, demanding State attention and State resources. Feminists have shown that women's "personal" needs—to know that their children are being well-cared for when they are at work; to know that taking care of sick relatives will not imperil jobs[93]—raise fundamentally political questions and require political action.[94]

At the same time, American feminists approach nurturing work with considerable ambivalence. Unlike battering, rape, incest, sexual harassment, and other forms of oppression, nurturing work is not necessarily painful or embarrassing. Indeed, it is often a source of great satisfaction. Feminist views on nurturing work, accordingly, range over a broad spectrum, from nurturing work as an art form[95] to nurturing work as the lowest form of

---

89. As Wesley Newcomb Hohfeld explained, rights correspond to duties, and we cannot talk about rights without considering the mechanisms through which they are to be realized. Wesley Hohfeld, *Fundamental Legal Conceptions as Applied to Judicial Reasoning*, 26 YALE L.J. 710 (1921). While I rely on Hohfeld's general analytic framework, a rigorous examination of juridical opposites and correlatives in this context is beyond the scope of this essay. Nurturing rights may be defended as true "rights" even though, depending on the circumstances, their exercise may well fit more snugly in another of Hohfeld's categories. A *privilege* to fish in state waters may be all a person needs to feed herself and her family, for example, but if the fish all get eaten, she may still assert her underlying *right* to food under the Covenant. Moreover, as Joseph Singer has noted: "Hohfeld demonstrated that any supposed connection between liberties and duties did not result from logical necessity. Whether there should be such concomitant rights (or claims) is ultimately a question of justice and policy." Joseph Singer, *The Legal Rights Debate in Analytical Jurisprudence from Bentham to Hohfeld*, 1982 WISC. L. REV. 975, 1053. *See generally* J. M. Balkin, *The Hohfeldian Approach to Law and Semiotics*, 44 U. MIAMI L. REV. 1119 (1990).

90. Waring, *supra* note 55, at 182 ("[I]t seems to me that one of the most glaring tools of continual enslavement of more than half of the human species finds its focus in the inadequate international patriarchal concept of 'work'....").

91. For a thoughtful and wide ranging collection of papers analyzing household resource distribution issues from the perspectives of anthropology, economics, and psychology, *see* INTRA-HOUSEHOLD RESOURCES ALLOCATION: ISSUES AND METHODS THAT DEVELOP IN POLICY AND PLANNING (Beatrice Lourge Rogers & Nina B. Schlossman eds., 1983).

92. *Feminist Legal Methods, supra* note 66, at 864 n. 143.

93. *See* Nadine Taub, *From Parental Leaves to Nurturing Leaves*, 13 N.Y.U. REV. L. & SOC. CHANGE 81 (1984–85).

94. This is a variation of a theme—the influx of women and "feminine" values into the public sphere —that resonates throughout feminist literature and movements. Women's movements have historically been expected to "inject social concerns" into the political agenda. WOMEN'S MOVEMENTS IN THE US AND WESTERN EUROPE 80 (M. Katzenstein & C. Mueller eds., 1987).

95. *See, e.g.,* Heidi Laing with Arlene Raven, *Selected Highlights from the Feminist Art Movement*, Ms., 68–72 (September 19, 1993) (describing "The Dinner Party," a sculptural installation by Judy Chicago, which opened at the San Francisco Museum of Art in 1979); *cf.* Arlene Raven, *Arts: The Archaic Smile*, Ms., 70 (September 19, 1993) (rejection by women artists of housework, as shown in works using "household metaphors such as sweeping a room or ironing clothes").

"dirty work."[96] This ambivalence makes nurturing work especially difficult to grapple with legally.[97] How can we develop coherent law when there is so little consensus as to the goals or purposes of such law? It may be even more difficult to generate norms about work that is not even seen.[98] Nurturing work is so deeply internalized in the individual[99] that women do it unconsciously, so deeply embedded in the culture that no one sees them doing it.[100] Underfunded public schools, for example, could hardly function without "parent" volunteers. These are almost exclusively women. Some argue that this shows the necessity of increasing the school budget. Others respond that children should not suffer until the needed teaching assistants can be hired. Still others contend that parents should be involved in the schools and that special efforts need to be made to involve fathers. ICE-SCR, again, would not resolve the debate. But it would re-situate it, providing a legal framework for challenging the system's *de facto* reliance on — and exploitation of — women.

THE STATE'S RELUCTANT RECOGNITION

The State resists recognizing women's nurturing work for several reasons.[101] First, the intrapsychic constructs of a gendered division of labor at the core of male experience,[102] as well as the self-serving oblivion of those who do not do the work, are deeply embedded in, and institutionalized by, the male State. Unless women become a self-conscious constituency and demand support or compensation for nurturing work, it remains easier and cheaper for the State to support an ideology of the family under which women provide nurturing services at no cost.

The State's refusal to recognize nurturing work is reflected in and reinforced by legal regimes which marginalize and distort it. Family law, for example, only considers the value of nurturing work at the time of divorce.[103] Tellingly, spousal support obligations are directly linked to the likelihood that the unsupported spouse will otherwise become

---

96. *See, e.g.*, Pat Mainardi, *The Politics of Housework*, *in* SISTERHOOD IS POWERFUL: AN ANTHOLOGY OF WRITING FROM THE WOMEN'S LIBERATION MOVEMENT 447 (Robin Morgan ed., 1970).

97. For a recent creative suggestion, *see* Cynthia Starnes, *Divorce and the Displaced Homemaker: A Discourse on Playing with Dolls, Partnership Buyouts and Disassociation Under No-Fault*, 60 U. CHI. L. REV. 67 (1993).

98. *Cf.* Charlesworth, *supra* note 73 (noting that the invisibility of women's work decreases women's claim to the basic necessities in some third world countries).

99. *See* Williams, *Gender Wars*, *supra* note 66, at 1571.

100. It becomes briefly, fleetingly visible when there is a gap between cultural and personal expectations, as there is when we are observers in another culture or sometimes between generations. *See, e.g.*, AMY TAN, THE KITCHEN GOD'S WIFE (1991).

101. Such "recognition" could be achieved in several ways, like any other binding interpretation of an international treaty provision. Vienna Convention on the Law of Treaties, Art. 19, Formulation of Reservations, Art. 31 *Interpretation of Treaties*. UN DOC. A/CONF. 39/27, (1969), 63 AM. J. INT'L L. 875 (1969), 8 I.L.M. 679 (1969). An "interpretive statement" or an "understanding" can be attached to a State's ratification, for example. *See generally* Belilos v. Switzerland 132 EUR. CT. H.R. (ser. A) 21–24 (1988); Derek W. Bowett, *Reservations to Non-Restricted Multilateral Treaties*, 48 BRIT. Y.B.I.L. 69 (1975). Alternatively, a domestic court can adopt the analysis of rights discussed here in the context of treaty-based litigation.

102. *See, e.g.*, Barbara Stark, *Psycho-Feminism and Divorce Law: "Oedipus Wrecks,"* *in* GENDER COMPARATIVE PERSPECTIVES (Barbara Stark ed., 1992) [hereinafter COMPARATIVE PERSPECTIVES].

103. McGuire v. McGuire, 59 N.W. 2d 336 (Neb. 1954); Barbara Stark, *Burning Down the House: Toward a Theory of More Equitable Distribution*, 40 RUTGERS L. REV. 1173 (1988) [hereinafter Burning Down the House]. *See generally* Pat Cain, *In Search of a Normative Principle for Property Division at Divorce*, (book review) 1 TEX. J. WOMEN & L. 249, 251–52 (1992) (noting benefits of equality rhetoric in the public sphere and urging its extension to the private sphere).

a public charge.[104] While social welfare law pays more attention to nurturing work, it devalues nonmarket labor by equating it with a bare subsistence allowance.[105] Employment law, similarly, has only recently acknowledged that workers may be nurturers as well.[106] It continues to privilege market labor over nonmarket work. While urging—and supporting—constructive reforms, feminists have stressed the limitations of any one approach.[107] If there is any consensus, it is on the need for a range of contextualized approaches perhaps including, but surely not limited to, those already developed.[108]

Under ICESCR

Where legal rights have value, as they do in this country, legal recognition effectively ascribes values to nurturing rights. This is necessary, but not sufficient, for ascribing value to women's work in securing these rights. The importance of ascribing value to the work done by women has already been recognized in a variety of domestic contexts.[109] Divorce and personal injury lawyers, for example, have sought to maximize benefits for the individual women they represented.[110] Some women's rights activists have argued that homemakers as a group will never attain parity until they are recognized—

---

104. Unander v. Unander, 506 P.2d 719 (Or. 1973) (provision in antenuptial agreement waiving alimony is unenforceable if spouse has no other source of income); cf. In re Wilson, 201 Cal. App. 3d 913 (1988) (affirming termination of support for disabled spouse where marriage was short and there were no children).

105. I am referring to the US welfare system. Those of some other nations are more generous. *Need for an Entirely New Strategy, supra* note 41, at 376 n. 49.

106. Family and Medical Leave Act of 1993, Pub. L. 103-3, Feb. 5, 1993; 107 Stat. 6. Feminists have also argued that the workplace should be restructured to accommodate nurturing work. *See, e.g.,* Lucinda Finley, *Transcending Equality Theory: A Way Out of the Maternity and the Workplace Debate,* 86 COLUM. L. REV. 1118 (1986); Nancy Dowd, *Work and Family: The Gender Paradox and the Limitations of Discrimination Analysis in Restructuring the Workplace,* 24 HARV. C.R.-C.L. L. REV. 79 (1989). They have pointed to the hostility of the workplace to nurturing work to expose its profound gender bias.

107. The former husband, for example, is often unable to support two households, even assuming he wanted to do so. In fact, as Lenore Wietzman has pointed out, most divorcing couples have very limited property. Alimony, moreover, has never been a solution for most divorcing women. *Burning Down the House, supra* note 103, at 1191–93. The welfare system is poorly funded, often poorly managed, and institutionally biased against single mothers. Martha Fineman, *The Concept of the Natural Family and the Limits of American Family Law, in* COMPARATIVE PERSPECTIVES, *supra* note 102, at 15. Employers, finally, may well be increasingly unresponsive to employee claims in an era of declining union influence and intense global competitiveness.

108. There seems to be a growing appreciation of the need for generating woman-focused law through the political process; that is, by electing feminists to office. *See, e.g.,* Richard Berke, *Women Discover the Political Power of Raising Money for Their Own,* N.Y. TIMES, May 31, 1992, §E, at 3 col. 1. This is at best a long-range proposition. Even assuming success, feminists will have to learn the ropes, "pay their dues" and work with non-feminist colleagues to develop appropriate law. It is impossible to predict how many will survive the process. *See generally,* Judith Resnik, *On the Bias: Feminist Reconsiderations of the Aspirations for Our Judges,* 61 S. CAL. L. REV. 1877 (1988).

109. There have been innumerable efforts to develop a method to calculate the market value of housework. In WOMEN'S CLAIMS: A STUDY IN POLITICAL ECONOMY (1983), for example, the authors, Lisa Peattie and Martin Rein, suggest three approaches. First, they provide two methods of calculating market cost, either "replacement cost" to hire individuals to do general housework, or "service cost" to hire market specialists, such as launderers or caterers. The third method is the "lost opportunity cost;" that is, what could have been earned by the houseworker had she been working for pay. *Id.* at 38. It is an open question whether the value of homemaker services can be adequately expressed in monetary terms. There are several reasons for this, including the tendency of household work to expand to fill all available time.

110. There is little consistency and less predictability in their methods, however. *See* Carl Schneider, *The Next Step: Definition, Generalization, and Theory in American Family Law,* 18 U. MICH. J. L.

and paid—as workers.[111] Advocates for the poor similarly have sought recognition of women's work as a way of securing benefits for the most significant segment of their constituency.

The recognition of nurturing rights as rights under the Covenant would facilitate feminist efforts to focus State attention on women's work, which would be taken into account in the State's self-monitoring reports.[112] The Committee recognizes State support of nurturing rights, and States include women's nurturing work (especially that which is State-supported) in their self-monitoring reports as evidence of their own compliance. State recognition of nurturing work, in turn, provides women with a basis for demanding State support. In conjunction with the participation of women effectively required in the reporting process,[113] State recognition of nurturing work—and women's self-consciousness regarding their role in providing it—are mutually reinforcing.

While ICESCR does not require the State to recognize the value of women's work, it gives women both the incentives to demand such recognition and the leverage to do so. The ICESCR process is structured so as to raise the consciousness of the State as well as the women involved.

Equally important, by requiring States to "take steps" to "progressively realize" nurturing rights, ICESCR implies some assumption of responsibility by the State and a corresponding decrease of the burden on women.[114] There are countless examples of States which have in fact relieved women of some burdens. Recent reports note, for example, that Sweden assures benefits for disabled children;[115] Norway has established an ombudsman (sic) for children "to deal with complaints of child abuse, physical conditions of children, child care, and schools;"[116] and Belarus provides subsidies for children's clothing.[117] Absent these State programs, women would have to cope individually with the needs of their disabled children in Sweden and the bureaucracy dealt with by the Norwegian ombudsman, and women would spend more time scrounging for children's clothing in Belarus.[118] Some of the work otherwise left to women is instead performed by the State.

Ref. 1039 (1985). More importantly, these methods are only applied if there is a divorce or an accident, and for the most part represent a very fact-specific determination.

111. The wages for housework movement attempted to make women's work visible by linking it to the national economy, by putting a dollar value on it. But who was supposed to pay? It would hardly be fair to have husbands pay, since the gap between the wages of a doctor's wife and those of a factory worker's wife would bear no relation to the respective work of each woman. *See* Silvia Federici, *Wages against Housework*, and Joan Landes, *Wages for Housework—Political and Theoretical Considerations*, *in* The Politics of Housework (Ellen Malos ed., 1980).

112. ICESCR, Art. 16. States parties to the Covenant already include benefits to women and families under Art. 10 in their reports. *See, e.g.*, Committee on Economic, Social, and Cultural Rights, Report on the Second Session E/1988/14, E/C.12/1988/4 at 26 (1988) [hereinafter Second Session Report](referring to high Swedish outlays in social and health sectors).

113. *See, e.g.*, Commentary on Art. 3 ("The positive measures needed in order to give effect to Article 3 require more than the enactment of legislation. Thus, reports should provide information as to the situation of women in practice in regard to the enjoyment of all of the rights recognized in the covenant."); Guidelines on Art. 11, 2(b)(ii) ("Please provide detailed information ... [on] any significant differences in the situation of men and women."), *in* Manual on Human Rights, *supra* note 56, at 48, 60.

114. This may increase women's tasks by requiring them to deal with State bureaucracy. *See, e.g.*, Fineman, *supra* note 107.

115. *Second Session Report*, *supra* note 112, at 28.

116. *Id.* at 41.

117. *Id.* at 32.

118. This does not directly answer the question posed by Anita Dahlberg and Nadine Taub—why are women invariably the ones coping with these problems? Anita Dahlberg & Nadine Taub, *Notions*

Support for the "Natural Family"

The "natural family" is not defined under the Covenant. Instead, the Article 10 Guidelines require the State to "indicate what meaning is given in your society to the term 'family.'"[119] Feminists have justly criticized human rights instruments for incorporating, and thereby legitimating and perpetuating, local patriarchal norms.[120] While it may be argued that the meanings given the term "family" in American society are far broader than those given the term in American law,[121] even under US law a considerable range is recognized. "Family" is defined differently for different purposes, and these definitions vary from state to state and in state and federal law. As the Supreme Court observed in *Moore v. East Cleveland*.[122]

> Ours is by no means a tradition limited to respect for the bonds uniting the members of a nuclear family.... The constitution prevents East Cleveland from standardizing its children—and its adults—by forcing all to live in certain narrowly defined family patterns.[123]

Given the broad mandate of Article 10, which requires that the "widest possible protection and assistance" be afforded to the family, *all* of the definitions contemplated under American law should arguably be included. Under the ICESCR reporting requirements, moreover, State support that privileged one form of family over another might have to be justified.

However the family is defined, State support is required under Article 10, which recognizes an affirmative duty to "protect and assist" the family, especially mothers and children.[124] This inverts the relationship of the family and the liberal State. This relationship is predicated on the notion of "privacy," that is, that the State stops at the threshold of the family home.[125] Whatever happens inside the family, unless it is clearly criminal, is the

---

of the Family in Recent Swedish Law, in Comparative Perspectives, *supra* note 102, at 133. But it could, over time, help alter this pattern.

119. Manual on Human Rights, *supra* note 56, at 57.

120. *See, e.g.*, Engle, *supra* note 48, at 597, citing Helen B. Holmes, *A Feminist Analysis of the Universal Declaration of Human Rights in* Beyond Domination: Perspectives on Women and Philosophy 250 (Carol C. Gould ed., 1983) (criticizing Art. 16(3) of the Universal Declaration of Human Rights as repressive to women); Waring, *supra* note 55, at 187 (arguing that "non-definition in international law is clarified by the use of the 'norm' that is, the insertion of the word 'patriarchal' before the word 'family'").

121. This is the theme of a recent Banana Republic advertising campaign, which shows sexually and racially mixed groups holding hands or arranging their untraditional selves in a traditional "family pose," accompanied only by the text, "My chosen family." "Family" is apparently a matter of preference for the targeted market, constrained only by the requirements that everyone be beautiful and well dressed.

A recent New Yorker Magazine cartoon makes a similar point, showing two adult fish in a glass bowl, surrounded by many baby fish. One of the adult fish says to the other: "I guess we'd be considered a family. We're living together, we love each other, and we haven't eaten the children yet." The New Yorker, February 15, 1993, at 51.

122. 431 US 494 (1977).

123. 431 US 494, 504–06; 97 S. Ct. 1932, 1938–39 (1977) (finding that plaintiff, her son, and her two grandsons—who were cousins, not brothers—constituted a family for purposes of a municipal housing ordinance limiting occupancy of a dwelling unit to members of a single family).

124. *But see* Wright, *supra* note 70, at 263 (arguing that the protection of the family under the analogous provision of the Universal Declaration is not synonymous with the protection of individual women and children within the family; rather, such protection is presumed to be unnecessary).

125. "A host of cases, tracing their lineage to *Meyer v. Nebraska* and *Pierce v. Society of Sisters*, have consistently acknowledged a 'private realm of family life which the state cannot enter.'" (citations omitted) Moore v. City of East Cleveland, 431 US 494, 499 (1977) (cited in Bartlett, *supra* note 66, at 875).

family's "own business," its "private" concern. Even if there is criminal abuse and neglect within the family, and even if the State has been called upon repeatedly to intervene, the State will not necessarily be held liable for its failure to do so.[126] This leaves the most vulnerable members of the family (usually women and children) at the mercy of the stronger (usually men), economically as well as physically.

OPEN QUESTIONS

Delegating responsibility for women's work to the State raises difficult and troubling questions. To what extent should women (or men) be paid for nurturing work? Should parents be paid hourly wages for taking care of their own children? Should the State subsidize childcare facilities to encourage mothers to seek "productive work" outside the home? Will State support commodify or dehumanize nurturing work? Who is doing the delegating? Will State support cushion nurturing work just enough to make it tolerable—and keep women from competing with men for other jobs?

The answers to these questions cannot be found in the Covenant's text. The "negative space"—what ICESCR does not do—may be as important as its affirmative directives. While ICESCR's mandate is clear, its specific substance, what it *particularly* requires, is not. This indeterminacy, in conjunction with the feminist floor described below, leaves room for women to explore and define their own needs.[127] As Charlotte Bunch has urged: "The specific experiences of women must be added to traditional approaches to human rights in order to make women more visible and to transform a concept and practice of human rights in our culture so that it takes better account of women's lives."[128] The question thus becomes one of women's role in this ongoing process, and how the process may be shaped to address women's diverse needs. As a practical matter women's participation in the ICESCR process is encouraged, if not assured, by ICESCR's hands-on, problem-solving approach.

CONCRETE OVER ABSTRACT[129]

The Economic Covenant inverts the usual hierarchy of rights instruments which privilege abstract rights over concrete ones. ICESCR focuses on actual "food," "shelter," and "health care," rather than on abstractions such as "liberty," "fairness," or "equality." This leads, moreover, to an inversion of the usual legal processes. Economic rights are realized through a process of "concretization:" how can a particular right be satisfied in a particular context?[130] As solutions are devised, modified, and improved upon, economic rights are progressively realized. The process of realizing rights is no longer the common law's "top down" process of conforming experience to an abstract paradigm.[131] Rather, it be-

---

126. DeShaney v. Winnebago County Dept. of Social Services, 489 US 189 (1989) (county agency could not be held liable under US Constitution for failure to remove child from the home of his violent and abusive father notwithstanding numerous complaints and ample evidence of abuse). Harm to women and children, while well-recognized and well-documented, may be ignored with impunity.

127. This assumes women's full participation in the process, as required under the Committee guidelines.

128. Charlotte Bunch, *Women's Rights as Human Rights: Toward a Re-Vision of Human Rights*, 12 HUM. RT. Q. 486, 487 (1990). *See also* Rende Eisler, *Human Rights: Toward an Integrated Theory for Action*, 9 HUM. RT. Q. 287 (1987).

129. Stark, *supra* note 32, at 33–38.

130. This is very similar to what Katharine Bartlett has called "feminist practical reasoning." *Feminist Legal Methods*, *supra* note 66, at 849–63.

131. *Cf.* Joan Williams' "new epistemology … perhaps the core element of [which] is its rejection of an absolute truth accessible through rigorous, logical manipulation of abstractions." Williams, *Deconstructing Gender*, *supra* note 87, at 805.

comes a process from the "bottom up," in which rights acquire meaning when they are given a concrete form. Economic rights are determined by practical problem-solving.

The Covenant's "enabling" process is a process of generating options, rather than finding truth. On both a daily operational level as well as over time, the Economic Covenant eschews the modern project of linear progression[132] in favor of a postmodern proliferation of options. These options are qualified, however, by a feminist floor in the form of two irreducible norms: (1) ICESCR prohibits discrimination, and (2) it requires the State to meet the subsistence needs of its people, particularly its women....

Conclusion[133]

The Economic Covenant inverts, rather than replicates, two of the hierarchies at the core of American jurisprudence. It is a feminist text because it privileges women over men, recognizing that discrimination requires compensatory measures and that women are sometimes entitled to special treatment. Because it is at the same time a postmodern text, it avoids rigid definitions which essentialize women,[134] instead offering a flexible framework through which solutions to economic problems may be tailored to the specific contexts in which needs arise. While irreducible norms prohibiting discrimination and mandating a "minimum core obligation" provide legal support for a feminist floor within each context, the ICESCR process is likely to generate multiple, even conflicting, "feminist" solutions.

Since the Covenant's inversions are profoundly destabilizing,[135] ratification of ICESCR would precipitate a normative shift, challenging that which is taken for granted and elevating unrecognized, even invisible, nurturing work to the status of protected rights. The Covenant could be used by American feminists to re-situate "women's work," placing it firmly in a political context. Women's participation in the ICESCR process, backed by law and by the State resources that back the law, is likely to produce substantive measures which benefit women. Equally important, although probably less demonstrable, it would contribute to a transformative process through which women increasingly[136] distance themselves from their present subordination.[137]

---

132. For a deeply humanistic appreciation of that project, *see* Marshall Berman, All That Is Solid Melts Into Air: The Experience of Modernity (1982).

133. Stark, *supra* note 32, at 38.

134. Joan C. Williams, *Dissolving the Sameness/Difference Debate: A Postmodern Path Beyond Essentialism in Feminist and Critical Race Theory*, 1991 Duke L.J. 296, 309 (1991).

135. Jane Flax, *Postmodernism and Gender Relations in Feminist Theory*, in Feminism/Postmodernism 39, 56 (Linda Nicholson ed., London, New York, Routledge 1990) [hereinafter Feminism/Postmodernism] ("Feminist theories, like other forms of postmodernism, should encourage us to tolerate and interpret ambivalence, ambiguity, and multiplicity as well as to expose the roots of our need for imposing order in structure no matter how arbitrary and oppressive these needs may be.... If we do our work well, reality will appear even more unstable, complex, and disorderly than it does now.").

136. *Id.* at 56 ("Any feminist standpoint will necessarily be partial.").

137. *See* Sandra Harding, *Feminism, Science, and the Anti-enlightenment Critiques*, in Feminism/Postmodernism, *supra* note 135, at 100–01. ("The feminist science and epistemology projects and the feminist enlightenment critiques should be understood as ... attempt[s] to escape damaging limitations of the dominant social relations and their conceptual schemes. These projects are incomplete—we haven't yet figured out how to escape such limitations. Most likely, we are not yet in an historical era when such visions should be possible. At this moment in history, feminists need both enlightenment and postmodernist agendas."). *Cf.* Guyora Binder, *Beyond Criticism*, 55 U. Chi. L. Rev. 888, 914–15 (1988) (discussing the "seeming paradox of undermining instrumental culture ... by proposing instrumental action").

C. The Importance of CEDAW for the Implementation of Women's Human Rights

1. UN Committee on the Elimination of Discrimination against Women: Concluding Comments of the Committee on the Elimination of Discrimination against Women: *China*[138]

A detailed process has developed over the years for examination of states' reports. The concern and recommendations set forth above for China and Guatemala come near the end of that process. Prior to the broad and general Concluding Comments, a meeting has taken place in which representatives of the state appear before the committee to respond to questions. Prior to this meeting, the committee has formulated and given to the state involved detailed questions based on the report, and has received (or at least should have received) the state's answers, to be sure of their quality depending on the state, ranging from the complete and responsive to the selective and evasive.

Review paragraphs 17 and 18 of the Concluding Comments for China's report. There appear below excerpts from the Committee's questions to China, during the meeting of China's representatives and Committee members, about part of the subject matter of those paragraphs, and from the answers provided by China.[139]

1. Excerpts from the Committees' questions and China's response on the question of sex-selective abortion follow:

19. In spite of China's recent efforts to combat sex-selective abortion infanticide of baby girls, the 2000 census in China showed 117 boys born for every 100 girls.... Please describe the concrete measures in place to ensure full adherence to the Law on Population and Family Planning of 2001, as well as cases brought under the law since 2001 and sanctions imposed on offenders.

...

(Response): ... [T]he Law on Population and Family Planning of 2001 again clearly stipulates that the identification of fetal gender for non-medical purposes or to bring about sex-selective pregnancy termination for non-medical purposes constitutes an unlawful act. In 2002, eleven Government ministries and committees ... collaborated in drawing up an official document clearly delineating each agency's operational responsibilities and duties in dealing comprehensively with problematic gender ratios in newborns....

Beginning in 2003, the Government began testing a campaign to promote caring for girl children in some areas around the country, with the purpose of fostering a social environment favorable to the lives and development of girls and eliminating the prejudice favoring male offspring in child-bearing through pro-

---

138. UN Comm. on the Elimination of Discrimination Against Women [CEDAW], *Concluding Comments of the Committee on the Elimination of Discrimination against Women: China*, UN Doc. CEDAW/C/CHN/CO/6 (Aug. 25, 2006), *available at* http://www.un.org/womenwatch/daw/cedaw/cedaw36/cc/CHINAadvance%20unedited.pdf.

139. The questions and responses can be found at the same website as the Concluding Comments: www.un.org/womenwatch/daw/cedaw. Responses to this list of issues and questions for consideration of the combined fifth and sixth periodic report of China, CEDAW/C/CHN/Q/6/Add. 1.

moting the equality of men and women, providing economic assistance to house-holds having only girl children, rigorously investigating and dealing with un-lawful fetal sex selection and gradually establishing a system of social guarantees for rural villages. In 2006, "Operation Caring for Girls" was launched nation-wide. In 2004, the Government formulated and began to implement a system of incentives and assistance for family planning in some rural villages, focusing on rural couples with only one child or with two daughters; for those age 60 and over, the Government provides lifetime incentives and financial assistance. A variety of local policies and measures benefiting girls' lives have also been drawn up in different localities; for example, families with daughters only are given priority in the deployment of development items and assistance, in the provision of educational, medical, and subsistence aid, and (for rural parents of daughters only) in being included in the basic social and old-age insurance system. With regard to cases on unlawful identification of fetal gender and the artificial termination of pregnancies for purposes of sex selection, [two Laws] both provide for penalizing those involved, confiscating the equipment used and suspending the operation of the business involved. Currently, some problems remain with regard to uncovering and verifying such unlawful activity, and concentrated laws and regulations to combat it are lacking. China is currently studying the legislative experiences of such countries as the Republic of Korea and India, and researching the issue of amending the relevant regulations of the Criminal Law. The Chinese government has set a goal of effectively abating the trend of higher ratios of male births and normalizing the gender ratios of newborns overall by the year 2010.

Excerpt from the Committee's question and China's response on the question of gender stereotypes and education follow:

The Committee, in the previous concluding comments, recommended that school textbooks and curricula be revised to eliminate gender stereotypes. Please provide an update on the implementation of this recommendation and, in particular, indicate how the principle of equality between women and men has been incorporated in the new curriculum referred to [in] the report.

(Response): ... [T]he Government has been carrying out a reform of the basic curriculum and teaching materials, and putting forward the need to fully incorporate the principle of equality between men and women.

...

(b). Close attention is paid to ensure that equality in education is an important component of curriculum content. For example, the standards for ideological and moral character education at the junior-secondary level call for students to understand that people are equal in dignity and their status before the law; to be able to treat people equally and refrain from mistreating the weak and bullying or cheating strangers; and to allow the differences of family background, physical appearance, or intellectual ability to give rise to feelings of excessive pride or inferiority.

(&). With regard to the compilation and evaluation of teaching materials, care is taken to increase content fostering equality awareness and action; to avoid exposing students to the imperceptible influences of mechanistic gender stereotypes in the illustrations for teaching materials; to preserve a numerical balance of males and females; and to chose literary compositions featuring female main characters in language-teaching materials and to introduce outstanding female historical figures in materials for history courses.

(d). Learning activities featuring education on the legal system and the protection of human rights have been developed; human-rights content is included in elementary and middle-school textbooks, with text and illustrations being equally high in quality; and laws are explained on the basis of actual cases. Excellent results have already been obtained in propagating knowledge of the law and human rights and forming a concept of equality between men and women among elementary and middle-school students.

2. UN Committee on the Elimination of Discrimination against Women: Concluding Comments of the Committee on the Elimination of Discrimination against Women: *Guatemala*[140]

1.   The Committee on the Elimination of Discrimination against Women considered the sixth periodic report of Guatemala (CEDAW/C/GUA/6) at its 725th and 726th meetings, on 18 May 2006 (see CEDAW/C/SR.725 and 726). The Committee's list of issues and questions is contained in document CEDAW/C/GUA/Q/6, and Guatemala's responses are contained in document CEDAW/C/GUA/Q/6/Add.1.

Introduction

Positive aspects

. . .

4.   The Committee welcomes the efforts of the State party to achieve greater coordination among the various institutions for the advancement of women, including the Presidential Secretariat for Women, the National Office for Women's Affairs, the Indigenous Women's Defense Unit and the First Lady's Social Work Secretariat.

5.   The Committee also welcomes the efforts of the State party to evaluate and update the National Policy for the Advancement and Development of Guatemalan Women: Equal Opportunity Plan 2001–2006 in order to ensure that it contributes effectively to the improvement of women's conditions in the areas of law, economy, health, education, personal security, labor, and political participation.

6.   The Committee further welcomes the adoption of the National Plan for Prevention and Eradication of Domestic Violence as well as the efforts to strengthen the National Coordinating Office for the Prevention of Domestic Violence and Violence against Women.

7.   The Committee welcomes the adoption of the Law on Universal Access to Family Planning Services and the Integration in the Programme on Reproductive Health, Decree 87-2005.

Principal areas of concern and recommendations

8.   While recalling the State party's obligation to systematically and continuously implement all the provisions of the Convention on the Elimination of All Forms of Dis-

---

140. UN Comm. on the Elimination of Discrimination against Women [CEDAW], *Concluding Comments of the Committee on the Elimination of Discrimination against Women;* Guatemala, UN Doc. C/GUA/CO/6 (June 2, 2006), *available at* http://www.un.org/womenwatch/daw/cedaw.

crimination against Women, the Committee views the concerns and recommendations identified in the present concluding comments as requiring the State party's priority attention between now and the submission of the next periodic report. Consequently, the Committee calls upon the State party to focus on those areas in its implementation activities and to report on action taken and results achieved in its next periodic report. It calls upon the State party to submit the present concluding comments and the Committee's concluding comments on the State party's combined third and fourth, and fifth periodic reports (see A/57/38) to Congress and to all relevant ministries so as to ensure their full implementation.

9.   The Committee is concerned that not all relevant government entities, in particular the legislative and judicial branches, may have been fully involved in the process of elaborating the report. As a result, the impact of the reporting process as an aspect of a holistic approach to the ongoing implementation of the Convention may be limited.

10.   The Committee calls upon the State party to strengthen the coordination among all relevant government entities, including representatives from the legislative and judicial powers, as a means to enhance the implementation of the provisions of the Convention, the follow-up to the concluding comments of the Committee and the preparation of future periodic reports under article 18 of the Convention.

11.   The Committee is concerned that the definition of discrimination contained in Decree 57-2002 that amends the Criminal Code is not in accordance with article 1of the Convention, which prohibits both direct and indirect discrimination, as well as article 2 (e), which explicitly requires measures to eliminate discrimination against women by private actors.

12.   The Committee encourages the State party to ensure that a definition of discrimination that encompasses both direct and indirect discrimination, in line with article 1 of the Convention, is explicitly reflected in all appropriate legislation and to include effective sanctions and remedies for the violation of rights by public and private entities, and actors. It urges the State party to carry out awareness-raising campaigns on the Convention and its Optional Protocol, including on the meaning and scope of substantive equality between women and men, aimed, *inter alia,* at the general public, legislators, the judiciary, and the legal profession. Such efforts should focus on the systematic use of the Convention to respect, promote, and fulfill women's human rights, and of the use of the Optional Protocol.

13.   While noting the efforts of the State party aimed at revising the existing discriminatory legislation in the Civil, Criminal, and Labor Codes, the Committee is concerned that, in spite of the recommendations it addressed to the State party on the occasion of the consideration of Guatemala's initial and second periodic reports in 1994 and its combined, third and fourth, and fifth periodic reports in 2002, the domestic legislation is still not in conformity with the Convention. It is also concerned about the lack of awareness about women's human rights among members of the legislature, which may be obstructing the adoption of required legislative reforms, in particular with regard to violence against women.

14.   The Committee urges the State party to put in place an effective strategy with clear priorities and timetables to achieve the required amendments to discriminatory provisions in the Civil, Criminal, and Labor Codes so as to bring them into conformity with the Convention as required by article 2. The Committee encourages the Government to ensure that the national machinery for the advancement of women has the necessary authority and human and financial resources to undertake awareness-raising initiatives for a full

understanding of women's human rights in light of the provisions of the Convention among the legislative and judicial branches.

15. While noting the adoption of the various laws and decrees aimed at protecting women and girls, including Decree 81-2002 aimed at promoting actions towards the elimination of discrimination on grounds of race and gender among all State ministries, the Committee is concerned about the lack of enforcement, coordination, effective implementation, and monitoring of those laws and decrees.

16. The Committee urges the State party to take all the appropriate measures to ensure the effective enforcement, implementation, and assessment of the application of those laws and decrees aimed at protecting women and girls. It recommends that the State party include the impact of those measures in its next periodic report.

17. While noting the steps taken by the State party to strengthen the national mechanism for the advancement of women, the Committee expresses its concern that the national machinery does not have enough human and financial resources to carry out its mandate and promote the advancement of women at the national and local levels. It is also concerned about the limited capacity of the Presidential Secretariat to undertake effective coordination and cooperation with the legislative and judicial branches. It is further concerned about the existing imbalance among the three branches of the State, which results in the resistance to adopt and modify legislation aimed at protecting women's human rights....

21. While appreciating the State party's efforts to combat the trafficking of women and girls, including the ratification of the Protocol to Prevent, Suppress and Punish Trafficking in Persons, Especially Women and Children, supplementing the United Nations Convention against Transnational Organized Crime, the Committee remains concerned about the absence of adequate measures to combat this phenomenon including its causes and extent, in particular from the State party's position as a country of origin, transit, and destination. It is further concerned at the insufficient information and awareness about the incidence of internal trafficking.

22. The Committee urges the State party to increase efforts to determine the causes and extent of trafficking of women and girls from its perspective as a country of origin, transit, and destination and the incidence of internal trafficking. It recommends that the State party strengthen the measures to combat and prevent trafficking in women and girls and provide detailed information about the impact of the measures taken in its next periodic report.

23. The Committee is deeply concerned about the continuing and increasing cases of disappearances, rape, torture, and murders of women, the engrained culture of impunity for such crimes, and the gender-based nature of the crimes committed, which constitute grave and systematic violations of women's human rights. It is concerned about the insufficient efforts to conduct thorough investigations, the absence of protection measures for witnesses, victims and victims' families, and the lack of information and data regarding the cases, the causes of violence, and the profiles of the victims.

24. The Committee urges the State party to take without delay all the measures necessary to put an end to the murders and disappearances of women and the impunity of perpetrators. In that regard, it suggests to the State party to take into account the recommendations made by the Committee in relation to its inquiry undertaken under article 8 of the Optional Protocol regarding the abduction, rape, and murder of women in the Ciudad Juarez area of Chihuahua, Mexico (CEDAW/C/2005/OP.8/MEXICO). It encourages the State party to institutionalize the Commission on Femicide as a permanent

body, with its own human and financial resources. It requests the State party to provide in its next periodic report detailed information on the causes, scope, and extent of the disappearances, rape, and murder of women and of the impact of measures taken to prevent such cases, to investigate occurrences, and prosecute and punish perpetrators, and to provide protection, relief and remedies, including appropriate compensation to victims and their families.

25. The Committee is concerned about the prevalence of domestic violence against women, the lack of effective access to justice for women, particularly indigenous women, who also face language barriers, and the lack of social awareness about and condemnation of violence against women and girls in the country.

26. The Committee urges the State party to accord priority attention to the adoption of a comprehensive and integrated approach to address violence against women and girls, taking into account the Committee's general recommendation 19 on violence against women. It urges the State party to enact the pending reforms to the Criminal Code to criminalize domestic violence and to allocate the necessary resources to implement the Plan for the Prevention and Eradication of Domestic Violence and Violence against Women 2004–2014. It recommends gender sensitivity training on violence against women for public officials, particularly law enforcement personnel, the judiciary, teaching personnel, and health service providers, so as to ensure that they are sensitized to all forms of violence against women and can adequately respond to it.

27. While noting the efforts to amend the Act on Elections and Political Parties to impose a quota of 44 per cent for women's participation, the Committee remains concerned about the underrepresentation of women, in particular indigenous women, in political and public positions at all levels. The Committee is also concerned about the persistence and pervasiveness of patriarchal attitudes and deep-rooted stereotypes regarding the roles and responsibilities of women and men in the family and society, which constitute a significant impediment to the participation of women in decisionmaking at all levels and a root cause of women's disadvantaged position in all spheres of life.

28. The Committee calls upon the State party to accelerate amending of the Act on Elections and Political Parties and strengthen the use of temporary special measures, including quotas, in accordance with article 4, paragraph 1, of the Convention and the Committee's general recommendation 25, to increase the number of women, in particular indigenous women, in political and public life and in decision-making positions. It suggests that the State party implement leadership training programmes aimed at women to help them participate in leadership and decision-making positions in society. The State party is urged to carry out awareness-raising campaigns aimed at women and men to help ensure the elimination of stereotypes associated with men's and women's traditional roles in the family and in society at large and enhance women's political empowerment.

29. The Committee is concerned about the significant gaps in the existing legislation pertaining to article 11 of the Convention, including the lack of provisions to address sexual harassment. It expresses concern about the violations of women's labor rights in the *maquiladora* industries, including the right to association, minimal wage, and maternity leave. The Committee is also concerned about the excessive hours of work and discriminatory practices against pregnant women. It is also concerned about the absence of legislative and policy measures to protect the rights of domestic workers despite the recommendations made by the Committee at the consideration of the previous periodic report....

D. Women as Caretakers of Persons with Disabilities

1. Susan Jones, *Obama Directs US to Sign 'First New Human Rights Treaty of the 21st Century'*[141]

President Barack Obama on Friday announced that the United States will sign the United Nations Convention on the Rights of Persons with Disabilities, a treaty that elevates disability beyond a health and social welfare issue to a human rights issue.

"Disability rights aren't just civil rights to be enforced here at home. They are universal rights to be recognized and promoted around the world," the President said at a White House ceremony. All treaties require Senate ratification.

Adopted by the UN General Assembly in December 2006, the lengthy treaty describes the human rights of persons with disabilities, including the right to equality under the law; the right to live in the community; the right to education, health, and work; and the right to participate in political, public, and cultural life.

The treaty also discusses disabled people's "right" to health care, saying that parties to the treaty "recognize that persons with disabilities have the right to the enjoyment of the highest attainable standard of health without discrimination on the basis of disability."

Countries signing on to the treaty agree to:

- Provide the disabled with the same "range, quality, and standard of free or affordable health care" as provided to other people, including in the area of sexual and reproductive health;
- Provide health services needed by the disabled specifically because of their disabilities, including early identification and intervention as well as services designed to minimize and prevent further disabilities;
- Provide health services as close as possible to people's own communities, including in rural areas;
- Require health professionals to provide the same quality of care to the disabled as to others;
- Prohibit discrimination against the disabled in the provision of health insurance and life insurance, "which shall be provided in a fair and reasonable manner";
- Prevent "discriminatory denial of health care or health services or food and fluids on the basis of disability."

Obama's announcement that he will direct US Ambassador to the UN Susan Rice to sign the treaty this week came on the 19th anniversary of the Americans with Disabilities Act. Attorney General Eric Holder said the UN treaty was inspired by the ADA and will "incorporate principles of empowerment and integration into international law."

According to the treaty's text, its goal is to "promote, protect, and ensure the full and equal enjoyment of all human rights and fundamental freedoms by all persons with disabilities, and to promote respect for their inherent dignity."

---

141. Susan Jones, *Obama Directs US to Sign 'First New Human Rights Treaty of the 21st Century,'* CNSNews.com, July 27, 2009, *available at* http://www.cnsnews.com/public/content/article.aspx?Rsrc ID-51614.

The treaty defines persons with disabilities as those with long-term physical, mental, intellectual, or sensory impairments which—in conjunction with various barriers—may hinder their full and effective participation in society on an equal basis with others.

Among other things, signatories to the treaty agree to protect and promote the human rights of persons with disabilities in all policies and programs; outlaw discrimination against the disabled; promote research and development of "universally designed goods, services, equipment, and facilities ... to meet the specific needs of a person with disabilities"; and promote "research and development of new technologies, including information and communications technologies, mobility aids, devices and assistive technologies, suitable for persons with disabilities, giving priority to technologies at an affordable cost."

WOMEN, TORTURE, REPRODUCTIVE SERVICES

Article 6 singles out women with disabilities. "State Parties recognize that women and girls with disabilities are subject to multiple discrimination, and in this regard shall take measures to ensure the full and equal enjoyment by them of all human rights and fundamental freedoms."

Article 15 grants disabled people "freedom from torture or cruel, inhuman or degrading treatment or punishment."

Article 23 guarantees the right of disabled people to marry—and "to found a family." It says disabled people have the right to decide on the number and spacing of their children—"and to have access to age-appropriate information, reproductive and family planning education."

It also says nations signing the treaty "shall render appropriate assistance to persons with disabilities in the performance of their child-rearing responsibilities."

The treaty "ensures equal access by persons with disabilities to clean water service"; and it ensures access—particularly for women, girls, and the elderly—to social protection and poverty reduction programs.

Article 30 deals with participation in cultural life, recreation, leisure, and sport. It says nations signing the treaty must take "appropriate measures" to ensure that the disabled enjoy access to television programs, films, theater, and other cultural activities "in accessible formats"; and enjoy access to places for cultural performances or services, such as theaters, museums, cinemas, libraries, and tourism services, and, as far as possible, enjoy access to monuments and sites of national cultural importance.

States must encourage and promote the participation of disabled people, to the fullest extent possible, in mainstream sporting activities at all levels. It says children with disabilities must have equal access to participate in play, recreation, and leisure and sporting activities, including those activities in the school system.

The treaty establishes a "Committee on the Rights of Persons with Disabilities," initially consisting of 12 "experts," who will receive reports submitted by nations that sign the treaty. Nations will be required to submit a report at least every four years, or whenever the Committee asks them to do so.

"Each report shall be considered by the Committee, which shall make such suggestions and general recommendations on the report as it may consider appropriate and shall forward these to the State Party concerned."

One hundred and forty nations already have signed the treaty.

Chapter 3

Views on Violence and Torture, the UN Convention against Torture, and Women's Human Rights

A. Different Views on Torture and the Impact of State-Sponsored Torture on Women

Women are particularly vulnerable to violence and torture, and they are frequently the victims of State-sponsored torture. The UN Declaration on the Elimination of Violence against Women[1] states that "violence against women means any act of gender-based violence that results in or is likely to result in physical, sexual or psychological harm or suffering to women, including threats of such acts, coercion or arbitrary deprivation of liberty, whether occurring in public or in private life." (Art. 1). States have an obligation to "exercise due diligence to prevent, investigate and, in accordance with national legislation, punish acts of violence against women, whether those acts are perpetrated by the State or by private persons." (Art. 4).

Violence against women is rampant in all corners of the world, and governments do little to prevent it. According to a Report of Amnesty International,[2] violence against women is manifested in a number of ways including: savage beating and rapes by prison guards; acid burning and dowry deaths by parents and relatives; "honor" killings; domestic violence; female genital mutilation; etc. Perpetrators of violence against women are rarely held accountable for their acts. Women who are victims of gender-related violence often have little recourse because many state agencies are themselves guilty of gender bias and discriminatory practices.

Torture is defined differently in the many legal documents that prohibit torture. For example, in Article 1 of the UN Convention against Torture and Other Cruel, Inhuman, or Degrading Treatment or Punishment, torture is defined as: "... any act by which severe pain or suffering, whether physical or mental, intentionally inflicted on a person for such purposes as obtaining from him or a third person information or a confession, punishing him for an act he or a third person has committed or is suspected of having committed, or intimidating or coercing him or a third person, or for any reason based on discrimination of any kind, when such pain or suffering is inflicted by or at the instiga-

---

1. UN Declaration on the Elimination of Violence against Women (1993), *available* at www.unhchr.ch/hutidoca.nsf/ ... /a.res.48.104.end.
2. Amnesty International, "Violence against Women: Information", *available* at http://www.amnestyusa.org/our-work/issues/women-s-rights/violence-against-women/violence-against-women-information.

tion of or with the consent or acquiescence of a public official or other person acting in an official capacity. It does not include pain or suffering arising only from, inherent in, or incidental to, lawful sanctions."

In Article 5 of the Inter-American Convention to Prevent and Punish Torture, acts constituting torture are "understood to be any act performed intentionally by which physical and mental pain or suffering is inflicted on a person for purposes of criminal investigation, as a means of intimidation, as a personal punishment, as a preventive measure, as a penalty or for any other purpose. Torture will also be understood to be [the] application to a person of methods designed to efface the victim's personality or to diminish his physical or mental capacity, even if they do not cause physical pain or mental anguish."

A State may employ torture as a method for terrorizing its population, discouraging dissent, or silencing opposition. Torture can be used by some states as a part of punishment itself, according to the criminal code. Some even argue that certain methods of capital punishment rise to the level of torture. Criminal punishment involving amputation of limbs is still used in countries that adhere to religious codes or *Shari'a* law. It is not unusual for a woman to be stoned to death for having sat next to a male from the wrong tribe or clan or simply for having an innocent flirtation with a boy.

Even if torture is expressly sanctioned by State consent, the practice of torture is a violation of human rights norms that are so fundamental as to be prohibited by *jus cogens*.[3] *Jus cogens* is considered a "peremptory norm" of international law, "from which no derogation is permitted and which can be modified only by a subsequent norm of general international law having the same character."[4] Furthermore, in 1992, the US Ninth Circuit ruled in the *Siderman* case that "the right to be free from official torture is fundamental and universal, a right deserving of the highest status under international law, a norm of *jus cogens*."[5]

Despite the universal prohibition against torture, the use of torture remains widespread and practiced by governments throughout the world, and especially on women, to achieve political or social goals. The prohibition against torture is stipulated prominently in the International Bill of Rights (Universal Declaration of Human Rights (Article 5) and the International Convention on Civil and Political Rights (Article 7)). The UN Convention against Torture and Other Cruel, Inhuman or Degrading Treatment or Punishment (CAT)[6] was enacted to give more force to the ban on State-sponsored torture.

It is generally accepted and encoded in the UN Convention against the Elimination of Discrimination against Women that women are particularly vulnerable and are frequently the victims of horrific State-inflicted torture. Typically, a government will torture a woman if it is primarily targeting that particular woman for an alleged crime, or if the government decides to use a woman in the family as an effective means of torturing a different family member. The wife or daughter of a suspect may be raped in front of a husband or

---

3. Vienna Convention on the Law of Treaties, adopted 23 May 1969, 1155 U.N.T.S. 331 (entered into force Jan. 27, 1980), *reprinted in* 8 I.L.M. 679 (1969), at art. 53, *available at* http://untreaty.un.org/ils/texts/instruments/english/conventions/1_1_1969.pdf (108 states parties).

4. *Id.* at art. 53.

5. Siderman de Blake v. Republic of Argentina, 965 F. 2d 699, 717 (9th Cir. 1992).

6. Convention against Torture and Other Cruel, Inhuman or Degrading Treatment or Punishment, adopted Dec. 10, 1984, 1465 U.N.T.S. 85 (entered into force June 26, 1987), *reprinted in* 23 I.L.M. 1027 (1984), minor changes *reprinted in* 24 I.L.M. 535 (1985), *available at* http://www.ohchr.org/english/law/cat/htm (146 states parties).

father who is the intended victim. Women may be tortured or raped to obtain information about a suspected dangerous family member's location.

If rape is a form of torture, then rape is also a violation of Article 11 of the American Convention on Human Rights, which guarantees the fundamental right to privacy by safeguarding the right to have one's "honor respected" and "dignity recognized." (Note the euphemistic language of "honor" referring to what women who are raped lose and suffer.) The groundbreaking jurisprudence of the International Tribunal for Crimes against the Former Yugoslavia in the Hague as well as the jurisprudence of the International Tribunal for Crimes Committed in Rwanda will use more objective language when defining the elements of rape by clearly and firmly establishing that rape is a war crime, a crime against humanity, an act of genocide, as well as torture and not simply a violation of a woman's "honor."

Despite the absolute prohibition by international and domestic laws against the use of torture, many States (more in authoritarian rather than liberal regimes) continue to use torture as a means to obtain critical information relating to national security. The use of torture for the protection of national security remains a controversial question. In the hope of protecting national security, some well-known legal scholars defend or rationalize torture[7] and the increasing use of "torture lite" or "enhanced interrogation techniques" such as sleep deprivation, standing or sitting in uncomfortable positions for days at a time, exploitation of phobias, cultural or sexual humiliation, prolonged isolation and water boarding. In the 18th century, Jeremy Bentham argued that torture is justified when it is instrumental in serving to further a goal, and he called it the price one pays for the right to dissent. This theory is akin to Macchiaveli's philosophy that the ends justify the means, which has generally been discredited by democratic nations of the world.

The events of September 11 led the Bush Administration to institutionalize a broad policy of counter-terrorism involving torture. A huge controversy issued forth a debate on the legitimate use of torture by the United States in times of emergency.[8] On August 1, 2002, the US Department of Justice issued a Memorandum from Jay Bybee, Assistant Attorney General to Alberto Gonzales, Counsel to President Bush, concerning standards of conduct for interrogation of detainees outside the United States under the US Torture Act, 18 U.S.C. Sections 2340–2340A. The memo concludes that according to the definitions of torture set forth in the statute, "pain or suffering must be of such a high level of intensity that the pain is difficult for the subject to endure." Moreover, "torture is a step far-removed from other cruel, inhuman or degrading treatment or punishment." The Bybee memo concludes that the US Convention against Torture reaches only "the most heinous acts." Such an interpretation gave the US military more freedom to use methods of interrogation involving torture.[9] President Bush and Vice President Cheney both openly approved of the use of water boarding in order to obtain vital information in the defense of national security.[10]

---

7. See Jeremy Bentham "On Torture" in W. L. Twining and P. E. Twining, *Bentham on Torture* (eds. and commentary, 24 N. IRELAND LEG. Q. 305 (1973)). Bentham wrote about the difference between "torture" and "punishment" in the mid 1770s, and he explained that the great objection against torture is that is liable to be abused. He did state that there were two cases in which torture may be applied with propriety.

8. See THE TORTURE DEBATE IN AMERICA (Karen J. Greenberg ed., 2006).

9. See Jordan J. Paust, *Executive Plans and Authorizations to Violate International Law*, 43 COLUM. J. TRANSNAT'L L. 811 (2005); *See also* Jordan J. Paust, *Prosecuting the President and His Entourage*, 14 ILSA J. INT'L & COMP. L. 539 (2007); Jordan J. Paust, *The Second Bybee Memo: A Smoking Gun*, THE JURIST (April 22, 2009).

10. See MARJORIE COHN, COWBOY REPUBLIC: SIX WAYS THE BUSH GANG HAS DEFIED THE LAW (2007). *See also* JORDAN J. PAUST, BEYOND THE LAW: THE BUSH ADMINISTRATION'S UNLAWFUL RE-

The United States has been accused of torturing individuals[11] by sending them to foreign countries where the laws on torture are more relaxed. This is known as "renditions."[12] Some seek justifications for the use of torture by the United States, claiming that the US Constitution and its amendments do not refer to torture as such. However, Article 16 of the US Constitution protects against cruel, inhuman or degrading treatment which is prohibited by the Fifth, Eighth, and/or Fourteenth Amendments. The United States is a State Party to the UN Torture Convention, but with reservations. The US has also signed the ICCPR which prohibits torture in Article 7. The United States is a State Party to the Geneva Conventions which prohibit torture.[13]

Despite the generally accepted human rights norm that all persons have the right to be free from torture and cruel and unusual punishment, some argue that torture may be excused by the "necessity" defense in a "ticking bomb" scenario in order to save the lives of many. Others argue for a universal ban on torture. Sanford Levinson claims that it is hard to avoid granting some degree of legitimacy to torture unless one is willing to adopt a "strict liability" concept for torture.[14] Absolutists argue that there should be a prohibition for any act that inflicts severe and devastating pain because torture has depraving and corrupting effects on individual torturers as well as on society at large. Moreover, absolutists argue that torture should be banned because the social costs of permitting the use of torture, even in narrowly defined exceptional circumstances, would always outweigh the social benefits that could be derived from applying torture.[15] Moreover, information obtained under torture is generally unreliable. Nevertheless, Alan Dershowitz proposed the unusual and rather unworkable suggestion that "torture warrants" be issued by judges on the theory that articulating a "necessity defense" for the use of torture in extreme cases is "not an adequate substitute for explicit advance approval."[16] Even though some believe that "torture lite" should be permitted to protect national security, the Geneva Conventions do not distinguish between torture and torture lite.

In 1996, the Inter-American Commission on Human Rights adopted a noteworthy decision on the issue of whether rape is a form of torture (*Raquel Martí de Mejía v. Perú*).[17] For the first time, the Inter-American Commission on Human Rights acknowledged that

---

SPONSES IN THE "WAR" ON TERROR (2007). *See also* MICHAEL P. SCHARF & PAUL R. WILLIAMS, SHAPING FOREIGN POLICY IN TIMES OF CRISIS (Cambridge 2010).

11. *See* MARK DANNER, TORTURE AND TRUTH: AMERICA, ABU GHRAIB, AND THE WAR ON TERROR (2004).

12. *See* Jordan J. Paust, *Above the Law: Unlawful Executive Authorizations Regarding Detainee Treatment, Secret Renditions, Domestic Spying, and Claims to Unchecked Executive Power* 2 UTAH L. REV. 345 (2007). *See also* Jordan J. Paust, *Civil Liability of Bush, Cheney, et al. for Torture, Cruel, Inhuman, and Degrading Treatment and Forced Disappearance*, 42 CASE W. RES. J. INT'L L. 359 (2009). On rendition, *see also* Leila Nadya Sadat, *Extraordinary Rendition, Torture, and Other Nightmares from the War on Terror*, 75 GEO. WASH. L. REV. 1200 (2007).

1200 (2007). *See also* Leila Nadya Sadat, *Ghost Prisoners and Black Sites: Extraordinary Rendition under International Law*, 37 CASE W. RES. J. INT'L L. 309 (2006).

13. *See generally* Jose E. Alvarez, *Torturing the Law*, 37 CASE W. RES. J. INT'L L. 175 (2006).

14. TORTURE: A COLLECTION 23 (Sanford Levinson ed., 2004).

15. Oren Gross, *The Prohibition on Torture and the Limits of Law* in TORTURE, *supra* note 14, at 229.

16. Alan Dershowitz, *Tortured Reasoning, in* TORTURE, *supra* note 14, at 257.

17. Raquel Marti de Mejia v. Peru, Inter-American Commission on Human Rights, Organization of American States, Report No. 5/96, Case 10.970, Peru (March 1, 1996). *See also* Salmond Masood, *Pakistani Court Upholds 5 Acquittals in Rape Case*, N.Y. TIMES, April 22, 2011, at A7.

rape could also rise to the level of torture, which is an aggravated form of inhumane treatment, that is prohibited by Article 5.2 of the American Convention on Human Rights.[18]

B. Rape Is a Form of Torture

1. Inter-American Commission on Human Rights Organization of American States: *Raquel Martí de Mejía v. Peru*

Report No. 5/96,
Case 10.970
Peru
March 1, 1996[19]

On October 17, 1991, the Inter-American Commission on Human Rights (hereinafter the Commission) received a petition reporting violations of the human rights of Fernando Mejía Egocheaga and of his wife Raquel Martí de Mejía....

Background

Fernando Mejía Egocheaga and his wife Raquel were living in Oxapampa, in the Department of Pasco, at the time the events reported to the Commission took place.

Dr. Mejía Egocheaga was a lawyer, journalist and political activist. At the time of his death he was President of the Oxapampa Bar Association and also Chairman of the Provincial Committee of Izquierda Unida (United Left), a Peruvian political party. He was also a member of the Peruvian Journalists' Association and worked as a journalist on the paper "Campanaria Oxapampa," which he had founded and of which he was editor. As a lawyer, Dr. Mejía Egocheaga concentrated mainly on defending the rights to land of the most disadvantaged groups in Peru. Between 1982 and 1986 he was legal adviser to the "Pichis Palcazu" special project, a rural development initiative launched under the auspices of the Presidency of the Republic. In 1986 he represented the indigenous peoples of the Amuesha Community in a land conflict with the Catholic Church. In his political activity, Dr. Mejía Egocheaga planned to run for mayor of Oxapampa and later possibly to make a bid for a seat in Congress. Mrs. Raquel Martí de Mejía was a teacher and worked as principal of a school for the handicapped in Oxapampa. She is presently living in Sweden, where she obtained political asylum in 1989.

In June 1989 some soldiers were killed by Sendero Luminoso (Shining Path) terrorists in Posuzo, a town not far from Oxapampa. A few days afterwards, about 100 military personnel from the "Batallón Nueve de Diciembre," based in Huancayo, were helicoptered

---

18. American Convention on Human Rights (Pact of San Jose), signed Nov. 22, 1969, 1144 U.N.T.S. 123 (entered into force July 18, 1978), OASTS 36, O.A.A. Off. Rec. OEA/Ser.L/V/11.23, doc. 21, rev. 6 (1979), *reprinted in* 9 I.L.M. 673 (1970), *available at* http://www.oas.org/juridico/english/treaties/b-32.html (24 states parties).

19. *Raquel Martí de Mejía v. Peru*, Inter-American Commission on Human Rights, Organization of American States, Report No. 5/96, case 10.970, Peru (March 1, 1996), *available at* http://www.cidh.oas.org/annualrep/95eng/Peru10970.htm.

into Oxapampa to conduct counterinsurgency operations in the region. These soldiers were billeted in the local Municipal Library....

Analysis

a. The repeated sexual abuse to which Raquel Mejía was subjected constitutes a violation of Article 5 and Article 11 of the American Convention on Human Rights

Current international law establishes that sexual abuse committed by members of security forces, whether as a result of a deliberate practice promoted by the State or as a result of failure by the State to prevent the occurrence of this crime, constitutes a violation of the victims' human rights, especially the right to physical and mental integrity.

In the context of international humanitarian law, Article 27 of the Fourth Geneva Convention of 1949 concerning the protection due to civilians in times of war explicitly prohibits sexual abuse. Article 147 of that Convention which lists acts considered as "serious offenses" or "war crimes" includes rape in that it constitutes "torture or inhuman treatment." The International Committee of the Red Cross (ICRC) has declared that the "serious offense" of "deliberately causing great suffering or seriously harming physical integrity or health" includes sexual abuse.

Moreover, Article 76 of Additional Protocol I to the 1949 Geneva Conventions expressly prohibits rape or other types of sexual abuse. Article 85(4), for its part, states that when these practices are based on racial discrimination they constitute "serious offenses." As established in the Fourth Convention and Protocol I, any act of rape committed individually constitutes a war crime.

In the case of non-international conflicts, both Article 3 common to the four Geneva Conventions and Article 4(2) of Protocol II additional to the Conventions, include the prohibition against rape and other sexual abuse insofar as they are the outcome of harm deliberately influenced on a person. The ICRC has stated that the prohibition laid down in Protocol II reaffirms and complements the common Article 3 since it was necessary to strengthen the protection of women, who can be victims of rape, forced prostitution or other types of abuse.

Article 5 of the Statute of the International Tribunal established for investigating the serious violations of international humanitarian law committed in the territory of the former Yugoslavia, considers rape practiced on a systematic and large scale a crime against humanity.

In the context of international human rights law, the American Convention on Human Rights stipulates in its Article 5 that:

1. Every person has the right to have his physical, mental, and moral integrity respected.

2. No one shall be subjected to torture or to cruel, inhuman or degrading punishment or treatment ...

The letter of the Convention does not specify what is to be understood by torture. However, in the Inter-American sphere, acts constituting torture are established in the Inter-American Convention to Prevent and Punish Torture, which states:

> ... torture will be understood to be any act performed intentionally by which physical and mental pain or suffering is inflicted on a person for purposes of criminal investigation, as a means of intimidation, as a personal punishment, as a preventive measure, as a penalty or for any other purpose. Torture will also

be understood to be [the] application to a person of methods designed to efface the victim's personality or to diminish his physical or mental capacity, even if they do not cause physical pain or mental anguish.

The following will be guilty of the crime of torture:

a. Public employees or officials who, acting in that capacity, order, instigate, induce its commission, commit it directly or, when in a position to prevent it, do not do so.

b. Persons who, at the instigation of the public officials or employees referred to in paragraph 1, order, instigate or induce its commission, commit it directly or are accomplices in its commission.

Accordingly, for torture to exist three elements have to be combined:

1. it must be an intentional act through which physical and mental pain and suffering is inflicted on a person;

2. it must be committed with a purpose;

3. it must be committed by a public official or by a private person acting at the instigation of the former.

Regarding the first element, the Commission considers that rape is a physical and mental abuse that is perpetrated as a result of an act of violence. The definition of rape contained in Article 170 of the Peruvian Criminal Code confirms this by using the phrasing "[h]e who, with violence or serious threat, obliges a person to practice the sex act ..." The Special Rapporteur against Torture has noted that sexual abuse is one of the various methods of physical torture. Moreover, rape is considered to be a method of psychological torture because its objective, in many cases, is not just to humiliate the victim but also her family or community. In this connection, the above-mentioned Special Rapporteur has stated that, particularly in Peru, "... rape would appear to be a weapon used to punish, intimidate, and humiliate."

Rape causes physical and mental suffering in the victim. In addition to the violence suffered at the time it is committed, the victims are commonly hurt or, in some cases, are even made pregnant The fact of being made the subject of abuse of this nature also causes a psychological trauma that results, on the one hand, from having been humiliated and victimized, and on the other, from suffering the condemnation of the members of their community if they report what has been done to them.

Raquel Mejía was a victim of rape, and in consequence of an act of violence that caused her "physical and mental pain and suffering." As she states in her testimony, after having been raped she "was in a state of shock, sitting there alone in her room." She was in no hurry to file the appropriate complaint for fear of suffering "public ostracism." "The victims of sexual abuse do not report the matter because they feel humiliated. In addition, no woman wants to publicly announce that she has been raped. She does not know how her husband will react. [Moreover], the integrity of the family is at stake, the children might feel humiliated if they know what has happened to their mother."

The second element establishes that for an act to be torture it must have been committed intentionally, i.e. to produce a certain result in the victim. The Inter-American Convention to Prevent and Punish Torture includes, among other purposes, personal punishment and intimidation.

Raquel Mejía was raped with the aim of punishing her personally and intimidating her. According to her testimony, the man who raped her told her that she, too, was wanted as a subversive, like her husband. He also told her that her name was on a list of persons connected with terrorism and, finally, warned her that her friendship with a former official in the previous government would not serve to protect her. On the second occasion, before leaving he threatened to come back and rape her again. Raquel Mejía felt terrorized not only for her own safety but also for that of her daughter who was sleeping in another room and for the life of her husband.

The third requirement of the definition of torture is that the act must have been perpetrated by a public official or by a private individual at the instigation of the former.

As concluded in the foregoing, the man who raped Raquel Mejía was a member of the security forces and was himself accompanied by a large group of soldiers.

Accordingly, the Commission, having established that the three elements of the definition of torture are present in the case under consideration, concludes that the Peruvian State is responsible for violation of Article 5 of the American Convention.

The petitioners have also asserted that the sexual abuse suffered by Raquel Mejía violates the provisions of Article 11 of the Convention.

Said article specifies that a State must guarantee everybody protection of their honor and dignity, within the framework of a broader right, namely the right to privacy. The relevant parts of paragraphs 1 and 2 of this article read as follows:

1.   Everyone has the right to have his honor respected and his dignity respected.

2.   No one may be the object of arbitrary or abusive interference with his private life....

The Special Rapporteur against torture has stated that "Rape is a particularly base attack against human dignity. Women are affected in the most sensitive part of their personality, and the long-term effects are perforce extremely harmful, since in the majority of cases the necessary psychological treatment and care will not and cannot be provided."

The Commission considers that sexual abuse, besides being a violation of the victim's physical and mental integrity, implies a deliberate outrage to their dignity. In this respect, it becomes a question that is included in the concept of "private life." The European Court of Human Rights has observed that the concept of private life extends to a person's physical and moral integrity, and consequently includes his sex life.

For the Commission, therefore, the rapes suffered by Raquel Mejía, in that they affected both her physical and her moral integrity, including her personal dignity, constituted a violation of Article 11 of the Convention, responsibility for which is attributable to the Peruvian State.

Article 1(1) of the Convention states:

The State Parties to this Convention undertake to respect the rights and freedoms recognized herein and to ensure to all persons subject to their jurisdiction the free and full exercise of those rights and freedoms.

The Inter-American Court of Human Rights has interpreted this article as establishing two obligations for the States Parties to the Convention: that of *respecting* the rights and freedoms recognized in it and that of *ensuring* their free and full exercise to individuals under their jurisdiction. According to the Court, any form of exercise of public power that violates the rights protected by the Convention is unlawful. Thus, when an organ or agent of the public authority violates any of these rights, this is a violation of the obligation to "respect," and consequently a violation of Article 1(1).

On the basis of these considerations, the Commission concludes that since the Peruvian State omitted to respect the rights to humane treatment and to protection of the honor and dignity of Raquel Mejía, the State is in violation of the obligation contained in Article 1(1).

b. THE IMPOSSIBILITY FOR RAQUEL MEJÍA TO ACCESS DOMESTIC RECOURSE FOR REMEDYING THE VIOLATIONS OF HER HUSBAND'S HUMAN RIGHTS AND OF HER OWN CONSTITUTES A VIOLATION OF ARTICLE 25 AND 8(1), IN RELATION TO ARTICLE 1(1) OF THE CONVENTION

Article 25 and 8(1) of the Convention respectively provide as follows:

Article 25

1. Everyone has the right to simple and prompt recourse, or any other effective recourse, to a competent court or tribunal for protection against acts that violate his fundamental rights recognized by the constitution or laws of the state concerned or by this Convention....

2. The States Parties undertake:

a. to ensure that any person claiming such remedy shall have his rights determined by the competent authority provided for by the legal system of the State;

b. to develop the possibilities of judicial remedy; and

c. to ensure that the competent authorities shall enforce such remedies when granted.

Chapter 4

Cultural Relativism and Conflicting Religious Values Harmful to Women and Children

A. Women's Human Rights and Cultural Relativism

Human rights are universal rights. Legal human rights documents define rights in hyperbolic terms in order to underline the universal nature of human rights norms (*e.g.,* "every human being" has the right to life, "everybody" has the right to liberty and security, "everyone" should be free from hunger, "no one" shall be subject to torture). Dame Roslyn Higgins, a great international law scholar, the former President of the International Court of Justice, and a well-respected human rights advocate, reminds us of the universality of the human spirit: "Individuals everywhere want the same essential things: to have sufficient food and shelter; to be able to speak freely; to practice their own religion or to abstain from religious belief; to feel that their person is not threatened by the state: to know that they will not be tortured, or detained without charge, and that, if charged, they will have a fair trial. I believe there is nothing in these aspirations that is dependent upon culture, or religions, or stage of development."[1]

However, there is a growing and persuasive movement in the human rights community that supports a more relativist position. In contrast to universalists, cultural relativists claim that there is no one transcendent notion of universal "rights" throughout the world and, therefore, no country or culture can impose its own notion of what is "right" or "wrong" on the rest of the world. Instead, respect for diversity and local customs should be observed, and local practices, as strange or even as harmful as they may seem, should receive greater understanding and autonomy from the international community.

The dichotomy between universalism and cultural relativism became prominent at the height of the Cold War between Western democracies and the communist world. With the collapse of the Soviet empire and the US policy of containment, the same debate shifted to the developed and less developed world. Some people in the less developed world, especially in the post-colonial era, view as sheer arrogance any attempt to impose on them a Judeo-Christian moral ideology or a liberal democratic political framework. Stated differently, the peoples of the less developed world view the application of international human rights laws on their local and indigenous practices as the continuation

---

1. Rosalyn Higgins, Problems and Process: International Law and How We Use It 96 1996).

95

of a pattern of cultural imperialism by the "haves" against the "have nots." This argument has merit. Nevertheless, certain traditions and cultural practices are sometimes the root causes of pervasive discrimination against women. Well-intended adherence to cultural relativism and respect for individual differences may actually foster a very detrimental pattern of discrimination against women.

The battle between adherence to universal standards for human rights norms and the respect for cultural differences specifically affects women, especially with regard to such highly controversial practices as honor killings, female genital mutilation, dowry deaths, the strictly enforced duty to wear a head scarf or full body covering, and widow burning, or *sati*. These cultural practices may conflict with overriding political philosophies such as secularism, which is the case in France, Turkey, Italy,[2] and Egypt, where either wearing of a full body covering (*burkha*) or even a simple headscarf in public institutions have been banned. Cultural practices like female genital mutilation may put women and girls in harm's way and result in the continuation of unfair sex discrimination that is justified in the name of "cultural tradition."

The term "culture" is not simple to define. In her book on *Human Rights and Gender Violence* (2006) Sally Engle Merry recognizes the conflict between universal human rights and cultural relativism, and she uses such terms as a "conundrum" or "paradox" or "contradiction" when discussing the relationship of human rights to culture. "Human rights promote ideas of individual autonomy, equality, choice, and secularism even when these ideas differ from prevailing cultural norms and practices." Merry explains that "there are several *conundrums* in applying human rights to local places. First, human rights law is committed to setting universal standards using legal rationality, yet this stance impedes adapting those standards to the particulars of local context. This perspective explains why local conditions often seem irrelevant to global debates. Second, human rights ideas are more readily adopted if they are packaged in familiar terms, but they are more transformative if they challenge existing assumptions about power and relationships. Activists who use human rights for local social movements face a *paradox*. Rights need to be presented in local cultural terms in order to be persuasive, but they must challenge existing relations of power in order to be effective. Third, to have local impact, human rights ideas need to be framed in terms of local values and images, but in order to receive funding, a wider audience, and international legitimacy, they have to be framed in terms of transnational rights principles...." Culture consists of "ideas and practices that are not homogenous but continually changing because of *contradictions* among them or because new ideas or institutions are adopted by members."[3]

Professor Abdullahi An-Na'im suggests that *Shari'a* law, as with all religious texts, should be open to interpretation, especially with regard to women's human rights. In order to protect and provide women's human rights in the Muslim world, An-Na'im hopes that human rights advocates there can "work within the framework of Islam to be effective" by finding interpretations that can be applied in a modern context and that can achieve cultural legitimacy. An-Na'im argues courageously for the possibility of the reinterpretation of tradition.

Tracy Higgins places in the feminist discourse the conflict between the universality of human rights and the need to respect cultural differences. She addresses the challenge of

---

2. Gaia Pianigiani, *Italy: Panel Approves Measure Banning Face Coverings*, N.Y. Times, Aug. 3, 2011, at A10. *See also* F. Brinley Bruton, *Headscarves Slam Brakes on Women's Careers*, MSNBC.com., April 20, 2011. "In secular Turkey, judges, teachers, and other officials are forbidden from wearing traditional Muslim head coverings in public buildings."

3. Sally Engle Merry, Human Rights and Gender Violence 3 (2006).

cultural relativism that has permeated the global political movement and the need to maintain women's rights, even when certain cultural practices tend to marginalize women. Women have much to lose in any movement away from a universal standard of human rights in favor of deference to culture. She points out the real tension that exists between universalism and cultural relativism in the women's rights discourse. On the one hand, women's rights advocates truly understand the value of universal human rights which they believe rightfully belong to all people including women. On the other hand, women's rights advocates also understand the need to respect women's individual differences and to hear women's voices about their own experiences. However, moving too much in the direction away from the equality of men and women toward a respect for women's individual difference may lead to a claim of women's "essentialism," which is a theory about women that may reinforce earlier patriarchal assumptions and further marginalize women. The dialectic of universalism and cultural relativism is tense and delicate.

Customary laws and cultural traditions may conflict with universalist prohibitions in the International Bill of Rights or in CEDAW. These legal instruments, and CEDAW in particular, specifically require States Parties to take "all appropriate measures" to modify or abolish customs and cultural patterns that constitute discrimination against women or that are based on the idea of the inferiority of women. In countries where such customs prevail, women are marginalized and often placed in stereotyped roles that prohibit their development. Thus, the human rights regime respects cultural differences while adhering to a universalist position that is dedicated to the protection and provision of women's basic and inalienable rights.

Female genital mutilation and the right of Muslim women to wear a headscarf in public institutions are two of the most controversial issues in the universalist/cultural relativist debate. The right to participate in one's own cultural life and the right to be free from harmful cultural practices are conflicting rights, and this conflict is manifested vividly in the practice of female genital mutilation. Similarly, the right to freedom of religion and to manifest one's own religion as well as the right to equality and the maintenance of public order are also conflicting rights vividly manifested in the current debate raging about the right to wear a headscarf in public institutions and the ban in France and Italy of the full body covering for women known as the *burkha*.

In this chapter, selections from the World Health Organization (WHO) and the CEDAW Committee outline the harmfulness of the practice of female genital mutilation. Nevertheless, failure to undergo this painful and dangerous procedure may result in a girl in Africa never being accepted as a full member of her community. She may never be eligible to marry and may face extreme economic hardship as a result of abstaining from or escaping the dangerous and painful procedure. Arguably, this procedure is forced torture, not unlike the horribly painful and dangerous foot-binding procedure that Chinese young girls had to endure for centuries, until it was effectively outlawed at the turn of the century.

In Turkey, France, and in several other countries in Europe and in the Middle East where secularism is valued and where there is a growing fear of pressure from fundamentalist Muslim groups, Muslim girls are not permitted to wear a headscarf in public schools (*Leyla Sahin v. Turkey*). In France all people are denied the right to wear a conspicuous religious symbol on their person. In Egypt the highest Muslim authority said in 2009 that he would issue a religious edict banning women from wearing full veils,'[4] referred

---

4. *Egypt Cleric 'To Ban Full Veils,'* BBC News.com, October 5, 2009, *available at* http://news.bbc.co.uk/go/pr/fr/-/2/hi/middle_east/8290606.stm.

to in Arabic as the *niqab* (where the woman is entirely covered from head to toe with only narrow slits for her eyes). Sheikh Mohamed Tantawi, the dean of Al-Azhar University in Egypt, called full-face veiling a custom that has nothing to do with the Islamic faith. However, increasing numbers of women in Egypt have adopted the *niqab*, which is a practice widely associated with the more radical trends of Islam. Sheikh Mohamed Tantawi stated that wearing the *niqab* was merely a tradition, with no connection to religion or the Koran.

Recently, President Nicolas Sarkozy of France succeeded in banning the *burkha* in public, particularly for reasons of national security and because of the disarming nature of a person whose face cannot be seen. Moreover, a woman wearing a *burkha* can hide weapons under her full body coverage. On the other hand, all women (whether Muslim or not) in Iran are forced to wear not only a headscarf but a *hejab* covering their body. Failure to wear this religious garb in Iran (and in Saudi Arabia) will result in public humiliation, severe punishment, and even incarceration.

In *Leyla Sahin v. Turkey,* the European Court of Human Rights ultimately upheld the Turkish law forbidding women to wear a headscarf in Turkish universities in order to protect the valued principle of secularism, "the rights and freedoms of others," as well as the "maintenance of public order and civil peace." In this case, the Court also upheld individual state's rights, referred to as a "margin of appreciation." Judge Tulken's dissent in this case sheds light on how and why this case flies in the face of the highly valued first amendment right of the US Constitution which protects freedom of speech and the fundamental right to manifest one's own religious beliefs.

Professor Tiefenbrun looks more deeply through the lens of semiotics at the symbolic significance of the act of wearing a headscarf and its underlying political significance in order to explain the reasons motivating this unusual court decision, which Americans find hard to understand.

In this chapter, Professor Tiefenbrun also discusses the negative impact on women's human rights in China of the ancient and still pervasive custom of male-child preference and the recent adoption in 1979 of a government one-child policy severely limiting the number of children permitted in a Chinese family. This policy has been enforced in a draconian fashion in order to combat the serious population explosion in China. Chinese women today face centuries of patterns of patriarchy and male domination in society. Even in modern China the existence of concubines and mistresses as well as trafficking of women and girl children are pervasive. It is quite common for the wealthy Chinese today to have several mistresses. One wealthy Chinese man stated: "Keeping a mistress is just like playing golf.... Both are expensive hobbies."[5] Liu Zhijun, a former railway minister, had 18 mistresses, and Xu Maiyong, a former vice mayor executed for embezzlement, reportedly had dozens. Thus, "as China has shed its chaste Communist mores for the wealth and indulgences of a market-oriented economy, the boom has bred a generation of nouveau riche lotharios yearning to rival the sexual conquests of their imperial ancestors."[6]

Chinese families want a baby boy, and this cultural tradition has lead to a disproportionate number of female infanticides, abandonment of baby girls, and sex-selective abortions. The male-child preference in conjunction with the implementation of the one-child

---

5. Dan Levin, *China's New Wealth Gives Old Status Symbol a Boost*, N.Y. TIMES, August 10, 2011, at A6.

6. *Id.*

policy has resulted in a recent decrease in the number of women in China. Despite the illegality of female infanticide and sex-selective abortions, these human rights violations persist in China due to the strength of the male-child preference in Chinese culture and the prominence of a one-child State policy that has been carefully and systematically enforced. This increase in sex trafficking in China, an effect of the one-child policy, is due to the increase in the demand for more women in Chinese society, especially by those men who wish to marry.

Sally Engle Merry views culture this way: "Seeing culture as contested and as a mode of legitimating claims to power and authority dramatically shifts the way we understand the universalism-relativism debate. It undermines those who resist changes that would benefit weaker groups in the name of preserving 'culture,' and it encourages human rights activists to pay attention to local cultural practices. This view of culture emphasizes that culture is hybrid and porous and that the pervasive struggles over cultural values within local communities are competitions over power. More recent anthropological scholarship explores processes by which human rights ideas are mobilized locally, adapted, and transformed and, in turn, how they shape local political struggles ... Rather than seeing universalism and cultural relativism as alternatives which one must choose, once and for all, one should see the tensions between the positions as part of the continuous process of negotiating ever-changing and interrelated global and local norms. Culture in this sense does not serve as a barrier to human rights mobilization but as a context that defines relationships and meanings and constructs the possibilities of action...."[7]

B. Women's Human Rights, Islam, and *Shari'a* Law

1. Abdullahi Ahmed An-Na'im, *Human Rights in the Muslim World*[8]

Introduction

Historical formulations of Islamic religious law, commonly known as *Shari'a*, include a universal system of law and ethics and purport to regulate every aspect of public and private life. The power of *Shari'a* to regulate the behavior of Muslims derives from its moral and religious authority as well as the formal enforcement of its legal norms. As such, *Shari'a* influences individual and collective behavior in Muslim countries through its role in the socialization processes of such nations regardless of its status in their formal legal systems. For example, the status and rights of women in the Muslim world have always been significantly influenced by *Shari'a*, regardless of the degree of Islamization in public life. Of course, *Shari'a* is not the sole determinant of human behavior nor the only formative force behind social and political institutions in Muslim countries....

I conclude that human rights advocates in the Muslim world must work within the framework of Islam to be effective. They need not be confined, however, to the particu-

---

7. Sally Engle Merry, Human Rights and Gender Violence 3 (2006).
8. Abdullahi Ahmed An-Na'im, *Human Rights in the Muslim World*, 13 Harv. Hum. Rts. J. 13, 15–16, 17–18, 19, 20–21, 22, 23–24, 36–37, 38, 39, 43, 45, 47, 49, 50 (1990).

lar historical interpretations of Islam known as *Shari'a*. Muslims are obliged, as a matter of faith, to conduct their private and public affairs in accordance with the dictates of Islam, but there is room for legitimate disagreement over the precise nature of these dictates in the modern context. Religious texts, like all other texts, are open to a variety of interpretations. Human rights advocates in the Muslim world should struggle to have their interpretations of the relevant texts adopted as the new Islamic scriptural imperatives for the contemporary world.

A. Cultural Legitimacy for Human Rights

The basic premise of my approach is that human rights violations reflect the lack or weakness of cultural legitimacy of international standards in a society. Insofar as these standards are perceived to be alien to or at variance with the values and institutions of a people, they are unlikely to elicit commitment or compliance. While cultural legitimacy may not be the sole or even primary determinant of compliance with human rights standards, it is, in my view, an extremely significant one. Thus, the underlying causes of any lack or weakness of legitimacy of human rights standards must be addressed in order to enhance the promotion and protection of human rights in that society.

… This cultural illegitimacy, it is argued, derives from the historical conditions surrounding the creation of the particular human rights instruments. Most African and Asian countries did not participate in the formulation of the Universal Declaration of Human Rights because, as victims of colonization, they were not members of the United Nations. When they did participate in the formulation of subsequent instruments, they did so on the basis of an established framework and philosophical assumptions adopted in their absence. For example, the preexisting framework and assumptions favored individual civil and political rights over collective solidarity rights, such as a right to development, an outcome which remains problematic today. Some authors have gone so far as to argue that inherent differences exist between the Western notion of human rights as reflected in the international instruments and non-Western notions of human dignity. In the Muslim world, for instance, there are obvious conflicts between *Shari'a* and certain human rights, especially of women and non-Muslims.

… In this discussion, I focus on the principles of legal equality and nondiscrimination contained in many human rights instruments. These principles relating to gender and religion are particularly problematic in the Muslim world.

Islam, *Shari'a* and Human Rights

A. The Development and Current Application of *Shari'a*

… To the over nine hundred million Muslims of the world, the Qur'an is the literal and final word of God and Muhammad is the final Prophet. During his mission, from 610 A.D. to his death in 632 A.D., the Prophet elaborated on the meaning of the Qur'an and supplemented its rulings through his statements and actions. This body of information came to be known as Sunna. He also established the first Islamic state in Medina around 622 A.D. which emerged later as the ideal model of an Islamic state....

While the Qur'an was collected and recorded soon after the Prophet Muhammad's death, it took almost two centuries to collect, verify, and record the Sunna. Because it remained an oral tradition for a long time during a period of exceptional turmoil in Muslim history, some Sunna reports are still controversial in terms of both their authenticity and relationship to the Qur'an.

Because *Shari'a* is derived from Sunna as well as the Qur'an, its development as a comprehensive legal and ethical system had to await the collection and authentication of Sunna. *Shari'a* was not developed until the second and third centuries of Islam....

Shari'a is not a formally enacted legal code. It consists of a vast body of jurisprudence in which individual jurists express their views on the meaning of the Qur'an and Sunna and the legal implications of those views. Although most Muslims believe *Shari'a* to be a single logical whole, there is significant diversity of opinion not only among the various schools of thought, but also among the different jurists of a particular school....

Furthermore, Muslim jurists were primarily concerned with the formulation of principles of *Shari'a* in terms of moral duties sanctioned by religious consequences rather than with legal obligations and rights and specific temporal remedies. They categorized all fields of human activity as permissible or impermissible and recommended or reprehensible. In other words, *Shari'a* addresses the conscience of the individual Muslim, whether in a private, or public and official, capacity, and not the institutions and corporate entities of society and the state.

... Whatever may have been the historical status of *Shari'a* as the legal system of Muslim countries, the scope of its application in the public domain has diminished significantly since the middle of the nineteenth century. Due to both internal factors and external influence, *Shari'a* principles had been replaced by European law governing commercial, criminal, and constitutional matters in almost all Muslim countries. Only family law and inheritance continued to be governed by *Shari'a*....

Recently, many Muslims have challenged the gradual weakening of *Shari'a* as the basis for their formal legal systems. Most Muslim countries have experienced mounting demands for the immediate application of *Shari'a* as the sole, or at least primary, legal system of the land. These movements have either succeeded in gaining complete control, as in Iran, or achieved significant success in having aspects of *Shari'a* introduced into the legal system, as in Pakistan and the Sudan. Governments of Muslim countries generally find it difficult to resist these demands out of fear of being condemned by their own populations as anti-Islamic. Therefore, it is likely that this so-called Islamic fundamentalism will achieve further successes in other Muslim countries.

The possibility of further Islamization may convince more people of the urgency of understanding and discussing the relationship between *Shari'a* and human rights, because *Shari'a* would have a direct impact on a wider range of human rights issues if it became the formal legal system of any country....

I believe that a modern version of Islamic law can and should be developed. Such a modern "*Shari'a*" could be, in my view, entirely consistent with current standards of human rights. These views, however, are appreciated by only a tiny minority of contemporary Muslims. To the overwhelming majority of Muslims today, *Shari'a* is the sole valid interpretation of Islam, and as such ought to prevail over any human law or policy.

B. *Shari'a* and Human Rights

In this part, I illustrate with specific examples how *Shari'a* conflicts with international human rights standards....

The second example is the *Shari'a* law of apostasy. According to *Shari'a*, a Muslim who repudiates his faith in Islam, whether directly or indirectly, is guilty of a capital offense punishable by death. This aspect of *Shari'a* is in complete conflict with the fundamental human right of freedom of religion and conscience. The apostasy of a Muslim may be inferred by the court from the person's views or actions deemed by the court to contravene the basic tenets of Islam and therefore be tantamount to apostasy, regardless of the accused's personal belief that he or she is a Muslim.

The *Shari'a* law of apostasy can be used to restrict other human rights such as freedom of expression. A person may be liable to the death penalty for expressing views held by the authorities to contravene the official view of the tenets of Islam. Far from being an historical practice or a purely theoretical danger, this interpretation of the law of apostasy was applied in the Sudan as recently as 1985, when a Sudanese Muslim reformer was executed because the authorities deemed his views to be contrary to Islam.[9]

A third and final example of conflict between *Shari'a* and human rights relates to the status and rights of non-Muslims. *Shari'a* classifies the subjects of an Islamic state in terms of their religious beliefs: Muslims, *ahl al-Kitab* or believers in a divinely revealed scripture (mainly Christians and Jews), and unbelievers. In modern terms, Muslims are the only full citizens of an Islamic state, enjoying all the rights and freedoms granted by *Shari'a* and subject only to the limitations and restrictions imposed on women. *Ahl al-Kitab* are entitled to the status of *dhimma*, a special compact with the Muslim state which guarantees them security of persons and property and a degree of communal autonomy to practice their own religion and conduct their private affairs in accordance with their customs and laws. In exchange for these limited rights, *dhimmis* undertake to pay *jizya* or poll tax and submit to Muslim sovereignty and authority in all public affairs....

According to this scheme, non-Muslim subjects of an Islamic state can aspire only to the status of *dhimma*, under which they would suffer serious violations of their human rights. *Dhimmis* are not entitled to equality with Muslims....

A Case Study: The Islamic Dimension of the Status of Women

... The present focus on Muslim violations of the human rights of women does not mean that these are peculiar to the Muslim world.[10] As a Muslim, however, I am particularly concerned with the situation in the Muslim world and wish to contribute to its improvement.

The following discussion is organized in terms of the status and rights of Muslim women in the private sphere, particularly within the family, and in public fora, in relation to access to work and participation in public affairs. This classification is recommended for the Muslim context because the personal law aspects of *Shari'a*, family law and inheritance, have been applied much more consistently than the public law doc-

---

9. The Salman Rushdie affair illustrates the serious negative implications of the law of apostasy to literary and artistic expression. Mr. Rushdie, a British national of Muslim background, published a novel entitled THE SATANIC VERSES, in which irrelevant reference is made to the Prophet of Islam, his wives, and leading companions. Many Muslim governments banned the book because their populations found the author's style and connotations extremely offensive. The late Imam Khomeini of Iran sentenced Rushdie to death *in absentia* without charge or trial.

10. It is difficult to distinguish between Islamic, or rather *Shari'a's*, factors and extra-*Shari'a's* actors affecting the status and rights of women. The fact that women's human rights are violated in all parts of the world suggests that there are universal social, economic, and political factors contributing to the persistence of this state of affairs. Nevertheless, the articulation and operation of these factors varies from one culture or context to the next. In particular, the rationalization of discrimination against the denial of equality for women is based on the values and customs of the particular society. In the Muslim world, these values and customs are supposed to be Islamic or at least consistent with the dictates of Islam. It is therefore useful to discuss the Islamic dimension of the status and rights of women.

trines.[11] The status and rights of women in private life have always been significantly influenced by *Shari'a* regardless of the extent of Islamization of the public debate.

Shari'a and the Human Rights of Women

... The most important general principle of *Shari'a* influencing the status and rights of women is the notion of *qawama*. *Qawama* has its origin in verse 4:34 of the Qur'an: "Men have *qawama* [guardianship and authority] over women because of the advantage they [men] have over them [women] and because they [men] spend their property in supporting them [women]." According to *Shari'a* interpretations of this verse, men as a group are the guardians of and superior to women as a group, and the men of a particular family are the guardians of and superior to the women of that family.

... For example, *Shari'a* provides that women are disqualified from holding general public office, which involves the exercise of authority over men, because, in keeping with the verse 4:34 of the Qur'an, men are entitled to exercise authority over women and not the reverse.

Another general principle of *Shari'a* that has broad implications for the status and rights of Muslim women is the notion of *al-hijab*, the veil. This means more than requiring women to cover their bodies and faces in public. According to *Shari'a* interpretations of verses 24:31, 33:33,[12] 33:53, and 33:59[13] of the Qur'an, women are supposed to stay at home and not leave it except when required to by urgent necessity. When they are permitted to venture beyond the home, they must do so with their bodies and faces covered. *Al-hijab* tends to reinforce women's inability to hold public office and restricts their access to public life. They are not supposed to participate in public life, because they must not mix with men even in public places.

... In family law for example, men have the right to marry up to four wives and the power to exercise complete control over them during marriage, to the extent of punishing them for disobedience if the men deem that to be necessary.[14] In contrast, the co-wives are supposed to submit to their husband's will and endure his punishments. While a husband is entitled to divorce any of his wives at will, a wife is not entitled to a divorce, except by judicial order on very specific and limited grounds. Another private law feature of discrimination is found in the law of inheritance, where the general rule is that women are entitled to half the share of men.

In addition to their general inferiority under the principle of *qawama* and lack of access to public life as a consequence of the notion of *al-hijab*, women are subjected to further specific limitations in the public domain. For instance, in the administration of

---

11. The private/public dichotomy, however, is an artificial distinction. The two spheres of life overlap and interact. The socialization and treatment of both men and women at home affect their role in public life and vice versa. While this classification can be used for analysis in the Muslim context, its limitations should be noted. It is advisable to look for both the private and public dimensions of a given *Shari'a* principle or rule rather than assume that it has only private or public implications.

12. "[O Consorts of the Prophet ...] And stay quietly in your houses, and make not a dazzling, like that of the former Times of Ignorance; and establish regular prayer, and give regular charity; and obey God and His Apostle. And God only wishes to remove all abomination from you, ye Members of the Family, and to make you pure and spotless."

13. "O Prophet! Tell thy wives and daughters, and the believing women, that they should cast their outer garments over their persons (when abroad): that is most convenient, that they should be known (as such) and not molested. And God is Oft-Forgiving, Most Merciful."

14. Polygamy is based on verse 4:3 of the Qur'an. The husband's power to chastise his wife to the extent of beating her is based on verse 4:34 of the Qur'an.

justice, *Shari'a* holds women to be incompetent witnesses in serious criminal cases, regardless of their individual character and knowledge of the facts. In civil cases where a woman's testimony is accepted, it takes two women to make a single witness. *Diya*, monetary compensation to be paid to victims of violent crimes or to their surviving kin, is less for female victims than it is for male victims.

... These overlapping and interacting principles and rules play an extremely significant role in the socialization of both women and men. Notions of women's inferiority are deeply embedded in the character and attitudes of both women and men from early childhood....

Muslim Women in Public Life

A similar and perhaps more drastic conflict exists between reformist and conservative trends in relation to the status and rights of women in the public domain. Unlike personal law matters, where *Shari'a* was never displaced by secular law, in most Muslim countries, constitutional, criminal, and other public law matters have come to be based on secular, mainly Western, legal concepts and institutions. Consequently, the struggle over Islamization of public law has been concerned with the reestablishment of *Shari'a* where it has been absent for decades, or at least since the creation of the modern Muslim nation states in the first half of the twentieth century. In terms of women's rights, the struggle shall determine whether women can keep the degree of equality and rights in public life they have achieved under secular constitutions and laws....

... Educated women and other modernist segments of society may not be able to articulate their vision of an Islamic state in terms of *Shari'a*, because aspects of *Shari'a* are incompatible with certain concepts and institutions which these groups take for granted, including the protection of all human rights. To the extent that efforts for the protection and promotion of human rights in the Muslim world must take into account the Islamic dimension of the political and sociological situation in Muslim countries, a modernist conception of Islam is needed.

Islamic Reform and Human Rights

... [T]he general principle of *qawama*, the guardianship and authority of men over women under *Shari'a*, is based on verse 4:34 of the Qur'an.... This verse presents *qawama* as a consequence of two conditions: men's advantage over and financial support of women. The fact that men are generally physically stronger than most women is not relevant in modern times where the rule of law prevails over physical might. Moreover, modern circumstances are making the economic independence of women from men more readily realized and appreciated. In other words, neither of the conditions—advantages of physical might or earning power—set by verse 4:34 as the justification for the *qawama* of men over women is tenable today.

The fundamental position of the modern human rights movement is that all human beings are equal in worth and dignity, regardless of gender, religion, or race. This position can be substantiated by the Qur'an and other Islamic sources, as understood under the radically transformed circumstances of today. For example, in numerous verses the Qur'an speaks of honor and dignity for "humankind" and "children of Adam," without distinction as to race, color, gender, or religion. By drawing on those sources and being willing to set aside archaic and dated interpretations of other sources, such as the one previously given to verse 4:34 of the Qur'an, we can provide Islamic legitimacy for the full range of human rights for women....

C. Tension in Women's Human Rights between Universalism, Cultural Relativism, and Essentialism

1. Tracy Higgins, *Anti-Essentialism, Relativism, and Human Rights*[15]

During the Fourth United Nations World Conference on Women [in 1995], cultural differences among women presented a series of practical and theoretical problems. The practical problems arose out of the enormous task of negotiating among a large group of people a single, albeit complex, document that would set an agenda for addressing the problems of women globally. Differences in culture, language, religion, and education presented complications at every stage of the process. As a theoretical matter, such differences presented a less immediate but in some ways more difficult and persistent problem: In the face of profound cultural differences among women, how can feminists maintain a global political movement yet avoid charges of cultural imperialism?

This theoretical dilemma has become a serious political hurdle for global feminism as the challenge of cultural relativism permeates the politics of any discussion of women's rights on the international stage. For example, at the 1994 United Nations Population Conference in Cairo, the Vatican joined with several Muslim governments to condemn what they viewed as the imposition of Western norms of sexual license and individual autonomy on the rest of the world....

Feminist responses to this charge are complicated and sometimes conflicting. On the one hand, feminists note that culture and religion are often cited as justifications for denying women a range of basic rights, including the right to travel, rights in marriage and divorce, the right to own property, even the right to be protected by the criminal law on an equal basis with men. Women have much to lose, therefore, in any movement away from a universal standard of human rights in favor of deference to culture. On the other hand, feminists acknowledge that feminism itself is grounded in the importance of participation, of listening to and accounting for the particular experiences of women, especially those on the margins of power. Indeed, much feminist criticism of traditional human rights approaches has focused on the tendency of international policymakers to exclude women's experiences and women's voices. Thus, the claim that Western concepts of women's equality are exclusionary or imperialist strikes at the heart of one of feminism's central commitments—respect for difference.

In short, both the move to expand universal human rights to include those rights central to women's condition and the move toward a relativist view of human rights are consistent with and informed by feminist theory. Indeed, the tension between them reflects a tension within feminism itself, between describing women's experience collectively as a basis for political action and respecting differences among women. Addressing this tension, this Article endeavors to sort out the degree to which feminism, by virtue of its own commitments, must take cultural defenses seriously, particularly when articulated by women themselves.

---

15. Tracy Higgins, *Anti-Essentialism, Relativism, and Human Rights,* 19 HARV. WOMEN'S L.J. 89 (1996).

... Despite the general consensus [over the universality of human rights that was reflected in the Declaration], differences have persisted over the scope and priorities of the international human rights agenda, differences that are translated with surprising frequency into the rhetoric of universality versus cultural relativism, and imperialism versus self-determination. Notwithstanding the language of universality, the question remains: To what extent may a state depart from international norms in the name of culture?

... The influence of the universalist/relativist divide on the politics of human rights is perhaps nowhere more evident than in debates over women's rights as human rights. Cultural relativists have targeted feminism itself as a product of Western ideology and global feminism as a form of Western imperialism. Ironically, cultural relativists have accused feminist human rights activists of imposing Western standards on non-Western cultures in much the same way that feminists have criticized states for imposing male-defined norms on women. The complexity of this debate has sown confusion among feminist human rights activists, undermining the effectiveness of the global feminist movement....

... Much incisive and insightful criticism, particularly by feminists of color, has revealed that treating gender difference as the primary concern of feminism has had the effect of reinforcing gendered categories and collapsing differences among women. These critics have argued convincingly that early feminist descriptions of women's experiences focused on white, middle-class, educated, heterosexual women. Consequently, the political priorities of the women's movement in the West (*e.g.,* equal access to education and employment, abortion rights) have reflected the most urgent concerns of a relatively more powerful group of women.... Accused of essentialism, feminists who theorized a commonality among women were criticized for committing the dual sin of reinforcing patriarchal assumptions about women as a group and marginalizing some women along the lines of race, class, and sexual orientation.

Despite its theoretical and political vulnerabilities, the practical appeal of essentialism, like the appeal of universalism, persists. Essentialist assumptions offer the promise of uniting women in a way that transcends or precedes politics....

Much feminist activism on the international level has been premised on two assumptions, both of which may be characterized as essentialist: first, that women share types of experiences and are oppressed in particular ways as women; and second, that these experiences are often different than those of men.... [F]eminist progress in reshaping the scope of the international human rights agenda is an important example of the power of organizing around assumptions of commonality....

Feminists have questioned arguments based on a simple assertion of cultural integrity for several reasons. First, cultural relativists may inadequately attend to the degree to which power relationships within the culture itself constrain the ability of individuals to renegotiate cultural norms. Yet, this inattention is inconsistent with a concern about coercion. The relativist cannot criticize Western imperialism and at the same time ignore non-Western states' selective use of the defense of culture in the service of state power. The risk of such intra-cultural coercion seems especially great when that selective invocation of culture has differential effects on groups within the state such as minority ethnic or racial groups or women.

Second, cultural relativist arguments may oversimplify the complexity and fluidity of culture by treating culture as monolithic and moral norms within a particular culture as readily ascertainable. Yet, a single, inward glance at Western culture reveals the absurdity of this assumption. The multiplicity of beliefs in the United States (or even within a single community or family) about the legitimacy of abortion or the role of women in the family illustrates the complexity of translating imperfectly shared assumptions into evaluative standards. Such oversimplification seems inconsistent with the very premises of cultural relativism. Indeed, cultural relativists' tendency to describe differences in terms of simple opposition—Western versus non-Western—without exploring how specific cultural practices are constituted and justified "essentializes" culture itself.

Treating culture as monolithic fails to respect relevant intra-cultural differences just as the assumption of the universality of human rights standards fails to respect cross-cultural differences. Cultural differences that may be relevant to assessing human rights claims are neither uniform nor static. Rather, they are constantly created, challenged, and renegotiated by individuals living within inevitably overlapping cultural communities.

This oversimplification of culture may lead relativists to accept too readily a cultural defense articulated by state actors or other elites on the international level, actors that tend not to be women. Yet, it seems unlikely that a cultural defense offered by the state will adequately reflect the dynamic, evolving, and possibly conflicting cultural concerns of its citizens.

Given the complexity and multiplicity of culture, the ability or inclination of heads of state to identify and translate cultural practices into specific defenses against the imposition of Western human rights norms is questionable. Feminists in particular have cited example after example in which culture has been selectively and perhaps cynically invoked to justify oppressive practices ...

Conclusion

Confronted with the challenge of cultural relativism, feminism faces divergent paths, neither of which seems to lead out of the woods of patriarchy. The first path, leading to simple tolerance of cultural difference, is too broad. To follow it would require feminists to ignore pervasive limits on women's freedom in the name of an autonomy that exists for women in theory only.

The other path, leading to objective condemnation of cultural practices, is too narrow. To follow it would require feminists to dismiss the culturally distinct experiences of women as false consciousness. Yet to forge an alternative path is difficult, requiring feminists to confront the risks inherent in global strategies for change.

Building upon women's shared experiences inevitably entails a risk of misdescription, or worse, cooptation but contains the promise of transforming and radicalizing women's understanding of their own condition. Emphasizing difference threatens to splinter women politically, undermining hard-won progress, but may simultaneously uncover new possibilities for re-creating gender relations. Forging a combined strategy that respects both commonality and difference requires feminists to acknowledge that we cannot eliminate the risk of coercion altogether, but the risk of inaction is also ever present.

D. Female Genital Mutilation: A Form of Torture and a Cultural Tradition

1. World Health Organization, Fact Sheet No. 241 (2000)
Views of Commentators about Female Genital Mutilation[16]

What Is Female Genital Mutilation?

Female genital mutilation (FGM), often referred to as 'female circumcision', comprises all procedures involving partial or total removal of the external female genitalia or other injury to the female organs whether for cultural, religious or other non-therapeutic reasons. There are different types of female genital mutilation known to be practiced today. They include:

- Type I—excision of the prepuce, with or without excision of part or all of the clitoris;

- Type II—excision of the clitoris with partial or total excision of the labia minora;

- Type III—excision of part or all of the genitalia and stitching/narrowing of the vaginal opening (infibulation);

- Type IV—pricking, piercing or incising of the clitoris and/or labia; stretching of the clitoris and/or labia; cauterization by burning of the clitoris and surrounding tissue;

- scraping of tissue surrounding the vaginal orifice (angurya cuts) or cutting of the vagina (gishiri cuts);

- introduction of corrosive substances or herbs into the vagina to cause bleeding or for the purpose of tightening or narrowing it; and any other procedure that falls under the definition given above.

The most common type of female genital mutilation is excision of the clitoris and the labia minora, accounting for up to 80% of all cases; the most extreme form is infibulation, which constitutes about 15% of all procedures.

Health Consequences of FGM

The immediate and long-term health consequences of female genital mutilation vary according to the type and severity of the procedure performed.

The immediate complications include severe pain, shock, haemorrhage, urine retention, ulceration of the genital region and injury to adjacent tissue. Haemorrhage and infection can cause death.

More recently, concern has arisen about possible transmission of the human immunodeficiency virus (HIV) due to the use of one instrument in multiple operations, but this has not been the subject of detailed research.

Long-term consequences include cysts and abscesses, keloid scar formation, damage to the urethra resulting in urinary incontinence, dyspareunia (painful sexual intercourse) and sexual dysfunction and difficulties with childbirth.

Psychosexual and psychological health: genital mutilation may leave a lasting mark on the life and mind of the women who have undergone it. In the longer term, women may suffer feelings of incompleteness, anxiety, and depression.

---

16. World Health Organization, Fact Sheet No. 241 (2000), *Views of Commentators about Female Genital Mutilation, available at* http://www.whoint/mediacentre/factsheets/fs241/en.

Who Performs FGM, at What Age, and for What Reasons?

In cultures where it is an accepted norm, female genital mutilation is practiced by followers of all religious beliefs as well as animists and non believers. FGM is usually performed by a traditional practitioner with crude instruments and without anesthetic. Among the more affluent in society, it may be performed in a health care facility by qualified health personnel. WHO is opposed to medicalization of all types of female genital mutilation.

The age at which female genital mutilation is performed varies from area to area. It is performed on infants a few days old, female children and adolescents and, occasionally, on mature women....

Prevalence and Distribution of FGM

Most of the girls and women who have undergone genital mutilation live in 28 African countries, although some live in Asia and the Middle East. They are also increasingly found in Europe, Australia, Canada, and the USA, primarily among immigrants from these countries.

Today, the number of girls and women who have undergone female genital mutilation is estimated at between 100 and 140 million. It is estimated that each year, a further 2 million girls are at risk of undergoing FGM.

2. UN CEDAW Committee General Recommendations on Female Circumcision[17]

[The Committee on the Elimination of Discrimination against Women, created by the Convention on the Elimination of all Forms of Discrimination against Women, is authorized to make general recommendations based on reports that it receives from the States parties.]

Recommends that States parties:

(a) Take appropriate and effective measures with a view to eradicating the practice of female circumcision. Such measures could include:

(i) The collection and dissemination by universities, medical or nursing associations, national women's organizations or other bodies of basic data about such traditional practices;

(ii) The support of women's organizations at the national and local levels working for the elimination of female circumcision and other practices harmful to women;

(iii) The encouragement of politicians, professionals, religious, and community leaders at all levels, including the media and the arts, to co-operate in influencing attitudes towards the eradication of female circumcision;

(iv) The introduction of appropriate educational and training programmes and seminars based on research findings about the problems arising from female circumcision;

(b) Include in their national health policies appropriate strategies aimed at eradicating female circumcision in public health care. Such strategies could include the special responsibility of health personnel, including traditional birth attendants, to explain the harmful effects of female circumcision;

---

17. UN Comm. on the Elimination of Discrimination against Women [CEDAW], Female Circumcision, General Recommendation No. 14, 9th Sess. (1990), UN Doc. A/45/38/1, 1 INT'L. HUM. RTS. REV. 21 (1994).

(c) Invite assistance, information, and advice from the appropriate organizations of the United Nations system to support and assist efforts being deployed to eliminate harmful traditional practices;

(d) Include in their reports to the Committee under articles 10 and 12 of the Convention on the Elimination of All Forms of Discrimination against Women information about measures taken to eliminate female circumcision.

E. Women's Right to Manifest Their Religion, to Wear a Headscarf in Turkey, and the Conflict of Secularism

1. *Leyla Sahin v. Turkey*

European Court of Human Rights, 2005
Judgment of Chamber, Application No. 44774/98[18]

[A]pplicant came from a traditional family of practicing Muslims, and considered it her religious duty to wear the Islamic headscarf. She did so during her four years studying medicine in a Turkish university. Applicant then transferred to Istanbul University to continue her studies. In a series of episodes beginning in 1998 she was censured by university authorities for refusing to comply with university circulars based on legislation banning students wearing headscarves from lectures and courses. After being denied enrollment and admission to lectures, she sought unsuccessfully relief from Turkish courts. Relevant provisions of the Turkish Constitution provide:

> Article 2: The Republic of Turkey is a democratic, secular(laic) and social State based on the rule of law that is respectful of human rights in a spirit of social peace.
>
> ...
>
> Article 10: All individuals shall be equal before the law without any distinction based on language, race, color, sex, political opinion, philosophical belief, religion, membership of a religious sect or other similar grounds.
>
> ...
>
> Article 13: Fundamental rights and freedoms may be restricted only by law and on the grounds set out in special provisions of the Constitution.... Any such restriction shall not conflict with the letter or spirit of the Constitution or the requirements of a democratic, secular social order and shall comply with the principle of proportionality.
>
> Article 14: The rights and freedoms set out in the Constitution may not be exercised with a view to undermining the territorial integrity of the State, the unity of the Nation or the democratic and secular Republic founded on human rights.
>
> ...

---

18. Sahin v. Turkey, European Court of Human Rights, Judgment of Chamber, Application No. 44774/98.

Article 24: Everyone shall have the right to freedom of conscience, belief, and religious conviction. Prayers, worship, and religious services shall be conducted freely, provided that they do not violate the provisions of art 14. No one shall be compelled to participate in prayers, worship, or religious services or to reveal his or her religious beliefs and convictions....

Ultimately, applicant abandoned her studies in Turkey and pursued her medical education at Vienna University. After failing to secure judicial relief in Turkey, she initiated proceedings against Turkey under the European Convention on Human Rights. In the 2004 judgment, a Chamber of the European Court of Human Rights held unanimously that there had been no violation of the Convention. Applicant's request that the case be referred to the Court's Grand Chamber was accepted. In its 2005 judgment, The Grand Chamber also ruled against applicant. [Excerpts from that opinion and a dissenting opinion follow.]

History and Background

30. The Turkish Republic was founded on the principle that the State should be secular. Before and after the proclamation of the Republic on 29 October 1923, the public and religious spheres were separated through a series of revolutionary reforms....

31. The principle of secularism was inspired by developments in Ottoman society in the period between the nineteenth century and the proclamation of the Republic.... Significant advances in women's rights were made during this period (equality of treatment in education, the introduction of a ban on polygamy in 1914, the transfer of jurisdiction in matrimonial cases to the secular courts that had been established in the nineteenth century).

32. The defining feature of the Republican ideal was the presence of women in public life and their active participation in society. Consequently, the ideas that women should be freed from religious constraints and that society should be modernized had a common origin.... [W]omen obtained equal political rights with men....

35. In Turkey wearing the Islamic headscarf to school and university is a recent phenomenon which only really began to emerge in the 1980s.... Those in favor of the headscarf see wearing it as a duty and/or a form of expression linked to religious identity. However, the supporters of secularism ... see the Islamic headscarf as a symbol of a political Islam....

[In the Turkish Constitutional Court's opinion that upheld the university's position, the judges stated that secularism had achieved so important a position among constitutional values because of the country's historical experience and the particularities of Islam compared to other religions; secularism was an essential condition for democracy and acted as a guarantor of freedom of religion and of equality before the law. Students must be allowed to work in a tolerant atmosphere without being deflected from their goals by signs of religious affiliation such as the headscarf.

The ECHR opinion included a comparative survey about laws about headscarves in a number of European countries. The survey indicated that the state legislation varied on many details—for example, how if at all the headscarf was regulated, and the level of school/university that was covered by any regulation.]

Alleged Violation of Article 9 of the Convention

70. The applicant submitted that the ban on wearing the Islamic headscarf in institutions of higher education constituted an unjustified interference with her right to freedom

of religion, in particular, her right to manifest her religion. She relied on art 9 of the Convention, which provides:

> 1. Everyone has the right to freedom of thought, conscience, and religion; this right includes freedom to change his religion or belief and freedom, either alone or in community with others and in public or private, to manifest his religion or belief, in worship, teaching, practice, and observance.

> 2. Freedom to manifest one's religion or beliefs shall be subject only to such limitations as are prescribed by law and are necessary in a democratic society in the interests of public safety, for the protection of public order, health or morals, or for the protection of the rights and freedoms of others....

104. The Court reiterates that as enshrined in art. 9, freedom of thought, conscience and religion is one of the foundations of a "democratic society" within the meaning of the Convention. This freedom is, in its religious dimension, one of the most vital elements that go to make up the identity of believers and their conception of life, but it is also a precious asset for atheists, agnostics, skeptics, and the unconcerned. The pluralism indissociable from a democratic society, which has been dearly won over the centuries, depends on it. That freedom entails, *inter alia*, freedom to hold or not to hold religious beliefs and to practice or not to practice a religion.

105. While religious freedom is primarily a matter of individual conscience, it also implies, *inter alia*, freedom to manifest one's religion, alone and in private, or in community with others, in public and within the circle of those whose faith one shares. Article 9 lists the various forms which the manifestation of one's religion or belief may take, namely worship, teaching, practice, and observance....

106. In democratic societies, in which several religions coexist within one and the same population, it may be necessary to place restrictions on freedom to manifest one's religion or belief in order to reconcile the interests of the various groups and ensure that everyone's beliefs are respected....

107. The Court has frequently emphasized the State's role as the neutral and impartial organizer of the exercise of various religions, faiths, and beliefs, and stated that this role is conducive to public order, religious harmony, and tolerance in a democratic society. It also considers that the State's duty of neutrality and impartiality is incompatible with any power on the State's part to assess the legitimacy of religious beliefs or the ways in which those beliefs are expressed....

29. Where questions concerning the relationship between State and religions are at stake, on which opinion in a democratic society may reasonably differ widely, the role of the national decision-making body must be given special importance. This will notably be the case when it comes to regulating the wearing of religious symbols in educational institutions, especially in view of the diversity of the approaches taken by national authorities on the issue. It is not possible to discern throughout Europe a uniform conception of the significance of religion in society and the meaning or impact of the public expression of a religious belief will differ according to the time and context. Rules in this sphere will consequently vary from one country to another according to national traditions and the requirements imposed by the need to protect the rights and freedom of others and maintain public order....

30. This margin of appreciation goes hand in hand with a European supervision embracing both the law and the decisions applying it. The Court's task is to determine whether the measures taken at the national level were justified in principle and propor-

tionate. In delimiting the extent of the margin of appreciation in the present case, the Court must have regard to what is at stake, namely the need to protect the rights and freedoms of others, to preserve public order, and to secure civil peace and true religious pluralism, which is vital to the survival of a democratic society....

115. After examining the parties' arguments, the Grand Chamber sees no good reason to depart from the approach taken by the Chamber as follows [Ed. Indented paragraphs are quotations from the 2004 judgment of the Chambers]:

> ... The Court ... notes the emphasis placed in the Turkish constitutional system on the protection of the rights of women.... Gender equality—recognized by the European Court as one of the key principles underlying the Convention and a goal to be achieved by member States of the Council of Europe—was also found by the Turkish Constitutional Court to be a principle implicit in the values underlying the Constitution.

> ... In addition, like the Constitutional Court..., the Court considers that, when examining the question of the Islamic headscarf in the Turkish context, there must be borne in mind the impact which wearing such a symbol, which is presented or perceived as a compulsory religious duty, may have on those who choose not to wear it. As has already been noted, the issues at stake include the protection of the "rights and freedoms of others" and the "maintenance of public order" in a country in which the majority of the population, while professing a strong attachment to the rights of women and a secular way of life, adhere to the Islamic faith. Imposing limitations on freedom in this sphere may, therefore, be regarded as meeting a pressing social need by seeking to achieve those two legitimate aims, especially since, as the Turkish courts stated ... this religious symbol has taken on political significance in Turkey in recent years. (2004 Judgment of the Chamber).

> ... The Court does not lose sight of the fact that there are extremist political movements in Turkey which seek to impose on society as a whole their religious symbols and conception of a society founded on religious precepts.... It has previously said that each Contracting State may, in accordance with the Convention provisions, take a stance against such political movements, based on its historical experience. The regulations concerned have to be viewed in that context and constitute a measure intended to achieve the legitimate aims referred to above and thereby to preserve pluralism in the university. (2004 Judgment of the Chamber)....

117. The Court must now determine whether in the instant case there was a reasonable relationship of proportionality between the means employed and the legitimate objectives pursued by the interference.

118. Like the Chamber..., the Grand Chamber notes at the outset that it is common ground that practicing Muslim students in Turkish universities are free, within the limits imposed by educational organizational constraints, to manifest their religion in accordance with habitual forms of Muslim observance. In addition, the resolution adopted by Istanbul University on 9 July 1998 shows that various other forms of religious attire are also forbidden on the university premises....

121. ... By reason of their direct and continuous contact with the education community, the university authorities are in principle better placed than an international court to evaluate local needs and conditions or the requirements of a particular course....

122. In the light of the foregoing and having regard to the Contracting States' margin of appreciation in this sphere, the Court finds that the interference in issue was justified in principle and proportionate to the aim pursued.

123. Consequently, there has been no breach of art. 9 of the Convention.

Alleged Violation of Article 2 of Protocol No. 1

[Applicant also argued that Article 2, of Protocol No. 1 of the European Convention should be interpreted to uphold her right to wear a headscarf while attending the university. That article provides:

> No person shall be denied the right to education. In the exercise of any functions which it assumes in relation to education and to teaching, the State shall respect the right of parents to ensure such education and teaching in conformity with their own religious and philosophical convictions. The Grand Chamber relied heavily on its reasoning with respect to freedom of religion in concluding that there had been no violation of Article 2 of Protocol No. 1.

157. ... [T]he Court is able to accept that the regulations on the basis of which the applicant was refused access to various lectures and examinations for wearing the Islamic headscarf constituted a restriction on her right to education, notwithstanding the fact that she had had access to the University and been able to read the subject of her choice in accordance with the results she had achieved in the university entrance examination. However, an analysis of the case by reference to the right to education cannot in this instance be divorced from the conclusion reached by the Court with respect to Article 9....

158. ... The obvious purpose of the restriction was to preserve the secular character of educational institutions.

159. As regards the principle of proportionality, the Court found in paras. 118 to 121 above that there was a reasonable relationship of proportionality between the means used and the aim pursued. In so finding, it relied in particular on the following factors which are clearly relevant here. Firstly, the measures in question manifestly did not hinder the students in performing the duties imposed by the habitual forms of religious observance. Secondly, the decision-making process for applying the internal regulations satisfied, so far as was possible, the requirement to weigh up the various interests at stake. The university authorities judiciously sought a means whereby they could avoid having to turn away students wearing the headscarf and at the same time honor their obligation to protect the rights of others and the interests of the education system. Lastly, the process also appears to have been accompanied by safeguards—the rule requiring conformity with statute and judicial review—that were apt to protect the students' interests....

161. Consequently, the restriction in question did not impair the very essence of the applicant's right to education....

Dissenting Opinion of Judge Tulkens

...

2. Underlying the majority's approach is the margin of appreciation which the national authorities are recognized as possessing and which reflects, *inter alia*, the notion that they are "better placed" to decide how best to discharge their Convention obligations in what is a sensitive area. The Court's jurisdiction is, of course, subsidiary and its role is not to impose uniform solutions, especially "with regard to establishment of the delicate relations between the Churches and the State." ...

3. I would perhaps have been able to follow the margin-of-appreciation approach had not two factors drastically reduced its relevance in the instant case. The first concerns the

argument the majority used to justify the width of the margin, namely the diversity of practice between the States on the issue of regulating the wearing of religious symbols in educational institutions and, thus, the lack of a European consensus in this sphere. The comparative law materials do not allow for such a conclusion, as in none of the member States has the ban on wearing religious symbols extended to university education, which is intended for young adults, who are less amenable to pressure. The second factor concerns the European supervision that must accompany the margin of appreciation.... [O]ther than in connection with Turkey's specific historical background, European supervision seems quite simply to be absent from the judgment. However, the issue raised in the application, whose significance to the right to freedom of religion guaranteed by the Convention is evident, is not merely a "local" issue, but one of importance to all the member States. European supervision cannot, therefore, be escaped simply by invoking the margin of appreciation.

4. On what grounds was the interference with the applicant's right to freedom of religion through the ban on wearing the headscarf based? In the present case, relying exclusively on the reasons cited by the national authorities and courts, the majority put forward, in general and abstract terms, two main arguments: secularism and equality.... In a democratic society, I believe that it is necessary to seek to harmonize the principles of secularism, equality, and liberty, not to weigh one against the other.

5. As regards, firstly, secularism ... Religious freedom is, however, also a founding principle of democratic societies. Accordingly, the fact that the Grand Chamber recognized the force of the principle of secularism did not release it from its obligation to establish that the ban ... met a "pressing social need".... [W]here there has been interference with a fundamental right, the Court's case law clearly establishes that mere affirmations do not suffice: they must be supported by concrete examples....

6. Under Article 9 of the Convention, the freedom with which this case is concerned is not freedom to have a religion (the internal conviction) but to manifest one's religion (the expression of that conviction). If the Court has been very protective (perhaps overprotective) of religious sentiment ... it has shown itself less willing to intervene in cases concerning religious practices ... which only appear to receive a subsidiary form of protection....

7. The majority thus consider that wearing the headscarf contravenes the principle of secularism. In so doing, they take up position on an issue that has been the subject of much debate....

In the present case, a generalized assessment of that type gives rise to at least three difficulties. Firstly, the judgment does not address the applicant's argument—which the Government did not dispute—that she had no intention of calling the principle of secularism, a principle with which she agreed, into doubt. Secondly, there is no evidence to show that the applicant, through her attitude, conduct or acts, contravened that principle.... Lastly, the judgment makes no distinction between teachers and students, whereas in the *Dahlab v. Switzerland* decision of 15 February 2001, which concerned a teacher, the Court expressly noted the role-model aspect which the teacher's wearing the headscarf had.... [T]he position of pupils and students seems to me to be different.

8. Freedom to manifest a religion entails everyone being allowed to exercise that right, whether individually or collectively, in public or in private, subject to the dual condition that they do not infringe the rights and freedoms of others and do not prejudice public order.

As regards the first condition, this could have been satisfied if the headscarf the applicant wore as a religious symbol had been ostentatious or aggressive or was used to exert pressure, to provoke a reaction, to proselytize or to spread propaganda and undermine—or was liable to undermine—the convictions of others. However, the Government did not argue that this was the case, and there was no evidence before the Court to suggest that Ms. Sahin had any such intention. As to the second condition, it has been neither suggested nor demonstrated that there was any disruption in teaching or in everyday life at the University ...

9. .... [T]the possible effect which wearing the headscarf, which is presented as a symbol, may have on those who do not wear it does not appear to me, in the light of the Court's case law, to satisfy the requirement of a pressing social need....

10. In fact, it is the threat posed by "extremist political movements" seeking to "impose on society as a whole their religious symbols and conception of a society founded on religious precepts" which, in the Court's view, serves to justify the regulations in issue, which constitute "a measure intended ... to preserve pluralism in the university"....

While everyone agrees on the need to prevent radical Islamism, a serious objection may nevertheless be made to such reasoning. Merely wearing the headscarf cannot be associated with fundamentalism, and it is vital to distinguish between those who wear the headscarf and "extremists" who seek to impose the headscarf as they do other religious symbols. Not all women who wear the headscarf are fundamentalists, and there is nothing to suggest that the applicant held fundamentalist views.... [T]he judgment fails to provide any concrete example of the type of pressure concerned....

11. Turning to equality, the majority focus on the protection of women's rights and the principle of sexual equality.... By converse implication, wearing the headscarf is considered synonymous with the alienation of women. The ban on wearing the headscarf is therefore seen as promoting equality between men and women. However, what, in fact, is the connection between the ban and sexual equality? ... [W]earing the headscarf has no single meaning; it is a practice that is engaged in for a variety of reasons. It does not necessarily symbolize the submission of women to men, and there are those who maintain that, in certain cases, it can even be a means of emancipating women. What is lacking in this debate is the opinion of women, both those who wear the headscarf and those who choose not to.

12. On this issue, the Grand Chamber refers in its judgment to the *Dahlab v. Switzerland* decision of 15 February 2001, citing what to my mind is the most questionable part of the reasoning in that decision, namely that wearing the headscarf represents a "powerful external symbol", which "appeared to be imposed on women by a religious precept that was hard to reconcile with the principle of gender equality" and that the practice could not easily be "reconciled with the message of tolerance, respect for others and, above all, equality and non-discrimination that all teachers in a democratic society should convey to their pupils."

... The applicant, a young adult university student, said—and there is nothing to suggest that she was not telling the truth—that she wore the headscarf of her own free will. In this connection, I fail to see how the principle of sexual equality can justify prohibiting a woman from following a practice which, in the absence of proof to the contrary, she must be taken to have freely adopted....

13.... In these circumstances, there has been a violation of the applicant's right to freedom of religion, as guaranteed by the Convention.

[[T]he dissenting opinion also disagreed on several grounds with the majority's disposition of applicant's claim based on Article 2 of Protocol No. 1.]

... I end by noting that all these issues must also be considered in the light of the observations set out in the annual activity report published in June 2005 of the European Commission against Racism and Intolerance (ECRI), which expresses concern about the climate of hostility existing against persons who are or are believed to be Muslim and considers that the situation requires attention and action in the future. Above all, the message that needs to be repeated over and over again is that the best means of preventing and combating fanaticism and extremism is to uphold human rights.

F. The Symbolic Significance of the Headscarf in Muslim Countries

1. Susan Tiefenbrun, *Semiotics of Women's Human Rights in Iran*[19]

...

The Iranian Family Laws: Then and Now

Iranian family law in post-Revolutionary Iran is based on *Shari'a* law, as interpreted according to the Ja'fari School of *Shi'a* law.[20] *Shari'a* law is not very favorable to women. The implementation of *Shari'a* law is arguably one of the causes for the establishment of gender inequality leading to a "gender apartheid"[21] in Iran. Family law in Iran has changed several times, once under the Pahlavi monarchy in 1925 and again in 1979 under the Islamic Republic. According to Donna Hughes, "[n]ew laws strengthening gender apartheid and repression of women are not a thing of the past."[22] Even under Khatami's reformist regime in 1997, new restrictive laws and policies were enacted in order to segregate women and men in the fields of medicine and healthcare.[23] Until the 1930s, the *Shi'a* clergy performed marriages and divorces in *Shari'a* courts that had jurisdiction in all family matters. Under Reza Shah's reign there was a move to create a more centralized judicial system based on a Western model, establishing new courts and new laws reminiscent of European legal concepts and codes. A Civil Code was enacted between 1927 and 1935.[24] However, Iranian Civil Code (ICC) Articles 1034 to 1206 on marriage, divorce, family affairs, and children "retain the patriarchal bias of the *Shari'a*."[25] In ICC Article 1129 an attempt was made to extend the grounds upon which a woman could obtain a judicial divorce to include the husband's refusal or his inability to provide for her, his refusal to perform his sexual duties, his mistreatment of her, and his

---

19. Susan Tiefenbrun, *Semiotics of Women's Human Rights in Iran*, 23 Conn. J. Int'l L. 1 (2007).

20. *See* Ziba Mir-Hosseini, *Family Law in Modern Persia, in* 9 Encyclopedia Iranica 192–96 (1999).

21. *See generally* Donna Hughes, *Women and Reform in Iran* (Feb. 2000), *available at* http://www.uri.edu/artsci/wms/hughes/reform.htm.

22. *Id.*

23. *Id.*

24. Mir-Hosseini, *supra* note 20, at 192.

25. *Id. See also* Quanun-i Madani [Civil Code] Tehran 1314 [1935], articles 1034–1206 (Iran), *translated in* Iran Human Rights Documentation Center, http://iranhrdc.org/english/pdfs/Codes/TheCivilCode.pdf (last visited on Dec. 5, 2007).

affliction with a disease that could harm her life (Article 1130).[26] The Civil Code departed from *Shari'a* law by prohibiting the marriage of girls under thirteen in Article 1041.[27]

The 1931 Marriage Law consisting of twenty articles and two notes reduced the administrative and judicial functions of the clergy.[28] The Iranian Marriage Law also established financial penalties and a prison term for anyone involved in the marriage of girls under thirteen (Article 3). ICC Articles 4 and 8 to 17 provide the wife with a right to maintenance and the right to initiate divorce proceedings in a civil court.[29]

In 1967 a big change in family law occurred when the Iranian Family Protection Law was enacted.[30] This law, which prohibited men's right to an automatic divorce and to the practice of polygamy, was written into the Civil Code as well.[31] The Family Protection Law set up new court procedures for family disputes.[32] Divorcing couples were required to appear in courts presided over by civil judges, some of whom were women.[33] If both parties do not agree to a divorce, the court can issue a Certificate evidencing "Impossibility of Reconciliation."[34] Men and women could appoint arbitrators to try to bring about reconciliation, but the final decision rested with the court (Articles 6 to 13).[35] The Family Protection Law included many other provisions that are favorable to women's rights to a divorce in Iran.[36]

In 1975 the Family Protection Law was amended, and the minimum age for marriage was increased from fifteen to eighteen for females and from eighteen to twenty for males.[37] The new law also provided more rights to women seeking a divorce and child custody.[38] Many clergy opposed this law, viewing it as the destruction of Muslim values and dissolution of the entire Iranian family structure.[39] "Ayatollah Khomeini denounced it [the Family Protection Law] as contrary to Islam, declaring divorces issued under the FPL to be void,"[40] retroactively.

Khomeini and the Islamic Republic reinstated strict *Shari'a* law and special civil courts presided over by religious judges who were "free" from the Civil Procedure Code.[41] During this period, Khomeini instituted certain contradictory policies resulting in the reduction in restrictions imposed on men's rights to divorce and polygamy and the increase in compensation to women who are harmed by divorce and polygamy.[42] The Council of Guardians was now required to revise any laws found to be in contradiction with *Shari'a* law.[43] Thus, for example, Article 1041, which formerly set a minimum age for marriage at thirteen for females and fifteen for males, was amended in

26. Mir-Hosseini, *supra* note 20, at 192.
27. Iranian Civil Code, *supra* note 25.
28. *Id.*
29. *Id.*
30. *Id.*
31. *Id.*
32. *Id.*
33. *Id.*
34. *Id.*
35. *Id.*
36. *See* Mir-Hosseini, *supra* note 20 (providing an in-depth analysis of Iranian Family Law).
37. *Id.*
38. *Id.*
39. *Id.*
40. *Id. at* 194.
41. *Id.*
42. *Id.*
43. *Id.*

1982 to prohibit marriage prior to the age of nine for girls and fifteen for boys.[44] Legalizing marriage for nine-year old girls is a serious step backwards for women's human rights because these young girls are generally forced into marriage by their parents.[45] Incidentally, Article 3 of the 1931 Marriage Law makes it illegal and punishable by six months to two years imprisonment to marry a girl under thirteen.[46] Similarly contradictory rules exist in Iran for polygamy.

Temporary marriage (*sigheh*, a custom that allows a married man to have sex with another woman by temporarily "marrying" her and unmarrying her after the sex is completed) is recognized as a valid marriage under the Iranian Civil Code, but the 1931 Marriage Laws are silent as to the legality of this temporary marriage.[47] After 1979, Special Civil Courts heard disputes involving the temporary marriage and even authorized their registration, thus giving legal status to the temporary marriage and to the legitimization of extramarital sex.[48]

Women's custody rights were also curtailed in 1979. The Iranian Civil Code gives a mother the right to the custody of her daughter only until the age of seven and to the custody of her son only until the age of two (Article 1169).[49] In the case of the husband's death, a woman naturally acquires custody of her children (Article 1170) but loses custody if she remarries (Article 1171), in which case the child is then raised by the child's paternal grandfather (Article 1180).[50] Mothers of martyrs have the right to receive their deceased husband's salary and to keep custody of their children under a new legislation that was passed on 6 Mordad 1365 (Islamic year).[51]

In 1982 new stipulations were added to the marriage contract entitling women to claim half the wealth acquired by her husband during the marriage (provided that she does not initiate the divorce) and enabling women to seek a judicial divorce, without the signature of her husband.[52] Article 1130 of the Civil Code was amended in 1982 to give the judge in the court the power to grant or withhold a divorce requested by a woman.[53] Article 1130 was again amended in 2002 to empower a judge to issue a divorce when a woman establishes that the continuation of the marriage would entail intolerable suffering or hardship.[54] The enforcement of Islamic jurisprudence rules (*figh*) in Iran since the 1979 Revolution resulted in these two favorable amendments to Article 1130 of the Civil Code; however, there are serious gaps between legal theory and social practice in Islamic law as enforced in Iran.[55] These gaps have "made the unequal construction of gender relations a site of contestation."[56]

In 1992, Amendments to Divorce Regulation (ADR) were passed in order to reinstate some of the elements of the Family Protection Law's divorce provisions that were rejected earlier.[57] ADR "requires all divorcing couples ... to go through a process of ar-

---

44. *Id.*
45. *Id.*
46. *Id.*
47. *Id.*
48. *Id.*
49. *Id.*
50. *Id.*
51. *Id.*
52. *Id.*
53. *Id.*
54. Ziba Mir-Hosseini, *When a Woman's Hurt Becomes an Injury: 'Hardship' as Grounds for Divorce in Iran*, 5 Hawaa 111, 111 (2007).
55. *Id.*
56. *Id.*
57. Mir-Hosseini, *Family Law in Modern Persia,*, *supra* note 20, at 196.

bitration," and if the arbiters fail to reconcile the couple in dispute, then "the court allows the man to effect and register a divorce, after he has paid his wife "what she has a legal right to receive."[58] ADR note 6 "enables the court to place a monetary value on women's housework and to force the husband to pay her 'wages in kind' for her work done during her marriage" (provided that the wife does not initiate the divorce and provided that the divorce is not caused by any fault of hers).[59] Thus, if the woman decides to divorce her husband, she loses her right to the housework wages.[60] If wages for housework are not possible, the husband must provide the wife with a marriage gift, "the amount [of which is] to be decided by the court" on the basis of the husband's financial need.[61]

A new Law of Formation of General Courts, enacted in June 1994, is designed to bring about a restructuring of the courts in Iran.[62] The Special Civil Courts governing family law matters will disappear.[63] In the future family disputes must appear in General Courts presided over by either a *mojtahed* or a civil judge who has jurisdiction over all penal and family law cases.[64] [Currently, the political regime in Iran is very repressive, and women's rights in Iranian courts have taken a turn for the worst. (author's note)]

Concept of Marriage in Iran: The Marriage Contract

Marriage in Iran is a contract regulated by a code of law that is deeply rooted in religious precepts and based on a "patriarchal ethos."[65] The three elements of an Iranian marriage contract constitute (1) the offer of marriage made by the woman or her guardian, (2) the acceptance by the man, and (3) the payment of a dower (*mahr*) called the "marriage gift," which is "money or any valuable that the husband pays or pledges to pay the wife on consummation of the marriage."[66] Polygamy is a man's legal right to marry more than one woman.[67] Therefore, one man can enter into more than one marriage at a time, "up to four permanent unions and as many temporary ones as he desires or can afford," by virtue of the "temporary marriage" (*mut'a*).[68]

The marriage contract sets forth certain rights and duties for the man and for the woman, such as *tamkin* (sexual submission, obedience) and *nafaqa* (maintenance).[69] The husband has the right to demand the woman's sexual submission because this is the wife's duty.[70] The husband must provide shelter, food, and clothing, and the wife has a right to this maintenance.[71] According to the Iranian marriage contract, a wife possesses nothing more than her marriage gift and her own personal wealth.[72] Only the husband has the unilateral right to terminate the contract, which he can do without any grounds and with-

---

58. *Id.*
59. *Id.*
60. *Id.*
61. *Id.*
62. *Id.*
63. *Id.*
64. *Id.*
65. *See* Ziba Mir-Hosseini, *Tamkin: Stories from a Family Court in Iran, in* EVERYDAY LIFE IN THE MIDDLE EAST 136, 137–38 (Donna Lee Brown & Evelyn A. Early eds., 2nd ed. 2002) [hereinafter Tamkin].
66. *Id.* at 137.
67. *Id.*
68. *Id.*
69. *Id.*
70. *Id.*
71. *Id.*
72. *See id.*

out the wife's consent or even her presence.[73] The inherently patriarchal discrimination and the lack of equality established by this contract are vividly portrayed in *Divorce Iranian Style*, a film that illuminates the vagaries of Iranian family law[74] and the procedural difficulties of divorce cases initiated by women in Iran.

> A large majority of divorce cases initiated by women never reach a decision [because] they are [either] abandoned after two or three hearings [or the] couple succeed[s] in reaching an out-of-court agreement or they give up [because of] the futility of their efforts. More than 70 percent of all divorces registered in any given year in Tehran are ... by mutual consent [involving] the wife waiving her claim to *mahr* [the marriage gift] in exchange for the husband's consent [to divorce].[75]

The marriage gift is, thus, a bargaining chip used by women to get the husband to consent to the divorce....

International Human Rights Laws Protecting Women's Rights

"Respect for basic human rights in Iran, especially freedom of expression and opinion, deteriorated considerably in 2005."[76] Human Rights Watch reports routine use by the [Iranian] government of torture, ill treatment in detention, and prolonged solitary confinement where the judiciary commits serious human rights violations.[77] Abuses are perpetrated by parallel institutions like paramilitary groups, plainclothes men, and intelligence services that attack protestors.[78] Iran has signed and is bound by certain international human rights treaties that, if enforced, would provide protection against these abuses and give women the justice and equality they deserve.

The Convention on the Elimination of All Forms of Discrimination against Women (CEDAW)

The Convention on the Elimination of All Forms of Discrimination against Women (CEDAW) was adopted in 1979 by the UN General Assembly and is considered to be the international bill of rights for women.[79] This comprehensive treaty codifies human rights as they specifically apply to women and girls. It defines discrimination against women and sets up a program for nations to eradicate discrimination domestically. Since there are currently 183 states party to the Convention, and the treaty has been in existence for more than twenty-seven years, arguably the provisions of CEDAW can be considered "customary international law" and applicable to even non-signatory States.[80] Iran, along with the United States, has not signed CEDAW.

---

73. *See id.*

74. DIVORCE IRANIAN STYLE (20th Century Vixen 1998), *described at* http://www.wmm.com/filmcatalog/pages/c454.shtml; *see also* ELAINE SCIOLINO, PERSIAN MIRRORS 264 (2000) ("'In our country, the problem is the law,' Hashemi says. 'All the judges are men, and they don't understand the problems of women.'").

75. *Tamkin, supra* note 65, at 149.

76. Human Rights Watch, *Essential Background: Overview of Human Rights in Iran* (Dec. 31, 2005), http://hrw.org/english/docs/2006/01/18/iran12214.htm (last visited Sept. 25, 2007).

77. *Id.*

78. *Id.*

79. UN Convention on the Elimination of All Forms of Discrimination against Women, Dec. 18, 1979, 1249 U.N.T.S. 14 [hereinafter CEDAW], *available at* http://www.un.org/womenwatch/daw/cedaw/index.html.

80. *See* HENRY J. STEINER & PHILLIP ALSTON, INTERNATIONAL HUMAN RIGHTS IN CONTEXT: LAW, POLITICS, MORALS 69, 72 (2d ed. 2000) ("Customary law refers to conduct, or the conscious abstention from certain conduct, of states that becomes in some measure a part of international legal order.")

CEDAW provides the foundation for achieving equality for women publicly, politically and privately.[81] CEDAW protects equality in voting, education, health, employment, access to the legal system, nationality, and many other fundamental freedoms. Although Iran's Parliament approved CEDAW in August 2003, the hard-line clerics in the Guardian Council ultimately refused to sign the treaty, stating that it went against Islamic law and was unconstitutional.[82] Nevertheless, since CEDAW has risen to the level of customary international law, Iran, arguably, may not take any action inconsistent with the treaty.[83]

Article 2 of CEDAW requires states to implement policies of equality between men and women within their national constitutions and legal systems.[84] All forms of discrimination against women are forbidden, whether by public or private entities, and "penal provisions which constitute discrimination against women" must be repealed.[85] Discrimination against women exists on many levels of the public and private sphere in Iran.[86] Women are not given as many rights as men,[87] and they are under the constant domination and control of their husbands or fathers.[88] Women in Iran cannot travel without their husband's permission[89] and must sit in the back of gender-segregated buses.[90] A woman's testimony in court is worth only half as much as a man's[91] and judges frequently give preference to men in domestic matters, even if the man has a history of domestic violence.[92] Women are punished more severely than men in criminal matters—such as stoning women for adultery while they are buried from the neck down, while men are buried from the waist down, thus arguably giving men a greater opportunity for escape.[93] Women are rarely given the promotions they deserve; even when they work tirelessly, and women cannot reach their full potential[94] in a stultifying, patriarchal system that looks down on working women. For example, the Islamic Republic applies "blood money" (compensation to the victim) in criminal cases, and the family of a victim of homicide or manslaughter has the right to choose between legal punishment or blood money.[95] Under the Iranian code, the worth of a woman's life equals half of a man's.[96] In one case a judge ruled that the blood money for two men was worth more than the life of the murdered nine-year-

---

(inferring that CEDAW is accepted as customary law because more than 140 states have adopted it since its inception).

81. *See* CEDAW, *supra* note 79.

82. Nazila Fathi, *Iran's Hard-Liners Reject Reform Bills Approved by Parliament*, N.Y. Times, Aug. 14, 2003, at A11; *see also* CEDAW, *supra* note 79 (showing that Iran has not adopted CEDAW—Country Reports section).

83. *See* Steiner & Alston, *supra* note 80.

84. CEDAW, *supra* note 79, at 16.

85. *Id.*

86. *See* Azar Nafisi, Reading Lolita in Tehran 261 (2004).

87. *Id.*

88. *See* Hughes, *supra* note 21; *see also* Geraldine Brooks, Nine Parts of Desire: The Hidden World of Islamic Women 106 (1995) (using the main character in that chapter as an example of the extraordinary amount of control that a man in Iran has over his wife's life).

89. *See* Nafisi, *supra* note 86, at 286 ("Azin had applied for a visa to Canada, but even if her application was accepted, she couldn't leave the country without her husband's permission.").

90. *Id.* at 27.

91. *Id.* at 261.

92. *Id.* at 273.

93. Brooks, *supra* note 88, at 46.

94. *See* Shirin Ebadi, Iran Awakening: A Memoir of Revolution and Hope 75 (2006).

95. *Id.* at 113–14.

96. *Id.* at 114.

old girl, and the judge demanded that her family pay thousands of dollars to finance the execution of the male criminals, unjustly punishing the female victim's family.[97]

States are obligated by Article 5 of CEDAW "to modify the social and cultural patterns of conduct of men and women" to eliminate the idea that women are inferior to men or that men are their superiors.[98] In Iran, women are blamed for their beauty and sexuality, forced to bear the responsibility of a man's lustful looks, thoughts or behavior.[99] In order to "protect" the men after the Revolution, women were forced to veil themselves,[100] and women could not even maintain eye contact with a man.[101] After the Revolution women could not sing publicly because a woman's voice is considered provocative.[102] Because "family honor rests on the virtue of women," the shame of a woman's rape could only be erased by execution of the perpetrator, for which the family of the woman would have to pay "blood money."[103]

Article 7 of CEDAW requires that women have equal access to voting rights and to run for election for public office.[104] CEDAW also requires that women participate equally "in the formulation of public office" and "perform all public functions at all levels of government."[105] Although women in Iran are allowed to vote, there are severe restrictions upon women who run for public office, and only approximately four percent of seats in Parliament are held by women.[106] Women in Iran who held ministerial positions at the time of the Revolution were stoned to death (i.e., the Minister of Education) or forced into exile (i.e., the Minister of Women's Affairs).[107] Female members of Parliament are segregated and forced to work in an empty room behind a curtain, without chairs, a table or even office equipment to make their attempts to legislate any easier.[108] Female government employees are regarded as a "nuisance," especially those who are vocal about their oppression.[109]

In Article 9 of CEDAW, women are assured their right "to acquire, change or retain their nationality."[110] A woman's nationality is protected because marriage does not "change the nationality of the wife, render her stateless or force upon her the nationality of the husband," and women shall be granted "equal rights with men with respect to the nationality of their children."[111] In Iran, women must convert to Islam in order to marry an Iranian.[112] Any children born to a non-Iranian mother and an Iranian father are considered Iranian, and the father has complete control over his wife and children.[113] Fathers

---

97. *Id.*
98. CEDAW, *supra* note 79, at art. 5.
99. *See* Nafisi, *supra* note 86, at 27.
100. *See id.* at 152.
101. *See id.* at 183.
102. *See id.* at 108; Ebadi, *supra* note 94, at 181.
103. Ebadi, *supra* note 94, at 114.
104. CEDAW, *supra* note 79, at art. 7.
105. *Id.*
106. UN Development Programme, Human Development Report 2005, 304 (2005, *available at* http://hdr.undp.org/en/media/hdr05_complete.pdf [hereinafter UNDP].
107. *See* Nafisi, *supra* note 86, at 262.
108. Ebadi, *supra* note 94, at 185–86.
109. *Id.* at 73.
110. CEDAW, *supra* note 79, at art. 9.
111. *Id.*
112. Brooks, *supra* note 88, at 92.
113. *See id.* at 106; *see* Nafisi, *supra* note 86, at 286.

and husbands even have the ability to notify the government and forbid their wives from leaving the country.[114]

Article 10 of CEDAW requires States to "take all appropriate measures to eliminate discrimination against women in order to ensure to them equal rights with men in the field of education …"[115] Education of women is one of the areas that has been gradually improving in Iran.[116] Immediately after the Revolution, some women were refused tenure,[117] forced out of universities and fired from teaching positions because of their refusal to wear the veil and conform to Khomeini's "ideal of a Muslim woman teacher."[118] University faculty and students were expelled, jailed, and purged for a variety of offenses, from being "too Western in … attitude"[119] to being "an enemy of God"[120] and for "using obscene language in class."[121] Nafisi's university did not allow women to enter through the main university entrance, so women had to use a separate door to the side.[122] It "segregate[d] men and women in classes"[123] and even segregated the cafeteria.[124] Professors extolled the differences between virtuous Muslim girls and promiscuous Christian girls,[125] and the faculty members were summoned to endless meetings and debates over "women's rights" and the government's "war against women."[126]

Women were also forbidden to have certain careers or study certain technical and experimental fields.[127] Other fields were restricted for women because of quotas ranging from twenty percent to fifty percent.[128] Women were not allowed to receive scholarships for study abroad programs without the permission of their husband or father.[129] Schools below the university level were segregated by gender.[130]

However, in the years following the Revolution, many changes occurred in the area of education for women.[131] Religious women were able to attend universities once they became "protected" by the veil.[132] Because of increased gender segregation in Iran, more female teachers, doctors and social workers were needed.[133] As the restrictions on women's study of science and technical subjects were lifted, the percentage of female university students also dramatically increased.[134] There was also a drive to improve the literacy rates

114. See NAFISI, supra note 86, at 286. In a personal interview Susan Tiefenbrun conducted on June 8, 2006 with Sonez Mashayekhi, a married Iranian woman who went to law school in Iran, Mashayekhi reported that when she attempted to leave the country to study in the United States, she was stopped by her husband who reported her to the CIA as a terrorist.

115. CEDAW, supra note 79, at art. 10.

116. Louise Halper, Law and Women's Agency in Post-revolutionary Iran, 28 HARV. J.L. & GENDER 85, 90 (2005).

117. See NAFISI, supra note 86, at 10.

118. Id. at 165.

119. Id. at 118.

120. Id. at 119.

121. Id. at 117.

122. See id. at 29.

123. Id. at 9.

124. EBADI, supra note 94, at 106.

125. See NAFISI, supra note 86, at 30.

126. Id. at 111.

127. Halper, supra note 116, at 90.

128. Id. at 106; see EBADI, supra note 94, at 108.

129. Halper, supra note 116, at 90.

130. Id. at 106.

131. Id. at 116.

132. See id. at 124; EBADI, supra note 94, at 106.

133. Halper, supra note 116, at 116.

134. Id. at 116.

of women in rural areas,[135] which cut the illiteracy rate of women from sixty percent in 1980 to thirty percent in 2005.[136] While these numbers are far from perfect, they do show an improving trend in the government's commitment to the education of women in Iran after the Revolution.

The right to equal employment rights, guaranteed in Article 11 of CEDAW,[137] is another area of fluctuation within the political tide of Iran's government.[138] After the Revolution, the government initially encouraged women to stay inside the home and to refrain from working.[139] However, during the Iran-Iraq War, working conditions for mothers improved significantly, such as the addition of daycares to workplaces and the availability of better benefits for women.[140] Once the war ended and the government began to rebuild its economy with greater global involvement, the need for women in the workplace continued.[141]

In Iran today improvements in the area of women's salary need to be made, since half of the women in Iran contribute to the family income, yet a woman typically earns less than a third of a man's salary.[142] With the increase in educational opportunities for women, many more women have earned university and graduate degrees, but the professional market has been unable to keep up.[143] The few jobs available usually go to men, and "[t]hough educated women outnumber educated men, the rate of women's unemployment is three times higher."[144]

Article 13(c) of CEDAW requires that women have "the right to participate in recreational activities, sports,[145] and all aspects of cultural life."[146] But after the Revolution, sports became segregated by gender,[147] and women's teams received far less funding, training or quality coaching.[148] Attendance at women's games or sporting events is limited to women only, so that they may participate without wearing the *hejab*.[149] In 2006, President Ahmadinejad made a surprising move towards allowing women to attend soccer games with men, but he was overruled by the Supreme Leader Ayatollah Khameini.[150] Women's participation in the arts was also severely curtailed after the Revolution.[151] Ballet and dancing were forbidden and eventually women singers were banned "because a woman's voice, like her hair, was sexually provocative and should be kept hidden."[152]

---

135. *Id.* at 113; EBADI, *supra* note 94, at 106.

136. United Nations Development Programme, Human Development Report 2005, 228, 308 (2005), http://hdr.undp.org/en/media/hdro5_complete.pdf [hereinafter UNDP].

137. CEDAW, *supra* note 79, at art. 11.

138. *See* NAFISI, *supra* note 86, at 275.

139. Halper, *supra* note 116, at 116.

140. *Id.*

141. *Id.* at 117.

142. UNDP, *supra* note 106, at 312.

143. EBADI, *supra* note 94, at 108.

144. *Id.*

145. *See* BROOKS, *supra* note 88, at 201–13 (discussing Iranian women in sports in pre- and post-Revolutionary Iran).

146. CEDAW, *supra* note 79, at art. 13(c). *See also* BROOKS, *supra* note 88, at 201–13.

147. Halper, *supra* note 116, at 106.

148. *See* Jenny Steel, *Sports and the Scarf*, BBC NEWS, Dec. 9, 2005, http://news.bbc.co.uk/go/pr/fr/-/2/i/middle east/4511680.stm.

149. *See id.*

150. *Iran Women Sports Ruling Vetoed*, BBC NEWS, May 8, 2006, *available* at http://newsvote.bbc.co.uk/mpapps/pagetools/print/news.bbc.co.uk/2/hi/middel east/4751033.stm.

151. NAFISI, *supra* note 86, at 108.

152. *Id.*; EBADI, *supra* note 94, at 181.

Equality with men before the law is guaranteed to women in Article 15 of CEDAW.[153] One of the first decisions of the new Islamic Republic, before even establishing a constitution or electing a parliament, was to abolish the Family Protection Law that guaranteed women equal rights in marriage, divorce, and child custody issues.[154] By abolishing this law the drafters of the post-Revolutionary penal code "turned the clock back fourteen hundred years" and imposed laws highly discriminatory towards women.[155] For example, a woman may not travel outside the country without the permission of her husband, and the husband may notify the government not to allow his wife to leave.[156] A "woman [must] ask her husband's permission for [a] divorce."[157] In some cases, physical and mental abuse of women is not considered sufficient grounds for a divorce, and the judge might even blame the woman for the husband's beatings.[158] In Iran, alimony is not given to women, and child custody is usually awarded to the father,[159] even if the father is "guilty of horrific abuse" of the child.[160] Women are given harsher sentences in criminal matters,[161] and their testimony is worth only half that of a man's.[162]

Finally, Article 16(f) of CEDAW gives women "[t]he same rights and responsibilities with regard to guardianship, wardship, trusteeship, and adoption of children."[163] However, when Khomeini declared that the Family Protection Law was un-Islamic, this decision quickly set a patriarchal precedent affirming that men and paternal family members would be given preference in child custody matters.[164] If divorced, women are allowed to retain guardianship of male children but only until the male child reaches the age of two and until the female child reaches the age of seven.[165] Although the pro-active demands of women during the Iran-Iraq war gave widows more physical custody over their children, guardianship is still technically held by paternal family members.[166] Women need the permission of their husbands to travel even just overnight with their children,[167] and parenting duties are heavily unequal, with the mother shouldering most of the responsibility.[168]

International Covenant on Civil and Political Rights (ICCPR)

The International Covenant on Civil and Political Rights (ICCPR)[169] is one of two major international human rights treaties that guarantee the rights of every individual to civil and political freedoms. The ICCPR codifies the first generation civil and political rights delineated in the Universal Declaration of Human Rights (UDHR),[170] such as freedom of speech,

---

153. CEDAW, *supra* note 79, at art. 15.
154. NAFISI, *supra* note 86, at 261.
155. EBADI, *supra* note 94, at 51.
156. NAFISI, *supra* note 86, at 286.
157. EBADI, *supra* note 94, at 51.
158. NAFISI, *supra* note 86, at 273.
159. *Id.* at 286; EBADI, *supra* note 94, at 111.
160. EBADI, *supra* note 94, at 123.
161. NAFISI, *supra* note 86, at 261.
162. *Id.*; EBADI, *supra* note 94, at 51.
163. CEDAW, *supra* note 79, at art. 16(f).
164. NAFISI, *supra* note 89, at 286; EBADI, *supra* note 94, at 53.
165. Halper, *supra* note 116, at 95.
166. *Id.* at 115.
167. EBADI, *supra* note 94, at 100.
168. *Id.* at 153.
169. International Covenant on Civil and Political Rights, G.A. Res. 2200A (XXI), UN Doc. A/6316 (Dec. 16, 1966), *available at* http://www.unhchr.ch/html/menu3/b/a_ccpr.htm [hereinafter ICCPR].
170. Universal Declaration of Human Rights, G.A. Res. 217A, UN Doc. A/810 (Dec. 12, 1948), *available at* http://www.unhchr.ch/udhr/lang/eng.htm [hereinafter UDHR].

the right to due process and a fair trial, and freedom of religion. Iran signed the ICCPR in 1968 and ratified it without reservations in 1975. Although there was a regime change in Iran in 1979, states parties are still obligated to respect their international treaty obligations.

After the Revolution, Ayatollah Khomeini faced criticism from many international human rights groups because of the large number of summary executions that followed the Revolution.[171] Khomeini's response was heartless and indicates a flagrant disrespect of traditional notions of human rights:

> Criminals should not be tried. The trial of a criminal is against human rights. Human rights demand that we should have killed them in the first place when it became known that they were criminals. They criticize us because we are executing the brutes.[172]

In direct violation of the right to life guaranteed by Article 6 of the ICCPR, executions became the rule rather than the exception in post-Revolutionary Iran.[173]

Dynamic interpretation of the Koran is the key to providing women with civil and political rights as well as human rights under Islam. While human rights of all persons men and women alike are often violated under a totalitarian regime such as the Islamic Republic of Iran, women's basic civil and political rights are particularly implicated in Iran because of the strict Islamist regulations set by the clerics,[174] who interpret the Koran more narrowly than feminists like Shirin Ebadi would like.[175] For Ebadi, Islam and women's rights are compatible as long as the Koran is interpreted in a manner to favor women.[176] Fundamentalists apply a literal interpretation of the Koran resulting in harsh sentences. For example, stoning is the punishment for adultery and prostitution.[177] Unfair show trials for suspected criminals are quite common.[178] For example, one woman was charged with "corruption on earth," "sexual offenses," and "violation of decency and morality," but her only real "crime" was her position under the Shah as the former Minister of Education. She was placed in a sack and either stoned or shot to death.[179] One official, whose only crime was to name his dogs after two clerics as an insult to them, was ordered to die.[180] So-called "enem[ies] of God" were murdered daily, whether or not they were former ministers and educators, prostitutes, leftist revolutionaries[181] or women of amazing beauty.[182]

In Iran, several sources report that Iranian girls believed to be virgins and convicted of a crime were often "married" off to prison guards who would rape them before executing them to deprive the girls of eternal bliss in heaven, confident that if the girls died as virgins they would go to heaven.[183] Khomeini issued a *fatwa* sanctioning the rape of girls be-

---

171. NAFISI, *supra* note 86, at 96.
172. *Id.*
173. EBADI, *supra* note 94, at 140–41.
174. NAFISI, *supra* note 86, at 108.
175. EBADI, *supra* note 94, at 122.
176. *Id.* at 187–88; *see also* Abdullahi Ahmed An-Na'im, *Human Rights in the Muslim World*, in INTERNATIONAL HUMAN RIGHTS IN CONTEXT 396 (Henry J. Steiner & Philip Alston eds., 2000).
177. NAFISI, *supra* note 86, at 261.
178. *Id.* at 101; EBADI, *supra* note 94, at 59.
179. NAFISI, *supra* note 86, at 112–13.
180. *Id.* at 137.
181. *Id.* at 119.
182. *Id.* at 212.
183. *Id.* at 212; EBADI, *supra* note 94, at 91.

fore their execution and another *fatwa* permitting the execution of pregnant women.[184] Minors were not exempt from this series of murders, and many teenagers and young children were killed without mercy or even a trial.[185] During the Iran-Iraqi war, young boys under the age of thirteen were abducted off the streets against their will and sent off to war to die in the minefields. But these boys died as martyrs, and their families boasted of their martyrdom with pride in a prevailing new cult of death. Iran became bloodthirsty—publishing the names, pictures, and crimes of those executed in the paper on a daily basis.[186] Rather than protests calling for an end to the killings, there were increasing demands and slogans calling "for more blood."[187] A female photojournalist, Zahra Kazemi, was imprisoned and tortured for taking pictures and defying a prison guard.[188] Her injuries from the torture and the beatings were so severe that she died only a few weeks after her imprisonment.[189]

Article 7 of the ICCPR forbids degrading treatment or punishment.[190] Like the villainous Humbert in Nabokov's *Lolita*, who regulated every step of Lolita's young life,[191] Ayatollah Khomeini forced women with threats of punishment and humiliation to live as he envisioned them—ideal Muslim women.[192] Failure to adhere to this vision with improper dress length, scarf thickness, wearing of nail polish, makeup[193] or even pink socks[194] subjected women to violent inspections, molestations,[195] detainment or public lashing.[196] When one girl was found in mixed company, she and the other girls were arrested for infractions on matters of morality and subjected to two brutal virginity tests, forced to sign confessions at a "trial" and sentenced to twenty-five lashes.[197]

The arbitrary nature of these arrests and the severe punishments meted out for minor infractions allegedly committed by women cannot remain unnoticed. For example, one girl traveling with her fiancé and two male companions was arbitrarily detained by the morality police, tried and sentenced to forty lashes; however, the punishment was given instead to her fiancé (who committed no crime or infraction at all) since there was no woman present to mete out her punishment.[198] Propaganda admonishing women to adhere to this vision of Khomeini's morality adorned the streets. In this repressive climate, women were reduced to "ethereal being[s] drifting soundlessly down the street."[199]

Arbitrary arrests and detentions are prohibited by Article 9 of the ICCPR.[200] However, during the days of the Revolution, many were unfairly arrested by the government simply for belonging to certain political groups,[201] speaking out or writing against the gov-

---

184. The Nat'l Council of Resistance of Iran Foreign Affairs Comm., *Islam: Beacon of Women's Emancipation, in* Women, Islam & Equality 37 (1995), *available at* http://www.iran-e-azard.org/english/book_on_women/wi&e.pdf.
185. Nafisi, *supra* note 86, at 191.
186. *Id.* at 102.
187. *Id.* at 100.
188. Ebadi, *supra* note 94, at 196.
189. *Id.* at 196–97.
190. ICCPR, *supra* note 169, at art. 7.
191. Nafisi, *supra* note 86, at 49.
192. *Id.* at 165.
193. *Id.* at 29; Ebadi, *supra* note 94, at 180.
194. Nafisi, *supra* note 86, at 76.
195. *Id.* at 168.
196. Ebadi, *supra* note 94, at 180.
197. Nafisi, *supra* note 86, at 73.
198. Ebadi, *supra* note 94, at 98–99.
199. Nafisi, *supra* note 86, at 168.
200. ICCPR, *supra* note 169, at art. 7.
201. Nafisi, *supra* note 86, at 31; Ebadi, *supra* note 94, at 67.

ernment,[202] or traveling with a man that was not a relative.[203] People were arrested just because the Revolutionary Guards had a search warrant, and even though they found no evidence of illegal activities, they couldn't let the warrant "go to waste."[204] The "frightening, thuggish"[205] morality police in later years roamed the city of Tehran in white jeeps, jailing any women they found for showing hair from underneath their scarves, wearing improper robes,[206] wearing makeup or even slippers.[207] A few of Nafisi's girls [*i.e.* private students she taught at her home] were imprisoned for several years after the Revolution because of their "political activities," and they reported being grateful that they were the lucky ones who were not executed.[208]

Article 12(2) of the ICCPR states that "everyone shall be free to leave any country, including his own."[209] Women in Iran do not have this basic human right. When one of Nafisi's girls struggled with a bad marriage, she applied for a visa to Canada, "but even if her application was accepted, she couldn't leave the country without her husband's permission."[210] Husbands could also forbid their wives from leaving the country by refusing to sign the papers that would allow them to travel.[211] Women who were granted scholarships to study abroad were also not allowed to leave the country without the accompaniment of their fathers or husbands.[212]

Article 18 of the ICCPR guarantees that "[e]veryone shall have the right to freedom of thought, conscience, and religion."[213] When the Revolution ended, the Islamic forces took power and made everyone wear a religious facade, regardless of their religious beliefs.[214] Women were forced to wear the *hejab*, whether or not they were practicing Muslims.[215]

> [Once] the mullahs ruled the land, religion was used as an instrument of power, an ideology. It was this ideological approach to faith that differentiated those in power from millions of ordinary citizens, believers like Mahshid, Manna, and Yassi, who found the Islamic Republic their worst enemy.[216]

In addition to forced religious garb, Iranian women were also required to support the war against Iraq. Iranians were forbidden to protest the war or to show grief when loved ones were killed or when a neighbor's house was bombed.[217] Censorship was then and is now everywhere in Iran. Nafisi reports that "certain books had been banned as morally harmful"[218] or "politically objectionable."[219] "Fires were set to publishing houses and

---

202. Nafisi, *supra* note 86, at 116.

203. Ebadi, *supra* note 94, at 98.

204. Nafisi, *supra* note 86, at 72–73.

205. Ebadi, *supra* note 94, at 102.

206. Nafisi, *supra* note 86, at 275; Ebadi, *supra* note 94, at 102–03.

207. Ebadi, *supra* note 94, at 102–03.

208. Nafisi, *supra* note 86, at 323 ("There, in jail, I like the rest of them thought we would be killed and that would be the end.").

209. ICCPR, *supra* note 169, at art. 12(2).

210. Nafisi, *supra* note 86, at 286.

211. *Id.*; Brooks, *supra* note 88, at 106.

212. *See* Halper, *supra* note 116, at 88.

213. ICCPR, *supra* note 169, at art. 18(1).

214. Ebadi, *supra* note 94, at 40. *See* Nafisi, *supra* note 86, at 112 (discussing the reimposition of the veiling of women signifying the "victory of the Islamic aspect of the revolution").

215. Nafisi, *supra* note 86, at 152; *see* Ebadi, *supra* note 94, at 72.

216. Nafisi, *supra* note 86, at 273.

217. *Id.* at 211.

218. *Id.* at 108.

219. Ebadi, *supra* note 94, at 66.

bookstores for disseminating immoral works of fiction."[220] Iran's xenophobia spread from inside Iran to the rest of the world. In Iran discriminatory treatment of religious minorities, such as Bahias and Armenians, is pervasive. Minorities face constant threats, and they cannot even be buried in the same graveyard as Muslims.[221] Anti-semitism also abounds in Iran, and the recent case of thirteen Iranian Jews accused and convicted unjustly for their alleged spying and affiliation with Israel aroused suspicion and controversy worldwide.

According to Article 19 of the ICCPR, "[e]veryone shall have the right to hold opinions without interference" and "have the right to freedom of expression orally, in writing or in print, in the form of art, or through any other media of his choice."[222] Protestors during the Revolution were often beaten or arrested for passing out leaflets.[223] Any critics of the new regime or of its laws were deemed "enemies," "against Islam," and "counterrevolutionar[ies]," and these victims of oppression "faced, often as not, the firing squad."[224] Secular women who initially refused to wear the veil were fired from their positions[225] and then pushed out because of their ideological beliefs and expressed opinions.[226] Today all women in Iran must wear at least the headscarf, if not the *chador* (a loose, usually black robe covering the body from head to toe) (also called *hejab*).

The Iranian post-Revolutionary regime understood the power of the word. Those who did not support the war and wrote or even spoke about it were considered unpatriotic and faced severe consequences.[227] As in the repressive Soviet regime, the Iranian government actually killed writers and poets such as Ahmad Mir Alai and Jahangir Tafazoli.[228] The government made attempts to kill any intellectual who did not support the Islamic regime.[229] On a manhunt, the Islamic Republic began searching for writers, poets and intellectuals, sending death squads to assassinate them one by one.[230] Some were detained, tortured, and imprisoned for several years[231] while many others died under mysterious circumstances[232] or were even blatantly murdered.[233] "Reporters were jailed, magazines and newspapers closed, and some of our best classical poets, like Rumi and Omar Khayyam, were censored or banned."[234]

In Article 21 of the ICCPR, "the right of peaceful assembly shall be recognized."[235] After the Revolution, the ability for writers and intellectuals to meet in public or in private was drastically curtailed by the government.[236] Unmarried men and women were

---

220. NAFISI, *supra* note 86, at 136.
221. *See e.g.*, NAFISI, *supra* note 86, at 230.
222. ICCPR, *supra* note 169, at art. 19.
223. NAFISI, *supra* note 86, at 191.
224. EBADI, *supra* note 94, at 52.
225. NAFISI, *supra* note 86, at 152–53.
226. *Id.*
227. *Id.* at 158–59.
228. *Id.* at 310.
229. NAFISI, *supra* note 86, at 308; EBADI, *supra* note 94, at 128–29.
230. *See* EBADI, *supra* note 94, at 129–32.
231. *Id.* at 134–35.
232. *See id.* at 132.
233. *Id.* at 137.
234. NAFISI, *supra* note 86, at 136.
235. ICCPR, *supra* note 169, at art. 21.
236. NAFISI, *supra* note 86, at 309; EBADI, *supra* note 94, at 130.

not allowed to be alone together, so dating couples often "borrow[ed] a young niece or nephew on their evenings out, to appear as a family and pass through checkpoints unmolested."[237] "Young people risked being intercepted by the morality police simply for venturing into the mountains together for a hike."[238] Nafisi herself was forced to cut short her meetings with her "magician" during police raids of a public cafe.[239] Even Nafisi's class with her girls had to remain a secret.[240]

Article 23 of the ICCPR refers to marriage and family rights, declaring that "no marriage shall be entered into without the free and full consent of the intending spouses."[241] Once the Islamic Regime took power, Khomeini lowered the acceptable age of marriage from eighteen to nine.[242] This increased forced marriages in post-Revolutionary Iran. While women of Nafisi's age had been able to choose a spouse for love, the women students in her class now had little choice, and their younger sisters would have even less.[243] Fathers often chose husbands for their daughters, confining them to perpetual domestic life rather than letting them pursue their education.[244] Marriage became more of a family agreement with the parents making the important decisions, rather than a decision of the intended bride and groom. Women cannot easily obtain a divorce by initiating the procedures in a family law court. One woman was so miserable in her marriage that when her husband would not grant her a divorce, she "doused herself with gasoline and lit herself ablaze."[245] Self-immolation by women in Iran is a much too common occurrence, a sign of the hopelessness of women in search of basic human rights that are provided by international treaties but unavailable to them because of failed enforcement by the Iranian State.

Finally, according to Article 26 of the ICCPR, "all persons are equal before the law and are entitled without any discrimination to the equal protection of the law."[246] As noted above, women "under law, [a]re considered to have half the worth of men,"[247] and they are often treated unfairly by family court judges.[248] Women, including Shirin Ebadi, were removed from their positions of power as judges[249] or from ministerial positions, merely because they are women.[250] Women are also treated far more harshly by the criminal system than are men accused of committing the same crimes.[251] After the Revolution, as women became more aware of their rights and also of their oppression, the suicide rate of women rose, "commonly taking the form of self-immolation."[252]

---

237. EBADI, *supra* note 94, at 96.
238. *See id.* at 180.
239. NAFISI, *supra* note 86, at 312–13.
240. *Id.* at 3.
241. ICCPR, *supra* note 169, at art. 23.
242. NAFISI, *supra* note 86, at 261.
243. *Id.* at 259.
244. EBADI, *supra* note 94, at 106–07.
245. *Id.* at 108–09.
246. ICCPR, *supra* note 169, at art. 26.
247. NAFISI, *supra* note 86, at 261.
248. *Id.* at 273.
249. EBADI, *supra* note 94, at 48.
250. NAFISI, *supra* note 86, at 261–62.
251. *Id.* at 261.
252. EBADI, *supra* note 94, at 109.

International Covenant on Economic, Social, and Cultural Rights (ICESCR)

The International Covenant on Economic, Social, and Cultural Rights[253] (ICESCR) is the second of the two major international human rights treaties that embodies many of the principles found in the Universal Declaration of Human Rights.[254] The ICESCR sets forth the second generation economic, social, and cultural rights, such as the right to work, the right to social welfare programs, and the right to take part in the cultural life of the country.[255] Iran signed the ICESCR in 1968 and ratified it without reservations in 1975. Thus, Iran may not take any actions that are inconsistent with the object and purpose of the ICESCR.[256]

States parties to the ICESCR must "guarantee that the rights enunciated in the present Covenant will be exercised without discrimination of any kind as to race, color, sex, language, religion, political or other opinion, national or social origin, property, birth or other status."[257] In Iran, preferential treatment of men begins at an early age. Men and boys "enjoy an exalted status" in the household, and they remain at "the center of the family's orbit."[258] As children grow older, the rights of boys expand "while the girls' contract[ed]."[259] Men have relative autonomy in Iranian society while women are given fewer rights than men,[260] and women are considered inferior to men in the workplace.[261] Women in Iran may only travel with their husband's permission.[262] Judges often treat men with preference in domestic matters, even if the men have a past record of domestic violence.[263] In addition, women are punished more severely than men in criminal matters and crimes such as "adultery and prostitution [which are] punished by stoning to death."[264]

Article 3 of the ICESCR requires that "States undertake to ensure the equal right of men and women to the enjoyment of all social and cultural rights...."[265] After the Revolution, women's participation in the arts was severely restricted.[266] In a country where all people love Persian poetry and music, it is amazing that dancing and singing were gradually eliminated altogether.[267] Women now are still unable to participate in sports and unable even to be spectators at men's events.[268] At a music concert, the management admonished the crowd that "if anyone acted in an un-Islamic manner, he or she would be kicked out. He went on to instruct women to observe the proper rules and regulations re-

---

253. International Covenant on Economic, Social, and Cultural Rights, G.A. Res. 2200 (XXI) UN Doc. (Dec. 16, 1966) *available at* http://www.unhchr.ch/html/menu3/b/a_cescr.htm [hereinafter ICESCR].

254. UDHR, *supra* note 170.

255. *See generally* Barbara Stark, *The "Other" Half of the International Bill of Rights as a Postmodern Feminist Text, in* THE AMERICAN SOCIETY OF INTERNATIONAL LAW, RECONCEIVING REALITY: WOMEN AND INTERNATIONAL LAW 19, 21 (1993).

256. Vienna Convention on the Law of Treaties, 1155 U.N.T.S. 331, 8 I.L.M. 679, UN Doc. A/CONF. 39/29 (May 23, 1155 U.N.T.S. 331, 8 I.L.M. 679, (1969)).

257. ICESCR, *supra* note 253, at art. 2 (emphasis added).

258. EBADI, *supra* note 94, at 11.

259. *Id.* at 11.

260. NAFISI, *supra* note 86, at 261.

261. *Id.* at 261; EBADI, *supra* note 94, at 75.

262. *See* NAFISI, *supra* note 86, at 286.

263. *Id.* at 273; EBADI, *supra* note 94, at 123.

264. NAFISI, *supra* note 86, at 261.

265. ICESCR, *supra* note 253, at art. 3 (emphasis added).

266. *See e.g.*, NAFISI, *supra* note 86, at 108.

267. *Id.*; EBADI, *supra* note 94, at 181.

268. *Iran Women Sports Ruling Vetoed, supra* note 150.

garding the use of the veil."[269] Women may not socialize with men in public, and women are not permitted to sit in the same classrooms with men.[270] "[E]ven the lunch tables in the [university] cafeteria were segregated."[271]

Article 7 of the ICESCR addresses "the right of everyone to the enjoyment of just and favorable conditions of work."[272] Section (a)(i) of Article 7 further provides that all workers are entitled to "[f]air wages and equal remuneration for work of equal value without distinction of any kind, in particular women being guaranteed conditions of work not inferior to those enjoyed by men."[273] Section (c) of Article 7 guarantees "equal opportunity for everyone to be promoted in his employment to an appropriate higher level, subject to no considerations other than those of seniority and competence."[274] During the Iran-Iraq war, women worked for free, but now women in Iran are demanding pay to cover the rising cost of living.[275] After the Revolution, women were forced out of positions of prominence within the government, such as judges[276] and cabinet ministers,[277] and they were reduced to accept only administrative and clerical positions.[278] Women were then and are now still denied "promotion[s] and permanence" at work because of their past political affiliations[279] or simply because they are women.[280] "[M]ale superiors will not look [women] in the eye,"[281] and they "reward [women's] exceptional work with something akin to envy."[282]

Conclusion

There is no doubt that without the popular support of the women in Iran, Ayatollah Khomeini would never have succeeded in leading the Revolution.[283] Disgusted by the Shah's excesses, repression, compromises, and conformity to the ideals of the West, all of which seemed contrary to the moral values of Islam, various political forces in Iran struggled to bring about a revolution that could bring the Iranian society back to its traditional values.[284] In the early days of the Revolution, it was not clear whether the leftist movement or the Islamic movement would take control, and the Islamists, with the support of the US government, gradually eliminated any opposition from the left, the intellectuals, or secular voices within the government structures.[285]

Khomeini continued to listen to the demands of his women constituents whose rights were being paradoxically expanded on certain levels and drastically reduced on other levels....

The status of women's human rights in Iranian society is conditioned by contradictions in the legal and political system of this totalitarian theocracy. Paradoxically, women's

---

269. NAFISI, *supra* note 86, at 300.
270. EBADI, *supra* note 94, at 106.
271. *Id.*
272. ICESCR, *supra* note 253, at art. 7.
273. *Id.* at art. 7(a)(i).
274. *Id.* at art. 7(c).
275. Roksana Bahramitash, *Revolution, Islamization, and Women's Employment in Iran*, 9 BROWN J. WORLD AFFAIRS 235 (2002).
276. EBADI, *supra* note 94, at 48.
277. NAFISI, *supra* note 86, at 262.
278. *See* EBADI, *supra* note 94, at 48.
279. NAFISI, *supra* note 86, at 270.
280. *See* EBADI, *supra* note 94, at 75.
281. NAFISI, *supra* note 86, at 328.
282. *Id.* at 288.
283. Halper, *supra* note 116, at 328.
284. *Id.* at 104.
285. *Id.* at 109.

rights in Iran today are both expanding and diminishing at the same time.... Only a dynamic interpretation[286] of the Koran together with radical transformations of the Iranian legal system and its procedures, and a systematic attempt to enforce the international treaties to which Iran is bound by ratification or by customary international law can provide hope for women's equality.

If justice and equality are intrinsic values in Islam and the *Shari'a*, why are justice and equality not reflected in the Iranian family laws that treat women as second class citizens, put women under men's domination, and strictly regulate gender relations and the rights of men and women unfairly?[287] Despite the movement backwards since 1979, particularly with regard to the enactment of family laws that discriminate against women in Iran, there is intense social pressure in Iran to change these laws and customs. Demographic developments in Iran constitute hope for the protection of human rights for women. Seventy percent of the population in Iran is below the age of thirty, and the young people in Iran want more freedom. There are twenty-two million students in Iran, and seventy percent of university students are women. Educated Iranian women who cannot find expression for their learning and young Iranian people who are frustrated by oppression make a volatile combination poised for transformation, if not revolution!

The burgeoning feminist movement in Iran wants more rights for women and more protective laws. Ideally, this feminist movement should be engaged more systematically in demanding the enforcement of the international human rights treaties to which Iran is a signatory. The populist movement in Iran wants to separate religion and the State, which could result in a diminution of the appreciation of *Shari'a* law and its application in private family matters directly affecting women. The development of a new gender discourse and the rise of a popular reformist movement in Iran are positive signs of the emergence of more equality for women within an Islamic framework.

In the 1990s, feminist readings of Islam were tolerated as the process of the Islamization of Iran continued to take place. While the ruling clerics continue to validate a patriarchal interpretation of the Koran and its translation into the laws of the Iranian courts, there is movement in Iran today to consider the legitimacy of a more dynamic interpretation of the Koran that would extend more protection to women and expand their rights through the laws. While Khomeini's office restored the *Shari'a* in order to "protect the family" and to realize women's "high status" in Islam, women are treated as second class citizens in the law, in society, and in the family structure that is decidedly patriarchal in Iran. Women cannot understand why husbands can divorce them automatically without even first securing their consent. Iranian women are justified in asking, "Is this what the *Shari'a* says? ... Is this how Islam honors women? Is this the justice of Islam?"[288] Rather than "producing the intended marital harmony or a generation of docile wives," the return to *Shari'a* in 1979 "further exposed and accentuated the gap between the patriarchal assumptions [about] marriage [and the kind of] egalitarian marriage lived and experienced by most people today."[289]

There is hope for women's human rights in Iran. Change will likely happen in Iran because of the emergence of a "sustained, indigenous feminism." The rise of an activist

---

286. "... *Shari'a* is not inherently inimical to women's rights ... the question of who gets to interpret *Shari'a* is critical." Isobel Coleman, *Women, Islam, and the New Iraq*, 85 FOREIGN AFF. 24, 26 (2006).

287. Mir-Hosseini, *Muslim Women's Quest for Equality: Between Islamic Law and Feminism* 32 CRITICAL INQUIRY 629, 629 (2006).

288. *Id.* at 635.

289. *Id.* at 636.

feminist movement in Iran has been delayed for many reasons other than the obvious fear of repression and reprisals. Women in Islam and in Iran are the symbols of cultural authenticity, the carriers of a religious tradition and a way of life. Thus, any form of dissent by women could be construed as a betrayal of their Muslim and/or Iranian identity,[290] and protest could, by extension, be construed as treasonous and pro-Western. Because of compulsory *hejab* and the multiplicity of meanings underlying women's dress wear, women in Iran have to choose between their Muslim identity and their new gender awareness.[291] This is a hard and dangerous choice that is unfairly imposed on women alone.

Islamic feminists are now engaged in finding the sources for so-called Islamic traditions that discriminate against them and force women to wear clothing that is cumbersome and renders them all the more dependent on men. Many studies show that men's unilateral rights to divorce and polygamy are not textually granted to them by the Koran or by God but were given to men by Muslim male jurists.[292] Iranian feminists[293] now focusing attention on Koranic interpretation (*tafsir*) have successfully uncovered the Koran's egalitarian message.[294] If continued, this belief in the power of interpretation is the clearest sign of hope for equality of women in Iran. The work of the Islamic feminists[295] should be examined in this light. By both uncovering a hidden history[296] and by rereading textual sources, women will come to see that there are two opposing views of Islam. One view is absolutist and legalistically inflexible with regard to the acceptance of modernity. The other view is pluralistic and tolerant, especially of equality between men and women. The new emphasis on interpretation of the original sacred texts will reveal that the inequalities embedded in Iranian law are not the manifestations of a divine will written into the Koran. Iranian jurisprudence is not the product of an inseparable bond between religion and the State. Iranian jurisprudence is not the product of a primitive, backward social system. The law and its system are human constructions that reflect political and ideological agendas of the controlling class. When Khomeini called back *Shari'a* law in Iran, this came with a forceful attempt "to impose anachronistic jurisprudential constructions of gender relations"[297] upon Iranian society

---

290. *Id.* at 639.

291. *Id.*

292. *Id.* at 642.

293. *See id.*, at n. 22 for a list of works showing how the Koran and Islam's sacred texts have been tainted by "the ideologies of their interpreters." *See generally*, Azizah Al-Hibri, *Islam, Law, and Custom: Redefining Muslim Women's Rights*, 12 Am. U. J. Int'l L. & Pol'y, 1–44 (1997), Kecia Ali, *Progressive Muslims and Islamic Jurisprudence: The Necessity for Critical Engagement with Marriage and Divorce Law*, in Progressive Muslims 163, 163–89 (Omid Safi ed., 2003), Asghar Ali Engineer, The Rights of Women in Islam (St. Martin's Press 1992), Farid Esack, *Islam and Gender Justice: Beyond Simplistic Apologia*, in What Men Owe to Women: Men's Voices from World Religions 187, 187–210 (John C. Rianes & Daniel C Maguire eds., 2001). Haifaa Jawad, The Rights of Women in Islam: An Authentic Approach (St. Martin's Press 1998), Ziba Mir-Hosseini, *The Construction of Gender in Islamic Legal Thought and Strategies for Reform*, 1 HAWWA 1, 1–18 (2003), *and* Amira El-Azhary Sonbol, *Rethinking Women and Islam*, in Daughters of Abraham: Feminist Thought in Judaism, Christianity, and Islam 108, 108–46 (Yvonne Yazbeck Haddad & John L. Esposito eds., 2001). *See also* Mir-Hosseini, *Women's Quest*, *supra* note 287, at n. 19 (providing a list of literature on Islamic feminism and its politics).

294. Mir-Hosseini, *Women's Quest*, *supra* note 287, at 642.

295. To some, the term "Islamic feminism" is an oxymoron. *See* Nayereh Tohidi, *Islamic Feminism: Perils and Promises*, 16 Mews Review 1 (2001), *available at* http://www.amews.org/review/reviewarticles/tohidi.htm.

296. Mir-Hosseini, *Women's Quest*, *supra* note 287, at 642.

297. *Id.* at 644.

whose women, unfortunately, suffer the most in the name of the preservation of tradition and national identity.

Why should women's equality be dependent upon ideological influences and patriarchal beliefs that filter people's personal and politically-charged interpretations of sacred texts? Rigid originalist interpretations put Islam and women's rights into a closed, static, and inflexible legal system that breeds unfairness to women, gender inequality, and unhealthy social relationships between men and women. To open this closure and liberate women in Iran, the feminists must overcome specious dichotomies,[298] established for self-serving reasons by men, between Islam and feminism, tradition and modernity, the quest for protection of Iranian national/religious identity, and the fear of equality that comes from integration and exposure to cultural difference in the course of international relations. Women's liberation from human rights abuse in Iran is an issue deeply entrenched in semiotics and a serious matter of interpretation.

G. Relation of Children's Human Rights and Women's Rights

How are children's rights related to women's human rights? In some cultures women have been reduced to the stereotype of mere child breeders and child caretakers. Women and children are frequently linked together in treaties[299] as a group that is in special need of protection, especially in wartime. There is no doubt that any deep understanding of women's rights must cover the rights of the people and groups she is associated with on a regular basis, including her children, and the persons she takes care of in her family.

As minors by law, children do not have autonomy or the right to make decisions on their own for themselves in any known jurisdiction of the world. Instead their adult caregivers, including parents, social workers, teachers, youth workers and others, most of whom are women, are vested with the authority to make decisions for the child, in most circumstances. Repressive caretakers of children can cause them to be particularly vulnerable. Therefore, children's rights and responsibilities must be recognized at all ages.

1. Children's Human Rights

a. Definition of a Child and a Child's Rights

A child is defined as any human being below the age of eighteen years, unless under the law applicable to the child, majority is attained earlier. Children's rights include their

---

298. *See* Abdullahi An-Na'im, *The Dichotomy Between Religious and Secular Discourse in Islamic Societies, in* FAITH AND FREEDOM: WOMEN'S HUMAN RIGHTS IN THE MUSLIM WORLD 51, 51–60 (Mahnaz Afkhami ed., 1995).

299. *See, e.g.,* Universal Declaration of Human Rights, Article 25(2): "Motherhood and childhood are entitled to special care and assistance. All children, whether born in or out of wedlock, shall enjoy the same social protection." *See also* ICCPR, Article 6(5): "Sentence of death shall not be imposed for crimes committed by persons below eighteen years of age and shall not be carried out on pregnant women."

rights to special protection and care. These rights include: the right of association with both of their biological parents, the right to a human identity, and the right to fulfill their basic needs for food, universal state-paid education, health care, and the kind of protection under the criminal laws that is appropriate for their age and development. Children have the right to be physically, mentally, and emotionally free from violence and abuse, and the right to receive care and nurturing.

Children's rights can be defined in different ways. Children's right advocates claim that children are endowed with the traditional civil, political, cultural, economic, and social rights. Moreover, some would like to give children the "right of empowerment" as well as the "right of protection." Children's rights can fall under a three-fold category: provision, protection, and participation. Children have the right to be provided with an adequate standard of living, heath care, education, services, and the right to play and have recreation. They have the right to be provided with a balanced diet, a warm bed to sleep in, and access to schooling (provision). Children also have the right to protection from violence and abuse, neglect, exploitation, and discrimination. They have the right to live and play in a safe place, to be subject to constructive child rearing behavior, and to have society acknowledge the evolving capacities of children (protection). Children have the right to participate in communities and services appropriate for themselves and their age. This includes children's involvement in libraries and community programs, and youth activities involving children as decision-makers (participation).

Amnesty International advocates four basic children's rights including the end to juvenile incarceration without parole, the end to the use of child soldiers, the end of the death penalty for people under 21, and raising awareness of human rights in the classroom. Human Rights Watch, another international NGO, focuses on the human rights issues involving child labor, juvenile justice, orphans and abandoned children, refugees, street children, and corporal punishment.

b.   Children's Rights Laws

Parents seriously impact the lives of children and have a direct relationship to the crimes of child neglect, child abuse, and excessive corporal punishment. Children's rights must be protected by law. The Universal Declaration of Human Rights is the basis for all international legal standards for children's rights. The Convention on the Rights of the Child is the most specific international instrument providing and protecting children's rights. The United States has not signed the CRC for many reasons. Children in the United States are afforded their basic rights embodied in the Constitution under the Fourteenth Amendment. The Equal Protection Clause of that amendment applies to children.

1.   The UN Convention on the Rights of the Child

The UN Convention on the Rights of the Child (CRC)[300] was adopted by the UN General Assembly on November 20, 1989 and entered into force less than a year later, on September 2, 1990. The CRC currently has 193 State parties, with the United States and

---

300. Convention on the Rights of the Child, adopted 20 Nov. 1989, entered into force 2 Sept. 1990, 1577 U.N.T.S. 3, *reprinted in* 28 I.L.M. 1448 (1989), *available at* http://www.ohchr.org/english/law/crc.htm. *See also* Optional Protocol to the Convention on the Rights of the Child on the Involvement of Children in Armed Conflicts, G.A. Res. 54/263, Annex I, UN GAOR, 54th Sess., UN Doc. A/RES/54/263 (May 25, 2000). *See also* Optional Protocol to the Convention on the Rights of the

Somalia as the only exceptions. Much controversy exists about the CRC. The US has refused to sign it primarily because of the belief that adherence to the provisions and protections of this treaty would be a serious threat to the sovereignty of the parent. The CRC was enacted in order to protect minors under the age of 18 who are undeniably in need of special protection and care. The CRC is comprehensive and provides children with all of the traditional human rights equally without hierarchy including civil, political, economic, social, and cultural rights. The CRC underscores the indivisibility, mutual reinforcement, and equal importance of all human rights. The CRC offers children protection, provision of services and material benefits, and participation in society and in decisions affecting children.

The CRC codifies many important legal principles as they pertain to children. For example, Article 3 stipulates that the child's best interests must be the primary consideration of all actions concerning the child. Article 8 seeks to preserve the identity of the child, in order to combat the large number of child "disappearances." Article 12 gives children the right to express an opinion and have that opinion taken into account in decisions that affect them. Article 19 especially protects children from intra-familial abuse and neglect. Article 21 places emphasis on safeguards for the adoption of children. Article 24 refers to the State's obligation to work towards the abolition of female genital mutilation (FGM) and other cultural practices and traditions such as male child preference which lead to the murder and disappearance of many girl babies and the increased trafficking of women. Article 37 declares that the imprisonment of children must be imposed only as a last resort and incarceration must be limited to the shortest possible period. Article 40 upgrades international norms with regard to children accused of crimes. Finally, Article 42 recognizes that children need and deserve to receive information about their rights.

c.   Basis of the Controversy over the CRC

The most controversial articles in the CRC are the following: Article 13 (a child's right to "freedom of expression including freedom to seek, receive, and impart information and ideas of all kinds regardless of frontiers, either orally, in writing or in print, in the form of art, or through any other media of the child's choice"); Article 14 (a child's right to "freedom of thought, conscience, and religion"); Article 15 (a child's right to "freedom of association"); Article 16 (a child's right to be free from "arbitrary or unlawful interference with his or her privacy, family, home or correspondence, nor to unlawful attacks on his or her honor and reputation"); and Article 43 (the establishment of a Committee on the Rights of the Child composed of ten experts to oversee implementation of the protections and provisions of the treaty).

The United States has refused to sign and ratify this treaty because of its general suspicion of the United Nations, its fear of losing its own sovereignty and the sovereignty of parents, and its objection to the probable increase in violations of states' rights and resultant damage to the US system of federalism. Some claim the CRC strips parents of rights and dangerously empowers children with decision-making functions, even though children are sometimes not ready or really able to make reasoned and reasonable decisions for themselves. Some of these fears may be based on misunderstandings about the implementation process or misreadings of the text of the treaty itself. For example, some fear that under Article 13 parents could be sued by their own children for any attempt to pre-

---

Child on the Sale of Children, Child Prostitution, and Child Pornography, G.A. Res. 54/263, UN GAOR, 54th Sess., Annex II, UN Doc. A/ RES/54/263 (January 18, 2002).

vent them from interaction with pornography or other inappropriate communication on television. Some fear that under Article 14 children may assert their right against parental objections to participate in occult religions. Under Article 15 parents are arguably prevented from forbidding their children to associate with objectionable people in gangs, cults, racist organizations, etc. Article 16 appears to give children an absolute "right of privacy" and may include the right to have an abortion without parental consent, the right to fornication, the right to view obscenity within the home, and the right to obtain and use birth control without parental involvement or consent. Finally, Article 43 calls for a Committee of 10 experts of high moral stature whom some fear may end up investigating and prosecuting any and all parents who violate their children's rights. Most of these readings are inaccurate, but several of the opposition points are merit-worthy. These objections need special consideration if there is any hope to encourage the US to sign and ratify this treaty, with or without reservations.

d.   Reservations to the CRC

Despite the overwhelming number of countries that have signed and ratified the CRC, many of them have chosen to make declarations and reservations to the treaty, which are legal but serve to weaken the overall impact of the treaty. A reservation is defined as "a unilateral statement" made by a state when ratifying a treaty "whereby it purports to exclude or to modify the legal effect of certain provisions of the treaty in their application to that State."[301] Any State ratifying a treaty may make a reservation unless it is "prohibited by the treaty" or "is incompatible with the object and purpose of the treaty."[302] A declaration can be made "by a State as to its understanding of some matter covered by a treaty or its interpretation of a particular provision. Unlike reservations, declarations merely clarify a State's position and do not purport to exclude or modify the legal effect of a treaty."[303]

2.   Conclusion

Children are vulnerable and need special protection from excessive force that may be used on them as corporal punishment both at home and in public institutions. For example, the practice of caning is still done customarily to children in Kenyan schools, despite Kenyan laws that prohibit corporal punishment in schools.[304] "For most Kenyan children, violence is a regular part of the school experience. Teachers use caning, slapping, and whipping to maintain classroom discipline and to punish children for poor academic performance. The infliction of corporal punishment is routine, arbitrary, and often brutal. Bruises and cuts are regular by-products of school punishments, and more severe injuries (broken bones, knocked-out teeth, internal bleeding) are not infrequent. At times, beatings by teachers leave children permanently disfigured, disabled or dead."[305] Many children all over the world are forced into becoming child soldiers or trafficked into a life

---

301. Vienna Convention on the Law of Treaties, *supra* note 256, at art. 2(d).

302. *Id.* at art. 19.

303. United Nations, Office of Legal Affairs, Treaty Handbook, Glossary, *available at* http://untreaty.un.org/english/treatyhandbook/glossary.htm.

304. Human Rights Watch, *Spare the Child: Corporal Punishment in Kenyan Schools* 3 (1999), *in* HENRY J. STEINER & PHILIP ALSTON, INTERNATIONAL HUMAN RIGHTS IN CONTEXT: LAW POLITICS MORALS 524 (Oxford, 2nd ed. 2000).

305. *Id.*

of slavery and prostitution. The Lord's Resistance Army in Northern Uganda systematically kidnaps girls and boys as young as eight and forces them through brutal indoctrination and brainwashing to commit murder and other grave atrocities. Some countries show blatant discrimination against girl children because of a deeply engrained cultural practice of male-child preference that leads to the murder of girl babies, the increase of trafficked girls from other countries into the country practicing female child infanticide, and the general marginalization of women in these societies. This chapter will examine the horrific effect that the tradition of male-child preference and the State-sponsored one-child policy have had on the increase of trafficking of women and girls in China.

H. The Male-Child Preference, the One-Child Policy, and the Increase of Trafficking of Women in China

1. Susan Tiefenbrun, *Human Trafficking in China*[306]
Introduction

A. BACKGROUND OF CHINA'S DEMOGRAPHIC CRISIS

Several factors work independently to cause a serious shortage of women in China. Women are bought and sold, murdered and made to disappear in China, in order to comply with a governmental policy that reflects the cultural phenomenon of male-child preference. In 1979, the Chinese government instituted a One-Child Policy (OCP) to control the enormous population expansion. In order to comply with the OCP and to ensure that the family has a coveted boy child, millions of people in China have committed sex-selective abortions, infanticide of their own baby girls, non-registration of the first or second infant in the family, and the abandonment or sale of their own girl children. Women are disappearing because of the social pressures of male-child preference, the zealous enforcement of the OCP by local government authorities, and the murderous responses to this policy undertaken by millions of ordinary people in China who are desperate to have a son. The scarcity of women has produced a gender imbalance and an increase in prostitution and human trafficking in China. Trafficking in China has many forms: the purchase of women for brides, the purchase of a male son, the sale of unwanted female children, and the use of people for slave labor, commercial sex, or forced prostitution. Men, primarily in rural China, are desperately seeking a bride in a country where women are in short supply. These men will resort to purchasing a trafficked woman for marriage. Couples seeking a male child will sell, drown, or even murder their girl child in order to make room for the purchase of a trafficked baby boy. Young adult women and boy infants are bought and sold like cargo in China. Human trafficking in China is a lucrative international business that is expanding due to the aggressive implementation of the OCP, a faulty legal system, and the blind adherence to long standing cultural traditions that devalue women. Moreover, in China, Communist Party directives overshadow

---

306. Susan Tiefenbrun, *Human Trafficking in China*, 6 U. St. Thomas L.J. 247 (2008).

the legislative and judicial process. The primacy of government policy results in the ineffectiveness of laws that theoretically protect women and female children in China.[307]

B. Chinese Culture

Women's inferiority is deeply ingrained in the Chinese culture and is reflected in the *Five Classics*, a canonical literary text ascribed to Confucius. The Confucian view of woman is clearly stated: "The female was inferior by nature, she was dark as the moon and changeable as water, jealous, narrow-minded, and insinuating. She was indiscreet, unintelligent, and dominated by emotion. Her beauty was a snare for the unwary male, the ruination of states."[308]

In Chinese culture, girls typically marry into the husband's family, leave home, and take care of their husband's parents. In the past, China's feudal tradition continuously subjected women to subordination by their father, husband, and even their son due to a patriarchal and patrilineal system. In addition, according to the rules of primogeniture, only the first male born traditionally inherited the parents' fortune. Moreover, only boys could continue the patrilineal family line. Thus, even today girl babies are considered financial burdens because they are unavailable to take care of their elderly parents who, upon retirement, do not receive enough money from the inadequate social services system in China. If only one child is allowed, the general consensus in China is that it better be a boy!

C. Trafficking in China

Trafficking of women and boy children in China is a serious human rights violation. According to the US Department of State's Annual Trafficking in Persons Report (TIP Report), domestic trafficking is "the most significant problem in China,"[309] and an estimated ten thousand to twenty thousand victims are trafficked internally each year.[310] China is designated as a source, transit, and destination country for women and children trafficked for the purpose of sexual exploitation and forced labor.[311] Trafficking occurs mainly within China's borders, but Chinese citizens are also trafficked out of China into Africa, Asia, Europe, Latin America, the Middle East, and North America.[312] Poor and desperate Chinese women are lured abroad with false promises of legitimate work only to be forced into prostitution and commercial sexual exploitation. They are trafficked typically into Taiwan, Thailand, Malaysia, and Japan. Foreign women and children are trafficked into China from Mongolia, Burma, North Korea, Russia, and Vietnam for purposes of forced labor, marriage, and prostitution.[313]

---

307. Xiaorong Li, *License to Coerce: Violence against Women, State Responsibility, and Legal Failures in China's Family Planning Program*, 8 Yale J.L. & Feminism 145, 184 (1996). *See also* Andrew Jacobs, *Abuses, cited in Enforcing China Policy of One Child*, N.Y. Times, December 22, 2010, at A 11.

308. Richard W. Guisso, *Thunder Over the Lake: The Five Classics and the Perception of Women in Early China*, *in* Women in China: Current Directions in Historical Scholarship 59 (Richard W. Guisso & Stanley Johannesen eds., 1981). *See also* Dan Levin, *"China's New Wealth Gives Old Status Symbol a Boost,"* N.Y. Times, August 10, 2011, at A6, discussing the role of women as mistresses to the rich in modern China.

309. US Dep't of State, Trafficking in Persons Report 91 (2008), *available at* http://www.state.gov/documents/organization/105501.pdf [hereinafter TIP Report 2008].

310. US Dep't of State, Trafficking in Persons Report 80 (2007), *available at* http://www.state.gov/documents/organization/82902.pdf [hereinafter TIP Report 2007].

311. TIP Report 2008, *supra* note 309, at 91.

312. *Id.*

313. *Id.* at 92.

Experts believe that China's OCP has resulted in a male-female birth ratio imbalance, and the scarcity of women has contributed mightily to the increase in trafficking of women for brides.[314] The government of China is making efforts to comply with minimum standards for the elimination of trafficking, but it fails to adequately punish traffickers or protect Chinese and foreign victims of trafficking.[315] China still continues to treat trafficked women as criminals and regularly deports North Korean trafficked women back to horrendous conditions in their home country.[316] In December 2007, China released a National Action Plan to Combat Trafficking, but the government has not allocated enough funds to implement the plan.

Trafficking laws around the world, including China's, are either weak or nonexistent, and those that exist are either not enforced or often enforced to the detriment of the victim, rather than the perpetrator.[317] China has a trafficking law, but it is not well enforced.[318] In addition, prostitution is illegal in China, and victims of trafficking are treated there like criminals engaging in prostitution. National laws that prohibit prostitution often discourage victims from seeking help from the authorities who might either throw the trafficking victims in jail for engaging in illegal prostitution or deport them to their home countries, where they are forced to live as social outcasts in horrific conditions.[319] However, I do not believe that legalizing prostitution helps trafficked victims. Legalized prostitution simply facilitates trafficking because the trafficked woman forced to engage in sex work against her will cannot be distinguished from the voluntary prostitute. A better approach is to increase the criminal penalties for trafficking. Since the criminal penalties for trafficking in women are typically very light, international crime syndicates are drawn to the sex trade industry.[320] Sex trafficking is the third-most-lucrative international crime, after the traffic of arms and drugs.[321] In China, however, human trafficking earns more money annually than the trafficking of weapons or drugs. The economic benefits of human trafficking make it all the more difficult to eradicate.

This article will address human trafficking in China and the root causes of this human rights violation that has developed from the strict enforcement of a governmental OCP and the persistence of a cultural phenomenon of male-child preference. The article is organized in five parts. Part II will examine the laws prohibiting trafficking in China; Part III will discuss the US trafficking law; Part IV will identify specific problems related to trafficking in China; Part V will unearth root causes of trafficking in China based on the OCP and the increasing scarcity of women; Part VI will offer policy suggestions to combat the growth of trafficking in China. The purpose of this article is to encourage the Chinese government to further protect the lives and rights of women.

D. Chinese Trafficking Laws

In addition to China's marriage law,[322] family planning policies, and inheritance laws, which do theoretically protect women and children, China has enacted several laws that

---

314. *Id.*

315. *Id.*

316. *Id.*

317. Susan Tiefenbrun, *The Saga of Susannah—A US Remedy for Sex Trafficking in Women: The Victims of Trafficking and Violence Protection Act of 2000*, 2002 Uтaн L. Rev. 107, 114 (2002).

318. TIP Report 2008, *supra* note 309, at 93.

319. Tiefenbrun, *supra* note 317, at 113–14.

320. *Id.* at 114.

321. *Id.* at 137.

322. Marriage Law (promulgated by Order No. 9 of the Chairman of the Standing Comm. Nat'l People's Cong., Sept. 10, 1980, effective Jan. 1, 1981) (P.R.C.), *available at* http://www.unescap.org/esid/psis/population/database/poplaws/law_china/ch_record003.htm [hereinafter Marriage Law].

specifically address trafficking, kidnapping, and sexual exploitation of women and children. In 1991, the National People's Congress Standing Committee criminalized the purchase of women by enacting a "Decision Relating to the Severe Punishment of Criminal Elements Who Abduct and Kidnap Women and Children" (Decision), making the abduction and the sale of women and children separate offenses.[323] Prior to the promulgation of this Decision, many traffickers who sold women whom others had kidnapped were released by the courts.[324] Now both the kidnapper and the seller are prosecuted under this Decision. The use of force to prevent the rescue of trafficked women was also specifically criminalized.[325] In 1992, the Law on the Protection of Women's Rights and Interests (LPWRI)[326] was passed. This was the first basic law to protect women's rights and interests in China.[327] The LPWRI prohibits kidnapping, trafficking, and buying women, though it fails to prescribe any specific penalties for these offenses.[328] The LPWRI also fails to provide a definition of discrimination against women.[329] However, those who buy abducted women and force them to have sex may be tried for the crime of rape under the Chinese Criminal Code.[330] Other types of violence against abducted women are subject to penalties under the Chinese Criminal Code.[331] The rights of women in Hong Kong are protected by the Sex Discrimination Ordinance (1995) and the Family Status Ordinance (1997).[332]

Article 236 of the Chinese Criminal Code provides a three- to ten-year sentence for rape, while sexual exploitation of girls under the age of fourteen can receive a sentence of life imprisonment or the death penalty.[333] Article 240 prohibits abducting and trafficking a woman or child and specifies a five- to ten-year sentence for this crime.[334] A ten-year to lifetime sentence or the death penalty may be imposed on those who abduct and traffic a woman or child, rape or prostitute the woman, steal an infant for the purpose of selling the victim, or sell the victim outside of China.[335] Purchasing an abducted woman or child carries a punishment of up to three years, although the punishment can be combined with other provisions in instances of rape or other crimes in order to give the perpetrator a longer sentence.[336] China's Criminal Code does not

---

323. Decision Regarding the Severe Punishment of Criminals Who Abduct and Traffic in or Kidnap Women or Children (promulgated by the Standing Comm. Nat'l People's Cong., Sept. 4, 1991, effective Sept. 4, 1991) (P.R.C.), *available at* http://english.mofcom.gov.cn/article/lawsdata/chinese law/200211/20021100053260.html.

324. Human Rights in China, *Caught between Tradition and the State: Violations of the Human Rights of Chinese Women*, 17 Women's Rts. L. Rep. 285, 290 (1996).

325. *Id.*

326. Law Protecting Women's Rights and Interests (promulgated by Order No. 58 of the President of the P.R.C. on Apr. 3, 1992, effective Oct. 1, 1992), *available at* http://www.unescap.org/esid/psis/ population/database/poplaws/law_china/ch_record002.htm [hereinafter LPWRI].

327. Chairperson, Comm. on the Elimination of Discrimination against Women, *Report of the Comm. on the Elimination of Discrimination against Women*, §272, *delivered to the UN General Assembly*, UN Doc. A/54/38 (Feb. 5, 1999) [hereinafter CEDAW Report].

328. LPWRI, *supra* note 326.

329. CEDAW Report, *supra* note 327, at §283.

330. Criminal Law (adopted by Nat'l People's Cong., July 1, 1979, revised March 14, 1997), arts. 236, 241 (P.R.C.), *available at* http://www.unescap.org/esid/psis/population/database/poplaws/law_ china/ch_record010.htm [hereinafter Criminal Law].

331. Human Rights in China, *supra* note 324, at 290.

332. CEDAW Report, *supra* note 327, at §260.

333. Criminal Law, *supra* note 330, at art. 236.

334. *Id.* at art. 240.

335. *Id.*

336. *Id.* at art. 241.

prohibit commercial sexual exploitation involving coercion or fraud, nor does it prohibit all forms of trafficking, such as debt bondage.[337] Chinese law enforcement efforts to arrest and prosecute perpetrators of these crimes are seriously lacking, and China does not even report statistics on prosecutions, convictions, or sentences for these crimes.[338]

The Law on the Protection of Minors, adopted in 1991, was revised in 2006 and became effective in June 2007.[339] This law specifically prohibits the trafficking, kidnapping, and sexual exploitation of minors.[340] The chairman of the Standing Committee of the National People's Congress has "urged tighter supervision on the implementation of the law," and warned that inspection teams would be visiting several provinces in the summer of 2008 to investigate compliance with the law.[341]

In December 2007, the Chinese government established a new Office for Preventing and Combating Crimes of Trafficking in Women and Children.[342] At that time, China also released its much-anticipated National Action Plan to Combat Trafficking, but "there are no plans for resources to be allocated to local and provincial governments for the implementation of the plan. Additionally, the action plan covers only sex trafficking of females, and does not address labor trafficking or male victims of sex trafficking."[343]

E. US Trafficking Law

The Trafficking Victims Protection Act of 2000 (TVPA)[344] is the US law with an international prong that is designed to combat human trafficking by punishing traffickers, protecting victims, and preventing trafficking.[345] On October 28, 2000, President William Clinton signed the TVPA in order to provide an international solution to an international crime. This law severely punishes sex trafficking as if it were a crime as serious as rape. Trafficking is punishable by a sentence of twenty years to life imprisonment.[346] The TVPA has been hailed as the "most significant human rights legislation of [the US] Congress."[347]

In addition to providing protection for victims, prosecution for perpetrators, and prevention of the crime of trafficking, the TVPA also intends to "encourage foreign governments to take effective actions to counter all forms of trafficking in persons" by enacting

---

337. TIP Report 2007, *supra* note 310, at 80.

338. TIP Report 2008, *supra* note 309, at 93.

339. Law on the Protection of Minors (adopted by the Standing Comm. Nat'l People's Cong., Sept. 4, 1991, *revised* December 29, 2006, *effective* June 1, 2007) (P.R.C.), *available at* http://www.npc.gov.cn/englishnpc/Law/2007-12/12/content_1383869.htm.

340. *Id.* at art. 41.

341. Embassy of the People's Republic of China in the United States of America, *China's Top Legislator Urges Better Protection of Minors*, June 2, 2008, *available at* http://www.china-embassy.org/eng/xw/t443171.htm.

342. TIP Report 2008, *supra* note 309, at 92.

343. *Id.*

344. Trafficking Victims Protection Act of 2000, 22 U.S.C.A. §7101 (West 2000).

345. *Id.*

346. Trafficking with Respect to Peonage, Slavery, Involuntary Servitude or Forced Labor, 18 U.S.C. §1590 (2000).

347. Press Release, Eric Hotmire, *Senate Passes Brownback, Wellstone Trafficking Victims Protection Act* (July 27, 2000), *available at* http://brownback.senate.gov/pressapp/record.cfm?id=175961&&year=2000&. President Clinton stated that the TVPA was "the most significant step we've ever taken to secure the health and safety of women at home and around the world." Leah Platt, *Regulating the Global Brothel*, Am. Prospect Mag., Summer 2001, *available at* http://www.thirdworldtraveler.com/Women/Regulate_Global_Brothel.html.

or amending sex trafficking legislation.[348] The TVPA seeks to strengthen enforcement policies and coordinate international anti-trafficking efforts through the publication of the annual TIP Report by the US State Department.[349]

F. Trafficking in China

1. Domestic Trafficking of Women within China

According to the 2008 US State Department TIP Report, China remains "a source, transit, and destination country for men, women, and children trafficked for the purposes of sexual exploitation and forced labor."[350] After spending four years on Tier 2[351] of the TIP rankings from 2001 to 2004, China was dropped to the Tier 2 Watch List in 2005, where it has remained up to the present due to its noncompliance "with the minimum standards for the elimination of trafficking."[352] Some of the factors impeding progress in China's anti-trafficking efforts include "tight controls over civil society organizations, restricted access of foreign anti-trafficking organizations, and the government's systematic lack of transparency," as well as its failure to "address labor trafficking or male victims of sex trafficking."[353]

Because of the scarcity of women in China due to the impact of the OCP and the cultural force of the male-child preference, domestic trafficking is one of the leading problems in China today. In 2007, the TIP Report stated that there are a minimum of ten thousand to twenty thousand victims trafficked internally per year.[354] The profit earned in human trafficking in China is more than seven billion dollars annually, more than arms trafficking or drug trafficking.[355] International organizations state that 90 percent of the trafficking victims are women and children from the Anhui, Henan, Hunan, Sichuan, Yunnan, and Guizhou Provinces who are sent to wealthier provinces in the East and trafficked primarily for sexual exploitation.[356]

The abducted women are usually between the ages of thirteen and twenty-four.[357] While many women are sold into forced and exploitative prostitution, most are purchased as brides in rural parts of China.[358] As the number of available women decreases and the number of peasant families moving to urban areas for jobs increases, peasant men look to traffickers to supply them with a wife.[359] Some say it is economically cheaper to purchase a wife than to pay for a wedding and dowry gifts.[360] Local villagers often sympathize with the husband whose bought bride tries to escape, and villagers sometimes will return the purchased wife to her husband even if she complains of abuse.[361]

---

348. TIP Report 2008, *supra* note 309, at 5.

349. *Id.*

350. *Id.* at 91.

351. *Id.* at 93.

352. *Id.* at 92.

353. *Id.*

354. TIP Report 2007, *supra* note 310, at 80.

355. Hong Ju, Jianhong Liu & Alicia Crowther, *Female Criminal Victimization and Criminal Justice Response in China*, 46 Brit. J. Criminology 859, 863 (2006). Note that statistics on income from trafficking can be unreliable. The 2008 TIP Report states that the total annual income earned internationally in trafficking is thirty-two billion dollars. Therefore, the seven billion dollar figure for China appears to be misleading and inaccurate. TIP Report 2008, *supra* note 309, at 34.

356. TIP Report 2007, *supra* note 310, at 80.

357. Calum MacLeod, *Life Begins Again for Chinese Girl Sold as Slave at 12*, Independent (London), May 17, 2000, *available at* http://findarticles.com/p/articles/mi_qn4158/is_20000517/ai_n14313948.

358. *Id.*

359. *Id.*

360. *Id.*

361. *Id.*

2. International Trafficking Into and Outside of China

International trafficking of Chinese citizens to Africa, Asia, Europe, Latin America, the Middle East, and North America is increasing.[362] Many poor Chinese women are duped by false promises of legitimate jobs in Taiwan, Thailand, Malaysia, and Japan, only to be sold into prostitution upon their arrival.[363] Although trafficking remains illegal in China, this crime is inadequately enforced, especially in the vulnerable southern provinces near Thailand and Taiwan.[364] In relation to the number of women and children trafficked in China, there are relatively few investigations of trafficking and even fewer trials or convictions.[365] In 2006, in Anhui Province, one of the major sources of trafficking victims, only six traffickers were convicted and sentenced to life imprisonment.[366] In 2007, China did not report any country-wide conviction records for trafficking.[367]

In 2007, the Chinese government "reported investigating 2,375 cases of trafficking of women and children … which is significantly lower than the 3,371 cases it cited in 2006."[368] These figures are likely based on China's definition of the term "trafficking," which "does not include acts of forced labor, debt bondage, coercion, involuntary servitude, or offenses committed against male victims."[369] Although China "sustained its record of criminal law enforcement against traffickers," the US State Department reports that these government statistics are difficult to verify.[370] Finally, in 2007, "Chinese law enforcement authorities arrested and punished some traffickers involved in forced labor practices and commercial sexual exploitation, but did not provide data on prosecutions, convictions, or sentences."[371] The lack of transparency in the Chinese judicial system exacerbates the problem of data verification.

Trafficking is not only limited to women and children but also includes infant girls and boys.[372] In poor rural districts of China, the preference for male children is high, and family planning rules are strictly enforced. The OCP limits the number of children that women may bear, and many women prefer to sell their infant daughter for relatively large sums of money in order to try again for a son.[373] Many women are afraid of the social stigma as well as the large fines and penalties imposed on them for violating the one-child limit.[374] While many families are willing to pay the fines if a son is born, most "would never pay that kind of fine for a daughter."[375] The trafficked infant girls are often sold to childless urban parents or rural farmers who desire a girl to help with the housework. Some girls in China are even raised to be child brides for farmers in remote villages.[376]

---

362. TIP Report 2008, *supra* note 309, at 91–93.
363. *Id.* at 91–92.
364. TIP Report 2007, *supra* note 310, at 81.
365. TIP Report 2008, *supra* note 309, at 92.
366. TIP Report 2007, *supra* note 310, at 80–81.
367. TIP Report 2008, *supra* note 309, at 92.
368. *Id.* at 93.
369. *Id.*
370. *Id.* at 92.
371. *Id.* at 93.
372. Elisabeth Rosenthal, *Bias for Boys Leads to Sale of Baby Girls in China*, N.Y. Times, July 20, 2003, *available at* http://query.nytimes.com/gst/fullpage.htm.
373. *Id.*
374. *Id.*
375. *Id.*
376. *Id.*

G. Complicity of Corrupt Local Officials

One of the big issues facing the Chinese government's efforts to combat trafficking is "the significant level of corruption and complicity in trafficking by some local government officials."[377] In many cases, corrupt local officials participate in the sexual exploitation of women, making it difficult to combat the trafficking industry on a national level.[378] Many of these officials do not view trafficking as a serious crime and do not take steps to prevent it.[379] At times, officials even accept bribes in order to overlook trafficking.[380]

Slave labor is a variant of trafficking. In May and June 2007, several cases of slave labor in brick kilns in China's Henan and Shanxi Provinces were discovered. Over one thousand farmers, teenagers, and children were confined, subject to physical abuse, and forced to work without pay for their labor.[381] The brick kiln operators claim to have paid off local officials to turn a blind eye to the slave labor and sweat shop conditions.[382] There are unconfirmed press reports that some local officers have resold rescued children to similarly abusive factories in other districts.[383] According to the latest 2008 TIP Report, "[t]he Chinese government has not demonstrated concerted efforts to investigate, prosecute, and punish government officials for complicity in trafficking."[384] In addition, "Chinese law does not prohibit commercial sexual exploitation involving coercion or fraud, nor does it prohibit all forms of trafficking."[385] Chinese law recognizes only abduction as constituting a means of trafficking but does not recognize other forms of coercion.[386] Finally, Chinese law specifies only a three-year sentence for purchasers of women and children, but this light sentence is rarely implemented.[387]

H. Criminalization of and Reprisals against Trafficking Victims

One main obstacle to the eradication of trafficking in China is the criminalization and punishment of the victims rather than the traffickers.[388] Prostitution is illegal in China, and authorities often falsely or mistakenly accuse trafficked women of engaging in unlawful prostitution.[389] Authorities fail to distinguish between a trafficked woman who was forced into prostitution and a voluntary prostitute. China arrests trafficked women for prostitution and does not refer them to organizations providing services.[390] In other words, China treats the victims of trafficking as mere criminals.[391] "Victims are sometimes punished for unlawful acts that were committed as a direct result of their being trafficked — such as violations of prostitution or immigration/emigration controls."[392]

---

377. TIP Report 2008, *supra* note 309, at 92.
378. *Id.*; CEDAW Report, *supra* note 327, at §§ 291–92.
379. Human Rights in China, *supra* note 324, at 290.
380. *Id.*
381. TIP Report 2008, *supra* note 309, at 93.
382. *Id.*
383. *Id.*
384. *Id.*
385. *Id.*
386. *Id.*
387. Criminal Law, *supra* note 330, at art. 241; MacLeod, *supra* note 357.
388. TIP Report 2008, *supra* note 309, at 93.
389. *Id.*
390. *Id.*
391. *Id.*
392. *Id.* at 92.

In the southern border provinces, local authorities rely heavily upon nongovernmental organizations to identify trafficking victims and to provide victim protection services since the local governments there lack significant resources and are severely underfunded.[393] Many trafficking victims are returned home without any rehabilitation.[394] Foreign trafficking victims are forcibly evicted from China and sent back to their home countries, where they often face punishments and rejection.[395] North Korean trafficking victims are treated solely as illegal economic migrants, and a few hundred of them are deported each month to North Korea where they may face severe penalties.[396] Some Chinese trafficking victims also face punishments in the form of fines for leaving China without proper authorization, even if they were coerced to leave China by authorities.[397] China clearly continues to punish the victims of trafficking.

Trafficked women face discrimination from their own families and communities upon their release and return home.[398] Families feel that the trafficking victim has caused them shame and "a loss of face" by having sex with her purchaser, even if she was forced to do so.[399] A commonplace view in China is that the woman is at fault for being trafficked.[400] Moreover, people believe that a woman's virtue is the property of the man; if a woman's virtue is "used" by another, it loses its value.[401] These beliefs are a sign of the pervasiveness of feudal attitudes deeply entrenched within the Chinese culture, and these attitudes continue to marginalize women.[402]

I. Root Causes of Trafficking

1. One-Child Policy

In 1979, the "One-Child Policy" (OCP) was launched.[403] This policy was outlined in countless Communist Party directives, with hopes that the population would be slowed to 1.2 billion by the year 2000, rather than the projected 1.4 billion.[404] At first, only three children or more were prohibited, but the policy was revised after only a few years to forbid couples from having more than one child.[405] Vice Premier Deng Xiaoping declared, "In order to reduce the population, use whatever means you must, but do it! With the support of the Party Central Committee, you will have nothing to fear."[406] In 1980, the Chinese Marriage Law was enacted, requiring family planning for all married couples and prescribing age restrictions for marriage.[407] For example, according to this law, women cannot marry before they are twenty, and men cannot

---

393. *Id.* at 93.

394. *Id.*

395. *Id.*

396. *Id.* at 93–94.

397. *Id.* at 93.

398. Human Rights in China, *supra* note 324, at 291.

399. *Id.*

400. *Id.*

401. *Id.*

402. *Id.*

403. James Z. Lee & Wang Feng, One Quarter of Humanity: Malthusian Mythology and Chinese Realities, 1700–2000, 94 (1999).

404. Penny Kane & Ching Y. Choi, *China's One-Child Family Policy*, 319 Brit. Med. J. 992 (1999).

405. Lee & Feng, *supra* note 403, at 93.

406. Steven W. Mosher, A Mother's Ordeal: One Woman's Fight Against China's One-Child Policy 274 (1993).

407. Marriage Law, *supra* note 322.

marry before the age of twenty-two.[408] Late marriage and late childbirth are strongly encouraged.[409] The 1982 Chinese Constitution also requires all Chinese citizens to practice family planning.[410]

The OCP ... is a policy that has been strictly and even coercively enforced throughout the country since 1979 in order to limit couples as to the time and manner of conception.[411] The 1982 Chinese Constitution stipulates that the absolute leadership of the Central Communist Party is one of the four cardinal principles that govern China.[412] Therefore, adherence to Communist Party directives is equivalent or superior to codified legislation.[413] Individual rights are thus subordinate to the State's interest.[414] Although women and children are given some rights under the Law Protecting Women's Rights and Interests (LPWRI)[415] and the Maternal and Infant Health Care Law (MIHCL),[416] the family planning policies of the State necessarily infringe on the reproductive rights of all Chinese women.

. . .

2. Forced Abortions

Chinese officials also force abortions upon women who have conceived outside of the quota system.[417] While official government policy states that participation in family planning must be voluntary and that coercion is forbidden, actual practice within the country is reportedly in direct contrast to the government policy.[418]

Women who are illegally pregnant are typically subjected to weeks of high pressure tactics by members of the Women's Federation and Communist Party leaders using threats, financial pressure, and public family planning "study sessions."[419] Women are actually escorted by officials to abortion clinics to ensure that they go through with the abortion procedure.[420] In order to avoid the coercive tactics of the government officials seeking to abort an over-quota child, some mothers choose "childbirth on the run."[421] These women flee their city or village where their pregnancy would be monitored in order to go to the home of a distant friend or relative who can keep the birth a secret.[422] On occasion, such women are caught and forced into a late-term abortion and forcibly "sterilized at the same time."[423]

---

408. *Id.*

409. *Id.*

410. Xian Fa art. 25 (1982) (P.R.C.), *available at* http://english.people.com.cn/constitution/constitution.html [hereinafter Chinese Constitution].

411. Xiaorong Li, *supra* note 307, at 151.

412. *Id.* at 150; Chinese Constitution, *supra* note 410, at Preamble para. 3 ("Under the leadership of the Communist Party of China and the guidance of Marxism-Leninism and Mao Zedong, the Chinese people of all nationalities will continue to adhere to the people's democratic dictatorship....").

413. Xiaorong Li, *supra* note 307, at 150.

414. *Id.* at 152.

415. LPWRI, *supra* note 326; Xiaorong Li, *supra* note 307, at 152.

416. Maternal and Infant Health Care Law (promulgated by Order No. 33 of the President of the P.R.C., Oct. 27, 1994, effective June 1, 1995), *available at* http://www.unescap.org/esid/psis/population/database/poplaws/law_china/ch_record006.htm [hereinafter MIHCL]; Xiaorong Li, *supra* note 307, at 152.

417. *Id.* at 250–51.

418. John S. Aird, Slaughter of the Innocents: Coercive Birth Control in China 30–31 (1990).

419. *Id.* at 17; Mosher, *supra* note 406, at 268.

420. *See* Aird, *supra* note 418, at 17.

421. Mosher, *supra* note 406, at 280; Aird, *supra* note 418, at 30–31.

422. Mosher, *supra* note 406; Aird, *supra* note 418, at 17.

423. Mosher, *supra* note 406, at 284–85.

The term "remedial measures" is a common Chinese euphemism for mandatory abortions.[424] Suction abortions can be performed in the first few months of pregnancy. Chinese doctors have also used far more inhumane methods to abort babies, such as inducing premature labor and "inject[ing] pure formaldehyde into the fetal brain through the fontanel, or soft spot" before the baby comes through the birth canal; doctors have also been known to "reach in with forceps [to] crush the baby's skull."[425]

3. Forced Sterilizations

For women in China who are caught giving birth to over-quota children, forced sterilizations in addition to abortions are required.[426] At the height of the coercive population planning campaigns, "sterilization presently emerged as the principal 'technical measure'" to control the population growth.[427] One woman who chose "childbirth on the run" in order to carry her third pregnancy to full term was immediately arrested by birth planning authorities after her return home, "taken under guard to the commune medical clinic ... [and] given a tubal ligation the same day."[428]

4. Carrot-and-Stick Coercion for Compliance

A strong sense of egalitarianism in family planning has produced a highly effective atmosphere of public intimidation in order to implement population controls.[429] Punitive coercive measures for disobedience of the OCP also exist and are used to implement the policy.[430] State officials at all levels are responsible for their own compliance and for the compliance of all those under their jurisdiction.[431] Failing to meet the birth quota limits in an official's jurisdiction can result in his or her demotion or even dismissal.[432] Therefore, officials use any means possible to enforce the family planning program to ensure the success of their own careers.[433]

Far more extreme measures have also been reported to retaliate against families with over-quota births or even those who refuse to sign the One-Child Agreement.[434] These people are denied food, given less drinking water and electricity,[435] see their homes destroyed, refused shelter because their friends are forbidden to help them, fired from jobs, fined up to several times their annual salaries, and denied the right to register their child's birth.[436] A child who is not registered cannot receive healthcare or education services.[437] In 1995, in a village called Xiaoxi, a man named Huang Fuqu, along with his wife and children, was ordered out of his house, which was then blown up with dynamite by gov-

---

424. AIRD, *supra* note 418, at 12.
425. MOSHER, *supra* note 406, at 255.
426. *See* Kay Johnson *et al.*, *Infant Abandonment and Adoption in China*, 24 POPULATION & DEV. REV. 469, 477 (1998).
427. AIRD, *supra* note 418, at 33.
428. MOSHER, *supra* note 406, at 243.
429. LEE & FENG, *supra* note 403, at 134–35.
430. *Id.* at 135.
431. *Id.* at 132.
432. *Id.*
433. *Id.*
434. Trent Wade Moore, *Fertility in China 1982–1990: Gender Equality as a Complement to Wealth Flows Theory*, 17 POPULATION & DEV. REV. 197, 198 (1998).
435. AIRD, *supra* note 418, at 16.
436. *Id.* at 72–73.
437. *See id.* at 73.

ernment officials.[438] On a nearby wall, the officials painted a warning: "Those who do not obey the family planning police will be those who lose their fortunes."[439] In 1996, in the town of Shenzhen, 906 families were given fifteen days to leave because they had produced too many children.[440] Government officials confiscated their residence permits, revoked their licenses to work, and ordered the housing department not to rent them houses or shops.[441]

By contrast, parents who comply with the OCP are rewarded with economic incentives. They receive a "signing bonus," after they sign the "One-Child Agreement."[442] Parents receive monthly healthcare cash payments until their child turns fourteen, milk subsidies for young children, childcare subsidies, and priority in free healthcare and education.[443]

5. Scarcity of Women

Since the inception of the OCP in 1979, population statisticians estimate that millions of infant girls are missing from projected birth rates.[444] In September 1997, the World Health Organization's Regional Committee for the Western Pacific released a report stating that "more than 50 million women are 'missing' in China, victims of female feticide,[445] selective malnourishment of girls, lack of investment in women's health and various forms of violence."[446] Other reports project even higher estimates of missing women—up to one hundred million.[447]

6. Abandonment of Infant Girls

One of the major sources of the decimation of the female population in China is the abandonment of infant girls. Infanticide has been practiced in China for centuries, and the strict birth planning controls of the 1980s revitalized the problems of abandonment and infanticide of female children.[448] There is a longstanding "tradition" of "throwing away" very young children in the Hubei province.[449] In a Chinese/American study that examined parents who abandoned babies and those that adopted them, the majority of children that parents admitted to abandoning were first- or second-born daughters.[450] Many hoped that by abandoning their newborn daughter, they would be permitted to try again for a son.[451] Child abandonment, particularly of girls and children with dis-

---

438. Patrick Tyler, *Birth Control in China: Coercion and Evasion*, N.Y. TIMES, June 25, 1995, *available at* http://query.nytimes.com/gst/fullpage.html.

439. *Id.*

440. Graham Hutchings, *Chinese Town Expels 906 Families for Over-Breeding*, ELECTRONIC TELEGRAPH, December 4, 1996, *available at* http://www.telegraph.co.uk/html.

441. *Id.*

442. CECELIA NATHANSEN MILWERTZ, ACCEPTING POPULATION CONTROL: URBAN CHINESE WOMEN AND THE ONE-CHILD FAMILY POLICY 90 (1997).

443. *Id.* at 90–91.

444. REG'L OFFICE FOR THE W. PAC., WORLD HEALTH ORG., WOMEN'S HEALTH IN A SOCIAL CONTEXT IN THE WESTERN PACIFIC REGION 27 (1997) [hereinafter WOMEN'S HEALTH].

445. This term refers to the killing of the girl fetus.

446. WOMEN'S HEALTH, *supra* note 444, at 27.

447. *See* MacLeod, *supra* note 357.

448. Johnson, *supra* note 426, at 472.

449. Kay Johnson, *The Politics of the Revival of Infant Abandonment in China, with Special Reference to Hunan*, 22 POPULATION & DEV. REV. 77, 78 (1996).

450. Johnson, *supra* note 426, at 475.

451. *Id.* at 476.

abilities, is a huge problem throughout China, in both rural and urban areas.[452] One official in the district of Shenyang stated, "[E]very year, no fewer than 20 abandoned baby girls are found in dustbins and corners."[453]

Over 92 percent of babies in state-run orphanages are healthy baby girls.[454] However, due to the poor conditions of the orphanages, a high percentage of the baby girls die within months.[455] In 1995, Human Rights Watch published "Death by Default," a report that chronicled the horrifying conditions of Chinese orphanages, including "waiting for death" where undesired infant girls were left to starve to death or died from neglect.[456] A British documentary entitled "The Dying Room" chronicled many orphanages where baby girls sit on bamboo benches in the middle of a courtyard with their wrists and ankles tied to the armrests and legs of the bench, rocking listlessly back and forth.[457]

According to the Marriage Law of 1980 and in the omnibus Law Protecting the Rights and Interests of Women and Children,[458] child abandonment is illegal but has become endemic in Chinese society since the promulgation of the OCP nearly thirty years ago.[459] Parents who have abandoned their children are subject to fines, sanctions, and even forced sterilizations.[460] Even though the laws make child abandonment illegal, there are few provisions for the prosecution of parents who abandon their children.[461]

In the rural Yunnan province, rather than merely abandoning their babies, many women sell their newborns on the black market to smugglers. They resell the babies to wealthier or childless parents in eastern China who need an extra set of hands to work on farms or who do not want to wait through China's endless adoption system.[462] The mothers who sell their daughters do so for many reasons: the fear of exceeding the limits set forth in the OCP, their hope to have a male child in a future pregnancy, or their need for extra money to pay off their debts.[463] Highly coveted male babies are also sold if the mother has exceeded the OCP or wants to make extra money.[464]

The Adoption Law of China[465] requires adoptive parents to be childless and over the age of thirty.[466] Childless adoptive parents who do not meet the thirty-year age requirement are not usually subjected to fines. Nevertheless, many people report that they can-

---

452. HUMAN RIGHTS WATCH, DEATH BY DEFAULT: A POLICY OF FATAL NEGLECT IN CHINA'S STATE ORPHANAGES 132 (1996).

453. Graham Hutchings, *Female Infanticide 'Will Lead to Army of Bachelors,'* ELECTRONIC TELEGRAPH, Apr. 11, 1997, *available at* http://www.telegraph.co.uk/htmlContent.jhtml?html=/archive/1996/12/04/wchin04.htm.

454. Johnson, *supra* note 426, at 475.

455. Kate Blewett & Brian Woods, *The Dying Room* (Lauderdale Productions 1995), *available at* http://www.channel4.com/fourdocs/archive/the_dying_room.html.

456. HUMAN RIGHTS WATCH, *supra* note 452, at 136.

457. Blewett & Woods, *supra* note 455.

458. Marriage Law, *supra* note 322; LPWRI, *supra* note 326.

459. Johnson, *supra* note 426.

460. *Id.* at 477–88.

461. *Id.* at 479.

462. Hannah Beech Xicheng, *China's Infant Cash Crop*, TIME PAC., Jan. 29, 2001, *available at* http://www.time.com/time/pacific/magazine/20010129/china.html.

463. *Id.*

464. *Id.*

465. Adoption Law (adopted by the Standing Comm. Nat'l People's Cong., Dec. 29, 1991, revised November 4, 1998) (P.R.C.), *available at* http://www.unescap.org/esid/psis/population/database/poplaws/law_china/ch_record008.htm.

466. Johnson, *supra* note 426, at 492.

not in fact register their adoption or obtain a proper household registration until they reach thirty years of age.[467] This delay subjects the child to an unregistered status, which deprives the child of benefits and human and civil rights protections.[468] Adoption of abandoned babies also carries risks for the adoptive parents who have other children. These adoptive parents are subjected to steep fines and even sterilizations because the Adoption Law requires the adoptive parent to have no other children.[469] A few families were even forced to give up their adoptive children to a State-run orphanage, where, paradoxically, the State incurred the cost of raising the child until another adoptive family could be found.[470]

7. Infanticide

Infanticide has been practiced in China since the early part of the first millennium by all classes of society.[471] While male infants also suffered from infanticide, the majority of victims have been female infants due to the traditional Chinese preference for male children to carry on the bloodline and for ancestor worship.[472] Today, infanticide is generally considered immoral in China and also illegal under Chinese law.[473]

Despite its illegality, female infanticide has increased dramatically since the OCP was put into practice in 1979. The doctors were allowed to use any method to kill the babies, even strangulation.[474] In 1989, another report was uncovered disclosing infants being killed by having gauze stuffed into their mouth and being given alcohol or ether injections.[475] In rural clinics, there are reports that babies were "thrown into boiling water and scalded to death or placed in airtight jars and smothered."[476]

Reports of prosecutions for infanticide are extremely rare because no enforcement mechanism exists for the relevant laws prohibiting infanticide.[477] Under Chinese law, the government typically fails to act unless the victim presses charges.[478] Since the victims here are infants, it is unlikely that charges could be brought, especially if the perpetrators are the infant's parents. Family planning measures take precedence over individual rights. This protection typically exempts physicians from prosecution for infanticide because they are deemed to be carrying out the State's birthrate goals.[479]

8. Sex-Selective Abortions

The strong preference for male children in China has increased the use of ultrasound machines.[480] Although it has been forbidden by law since 1998 for ultrasound technicians or doctors to reveal the sex of the fetus,[481] many doctors will perform this service

---

467. *Id.*
468. *Id.*
469. *Id.*
470. *Id.*
471. Lee & Feng, *supra* note 403, at 47.
472. *Id.*
473. *Id.* at 61.
474. Aird, *supra* note 418, at 91.
475. *Id.* at 92.
476. Mosher, *supra* note 406, at 255.
477. LPWRI, *supra* note 326; Criminal Law, *supra* note 330, at art. 241.
478. Xiaorong Li, *supra* note 307, at 167.
479. *Id.* at 169.
480. Milwertz, *supra* note 442, at 61.
481. *Id.*; Regulation on Prohibiting Fetal Sex Identification and Selective Termination of Pregnancy for Non-Medical Reasons (adopted by the Standing Comm. Nat'l People's Cong., Nov. 21,

for a small fee or as a favor to friends and family.[482] Enforcement of the laws prohibiting the use of sonograms for sex selection is practically nonexistent, and law enforcement agents seem to be unable or unwilling to implement them.[483] Several factors contribute to the lack of enforcement, including widespread participation by the medical community, strict birth control measures, and the strong desire by couples for a son....[484]

K. Policy Suggestions to Combat Trafficking in China

... [T]he One-Child Policy must be drastically revised in order to comport with the basic international human rights laws to which China is a signatory.[485] The population growth can be checked by providing incentives to limit the number of children, not by inflicting coercive or harsh persuasive tactics. China must begin to address effectively the long-standing cultural prejudices against women. Government practices that promote active discrimination against women in the country must be stopped. If strict enforcement of the existing laws in China were a government priority, women in China could be given equality in their inheritance rights, as well as wage parity and job opportunities, so that men and women alike are able to sufficiently care for their parents in later years. Substantial pension systems or retirement plans should also be established for people in rural as well as urban areas in China in order to alleviate the elderly's high level of economic dependence upon their children for financial security in agricultural communities. Finally, China must address the illiteracy rate of over one hundred million women by abolishing school fees which exclude rural girls from the right to an education.[486] Textbooks in China must be revised to eliminate gender stereotypes. The implementation of these measures could pave the way toward cultural reform in China. The revision of the One-Child Policy, the eradication of male-child preference, and the elimination of discrimination against women in Chinese society will reduce human trafficking in China.

L. Conclusion

In order to reverse the deleterious effects of the One-Child Policy and the marginalization of women in China, the Chinese government must make a commitment to implement laws and policies that can reverse long-standing cultural trends and combat discriminatory traditions against women. Civil rights laws enacted in the United States in the 1960s have had a profoundly ameliorative effect on reducing discrimination against African Americans in American society. There is no reason why the adoption and strict enforcement of Chinese civil rights and trafficking laws could not similarly result in profound cultural change and equality for women in a traditionally male-dominated society now in transition. Since 1979, China has instituted economic reform policies that mirac-

---

1998) (P.R.C.), *available at* http://www.unescap.org/esid/psis/population/database/poplaws/law_china/ch_record021.htm.

482. Xiaorong Li, *supra* note 307, at 170.

483. *Id.*

484. *Id.*

485. China has not signed the International Covenant on Civil and Political Rights or the International Covenant on Economic, Social, and Cultural Rights, but is a signatory to the Convention on the Elimination of All Forms of Discrimination against Women and the Convention on the Rights of the Child. International Covenant on Civil and Political Rights, *opened for signature* December 16, 1966, 999 U.N.T.S. 171; International Covenant on Economic, Social, and Cultural Rights, *opened for signature* December 16, 1966, 993 U.N.T.S. 3; Convention on the Elimination of All Forms of Discrimination against Women, *opened for signature* March. 1, 1980, 1249 U.N.T.S. 13; Convention on the Rights of the Child, *opened for signature* November 20, 1989, 1577 U.N.T.S. 3.

486. CEDAW Report, *supra* note 327, at § 257.

ulously work in harmony with a Communist political system. Now China needs to perform another miracle: the adoption of cultural reforms that produce gender parity and that stop the marginalization of women in Chinese society. Only then will the lucrative business of human trafficking be reduced, if not eliminated entirely.

Chapter 5

Human Trafficking

A. The Crime of Human Trafficking and the US Trafficking Law with Extraterritorial Reach to Prevent Trafficking of Women Worldwide

Trafficking in women and children is a huge and very profitable international industry run by organized crime. Trafficking in human beings is the third most lucrative international crime after the traffic of weapons and the traffic of drugs.[1] Trafficking in persons is associated with other industries such as sex tourism, child pornography, mail order brides, forced prostitution, forced child prostitution, and the sale of women and children via the Internet. Each year more than 32 billion dollars is earned from the purchase and sale of women and children for the purposes of sexual exploitation.[2]

Trafficking is a contemporary form of slavery and is defined as "the recruitment, harboring, transfer, sale or receipt of persons within national or across international borders through the use of fraud, force, coercion, or kidnapping for the purpose of placing persons in situations of slavery-like conditions, forced labor or services, domestic servitude, bonded sweatshop labor, or other debt bondage."[3] While trafficking has been defined as the "trade of women for the purpose of prostitution,"[4] most of the trafficked women never see the money they earn from prostitution because they are enslaved and indebted to their trafficker for the purchase of their immigration documents, transportation, and living quarters in a brothel oftentimes run and owned by police who are complicit in the trafficking. This form of women's illegal and involuntary servitude in satisfaction of a debt is referred to as debt bondage and "peonage."

Statistics about trafficking are notoriously unreliable. One report states that more than 2.4 million victims of sex trafficking are bought and sold each year for the purpose of sexual exploitation.[5] Other reports indicate that each year anywhere from 4 million to 27

---

1. Susan Tiefenbrun, *Saga of Susannah—A U.S. Remedy for Sex Trafficking in Women: The Victims of Trafficking and Violence Protection Act of 2000*, 2002 UTAH L. REV. 107, 114 (2002).

2. US DEP'T OF STATE, TRAFFICKING IN PERSONS REPORT 34 (2008), *available at* http://www.state.gov/documents/organization/105501.pdf [hereinafter TIP REPORT 2008].

3. CIA Report, Amy O'Neill Richard, *International Trafficking in Women to the United States: A Contemporary Manifestation of Slavery and Organized Crime*, DCI EXCEPTIONAL INTELLIGENCE ANALYST PROGRAM: AN INTELLIGENCE MONOGRAPH, November 1999, 3 (Central Intelligence Agency, April, 2000); *see also* Tiefenbrun, *supra note* 1, at 120.

4. Roelof Haveman, *Traffic in Persons as a Problem, in* COMBATING TRAFFIC IN PERSONS 137, 139 (1994) [hereinafter Traffic in Persons].

5. UN International Labor Organization, *A Global Alliance against Forced Labor* 10 (2005), *available at* http://www.ilo.org/dyn/declaris/DECLARATIONWEB.DOWNLOAD_BLOB?Var_Document ID=5059.

million people are trafficked.[6] Trafficking exists all over the world, especially in war-torn countries and poverty stricken areas, but it also exists in the rich countries like the United States. Each year, from 17,500 to more than 50,000 women are trafficked within or into the United States for the purpose of sexual exploitation or forced labor. Trafficking typically involves the transportation of a woman across an international border, [7] but it is not smuggling. The crime of trafficking does not stop once the person is brought over the border. Human trafficking involves the movement of people with force, fraud, or coercion in order to make them engage in exploitative, slave-like labor. Forced labor is also a form of trafficking, and it is a significant problem in many countries including India and China.

Although there is no consensus among scholars or governments on the definition of trafficking, in 1995 the United Nations General Assembly defined trafficking broadly in this way:

> [Trafficking is] "the illicit and clandestine movement of persons across national and international borders, largely from developing countries and some countries with economies in transition, with the end goal of forcing women and girl children into sexually or economically oppressive and exploitative situations for the profit of recruiters, traffickers and crime syndicates, as well as other illegal activities related to trafficking, such as forced domestic labor, false marriages, clandestine employment and false adoption."[8]

The United Nations Protocol to Prevent, Suppress and Punish Trafficking in Persons, Especially Women and Children, Supplementing the United Nations Convention Against Transnational Organized Crime [Palermo Protocol] defines "trafficking in persons" as a form of slavery, forced labor, and forced prostitution:

> [Trafficking is] [t]he recruitment, transportation, transfer, harboring or receipt of persons, by means of the threat or use of force or other forms of coercion, of abduction, of fraud, of deception, of the abuse of power or of a position of vulnerability or of the giving or receiving of payments or benefits to achieve the consent of a person having control over another person, for the purpose of exploitation. Exploitation shall include, at a minimum, the exploitation of the prostitution of others or other forms of sexual exploitation, forced labor or services, slavery or practices similar to slavery, servitude or the removal of organs.[9]

In 2000, under the leadership of President William Clinton, the United States enacted a sweeping trafficking law that has extraterritorial reach in an attempt to eradicate trafficking worldwide. This US trafficking law requires all nations of the world to submit a report each year describing their efforts to combat the crime and enforce their trafficking laws, if any. The US Trafficking Victims Protection Act of 2000[10] [TVPA] was reauthorized in 2003, 2005, and 2008 through the Trafficking Victims Reauthorization Act. The TVPA distinguishes between sex trafficking and "severe forms of trafficking in persons."

---

6. TIP REPORT 2008, *supra* note 2, at 7.

7. *Traffic in Persons, supra* note 4, at 144.

8. The Secretary General, *Report of the Secretary-General on Traffic of Women and Girls,* ¶ 8, G.A. Res 49/166, UN Doc. A/50/369 (Aug. 24, 1995) *available at* http://daccessdds.un.org/doc/UNDOC/GEN/N95/260/58/PDF/N9526058.pdf?OpenElement.

9. Protocol to Prevent, Suppress and Punish Trafficking in Persons, Especially Women and Children, Supplementing the United Nations Convention against Transnational Organized Crime, art. 3(a), Dec. 12, 2000, G.A. Res. 55/25, UN Doc. A/55/383 (2000) [hereinafter Palermo Protocol].

10. Trafficking Victims Protection Act of 2000, 22 U.S.C.A. § 7101 (2000) [hereinafter TVPA].

Severe forms of trafficking, which provide victims when rescued with enhanced benefits, include trafficking of minors or persons with forced violence:

(A) sex trafficking in which a commercial sex act is induced by force, fraud, or coercion, or in which the person induced to perform such act has not attained 18 years of age; or

(B) the recruitment, harboring, transportation, provision, or obtaining of a person for labor or services, through the use of force, fraud, or coercion for the purpose of subjection to involuntary servitude, peonage, debt bondage, or slavery.

"Sex trafficking" is defined in the TVPA as: "the recruitment, harboring, transportation, provision, or obtaining of a person for the purpose of a commercial sex act."[11]

Trafficking involves the forced movement of human beings from poor or war-torn source countries through transition countries and into relatively rich destination countries, such as the United States, Western Europe, North America, Australia, China, and Japan.[12] Globalization, the advancement of technology, and the expansion of Internet use increase people's access to remote parts of the world and facilitate trafficking. The ease with which traffickers can transport their victims across international borders through modern technology also increases the incidence of trafficking.[13] According to the International Organization of Migration, women move because of poverty, economic disparity among nations, a general lack of economic opportunity for women (especially in poor, source or transition countries), and the cultural and political marginalization of women in source countries.[14] While the World Bank has encouraged the promotion of tourism as a development strategy, tourism has led to a rise in sex tourism which has contributed to the rise in trafficked women for prostitution.[15] Desperate women from developing countries are highly susceptible to the deception of traffickers who promise them high paying jobs or advantageous marriages in developed countries.[16] However, these women are duped and ultimately sold to brothel owners or to men who buy them as wives or concubines for the purpose of slave labor and exploitation.[17]

Sex trafficking laws around the world are either weak, poorly enforced, or non-existent. Nevertheless, more and more countries are paying attention to the trafficking of women and children. 142 countries have ratified the Palermo Protocol and 128 countries have enacted laws prohibiting all forms of human trafficking.[18] Pursuant to the US Trafficking Victims Protection Reauthorization Act of 2003 [TVPRA], foreign governments must provide the US Department of State with data on trafficking investigations, prosecutions, convictions, and sentences in order to be in full compliance with the TVPA's minimum standards for the elimination of trafficking. Globally, in 2010 there were 6,017 prosecutions; 3,619 convictions; 33,113 trafficking victims identified; and 17 new or

---

11. *See* Tiefenbrun, *supra* note 1, at 122 (discussing sex trafficking).

12. *Id.* at 111; Radhika Coomaraswamy & Lisa M. Kois, *Violence against Women, in* WOMEN AND INTERNATIONAL HUMAN RIGHTS LAW 177, 203 (1999) [hereinafter Violence against Women].

13. *Violence against Women, supra* note 12, at 202.

14. INTERNATIONAL ORGANIZATION OF MIGRATION, TRAFFICKING IN WOMEN TO COUNTRIES OF THE EUROPEAN UNION: CHARACTERISTICS, TRENDS & POLICY ISSUES 6 (1996).

15. *Violence against Women, supra* note 12, at 202.

16. *Id.* at 203.

17. *Id.*

18. *Letter from Ambassador Luis CdeBaca*, US DEP'T OF STATE, TRAFFICKING IN PERSONS REPORT (2011), *available at* http://www.state.gov/g/tip/rls/tiprpt/2011/14218.htm.

amended trafficking laws.[19] In 2009, there were 5,605 prosecutions; 4,166 convictions; 49,105 trafficking victims identified; and 33 new or amended laws. Thus, according to the TIP Report of 2011, there were more prosecutions but fewer convictions, fewer victims identified, and fewer new or amended laws in 2010.

Sometimes trafficking laws in other countries are enforced to the detriment of the victim, rather than the perpetrator.[20] Moreover, national laws that prohibit prostitution often discourage trafficked victims (who are lucky enough to escape) from seeking help from the law enforcement authorities who might either throw the trafficking victims in jail for engaging in illegal prostitution or deport them to their home countries, where they are forced to live as social outcasts in horrific conditions.[21] Legalizing prostitution will only facilitate trafficking because a trafficked woman who is forced to engage in sex work against her will cannot be easily distinguished from the voluntary prostitute. In many countries and in some states in the United States, despite the prominence of the US federal statute banning trafficking, the criminal penalties for trafficking in women are typically very light. Thus, international crime syndicates are drawn to the sex trade industry.[22] That is why sex trafficking is soon to become the second most lucrative international crime, even more profitable than the traffic in drugs. It is possible to use a woman more than thirty or forty times a day, but one can only use a drug once. The economic advantages of human trafficking make this crime difficult to eradicate.

Hillary Rodham Clinton's article "Partnering against Trafficking," which appeared in the Washington Post, clearly describes the plight of trafficked women held in bondage under the constant threat of violence. Under the US Trafficking Victims Protection Act, a Trafficking in Persons Report (TIP) is published every year in June and places all countries in the world on either Tier 1, Tier 2, Tier 2 Watchlist or Tier 3. A country on Tier 3 can be subject to non-humanitarian economic sanctions for failing to comply with minimum standards of the US Trafficking Victims Protections Act. Susan Tiefenbrun's article "Sex Sells but Drugs Don't Talk: Trafficking of Women Sex Workers and an Economic Solution" describes the need to develop an economic and international solution to the problems created by huge profits obtained from trafficking. Donna Hughes draws our attention to the extent of trafficking worldwide because of the demand for victims of sex exploitation. The demand includes not only the men who purchase sex acts but the exploiters, the traffickers, and the pimps, as well as the State. Laura Lederer, Senior Advisor on Trafficking in Persons, stresses the need for peacekeeping in order to reduce trafficking which is exacerbated by war. Mohamed Y. Mattar emphasizes the threat that trafficking in persons poses to human security. Mattar discusses the need to design appropriate legal responses to trafficking in persons that focus on the personal security and safety of the victims. He points out the need to protect the rights of the trafficking victim, to recognize all forms of trafficking, and the important involvement of NGOs and civil society in the fight against trafficking in persons.

Trafficking of women and children is particularly prevalent during wartime. The capture and use of girls as soldiers is a form of human trafficking which subjects little girls to violence, rape, torture, and even genocide. Susan Tiefenbrun discusses the increasing

---

19. US Dep't of State, Trafficking in Persons Report 38 (2011) [hereinafter TIP Report 2011].
20. Tiefenbrun, *supra* note 1, at 114.
21. *Id.* at 113–14.
22. *Id.* at 114.

use of child soldiers as a variant form of trafficking and its scourge on women and children in the world.

1. Hillary Rodham Clinton, *Partnering against Trafficking*[23]

Twenty-year-old Oxana Rantchev left her home in Russia in 2001 for what she believed was a job as a translator in Cyprus. A few days later, she was found dead after attempting to escape the traffickers who tried to force her into prostitution.

Oxana's story is the story of modern slavery. Around the world, millions of people are living in bondage. They labor in fields and factories under threat of violence if they try to escape. They work in homes for families that keep them virtually imprisoned. They are forced to work as prostitutes or to beg in the streets. Women, men, and children of all ages are often held far from home with no money, no connections, and no way to ask for help. They discover too late that they've entered a trap of forced labor, sexual exploitation, and brutal violence. The United Nations estimates that at least 12 million people worldwide are victims of trafficking. Because they often live and work out of sight, that number is almost certainly too low. More than half of all victims of forced labor are women and girls, compelled into servitude as domestics or sweatshop workers or, like Oxana, forced into prostitution. They face not only the loss of their freedom but also sexual assaults and physical abuses.

To some, human trafficking may seem like a problem limited to other parts of the world. In fact, it occurs in every country, including the United States, and we have a responsibility to fight it just as others do. The destructive effects of trafficking have an impact on all of us. Trafficking weakens legitimate economies, breaks up families, fuels violence, threatens public health and safety, and shreds the social fabric that is necessary for progress. It undermines our long-term efforts to promote peace and prosperity worldwide. And it is an affront to our values and our commitment to human rights.

The Obama administration views the fight against human trafficking, at home and abroad, as an important priority on our foreign policy agenda. The United States funds 140 anti-trafficking programs in nearly 70 countries, as well as 42 domestic task forces that bring state and local authorities together with nongovernmental organizations to combat trafficking. But there is so much more to do.

The problem is particularly urgent now, as local economies around the world reel from the global financial crisis. People are increasingly desperate for the chance to support their families, making them more susceptible to the tricks of ruthless criminals. Economic pressure means more incentive for unscrupulous bosses to squeeze everything they can from vulnerable workers and fewer resources for the organizations and governments trying to stop them.

The State Department's annual Trafficking in Persons Report, released this week, documents the scope of this challenge in every country. The report underscores the need to address the root causes of human trafficking — including poverty, lax law enforcement, and the exploitation of women — and their devastating effects on its victims and their families.

Since 2000, more than half of all countries have enacted laws prohibiting all forms of human trafficking. New partnerships between law enforcement and nongovernmental

---

23. Hillary Rodham Clinton, *Partnering against Trafficking*, WASH. POST, June 17, 2009, *available at* http://www.washingtonpost.com/wp-dyn/content/article/2009/06/16/AR2009061602628.html.

organizations, including women's shelters and immigrants' rights groups, have led to thousands of prosecutions, as well as assistance for many victims.

The 2009 report highlights progress that several countries have made to intensify the fight against human trafficking. In Cyprus, where Oxana Rantchev was trafficked and killed, the government has taken new steps to protect victims. Another example is Costa Rica, long a hub for commercial sex trafficking. This year, it passed an anti-trafficking law; trained nearly 1,000 police, immigration agents, and health workers to respond to trafficking; launched a national awareness campaign; and improved efforts to identify and care for victims. This progress is encouraging. Much of it is the result of the hard work of local activists such as Mariliana Morales Berrios, who founded the Rahab Foundation in Costa Rica in 1997 and has helped thousands of trafficking survivors rebuild their lives. Advocates such as Mariliana help spur change from the bottom up that encourages governments to make needed reforms from the top down.

We must build on this work. When I began advocating against trafficking in the 1990s, I saw firsthand what happens to its victims. In Thailand, I held 12-year-olds who had been trafficked and were dying of AIDS. In Eastern Europe, I shared the tears of women who wondered whether they'd ever see their relatives again. The challenge of trafficking demands a comprehensive approach that both brings down criminals and cares for victims. To our strategy of prosecution, protection, and prevention, it's time to add a fourth P: partnerships.

The criminal networks that enslave millions of people cross borders and span continents. Our response must do the same. The United States is committed to building partnerships with governments and organizations around the world, to finding new and more effective ways to take on the scourge of human trafficking. We want to support our partners in their efforts and find ways to improve our own.

Human trafficking flourishes in the shadows and demands attention, commitment, and passion from all of us. We are determined to build on our past success and advance progress in the weeks, months, and years ahead. Together, we must hold a light to every corner of the globe and help build a world in which no one is enslaved.

B. Sex Trafficking of Women

1. Susan Tiefenbrun, *Sex Sells but Drugs Don't Talk: Trafficking of Women Sex Workers and an Economic Solution*[24]

Introduction

Sex trafficking is a lucrative international business, second only in profits to the drug and weapons trade.[25] More than 2,000,000[26] women around the world are bought and

---

24. Susan Tiefenbrun, *Sex Sells but Drugs Don't Talk: Trafficking of Women Sex Workers and an Economic Solution*, 24 T. Jefferson L. Rev. 161 (2002).

25. "Traffic in human beings was estimated to generate some 6 billion dollars annually, according to a report of the International Organization of Migration." *UN Economic Alternatives to Illicit Drug Cultivation, Trafficking Must Be Created*, Presswire, Feb. 19, 1998, at M2 (Statement of Pino Arlacchi, Executive Director of the United Nations Office for Drug Control and Crime Prevention) [hereinafter Statement of Pino Arlacchi].

26. These numbers are difficult to verify, and some have reported as many as 4,000,000 women trafficked each year. *See* Becky Young, *Trafficking of Humans Across United States Borders: How United States Laws Can Be Used to Punish Traffickers and Protect Victims*, 13 Geo. Immigr. L.J. (1998). The

sold each year for the purpose of sexual exploitation,[27] and 50,000 of these women are trafficked into the United States in a modern-day form of slavery called non-consensual[28] sex work. The purpose of this article is twofold: to raise the public's awareness of this widespread, heinous crime perpetrated both in the United States and abroad, and to probe into some of the economic, social, cultural, and political reasons why this crime continues to spread like an uncontrollable disease, impervious to the plethora of international and domestic laws prohibiting slave trade.[29]

---

statistics that seem most closely documented are reported in a CIA Report. Amy O'Neill Richard, *International Trafficking in Women to the United States: A Contemporary Manifestation of Slavery and Organized Crime*, DCI EXCEPTIONAL INTELLIGENCE ANALYST PROGRAM: AN INTELLIGENCE MONOGRAPH 3, November 1999 (Central Intelligence Agency, April, 2000) [hereinafter CIA Report].

27. Statement of Pino Arlacchi, *supra* note 25.

28. *See infra* discussion of "consent," *in* The Victims of Trafficking and Violence Protection Act of 2000, PUB. L. No. 106-386, 114 Stat. 1464 (2000) [hereinafter Victims Protection Act], at § 102(2)(6); *see also* Joe Doezema, *Loose Women or Lost Women: The Re-emergence of the Myth of White Slavery in Contemporary Discourses of Trafficking in Women*, available at http://www.cc.columbia.edu/sec/dlc/ciao/isa/doj, *citing* GAATW, *A Proposal to Replace the Convention for the Suppression of the Traffic in Persons and of the Exploitation of the Prostitution of Others*, Utrecht: GAATW Bulletin, 1994. The GAATW is a group of feminists that does not place value judgments on a woman's career choice of sex work. *Cf.* IN HARM'S WAY: THE PORNOGRAPHY CIVIL RIGHTS HEARINGS 68, n. 23 (Catharine MacKinnon & Andrea Dworkin, eds., 2001): ("[a]t any rate, even when prostitution seems to have been chosen freely, it is actually the result of coercion ... all prostitution is forced prostitution."). *E.g.*, Kathleen Barry, founder of The Coalition Against Trafficking in Women (CATW) and author of FEMALE SEXUAL SLAVERY (1979), is of the neo-abolitionist belief that prostitution is violence against women, sexual exploitation, and an institution that victimizes all women. The neo-abolitionists claim that prostitution justifies the sale of women and reduces all women to sex (CATW 1998:2). The other feminist school draws a distinction between "forced prostitution" and "voluntary prostitution" and does not seek to place a value judgment on women who choose prostitution or sex work for their livelihood. The Global Alliance Against Trafficking in Women (GAATW) is the primary exponent of this other feminist position. *See also* CIA Report, *supra* note 26, at VI.

See CATHARINE A. MACKINNON, SEX EQUALITY: RAPE LAW, 817–18 (2001) for an enlightening discussion of "consent" to sex as applied in the law of rape: "... any form of force ... can make submission to sex unfree."

29. Numerous international conventions have attempted, without much success, to eradicate sex trafficking. *See, e.g.*, International Agreement for the Suppression of the White Slave Traffic, May 18, 1904, 35 Stat. 426, 1 U.N.T.S. 83 (amended 1910, 1949, 1997); International Convention for the Suppression of Traffic in Women and Children, Sept. 30, 1921, 9 U.N.T.S. 416; International Convention for the Suppression of the Traffic in Women of Full Age, Oct. 11, 1933, 150 U.N.T.S. 431; Convention to Suppress the Slave Trade and Slavery, Sept. 24, 1926, 46 Stat. 2183; Forced Labor Convention. Adopted on June 28, 1930 by the General Conference of International Labor Organization at its fourteenth session; Supplementary Convention on the Abolition of Slavery, the Slave Trade, and Institution and Practices Similar to Slavery, Sept. 7, 1956, 18 U.S.T. 3201; 266 U.N.T.S. 3; U.N. CHARTER (as amended) June 26, 1945, 59 Stat. 1031, U.N.T.S. No. 933, 3 Bevans 1153; Universal Declaration of Human Rights, *adopted and opened for signature, ratification and accession* by General Assembly Resolution 217A (III) of Dec. 10, 1948, G.A. Res. 217, UN GAOR, 3rd Sess. UN Doc A/810 (1948). International Covenant on Civil and Political Rights, *adopted and opened for signature, ratification and accession by* General Assembly Resolution 2200A (XXI) of Dec. 16, 1966; Convention on the Rights of the Child. General Assembly Resolution 44/25 of Nov. 20, 1989, *entered into force* Sept. 2, 1990; Convention on the Elimination of All Forms of Discrimination against Women, *adopted and opened for signature, ratification and accession* Mar. 1, 1980, G.A. Res. 34/180, 34 UN GAOR Supp. (No. 46), UN Doc. A/34/36 (Dec. 18, 1979) [hereinafter CEDAW]; Convention against Torture and Other Forms of Cruel, Inhuman or Degrading Treatment or Punishment 1984, G.A. Res. 39/46, Annex, A/39/51.

The international community has condemned slavery, involuntary servitude, violence against women and other elements of trafficking in the form of declarations, treaties, and United Nations resolutions and reports. These include the Universal Declaration of Human Rights of 1948; the 1956 Supplementary Convention on the Abolition of Slavery, the Slave Trade, and Institutions and Prac-

...

Statistics on Trafficking

Statistics on trafficking are admittedly not very reliable because of the clandestine nature of the crime and the social stigma attached to sex worker activity. There are documented reports claiming that 2,000,000 women are trafficked each year around the world, but other reports cite as many as 4,000,000. Failure to obtain accurate statistics should not in any way justify the view that sex trafficking is a "cultural myth."[30] This is an untenable position, reminiscent of the argument that the Holocaust and the annihilation of 6,000,000 Jews simply never happened. The many horrifying stories these women tell of their enslavement[31] are documented in the voluminous body of literature on sex trafficking and constitute vivid evidence that this crime is real and not a cultural myth. The numbers of women and children trafficked today for the purpose of forced prostitution may soon be as high as those of the African slave trade of the 1700s.[32]

Statistics about the profits earned from sex trafficking also vary. Traffickers in some countries can buy a woman for $15,000, and traffickers in other countries charge as much as $40,000.[33] In Japan, for example, the usual pay received for the sale of a woman is 2 million yen, or approximately $14,000 to $15,000.[34] Traffic in human beings designated for sex work is estimated to generate somewhere between $7 to $12 billion dollars annually.[35]

Countries Engaging in the Crime of Trafficking Sex Workers

The United States is one of the primary destination points for trafficked women, especially from war torn countries and the former Soviet Union.[36] Other popular destina-

---

tices Similar to Slavery; the 1948 American Declaration on the Rights and Duties of Man; the 1957 Abolition of Forced Labor Convention; the International Covenant on Civil and Political Rights; the Convention against Torture and Other Cruel, Inhuman or Degrading Treatment or Punishment; United Nations General Assembly Resolutions 50/67, 51/66, and 52/98; the Final Report of the World Congress against Sexual Exploitation of Children (Stockholm, 1996); the Fourth World Conference on Women (Beijing, 1995); the 1991 Moscow Document of the Organization for Security and Cooperation in Europe; the UN Convention against Transnational Organized Crime: Protocol to Prevent, Suppress and Punish Trafficking in Persons, Especially Women and Children and the Protocol against Smuggling of Migrants by Land, Sea and Air (November 15, 2000).

30. Doezema, *supra* note 28, at 7–8. Professor Doezema calls "White Slavery" a racist concept and calls sex trafficking in women a "cultural myth." Professor Doezema frequently states that he is not trying to infer that sex trafficking doesn't exist; he only means to underline that many women choose to do sex work willingly and, therefore, they should not be condemned for that choice. From this fact Professor Doezema concludes, without proof, that the majority of sex trafficked women go into sex work willingly! This view does serious damage to the cause of eradicating sex trafficking.

31. *See, e.g.*, Timothy Pratt, *UN Moves to Slay Human Trafficking 'Beast,'* SUNDAY HERALD, December 31, 2000, at 12. "Viviana still remembers the night she fell "into the jaws of a beast." It is a monster which snares as many as 35,000 women out of her native Colombia every year ... and leads to untold misery, disease, and death. The "beast" is the sex slave trade, a growing international crime with profits second only to drugs and arms." The article goes on to describe the plight of Viviana, a Colombian woman of 23, who successfully escaped a bordello in Spain, where she was kept in bondage until she paid off her $4000 debt to her trafficker.

32. Dr. Laura Lederer's Statement [This story is a variation of Lydia's story told by Dr. Laura Lederer in her testimony to the House of Representatives Subcommittee on International Operations and Human Rights on Sept. 14, 1999], 1999 WL 717872, at 24.

33. *Id.* at 57.

34. CIA Report, *supra* note 26, at 56.

35. John Daniszewski, *Russian Coalition Fights Sex Slavery*, L.A. TIMES, May 17, 2001, at A3.

36. Sex Trade Hearing, Opening Statement of Hon. Christopher H. Smith, at 2 [hereinafter Christopher Smith Opening Statement].

tion countries include Israel, Japan, Holland, Germany, and Italy.[37] Trafficking instances were reported in at least 20 different states in the United States, with most cases occurring in New York, California, and Florida.[38] The Immigration and Naturalization Service (I.N.S.) has discovered over 250 brothels likely to be involved in trafficking in 26 different cities of the United States.[39] The primary source countries for sex trafficking in the United States are Thailand, Vietnam, China, Mexico, Russia, Ukraine, and the Czech Republic.[40] But women have also been trafficked to the US from the Philippines, Korea, Malaysia, Latvia, Hungary, Poland, Brazil, and Honduras, among other countries.[41] Examples of sex trafficking in the United States abound: Latvian women were threatened and forced to dance nude in Chicago; Thai women were brought to the United States for the sex industry and then forced to be virtual sex slaves; ethnically Korean-Chinese women were held as indentured servants in the Commonwealth of the Northern Mariana Islands, which is governed by US law;[42] and hearing-impaired and mute Mexicans brought to the United States were enslaved, beaten, and forced to peddle trinkets in New York City.[43]

The Role of International Crime Organizations in Trafficking and Related Crimes

International crime organizations[44] are allegedly running the sex trafficking industry through powerful networks that trade and traffic impoverished women by the use of force,[45] fraud, and coercion for commercial gain.[46] Profits earned from sex trafficking are often applied to the illegal narcotics industry, which is also protected by international crime organizations. Thus, there is a direct link between sex trafficking and drugs. The trafficking industry is also closely intertwined with other related criminal activities, such as extortion, racketeering, money laundering, bribery of public officials, drug use, gambling, smuggling, loan sharking, conspiracy, document forgery, visa, mail, and wire fraud.[47] Other industries related to trafficking include mail order bride companies, maid schemes, domestic servant schemes, and illicit foreign adoptions.[48]

International organized crime networks engage in sex trafficking all over the world, but the source of the criminal activity is usually in poor, war-torn, or transition countries from which women are sent to richer, developed countries to do sex work.[49] The involvement of the organized crime networks in the sex trafficking industry is extensive because the sex work industry is lucrative. Profits from sex trafficking are second only to drugs

---

37. *Id.*, at 4.

38. CIA Report, *supra* note 26, at 3.

39. *Id.*

40. *Id.*

41. *Id.*

42. *See* Marybeth Herald, *The Northern Mariana Islands: A Changing Course under Its Covenant with the United States*, 71 Or. L. Rev. 127 (1992).

43. CIA Report, *supra* note 26, at V.

44. *Id.* at VII ("International criminal organization" is defined in the CIA Report. "[A]n organized criminal group is a structured group of three or more persons existing for a period of time and having the aim of committing a serious crime in order to, directly or indirectly, obtain a financial or other material benefit.").

45. Victims Protection Act, *supra* note 28, at § 102(6) ("Such force includes rape and other forms of sexual abuse, torture, starvation, imprisonment, threats, psychological abuse and coercion.").

46. For example, in China, the Sun Yee On, the 14K, the Big Circle Boys, and Wo On Lok Triads have been linked repeatedly to smuggling illegal immigrants and prostitution rackets. Japanese organized crime or the Yakuza are involved in trafficking in women and in the adult entertainment industry. CIA Report, *supra* note 26, at 55.

47. *Id.* at 14, 57.

48. *Id.* at 27–31.

49. *Id.* at 1.

and arms.[50] At least seven crime "families" in Bangkok, Thailand, recruit, sell, and smuggle Asian women throughout the world, including the US, to serve as prostitutes.[51] Russian organized crime is widespread and provides "the roof," or cover for trafficking operations, while lower-level Russian criminals manage recruitment of women and the logistics of sex work.[52] Russian criminals often operate behind the disguise of employment, travel, modeling, or matchmaking agencies[53] sometimes listed on the Internet in order to reach a global market.[54] Ukrainian criminal syndicates typically buy the favors of domestic immigration officials. Bribery makes enforcement of immigration laws weak in the Ukraine and in other Eastern European and Asian areas of the world. Immigration officials are paid off handsomely to look the other way or facilitate the illegal entry or exit of undocumented or improperly documented women.[55] In Poland traffickers sink huge profits from their prostitution rings into illegal narcotics, weapons, or stolen cars.[56] Albanian criminal groups include prostitution rings that operate in northern Italy.[57] Albanian criminals also take advantage of war-torn Eastern Europe, the migration of women and children, broken-up families and confusion in the refugee camps in neighboring countries to target and traffic Kosovo women into the sex industry.[58] These girls end up in prostitution and child exploitation rings in northern Italy, especially Turin and Milan. There is evidence of torture and terror by the Albanian criminals in order to keep these girls in line. Some uncooperative girls have reportedly been tortured by burning or tattooing the crime group's symbols on their body. Some less lucky girls have been killed by Albanian crime organizations.[59]

The composition of the international crime organizations varies from country to country. In the United States, the sex trafficking perpetrators tend to be smaller crime groups, smuggling rings, gangs, loosely linked criminal networks, and corrupt individuals.[60] In contrast, European and Asian trafficking involves large, hierarchical structures of the criminal group.[61] Asian and Russian organized crime groups and large criminal syndicates present in the US are involved in alien smuggling and/or prostitution, and are likely to become more immersed in trafficking to the US given the industry's extensive profits.[62]

Profits from the Industry of Trafficking Sex Workers

"Profit ... is at the root of the whole business" of sex trafficking.[63] Profits from the trafficking industry contribute to the expansion of organized crime in the United States and worldwide.[64] Women are cheap products that can be used and reused. The mantra in the trafficking industry is that women provide good cheap labor for the slave trade industry because selling a woman is no great loss to society. By contrast, in the drug trafficking industry, the high priced and highly sought after narcotics product can be sold

---

50. Daniszewski, *supra* note 35.
51. CIA Report, *supra* note 26, at 57.
52. *Id.*
53. *Id.*
54. Sex Trade Hearing, *supra* note 36, at 20. *See also* Daniszewski, *supra* note 35.
55. CIA Report, *supra* note 26, at 57.
56. *Id.* at 60.
57. *Id.*
58. *Id.*
59. *Id.* at 61.
60. *Id.* at VII.
61. *Id.*
62. *Id.*
63. *Id.* at 22.
64. Victims Protection Act, *supra* note 28, at § 102(6)

only once, but when you commodify a human being, she can be sold over and over again; thus, the potential profits in the sex trade industry are high, and the risk for the perpetrators is low. To the traffickers women are expendable, reusable, and resalable cheap commodities that offer a highly desirable service of sex work.[65]

People know and understand that there are big profits in the illegal drugs and arms industries, but few understand that sex trafficking is almost as profitable. Traffickers make anywhere from one to eight million dollars in a period ranging from one to six years.[66] Thai traffickers who enslaved Thai women in a New York brothel made $1.5 million over roughly a year and three months, while the women earned nothing because they were made to pay debts ranging from $30,000 to $50,000.[67] In order to eradicate sex trafficking, it will be necessary to reduce the lure of big profits which only the heads of organized crime, not the traffickers, earn in a complex network known as the sex work industry....

C. Human Trafficking Laws in Other Countries and the Need to Address the Demand, the International Scope of the Crime, and Its Effects on State Security

1. Donna M. Hughes, *The Demand for Victims of Sex Trafficking*[68]

Introduction

Each year, hundreds of thousands of women and children around the world become victims of the global sex trade. They are recruited into prostitution and other forms of sexual exploitation, often using tactics involving force, fraud, or coercion. Criminals working in organized networks treat the victims like commodities, buying and selling them for profit. This modern-day form of slavery is called sex trafficking.

The transnational sex trafficking of women and children is based on a balance between the supply of victims from sending countries and the demand for victims in receiving countries. Sending countries are those from which victims can be relatively easily recruited, usually with false promises of jobs. Receiving or destination countries are those with sex industries that create the demand for victims. Where prostitution is flourishing, pimps cannot recruit enough local women to fill up the brothels, so they have to bring in victims from other places.

Analyzing trafficking and prostitution as parts of an interlocking system reveals how the components are linked, and studying the dynamics of supply and demand for victims reveals what keeps the system working. The trafficking process begins with the demand for women to be used in prostitution.

---

65. CIA Report, *supra* note 26, at 1. *See also* CATHARINE A. MacKINNON, SEXUAL HARASSMENT OF WORKING WOMEN 9 (1979) ("Women work 'as women.' ... Women tend to be employed in occupations that are considered 'for women,' to be men's subordinates on the job, and to be paid less than men both on the average and for the same work."). Sex workers are paid nothing, and are asked to repay a debt to the traffickers.

66. CIA Report, *supra* note 26, at 19.

67. *Id.*

68. Donna M. Hughes, *The Demand for Victims of Sex Trafficking*, June, 2005, *available at* http://www.uri.edu/artsci/wms/hughes/demand_for_victims.pdf.

To date, discussion of the "demand side" of sex trafficking has focused on the men who purchase sex acts.[69] This report will expand the conceptualization of "the demand" to include two additional components: the exploiters—the traffickers and pimps—and the state. The purpose is to bring a better understanding to the factors that lead to the exploitation and sexual enslavement of women and children around the world.

The movement to abolish trafficking and sexual exploitation needs a more comprehensive approach, one that includes analyses of the demand side of trafficking, and develops comprehensive practices to combat the demand in receiving countries.[70] The goal of this report is to analyze the exploiters' demand for victims and how states facilitate or suppress the flow of women and children for commercial sexual exploitation. It describes how and why exploiters create a demand for victims by examining sex trafficking as a money-making activity. It examines state policies on immigration and the sex trade that impact the relative ease or difficulty with which traffickers operate in the country. Policies set by some countries are more effective in combating the demand for victims and consequently deter the trafficking of victims.

What Is the Demand?

Although trafficking is usually associated with poverty, it is often the wealthier countries that create the demand for victims for their sex industries. To fully understand and combat sex trafficking it is important to identify what is meant by "the demand" and to define and characterize each component so that policies and laws can be created to address it.

There are four components that make up the demand: 1) the men who buy commercial sex acts, 2) the exploiters who make up the sex industry, 3) the states that are destination countries, and 4) the culture that tolerates or promotes sexual exploitation.

The Men

Typically, when prostitution and sex trafficking are discussed, the focus is on the women and children victims. The men who purchase the sex acts are usually faceless and nameless. The men, the buyers of commercial sex acts, are the ultimate consumers of trafficked and prostituted women and children. They use them for entertainment, sexual gratification, and acts of violence.

Research on men who purchase sex acts has found that many of the assumptions we make about them are myths. Seldom are the men lonely or have sexually unsatisfying relationships. In fact, men who purchase sex acts are more likely to have more sexual partners than those who do not purchase sex acts. They often report that they are satisfied with their wives or partners. They say that they are searching for more—sex acts that their wives will not do or the excitement that comes with the hunt for a woman they can buy for a short time. They are seeking sex without relationship responsibilities. Men who purchase sex acts do not respect women, nor do they want to respect women. They are seeking control and sex in contexts in which they are not required to be polite or nice, and where they can humiliate, degrade, and hurt the woman or child, if they want.

---

69. Donna M. Hughes, *Best Practices to Address the Demand Side of Sex Trafficking*, June, 2005, *available at* http://www.hks.harvard.edu/cchrp/isht/study_group/2010/pdf/BestPracticesToAddress TheDemandSide.pdf.

70. Donna M. Hughes, *The 2002 Trafficking in Persons Report: Lost Opportunity for Progress, in* Foreign Government Complicity in Human Trafficking: A Review of the State Department's 2002 Trafficking in Persons Report, House Committee on International Relations, Wednesday, June 19, 2002.

For an in depth look at the demand created by men's decision to purchase sex acts, and efforts to discourage and punish their behavior see "Best Practices to Address the Demand Side of Sex Trafficking."[71]

The Exploiters

The exploiters, including traffickers, pimps, and brothel owners, make-up what is known as the sex industry. Traffickers and organized crime groups are the perpetrators that have received most of the attention in discussions about the sex trafficking. They operate the business of sexual exploitation. They make money from the sale of sex as a commodity. The exploiters include individual perpetrators, organized crime networks, and corrupt officials. Secondary profiteers include hotels, restaurants, taxi services, and other businesses that provide support services to the sex industry.

The State

By tolerating or legalizing prostitution, the state, at least passively, is contributing to the demand for victims. The more states regulate prostitution and derive tax revenue from it, the more actively they become part of the demand for victims.

If we consider that the demand is the driving force of trafficking, it is important to analyze the destination countries' laws and policies. Officials in destination countries do not want to admit responsibility for the problem of sex trafficking or be held accountable for creating the demand for victims. In destination countries, strategies are often devised to protect the sex industries that generate millions, even billions, of dollars per year for the economy. When prostitution is legal, governments expect to collect tax revenue. Where prostitution is illegal, criminals, organized crime groups and corrupt officials profit.

In the destination countries, exploiters exert pressure on the lawmakers and officials to create conditions that allow them to operate. They use power and influence in order to shape laws and policies that maintain the flow of women to their sex industries. They do this through the normalization of prostitution.

The Culture

The culture, particular mass media, is playing a large role in normalizing prostitution by portraying prostitution as glamorous, empowering, or a fast, easy way to make money.[72]

The Internet and other types of new information and communications technologies are increasing the global sexual exploitation of women and children. Sex industry sites on the Internet are popular and highly profitable. The growth and expansion of the sex industry is closely intertwined with new technologies. Although trafficking for prostitution is widely recognized, trafficking of women and children for the production of pornography receives less attention. Increasingly, the pornographers are traveling to poor countries where they can abuse and exploit women and children with fewer risks. They use new information technologies to transmit the live images around the world.

---

71. Donna M. Hughes, *Best Practices to Address the Demand Side of Sex Trafficking*, 2004, *available at* http://www.uri.edu/artsci/wms/hughes/demand_sex_trafficking.pdf.

72. *See* Jillian Blume, *Prostitution Gives Me Power*, Marie Claire (July 2005) (*Marie Claire* is a magazine for young women and teens, and in this article women claim that being a prostitute is empowering. The women liken themselves to being therapists and social workers for men.).

2. Laura J. Lederer, *In Modern Bondage: An International Perspective on Human Trafficking in the 21st Century*[73]

…

Peacekeeping and Trafficking

We are often asked, "which countries are the worst offenders?" The answer is that almost every country has a trafficking problem, whether it is a country of origin, transit or destination. Trafficking thrives when there is poverty, political and economic instability, low status of women and girls, official corruption, weak laws and enforcement, demand for cheap labor, and high profits. These conditions are all the more acute during humanitarian crises and civil conflict. Where there is an international humanitarian or peacekeeping/military presence, there tends to be an increase in prostitution leading to a rise in sex trafficking. This is because there is demand for commercial sexual exploitation with ready cash, and these operations take place in countries with heightened conditions for victimization. Crime groups set up brothels or nightclubs and provide a steady supply of local and foreign women and girls who are forced to service the influx of visitors and deployed personnel. We've seen this recently, for example, in Bosnia, Liberia, and the Democratic Republic of Congo. Unfortunately, as Secretary Rice has noted, "traffickers prey on the most vulnerable and turn a commercial profit at the expense of innocent human lives."

Humanitarian and peacekeeper/military personnel are entrusted to provide assistance and protection to the local population. There have been too many instances where some of these personnel end up exploiting young women and children as young as 5 years old—offering food, money, and promises of education in exchange for sexual favors. This is an abuse of power. Instead of reducing human suffering, they have extended it.

The Efforts of the UN and Other Organizations Engaged in Peace Operations

Over the last few years, the UN has been grappling with this type of exploitation. Currently it is instituting system-wide reforms including a zero-tolerance policy. They have begun trainings for peacekeepers and are sending home offending personnel. But enforcement and accountability ultimately rest with countries providing personnel to humanitarian and peacekeeping operations. The UN needs to do more to press troop contributing countries to ensure that they train their personnel on the front end, and discipline them if they engage in or enable human trafficking.

The US Government has taken a strong stand against human trafficking within the UN, NATO, and the Organization for Security and Cooperation in Europe (OSCE). For example, in early 2005, then-Secretary of State Colin Powell, and his Japanese counterpart, representing the two largest donor countries to the UN, sent a joint letter to the UN Secretary General expressing concern about continued sexual misconduct by peacekeepers in light of the UN's zero-tolerance policy. We continue to press the UN for reforms and accountability of personnel. In 2004, we co-led an effort with Norway to get a NATO Policy on Combating Trafficking in Human Beings adopted by member states. In 2005, the OSCE adopted a US-initiated resolution entitled "Ensuring the Highest Standards of Conduct and Accountability of Persons serving on International Forces and Missions."

---

73. Laura Lederer, *In Modern Bondage: An International Perspective on Human Trafficking in the 21st Century*, Remarks at the Federal Acquisition Regulation Compliance Training for Government Contractors, July 17, 2007.

US Prevention Efforts with Military and Civilian Personnel

We acknowledge that, unfortunately, some of our own personnel and contractor staff have also contributed to the problem of trafficking in persons both for sexual and labor exploitation, and we have developed new laws and regulations to address this. For example, as Colonel Hansen described, in 2004, DOD [Department of Defense] adopted an aggressive anti-trafficking approach that includes zero-tolerance of prostitution and human trafficking. In addition, in 2005, President Bush signed an executive order to amend the Manual for Courts Martial that makes patronizing a prostitute a chargeable offense under the military justice system. DOD contracts now include anti-trafficking language laying out the responsibilities of contractors. The Department of State is also working closely with its contractors to educate civilian police about human trafficking and the US Government's strong stance on this matter. The 2005 Trafficking Victims Protection Reauthorization Act extends extraterritorial jurisdiction over persons employed by or accompanying the Federal Government overseas for certain trafficking crimes.

Contractor Role in Fighting Human Trafficking

US contractors have an important role in our fight against human trafficking. Three ways you can help:

1. Don't create demand for victims of sex trafficking and slave labor;

2. Educate foreign counterparts (this applies primarily to police officers and prosecutors); and

3. Establish procedures for reporting possible human trafficking situations and addressing violations.

Taking each of these in order, here are a few suggestions:

1. Ways to help curb demand:

    • Provide training to employees and sub-contractors about trafficking, including how prostitution contributes to the phenomenon of trafficking, and related US policies and laws;

    • Have employees and sub-contractors sign an agreement that they understand the requirements and the ramifications for violations;

    • Provide adequate housing and legitimate recreation facilities.

2. Educate foreign counterparts (in coordination with foreign governments) about trafficking and how to recognize and treat potential victims.

    • Utilize US Government materials such as our "Fact Sheet on Human Trafficking" and our Annual Trafficking in Persons Report for detailed information on trafficking. Hold workshops and seminars on how to recognize trafficking victims.

    • Work with the US Departments of State and Justice to organize international visitor programs and training for foreign national police, prosecutors, and judges.

3. Establish monitoring and reporting procedures that allow employees to report a possible trafficking scenario or violation.

    • Contractors should identify off-limits areas (bars, nightclubs, brothel areas) and inform employees.

    • Employees should not try to take matters into their own hands by trying to rescue or shelter a trafficked victim.

- Contractors working in the field should find out what non-governmental or international organizations are in place that can provide shelter and assistance to trafficked victims. International organizations such as the International Organization for Migration, UNICEF and Save the Children have anti-trafficking programs in major post-conflict areas. The US embassy or non-governmental organizations generally should know who in the local government is reliable to assist in a victim rescue. Confidentiality and protection of a whistleblower is essential to encouraging reporting of any violations.

Participants need to be aware that the Trafficking Victims Protection Act requires that the US Government shall include a provision that authorizes a Federal department or agency to terminate any grant, contract or cooperative agreement (regardless of whether or not it is related to human trafficking) if the recipients or their sub-recipients: 1) engage in severe forms of trafficking in persons or have procured a commercial sex act during the time of the US Government-funded activity, or 2) use forced labor in carrying out US Government-funded activities.

The FAR [Federal Acquisition Regulation] Council and relevant agencies such as the Office of Management and Budget are in the process of establishing uniform government procedures for the inclusion of such a provision.

US Government's Response to Stop Trafficking in Persons

In response to this growing awareness of the phenomenon of human trafficking, a broad-based coalition of women's rights organizations, faith-based organizations, children's groups, labor unions, and others came together to help Congress draft and pass our Trafficking Victims Protection Act.

The law does a number of things. I only want to mention four briefly because we are going to hear in more detail from the Department of Justice about the use of our new law to prosecute human traffickers. Why is the Trafficking Victims Protection Act so important?

First, it broadens the definition of trafficking to include recruiter, transporter, buyer, seller, harborer, brothel owner, manager, and guards. This is important because it gets to the whole pipeline of activity in trafficking.

Second it increases penalties from 20 years to life imprisonment. This is important because it sends a message to traffickers that we take human trafficking as seriously as drug trafficking — and that the penalties will be commensurate with the crime.

Third, it has a victim-centered approach, including a "T visa" for victims of severe forms of trafficking — which allows the victim to stay in the US temporarily for up to 4 years and apply for permanent residency status, and allows access to benefits, including food, clothing, and shelter, medical, legal, and other forms of assistance, and finally, education and employment assistance.

Fourth, the law also mandated the creation of a President's Interagency Task Force on Trafficking in Persons. This cabinet level task force is chaired by the Secretary of State, and includes the Attorney General, the Secretary of Homeland Security, the Director of National Intelligence, Secretary of Health and Human Services, Secretary of Labor, the Secretary of Defense, the US Agency for International Development Administrator, and other officials as designated by the President. This Cabinet-level Task Force is important because it creates political will at the highest levels, which streams down into each agency.

Implementation of the Law

In the last 5 years, since the law passed, the US Government, through all its agencies, has worked hard to implement the law, for example:

- The US Department of Justice formed 42 state and local task forces that link federal officials, local law enforcement, and NGO service providers to create pro-active law enforcement programs at the grass roots level to identify and rescue victims, arrest, prosecute, and convict traffickers. (www.usdoj.gov/whatwedo/whatwedo_ctip.html)

- The US Department of Health and Human Services created a new education and awareness campaign entitled "Look Beneath the Surface." This campaign, aimed both at the general public, but also at immigrant communities in cities and rural areas, helps identify, rescue, rehabilitate, and restore trafficking victims. (www.acf.hhs.gov/trafficking)

- The US Department of Labor has created a program to address the worst forms of child labor in countries around the world. This program supports organizations working to combat child labor and child sex trafficking in over forty countries. DOL's Wage and Hour Division (WHD) has a program to help investigators identify potential trafficking victims in its regular investigations. (www.dol.gov/esa/whd and www.dol.gov/ILAB)

- The Department of Homeland Security [DHS] has created a special unit at its Center in Vermont to issue T visas to foreign survivors of severe forms of trafficking identified in the US. DHS also investigates severe forms of trafficking in the US and child sex tourism cases in countries abroad and seeks the return of alleged child predators for prosecution in the US (www.ice.gov)

- DOJ [Department of Justice] and DHS have Victim-Witness Coordinators responsible for working with victims discovered in the US throughout the investigation and prosecution of alleged traffickers.

- The Department of Defense [DOD] has instituted a new TIP [Trafficking in Persons] training program for all military personnel to prevent trafficking in persons. They have also instituted a "zero tolerance policy" of human trafficking. In addition, DOD amended its military justice system in an effort to prevent US military personnel from fueling sex trafficking and published a regulation requiring TIP prevention provisions for all DOD contracts. (www.dodig.mil/Inspections/IPO/combatinghuman.htm)

- The Department of State has established the Office to Monitor and Combat Trafficking in Persons (TIP Office) to lead the diplomatic effort to address trafficking in persons around the world. It does this through high-level meetings with Ambassadors and other senior policy officials, through international programs, and through public awareness campaigns here and abroad. The TIP Office also produces an annual Trafficking in Persons Report. The TIP Report, as it is known, assesses and rates government progress of most countries around the world in addressing human trafficking. This TIP Report is a foreign policy tool, utilized to help increase dialogue with other countries and to provide an impetus for serious action. (www.state.gov/g/tip)

Trafficking as a Transnational Crime

In the last decades, marred by wars, ethnic cleansing, and the forced displacement of millions of people around the world, many have suffered tremendously. The horror of trafficking in human beings is one of the problems that has flourished in regions where there is economic, political, or social instability.

Taking advantage of the chaos, poverty, and vulnerability of people, traffickers have set up and solidified sophisticated regional and global trafficking networks that include recruiters, transporters, harborers, buyers, sellers, and others. These networks operate across national, ethnic, language, and geographic barriers. With estimates in the millions of people being moved across borders, the transnational crime of trafficking has created significant challenges for countries of origin, transit, and destination. Those working to help victims see on a daily basis the lives shattered by the terrible exploitation of innocent people. Countless men, women, and children are subjected to abuse we cannot begin to imagine. People seeking better lives are tricked, forced, and coerced into slavery and slavery-like situations. The stories of young women and children trafficked into sexual slavery are especially horrifying.

- Because trafficking is a transnational problem, it requires a transnational solution. Organized crime doesn't stop at the borders — neither can our law enforcement efforts. We need to find answers to an especially thorny set of questions:

- How can we build bridges between our countries and our regions to combat trafficking in persons?

- How can we insure that a victim rescued in one country is safely returned and reintegrated in another?

- If a child cannot go home, how can we insure her safe settlement in the new, or possibly a third, country?

- How can we forge closer ties among law enforcement agencies, service providers, civic and religious leaders, and lawmakers to ensure that we are maximizing efforts?

- In short, how can we cooperate and collaborate to stop trafficking?

The United States has developed a framework of three Ps: prevention, prosecution, and protection (and assistance) to help combat trafficking in persons. For prosecution, we have made reducing corruption and enhancing transparency a top foreign policy priority because we believe both are central to stable democracies, sustainable development, and national security. We have also passed new legislation making document fraud intended to further trafficking in persons a crime. We are also working with countries to encourage them to draft and pass their own laws prohibiting trafficking in persons, corruption, money laundering, document tampering, and other related crimes. We do this because we believe that a counter-crime approach that connects trafficking to corruption, border patrol, document forgery, money-laundering, terrorism, and other transnational criminal activities is essential.

For protection, we encourage victim-centered programs that include rescue of victims, witness protection, shelters, and a comprehensive set of services for trafficking victims, as well as repatriation, resettlement, and reintegration programs where necessary. The victim-centered approach to trafficking does not prosecute the victims of sex trafficking for prostitution, for example. Rather it offers them a place of safety while addressing their physical, psychological, and vocational needs. These assistance programs are basic humanitarian responses to a global problem.

But perhaps most important of the three Ps are the prevention programs. Prevention is primary. Why? Because once a human being has been trafficked, the devastation is so great that rehabilitation is a lengthy effort with highly uncertain prospects for success. While we have victims we will support assistance programs, but in almost every country we are encouraging education and awareness campaigns to reach vulnerable communities and individuals. We are also interested in addressing issues of property and inheritance rights for women and suggesting legal as well as social reforms to combat practices and attitudes that discriminate against women and girls. These prevention programs are critical. After all, which would you rather have: a hospital at the bottom of the cliff or a fence at the top? Prevention programs are the fence at the top.

While we have come a long way, we still have much to do. Winston Churchill once said "Give us the Tools and we will finish the Job." This training, which I hope will be the first of many that contractors undertake, will give your people the information—the tools—they need to conduct themselves properly in the field, as well as to help combat trafficking in persons. The United States Government looks forward to working with you to insure excellence in peacekeeping operations, including abolishing human trafficking and related transnational criminal activities. If we share a common goal and a common determination, together we can finish the job.

3. Mohamed Y. Mattar, *Human Security or State Security? The Overriding Threat in Trafficking in Persons*[74]

Introduction

Trafficking in persons[75] is a violation of human rights that mainly affects women and children. For this reason, it should be recognized not only as a crime against the state but as a crime against the individual that poses a threat to human security. This paper will inquire into how national legal systems take into consideration the concept of human security in designing the appropriate legal response to trafficking in persons.[76] This paper will focus on the following issues: personal security and safety versus human security; the methods that can be employed by legislation to protect the rights of a trafficking victim; causes of human insecurity; trafficking in persons as a threat against the individual, not the state; recognition of all forms of trafficking; confronting all actors in the trafficking enterprise; and the involvement of NGOs and civil society in the fight against trafficking in persons. I will argue that understanding the real threat in cases of trafficking in persons affects the rules that a legal system must incorporate to combat the problem....

How Can Legislation Protect the Rights of a Trafficked Victim?

The right to safety of the trafficked person may be protected by defining trafficking in persons as a violent crime. In many cases, trafficking in persons involves violent commodities, where those who demand or supply a particular commodity frequently practice violence in order to satisfy their demand or to protect their supply.[77] Typically, this

---

74. Mohamed Y. Mattar, *Human Security or State Security? The Overriding Threat in Trafficking in Persons*, 1 INTERCULTURAL HUM. RTS. L. REV. 249 (2006).

75. This concept is also commonly referred to as "human trafficking" or "trafficking in human beings." For an overview of various definitions of trafficking, *see generally* Daan Everts, *Human Trafficking: The Ruthless Trade in Human Misery*, 10 BROWN J. WORLD AFF. 149 (2003), Aiko Joshi, *The Face of Human Trafficking*, 13 HASTINGS WOMEN'S L.J. 31 (2002), and Alison N. Stewart, *Report From the Roundtable on the Meaning of "Trafficking Persons,"* 20 WOMEN'S RTS. L. REP. 11 (1998).

76. This paper analyzes one level of government responses to trafficking in persons as a human security. *See* Commission on Human Security, Human Security Now 7–11 (2003), *available at* http://www.humansecurity-chs.org/finalreport/ (last visited March 25, 2006), for a discussion on the suggestion that human insecurities comprise a five-level vertical structure consisting of insecurities at the individual, community, national, regional, and global levels.

77. *See generally* Alex Y. Seita, *Conceptualizing Violence: Present and Future Developments in International Law: Panel I: Human Rights & Civil Wrongs at Home and Abroad: Old Problems and New Paradigms:*

occurs in the so-called violent entrepreneur model of trafficking, where the trafficker relies on violence in all stages of the trafficking operation.[78] Trafficking in persons, as well as many of its aspects such as forced prostitution, necessarily involves violence against women. Therefore, under the UN Declaration on the Elimination of Violence against Women, violence against women is defined to include trafficking in persons.[79] Consequently, a national legal system may protect the right to personal security and personal safety of the trafficked person by making violence, or the threat of violence, an illegal means, the existence of which makes trafficking in persons a crime.[80]

The legislation may also protect the right to safety of the trafficked person by making violence and the threat of violence, as well as bodily harm or death, an aggravated circumstance that enhances the penalty for the crime of trafficking.[81] Further, fear of violence may be designated as a ground for enrolling a trafficked person in a witness protection program. Finally, the right to safety of the trafficked person may be protected by making

---

The Role of Market Forces in Transnational Violence, 60 ALB. L. REV. 635 (1997) (analyzing how the market forces of supply and demand can lead to transnational violence).

78. *See generally* Louise Shelley, *Trafficking in Women: The Business Model Approach*, 10 BROWN J. WORLD AFF. 119 (2003) (presenting various business models of trafficking in women).

79. Declaration on the Elimination of Violence against Women, art. 2(b), G.A. Res. 48/104, UN GAOR, 48th Sess., UN Doc. A/48/49 (December 20, 1993) ("[v]iolence against women shall be understood to encompass, but not be limited to, the following: ... (b) Physical, sexual, and psychological violence occurring within the general community, including ... trafficking in women and forced prostitution....").

80. "Illegal means" should be defined very broadly to include debt bondage, disclosure of confidential information to the victim's family or to other persons, confiscation of travel documents, abuse of power, abuse of office, bribery, abuse of a position of vulnerability, and other illegal or improper means. *For example*, Article 3(a) of the 2000 UN Protocol to Prevent, Suppress, and Punish Trafficking in Persons, Especially Women and Children, supplementing the United Nations Convention against Transnational Organized Crime defines "illegal means" to include the threat or use of force or other forms of coercion, abduction, fraud, deception, abuse of power or of a position of vulnerability, or giving or receiving of payments or benefits to achieve the consent of a person having control over another person. Protocol to Prevent, Suppress, and Punish Trafficking in Persons, Especially Women and Children, Supplementing the United Nations Convention against Transnational Organized Crime, *opened for signature*, Dec. 12, 2000, art. 2(b), G.A. Res. 55/25, at 60, UN GAOR, 55th Sess., Supp. No. 49, Annex II, UN Doc. A/RES/55/383 (Nov. 15, 2000) (*entered into force* September 29, 2003) [hereinafter UN Protocol]. Under section 103 of the United States Trafficking Victims Protection Act of 2000, "illegal means" include the use of force, fraud, or coercion, and "coercion" is further defined to include "(A) threats of serious harm to or physical restraint against any person; (B) any scheme, plan, or pattern intended to cause a person to believe that failure to perform an act would result in serious harm to or physical restraint against any person; or (C) the abuse or threatened abuse of the legal process." Victims of Trafficking and Violence Protection Act of 2000, PUB. L. No. 106-386, 114 Stat. 1464 (codified as amended at scattered sections of 8, 20, 22, 27, 28, and 42 U.S.C.) [hereinafter VTVPA]. Division A of the VTVPA is further identified as the Trafficking Victims Protection Act of 2000 (codified as amended at 22 U.S.C. §§ 7101–7110 (2000), which incorporates 18 U.S.C. §§ 1589–1594 (2000)) [hereinafter TVPA].

81. The new anti-trafficking articles in the criminal codes of many countries contain such provisions. This is the case, for instance, under Article 217 of the Criminal Code of Austria, Article 181 of the Criminal Code of Belarus, Article 204 of the Criminal Code of the Czech Republic, Article 181 of the Criminal Code of Germany, Article 165 of the Criminal Code of Moldova, Article 201a of the Criminal Code of Montenegro, Article 250a of the Criminal Code of the Netherlands, Article 127-a of the Criminal Code of the Russian Federation, Article 111b of the Criminal Code of Serbia, and Article 167 of the Criminal Code of Tajikistan. *See* 2005 Human Rights Reports, The Protection Project, *available at* http://www.protectionproject.org/pub.htm (follow "Navigate" drop-down box to "Human Rights Reports"). Translations of all of the aforementioned criminal code provisions are on file with the author.

the fear of reprisal from the trafficker a ground for granting the victim a residency status in the country of destination.

Causes of Human Insecurity

Applying the extended concept of human security means that it is necessary to address not only the right of the trafficked person to personal safety, but the other aspects of human security as well, including economic security, political security, legal security, and community or cultural security. Thus, it is imperative that the causes of insecurity of the trafficked person be explored. In the context of trafficking in persons, the primary causes of insecurity are economic, social, cultural, legal, and political insecurities.

Economic insecurity is addressed directly in the UN Protocol to Prevent, Suppress, and Punish Trafficking in Persons, Especially Women and Children, Supplementing the United Nations Convention against Transnational Organized Crime ("UN Protocol"), which mentions poverty, underdevelopment, and lack of equal opportunities as being among the root causes of trafficking in persons.[82] Economic insecurities may also be extended to include unemployment and the lack of access to basic health care, education, and social welfare.

Social insecurity is concerned with the low status of women in society. This involves gender inequality and sex discrimination in education, employment, access to legal and medical services, and access to information. This also includes violence against women, sexual violence or abuse, and domestic violence.

Cultural insecurity is related to social insecurity in a number of ways. For example, in many societies there exist harmful cultural practices, such as arranged marriages, early marriages, temporary marriages, marriages by catalog or mail order, and other forms of sexual exploitation which contribute to the trafficking infrastructure.[83] Further, in many societies, cultural norms affect the manner in which women respond to trafficking. For instance, women from Muslim countries who are trafficked into prostitution would find it more difficult to reintegrate into their families and communities after being freed from exploitation.[84] Many trafficked women may also have contracted HIV/AIDS or other sexually transmitted diseases, reporting of which is considered shameful in these traditional societies.

Legal insecurity is manifested in the lack of access to the criminal justice system, which occurs either because the trafficked person is a foreigner, lacks access to legal representation, or the system itself does not offer an appropriate remedy. In addition, the insecurity is fostered by the Double Witness Rule or the Corroborative Evidence Rule, which is still applied in the criminal procedure of many countries. The Double Witness Rule or the Corroborative Evidence Rule does not allow treating victims of trafficking as credible witnesses. It prohibits the admission of evidence of only one witness unless her testimony is corroborated by another witness or other material evidence implicating the accused. As a result of this insecurity, trafficked persons are not afforded the opportunity to be heard in court.

---

82. *See* UN Protocol, *supra* note 80, art. 9.4.

83. *See* Mohamed Y. Mattar, *Trafficking Persons, Especially Women and Children, in Countries of the Middle East: The Scope of the Problem and the Appropriate Legislative Responses*, 26 FORDHAM INT'L L J. (721, 730–33 (2003) (discussing the Islamic institutions of early marriage and temporary marriage and their role in the trafficking infrastructure of some countries of the Middle East)).

84. *See, e.g.*, Nicole Ball, *Report of a Conference Organized by the Programme for Strategic and International Studies, Graduate Institute of International Studies* (2001), *available at* http://www.humansecuritynetwork.org/docs/report_may2001_3-ephp.

In addition to economic, social, cultural, and legal insecurity, political insecurity may be a reason behind trafficking in persons. This is particularly the case in the former Soviet republics, where transition from communism to democracy, civil unrest, loss of national identity, and political instability have all created a favorable environment for organized crime, including trafficking in persons.[85]

Trafficking in Persons: From Prohibition to Prevention and Protection

A human security approach to the problem of trafficking in persons requires addressing the aforementioned causes of insecurity and taking the appropriate steps to eliminate those causes. In this respect, prevention of the contributing factors to trafficking in persons, or of the causes of human insecurity that make women and children vulnerable to trafficking, becomes the key. Prevention and protection are implied by a broad definition of human security, as opposed to the prohibition approach which is the focus of a limited concept of personal safety.[86]

The limited prohibition approach to trafficking in persons was reflected in the traditional international law that existed prior to the UN Protocol. For instance, UDHR stated that "[n]o one shall be held in slavery or servitude; slavery and the slave trade shall be prohibited in all their forms."[87] The 1956 Supplementary Convention on the Abolition of Slavery, the Slave Trade, and Institutions and Practices Similar to Slavery outlawed practices such as debt bondage, serfdom, bride price, and exploitation of child labor.[88] The Convention on the Elimination of All Forms of Discrimination against Women ("CEDAW") prohibits "exploitation of prostitution of women" and "all forms of traffic in women."[89] The UN Convention on the Rights of the Child mandates that state parties prohibit "the abduction of, the sale of or traffic in children for any purpose or in any form."[90] Similarly, ILO Convention No. 182 on the Elimination of the Worst Forms of Child Labor prohibits

---

85. It has been suggested that threats to human security of the former Soviet countries arise from four interrelated transitions: "1) identity and nation-state building, 2) economic liberalization, 3) social reform, and 4) political liberalization." *See* Dr. Kathleen Collins, Commission on Human Security, *Human Security in Central Asia: Challenges Posed by a Decade of Transition (1991–2002)* 2 (2002).

86. Numerous writings have suggested that prevention of human insecurities and protection of human security should be the preferred responses to these issues. *See, e.g.,* Kofi A. Annan, United Nations, *"We the Peoples": The Role of the United Nations in the 21st Century* 44–45 (2000) ("[t]here is near-universal agreement that prevention is preferable to cure, and that strategies of *prevention* must address the root causes of conflicts, not simply their violent symptoms") (emphasis added); Canada Department of Foreign Affairs and International Trade, Freedom from Fear: Canada's Foreign Policy for Human Security 7 (2002), *available at* http://www.humansecurity.gc.ca/pdf/freedo_from_fear-en.pdf, (stating that "the responsibility to protect has three dimensions: to prevent, to react, and to rebuild, "the most important of them being prevention) (emphasis added); International Commission on Intervention and State Sovereignty, THE RESPONSIBILITY TO PROTECT 6 (2001), ("there is growing recognition worldwide that the *protection* of human security, including human rights and human dignity, must be one of the fundamental objectives of modern international institutions") (emphasis added).

87. Universal Declaration of Human Rights, art. 3, G.A. Res. 217A (III), at 71, UN GAOR, 3d Sess., 1st plen. mtg., UN Doc. A/810 (December 12, 1948) [hereinafter UDHR].

88. Supplementary Convention on the Abolition of Slavery, the Slave Trade, and Institutions and Practices Similar to Slavery art. 1, September 7, 1956, 226 U.N.T.S. 3.

89. Convention on the Elimination of All Forms of Discrimination against Women, Dec. 18, 1979, 1249 U.N.T.S. 13 [hereinafter CEDAW].

90. Convention on the Rights of the Child, art. 35, G.A. Res. 44/25, UN Doc. A/Res/44/25 (November 20, 1989). Sale of children, child prostitution, and child pornography are also prohibited pursuant to the Optional Protocol to the Convention on the Rights of the Child on the Sale of Children, Child Prostitution, and Pornography, art. 1, G.A. Res. 54/263, UN Doc. A/Res/54/263 (May 25, 2000).

"the use, procuring or offering of a child for prostitution … [.]"[91] Finally, the Optional Protocol to the Convention on the Rights of the Child on the Involvement of Children in Armed Conflict prohibits "recruit[ment] and use in hostilities [of] persons under the age of 18 years."[92]

However, it was the UN Protocol[93] that shifted the focus from prohibition to the prevention of the act of trafficking and the protection of victims. The UN Protocol became international law in December 2003, after it was ratified by forty countries.[94] It is necessary to urge more countries not only to ratify the UN Protocol, but to also change their law and policy to meet international obligations. This is especially important given that the UN Protocol had a significant impact in various countries in creating the international consensus as to what should be considered trafficking. In addition, the UN Protocol will create a reporting mechanism different from the sanctions that are now being imposed by the United States under the Victims of Trafficking and Violence Protection Act of 2000 ("TVPA").[95]

Threat against the Individual, Not the State

While addressing the issue of trafficking in persons as a threat to human security requires focusing on prevention in addition to prohibition, such approach also requires recognizing trafficking in persons not only as a crime against the state, but also as a crime against the individual.[96] Such recognition would shift the concept of security from the state security to human security.[97] Several important questions arise in this respect. Should internal trafficking acquire the same importance as international trafficking? Should victims of trafficking be eligible to receive residency status on a humanitarian basis even if it places a burden on the state's immigration policy? Should they be penalized for commission of unlawful acts that are incident to their trafficking? Should they be eligible for witness protection programs if they agree to testify against their traffickers? The answers to these questions depend on the type of protected interest threatened by trafficking in persons.

Internal Trafficking

If trafficking in persons is considered mainly as a threat to the state, then addressing internal trafficking becomes less important. Although, in many cases internal trafficking poses a real threat to human security. For instance, it is estimated that 100,000 women

---

91. International Labor Organization Convention No. 182 Concerning the Prohibition and Immediate Action for the Elimination of the Worst Forms of Child Labor, June 17, 1999, art. 3(b), 38 I.L.M. 1207.

92. Optional Protocol to the Convention on the Rights of the Child on the Involvement of Children in Armed Conflict, May 25, 2000, art. 4, UN Doc. A/Res/54/263.

93. UN Protocol, *supra* note 80.

94. At present, 54 countries have ratified the U.N Protocol. The information regarding the status of the UN Protocol is *available at* http://www.unodc.org/unodc/en/crime_cicp_signatures_trafficking.html.

95. TVPA, *supra* note 80.

96. It should be emphasized that trafficking in persons has to be classified as a crime that threatens two distinct protected interests: the human security of women and children, and the state security.

97. It should be noted that until recently, the notion of security in international law has most commonly been presented in terms of nation states protecting their borders, people, institutions, and values from foreign military aggression. This notion of security assumed that achieving state security automatically assured the security of the citizens and disregarded the fact that states can be "both a major threat to human security and a major vehicle for guaranteeing human security." Ball, *supra* note 84. Therefore, a more appropriate approach is to look at human security as complementary to state security.

and children are sexually exploited annually within the borders of Brazil, and 40,000 children are trafficked and sold every year for work in domestic service or in agriculture.[98] Also, it is commonly known that there are incidents of internal trafficking in such countries as Afghanistan, Haiti, India, the Philippines, Russia, and Thailand. Nevertheless, many countries still only consider trans-border trafficking to be an offense and refuse to recognize internal trafficking.[99] While crossing international borders should not be an element of the crime of trafficking, it may warrant a different response, such as transnational cooperation or an enhanced penalty.[100]

From Deportation to a Residency Status

If trafficking in persons is considered as a crime against the state, then the state should have the right to deport the trafficked persons. This deportation policy is the policy that is followed in most countries today.[101] Immigration laws in most countries still treat the victim of trafficking as a prohibited immigrant and provide for her deportation, ignoring the distinction between smuggling of migrants and trafficking in persons.

By contrast, if trafficking in persons is considered a threat to the person, then reconsideration or a review of this deportation policy is warranted as a matter of principle. Indeed, about thirty countries have changed their immigration policy to grant a victim of trafficking some kind of residency status (temporary or permanent).[102] However, in most of these countries the underlying basis for this status is the protection of state security and not the security of the trafficked person. Such an approach is manifested in the laws of many countries such as Belgium, where the residency status is dependent upon the legal proceedings and is temporary in nature.[103] Once the legal proceedings are concluded, the victims return to their countries of origin. The same is true in Germany, although permanent residency may be granted on very rare occasions where the victims' return to their countries of origin would present a risk to their lives.[104] In all of these cases, the focus is on trafficking as a threat to state security and the need to protect the state. However, if trafficking is considered as a crime against the individual and as a threat to human

---

98. Louise Corradini, *Children in Chains*, THE UNESCO COURIER, June 2001, at 38.

99. The examples include Article 217 of the Criminal Code of Austria, Article 187 of the Criminal Code of Bosnia and Herzegovina, Article 177 of the Criminal Code of Croatia, Article 246 of the Criminal Code of the Czech Republic, Article 81-2 of the Criminal Code of Estonia, Article 246 of the Criminal Code of Slovakia, and Article 149 of the Criminal Code of Ukraine. *See supra* note 97 and accompanying text.

100. Crossing national borders as an aggravated circumstance for trafficking in persons is provided, for instance, under Article 173 of the Criminal Code of Azerbaijan, Articles 128 and 133 of the Criminal Code of Kazakhstan, Article 124 of the Criminal Code of the Kyrgyz Republic, and Article 127-1 of the Criminal Code of Russian Federation. *See supra* note 81and accompanying text.

101. In fact, it has been estimated that as of 2001, 44 percent of developed countries and 39 percent of developing countries had restrictive immigration policies. *See* Commission on Human Security, *supra* note 85, at 42.

102. These include, for example, Australia, Austria, Bahrain, Belgium, Bosnia and Herzegovina, Bulgaria, the Canada, Czech Republic, Denmark, France, Germany, Hong Kong, Hungary, Israel, Italy, Macedonia, Moldova, the Netherlands, Norway, Pakistan, Portugal, Romania, Russian Federation, Spain, Sweden, Switzerland, Turkey, the United Kingdom, and the United States. For the trafficking reports of these countries, *see* http://www.protectionproject.org/allreports.htm.

103. Details on Belgium's requirements and procedure for granting the temporary residence status to victims of trafficking are available from the Daphne Programme's Committee against Modern Slavery, *available at* http://victimsoftrafficking.esclavagemoderne.or/UK/index.html.

104. Ausländergesetz [AuslG, Aliens Act], January 1, 2000, B.G.B.L. I at 1620, §§54–56 (F.R.G.). Details on Austria's procedure for granting the temporary residence status to victims of trafficking are available from the Daphne Programme's Committee against Modern Slavery, *available at* http://victims oftrafficking.esclavagemoderne.or/UK/index.html [hereinafter Aliens Act].

security, it is necessary to consider granting a victim of trafficking temporary or permanent immigration status on a humanitarian basis. Moreover, once the victim of trafficking has been identified, the benefits granted to them should not depend on their immigration status, but nevertheless, in many cases, foreign victims of trafficking fall outside the protection of the national legal system of the destination countries.

The humanitarian approach to the residency status of victims of trafficking is manifested in the UN Protocol stating that "each State Party shall consider adopting legislative or other appropriate measures that permit victims of trafficking to remain in its territory, temporarily or permanently, in appropriate cases ... giv[ing] appropriate consideration to humanitarian and compassionate factors."[105] Such approach is taken by the Netherlands, which may grant a victim a residency permit on humanitarian grounds. These humanitarian grounds may include the risk of reprisals against the victim or their families, the risk of persecution in the victim's country of origin for committing an offense related to prostitution, and the difficulty of social reintegration in the country of origin.[106] This approach is also reflected in the TVPA, as amended by the Trafficking Victims Protection Reauthorization Act ("TVPRA") of 2003.[107] The TVPA uses the term extreme hardship upon removal from the United States as the human insecurity that constitutes the basis for granting a victim of trafficking a special T visa.[108] While the T visa is temporary in nature and lasts for three years, it may be adjusted to provide permanent residency status.[109]

One can interpret the extreme hardship standard of the TVPA as one that is based on the concept of human insecurity, whether this means medical, legal, personal, or social insecurity. Medical insecurity refers to the medical status of a victim of trafficking and implies that the required medical care is not available in the victim's country of origin. Legal insecurity means that if a victim is denied access to the US legal system, they would be left without any effective legal remedy. Personal insecurity refers to the issue of the victim being subjected to reprisals from their trafficker or to criminal or other punishment because their countries of origin penalize the trafficked person. Finally, social insecurity means the likelihood of a victim's re-victimization, especially in the absences of any assistance to her in her country.[110]

Ultimately, whether trafficking in persons is considered to be a threat to state security or to human security, this determination will affect the approach taken in immigration law to trafficking in persons, including the granting of immigration status to the victim.

The Principle of Non-Criminalization

The distinction between state security and human security also affects criminal justice policies. Among these policies is the application of the principle of non-criminalization of the acts of trafficked victims that are incident to trafficking, such as illegal entry, falsification of travel documents, or prostitution. Unfortunately, existing domestic laws in

---

105. *See* UN Protocol, *supra* note 80, at art. 7.

106. *See generally* Aliens Act, *supra* note 104.

107. Trafficking Victims Protection Reauthorization Act of 2003, PUB. L. No. 108-193, 117 Stat. 2875 (codified in scattered sections of 8, 18, and 22 U.S.C.A) [hereinafter TVPRA].

108. TVPA, *supra* note 80, 22 U.S.C. §7105(e)(1)(C), (f) (amending the Immigration and Nationality Act).

109. TVPA, *supra* note 80, 22 U.S.C. §7105(f).

110. The eligibility criteria for a T visa are specified in Immigration and Naturalization Service's Final Rule on New Classification for Victims of Severe Forms of Trafficking in Persons: Eligibility for "T" Non-immigrant Status, Jan. 31, 2002, Section 9 (adding Part 214.11(i) to Title 8, Code of Federal Regulations), 8 C.F.R. §214.11 (2002).

most countries fall short of applying these principles. The use of the above-mentioned traditional immigration law approach results in punishing the victims through deportation. Further, in countries where prostitution is illegal, victims may also be held criminally responsible for engaging in this unlawful act. For example, in August 2002, 10 Vietnamese girls ranging from ages 12 to 18 were arrested and convicted on immigration violations in Cambodia. The girls were sentenced to three months in prison and subsequently deported, even though they were trafficked into the country against their will and forced to engage in prostitution.[111]

The human security approach to the victims of trafficking implies that they should not be penalized for unlawful acts committed as a direct result of being trafficked. This is the rule exemplified in the UN Regulation on the Prohibition of Trafficking in Persons in Kosovo, stating that "[a] person is not criminally responsible for prostitution or illegal entry, presence or work in Kosovo if that person provides evidence that supports a reasonable belief that he or she was the victim of trafficking."[112] Likewise, this rule was introduced into the US criminal justice system in accordance with TVPA, which provides for 5 years of imprisonment for the trafficker who falsifies immigration documents and explicitly provides that this rule "does not apply to the conduct of a person who is or has been a victim of a severe form of trafficking in persons if that conduct is caused by, or incident to, trafficking."[113]

Still interpreting trafficking in persons as a crime against a state, some countries make the application of the principle of non-criminalization contingent upon the victim's willingness to cooperate with the state law enforcement officials in investigating and prosecuting the trafficking offense and testifying against the traffickers. This is the case under Article 165(4) of the Criminal Code of Moldova,[114] Article 124 of the Criminal Code of the Kyrgyz Republic,[115] and Article 8 of the Dominican Republic's Law No. 137-03 Regarding Illegal Trafficking of Migrants and Trade in Persons.[116] These laws do not reflect the rule that the victim's immunity from liability for trafficking-related offenses should not be contingent upon the victim serving as a witness on behalf of the state. While the victim's testimony should be encouraged, it should not be a requirement for granting immunity.

---

111. Feminist Majority Foundation, *Victims of Sex Trafficking Imprisoned for Immigration Violations*, FEMINIST DAILY NEWS WIRE, Aug. 8, 2002, *available at* http://www.feminist.org/news/news-byte/uswirestory.asp?id=6774.

112. United Nations Interim Administration Mission in Kosovo, Regulation No. 2001/4, on the Prohibition of Trafficking in Persons in Kosovo, UN Doc. UNMIK/REG/2001/4, §8 (January 12, 2001), *available at* http://www.unmikonline.org/regulations/2001/reg04-01.html.

113. TVPA, *supra* note 80, 22 U.S.C. §7109(a)(2) (adding §1592 to Chapter 77, Title 18, United States Code). Note that according to the draft TVPA as introduced in the House of Representatives, victims of trafficking could not be imprisoned, fined or otherwise penalized merely because they were trafficked. However, under the TVPA as passed by the Senate and signed into law by the President, victims are not to be detained in facilities inappropriate to their status as crime victims. It was concluded during the deliberations that the original provision that prohibited penalizing victims of trafficking by virtue of their status as crime victims or for conduct committed under duress incident to such status restated existing criminal law and, therefore, was unnecessary. *See* Chris Smith, *Victims of Trafficking and Victims Protection Act*, H.R. Doc. No. 106-939, at 93 (2000) (Conf. Rep.).

114. Article 165(4) of the Criminal Code of Moldova. *See supra* note 81 and accompanying text.

115. Article 124 of the Criminal Code of the Kyrgyz Republic. *See supra* note 81 and accompanying text.

116. Dr. Mohamed Y. Mattar, *The Birth of a New Anti-Trafficking Legislation: The Dominican Republic's Law Number 137-03 Regarding Illegal Trafficking of Migrants and Trade in Persons*, Speech given at the Conference on New Steps in Path Breaking Strategies in the Global Fight against Sex Trafficking (Santo Domingo, Dominican Republic, December 8–9, 2003) transcript *available at* http://www.protectionproject.org/pub.htm.

D. Human Trafficking of Women and Girls in War and Their Use as Child Soldiers

1. Susan Tiefenbrun, *Child Soldiers, Slavery, and the Trafficking of Children*[117]

Introduction

A. Definitions

The prevalent use of children in armed combat is a contemporary manifestation of slavery and a form of human trafficking that is as serious and as lucrative as the international crimes of trafficking in weapons and drugs.[118] Both boys and girls are abducted and trafficked into paramilitary units engaged in armed combat. Girls are trafficked into armed combat and are also used as sex slaves for leaders in the army. Trafficking is defined as the illegal trade of contraband goods, usually across borders, in order to make a profit.[119]

Trafficking in persons, especially women and children, is the purchase and sale of human beings as cargo for the purpose of engaging in exploitative forms of labor such as sex work[120] or participation in armed conflict. Trafficking in children for their use on the battlefield is a human rights violation that rises to the level of slavery.[121]

The United Nations Protocol to Prevent, Suppress, and Punish Trafficking in Persons, Especially Women and Children, Supplementing the United Nations Convention Against Transnational Organized Crime ("Palermo Protocol")[122] defines trafficking as:

---

117. Susan Tiefenbrun, *Child Soldiers, Slavery, and the Trafficking of Children*, 31 Fordham Int'l. L.J. 415 (2008).

118. *See generally* Susan Tiefenbrun, *Sex Sells but Drugs Don't Talk: Trafficking of Women Sex Workers and an Economic Solution*, 24 T. Jefferson L. Rev. 161 (2002).

119. *See* Sandrine Valentine, *Trafficking of Child Soldiers: Expending the United Nations Convention on the Rights of the Child and Its Optional Protocol on the Involvement of Children in Armed Conflict*, 9 New Eng. J. Int'l & Comp L. 109. *See also* U.N. Children's Fund ("UNICEF"), Child Protection Information Sheets 27 (2006), *available at* http://www.unicef.org/publications/files/ Child_Protection_Information_Sheets.pdf [hereinafter UNICEF].

120. *See* Tiefenbrun, *supra* note 118, at 167; *see also* Valentine, *supra* note 119, at 109.

121. *See* Victims of Trafficking and Violence Protection Act of 2000, 22 U.S.C. §7105 (2006) [hereinafter TVPA], for the link between trafficking of persons and slavery. The Rome Statute that founded the International Criminal Court ("ICC") also recognizes trafficking in persons as "enslavement" (Article 7) which is considered a "crime against humanity." Rome Statute of the International Criminal Court, United Nations Diplomatic Conference of Plenipotentiaries on the Establishment of an International Criminal Court, Rome, Italy, June 1, 2002) [hereinafter Rome Statute]. On this issue of trafficking of persons as a contemporary form of slavery, *see generally* Susan Tiefenbrun, *The Cultural, Political, and Legal Climate Behind the Fight to Stop Trafficking in Women: William J. Clinton's Legacy to Women's Rights*, 12 Cardozo J. L. & Gender 855 (2006); Susan Tiefenbrun, *The Domestic and International Impact of the US Victims of Trafficking Protection Act of 2000: Does Law Deter Crime?* 2 Loy. U. Chi. Int'l L. Rev. 193 (2005), *reprinted and completely updated in* 38 Case W. Res. J. Int'l L. 249 (2007); Susan Tiefenbrun, *Sex Slavery in the United States and Its Law to Stop It Here and Abroad*, 11 Wm. & Mary J. Women & L. 317 (2005); Susan Tiefenbrun, *Copyright Infringement, Sex Trafficking, and Defamation in the Fictional Life of a Geisha*, 10 Mich. J. Gender & L. 327 (2004); Susan Tiefenbrun, *The Saga of Susannah: A US Remedy for Sex Trafficking in Women: The Victims of Trafficking and Violence Protection Act of 2000*, 2002 Utah L. Rev. 107 (2002); Tiefenbrun, *supra* note 118, at 161.

122. UN Protocol to Prevent, Suppress, and Punish Trafficking in Persons, Especially Women and Children, supplementing the United Nations Convention against Transactional Organized Crime, G.A. Res. 55/25, Annex II, UN GAOR, 55th Sess., UN Doc. A/RES/55/25 (2001) [hereinafter Palermo Protocol].

the recruitment, transportation, transfer, harboring or receipt of persons, by means of the threat or use of force or other forms of coercion, of abduction, of fraud, of deception, or the abuse of power or of a position of vulnerability or of the giving or receiving of payments or benefits to achieve the consent of a person having control over another person, for the purpose of exploitation.[123]

The recruitment of a child (*i.e.*, a person under the age of eighteen) for the purpose of sexual exploitation or participation in armed conflict falls under the ambit of "trafficking in persons."[124]

The international definition of the trafficking of child soldiers involves three necessary elements: consent, exploitation, and movement within a country or across a border.[125] A child soldier is "trafficked" when there is forced recruitment or no genuine voluntary recruitment; when the recruitment is done without the informed consent of the person's parent or legal guardians; and when such persons were not fully informed of the duties involved in the military service.[126] Child soldiering is a form of child trafficking because the acts required of a child soldier are dangerous enough to interfere with a child's fundamental human right to education, health, and development.[127]

The abduction and employment of children as soldiers is a form of exploitative labor that is tantamount to slavery. Child soldiering is listed as "one of the worst forms of child labor" in the Convention Concerning the Prohibition and Immediate Action for the Elimination of the Worst Forms of Child Labor ("ILO Worst Forms of Child Labor Convention 182").[128] In the ILO Worst Forms of Child Labor Convention 182, child soldiering is included as a form of slavery on the same list as "all forms of slavery or practices similar to slavery, such as the sale and trafficking of children, debt bondage and serfdom, and forced or compulsory labor, including forced or compulsory recruitment of children for use in armed conflict."[129]

The trafficking of child soldiers is directly connected to sexual violence and the sexual exploitation of children who are mainly, but not exclusively, young girls.[130] "Child sexual exploitation" is defined as a situation in which an individual takes "unfair advan-

---

123. *Id.* art. 3(a).

124. *Id.* art. 3(c)–(d). In the Palermo Protocol a "child" is any person under eighteen years of age, however, the definition of a "child" is controversial because the age that determines when a child becomes an adult differs in several international treaties.

125. *See* Valentine, *supra* note 119, at 116–19.

126. *See* Optional Protocol to the Convention on the Rights of the Child on the Involvement of Children in Armed Conflict, G.A. Res. 54/263, Annex I, art. 3, UN GAOR, 54th Sess., Supp. No. 49, UN Doc. A/54/49 (2000) (entered into force February 12, 2002) [hereinafter Children in Armed Conflict Protocol]. *See also* Jisha S. Vachachira, UN Reports, *Report 2002: Implementation of the Optional Protocol to the Convention on the Rights of the Child on the Involvement of Children in Armed Conflict*, 18 N.Y.L. Sch. J. Hum. Rts. 543 (2002).

127. *See generally* Rebecca Rios-Kohn, *The Convention on the Rights of the Child: Progress and Challenges*, 5 Geo. J. on Fighting Poverty 139 (1998).

128. Convention Concerning the Prohibition and Immediate Action for the Elimination of the Worst Forms of Child Labor (I.L.O. No. 182), arts. 1–3, June 17, 1999, 38 I.L.M. 1207, 1208 (1999) [hereinafter ILO Worst Forms of Child Labor Convention 182].

129. *See id.* art. 3; *see also* Recommendation Concerning the Prohibition and Immediate Action for the Elimination of the Worst Forms of Child Labor (Recommendation 190), art. 12(a), June 17, 1999, 38 I.L.M. 1211, 1213 *available at* http://www.ilo.org/public/english/standards/relm/ilc/ilc87/comchir.htm [hereinafter ILO Recommendation 190].

130. *See* Uzodinma Iweala, Beasts of No Nation 83–85 (2005) for a description of a young boy soldier who is sodomized and forced to engage in sex with his male Commander on a regular basis.

tage of some imbalance of power between themselves and another person under the age of eighteen in order to sexually use them."[131] The United Nations Children's Fund ("UNICEF") draws attention to the economic benefits of child sexual exploitation when "a second party benefits, through making a profit or through a *quid pro quo*, through sexual activity involving a child."[132] The exploitation of child soldiers is typically accompanied by brutality and sexual violence. "Child soldiers serve within militaries and armed groups in which complete cooperation and obedience is demanded, in contexts where moral and legal safeguards against their abuse may have broken down. In this context sexual violence becomes sexual exploitation."[133]

Very often children are abducted from one place to another (from their home to a camp where they are trained and then to a field of combat).[134] But children do not have to actually cross a border to be trafficked. If they are moved within their own country and forced to engage in exploitative labor like dangerous armed combat, this constitutes child trafficking.[135]

Thus, using children against their will to engage in armed combat involves human trafficking and unfair labor practices that rise to the level of child slavery. Slavery is one of the most heinous crimes imaginable, especially when it is inflicted on the most vulnerable victims — our children.

B. Extent of Child Soldiering Worldwide

Children who are on the move because they are displaced and impoverished by war or civil unrest are particularly vulnerable for abduction and forced child soldiering. In 2000, about thirteen million children were displaced as a result of warring conflicts.[136] During the civil war that lasted seventeen years in Sierra Leone, more than one million children were displaced, and twenty-five thousand children (some as young as six)[137] were abducted and forced to become members of armed groups.[138] The recruitment of children into armed conflict has claimed the lives of more than two million children, left more than six million children maimed or permanently disabled, caused one million children to be orphaned, afflicted ten million children with serious psychological trauma, and made twelve million children refugees.[139] Currently, over three hundred thousand children, most of them ranging in ages from eleven to fifteen, are serving as child soldiers in

---

131. Julia O'Connell Davidson, *The Sex Exploiter, in* Second World Congress against the Sexual Exploitation of Children 8, 8–9 (2001), *available at* http://www.csecworldcongress.org/PDF/en/Yokohama/Background_reading/Theme_papers/Theme%20paper%20The%20Sex%20Exploiter.pdf.

132. UNICEF, *supra* note 119, at 27

133. Lisa Alfredson, Sexual Exploitation of Child Soldiers: An Exploitation and Analysis of Global Dimensions and Trends 1 (2001), *available at* http://reliefweb.int/sites/reliefweb.int/files/resources/C216BEBEEF8597E1C1256DAB002D9450-csusc-exploit.pdf.

134. *See* Marsha L. Hackenberg, *Can the Optional Protocol for the Convention on the Rights of the Child Protect the Uganda Child Soldier?*, 10 Ind. Int'l & Comp. L. Rev. 417, 426 (2000).

135. *See* Valentine, *supra* note 119, at 116–19.

136. *See generally* Colin MacMullin & Maryanne Loughry, *Investigating Psychosocial Adjustment of Former Child Soldiers in Sierra Leone and Uganda*, 17 J. Refugee Stud. 460 (2004).

137. *See* Payam Akhavan, *The Lord's Resistance Army Case: Uganda's Submission of First State Referral to the International Criminal Court*, 99 Am. J. Int'l L. 403, 407 (2005). *See generally* Nsongurua J. Udombana, *War Is Not Child's Play! International Law and the Prohibition of Children's Involvement in Armed Conflicts*, 20 Temp. Int'l & Comp. L J. 57 (2006).

138. *See* MacMullin & Loughry, *supra* note 136, at 461.

139. *See* Udombana, *supra* note 137, at 67–68.

fifty countries in every region of the world.[140] With so many countries recruiting children by force, deception, and coercion to serve in armed conflicts, it is fair to say that children of today are "the world's most endangered species."[141]

While the participation of children in armed conflict is not new — it occurred in World War II[142] — child soldiering today is a widespread phenomenon, prevalent particularly in developing countries where political, economic, and social instability are more commonplace and where approximately half the population are children.[143] Save the Children reported that hundreds of thousands of under-age soldiers are currently being forced to fight around the world, despite guidelines set forth more than ten years ago in the Cape Town Principles[144] of 1997 that established eighteen as the minimum age for recruitment.[145] Children have served in government forces, paramilitaries or in opposition forces in Colombia, Mexico, Peru, Turkey, Yugoslavia, Algeria. Angola, Burundi, Chad, Democratic Republic of Congo, Eritrea, Ethiopia, Rwanda, Sierra Leone, Somalia, Sudan, Uganda, Afghanistan, Iran, Iraq, Israel and the Occupied Territories, Lebanon, India, Indonesia, Myanmar, Nepal, Pakistan, the Philippines, Solomon Islands, Papua New Guinea, Sri Lanka, East Timor, Tajikistan, and Uzbekistan.[146] The use of child soldiers is still occurring in the Western Hemisphere,[147] Europe,[148] Africa,[149] the Middle East, Central Asia,[150]

---

140. *See generally* Abigail Leibig, *Child Soldiers in Northern Uganda: Do Current Legal Frameworks Offer Sufficient Protection?*, 3 Nw. U. J. Int'l Hum. Rts. 6 (2005).

141. Udombana, *supra* note 137, at 68.

142. *See* P. W. Singer, Children at War 14–15 (2005). "The Hitler Jugend were young boys who had received quasi-military training as part of a political program to maintain Nazi rule through indoctrination ... Hitler's regime ordered these boys to fight as well.... Lightly armed and mostly sent out in small ambush squads, scores of Hitler Jugend were killed in futile skirmishes, all occurring after the war had essentially been decided." Udombana, *supra* note 137, at 68.

143. *See* MacMullin & Loughry, *supra* note 136, at 460.

144. UNICEF, Cape Town Annotated Principles and Best Practice on the Prevention of Recruitment of Children into the Armed Forces and Demobilization and Social Reintegration of Child Soldiers in Africa (1997), *available at* http://iggi.unesco.or.kr/web/iggi_docs/ 02/952579100.pdf [hereinafter Cape Town Annotated Principles].

145. *See* Nick Tattersall, *Child Soldiers Still Recruited 10 Years After Pact*, Reuters, Feb. 5, 2007, *available at* http://www.reuters.com/article/homepageCrisis/idUSL05604214._CH_.2400.

146. *See* Human Rights Watch, *Where Child Soldiers Are Being Used,* http://www.hrw.org/ campaigns/crp/where.htm (last visited Oct. 25, 2007).

147. *See* Singer, *supra* note 142, at 16. In the Americas since 1990, child soldiers have fought in Colombia, Ecuador, El Salvador, Guatemala, Mexico (in the Chiapas conflict), Nicaragua, Paraguay, and Peru. The most substantial numbers are in Colombia. There, more than eleven thousand children are being used as soldiers ... one out of every four irregular combatants is underage.... Child soldiers in Colombia are nicknamed 'little bells' by the military that use them as expendable sentries and 'little bees' by the FARC guerrillas, because they 'sting' their enemies before they know they are under attack.

148. *See id.* at 18–19. On the European continent, children under eighteen years of age have served in both British government forces and their opposition in Northern Ireland and on all sides in the Bosnian conflict.... It is in Turkey, though, where the most child soldiers in Europe are found, in the Kurdish Workers' Party ("PKK").... In 1998, it was reported that the PKK had three thousand underage children within its ranks, with the youngest reported PKK fighter being an armed seven-year-old. Ten percent of these were girls.

149. *See id.* at 19–21. Countries in Africa that employ child soldiers include Sierra Leone, Angola, Liberia, Uganda, Rwanda, Burundi, Kenya, Central African Republic, Tanzania, Congo-Brazzaville, Ivory Coast, Ethiopia, and Democratic Republic of the Congo.

150. *See id.* at 21–22, 24. Today, children are fighting in Algeria, Azerbaijan, Egypt, Iran (even though it is against *Shari'a* law), Iraq, Lebanon, Sudan, Tajikistan, and Yemen, including children younger than fifteen serving in a number of radical Islamic groups, and Palestine. Sudan has the

and Asia.[151] Today fighting forces still recruit child soldiers in Afghanistan, Chad, Colombia, Democratic Republic of Congo, Ivory Coast, Myanmar, Nepal, the Philippines, Sri Lanka, Somalia, Sudan, and Uganda.[152] Graca Machel, the former first lady of Mozambique and the wife of Nelson Mandela, who served as a special expert for the United Nations on the issue of child soldiers, wrote a ground breaking report on child soldiering, summing up the extent of the use of child soldiers and its significance:

> These statistics are shocking enough, but more chilling is the conclusion to be drawn from them: more and more of the world is being sucked into a desolate moral vacuum. This is a space devoid of the most basic human values; a space in which children are slaughtered, raped, and maimed; a space in which children are exploited as soldiers; a space in which children are starved and exposed to extreme brutality. Such unregulated terror and violence speak of deliberate victimization. There are few further depths to which humanity can sink.[153]

C. Abuses of Child Soldiers

Child soldiers are subjected daily to dehumanizing atrocities. They are often abducted from their own home, tortured, indoctrinated with brutality, forced to become intoxicated with mind-altering drugs, threatened with death and/or dismemberment if they don't fight, forced to return to their own village to witness or participate in the death or disfigurement of their own family members, required to kill friends who don't obey the commanders, and made to watch the punishment of other child soldiers who attempt in vain to escape.

Child soldiers are brainwashed thoroughly and brutally until their ethics and moral values become so distorted that they believe doing evil is good. One twelve-year-old child in Columbia described the leadership's obsession with the virtues of killing:

> If you join the paramilitaries [the AUC in Colombia,] your first duty is to kill. They tell you, 'Here you are going to kill.' From the very beginning, they teach you how to kill. I mean when you arrive at the camp, the first thing they do is kill a guy, and if you are a recruit they call you over to prick at him, to chop off his hands and arms.[154]

Brainwashing is accomplished by desensitizing children to the sight and commission of atrocities. Some children who try to escape are reportedly boiled alive, and the other child soldiers are then forced to eat the human flesh as part of their training.[155] Other child soldiers who manage to escape reported that while they were at the training camp they were forced to beat the dead body of a captured escapee and "smear themselves with

---

largest use of child soldiers in the region, and as many as 100,000 children have served on both sides of the civil war.

151. *See id.* at 26–27. The practice of child soldiers is highly prevalent in Asia especially in Cambodia, East Timor, India, Indonesia, Laos, Myanmar, Nepal, Pakistan, Papua New Guinea, the Philippines, Sri Lanka, and the Solomon Islands. Myanmar alone has more than 75,000 child soldiers, one of the highest numbers of any country in the world with some as young as eleven.

152. *See* Tattersall, *supra* note 145, at 1.

153. Expert of the Secretary-General, Ms. Graca Machel, *Impact of Armed Conflict on Children*, §5, *delivered to the General Assembly*, UN Doc. A/51/306 (Aug. 26, 1996), [hereinafter Machel Report].

154. Human Rights Watch, You'll Learn Not to Cry: Child Combatants in Columbia 95 (2003), *available at* http://www.hrw.org/reports/2003/colombia0903/columbia0903.pdf.

155. *See Justice Versus Reconciliation: Hunting Uganda's Child-Killers*, Economist, May 7, 2005, at 41.

his blood."[156] Rebels keep the children obedient through frequent beatings, threats of death, and threats of death against the children's family members.[157]

Young girls are abducted as well and make up forty percent of the ranks of armed groups in some countries.[158] In El Salvador, Ethiopia, and Uganda, almost a third of the child soldiers are young girls,[159] who are raped, enslaved, given to military commanders as "wives," and victimized by sexual violence on a daily basis. Girl soldiers encounter serious abuse, including forced pregnancy. During the 1990s over eight hundred children were born to the Lord's Resistance Army ("LRA") "wives" who were concentrated at Jabelein camp in southern Sudan.[160] Girl soldiers are often used as domestic servants and sex slaves during conflict, and when they become infected with HIV they are usually not treated. These victimized girl soldiers require rehabilitation and special attention after their demobilization.[161]

These children who are trained to be fearless actually become dangerous, killing machines. Anyone seeing them in action is naturally stunned into disbelief and is likely to wonder why these children kill, maim, and dismember their own friends and relatives. The answer is quite simple. Child soldiers are pumped up on drugs to make them fearless.[162] These drugs are no doubt trafficked into the country for a hefty sum. Powerless and abandoned children are empowered with small, light weapons and brutally indoctrinated into the virtues of committing wartime atrocities. These small weapons are trafficked into the country at a substantial cost. Young girls are also trafficked to service the commanders and even the boy child soldiers. The money earned from one form of trafficking typically supplies the goods and services of the other form of trafficking in a complex network that constitutes a lucrative trafficking industry run by international organized crime groups.

These children are victims of inhumane brainwashing and merciless combat training that makes them robotically obey orders to kill innocent victims, just to stay alive. These children undergo a terrifying initiation that consists of killing or raping a close relative. They are forced to participate in acts of extreme violence and barbarity including beheadings, amputations, rape, and the burning of people alive.[163] The LRA in Uganda initiates children into its gang by forcing them "to club, stamp or bite to death their friends and relatives, and then to lick their brains, drink their blood and even eat their boiled flesh."[164] The LRA slices off the lips and noses of children it suspects of disloyalty.[165] The children of Uganda are reportedly so frightened about being abducted and enslaved by the

---

156. *See I Don't Know Why They Did It,* News 24 (S. Afr.), Oct. 6, 2005, *available at* http://www.news24.com/News24/Africa/Features/0,,2-11-37_1719250,00.html.

157. *See* Human Rights Watch, The Scars of Death 37 (1997), *available at* http://www.hrw.org/reports97/uganda.

158. *See* UN Office for the Coordination of Humanitarian Affairs, *AFRICA: Fighting for Children,* IRIN, February 7, 2007, http://irinnews.org/report.aspx?reportid=70016 [hereinafter AFRICA: Fighting for Children].

159. *See* Leibig, *supra* note 140, at 6.

160. *See* Akhavan, *supra* note 137, at 408.

161. *See* AFRICA: Fighting for Children, *supra* note 158.

162. *See* Ishmael Beah, *The Making, and Unmaking of a Child Soldier,* N.Y. Times Mag., January 14, 2007, at 7 ("I smoked marijuana, ate and snorted cocaine and brown brown. That was all I did for a few days before we went back to the new base we had captured.").

163. *See* Akhavan, *supra* note 137, at 408; *see also* Ishmael Beah, A Long Way Gone: Memories of a Boy Soldier (2007); *Justice Versus Reconciliation: Hunting Uganda's Child-Killers, supra* note 155, at 41.

164. *See Justice Versus Reconciliation: Hunting Uganda's Child-Killers, supra* note 155; *see also* Udombana, *supra* note 137, at 68.

165. *See Justice Versus Reconciliation: Hunting Uganda's Child-Killers, supra* note 155.

LRA that they do not sleep at home, preferring instead to become "night commuters"[166] who travel alone or in groups every night to "protected villages" where "they sleep on verandas, in bus parks, or on church grounds" for safety....[167]

Conclusion and Some Proposals for Solutions

A. So Many Laws

Forty percent of the children abducted into soldiering are girls. Despite a profusion of domestic and international laws that prohibit the use of child soldiers, this inhumane and widespread practice continues today and is likely to increase in the future due to the economics of war. Considering that the use of child soldiers is "rooted in the endemic competition for economic resources"[168] and fueled by the huge profits from the traffic in drugs, weapons, and human beings, any proposal to eradicate child soldiering must necessarily involve economic solutions in order to effectuate real change in this hideous practice and to firmly re-establish traditional ethics relating to the protection and preservation of women and children's rights.

I would like to propose some solutions that might make the practice of using child soldiers more difficult and thus pave the way towards its eradication. Stated differently, I believe we need to destabilize the cost/benefit ratio and decrease the economic benefits of child trafficking by increasing the business costs and the legal risk.

B. Prevention

The key to the elimination of child soldiering and trafficking is prevention, which can be accomplished by raising public awareness of the extent of this international crime and its impact on the society at large. Consciousness raising can be accomplished through education, effective use of the media, State support for NGOs, publicity about international conferences, and publications that disseminate information widely about the following issues: children's rights, recruitment guidelines,[169] new anti-trafficking and anti-child soldiering legislation, and the dangers of child soldiering. States should publicize information widely through the media about women's rights and children's rights and recruitment guidelines[170] in order to educate the public at large. Governments and people must be made aware of children's rights and the international agreements that protect children against their engagement and enslavement as child soldiers. Education of the most vulnerable children such as refugees and street children must be made more available so that parents and children can avoid being duped into thinking that the life of a child soldier provides security and stability.

Awareness about the use of child soldiers can be raised by holding and widely publishing international conferences on child soldiering like the "Free Children from War" Con-

---

166. *See* Amnesty Int'l, *UGANDA: Child "Night Commuters,"* AI Index AFR 59/013/2005, November 18, 2005, *available at* http://web.amnesty.org/library/print/ENGAFR590132005. "We come to the shelter because I fear being abducted again. I was eight years old then. I do not want my brothers and sisters to be abducted as I was. We walk fast in the night to be here.... Some walk for several kilometers, without the protection of adult family members.... All risk harassment, physical abuse, sexual exploitation, and rape on the way."

167. Akhavan, *supra* note 137, at 409.

168. Udombana, *supra* note 137, at 107.

169. For example, The Principles and Best Practices on the Prevention of Recruitment of Children into the Armed Forces and on Demobilization and Social Reintegration of Child Soldiers in Africa, adopted in April 1997, provide a strategy to address the factors that contribute to the use of children as soldiers. *See generally,* Cape Town Annotated Principles, *supra* note 144.

170. *Id.*

ference that took place in Paris on February 6, 2007.[171] African nations participating in that international conference on child soldiers pledged to do their utmost to prevent children from being used as fighters, although the commitment is not legally binding. This conference was hosted by France and UNICEF and included delegates from nearly sixty nations, other UN agencies and thirty non-governmental organizations [NGOs], all of whom vowed "to spare no effort to put an end to the illegal use and recruitment of children by groups of armed forces."[172] This Conference should have been picked up by the media, televised on C-SPAN, and covered by CNN International to disseminate the message that our children are in danger worldwide.

The international community must raise awareness worldwide of the extent and impact of the crime of child soldiering in order to create the political will to eradicate the crime and to shame government leaders into implementing legislative protection of children. The media can and should draw more attention to the plight of boys and girls in armed conflict. For example, in May 2001, sixty Angolan children were abducted by the National Union for the Total Independence of Angola ("UNITA"), and the documentation available on the abducted children, including their names, ages, and photographs, enabled UNICEF and the United Nations Humanitarian Coordinator in Angola to launch an international publicity campaign that prompted the release of children to a Catholic Mission after twenty days.[173]

States must show support for non-governmental organizations as well as religious and community leaders who do work on the ground to educate the public. NGOs can change values and influence ethics by appealing to the people to adhere to local values and to customs that validate children and their basic human rights.[174] However, in the past many of the non-governmental organizations groups and the international coalitions[175] created to stop the use of child soldiers have been distracted or misdirected by anti-American sentiment that thwarts their mission to stop the use of child soldiers.[176] The international community must help create the political will to eradicate child soldiering by shaming government leaders into implementing legislative protection of children.

C. Protection of Child Victims

In order to eliminate child soldiering, the global community must address the protection of the child victims by strengthening compliance and implementation[177] of international humanitarian laws, human rights norms, slavery conventions, trafficking conventions, international criminal laws, and fair labor laws that are applicable to children's rights and child soldiering. Implementation starts by abolishing the general per-

---

171. *See generally,* AFRICA: Fighting for Children, *supra* note 158.
172. *Id.*
173. *See* Amnesty Int'l, *Innocent Victims of Angola's Cruel War,* Wire, Nov. 2001, *available at* http://web.amnesty.org/wire/November2001/Angola; *see also* Justin Pearce, *UNITA Attack East of Luanda,* BBC News, May 22, 2001, *available at* http://news.bbc.co.uk/2/hi/africa/1345364.stm.
174. *See* Singer, *supra* note 142, at 146.
175. *See id.* at 148 ("The Coalition to Stop the Use of Child Soldiers has wasted its political capital by engaging in a long-drawn-out public relations war with the US and British governments.").
176. *Id.*
177. If a State is not a party to the relevant treaties protecting children, they may be obligated to enforce the provisions anyway because the provisions have become part of international custom. *See* Vienna Convention on the Law of Treaties art. 38, 1155 U.N.T.S. 331, 8 I.L.M. 679, UN Doc. A/CONF. 39/29 (May 23, 1155 U.N.T.S. 331, 8 I.L.M. 679, (1969)).

"Nothing in articles 34 to 37 precludes a rule set forth in a treaty from becoming binding upon a third State as a customary rule of international law, recognized as such."

ception of impunity for crimes related to child soldiering.[178] The Rome Statute of the International Criminal Court established child soldiering as a war crime in 2002. International *ad hoc* tribunals and the permanent International Criminal Court should prosecute individuals and States Parties engaging in child soldiering and widely publicize the outcome of these cases. Foreign victims of child soldiering should be informed that they can also file lawsuits under the Alien Tort Claims Act in the US federal courts.

In order to protect the child victims, the international community must support the availability of birth records. This would better document the age of children and avoid inadvertent underage recruitment.[179] States should provide rescue missions, financial aid, health and psychological assistance, meaningful rehabilitation to child victims of war, and carefully planned reintegration programs so that abducted children can live again in the community that once welcomed them as children.

D. Economic Solutions

Shaming States and engaging in a universal moral outcry is necessary and helpful, but the most effective form of deterrence is linked to economic solutions affecting trade and international aid that do not negatively impact women and children. The international community should limit small arms trade to non-State actors and target trading partners of States engaging in child soldiering. States should withhold recognition and financial benefits to any groups that seize power through the use of child soldiers or to States that aid them.[180] States should reduce international aid and trade or implement divestiture policies in countries engaging in child soldiering. "International aid donors should make compliance with the Children's Rights Convention (CRC) Protocol a condition for development assistance."[181]

UN Resolution 1612[182] requires States to monitor and report on the recruitment and use of child soldiers, and any State engaging in child soldiering could be subject to a ban on the export and supply of small arms and light weapons and other military equipment. States should also develop a policy that targets the external support structures providing donations to the groups or States that engage in child soldiering. Any State engaging in human rights violations such as the use of child soldiers could be deprived of their Most Favored Nation status in the General Agreement on Tariffs and Trade and the World Trade Organization, pursuant to the Jackson-Vanick amendment. Other effective measures to eliminate child soldiering might include taking away seats at the United Nations for States engaging in or aiding and abetting this crime.

E. Prosecution of Perpetrators

The next step in the process of eliminating child soldiering is the effective prosecution of perpetrators. Governments should be held accountable for their deliberate decision to use children as human shields and combatants. States must establish and implement laws that criminalize perpetrators with a severe sentence of imprisonment for thirty or more years for anyone who employs child soldiers. This increased sentence would act as a deterrence measure and provide victims with a sense of justice and retribution. For exam-

---

178. Udombana, *supra* note 137, at 102 ("The referral of LRA leaders to the ICC by the Ugandan Government provided the first experiment of the ICC's ability to suppress impunity. In December 2003, the Ugandan Government referred the LRA atrocities committed in Northern Uganda to the ICC Prosecutor.").
179. *See* SINGER, *supra* note 142, at 146.
180. *See id.* at 160.
181. Udombana, *supra* note 137, at 105.
182. S.C. Res. 1612, §9, UN Doc. S/RES/1612 (July 26, 2005).

ple, on December 16, 2003, Uganda referred the situation concerning the Lord's Resistance Army to the prosecutor of the International Criminal Court.[183] The referral was an attempt by Uganda to engage an "otherwise aloof international community"[184] to stop this inhumane practice and to address the moral outrage of using children as soldiers. The prosecution of perpetrators of child soldiering with a severe sentence would increase the risk and thus the cost of doing the business of child soldiering.

Leaders may know that child soldiering is a war crime, but they seem to believe they will never be brought to justice because of a sense of "rampant impunity."[185] Criminalizing the practice could be accomplished by prosecuting former leaders of groups that used child soldiers in *ad hoc* international tribunals like the war crimes tribunal in Sierra Leone or in the permanent International Criminal Court. Local communities should increase their level of financial support for the *ad hoc* tribunals that are plagued by limited funds.

One of the problems associated with implementing accountability for atrocities associated with child soldiering is the possibility that child soldiers themselves will be prosecuted unfairly. The prospect of prosecuting children for war crimes is controversial. Sierra Leone seems to have found a good solution to this problem. The Statute of the Special Court of Sierra Leone does allow for the prosecution of children between the ages of fifteen and eighteen, but the prosecutor has not taken such action yet, focusing instead on the adult leaders.[186] Children implicated in these crimes are given hearings in special closed juvenile chambers so that their identities are not revealed. Children are also given psychological counseling and other assistance. Moreover, children are not sentenced to prison with adult perpetrators but rather they are placed in special custody and rehabilitation/demobilization programs, as well as foster care. This kind of response recognizes that child soldiering is a unique crime because perpetrators are oftentimes themselves the victims.[187]

In view of the uniqueness of the crime of child soldiering, the UN Security Council should consider establishing a new *ad hoc* tribunal specifically centered on the crime of child soldiering. In addition, the rules of the ICC might be modified to allow children to testify before the court[188] and thereby create a more accurate historical record that should be publicized widely.

Three years after the CRC Protocol on Children in Armed Combat entered into force, the UN Security Council expressed deep concern "over the lack of overall progress on the ground, where parties to conflict continue to violate with impunity the relevant provisions of applicable international law relating to the rights and protection of children in armed conflict."[189] The use of children as soldiers in armed combat is nothing less than a contemporary form of slavery that must be eradicated by carefully implemented measures to re-establish ethical norms that valorize children.

Hope is not dead in this campaign against the enslavement of child soldiers. Recently, fifty-eight countries and non-governmental agencies signed a treaty to free current and potential child soldiers from peril.[190] On January 29, 2007, the International Criminal

---

183. *See* Akhavan, *supra* note 137, at 403.

184. *Id.*

185. *See* Singer, *supra* note 142, at 149.

186. *Id.* at 155.

187. *Id.*

188. *Id.* at 153.

189. *See generally,* S.C. Res. 1612, *supra* note 182.

190. *See* Ann O'Neil, *Stolen Kids Turned Into Terrifying Killers*, CNN, February 12, 2007, http://www.cnn.com/2007/WORLD/africa/02/12/child.soldiers/index.html.

Court forged ahead with its first war crimes prosecution targeting the leader of the Congolese militia with charges of recruiting child soldiers. The act was declared a war crime when the International Criminal Court was established in 2002. Radhika Coomaraswamy, the United Nations envoy for children and armed conflict, stated: "We've come a long way. Ten years ago this was an invisible issue."[191] Last summer groups in Burundi, Ivory Coast, Myanmar, the Democratic Republic of the Congo, Sudan and Somalia were referred to the UN Security Council for possible sanctions related to their use of children as soldiers. Individual commanders are being held responsible for their war crimes. [In 2008, the United States enacted a federal statute, The Protection of Child Soldiers Act, which, like the US federal statute for trafficking, The Trafficking Victims Protection Act, has extraterritorial reach.]

But in order to do more to eradicate this crime, funds must be found and steps must be taken to restore normal life to the children victimized by this atrocity. Many of these children need rehabilitation and serious counseling in improved rehabilitation and transit centers.[192] Many of the escapees, and especially the girls, who return home are rejected by their own families and shunned by villagers who view them as killers or prostitutes. Changing community and family norms to safeguard the reintegration of these victims is no easy task and can only be done through a widespread information and education campaign, as well as a serious attempt to eradicate poverty which is at the source of many of the armed conflicts that produce and perpetuate the use of child soldiers as a military strategy. The fact is that children, especially girls, are devalued, viewed as expendable, and a convenient natural resource for economic efficiency during war. Public condemnation of this kind of perverse thinking and of the leaders who recruit children into armed combat can help to reduce future recruitment. Imposing sanctions on corporations that trade with leaders of groups that use children as soldiers is more effective than imposing sanctions on the State as a whole. Without the moral outcry and the effective intervention of the community, these children could become a lost generation of migratory professional killers and sex slaves who perpetuate conflict and war.

---

191. *Id.*

192. *See* Naomi Cahn, *Poor Children: Child "Witches" and Child Soldiers in Sub-Saharan Africa*, 3 Ohio St. J. Crim. L. 413, 442 (2006).

Chapter 6

Effects of International *Ad Hoc* and Permanent Tribunals and Truth Commissions on Women's Rights

A. Introduction to the Laws of War and the Crime of Rape in the Jurisprudence of the ICTY and ICTR

The jurisprudence of the United Nations *ad hoc* tribunals such as the International Tribunal for Crimes against the Former Yugoslavia (ICTY) and the International Tribunal for Crimes against Rwanda (ICTR) evidences the enormous strides that have been made to protect women against sexual violence and rape during war.[1] For hundreds of years rape has been considered booty, the natural byproduct of war, and the "spoils of war."[2] In the past, people simply have turned a blind eye to the rape of women by victorious soldiers. Rape was used as an incentive to boost the morale of weary soldiers. After World War II and especially during the wars in Bosnia-Herzegovinia and Rwanda, rape became a weapon of war, a symbol of domination, an instrument of terror, torture, a crime against humanity, and genocide, as well as an effective means to dehumanize women.

1. Rape as a Weapon of War

During the Bosnia-Herzegovinian war, rape was used systematically as a weapon of war and with the intent to impregnate Muslim women with Serbian babies in order to destroy the entire Muslim culture and fulfill the goal of ethnic cleansing and genocide. As a result of the judicial decisions of the ICTY and ICTR,[3] rape finally became recognized as a war crime, a crime against humanity, a form of genocide, and an instrument of torture.

---

1. *See* Christine Strumpen-Darrie, "Rape: A Survey of Current International Jurisprudence," *available at* http://www.wcl.american.edu/hrbrief/v7i3rape.htm.

2. Theodor Meron, *Rape as a Crime Under International Humanitarian Law*, 87 Am. J. Int'l L. 424 (1993).

3. Richard J. Goldstone was the first Prosecutor of the ICTY and ICTR. *See* Richard J. Goldstone and Estelle A. Dehon, *Engendering Accountability: Gender Crimes under International Criminal Law*, 19 New Eng. J. Pub. Pol. 121, 123 (2003). *See also* Kelly D. Askin, *A Decade of the Development of Gender Crimes in International Courts and Tribunals: 1993 to 2003*, 3 Hum. Rts. Brief 16, 17 (2004).

2. Jurisprudence of the ICTY and ICTR

Several key cases regarding sexual violence and rape have emanated out of these two *ad hoc* tribunals. *Prosecutor v. Jean-Paul Akayesu* was decided in the ICTR in 1998, and the court attributed individual criminal responsibility to Akayesu for crimes against humanity. The facts of this case will be discussed later in this chapter. The *Akayesu* court recognized that rape is a form of genocide, prohibited under Article 2 of the ICTR Statute. *Prosecutor v. Tadic*,[4] was the first ICTY judgment that provided horrifying evidence of sexual assault perpetrated with a "common purpose," a term which was further defined in the appeal judgment of this case. *Prosecutor v. Delalic et al.* (*Celebici*) (Case No. IT-96-21-A.) was decided in 1998 in the ICTY, and the court held that rape is a form of torture (committed by a Serbian prison camp guard who repeatedly raped two non-Serbian female prisoners) in violation of Articles 2 and 3 of the ICTY Statute. The ICTY convicted Delalic to four 15-year sentences for rape. *Prosecutor v. Furundzija*,[5] was issued in 1998 in the ICTY, and it expanded the legal definition of rape.[6] Furundzija did not personally commit the rapes but was nevertheless held to be a co-perpetrator of rape which the court considered to be a form of torture. He was found guilty of the law or customs of war (torture) and of violating Article 3 of the ICTY Statute. He was sentenced to eight years in prison. Other important cases involving rape are the *Kvocka*[7] case (about the infamous Omarska rape camp) in which the court held that rape is a joint criminal enterprise. The *Kunarac, Kovac and Vukovic (Foca)*[8] case, concerning the Foca massacres, mass killings, and rapes against non-Serb Bosnian Muslim civilians for purposes of ethnic cleansing, uncovered evidence about hundreds of women in the Foca so-called detention centers who were tortured and raped. The women had to live in intolerably unhygienic conditions and were mistreated by being repeatedly raped violently. Serb soldiers and policemen would come to the detention centers, which were nothing more than camps for the sole purpose of raping women, select one or more women, take them outside, and rape them in full view, with the direct involvement of the Serb local authorities, particularly the police force. For example, Kovac kept four young Muslim girls in his apartment, sexually abusing and repeatedly raping them, and he invited his friends to rape the girls in his home. Kovac also sold three of the girls who were his Muslim sex slaves. Prior to selling them, he gave them to other Serb soldiers who gang raped them for more than three weeks. This case provided a new definition of rape where "resistance" is no longer required to fulfill the elements of the crime of rape. The *Foca* case involved sexual enslavement and rape as crimes against humanity. Kunarac was convicted and sentenced to 28 years in prison. Kovac was convicted and sentenced to 20 years in prison. Vukovic was convicted and sentenced to 12 years in prison. The *Krstic*[9] case found a direct link between rape and ethnic cleansing.

---

4. Prosecutor v. Tadic, Judgment, Case No. IT-94-1-T (May 7, 1997).

5. Prosecutor v. Anto Furundzijia, Judgment, Case No. IT-95-17/1-T, (Dec. 10, 1998).

6. In Prosecutor v. Furundzija, the ICTY concluded that the elements of the crime of rape are: "1) sexual penetration, however slight; a) of the vagina or anus of the victim by the penis of the perpetrator or any other object used by the perpetrator or b) of the mouth of the victim by the penis of the perpetrator; 2) by coercion or force or threat of force against the victim or a third person."

7. Prosecutor v. Kvocka *et al.,* Judgment, Case No. IT-98-30/1-T (Nov. 2 2001), *available at* http://www.icty.org/case/kvocka/4.

8. Prosecutor v. Kunarac, Kovac and Vukovic, Judgment International Criminal Tribunal for the former Yugoslavia, *available at* www.icty.org/cases/kunarac/cis.

9. Prosecutor v. Radislav Krstic, Judgment International Criminal Tribunal for the former Yugoslavia, case No. IT-98-33-T. Judgment (Aug. 2, 2001).

The use of rape as a weapon of war has expanded exponentially during the last twenty years. Catharine MacKinnon states that "[t]hese rapes are to everyday rape what the Holocaust was to everyday anti-Semitism."[10]

3. Humanitarian Laws and the Protection of Women against Rape

The protection of women against rape and sexual violence during armed conflict is not well established in the international laws of war. In the Lieber Code of 1863 "all rape" was prohibited, but the protection of women's rights was not adequately enforced. The Hague Regulations[11] provide only indirect and partial protection against rape [in Article 46]. The 1929 Geneva Convention on Prisoners of War contains a general provision that is too vague to effectively protect women prisoners [Article 3]. During the Second World War, rape was tolerated and even utilized as an instrument of policy. In occupied Europe, thousands of women were subjected to rape and forced to service Nazi troops in brothels. The Fourth Geneva Convention of 1949 contains a clear prohibition of rape in Art. 27. Nevertheless, infringement of this prohibition of rape was not listed among the 'grave breaches' of the Convention. Grave breaches of the Geneva Convention typically require penal sanctions or extradition. Rape still continues relatively unchecked in armed combat. The huge number of rapes committed in recent armed conflicts (Kuwait, Rwanda, Sierra Leone, Bosnia-Herzegovina, among others) is proof of the prevalence of this international crime.

Many horrific atrocities were committed by the Nazis throughout World War II. After the war, legal scholars realized that the original Geneva Conventions of 1929[12] were inadequate. They were amended in 1949, resulting in four Geneva Conventions.[13] The Fourth Geneva Convention specifically protects civilians during periods of war. This convention protects women in particular by explicitly prohibiting rape, forced prostitution, or any form of indecent assault.[14] However, Article 27 of the Fourth Geneva Convention refers to rape as an attack on women's "honor," a euphemism that reflects the failure of the international community to take rape of women seriously. Two Additional Protocols[15] to the Geneva Conventions of 1949 were enacted in 1977 to prohibit these crimes

---

10. Catharine MacKinnon, *Rape, Genocide, and Women's Human Rights, in* MASS RAPE: THE WAR AGAINST WOMEN IN BOSNIA-HERZEGOVINA 184 (Alexandra Stiglmayer ed., 1994).

11. Hague Regulations annexed to Convention (No. IV), Respecting the Laws and Customs of War on Land, Art. 23 (c)–(d) October 18, 1907, 36 Stat. 2277, TS No. 539, 1 Bevans 631.

12. Convention Relative to the Treatment of Prisoners of War, Geneva, 27 July 1929, *available at* http://www.icrc.org/ihl.nsf/FULL/305?OpenDocument.

13. The four Geneva Conventions (signed 12 August 1949, and entered into force 21 October 1950) are the Geneva Convention (I) for the Amelioration of the Condition of the Wounded and Sick in Armed Forces in the Field, 75 U.N.T.S. 31; Geneva Convention (II) for the Amelioration of the Condition of the Wounded, Sick and Shipwrecked Members of Armed Forces at Sea, 75 U.N.T.S. 85; Geneva Convention (III) Relative to the Treatment of Prisoners of War, 75 U.N.T.S. 135; and Geneva Convention (IV) Relative to the Protection of Civilian Persons in Time of War, 6 U.S.T. 3516, 75 U.N.T.S. 287 (1949).

14. Geneva Convention (IV) Relative to the Protection of Civilian Persons in Time of War, 6 U.S.T. 3516, 75 U.N.T.S. 287, art. 27 (1949) [hereinafter Fourth Geneva Convention].

15. Protocol Additional to the Geneva Convention, Relating to the Protection of Victims of International Armed Conflicts (Protocol I) of 8 June 1977. Article 76 (1) of Protocol I includes under the *Protection of Women* the crime of rape, forced prostitution, and any other form of indecent assault. *See also* Protocol Additional to the Geneva Conventions of 12 August 1949, and relating to the pro-

in both international and non-international conflicts.[16] Article 76 of Protocol I states that "[w]omen shall be the object of special respect and shall be protected in particular against rape, forced prostitution, and any other form of indecent assault." Since many of the conflicts that occurred and are still occurring are considered internal or civil wars, it is important to note that article 3 common to the Geneva Conventions and Protocol I and Protocol II of the Geneva Conventions are applicable to non-international conflicts. In non-international armed conflicts, rape has been specifically outlawed in two provisions of Protocol II: Articles 4(2)(e) and 6. There is no specific mention of rape in common Article 3 to the Geneva Conventions.

International humanitarian laws relating to the protection of women against sexual violence and rape committed against them during periods of armed conflict offered less protection than required to prevent the ultimate establishment of rape as a weapon of war in more recent wars. Moreover, if domestic criminal laws expressly forbid rape crimes, enforcement of these laws prohibiting rape has been weak in many countries due to custom and cultural traditions that marginalize and devalue women. International humanitarian law has set forth detailed rules of engagement and comprehensive regulations protecting combatants, civilians, and prisoners of war, but these laws of war make little specific mention of crimes against female combatants or civilians, except in Additional Protocol I (Article 76(1)), Protocol II (Articles 4(2)(e) and 6), and Article 27 of the Fourth Geneva Convention of 1949. The statutes establishing the *ad hoc* war crimes tribunals illustrate the weakness of protection of women against rape and sexual violence.[17]

4. International Military Tribunals and the Crime of Rape: Nuremberg and Tokyo

After World War II, the international military tribunal at Nuremberg was established to prosecute individuals for crimes against the peace, (*i.e.*, *jus ad bello*), war crimes, and crimes against humanity, as set forth in the Nuremberg Charter.[18] The trial and the judgment at Nuremberg applied international law doctrines to impose criminal punishment on individuals for their commission of the crimes (not including rape and not including genocide) set forth and defined below in Article 6 of the Nuremberg Charter:

---

tection of victims of non-international armed conflicts (Protocol II). Protocol II was enacted on June 8, 1977. Protocol II art. 4(e)–(f) includes "rape, enforced prostitution, and any form of indecent assault ... slavery and the slave trade in all their forms."

16. *Id.*

17. The Statute of the ICTY, UN S.C. Res. 827 (1993), including rape as a crime against humanity in Art. 5(g). The Statute of the ICTR, UN S.C. Res. 955 (8 November 1994), including rape as a crime against humanity in Art. 3(g) and referring to rape as a violation of Additional Protocol II in Art. 4 (e): "outrages upon personal dignity, in particular humiliating and degrading treatment of rape, enforced prostitution and any form of indecent assault.".

18. Charter of the International Military Tribunal at Nuremberg, Agreement for the Prosecution and Punishment of the Major War Criminals of the European Axis, Aug. 8, 1945, 82 U.N.T.S, 279, *available at* http://www.gonzagajil.org/pdf/volume10/Nuremberg/Nuremberg%20Charter.pdf (Article 6 defines crimes against the peace (otherwise referred to as *jus ad bello*), war crimes, and crimes against humanity. It does not refer to rape as a crime, and it does not refer to "genocide." Crimes against humanity are similar to "genocide" and easier to prove because there is no need to prove "intent" for a crime against humanity.).

Article 6

The Tribunal established by the Agreement referred to in Article 1 hereof for the trial and punishment of the major war criminals of the European Axis countries shall have the power to try and punish persons who, acting in the interests of the European Axis countries, whether as individuals or as members of organizations, committed any of the following crimes.

The following acts, or any of them, are crimes coming within the jurisdiction of the Tribunal for which there shall be individual responsibility:

(a) *Crimes against Peace:* namely, planning, preparation, initiation or waging of a war of aggression, or a war in violation of international treaties, agreements or assurances, or participation in a common plan or conspiracy for the accomplishment of any of the foregoing;

(b) *War Crimes:* namely, violations of the laws or customs of war. Such violations shall include, but not be limited to, murder, ill-treatment or deportation to slave labor for any other purpose of civilian population of or in occupied territory, murder or ill-treatment of prisoners of war or persons on the seas, killing of hostages, plunder of public or private property, wanton destruction of cities, towns or villages, or devastation not justified by military necessity;

(c) *Crimes against Humanity:* namely, murder, extermination, enslavement, deportation, and other inhumane acts committed against any civilian population, before or during the war, or persecutions on political, racial or religious grounds in execution of or in connection with any crimes within the jurisdiction of the Tribunal, whether or not in violation of the domestic law of the country where perpetrated.

While the Nuremberg Tribunal did establish individual responsibility for crimes committed during armed conflict, the Nuremberg Charter did not include sexual violence or rape as crimes. Moreover, the Nuremberg Tribunal did not prosecute perpetrators of sexual violence or rape, even though the trial records contain extensive evidence of sexual violence and rape. These crimes were simply included as evidence of broader war crimes.

Another international military tribunal was established in Tokyo after the end of World War II. Like the Nuremberg Charter, sex crimes were not specifically detailed in the Tokyo Charter,[19] but the Tokyo Indictment did include allegations of gender-related crimes and, to a limited extent, expressly prosecuted rape crimes committed in conjunction with other crimes. However, the prolonged sexual enslavement of the "comfort women" in Japan was ignored by the Tokyo Tribunal, until the Women's International War Crimes Tribunal found Emperor Hirohito and other leaders guilty of crimes against humanity for the use of women as sexual slaves during the war. Nevertheless, Japan has not officially admitted to having committed these crimes.

5. Protection of Women in Armed Conflict

Do women have equal protection under the law of armed conflict? Combatants are predominantly male, and most women in war are non-combatants. One scholar, Judith

---

19. Charter of the International Military Tribunal for the Far East, Tokyo, 19 January 1946, *available at* http://www.isabelle-walther.de/texts/IMT%20Far%20East.htm.

Gail Gardam, has argued persuasively that the laws of armed conflict are gendered by their very nature.[20] For example, when hundreds of Iraqi civilian women and children were wounded and died after "precision bombing" of military targets occurred by the Coalition forces, this deplorable outcome "attracted almost no scholarly analysis and even less press coverage." While two US bomber pilots were convicted of hitting the wrong target and unintentionally killing nine British soldiers during the Gulf conflict, Gardam remarks that not many soldiers have been brought to justice for killing women non-combatants. Rape in warfare has been generally unreported and unrecorded, even though it has resulted in massive deaths and suffering to women since the beginning of time. During the war in Bosnia-Herzegovina and in Rwanda, rape was not only a weapon of war but an integral part of a system designed to ensure the maintenance of the subordination of women.

Rape and indiscriminate aerial bombardment are two practices in warfare that have had the most impact on women. The fact that rape has never been regarded as a method of warfare causing prohibited "unnecessary suffering" is arguably due to discrimination against women in wartime. Gardam concludes that "until recently, despite the scale on which it is perpetrated in warfare, rape rarely has been taken seriously as an offence."

6. Economic Sanctions, Women, Humanitarian Law, and Human Rights

Just as aerial bombardment may have good intentions but bad results by inflicting unnecessary pain and suffering on women and children, so, too, economic sanctions, which have become a frequent response to transgressions by States,[21] may cause undue harm to women and children.[22] The four basic principles of the laws of war include military necessity, proportionality, humanity, and distinction. Economic sanctions are arguably disproportionate to the purpose of the military objectives, lacking in distinction between combatants and non-combatants, and inhumane towards the most vulnerable populations including women and children civilians:[23]

"Violations of humanitarian norms have been invoked as a ground for resorting to sanctions in such cases as Iraq, for its treatment of the Kurdish population, Serb-controlled areas in the former Yugoslavia and the Federal Republic of Yugoslavia, for violations of humanitarian norms, and Haiti, for violation of human rights."[24] Nevertheless,

---

20. Judith Gail Gardam, *The Law of Armed Conflict: A Gendered Regime?, in* Reconceiving Reality: Women & International Law 171–75, 177–79, 183–88 (Dorinda Dallmeyer ed., Washington DC, Am. Soc'y of Int'l Law 1993). *See also* Jesse Ellison, *The Military's Secret Shame,* Newsweek, April 11, 2011, at 40 (discussing the frequency of men in the military raping other men in the ranks).

21. Christine Gray, International Law and the Use of Force 154–56 (2000).

22. *See* Theodor Meron, *Humanization of International Law in* Hague Academy of International Law Monographs, Chapter 8, 497–501, 502–09 (2006).

23. Theodor Meron, Henry's Wars and Shakespeare's Laws: Perspectives on the Law of War in the Later Middle Ages 112–13 (Clarendon Press Oxford 1993). Professor Theodor Meron served as a judge of the Appeals Chambers of the International Criminal Tribunal for Rwanda and the Former Yugoslavia (ICTR and ICTY). He also served as President of these Tribunals until 2005.

24. *Id.*

"any decision on economic sanctions must ... necessarily take human rights into account."[25] Economic sanctions have resulted in increased infant mortality rates, decreased access to clean drinking water, lack of access to medical care, and malnutrition, as well as to negative social and political consequences, including the development of a black market in basic goods, and the increased power of oppressive elites who control access to basic goods.[26] If sanctions harm mostly civilians and in particular women and children, how can they be justified as a response to transgressions by States?

With respect to human rights, there are humanitarian exemptions which allow essential items to pass through an economic sanctions program. For example, Article 23 of the Fourth Geneva Convention requires the free passage of medical supplies "intended only" for civilians and of essential foodstuffs and clothing for women and children. This exemption is not enough to protect innocent civilians during war, and the exemption is applicable only for international armed conflicts. The UN Committee on Economic, Social, and Cultural Rights has observed that "[i]t is commonly assumed that these exemptions ensure basic respect for economic, social, and cultural rights within the targeted country.... However, a number of recent United Nations and other studies which have analyzed the impact of sanctions, have concluded that these exemptions do not have this effect. Moreover, the exemptions are very limited in scope. They do not address, for example, the question of access to primary education, nor do they provide for repairs to infrastructures which are essential to provide clean water, adequate health care, etc."[27] In fact, two highly respected scholars, W. Michael Reisman and Douglas L. Stevick, stated that "[e]conomic sanctions may, however, cause greater collateral damage than military strikes."[28]

Lori Damrosch has proposed a solution to the problematic use of economic sanctions that appears to be in violation of basic human rights, especially for women and children. She believes that "a program of economic sanctions should not diminish the standard of living of a significant segment of society below the subsistence level."[29]

Examples of preferred types of economic sanctions which would minimally impact women and children are those imposed on the Haitian military leaders, restricting their personal ability to travel, or freezing assets, as was done in the case of Libya.[30] One can also limit sanctions to a geographic area, as was done in the Bosnian-Serb controlled areas in the former Yugoslavia,[31] but this limitation will not significantly relieve the suffering of women and children in the targeted area.

---

25. Hans-Peter Gasser, *Collective Economic Sanctions and International Humanitarian Law, An Enforcement Measure under the United Nations Charter and the Right of Civilians to Immunity: An Unavoidable Clash of Policy Goals?*, 56 Z.a.o.R.V, 871, 881 (1996).

26. *See* Theodor Meron, *supra* note 22, *citing* F. Gregory Gause III, *Getting It Backward on Iraq*, Foreign Affairs, May/June 1999, at 54, 58 [A-66]; John Mueller, *Sanctions of Mass Destruction*, Foreign Affairs, May/June 1999, at 43, 48–50.

27. Committee on Economic, Social, and Cultural Rights, General Comment No. 8 (1997): The relationship between economic sanctions and respect for economic, social, and cultural rights, UN Doc. E/C/12/1997/8, at paras. 4–5 (1997).

28. W. Michael Reisman & Douglas L. Stevick, *The Applicability of International Law Standards to United Nations Economic Sanctions Programmes*, 9 Eur. J. Int'l L. 86, 93–94 (1998).

29. Lori Fisler Damrosch, *The Civilian Impact of Economic Sanctions, in* Enforcing Restraint: Collective Intervention in Internal Conflicts 274, 281–82 (Lori Fisler Damrosch ed., 1993).

30. Adam Winkler, *Just Sanctions*, 21 Hum. Rts. Q. 133, 149–50 (1999).

31. *See* Damrosch, *supra* note 29, at 297.

7.   Rape and the *Akayesu* Case in the ICTR

Fifty years after World War II, a massive genocide occurred in Rwanda during the course of ninety days in 1994. The Hutu mayor of a small village called Taba, Jean-Paul Akayesu, knowingly permitted the mass rapes of Tutsi women in order to wipe out the Tutsis. As mayor, he controlled the police and could have stopped the attacks, yet he failed to do so. When Tutsi women sought refuge in the village's communal center, they were regularly taken by armed local militia and/or the police in order to endure humiliation, sexual violence, and beatings on or near the bureau communal premises. Many women were subjected to multiple acts of sexual violence by more than one attacker. The acts against these women were usually accompanied by threats of death or bodily harm.

The genocide in Rwanda might have been avoided if the United Nations, then under the leadership of Kofi Annan, would have intervened. The United Nations is bound by the UN Charter and by the doctrines of sovereignty and non-intervention. Humanitarian intervention is not officially permitted, even if intervention is exercised in order to prevent the kind of massive death and destruction that occurred in Rwanda where more than 800,000 civilians including women and children were raped, violated sexually, and tortured before they died.

When the International Criminal Tribunal for Rwanda was formed by UN Resolution 955[32] to prosecute the perpetrators of human rights violations and other war crimes committed in Rwanda, Akayesu was tried and convicted of genocide and crimes against humanity for his encouragement of the rapes of Tutsi women in Rwanda.[33] His case focuses attention on the element of "intent" required to prove genocide and on the "command responsibility" of a State official.

The *Prosecutor v. Akayesu*[34] decision of the ICTR is historically significant because it constitutes the first time a defendant was actually tried and convicted by an international tribunal for rape-based genocide. The ICTR developed the first international definition of rape and established that a criminal could receive multiple convictions for the same act. Thus, the perpetrator of a particular act like rape could be tried for genocide (requiring proof of intent and systematic occurrences), torture, and a crime against humanity.[35] The *Akayesu* case played an important role in the jurisprudence of crimes involving rape under international law, and it laid a foundation for further rape-related decisions in the International Criminal Tribunal for the Former Yugoslavia. Prosecutor Louise Arbour (of both the ICTY and the ICTR) stated, "... the judgment [in *Akayesu*] is truly remarkable in its breadth and vision, as well as in the detailed legal analysis on many issues that will be critical to the future of both the ICTR and the ICTY, in particular with respect to the law of sexual violence."[36]

---

32. UN Security Council Resolution 995, S/RES/955 (1994), *available at* http://www.un.org/ictr/english/Resolutions/955e.htm.

33. Prosecutor v. Akayesu, Judgment, Case No. ICTR-96-4 (ICTR Sept. 2, 1998) *reprinted* in 37 I.L.M. 1399, 1401 (1998) *available at* http://www.ictr.org/english/cases/Akayesu/judgement/akay001.htm [hereinafter Akayesu Judgment] (summarizing that Akayesu was indicted on 13 counts of genocide, crimes against humanity, and violations of the Geneva Conventions, including extermination, murder, torture, and rape).

34. *Id.*

35. *Id.* at 1406.

36. Press Release, ICTY Office of the Prosecutor, Statement by Justice Louise Arbour, ICTY Doc. CC/PIU/342-E (Sept. 4, 1998).

8. More on the Crime of Rape and the Jurisprudence of the ICTY

The *ad hoc* international tribunals have broadened the definitions of rape and sexual violence to successfully prosecute perpetrators.[37] The ICTY prosecuted Kunarac, Kovac, and Vukovic, the leaders of the Foca rape camp, for the crimes of rape and for enslavement which were found to be crimes against humanity. The *Celebici* case in the ICTY also established that superior officers can be criminally liable for rape crimes committed by their subordinates. *Celebici* also established that sexual violence may constitute torture if the sexual violence fits the definition of torture contained in the UN Convention against Torture.[38] The *Tadic, Furundzija, Krstic,* and *Kvocka* decisions of the ICTY involving sexual violence and rape are of major importance because they finally provide protection to the huge numbers of women sexually violated and raped during armed conflict.

9. The Crime of Rape in the Rome Statute of the ICC

The laws of war, which were defined in the Nuremberg Charter and in earlier humanitarian laws, were expanded in the Rome Statute establishing the permanent International Criminal Court (see Appendix), which is the first and only permanent and universal international crimes tribunal. The International Criminal Court (ICC) was established by the Rome Statute of the ICC[39] in 1998, and the Rome Statute[40] includes rape as a war crime and as a crime against humanity.[41]

In Article 7(6) rape and sexual violence are listed specifically as crimes against humanity: "Rape, sexual slavery, enforced prostitution, forced pregnancy, enforced sterilization, or any other form of sexual violence of comparable gravity." The Rome Statute includes rape under the following categories: "(b) Other serious violations of the laws and customs applicable *in international armed* conflict, within the established framework of international law, namely, any of the following acts: ... (xxii) Committing rape, sexual slavery, enforced prostitution, forced pregnancy, as defined in article 7, paragraph 2(f), enforced sterilization, or any other form of sexual violence also constituting a grave breach of the Geneva Conventions." Rape is again proscribed in Section (e)(vi) of the Rome Statute establishing the ICC, which applies to: "Other serious violations of the laws and customs applicable in armed conflicts *not of an international character,* within the established framework of international law...." Article (e)(vi) prohibits "Committing rape, sexual slavery, enforced prostitution, forced pregnancy, as

---

37. Kelly D. Askin, *Prosecuting Wartime Rape and Other Gender-Related Crimes under International Law: Extraordinary Advances, Enduring Obstacles,* 21 Berkeley J. Int'l L. 288, 307 (2003).

38. UN Convention against Torture and Other Forms of Cruel, Inhuman or Degrading Treatment or Punishment 1984, G.A. Res. 39/46, Annex, A/39/51.

39. Rome Statute of the International Criminal Court, Rome, (Jul. 17, 1998), A/CONF.183/9, *available at* http://www.icc-cpi.int/NR/rdonlyres/EA9AEFF7-5752-4F84-BE94-0A655EB30E16/0/Rome_Statute_English.pdf. The United States is not a signatory to the Rome Statute and, therefore, is not a member of the ICC.

40. William A. Schabas, An Introduction to the International Criminal Court (2011).

41. *See* M. Cherif Bassiouni, Crimes against Humanity: Historical Evolution and Contemporary Application (Leila Nadya Sadat ed., 2011); Forging a Convention for Crimes against Humanity (Leila Nadya Sadat ed., 2011).

defined in article 7, paragraph 2(f), enforced sterilization, and any other form of sexual violence also constituting a serious violation of article 3 common to the four Geneva Conventions."

The United States has refused to ratify the ICC. In this chapter we present Kenneth Roth's article discussing reasons "Why the US Is Not a Member of the International Criminal Court." The Rome Statute establishing the ICC defines the crime of aggression, war crimes, crimes against humanity, and genocide, and it specifically lists rape and sexual violence as a war crime and as a crime against humanity. The Rome Statute adopts provisions and protections specifically for women. Despite the principle of complementarity in which a State can choose first to try war criminals in its own national courts, the United States has refused to become a member of the International Criminal Court, and Kenneth Roth examines the validity of US objections to the Rome Statute.

In this chapter Patricia Viseur Sellers, the Legal Advisor for Gender-related Crimes in the Office of the Prosecutor for the ICTY, discusses the need to charge individuals for the collective sexual violence that occurred in Yugoslavia. Thus, the former Serbian President Slobodan Milosevic, members of the Bosnian-Serb Presidency, and the infamous Biljana Plavsic, the woman who designed the discriminatory "ethnic cleansing" campaign in the former Yugoslavia, were all indicted and prosecuted at the ICTY (with the exception of Milosevic who died just prior to his conviction). Sellers discusses the two types of individual's liability that exist for collective sexual violence and rape that were committed systematically during the Bosnian-Herzegovinian war. These are direct criminal individual responsibility and indirect or superior individual responsibility. The traditional military doctrine of command responsibility is the most commonly used form of indirect individual liability.

10. Truth and Reconciliation Commissions

During the ten-year civil war in Sierra Leone, an overwhelming number of women and girls suffered from sexual abuse, rape, and assault. After the conflict, the Truth and Reconciliation Commission (TRC) and the Special Court for Sierra Leone were set up to address the issues of violence against women. Truth and Reconciliation Commissions help victims and perpetrators relate the details of the atrocities they suffered or committed during the conflict. But Truth and Reconciliation Commissions alone cannot provide justice to the victims who inevitably seek revenge and retribution. During the TRC Special Thematic Hearings on Women in 2003, testimony was presented by women who had suffered sexual violations. The Truth and Reconciliation Steering Committee Report on Women and Armed Conflict in Sierra Leone contained in this chapter provides vivid details about terrorizing abduction, mutilation, detention, assault, torture, forced drugging, killing, amputation, forced cannibalism, sexual violation, rape, sexual slavery, and other horrendous crimes perpetrated particularly on women and children.

B. Women's Human Rights and the Crime of Rape in the Jurisprudence of the ICTR

1. *Prosecutor v. Akayesu*

International Criminal Tribunal for Rwanda, 1998
Trial Chamber Judgment, Case No. ICTR-96-4-T[42]

[The trial of Jean-Paul Akayesu resulted in the first conviction for genocide by an international court.] The indictment charged Akayesu, a Hutu, with genocide, crimes against humanity, and violations of Article 3 common to the Geneva Conventions, punishable under Articles 2–4 of the ICTR Statute. All alleged acts took place in Rwanda during 1994. The country is divided into 11 prefectures, which are subdivided into communes placed under the authority of bourgmestres (mayors). From April 1993 to June 1994, Akayesu served as bourgmestre of the Taba commune.

There were 15 counts in the indictment. Some illustrative charges follow: (1) At least 2,000 Tutsis were killed in Taba from April to June 1994. Killings were so open and widespread that the defendant 'must have known about them,' but despite his authority and responsibility, he never attempted to prevent the killings. (2) Hundreds of displaced Tutsi civilians sought refuge at the bureau communal. Females among them were regularly taken by the armed local militia and subjected to sexual violence, including multiple rapes. Civilians were frequently murdered on or near the communal premises. Akayesu knew of these events and at times [he] was present during their commission. That presence and his failure to attempt to prevent actually 'encouraged these activities.' (3) At meetings, Akayesu 'urged the population to eliminate accomplices of the RPF, which was understood by those present to mean Tutsis.... The killing of Tutsis in Taba began shortly after the meeting.' He also 'named at least three prominent Tutsis ... who had to be killed because of their alleged relationships with the RPF.' Two of them were soon killed. (4) Akayesu ordered and participated in the killing of three brothers, and took eight detained men from the bureau communal and ordered militia members to kill them. (5) He ordered local people to kill intellectual and influential people. On his instructions, five secondary school teachers were killed.

The Trial Chamber found it 'necessary to say, however briefly, something about the history of Rwanda, beginning from the pre-colonial period up to 1994.' Prior to and during colonial rule (first under Germany, and from 1917 until independence under Belgium), Rwanda was an advanced monarchy ruled by the monarch's representatives drawn from the Tutsi nobility. The Trial Chamber further explained:

> In those days, the distinction between the Hutu and Tutsi was based on lineage rather than ethnicity. Indeed, the demarcation line was blurred: one could move from one status to another, as one became rich or poor, or even through marriage.

> Both German and Belgian colonial authorities, if only at the outset as far as the latter are concerned, relied on an elite essentially composed of people who referred to themselves as Tutsi, a choice which, according to Dr. Alison Desforges, was born of racial or even racist considerations. In the minds of the colonizers,

---

42. Prosecutor v. Akayesu, Trial Chamber Judgment, International Criminal Tribunal for Rwanda, 1998, Case No. ICTR-96-4-T.

the Tutsi looked more like them, because of their height and color, and were, therefore, more intelligent and better equipped to govern.

In the early 1930s, Belgian authorities introduced a permanent distinction by dividing the population into three groups which they called ethnic groups, with the Hutu representing about 84% of the population, while the Tutsi (about 15%) and Twa (about 1%) accounted for the rest. In line with this division, it became mandatory for every Rwandan to carry an identity card mentioning his or her ethnicity....

The Chamber explained that the Tutsi were more willing to be converted to Christianity; hence the Church too supported their monopoly of power....

When the Tutsi led campaigns for independence, the allegiance of the colonizer shifted to the Hutu. In the 1950s, elections were held and political parties were formed. The Hutu held a clear majority in voting power. Violence broke out between Hutu and Tutsi. Independence was attained in 1962. In 1975, a one-party system was instituted under (Hutu) President Habyarimana, whose policies became increasingly anti-Tutsi through a discriminatory quota system and other methods. In 1991, following violence and growing pressures, Habyarimana accepted a multi-party system.

Many Tutsi in exile formed a political organization and a military wing, the Rwandan Patriotic Army (RPA). Their aim was to return to Rwanda. Violence, negotiations, and accords led to the participation of the Tutsi political organization (RPF) in the government institutions. Hard-line Hutu formed a radical political party, more extremist than Habyarimana. There were growing extremist calls for elimination of the Tutsi.

The Arusha accords between the Government and the RPF in 1993 brought temporary relief from the threat of war. The climate worsened with assassinations, and the accords were denounced. Habyarimana died in an air crash, of unknown cause, in April 1994. The Rwandan army, Presidential Guard and militia immediately started killing Tutsi, as well as Hutu who were sympathetic to the Arusha accords and to power-sharing between Tutsi and Hutu. Belgian soldiers and a small UN peacekeeping force were withdrawn from the country. RPF troops resumed open war against Rwandan armed forces. The killing campaign against the Tutsi reached its zenith in a matter of weeks, and continued to July. The estimated dead in the conflict at that time, overwhelmingly Tutsi, ranged from 500,000 to 1,000,000....

112. As regards the massacres which took place in Rwanda between April and July 1994, as detailed above in the chapter on the historical background to the Rwandan tragedy, the question before this Chamber is whether they constitute genocide. Indeed, it was felt in some quarters ... that the tragic events which took place in Rwanda were only part of the war between the Rwandan Armed Forces (the RAF) and the Rwandan Patriotic Front (RPF)....

118. In the opinion of the Chamber, there is no doubt that considering their undeniable scale, their systematic nature and their atrociousness, the massacres were aimed at exterminating the group that was targeted.... In this connection, Alison Desforges, an expert witness, in her testimony before this Chamber ... stated as follows: "on the basis of the statements made by certain political leaders, on the basis of songs and slogans popular among the Interahamwe, I believe that these people had the intention of completely wiping out the Tutsi from Rwanda so that—as they said on certain occasions—their children, later on , would not know what a Tutsi looked like, unless they referred to history books." ...

119. ... Dr. Zachariah also testified that the Achilles' tendons of many wounded persons were cut to prevent them from fleeing. In the opinion of the Chamber, this demonstrates the resolve of the perpetrators of these massacres not to spare any Tutsi....

120. Dr. Alison Desforges testified that many Tutsi bodies were often systematically thrown into the Nyabarongo river, a tributary of the Nile. Indeed, this has been corroborated by several images shown to the Chamber throughout the trial....

121. ... [E]ven newborn babies were not spared. Even pregnant women, including those of Hutu origin, were killed on the grounds that the foetuses in their wombs were fathered by Tutsi men, for in a patrilineal society like Rwanda, the child belongs to the father's group of origin....

122. In light of the foregoing, it is now appropriate for the Chamber to consider the issue of specific intent that is required for genocide (*mens rea* or *dolus specialis*). In other words, it should be established that the above-mentioned acts were targeted at a particular group as such. In this respect also, many consistent and reliable testimonies ... agree on the fact that it was the Tutsi as members of an ethnic group ... who were targeted during the massacres.

123. ... [T]he propaganda campaign conducted before and during the tragedy by the audiovisual media, ... or the print media, like the Kangura newspaper ... overtly called for the killing of Tutsi, who were considered as the accomplices of the RPF and accused of plotting to take over the power lost during the revolution of 1959....

126. Consequently, the Chamber concludes from all the foregoing that genocide was, indeed, committed in Rwanda in 1994 against the Tutsi as a group....

127. ... [A]s to whether the tragic events that took place in Rwanda in 1994 occurred solely within the context of the conflict between the RAF and the RPF, the Chamber replies in the negative, since it holds that the genocide did indeed take place against the Tutsi group, alongside the conflict. The execution of this genocide was probably facilitated by the conflict, in the sense that the fighting against the RPF forces was used as a pretext for the propaganda inciting genocide against the Tutsi....

128. ... The accused himself stated during his initial appearance before the Chamber, when recounting a conversation he had with one RAF officer and ... a leader of the Interahamwe, that the acts perpetrated by the Interahamwe against Tutsi civilians were not considered by the RAF officer to be of a nature to help the government armed forces in the conflict with the RPF.... The Chamber's opinion is that the genocide was organized and planned not only by members of the RAF, but also by the political forces who were behind the "Hutu-power," that it was executed essentially by civilians including the armed militia and even ordinary citizens, and above all, that the majority of the Tutsi victims were non-combatants, including thousands of women and children, even fetuses....

Factual Findings

[The Chamber noted that in addition to witnesses, it would take 'judicial notice' of UN reports extensively documenting the massacres of 1994. Its listing included reports of a Commission of Experts established by a Security Council resolution, of a special rapporteur of the Secretary General, and of the High Commissioner for Human Rights. Note that the 'factual findings' *infra* are relevant to determining whether the conditions stated in several articles of the ICTR Statute were met.] ...

178. The Chamber now considers paragraph 12 of the Indictment, which alleges the responsibility of the Accused, his knowledge of the killings which took place in Taba between 7 April and the end of June 1994, and his failure to attempt to prevent these killings or to call for assistance from regional or national authorities....

188. The Chamber recognizes the difficulties a bourgmestre encountered in attempting to save lives of Tutsi in the period in question. Prosecution witness R, who was the

bourgmestre of another commune, ... He averred that a bourgmestre could do nothing openly to combat the killings after that date or he would risk being killed; what little he could do had to be done clandestinely. The Defense case is that this is precisely what the accused did.

189. Defense witnesses, DAAX, DAX, DCX, DBB and DCC, confirm that the accused failed to prevent killings after 18 April 1994 and expressed the opinion that it was not possible for him to do anything with ten communal policemen at his disposal against more than a hundred Interahamwe....

449. ... Chamber finds that there is sufficient credible evidence to establish beyond a reasonable doubt that during the events of 1994, Tutsi girls and women were subjected to sexual violence, beaten, and killed on or near the bureau communal premises, as well as elsewhere in the commune of Taba.... Hundreds of Tutsi, mostly women and children, sought refuge at the bureau communal during this period and many rapes took place on or near the premises of the bureau communal.... Witness JJ was also raped repeatedly on two separate occasions in the cultural center on the premises of the bureau communal, once in a group of fifteen girls and women and once in a group of ten girls and women.... The Chamber notes that much of the sexual violence took place in front of large numbers of people, and that all of it was directed against Tutsi women....

452. On the basis of the evidence set forth herein, the Chamber finds beyond a reasonable doubt that the Accused had reason to know and in fact knew that sexual violence was taking place on or near the premises of the bureau communal, and that women were being taken away from the bureau communal and sexually violated. There is no evidence that the Accused took any measures to prevent acts of sexual violence or to punish the perpetrators of sexual violence. In fact there is evidence that the Accused ordered, instigated and otherwise aided and abetted sexual violence.... On the two occasions Witness JJ was brought to the cultural center of the bureau communal to be raped. She and the group of girls and women with her were taken past the Accused, on the way. On the first occasion he was looking at them, and on the second occasion he was standing at the entrance to the cultural center. On this second occasion, he said, "Never ask me again what a Tutsi woman tastes like." Witness JJ described the Accused in making these statements as "talking as if someone were encouraging a player." More generally she stated that the Accused was the one "supervising" the acts of rape....

The Law

471. The Accused is charged under Article 6(1) of the Statute of the Tribunal with individual criminal responsibility for the crimes alleged in the Indictment. With regard to Counts ... on sexual violence, the Accused is charged additionally, or alternatively, under Article 6(3) ... Article 6(1) sets forth the basic principles of individual criminal liability, which are undoubtedly common to most national criminal jurisdictions. Article 6(3), by contrast, constitutes something of an exception to the principles articulated in Article 6(1), as it derives from military law, namely the principle of the liability of a commander for the acts of his subordinates or "command responsibility." ...

488. There are varying views regarding the *mens rea* required for command responsibility....

489. ... [I]t is certainly proper to ensure that there has been malicious intent, or, at least, ensure that negligence was so serious as to be tantamount to acquiescence or even malicious intent.

490. As to whether the form of individual criminal responsibility referred to Article 6(3) of the Statute applies to persons in positions of both military and civilian authority, it should be noted that during the Tokyo trials, certain civilian authorities were convicted of war crimes under this principle. Hirota, former Foreign Minister of Japan, was convicted of atrocities—including mass rape—committed in the "rape of Nanking," under a count which charged that he had "recklessly disregarded their legal duty by virtue of their offices to take adequate steps to secure the observance and prevent breaches of the law and customs of war." ...

It should, however, be noted that Judge Röling strongly dissented from this finding, and held that Hirota should have been acquitted. Concerning the principle of command responsibility as applied to a civilian leader, Judge Röling stated that:

> Generally speaking, a Tribunal should be very careful in holding civil government officials responsible for the behavior of the army in the field. Moreover, the Tribunal is here to apply the general principles of law as they exist with relation to the responsibility for omissions. Considerations of both law and policy, of both justice and expediency, indicate that this responsibility should only be recognized in a very restricted sense.

491. The Chamber therefore finds that in the case of civilians, the application of the principle of individual criminal responsibility, enshrined in Article 6(3), to civilians remains contentious. Against this background, the Chamber holds that it is appropriate to assess on a case by case basis the power of authority actually devolved upon the Accused in order to determine whether or not he had the power to take all necessary and reasonable measures to prevent the commission of the alleged crimes or to punish the perpetrators thereof.

Genocide

498. Genocide is distinct from other crimes in as much as it embodies a special intent or *dolus specialis*. Special intent of a crime is the specific intention, required as a constitutive element of the crime, which demands that the perpetrator clearly seeks to produce the act charged. Thus, the special intent in the crime of genocide lies in "the intent to destroy, in whole or in part, a national, ethnical, racial or religious group, as such." ...

523. On the issue of determining the offender's specific intent, the Chamber considers that intent is a mental factor which is difficult, even impossible, to determine. This is the reason why, in the absence of a confession from the accused, his intent can be inferred from a certain number of presumptions of fact. The Chamber considers that it is possible to deduce the genocidal intent inherent in a particular act charged from the general context of the perpetration of other culpable acts systematically directed against that same group, whether these acts were committed by the same offender or by others. Other factors, such as the scale of atrocities committed, their general nature, in a region or a country, or furthermore, the fact of deliberately and systematically targeting victims on account of their membership of a particular group, while excluding the members of other groups, can enable the Chamber to infer the genocidal intent of a particular act.

524. Trial Chamber I of the International Criminal Tribunal for the former Yugoslavia also stated that the specific intent of the crime of genocide:

> may be inferred from a number of facts such as the general political doctrine which gave rise to the acts possibly covered by the definition in Article 4, or the repetition of destructive and discriminatory acts. The intent may also be inferred from the perpetration of acts which violate, or which the perpetrators them-

selves consider to violate, the very foundation of the group—acts which are not in themselves covered by the list in Article 4(2) but which are committed as part of the same pattern of conduct....

Complicity in Genocide

525. Under Article 2(3)(e) of the Statute, the Chamber shall have the power to prosecute persons who have committed complicity in genocide....

530. Consequently, the Chamber is of the opinion that in order for an accused to be found guilty of complicity in genocide, it must, first of all, be proven beyond a reasonable doubt that the crime of genocide has, indeed, been committed....

547. Consequently, where a person is accused of aiding and abetting, planning, preparing or executing genocide, it must be proven that such a person acted with specific genocidal intent, *i.e.,* the intent to destroy, in whole or in part, a national, ethnical, racial or religious group as such, whereas, as stated above, there is no such requirement to establish accomplice liability in genocide....

[Crimes against Humanity—Rape and Other Inhuman Acts]

691. The Tribunal has found that the Accused had reason to know and in fact knew that acts of sexual violence were occurring on or near the premises of the bureau communal and that he took no measures to prevent these acts or punish the perpetrators of them. The Tribunal notes that it is only in consideration of Counts 13, 14, and 15 that the Accused is charged with individual criminal responsibility under Section 6(3) of its Statute.... Although the evidence supports a finding that a superior/subordinate relationship existed between the Accused and the Interahamwe who were at the bureau communal, the Tribunal notes that there is no allegation in the Indictment that the Interahamwe, who are referred to as "armed local militia," were subordinates of the Accused. This relationship is a fundamental element of the criminal offence set forth in Article 6(3). The amendment of the Indictment with additional charges pursuant to Article 6(3) could arguably be interpreted as implying an allegation of the command responsibility required by Article 6(3). In fairness to the Accused, the Tribunal will not make this inference. Therefore, the Tribunal finds that it cannot consider the criminal responsibility of the Accused under Article 6(3)....

694. The Tribunal finds, under Article 6(1) of its Statute, that the Accused, having had reason to know that sexual violence was occurring, aided and abetted the following acts of sexual violence, by allowing them to take place on or near the premises of the bureau communal and by facilitating the commission of such sexual violence through his words of encouragement in other acts of sexual violence which, by virtue of his authority, sent a clear signal of official tolerance for sexual violence, without which these acts would not have taken place....

[Genocide and Complicity in Genocide]

704. The Chamber finds that, as pertains to the acts alleged in paragraph 12, it has been established that, throughout the period covered in the Indictment, Akayesu, in his capacity as bourgmestre, was responsible for maintaining law and public order in the commune of Taba and that he had effective authority over the communal police. Moreover, as "leader" of Taba commune, of which he was one of the most prominent figures, the inhabitants respected him and followed his orders. Akayesu himself admitted before the Chamber that he had the power to assemble the population and that they obeyed his instructions. It has also been proven that a very large number of Tutsi were killed in Taba between 7 April and the end of June 1994, while Akayesu was bourgmestre of the Com-

mune. Knowing of such killings, he opposed them and attempted to prevent them only until 18 April 1994, date after which he not only stopped trying to maintain law and order in his commune, but was also present during the acts of violence and killings, and sometimes even gave orders himself for bodily or mental harm to be caused to certain Tutsi, and endorsed and even ordered the killing of several Tutsi.

705. In the opinion of the Chamber, the said acts indeed incur the individual criminal responsibility of Akayesu for having ordered, committed, or otherwise aided and abetted in the preparation or execution of the killing of and causing serious bodily or mental harm to members of the Tutsi group. Indeed, the Chamber holds that the fact that Akayesu, as a local authority, failed to oppose such killings and serious bodily or mental harm constituted a form of tacit encouragement, which was compounded by being present to such criminal acts....

728. ... The Chamber is of the opinion that it is possible to infer the genocidal intention that presided over the commission of a particular act, *inter alia*, from all acts or utterances of the accused, or from the general context in which other culpable acts were perpetrated systematically against the same group, regardless of whether such other acts were committed by the same perpetrator or even by other perpetrators....

731. With regard, particularly, to ... rape and sexual violence, the Chamber wishes to underscore the fact that in its opinion, they constitute genocide in the same way as any other act as long as they were committed with the specific intent to destroy, in whole or in part, a particular group, targeted as such. Indeed, rape and sexual violence certainly constitute infliction of serious bodily and mental harm on the victims and are even, according to the Chamber, one of the worst ways of inflicting harm on the victim as he or she suffers both bodily and mental harm. In light of all the evidence before it, the Chamber is satisfied that the acts of rape and sexual violence described above, were committed solely against Tutsi women, many of whom were subjected to the worst public humiliation, mutilated, and raped several times, often in public, in the Bureau Communal premises or in other public places, and often by more than one assailant. These rapes resulted in physical and psychological destruction of Tutsi women, their families and their communities. Sexual violence was an integral part of the process of destruction, specifically targeting Tutsi women and specifically contributing to their destruction and to the destruction of the Tutsi group as a whole.

732. The rape of Tutsi women was systematic and was perpetrated against all Tutsi women and solely against them. A Tutsi woman, married to a Hutu, testified before the Chamber that she was not raped because her ethnic background was unknown. As part of the propaganda campaign geared to mobilizing the Hutu against the Tutsi, the Tutsi women were presented as sexual objects. Indeed, the Chamber was told, for an example, that before being raped and killed, Alexia, who was the wife of the Professor, Ntereye, and her two nieces, were forced by the Interahamwe to undress and ordered to run and do exercises "in order to display the thighs of Tutsi women." The Interahamwe who raped Alexia said, as he threw her on the ground and got on top of her, "let us now see what the vagina of a Tutsi woman tastes like." As stated above, Akayesu himself, speaking to the Interahamwe who were committing the rapes, said to them: "don't ever ask again what a Tutsi woman tastes like." This sexualized representation of ethnic identity graphically illustrates that Tutsi women were subjected to sexual violence because they were Tutsi. Sexual violence was a step in the process of destruction of the Tutsi group—destruction of the spirit, of the will to live, and of life itself.

733. On the basis of the substantial testimonies brought before it, the Chamber finds that in most cases, the rapes of Tutsi women in Taba, were accompanied with the intent

to kill those women. Many rapes were perpetrated near mass graves where the women were taken to be killed. A victim testified that Tutsi women caught could be taken away by peasants and men with the promise that they would be collected later to be executed. Following an act of gang rape, a witness heard Akayesu say "tomorrow they will be killed" and they were actually killed. In this respect, it appears clearly to the Chamber that the acts of rape and sexual violence, as other acts of serious bodily and mental harm committed against the Tutsi, reflected the determination to make Tutsi women suffer and to mutilate them even before killing them, the intent being to destroy the Tutsi group while inflicting acute suffering on its members in the process.

734. In light of the foregoing, the Chamber finds firstly that the acts described *supra* are indeed acts as enumerated in Article 2(2) of the Statute, which constitute the factual elements of the crime of genocide, namely the killings of Tutsi or the serious bodily and mental harm inflicted on the Tutsi. The Chamber is further satisfied beyond reasonable doubt that these various acts were committed by Akayesu with the specific intent to destroy the Tutsi group, as such....

[Akayesu appealed the trial Chamber decision, though primarily on evidentiary and procedural grounds. In a decision issued in 2001, the Appeals Chamber affirmed the guilty verdict of all counts.]

C. Women's Rights and Sexual Violence

1. Patricia Viseur Sellers,[43] *Individual(s') Liability for Collective Sexual Violence*[44]

War, systematic attacks against civilians, or the eruption of genocide entail and breed collective criminal conduct. Collective conduct denotes crimes dependent upon the coordinated or simultaneous acts of multiple perpetrators and crimes that often ensnare multiple victims, notably massacres, large-scale deportations, or prolonged civilian detention. Whether by sexual threats or actual sexual assaults, the susceptibility of sexual violence to collective conduct seems predictable. The individuals eventually charged and tried for these crimes, in truth, only hint at the number of perpetrators.

For accused who appear before the International Criminal Tribunal for the Former Yugoslavia (ICTY),[45] the Statute[46] obliges the Prosecutor to prove, regardless of the collective nature of the acts, the underlying crime. Accordingly, Tribunal judgments and decisions have defined and interpreted the elements of crimes accepted as serious violations of international humanitarian law. The Trial Chambers and the Appeal Chamber have

---

43. Ms. Seller is the Legal Advisor for Gender-related Crimes in the Office of the Prosecutor for the ICTY. The opinions expressed in this article are solely those of the author and are not intended to represent the official views or policies of the Office of the Prosecutor of the ICTY, nor those of the United Nations.

44. Patricia Viseur Sellers, *Individual(s') Liability for Collective Sexual Violence, in* GENDER HUMAN RIGHTS 153–94 (Karen Knop ed., Oxford University Press 2004).

45. S.C. Res. 827 (May 25,1993) (establishing the International Criminal Tribunal for the Former Yugoslavia).

46. Statute of the ICTY, attached to the report of the Secretary General Pursuant to Paragraph 2 of the Security Council Resolution 808, UN Doc. S/25704, Annex (1993), *reprinted in* 32 I.L.M. 1159 (1993).

germinated a similar, yet less acknowledged examination of an accused's form of participation in a crime, otherwise known as the individual mode of liability.

Security Council Resolution 808[47] recalled that persons who commit or order the commission of grave breaches of the Geneva Conventions[48] are individually responsible or liable in respect of such breaches. Flowing from the international law principle of individual responsibility for international crimes, Article 6 of the ICTY Statute sets forth the Tribunal's competence *ratione personae* or personal jurisdiction. The ICTY Appeals Chamber has consequently ruled that no one who participates in a serious violation of humanitarian law escapes the Tribunal's jurisdiction.[49]

The Tribunal limits attribution of personal culpability to natural persons, parties, associations, or groups.[50] Nevertheless, personal jurisdiction is triggered for individuals accused who, by means of formal or informal groups, participate in collective criminal conduct.[51]

An accused's participation or liability must satisfy the specificities of Article 7(1) or (3) of the ICTY Statute. Two broad types of individual liability exist: direct criminal responsibility, and indirect or superior responsibility. Direct responsibility implicates any accused who has planned, instigated, committed, ordered, or aided or abetted the execution of crimes within the jurisdiction of the Statute. Indirect criminal responsibility attributes liability to a person in a position of superior authority, whether military, political, business, or any hierarchical status, for acts directly committed by his or her subordinates. The traditional military doctrine of command responsibility is the most commonly used mode of indirect liability.

Proof of the form of liability fulfills a crucial part in constructing an accused's individual criminal responsibility. Direct and indirect liability apply to all crimes within the competence *ratione materiae* or subject matter jurisdiction listed in the provisions of Articles 2–5 of the ICTY Statute. Either form of liability amply covers justiciable sexual assault conduct.

The issuance of sound, reasoned sexual assault jurisprudence is an acknowledged achievement of the ICTY.[52] In the 'early days' of the 1990s, reservations persisted as to whether the prohibition of rape, strikingly absent from the grave breach provisions of each Geneva Convention, constituted a *serious* violation of the laws and customs of war, that compelled prosecution. Upon deliberation of sexual assault evidence, the ICTY Trial and Appeals Chambers have repeatedly confirmed that several acts of sexual violence, not just the enumeration of rape as a crime against humanity, were serious violations of in-

---

47. S.C. Res. 808, 22 February 1993.

48. The four Geneva Conventions, *signed* Aug. 12, 1949, *in force* Oct. 21, 1950, are the Geneva Convention (I) for the Amelioration of the Condition of the Wounded and Sick in Armed Forces in the Field, 75 U.N.T.S. 31; Geneva Convention (II) for the Amelioration of the Condition of the Wounded, Sick and Shipwrecked Members of Armed Forces at Sea, 75 U.N.T.S. 85; Geneva Convention (III) Relative to the Treatment of Prisoners of War, 75 U.N.T.S. 135; and Geneva Convention (IV) Relative to the Protection of Civilian Persons in Time of War, 75 U.N.T.S. 287.

49. Prosecutor v. Dusko Tadic, Decision on the Defence Motion for Interlocutory Appeal on Jurisdiction, 2 October 1995, Case No. IT-94-AR72, para. 92 (hereinafter Tadic Jurisdiction Decision).

50. Report of the Secretary-General Pursuant to Paragraph 2 of Security Council Resolution 808, UN Doc. S/25704 (1993), *reprinted in* 32 I.L.M. 1159 (1993) (hereinafter Report).

51. *Id.* at para. 51. Paragraph 51 concludes by stating that: "[T]he ordinary meaning of the term 'persona; responsibility for serious violations of international humanitarian law' would be natural persons to the exclusion of juridical persons."

52. J.G. Gardam and M. J. Jarvis, *Women, Armed Conflict, and International Law* (2001), at 208–18.

ternational humanitarian law and, thus, within the subject matter jurisdiction of the Statute.

In a like fashion, the Trial Chambers and Appeals Chamber have confirmed direct liability to encompass a form of criminal liability not expressed in Article 7(1). Co-perpetration or joint criminal enterprise is a form of direct liability based upon a perpetrator undertaking to participate in criminal conduct with a plurality of actors. In regard to sexual assault evidence, this implied form of liability emerged starting with the cryptic language of common purpose in the first ICTY judgment, *Prosecutor v. Tadic*,[53] and with the subsequent differentiation of a co-perpetrator from an aider and abettor in the *Prosecutor v. Furundzija* decision.[54] It progressed through the defining *Tadic*[55] and *Furundzija*[56] appeal judgments and then received noteworthy application in the *Krstic*[57] and *Kvocka*[58] trial judgments.

In this 'midlife' stage of the Tribunal's existence,[59] the Prosecutor has increasingly indicted superiors in positions of military or political leadership for collective criminal conduct. The indictments against former Serbian President, Slobodan Milosevic, and the former members of the Bosnian-Serb Presidency, Momcilo Krajisnik and Ms. Biljana Plavsic, allege they were co-perpetrators who, with other participants, ethnically cleansed the former Yugoslavia. The primary mode of liability is joint criminal enterprise, governed by Article 7(1) of the ICTY Statute.

D. Truth and Reconciliation Commissions

1. Truth and Reconciliation Commission of Sierre Leone, *Women and the Armed Conflict in Sierra Leone*[60]

...

Abduction

211. A former abductee of the RUF testified to the Commission of her experiences:

> I was forcefully conscripted into the rebel army to become a sex instrument for the rebel commanders, though I was a virgin ... during our stay in the camp, we were visited by Corporal Foday Sankoh, whom we referred to, as "Popay" ...

---

53. Prosecutor v. Tadic, Judgment, Case No. IT-94-1-T 7 May 1997, 536 [hereinafter Tadic Judgment].

54. Prosecutor v. Anto Furundzija, Judgment, Case No. IT-95-17/1-T, 10 December 1998 [hereinafter Furundzija Judgment].

55. Prosecutor v. Tadic, Judgment, Case No. IT-94-1-A, 15 July 1999, 536 [hereinafter Tadic Appeal Judgment].

56. Prosecutor v. Furundzija, Judgment, Case No. IT-95-17/-A, 21 July 2000 [hereinafter Furundzija Appeal Judgment].

57. Prosecutor v. Krstic, Judgment, Case No. IT-98-33-T, 2 August 2001, para. 2 [hereinafter Krstic Judgment].

58. Prosecutor v. Kvocka *et al.*, Judgment, Case No. IT-98-30/&-T, 2 November 2001 [hereinafter Kvocka Judgment].

59. *See* the minutes from the S.C. 4429th Meeting, 27 November 2001, S/PV.4429 (discussing the Prosecutor's exit strategy for the ICTY and the ICTR).

60. Truth and Reconciliation Commission of Sierra Leone, *Women and the Armed Conflict in Sierra Leone*, in TRUTH HURTS BUT WAR HURTS MORE 85–162, Vol. Three B, Chapter Three.

My duties were to prepare food and to satisfy my "blush husband" anytime he needs me. After six months my "blush husband" Captain Kemokai left me to fight ... he got missing in action. At that time I was four months pregnant ... Later I became wife to another Commander named Mohammed. As usual, my duties were to prepare food and satisfy him sexually, any time he needs me. ...[61]

Mutilation

218. Women and girls abducted were compelled to remain with the fighting forces throughout the conflict. It was only with disarmament that they were able to leave. A number of women and girls told the Commission how they tried to escape. Punishment was harsh if they were recaptured. They suffered even further when the fighting force to which they belonged deliberately marked them on their chests by carving the initials of the particular fighting force on it. This was a deliberate strategy on the part of the RUF and the AFRC.[62] Marking abductees in this way prevented their escape, as to run the risk of being identified as a member of the RUF or AFRC would be to risk death. A girl who was 13 years old at the time she was abducted by the RUF told the Commission her story:

> I was captured together with five other girls and taken to their base at Mattru Jong. I was captured by a man called "Delawey" (a Sierra Leonean), who also had been captured and sent to Liberia for training ... When we attempted to escape, we were caught by another set of RUF members, who beat us and brought us back to the base. At the base we were trained to become fighters for six months ... If anyone becomes tired they shot the person dead. ... After the training, they forced people to take up guns and attack villages. ... All those who attempted to run were caught and labeled RUF with knife, blade or a very sharp stick. Also in the bush, I got a man whom I gave birth for. He is still my husband. ...[63]

Assault

243. Life for women with the armed groups was brutal. They were treated savagely and were constantly humiliated. Assaults and beatings were commonplace and were doled out for the slightest infraction. The frequent assaults and beatings were meant to sow terror, fear and complete insecurity of person. Women were cowed into submission. One of the victims indicated her sense of vulnerability in her statement to the Commission:

> "They (RUF) gave me a very serious beating ... then I was stripped naked. I only had a pant on. ..."[64]

245. Beatings were arbitrary with the deliberate intention of inflicting cruelty, humiliating and degrading the person concerned.[65] An abducted girl-child who lived with an RUF combatant couple testified to the Commission:

> The rebel wife I was staying with used to flog me every day and even requested for her husband to kill me as she did not want to see me. At that time they had already killed my mother and my father.[66]

---

61. TRC confidential statements from a female victim, recorded in Gbangbatoke, Feb. 5, 2003.
62. *See*, for example, TRC interviews with two former RUF juniors commandos who stayed in the movement from 1991 until the end of the conflict, interviews conducted in Kailahun, July 2003.
63. TRC confidential statement recorded in Cline Town, Freetown, Jan. 13, 2003.
64. Amie Kallon, TRC statement, Yoni, Kpanga Kabondeh Chiefdom, Feb. 26, 2003.
65. *See*, for example, Mariama Sam, TRC statement, Ngordohun Gbameh, Kono, Feb. 27, 2003.
66. Confidential testimony received before TRC Closed Hearings, Tonkolili District, July 9, 2003.

246. Of the 3,281 cases of assault recorded by the Commission, where the gender of the victims is known, 914 cases recorded women victims.[67]

247. The Commission finds that women and girls were subjected to cruel and inhuman treatment by all the armed perpetrator groups, with the deliberate intention of inflicting serious mental and physical suffering or injury....

Torture

248. Acts of torture, carried out on a systematic scale, are regarded as both a crime against humanity and a war crime. The requirements though are different. The right not to be tortured is one of the fundamental rights of a non-derogable nature, in other words it is a *jus cogens* norm. Rape and other forms of sexual violence are recognized both under international human rights law and humanitarian law as torture. Women experienced intense mental and physical torture in the hands of the armed forces, particularly the RUF. The intention was to strip them of any sense of identity or self worth. They were treated like animals with the clear purpose of dehumanizing them. Cruel and degrading treatment was extensively practiced on women and girls. A girl-child who lived with the RUF described some sordid acts she witnessed:

> ... They used to cook a lot of food and at the end of the day after they had eaten their own food, whatever remains, they will mix it with toilet and give it to civilians in the villages ... If you refuse to eat, they will in turn kill you. Those who will eat the toilet food they will ask them to carry their loads....[68]

251. Torture took a number of different forms. Women were put into a hole in the ground, which was filled with water that covered a greater portion of their bodies. They were made to stay like that for a number of days. Some women were forced onto cages smaller than their bodies.[69] Others had hot oil poured over them, burning the skin away. Others had their bodies and faces mutilated....

252. Of the 2,086 torture violations recorded in the Commission's database, women accounted for 538 violations where the gender of the victim is known.[70]

253. The Commission finds that all of the armed perpetrator groupings pursued a deliberate strategy of inflicting torture on women and girls, by inflicting or threatening to inflict sexual violence, other acts or violence and cruel and inhuman acts upon them or on a third person or persons close to them.

Forced Drugging

254. Statistics in terms of the violation of forced drugging, like forced labor, remain inadequate because it was generally under-reported by women. A major reason for the failure to report the abuse is that drugging became part of many women's daily experiences and assumed a semblance of normality. However, a close reading of statements made by women and girls, as well as almost all of the hearing testimony, confirms that forced drugging became the norm.

255. At the Special Hearings on Women held in Freetown, many women testified to the fact that in the course of their abduction and whilst living with the rebels they were given drugs every day. They also confirmed that drugs were on a daily basis added into

---

67. More detail on violation rates and the levels of different violations experienced by women can be found in the Statistical Report produced as an Appendix to this Report.

68. Confidential testimony received before TRC Closed Hearing, Tonkolili District, July 9, 2003.

69. TRC confidential statement for a female victim, recorded in Gbangbatoke, Feb. 9, 2003.

70. *See* the Statistical Report produced as an Appendix to this report.

their food.[71] Their abductors would add marijuana into some of the sauces normally eaten with rice, such as cassava or potato leaves. Marijuana and other drugs such as cocaine, heroin and "brown-brown" were administered to women in a number of different ways, including forced inhalation, or making incision on their bodies and rubbing the drugs into the wounds. Gunpowder was also administered to women, presumably as a stimulant....

Killing

259. Scores of thousands of Sierra Leoneans, including thousands of women, lost their lives in the conflict. There was a deliberate policy by certain of the armed forces, particularly the RUF and the AFRC, to target civilians in campaigns of killings. Many families and communities were massacred. One example is this mass killing of a family at Kangana, Gorama Chiefdom in 1994:

> ... The soldiers started asking my sisters, uncle, and mother's mate under threat to give them all that they had or they should buy them marijuana to smoke. My sisters in turn refused giving them anything. So the soldiers killed my mother's mate and my sisters; in all seven people were killed. Only two of us narrowly escaped the massive killing....[72]

Amputation

270. The conflict in Sierra Leone is most visibly associated with amputations. Pictures of amputees have been shown on television screens and newspapers all across the world. Amputation is also the violation that has had the most devastating effect on the morale of the population. Due to a variety of factors, the Commission has found that it has not been able to establish absolutely reliable statistics on how many people suffered amputations or died from their injuries. In terms of alternative sets of figures, the United Nations Mission in Sierra Leone (UNAMSIL) has relied in its reports on the statistics of the Norwegian Refugee Council, which estimates that there are currently 1,600 surviving amputees in Sierra Leone, with more than 40% of them being women.[73] Figures available for 2002, estimate that 19% of the 225 registered amputees in the Southern region were women....[74]

Sexual Violations

279. A victim of sexual violence testified to the TRC about her experiences:

> After the attacks on Bandajuma Sinneh, around 12.00 noon, the RUF rebels entered my village. On my way to my house I was captured by an RUF rebel called Allieu. He then told me to go with him, but I refused to go. He said if I didn't go with him, he will kill me. My mother was afraid of the rebel, so for him not to kill me, she then persuaded me to go with him. When we arrived in Bandajuma Sinneh, two RUF rebels joined us.... In Bandajuma, I was taken into house, laid on the bare ground under gunpoint. All three of these rebels had sexual intercourse with me. They did it one after the other—it was gang rape ... They were doing it with impunity, telling me they will rape me to death. After that I became unconscious....[75]

---

71. "First Witness" and "Second Witness"—confidential testimonies received before the TRC Special Thematic Hearings on Women, Freetown, May 22–24, 2003.

72. TRC confidential statements recorded in Kenema District, Dec. 7, 2002.

73. *See* United Nations Assistance Mission in Sierra Leone (UNAMSIL); *Amputee Report 2000*, produced using data from surveys conducted by the Norwegian Refugee Council.

74. *Id.*

75. TRC confidential statements from a female, recorded in Gbangbatoke, Feb. 5, 2003.

280. During the conflict in Sierra Leone, women were systematically raped and sexually violated. The Commission received more than 800 statements from women and girls reporting and describing acts of rape. Girls in the age group from ten to 18 years were most likely to be the victims of rape. Women were gang raped and suffered multiple rapes as well as being kept in sexual slavery. In instances where women and girls were abducted, their capture was often the prelude to being handed over to and assigned to one of the fighters with the sole purpose of being his sexual slave.

281. In a large number of cases, women were handed over to combatants and became their "bush wives" for the purpose of satisfying not only their sexual needs but also to perform a host of different duties including domestic chores.[76] Having analyzed the systematic and widespread use of rape during the conflict period, the Commission came to the conclusion that all of the armed forces systematically raped and sexually violated women.

282. While rape was the major violation perpetrated against women, other acts of sexual violence were additionally carried out indiscriminately on women of all ages, of every ethnic group and from all social classes. In the views of many Sierra Leoneans who testified to the TRC, just being a woman in Sierra Leone during the conflict period was enough to create the likelihood that you would be raped and sexually violated in the most horrible ways, regardless of whether you were a pre-pubescent girl, an elderly woman or pregnant....[77]

Rape

283. The conflict in Sierra Leone is characterized by the vast number of rape violations that were perpetrated. The Commission received more than 800 statements reporting and describing rape.[78] A review of all the statements dealing with rape suggests that at least 58% of all rape victims suffered multiple rapes.[79] An analysis of the rape statistics in the Commission's database confirms that where the gender and age of the victims is known, 50% of them were 18 or younger, with 25% of them being younger than 13 years.[80] The youngest victim in the Commission's statements was just four years old while the oldest was 69 years of age at the time of rape.[81]

284. While many of the women who made statements to the Commission did report that they had been victims of rape, rape as a violation still remains largely under-reported. Cultural taboos associated with rape and the societal stigma that attaches to women who disclose that they have been raped have constrained women from being completely open in their statements to the Commission. Women have been even more reticent about disclosing that they have been gang-raped, as they have not wanted family members or the society they live in to know the traumatic details. In a number of instances, spouses of women raped have not wanted their wives to disclose these details, fearing that it would bring shame on them and the family. A common feature of victims' reactions to rape vi-

---

76. *See* Physician for Human Rights, *War-Related Sexual Violence in Sierra Leone. See also* Human Rights Watch, *We'll Kill You If You Cry. See also* Mansaray, Binta, "The Invisible Human Rights Abuses in Sierra Leone," Freetown, June 2002. *See also* Federation of African Media Women, "The Girl Child during the Civil War in Sierra Leone," Freetown, October, 2002.

77. Theresa Blackie, TRC statement, Bo Kakua, Dec. 16, 2002.

78. *See* the Statistical Report produced as an Appendix to this report.

79. More detail on the manner and circumstances in which women suffered sexual violations can be found in the results of the Commission's special coding exercises on sexual violations included in the Statistical Report produced as an Appendix to this report.

80. *See* the Statistical Report produced as an Appendix to this report.

81. *Id.*

olations has been husbands and wives entering into a conspiracy of silence about what has happened....

Sexual Slavery

299. In terms of international law, the two essential elements unique to the crime of sexual slavery are the "exercise of any or all of the powers attaching to the right of ownership over one or more person" and the "forced participation in one or more acts of sexual violence."[82] In Sierra Leone, hundreds of abducted women and girls were compelled to endure the violation of "sexual slavery." The Commission identified the act of "forced marriage" as synonymous with "sexual slavery." This violation is colloquially referred to by Sierra Leoneans as being forced to become a "bush wife." In describing the experiences of what the Commission has termed "sexual slavery," the pattern that emerged was as follows: women were captured and abducted; they became part of the entourage of the armed group to which their captors belonged; and they were continuously sexually violated as their captors moved along with them. Again this violation was particularly prevalent for the RUF and the AFRC, who kept women as sexual slaves under what could only be termed "roaming detention," which could last for time periods ranging from one or two days to several months and years.

300. Another pattern identified as part of this violation was for women to be detained and kept locked up in a specific place, in order that their captors could violate them at any time they had the urge to do so. This pattern of violation was particularly characteristic of the SLA and the CDF functions, who were not as mobile as the RUF and the AFRC. CDF units were typically attached to specific towns and villages, while the SLA would normally be stationed in barracks or assigned to specific locations. The RUF and the AFRC on the other hand were highly mobile and as offensive forces were constantly on the move. A former abductee of the RUF, who was seven years old at the time of her first encounter, recounted her second encounter with the faction, which led to her abduction in 1994 at Pendembu:

> In March 1994, on a Sunday at about 10 o'clock in the morning, I was at the house waiting to see my mother return. Immediately I saw so many RUF rebels that I cannot state their number ... five of them ran after me and held me ... later I was taken away and I was kept in a locked room always ready for me to be sexed by the commander. Sometimes when he was away, his junior boys will come and open the door sometimes three, sometimes four men. They will force me, telling me if I refuse they will kill me.[83]

E. Why the US Is Not a Member of the International Criminal Court

1. Kenneth Roth, *The Court the US Doesn't Want*[84]

... In favor of the court were most of America's closest allies, including Britain, Canada, and Germany. But the United States was isolated in opposition, along with such dictatorships and enemies of human rights as Iran, Iraq, China, Libya, Algeria, and Sudan.

---

82. *See* the Rome Statute of the International Criminal Code, at Article 7(2)(c).

83. TRC confidential statement recorded in Upper Bambara Chiefdom, Jan. 24, 2003.

84. Kenneth Roth, *The Court the US Doesn't Want, in* NEW YORK REVIEW OF BOOKS, vol. 45, No. 18 (Nov. 19, 1998). *See also* David Kaye, *Who's Afraid of the International Criminal Court? Finding*

The Clinton administration's opposition to the ICC [International Criminal Court] stemmed in part from its fear, a plausible one, that hostile states like Cuba, Libya, or Iraq might try to convince the court to launch a frivolous or politically motivated prosecution of US soldiers or commanding officers. The Rome delegates adopted several safeguards against this possibility, most importantly, the so-called principle of complementarity. This gives the ICC jurisdiction over a case only if national authorities are 'unwilling or unable' to carry out a genuine investigation and, if appropriate, prosecution. The complementarity principle also reflects the widely shared view that systems of national justice should remain the front-line defense against serious human rights abuse, with the ICC serving only as a backdrop. (By contrast, the Yugoslav and Rwandan tribunals are empowered to supersede local prosecutorial authorities at their discretion and have done so repeatedly.)

According to the principle of complementarity, if an American soldier were to commit a serious war crime — say, by deliberately massacring civilians — he could be brought before the ICC only if the US government failed to pursue his case. Indeed, even a national decision not to prosecute must be respected so long as it is not a bad faith effort to shield a criminal from justice. Because of the strength of the US judicial system, an ICC prosecutor would have a hard time dismissing a US investigation or prosecution as a sham. And, under the treaty, any effort to override a nation's decision not to prosecute would be subject to challenge before one panel of international judges and appeal before another.

Much would still depend on the character and professionalism of the ICC prosecutor and judges. The record of the International Criminal Tribunals for Rwanda and the former Yugoslavia suggests that faith in them would be well placed....

There is every reason to believe that the ICC will be run by jurists of comparable stature.... But the Pentagon and its congressional allies were not satisfied with the principle of complementarity as a protection against unjustified prosecutions....

Efforts by the US to exempt its nationals from the ICC's jurisdiction contributed to four points in contention during the Rome conference.... The resulting concessions [by other states] weakened the court significantly; still the Clinton administration ended up denouncing it.

The first controversy concerned whether and, if so, how the UN Security Council should be permitted to halt an ICC prosecution. The US proposed that before the ICC could even begin an investigation the Security Council would have to expressly authorize it. Because the United States, as a permanent Council member, could single-handedly block Council approval by exercising its veto, this proposal would have allowed Washington to prevent any investigation, including of its own soldiers and those of its allies. The other four permanent Council members — Britain, France, China, and Russia — would necessarily have had the same veto power. As a result only criminals from a handful of pariah states would have been likely to face prosecution....

Singapore offered a compromise to the veto problem which ultimately prevailed. It granted the Security Council the power to halt an ICC prosecution for a one-year period, which could be renewed. But the Security Council would act in its usual manner — by the vote of nine of its fifteen members and the acquiescence of all five permanent members. Therefore no single permanent Council member could use its veto to prevent a prosecution from being initiated.... The third major controversy involved what restriction should be placed on the ICC's definition of war crimes.... Of special concern was the so-called rule of proportionality under international law, which prohibits a military attack causing an incidental loss of civilian life that is 'excessive' compared to the military advantage gained. This less precise rule could implicate activity that US military commanders consider lawful but the ICC might not. For example, the Gulf War bombing of Iraq's electrical grid was claimed to have killed a disproportionate number of civilians, including the thousands said to have died because of the resulting loss of refrigeration, water purification, and other necessities of modern life. What if the ICC had been in existence and had found such claims well founded? ...

To avoid prosecution in such borderline situations, US negotiators successfully redefined the proportionality rule to prohibit attacks that injure civilians only when such injury is 'clearly excessive' in relation to the military advantage....

The United States, joined by France, also proposed that governments be allowed to join the ICC while specifying that their citizens would be exempted from war crimes prosecutions.... [A]s a compromise, the treaty allows governments to exempt their citizens from the court's war crimes jurisdiction for a period of seven years. That would allow a hesitant government to reassure itself about the court's treatment of war crimes without permanently denying the court jurisdiction over its citizens.

The most divisive issue delegates faced was deciding how — once the ICC treaty was ratified by sixty countries — the court would get jurisdiction over a case that was referred by an individual government or initiated by the prosecutor. (This issue does not arise when the Security Council refers a matter for prosecution, since the Council has the power to impose jurisdiction.) ... South Korea put forward a more limited proposal which gained broad support. It would have granted the ICC jurisdiction when any one of four governments concerned with a crime had ratified the ICC treaty or accepted the court's jurisdiction over the crime. These were (1) the government of the suspect's nationality; (2) the government of the victims' nationality; (3) the government on whose territory the crime took place; or (4) the government that gained custody of the suspect. In any given case, some and perhaps all of these governments would be the same, but each separate category increases the possibility that the court could pursue a particular subject.

Speaking for the Clinton administration, Ambassador Scheffer vehemently insisted that the court should be empowered to act only if the government of the suspect's nationality had accepted its jurisdiction....

Clinton administration officials were not mollified by the fact that, under the doctrine of universal jurisdiction, American soldiers are already vulnerable to prosecution in foreign courts. The US government has many ways of dissuading governments from attempting to try an American — from diplomatic and economic pressure to the use of military force. But the administration fears such dissuasion would be less effective against the ICC. After all, the Pentagon could hardly threaten to bomb The Hague.

... Facing these extraordinary threats [from the United States], the Rome delegates gave in, but only partially. They got rid of two of Korea's proposed conditions for ICC jurisdiction: that the treaty would have to be ratified by the state of the victim's nationality or it would have to be ratified by the state that gained custody of the suspect.

This concession was damaging. Because a state could not give the ICC jurisdiction just by arresting a suspect, a leader who commits atrocities against his own country's citizens, such as a future Pol Pot or Idi Amin, could travel widely without being brought before the ICC — so long as his own government had not ratified the treaty (and assuming the Security Council does not act).... And if the victims' nationality cannot be used as grounds for ICC jurisdiction, then the ICC could not take action against the leader of a non-rat-ifying government that slaughters refugees from a ratifying state who seek shelter on its territory (again, assuming the Security Council fails to act)....

But the Rome delegates did not accept the Clinton administration's demands entirely. They retained two grounds for the ICC's jurisdiction: not only that the government of the suspect's nationality had ratified the treaty (the only ground acceptable to the US) but also that the government on whose territory the crime took place had ratified it. In the case of a tyrant who commits crimes at home, these two governments would be the same.... The United States, however, feared that the territorial hook might catch Amer-ican troops, or their commanders, for alleged crimes committed while they were abroad. If the country where US troops are present has ratified the treaty, the ICC could pursue a case against them even though the United States had not joined the court.... Can the ICC survive without US participation? The Clinton administration is betting that it can-not. Already Jesse Helms, having declared the ICC to be treated as 'dead on arrival' in the Senate, has vowed to sponsor legislation forbidding the US government to fund the court or do anything to give it legitimacy. The State Department said publicly it might put pres-sure on governments not to join the court; and it is considering renegotiating the bilat-eral treaties that govern the stationing of US forces overseas in order to protect them from the ICC.

The Clinton administration ... also contends that, small as the risk is of an American being brought before the court, the ICC will undermine humanitarian goals by making the United States reluctant to deploy troops in times of need.

[See Appendix for full text of Rome Statute.]

Appendix

Charter of the United Nations

We the Peoples of the United Nations Determined

to save succeeding generations from the scourge of war, which twice in our lifetime has brought untold sorrow to mankind, and

to reaffirm faith in fundamental human rights, in the dignity and worth of the human person, in the equal rights of men and women and of nations large and small, and

to establish conditions under which justice and respect for the obligations arising from treaties and other sources of international law can be maintained, and

to promote social progress and better standards of life in larger freedom,

And for these ends

to practice tolerance and live together in peace with one another as good neighbours, and

to unite our strength to maintain international peace and security, and

to ensure, by the acceptance of principles and the institution of methods, that armed force shall not be used, save in the common interest, and

to employ international machinery for the promotion of the economic and social advancement of all peoples,

Have resolved to combine our efforts to accomplish these aims

. . .

Chapter 1: Purposes and Principles

Article 1

The Purposes of the United Nations are:

1. To maintain international peace and security, and to that end: to take effective collective measures for the prevention and removal of threats to the peace, and for the suppression of acts of aggression or other breaches of the peace, and to bring about by peaceful means, and in conformity with the principles of justice and international law, adjustment or settlement of international disputes or situations which might lead to a breach of the peace;

2. To develop friendly relations among nations based on respect for the principle of equal rights and self-determination of peoples, and to take other appropriate measures to strengthen universal peace;

3. To achieve international co-operation in solving international problems of an economic, social, cultural, or humanitarian character, and in promoting and encouraging re-

spect for human rights and for fundamental freedoms for all without distinction as to race, sex, language, or religion; and

4. To be a centre for harmonizing the actions of nations in the attainment of these common ends.

Article 2

The Organization and its Members, in pursuit of the Purposes stated in Article 1, shall act in accordance with the following Principles.

1. The Organization is based on the principle of the sovereign equality of all its Members.

2. All Members, in order to ensure to all of them the rights and benefits resulting from membership, shall fulfill in good faith the obligations assumed by them in accordance with the present Charter.

3. All Members shall settle their international disputes by peaceful means in such a manner that international peace and security, and justice, are not endangered.

4. All Members shall refrain in their international relations from the threat or use of force against the territorial integrity or political independence of any state, or in any other manner inconsistent with the Purposes of the United Nations.

5. All Members shall give the United Nations every assistance in any action it takes in accordance with the present Charter, and shall refrain from giving assistance to any state against which the United Nations is taking preventive or enforcement action.

6. The Organization shall ensure that states which are not Members of the United Nations act in accordance with these Principles so far as may be necessary for the maintenance of international peace and security.

7. Nothing contained in the present Charter shall authorize the United Nations to intervene in matters which are essentially within the domestic jurisdiction of any state or shall require the Members to submit such matters to settlement under the present Charter; but this principle shall not prejudice the application of enforcement measures under Chapter VII.

Chapter 2: Membership

. . .

Article 4

1. Membership in the United Nations is open to all other peace-loving states which accept the obligations contained in the present Charter and, in the judgment of the Organization, are able and willing to carry out these obligations.

. . .

Chapter 3: Organs

Article 7

1. There are established as the principal organs of the United Nations: a General Assembly, a Security Council, an Economic and Social Council, a Trusteeship Council, an International Court of Justice, and a Secretariat.

2. Such subsidiary organs as may be found necessary may be established in accordance with the present Charter.

Article 8

The United Nations shall place no restrictions on the eligibility of men and women to participate in any capacity and under conditions of equality in its principal and subsidiary organs.

Chapter 4: The General Assembly

Article 9

1. The General Assembly shall consist of all the Members of the United Nations.

...

Article 13

1. The General Assembly shall initiate studies and make recommendations for the purpose of:

a. promoting international co-operation in the political field and encouraging the progressive development of international law and its codification;

b. promoting international co-operation in the economic, social, cultural, educational, and health fields, and assisting in the realization of human rights and fundamental freedoms for all without distinction as to race, sex, language, or religion.

...

Article 18

1. Each member of the General Assembly shall have one vote.

2. Decisions of the General Assembly on important questions shall be made by a two-thirds majority of the members present and voting. These questions shall include: recommendations with respect to the maintenance of international peace and security, the election of the non-permanent members of the Security Council, the election of the members of the Economic and Social Council, the election of members of the Trusteeship Council in accordance with paragraph 1 of Article 86, the admission of new Members to the United Nations, the suspension of the rights and privileges of membership, the expulsion of Members, questions relating to the operation of the trusteeship system, and budgetary questions.

3. Decisions on other questions, including the determination of additional categories of questions to be decided by a two-thirds majority, shall be made by a majority of the members present and voting.

Chapter 5: The Security Council

Article 23

1. The Security Council shall consist of fifteen Members of the United Nations. The Republic of China, France, the Union of Soviet Socialist Republics, the United Kingdom of Great Britain and Northern Ireland, and the United States of America shall be permanent members of the Security Council. The General Assembly shall elect ten other Members of the United Nations to be non-permanent members of the Security Council, due regard being specially paid, in the first instance to the contribution of Members of the United Nations to the maintenance of international peace and security and to the other purposes of the Organization, and also to equitable geographical distribution.

2. The non-permanent members of the Security Council shall be elected for a term of two years. In the first election of the non-permanent members after the increase of the

membership of the Security Council from eleven to fifteen, two of the four additional members shall be chosen for a term of one year. A retiring member shall not be eligible for immediate re-election.

...

Article 24

1. In order to ensure prompt and effective action by the United Nations, its Members confer on the Security Council primary responsibility for the maintenance of international peace and security, and agree that in carrying out its duties under this responsibility the Security Council acts on their behalf.

2. In discharging these duties the Security Council shall act in accordance with the Purposes and Principles of the United Nations. The specific powers granted to the Security Council for the discharge of these duties are laid down in Chapters VI, VII, VIII, and XII.

...

Article 25

The Members of the United Nations agree to accept and carry out the decisions of the Security Council in accordance with the present Charter.

...

Article 27

1. Each member of the Security Council shall have one vote.

2. Decisions of the Security Council on procedural matters shall be made by an affirmative vote of nine members.

3. Decisions of the Security Council on all other matters shall be made by an affirmative vote of nine members including the concurring votes of the permanent members; provided that, in decisions under Chapter VI, and under paragraph 3 of Article 52, a party to a dispute shall abstain from voting.

...

Chapter 6: Pacific Settlement of Disputes

Article 33

1. The parties to any dispute, the continuance of which is likely to endanger the maintenance of international peace and security, shall, first of all, seek a solution by negotiation, enquiry, mediation, conciliation, arbitration, judicial settlement, resort to regional agencies or arrangements, or other peaceful means of their own choice.

2. The Security Council shall, when it deems necessary, call upon the parties to settle their dispute by such means.

Article 34

The Security Council may investigate any dispute, or any situation which might lead to international friction or give rise to a dispute, in order to determine whether the continuance of the dispute or situation is likely to endanger the maintenance of international peace and security.

...

Article 36

1. The Security Council may, at any stage of a dispute of the nature referred to in Article 33 or of a situation of like nature, recommend appropriate procedures or methods of adjustment.

2. The Security Council should take into consideration any procedures for the settlement of the dispute which have already been adopted by the parties.

3. In making recommendations under this Article the Security Council should also take into consideration that legal disputes should as a general rule be referred by the parties to the International Court of Justice in accordance with the provisions of the Statute of the Court.

...

Chapter 7: Actions with Respect to Threat to the Peace, Breach of the Peace, and Acts of Aggression

Article 39

The Security Council shall determine the existence of any threat to the peace, breach of the peace, or act of aggression and shall make recommendations, or decide what measures shall be taken in accordance with Articles 4 and 42, to maintain or restore international peace and security.

...

Article 41

The Security Council may decide what measures not involving the use of armed force are to be employed to give effect to its decisions, and it may call upon the Members of the United Nations to apply such measures. These may include complete or partial interruption of economic relations and of rail, sea, air, postal, telegraphic, radio, and other means of communication, and the severance of diplomatic relations.

Article 42

Should the Security Council consider that measures provided for in Article 41 would be inadequate or have proved to be inadequate, it may take such action by air, sea, or land forces as may be necessary to maintain or restore international peace and security. Such action may include demonstrations, blockade, and other operations by air, sea, or land forces of Members of the United Nations.

Article 43

1. All Members of the United Nations, in order to contribute to the maintenance of international peace and security, undertake to make available to the Security Council, on its and in accordance with a special agreement or agreements, armed forces, assistance, and facilities, including rights of passage, necessary for the purpose of maintaining international peace and security.

2. Such agreement or agreements shall govern the numbers and types of forces, their degree of readiness and general location, and the nature of the facilities and assistance to be provided.

3. The agreement or agreements shall be negotiated as soon as possible on the initiative of the Security Council. They shall be concluded between the Security Council and Members or between the Security Council and groups of Members and shall be subject to ratification by the signatory states in accordance with their respective constitutional processes.

Article 44

When Security Council has decided to use force it shall, before calling upon a Member not represented on it to provide armed forces in fulfillment of the obligations assumed under Article 43, invite that Member, if the Member so desires, to participate in the decisions of the Security Council concerning the employment of contingents of that Member's armed forces.

Article 45

In order to enable the Nations to take urgent military measures, Members shall hold immediately available national air-force contingents for combined international enforcement action.

. . .

Article 48

1. The action required to carry out the decisions of the Security Council for the maintenance of international peace and security shall be taken by all the Members of the United Nations or by some of them, as the Security Council may determine.

2. Such decisions shall be carried out by the Members of the United Nations directly and through their action in the appropriate international agencies of which they are members.

. . .

Article 51

Nothing in the present Charter shall impair the inherent right of individual or collective self-defence if an armed attack occurs against a Member of the United Nations, until the Security Council has taken measures necessary to maintain international peace and security. Measures taken by Members in the exercise of this right of self-defence shall be immediately reported to the Security Council and shall not in any way affect the authority and responsibility of the Security Council under the present Charter to take at any time such action as it deems necessary in order to maintain or restore international peace and security.

Chapter 8: Regional Arrangements

Article 52

1. Nothing in the present Charter precludes the existence of regional arrangements or agencies for dealing with such matters relating to the maintenance of international peace and security as are appropriate for regional action, provided that such arrangements or agencies and their activities are consistent with the Purposes and Principles of the United Nations.

. . .

3. The Security Council shall encourage the development of pacific settlement of local disputes through such regional arrangements or by such regional agencies either on the initiative of the states concerned or by reference from the Security Council.

4. This Article in no way impairs the application of Articles 34 and 35.

Article 53

1. The Security Council shall, where appropriate, utilize such regional arrangements or agencies for enforcement action under its authority. But no enforcement action shall

be taken under regional arrangements or by regional agencies without the authorization of the Security Council, with the exception of measures against any enemy state, as defined in paragraph 2 of this Article, provided for pursuant to Article 107 or in regional arrangements directed against renewal of aggressive policy on the part of any such state, until such time as the Organization may, on request of the Governments concerned, be charged with the responsibility for preventing further aggression by such a state.

2. The term enemy state as used in paragraph 1 of this Article applies to any state which during the Second World War has been an enemy of any signatory of the present Charter.

Article 54

The Security Council shall at all times be kept fully informed of activities undertaken or in contemplation under regional arrangements or by regional agencies for the maintenance of international peace and security.

Chapter 9: International Economic and Social Co-Operation

Article 55

With a view to the creation of conditions of stability and well-being which are necessary for peaceful and friendly relations among nations based on respect for the principle of equal rights and self-determination of peoples, the United Nations shall promote:

a. higher standards of living, full employment, and conditions of economic and social progress and development;

b. solutions of international economic, social, health, and related problems; and international cultural and educational co-operation; and

c. universal respect for, and observance of, human rights and fundamental freedoms for all without distinction as to race, sex, language, or religion.

Article 56

All Members pledge themselves to take joint and separate action in co-operation with the Organization for the achievement of the purposes set forth in Article 55.

. . .

Chapter 10: The Economic and Social Council

Article 61

1. The Economic and Social Council shall consist of fifty-four Members of the United Nations elected by the General Assembly.

. . .

Article 62

1. The Economic and Social Council may make or initiate studies and reports with respect to international economic, social, cultural, educational, health, and related matters and may make recommendations with respect to any such matters to the General Assembly, to the Members of the United Nations, and to the specialized agencies concerned.

2. It may make recommendations for the purpose of promoting respect for, and observance of, human rights and fundamental freedoms for all.

3. It may prepare draft conventions for submission to the General Assembly, with respect to matters falling within its competence.

4. It may call, in accordance with the rules prescribed by the United Nations, international conferences on matters falling within its competence.

...

Article 68

The Economic and Social Council shall set up commissions in economic and social fields and for the promotion of human rights, and such other commissions as may be required for the performance of its functions.

...

Chapter 11: Declaration Regarding Non-Self-Governing Territories

Article 73

Members of the United Nations, which have or assume responsibilities for the administration of territories whose peoples have not yet attained a full measure of self-government, recognize the principle that the interests of the inhabitants of these territories are paramount, and accept as a sacred trust the obligation to promote to the utmost, within the system of international peace and security established by the present Charter, the well-being of the inhabitants of these territories, and, to this end:

a. to ensure, with due respect for the culture of the peoples concerned, their political, economic, social, and educational advancement, their just treatment, and their protection against abuses;

b. to develop self-government, to take due account of the political aspirations of the peoples, and to assist them in the progressive development of their free political institutions, according to the particular circumstances of each territory and its peoples and their varying stages of advancement;

c. to further international peace and security;

d. to promote constructive measures of development ...

...

Chapter 12: International Trusteeship System

Article 75

The United Nations shall establish under its authority an international trusteeship system for the administration and supervision of such territories as may be placed thereunder by subsequent individual agreements. These territories are hereinafter referred to as trust territories.

...

Chapter 14: The International Court of Justice

Article 92

The International Court of Justice shall be the principal judicial organ of the United Nations. It shall function in accordance with the annexed Statute, which is based upon the Statute of the Permanent Court of International Justice and forms an integral part of the present Charter.

...

Article 94

1. Each Member of the United Nations undertakes to comply with the decision of the International Court of Justice in any case to which it is a party.

2. If any party to a case fails to perform the obligations incumbent upon it under a judgment rendered by the Court, the other party may have recourse to the Security Council, which may, if it deems necessary, make recommendations or decide upon measures to be taken to give to the judgment.

. . .

Article 96

1. The General Assembly or the Security Council may request the International Court of Justice to give an advisory opinion on any legal question.

. . .

Chapter 15: The Secretariat

Article 97

The Secretariat shall comprise a Secretary-General and such staff as the Organization may require. The Secretary-General shall be appointed by the General Assembly upon the recommendation of the Security Council. He shall be the chief administrative officer of the Organization.

. . .

Article 99

The Secretary-General may bring to the attention of the Security Council any matter which in his opinion may threaten the maintenance of international peace and security.

Article 100

1. In the performance of their duties the Secretary-General and the staff shall not seek or receive instructions from any government or from any other authority external to the Organization. They shall refrain from any action which might on their position as international officials responsible only to the Organization.

2. Each Member of the United Nations undertakes to respect the exclusively international character of the responsibilities of the Secretary-General and the staff and not to seek to influence them in the discharge of their responsibilities.

. . .

Chapter 16: Miscellaneous Provisions

Article 103

In the event of a conflict between the obligations of the Members of the United Nations under the present Charter and their obligations under any other international agreement, their obligations under the present Charter shall prevail.

. . .

Chapter 18: Amendments

Article 108

Amendments to the present Charter shall come into force for all Members of the United Nations when they have been adopted by a vote of two thirds of the members of the General Assembly and ratified in accordance with their respective constitutional processes by two thirds of the Members of the United Nations, including all the permanent members of the Security Council.

...

Universal Declaration of Human Rights

Preamble

Whereas recognition of the inherent dignity and of the equal and inalienable rights of all members of the human family is the foundation of freedom, justice and peace in the world,

Whereas disregard and contempt for human rights have resulted in barbarous acts which have outraged the conscience of mankind, and the advent of a world in which human beings shall enjoy freedom of speech and belief and freedom from fear and want has been proclaimed as the highest aspiration of the common people,

Whereas it is essential, if man is not to be compelled to have recourse, as a last resort, to rebellion against tyranny and oppression, that human rights should be protected by the rule of law,

Whereas it is essential to promote the development of friendly relations between nations,

Whereas the peoples of the United Nations have in the Charter reaffirmed their faith in fundamental human rights, in the dignity and worth of the human person and in the equal rights of men and women and have determined to promote social progress and better standards of life in larger freedom,

Whereas Member States have pledged themselves to achieve, in cooperation with the United Nations, the promotion of universal respect for and observance of human rights and fundamental freedoms,

Whereas a common understanding of these rights and freedoms is of the greatest importance for the full realization of this pledge,

Now, therefore, The General Assembly Proclaims this Universal Declaration of Human Rights as a common standard of achievement for all peoples and all nations, to the end that every individual and every organ of society, keeping this Declaration constantly in mind, shall strive by teaching and education to promote respect for these rights and freedoms and by progressive measures, national and international, to secure their universal and effective recognition and observance, both among the peoples of Member States themselves and among the peoples of territories under their jurisdiction.

Article 1

All human beings are born free and equal in dignity and rights. They are endowed with reason and conscience and should act towards one another in a spirit of brotherhood.

Article 2

Everyone is entitled to all the rights and freedoms set forth in this Declaration, without distinction of any kind, such as race, colour, sex, language, religion, political or other opinion, national or social origin, property, birth or other status. Furthermore, no distinction shall be made on the basis of the political, jurisdictional or international status of the country or territory to which a person belongs, whether it be independent, trust, non-self-governing or under any other limitation of sovereignty.

Article 3

Everyone has the right to life, liberty and security of person.

Article 4

No one shall be held in slavery or servitude; slavery and the slave trade shall be prohibited in all their forms.

Article 5

No one shall be subjected to torture or to cruel, inhuman or degrading treatment or punishment.

Article 6

Everyone has the right to recognition everywhere as a person before the law.

Article 7

All are equal before the law and are entitled without any discrimination to equal protection of the law. All are entitled to equal protection against any discrimination in violation of this Declaration and against any incitement to such discrimination.

Article 8

Everyone has the right to an effective remedy by the competent national tribunals for acts violating the fundamental rights granted him by the constitution or by law.

Article 9

No one shall be subjected to arbitrary arrest, detention or exile.

Article 10

Everyone is entitled in full equality to a fair and public hearing by an independent and impartial tribunal, in the determination of his rights and obligations and of any criminal charge against him.

Article 11

(1) Everyone charged with a penal offence has the right to be presumed innocent until proved guilty according to law in a public trial at which he has had all the guarantees necessary for his defence.

(2) No one shall be held guilty of any penal offence on account of any act or omission which did not constitute a penal offence, under national or international law, at the time when it was committed. Nor shall a heavier penalty be imposed than the one that was applicable at the time the penal offence was committed.

Article 12

No one shall be subjected to arbitrary interference with his privacy, family, home or correspondence, nor to attacks upon his honour and reputation. Everyone has the right to the protection of the law against such interference or attacks.

Article 13

(1) Everyone has the right to freedom of movement and residence within the borders of each state.

(2) Everyone has the right to leave any country, including his own, and to return to his country.

Article 14

(1) Everyone has the right to seek and to enjoy in other countries asylum from persecution.

(2) This right may not be invoked in the case of prosecutions genuinely arising from non-political crimes or from acts contrary to the purposes and principles of the United Nations.

Article 15

(1) Everyone has the right to a nationality.

(2) No one shall be arbitrarily deprived of his nationality nor denied the right to change his nationality.

Article 16

(1) Men and women of full age, without any limitation due to race, nationality or religion, have the right to marry and to found a family. They are entitled to equal rights as to marriage, during marriage and at its dissolution.

(2) Marriage shall be entered into only with the free and full consent of the intending spouses.

(3) The family is the natural and fundamental group unit of society and is entitled to protection by society and the State.

Article 17

(1) Everyone has the right to own property alone as well as in association with others.

(2) No one shall be arbitrarily deprived of his property.

Article 18

Everyone has the right to freedom of thought, conscience and religion; this right includes freedom to change his religion or belief, and freedom, either alone or in community with others and in public or private, to manifest his religion or belief in teaching, practice, worship and observance.

Article 19

Everyone has the right to freedom of opinion and expression; this right includes freedom to hold opinions without interference and to seek, receive and impart information and ideas through any media and regardless of frontiers.

Article 20

(1) Everyone has the right to freedom of peaceful assembly and association.

(2) No one may be compelled to belong to an association.

Article 21

(1) Everyone has the right to take part in the government of his country, directly or through freely chosen representatives.

(2) Everyone has the right of equal access to public service in his country.

(3) The will of the people shall be the basis of the authority of government; this will shall be expressed in periodic and genuine elections which shall be by universal and equal suffrage and shall be held by secret vote or by equivalent free voting procedures.

Article 22

Everyone, as a member of society, has the right to social security and is entitled to realization, through national effort and international co-operation and in accordance with the organization and resources of each State, of the economic, social and cultural rights indispensable for his dignity and the free development of his personality.

Article 23

(1) Everyone has the right to work, to free choice of employment, to just and favourable conditions of work and to protection against unemployment.

(2) Everyone, without any discrimination, has the right to equal pay for equal work.

(3) Everyone who works has the right to just and favourable remuneration ensuring for himself and his family an existence worthy of human dignity, and supplemented, if necessary, by other means of social protection.

(4) Everyone has the right to form and to join trade unions for the protection of his interests.

Article 24

Everyone has the right to rest and leisure, including reasonable limitation of working hours and periodic holidays with pay.

Article 25

(1) Everyone has the right to a standard of living adequate for the health and well-being of himself and of his family, including food, clothing, housing and medical care and necessary social services, and the right to security in the event of unemployment, sickness, disability, widowhood, old age or other lack of livelihood in circumstances beyond his control.

(2) Motherhood and childhood are entitled to special care and assistance. All children, whether born in or out of wedlock, shall enjoy the same social protection.

Article 26

(1) Everyone has the right to education. Education shall be free, at least in the elementary and fundamental stages. Elementary education shall be compulsory. Technical and professional education shall be made generally available and higher education shall be equally accessible to all on the basis of merit.

(2) Education shall be directed to the full development of the human personality and to the strengthening of respect for human rights and fundamental freedoms. It shall promote understanding, tolerance and friendship among all nations, racial or religious groups, and shall further the activities of the United Nations for the maintenance of peace.

(3) Parents have a prior right to choose the kind of education that shall be given to their children.

Article 27

(1) Everyone has the right freely to participate in the cultural life of the community, to enjoy the arts and to share in scientific advancement and its benefits.

(2) Everyone has the right to the protection of the moral and material interests resulting from any scientific, literary or artistic production of which he is the author.

Article 28

Everyone is entitled to a social and international order in which the rights and freedoms set forth in this Declaration can be fully realized.

Article 29

(1) Everyone has duties to the community in which alone the free and full development of his personality is possible.

(2) In the exercise of his rights and freedoms, everyone shall be subject only to such limitations as are determined by law solely for the purpose of securing due recognition and respect for the rights and freedoms of others and of meeting the just requirements of morality, public order and the general welfare in a democratic society.

(3) These rights and freedoms may in no case be exercised contrary to the purposes and principles of the United Nations.

Article 30

Nothing in this Declaration may be interpreted as implying for any State, group or person any right to engage in any activity or to perform any act aimed at the destruction of any of the rights and freedoms set forth herein.

United Nations Genocide Convention

Article 1

The Contracting Parties confirm that genocide, whether committed in time of peace, or in time of war, is a crime under international law which they undertake to prevent and to punish.

Article 2

In the present Convention, genocide means any of the following acts committed with intent to destroy, in whole or in part, a national, ethical, racial or religious group as such:

(a) Killing members of the group;

(b) Causing serious bodily or mental harm to members of the group;

(c) Deliberately inflicting on the group conditions of life calculated to bring about its physical destruction in whole or in part;

(d) Imposing measures intended to prevent births within the group;

(e) Forcibly transferring children of the group to another group.

Article 3

The following acts shall be punishable:

(a) Genocide;

(b) Conspiracy to commit genocide;

(c) Direct and public incitement to commit genocide;

(d) Attempt to commit genocide;

(e) Complicity in genocide.

Article 4

Persons committing genocide or any of the other acts enumerated in Article 3 shall be punished, whether they are constitutionally responsible rulers, public officials or private individuals.

Article 5

The Contracting Parties undertake to enact, in accordance with their respective Constitutions, the necessary legislation to give effect to the provisions of the present Convention and, in particular, to provide effective penalties for persons guilty of genocide or of any of the other acts enumerated in Article 3.

Article 6

Persons charged with genocide or any of the other acts enumerated in Article 3 shall be tried by a competent tribunal of the State in the territory of which the act was committed, or by such international panel tribunal as may have jurisdiction with respect to those Contracting Parties which shall have accepted its jurisdiction.

Article 7

Genocide and the other acts enumerated in Article 3 shall not be considered as political crimes for the purpose of extradition. The Contracting Parties pledge themselves in such cases to grant extradition in accordance with their laws and treaties in force.

Article 8

Any Contracting Party may call upon the competent organs of the United Nations to take such action under the Charter of the United Nations as they consider appropriate for the prevention and suppression of acts of genocide or any of the other acts enumerated in Article 3.

. . .

International Covenant on Civil and Political Rights

Preamble

The States Parties to the present Covenant,

Considering that, in accordance with the principles proclaimed in the Charter of the United Nations, recognition of the inherent dignity and of the equal and inalienable rights of all members of the human family is the foundation of freedom, justice and peace in the world,

Recognizing that these rights derive from the inherent dignity of the human person,

Recognizing that, in accordance with the Universal Declaration of Human Rights, the ideal of free human beings enjoying civil and political freedom and freedom from fear and want can only be achieved if conditions are created whereby everyone may enjoy his civil and political rights, as well as his economic, social and cultural rights,

Considering the obligation of States under the Charter of the United Nations to promote universal respect for, and observance of, human rights and freedoms,

Realizing that the individual, having duties to other individuals and to the community to which he belongs, is under a responsibility to strive for the promotion and observance of the rights recognized in the present Covenant,

Agree upon the following articles:

Part 1

Article 1

1. All peoples have the right of self-determination. By virtue of that right they freely determine their political status and freely pursue their economic, social and cultural development.

2. All peoples may, for their own ends, freely dispose of their natural wealth and resources without prejudice to any obligations arising out of international economic cooperation, based upon the principle of mutual benefit, and international law. In no case may a people be deprived of its own means of subsistence.

3. The States Parties to the present Covenant, including those having responsibility for the administration of Non-Self-Governing and Trust Territories, shall promote the realization of the right of self-determination, and shall respect that right, in conformity with the provisions of the Charter of the United Nations.

Part 2

Article 2

1. Each State Party to the present Covenant undertakes to respect and to ensure to all individuals within its territory and subject to its jurisdiction the rights recognized in the present Covenant, without distinction of any kind, such as race, colour, sex, language, religion, political or other opinion, national or social origin, property, birth or other status.

2. Where not already provided for by existing legislative or other measures, each State Party to the present Covenant undertakes to take the necessary steps, in accordance with its constitutional processes and with the provisions of the present Covenant, to adopt such laws or other measures as may be necessary to give effect to the rights recognized in the present Covenant.

3. Each State Party to the present Covenant undertakes:

(a) To ensure that any person whose rights or freedoms as herein recognized are violated shall have an effective remedy, notwithstanding that the violation has been committed by persons acting in an official capacity;

(b) To ensure that any person claiming such a remedy shall have his right thereto determined by competent judicial, administrative or legislative authorities, or by any other competent authority provided for by the legal system of the State, and to develop the possibilities of judicial remedy;

(c) To ensure that the competent authorities shall enforce such remedies when granted.

Article 3

The States Parties to the present Covenant undertake to ensure the equal right of men and women to the enjoyment of all civil and political rights set forth in the present Covenant.

Article 4

1. In time of public emergency which threatens the life of the nation and the existence of which is officially proclaimed, the States Parties to the present Covenant may take measures derogating from their obligations under the present Covenant to the extent strictly required by the exigencies of the situation, provided that such measures are not inconsistent with their other obligations under international law and do not involve discrimination solely on the ground of race, colour, sex, language, religion or social origin.

2. No derogation from articles 6, 7, 8 (paragraphs 1 and 2), 11, 15, 16 and 18 may be made under this provision.

3. Any State Party to the present Covenant availing itself of the right of derogation shall immediately inform the other States Parties to the present Covenant, through the intermediary of the Secretary-General of the United Nations, of the provisions from which it has derogated and of the reasons by which it was actuated. A further communication shall be made, through the same intermediary, on the date on which it terminates such derogation.

Article 5

1. Nothing in the present Covenant may be interpreted as implying for any State, group or person any right to engage in any activity or perform any act aimed at the destruction of any of the rights and freedoms recognized herein or at their limitation to a greater extent than is provided for in the present Covenant.

2. There shall be no restriction upon or derogation from any of the fundamental human rights recognized or existing in any State Party to the present Covenant pursuant to law, conventions, regulations or custom on the pretext that the present Covenant does not recognize such rights or that it recognizes them to a lesser extent.

Part 3

Article 6

1. Every human being has the inherent right to life. This right shall be protected by law. No one shall be arbitrarily deprived of his life.

2. In countries which have not abolished the death penalty, sentence of death may be imposed only for the most serious crimes in accordance with the law in force at the time of the commission of the crime and not contrary to the provisions of the present Covenant and to the Convention on the Prevention and Punishment of the Crime of Genocide. This penalty can only be carried out pursuant to a final judgement rendered by a competent court.

3. When deprivation of life constitutes the crime of genocide, it is understood that nothing in this article shall authorize any State Party to the present Covenant to derogate in any way from any obligation assumed under the provisions of the Convention on the Prevention and Punishment of the Crime of Genocide.

4. Anyone sentenced to death shall have the right to seek pardon or commutation of the sentence. Amnesty, pardon or commutation of the sentence of death may be granted in all cases.

5. Sentence of death shall not be imposed for crimes committed by persons below eighteen years of age and shall not be carried out on pregnant women.

6. Nothing in this article shall be invoked to delay or to prevent the abolition of capital punishment by any State Party to the present Covenant.

Article 7

No one shall be subjected to torture or to cruel, inhuman or degrading treatment or punishment. In particular, no one shall be subjected without his free consent to medical or scientific experimentation.

Article 8

1. No one shall be held in slavery; slavery and the slave-trade in all their forms shall be prohibited.

2. No one shall be held in servitude.

...

Article 9

1. Everyone has the right to liberty and security of person. No one shall be subjected to arbitrary arrest or detention. No one shall be deprived of his liberty except on such grounds and in accordance with such procedure as are established by law.

2. Anyone who is arrested shall be informed, at the time of arrest, of the reasons for his arrest and shall be promptly informed of any charges against him.

3. Anyone arrested or detained on a criminal charge shall be brought promptly before a judge or other officer authorized by law to exercise judicial power and shall be entitled to trial within a reasonable time or to release. It shall not be the general rule that persons awaiting trial shall be detained in custody, but release may be subject to guarantees to appear for trial, at any other stage of the judicial proceedings, and, should occasion arise, for execution of the judgment.

4. Anyone who is deprived of his liberty by arrest or detention shall be entitled to take proceedings before a court, in order that that court may decide without delay on the lawfulness of his detention and order his release if the detention is not lawful.

5. Anyone who has been the victim of unlawful arrest or detention shall have an enforceable right to compensation.

Article 10

1. All persons deprived of their liberty shall be treated with humanity and with respect for the inherent dignity of the human person.

2. (a) Accused persons shall, save in exceptional circumstances, be segregated from convicted persons and shall be subject to separate treatment appropriate to their status as unconvicted persons;

(b) Accused juvenile persons shall be separated from adults and brought as speedily as possible for adjudication.

3. The penitentiary system shall comprise treatment of prisoners the essential aim of which shall be their reformation and social rehabilitation. Juvenile offenders shall be segregated from adults and be accorded treatment appropriate to their age and legal status.

Article 11

No one shall be imprisoned merely on the ground of inability to fulfill a contractual obligation.

Article 12

1. Everyone lawfully within the territory of a State shall, within that territory, have the right to liberty of movement and freedom to choose his residence.

2. Everyone shall be free to leave any country, including his own.

3. The above-mentioned rights shall not be subject to any restrictions except those which are provided by law, are necessary to protect national security, public order (ordre public), public health or morals or the rights and freedoms of others, and are consistent with the other rights recognized in the present Covenant.

4. No one shall be arbitrarily deprived of the right to enter his own country.

Article 13

An alien lawfully in the territory of a State Party to the present Covenant may be expelled therefrom only in pursuance of a decision reached in accordance with law and shall, except where compelling reasons of national security otherwise require, be allowed to submit the reasons against his expulsion and to have his case reviewed by, and be represented for the purpose before, the competent authority or a person or persons especially designated by the competent authority.

Article 14

1. All persons shall be equal before the courts and tribunals. In the determination of any criminal charge against him, or of his rights and obligations in a suit at law, everyone shall be entitled to a fair and public hearing by a competent, independent and impartial tribunal established by law. The press and the public may be excluded from all or part of a trial for reasons of morals, public order (ordre public) or national security in a democratic society, or when the interest of the private lives of the parties so requires, or to the extent strictly necessary in the opinion of the court in special circumstances where publicity would prejudice the interests of justice; but any judgment rendered in a criminal case or in a suit at law shall be made public except where the interest of juvenile persons otherwise requires or the proceedings concern matrimonial disputes or the guardianship of children.

2. Everyone charged with a criminal offence shall have the right to be presumed innocent until proved guilty according to law.

3. In the determination of any criminal charge against him, everyone shall be entitled to the following minimum guarantees, in full equality:

(a) To be informed promptly and in detail in a language which he understands of the nature and cause of the charge against him;

(b) To have adequate time and facilities for the preparation of his defence and to communicate with counsel of his own choosing;

(c) To be tried without undue delay;

(d) To be tried in his presence, and to defend himself in person or through legal assistance of his own choosing; to be informed, if he does not have legal assistance, of this right; and to have legal assistance assigned to him, in any case where the interests of justice so require, and without payment by him in any such case if he does not have sufficient means to pay for it;

(e) To examine, or have examined, the witnesses against him and to obtain the attendance and examination of witnesses on his behalf under the same conditions as witnesses against him;

(f) To have the free assistance of an interpreter if he cannot understand or speak the language used in court;

(g) Not to be compelled to testify against himself or to confess guilt.

4. In the case of juvenile persons, the procedure shall be such as will take account of their age and the desirability of promoting their rehabilitation.

5. Everyone convicted of a crime shall have the right to his conviction and sentence being reviewed by a higher tribunal according to law.

6. When a person has by a final decision been convicted of a criminal offence and when subsequently his conviction has been reversed or he has been pardoned on the

ground that a new or newly discovered fact shows conclusively that there has been a miscarriage of justice, the person who has suffered punishment as a result of such conviction shall be compensated according to law, unless it is proved that the non-disclosure of the unknown fact in time is wholly or partly attributable to him.

7. No one shall be liable to be tried or punished again for an offence for which he has already been finally convicted or acquitted in accordance with the law and penal procedure of each country.

Article 15

1. No one shall be held guilty of any criminal offence on account of any act or omission which did not constitute a criminal offence, under national or international law, at the time when it was committed. Nor shall a heavier penalty be imposed than the one that was applicable at the time when the criminal offence was committed. If, subsequent to the commission of the offence, provision is made by law for the imposition of the lighter penalty, the offender shall benefit thereby.

2. Nothing in this article shall prejudice the trial and punishment of any person for any act or omission which, at the time when it was committed, was criminal according to the general principles of law recognized by the community of nations.

Article 16

Everyone shall have the right to recognition everywhere as a person before the law.

Article 17

1. No one shall be subjected to arbitrary or unlawful interference with his privacy, family, or correspondence, nor to unlawful attacks on his honour and reputation.

2. Everyone has the right to the protection of the law against such interference or attacks.

Article 18

1. Everyone shall have the right to freedom of thought, conscience and religion. This right shall include freedom to have or to adopt a religion or belief of his choice, and freedom, either individually or in community with others and in public or private, to manifest his religion or belief in worship, observance, practice and teaching.

2. No one shall be subject to coercion which would impair his freedom to have or to adopt a religion or belief of his choice.

3. Freedom to manifest one's religion or beliefs may be subject only to such limitations as are prescribed by law and are necessary to protect public safety, order, health, or morals or the fundamental rights and freedoms of others.

4. The States Parties to the present Covenant undertake to have respect for the liberty of parents and, when applicable, legal guardians to ensure the religious and moral education of their children in conformity with their own convictions.

Article 19

1. Everyone shall have the right to hold opinions without interference.

2. Everyone shall have the right to freedom of expression; this right shall include freedom to seek, receive and impart information and ideas of all kinds, regardless of frontiers, either orally, in writing or in print, in the form of art, or through any other media of his choice.

3. The exercise of the rights provided for in paragraph 2 of this article carries with it special duties and responsibilities. It may therefore be subject to certain restrictions, but these shall only be such as are provided by law and are necessary:

(a) For respect of the rights or reputations of others;

(b) For the protection of national security or of public order (ordre public), or of public health or morals.

Article 20

1. Any propaganda for war shall be prohibited by law.

2. Any advocacy of national, racial or religious hatred that constitutes incitement to discrimination, hostility or violence shall be prohibited by law.

Article 21

The right of peaceful assembly shall be recognized. No restrictions may be placed on the exercise of this right other than those imposed in conformity with the law and which are necessary in a democratic society in the interests of national security or public safety, public order (ordre public), the protection of public health or morals or the protection of the rights and freedoms of others.

Article 22

1. Everyone shall have the right to freedom of association with others, including the right to form and join trade unions for the protection of his interests.

2. No restrictions may be placed on the exercise of this right other than those which are prescribed by law and which are necessary in a democratic society in the interests of national security or public safety, public order (ordre public), the protection of public health or morals or the protection of the rights and freedoms of others. This article shall not prevent the imposition of lawful restrictions on members of the armed forces and of the police in their exercise of this right.

...

Article 23

1. The family is the natural and fundamental group unit of society and is entitled to protection by society and the State.

2. The right of men and women of marriageable age to marry and to found a family shall be recognized.

3. No marriage shall be entered into without the free and full consent of the intending spouses.

4. States Parties to the present Covenant shall take appropriate steps to ensure equality of rights and responsibilities of spouses as to marriage, during marriage and at its dissolution. In the case of dissolution, provision shall be made for the necessary protection of any children.

Article 24

1. Every child shall have, without any discrimination as to race, colour, sex, language, religion, national or social origin, property or birth, the right to such measures of protection as are required by his status as a minor, on the part of his family, society and the State.

2. Every child shall be registered immediately after birth and shall have a name.

3. Every child has the right to acquire a nationality.

Article 25

Every citizen shall have the right and the opportunity, without any of the distinctions mentioned in article 2 and without unreasonable restrictions:

(a) To take part in the conduct of public affairs, directly or through freely chosen representatives;

(b) To vote and to be elected at genuine periodic elections which shall be by universal and equal suffrage and shall be held by secret ballot, guaranteeing the free expression of the will of the electors;

(c) To have access, on general terms of equality, to public service in his country.

Article 26

All persons are equal before the law and are entitled without any discrimination to the equal protection of the law. In this respect, the law shall prohibit any discrimination and guarantee to all persons equal and effective protection against discrimination on any ground such as race, colour, sex, language, religion, political or other opinion, national or social origin, property, birth or other status.

Article 27

In those States in which ethnic, religious or linguistic minorities exist, persons belonging to such minorities shall not be denied the right, in community with the other members of their group, to enjoy their own culture, to profess and practise their own religion, or to use their own language.

Part 4

Article 28

1. There shall be established a Human Rights Committee (hereafter referred to in the present Covenant as the Committee). It shall consist of eighteen members and shall carry out the functions hereinafter provided.

2. The Committee shall be composed of nationals of the States Parties to the present Covenant who shall be persons of high moral character and recognized competence in the field of human rights, consideration being given to the usefulness of the participation of some persons having legal experience.

3. The members of the Committee shall be elected and shall serve in their personal capacity.

. . .

Article 40

1. The States Parties to the present Covenant undertake to submit reports on the measures they have adopted which give effect to the rights recognized herein and on the progress made in the enjoyment of those rights:

(a) Within one year of the entry into force of the present Covenant for the States Parties concerned;

(b) Thereafter whenever the Committee so requests.

2. All reports shall be submitted to the Secretary-General of the United Nations, who shall transmit them to the Committee for consideration. Reports shall indicate the factors and difficulties, if any, affecting the implementation of the present Covenant.

3. The Secretary-General of the United Nations may, after consultation with the Committee, transmit to the specialized agencies concerned copies of such parts of the reports as may fall within their field of competence.

4. The Committee shall study the reports submitted by the States Parties to the present Covenant. It shall transmit its reports, and such general comments as it may consider appropriate, to the States Parties. The Committee may also transmit to the Economic and Social Council these comments along with the copies of the reports it has received from States Parties to the present Covenant.

5. The States Parties to the present Covenant may submit to the Committee observations on any comments that may be made in accordance with paragraph 4 of this article.

. . .

1. A State Party to the present Covenant may at any time declare under this article that it recognizes the competence of the Committee to receive and consider communications to the effect that a State Party claims that another State Party is not fulfilling its obligations under the present Covenant. Communications under this article may be received and considered only if submitted by a State Party which has made a declaration recognizing in regard to itself the competence of the Committee. No communication shall be received by the Committee if it concerns a State Party which has not made such a declaration. Communications received under this article shall be dealt with in accordance with the following procedure:

[Article 41 spells out a procedure involving efforts toward resolution, referral of the matter to the Committee, and a report by the Committee to the States Parties concerned that is confined 'to a brief statement of the facts; written submissions and a record of the oral submissions made by the States Parties concerned shall be attached to the report.' Article 42 provides that if the matter is not resolved to the satisfaction of the States Parties concerned the Committee may, with the consent of those parties, appoint an *ad hoc* Conciliation Commission. If no amicable solution is reached, the Commission submits a report to the Chairman of the Committee. The report includes the Commission's finding on all relevant questions of fact, and its views on possibilities of an amicable solution.]

. . .

Article 45

The Committee shall submit to the General Assembly of the United Nations, through the Economic and Social Council, an annual report on its activities.

Part 5

Article 46

Nothing in the present Covenant shall be interpreted as impairing the provisions of the Charter of the United Nations and of the constitutions of the specialized agencies which define the respective responsibilities of the various organs of the United Nations and of the specialized agencies in regard to the matters dealt with in the present Covenant.

Article 47

Nothing in the present Covenant shall be interpreted as impairing the inherent right of all peoples to enjoy and utilize fully and freely their natural wealth and resources.

. . .

Protocols to the International Covenant on Civil and Political Rights

First Optional Protocol

The States Parties to the present Protocol,

Considering that in order further to achieve the purposes of the International Covenant on Civil and Political Rights (hereinafter referred to as the Covenant) and the implementation of its provisions it would be appropriate to enable the Human Rights Committee set up in part IV of the Covenant (hereinafter referred to as the Committee) to receive and consider, as provided in the present Protocol, communications from individuals claiming to be victims of violations of any of the rights set forth in the Covenant.

Have agreed as follows:

Article 1

A State Party to the Covenant that becomes a Party to the present Protocol recognizes the competence of the Committee to receive and consider communications from individuals subject to its jurisdiction who claim to be victims of a violation by that State Party of any of the rights set forth in the Covenant. No communication shall be received by the Committee if it concerns a State Party to the Covenant which is not a Party to the present Protocol.

Article 2

Subject to the provisions of article 1, individuals who claim that any of their rights enumerated in the Covenant have been violated and who have exhausted all available domestic remedies may submit a written communication to the Committee for consideration.

Article 3

The Committee shall consider inadmissible any communication under the present Protocol which is anonymous, or which it considers to be an abuse of the right of submission of such communications or to be incompatible with the provisions of the Covenant.

Article 4

1. Subject to the provisions of article 3, the Committee shall bring any communications submitted to it under the present Protocol to the attention of the State Party to the present Protocol alleged to be violating any provision of the Covenant.

2. Within six months, the receiving State shall submit to the Committee written explanations or statements clarifying the matter and the remedy, if any, that may have been taken by that State.

Article 5

1. The Committee shall consider communications received under the present Protocol in the light of all written information made available to it by the individual and by the State Party concerned.

2. The Committee shall not consider any communication from an individual unless it has ascertained that:

(a) The same matter is not being examined under another procedure of international investigation or settlement;

(b) The individual has exhausted all available domestic remedies. This shall not be the rule where the application of the remedies is unreasonably prolonged.

3. The Committee shall hold closed meetings when examining communications under the present Protocol.

4. The Committee shall forward its views to the State Party concerned and to the individual.

Article 6

The Committee shall include in its annual report under article 45 of the Covenant a summary of its activities under the present Protocol.

...

Second Optional Protocol

The States Parties to the present Protocol,

Believing that abolition of the death penalty contributes to enhancement of human dignity and progressive development of human rights,

Recalling article 3 of the Universal Declaration of Human Rights, adopted on 10 December 1948, and article 6 of the International Covenant on Civil and Political Rights, adopted on 16 December 1966,

Noting that article 6 of the International Covenant on Civil and Political Rights refers to abolition of the death penalty in terms that strongly suggest that abolition is desirable,

Convinced that all measures of abolition of the death penalty should be considered as progress in the enjoyment of the right to life,

Desirous to undertake hereby an international commitment to abolish the death penalty,

Have agreed as follows:

Article 1

1. No one within the jurisdiction of a State Party to the present Protocol shall be executed.

2. Each State Party shall take all necessary measures to abolish the death penalty within its jurisdiction.

Article 2

1. No reservation is admissible to the present Protocol, except for a reservation made at the time of ratification or accession that provides for the application of the death penalty in time of war pursuant to a conviction for a most serious crime of a military nature committed during wartime.

...

Article 3

The States Parties to the present Protocol shall include in the reports they submit to the Human Rights Committee, in accordance with article 40 of the Covenant, information on the measures that they have adopted to give effect to the present Protocol.

. . .

International Covenant on Economic, Social, and Cultural Rights

Preamble

The States Parties to the present Covenant,

. . .

Recognizing that these rights derive from the inherent dignity of the human person,

Recognizing that, in accordance with the Universal Declaration of Human Rights, the ideal of free human beings enjoying freedom from fear and want can only be achieved if conditions are created whereby everyone may enjoy his economic, social and cultural rights, as well as his civil and political rights,

. . .

Realizing that the individual, having duties to other individuals and to the community to which he belongs, is under a responsibility to strive for the promotion and observance of the rights recognized in the present Covenant,

Agree upon the following articles:

Part 1

Article 1

1. All peoples have the right of self-determination. By virtue of that right they freely determine their political status and freely pursue their economic, social and cultural development.

2. All peoples may, for their own ends, freely dispose of their natural wealth and resources without prejudice to any obligations arising out of international economic cooperation, based upon the principle of mutual benefit, and international law. In no case may a people be deprived of its own means of subsistence.

3. The States Parties to the present Covenant, including those having responsibility for the administration of Non-Self-Governing and Trust Territories, shall promote the realization of the right of self-determination, and shall respect that right, in conformity with the provisions of the Charter of the United Nations.

Part 2

Article 2

1. Each State Party to the present Covenant undertakes to take steps, individually and through international assistance and co-operation, especially economic and technical, to the maximum of its available resources, with a view to achieving progressively the full realization of the rights recognized in the present Covenant by all appropriate means, including particularly the adoption of legislative measures.

2. The States Parties to the present Covenant undertake to guarantee that the rights enunciated in the present Covenant will be exercised without discrimination of any kind as to race, colour, sex, language, religion, political or other opinion, national or social origin, property, birth or other status.

3. Developing countries, with due regard to human rights and their national economy, may determine to what extent they would guarantee the economic rights recognized in the present Covenant to non-nationals.

Article 3

The States Parties to the present Covenant undertake to ensure the equal right of men and women to the enjoyment of all economic, social and cultural rights set forth in the present Covenant.

Article 4

The States Parties to the present Covenant recognize that, in the enjoyment of those rights provided by the State in conformity with the present Covenant, the State may subject such rights only to such limitations as are determined by law only in so far as this may be compatible with the nature of these rights and solely for the purpose of promoting the general welfare in a democratic society.

Article 5

1. Nothing in the present Covenant may be interpreted as implying for any State, group or person any right to engage in any activity or to perform any act aimed at the destruction of any of the rights or freedoms recognized herein, or at their limitation to a greater extent than is provided for in the present Covenant.

2. No restriction upon or derogation from any of the fundamental human rights recognized or existing in any country in virtue of law, conventions, regulations or custom shall be admitted on the pretext that the present Covenant does not recognize such rights or that it recognizes them to a lesser extent.

Part 3

Article 6

1. The States Parties to the present Covenant recognize the right to work, which includes the right of everyone to the opportunity to gain his living by work which he freely chooses or accepts, and will take appropriate steps to safeguard this right.

2. The steps to be taken by a State Party to the present Covenant to achieve the full realization of this right shall include technical and vocational guidance and training programmes, policies and techniques to achieve steady economic, social and cultural development and full and productive employment under conditions safeguarding fundamental political and economic freedoms to the individual.

Article 7

The States Parties to the present Covenant recognize the right of everyone to the enjoyment of just and favourable conditions of work which ensure, in particular:

(a) Remuneration which provides all workers, as a minimum, with:

(i) Fair wages and equal remuneration for work of equal value without distinction of any kind, in particular women being guaranteed conditions of work not inferior to those enjoyed by men, with equal pay for equal work;

(ii) A decent living for themselves and their families in accordance with the provisions of the present

Covenant;

(b) Safe and healthy working conditions;

(c) Equal opportunity for everyone to be promoted in his employment to an appropriate higher level, subject to no considerations other than those of seniority and competence;

(d) Rest, leisure and reasonable limitation of working hours and periodic holidays with pay, as well as remuneration for public holidays

Article 8

1. The States Parties to the present Covenant undertake to ensure:

(a) The right of everyone to form trade unions and join the trade union of his choice, subject only to the rules of the organization concerned, for the promotion and protection of his economic and social interests. No restrictions may be placed on the exercise of this right other than those prescribed by law and which are necessary in a democratic society in the interests of national security or public order or for the protection of the rights and freedoms of others;

(b) The right of trade unions to establish national federations or confederations and the right of the latter to form or join international trade-union organizations;

(c) The right of trade unions to function freely subject to no limitations other than those prescribed by law and which are necessary in a democratic society in the interests of national security or public order or for the protection of the rights and freedoms of others;

(d) The right to strike, provided that it is exercised in conformity with the laws of the particular country.

2. This article shall not prevent the imposition of lawful restrictions on the exercise of these rights by members of the armed forces or of the police or of the administration of the State.

...

Article 9

The States Parties to the present Covenant recognize the right of everyone to social security, including social insurance.

Article 10

The States Parties to the present Covenant recognize that:

1. The widest possible protection and assistance should be accorded to the family, which is the natural and fundamental group unit of society, particularly for its establishment and while it is responsible for the care and education of dependent children. Marriage must be entered into with the free consent of the intending spouses.

2. Special protection should be accorded to mothers during a reasonable period before and after childbirth. During such period working mothers should be accorded paid leave or leave with adequate social security benefits.

3. Special measures of protection and assistance should be taken on behalf of all children and young persons without any discrimination for reasons of parentage or other conditions. Children and young persons should be protected from economic and social exploitation. Their employment in work harmful to their morals or health or dangerous to life or likely to hamper their normal development should be punishable by law. States should also set age limits below which the paid employment of child labour should be prohibited and punishable by law.

Article 11

1. The States Parties to the present Covenant recognize the right of everyone to an adequate standard of living for himself and his family, including adequate food, clothing and housing, and to the continuous improvement of living conditions. The States Parties will take appropriate steps to ensure the realization of this right, recognizing to this effect the essential importance of international co-operation based on free consent.

2. The States Parties to the present Covenant, recognizing the fundamental right of everyone to be free from hunger, shall take, individually and through international co-operation, the measures, including specific programmes, which are needed:

(a) To improve methods of production, conservation and distribution of food by making full use of technical and scientific knowledge, by disseminating knowledge of the principles of nutrition and by developing or reforming agrarian systems in such a way as to achieve the most efficient development and utilization of natural resources;

(b) Taking into account the problems of both food-importing and food-exporting countries, to ensure an equitable distribution of world food supplies in relation to need.

Article 12

1. The States Parties to the present Covenant recognize the right of everyone to the enjoyment of the highest attainable standard of physical and mental health.

2. The steps to be taken by the States Parties to the present Covenant to achieve the full realization of this right shall include those necessary for:

(a) The provision for the reduction of the stillbirth-rate and of infant mortality and for the healthy development of the child;

(b) The improvement of all aspects of environmental and industrial hygiene;

(c) The prevention, treatment and control of epidemic, endemic, occupational and other diseases;

(d) The creation of conditions which would assure to all medical service and medical attention in the event of sickness.

Article 13

1. The States Parties to the present Covenant recognize the right of everyone to education. They agree that education shall be directed to the full development of the human personality and the sense of its dignity, and shall strengthen the respect for human rights and fundamental freedoms. They further agree that education shall enable all persons to participate effectively in a free society, promote understanding, tolerance and friendship among all nations and all racial, ethnic or religious groups, and further the activities of the United Nations for the maintenance of peace.

2. The States Parties to the present Covenant recognize that, with a view to achieving the full realization of this right:

(a) Primary education shall be compulsory and available free to all;

(b) Secondary education in its different forms, including technical and vocational secondary education, shall be made generally available and accessible to all by every appropriate means, and in particular by the progressive introduction of free education;

(c) Higher education shall be made equally accessible to all, on the basis of capacity, by every appropriate means, and in particular by the progressive introduction of free education;

(d) Fundamental education shall be encouraged or intensified as far as possible for those persons who have not received or completed the whole period of their primary education;

(e) The development of a system of schools at all levels shall be actively pursued, an adequate fellowship system shall be established, and the material conditions of teaching staff shall be continuously improved.

3. The States Parties to the present Covenant undertake to have respect for the liberty of parents and, when applicable, legal guardians to choose for their children schools, other than those established by the public authorities, which conform to such minimum educational standards as may be laid down or approved by the State and to ensure the religious and moral education of their children in conformity with their own convictions.

4. No part of this article shall be construed so as to interfere with the liberty of individuals and bodies to establish and direct educational institutions, subject always to the observance of the principles set forth in paragraph I of this article and to the requirement that the education given in such institutions shall conform to such minimum standards as may be laid down by the State.

Article 14

Each State Party to the present Covenant which, at the time of becoming a Party, has not been able to secure in its metropolitan territory or other territories under its jurisdiction compulsory primary education, free of charge, undertakes, within two years, to work out and adopt a detailed plan of action for the progressive implementation, within a reasonable number of years, to be fixed in the plan, of the principle of compulsory education free of charge for all.

Article 15

1. The States Parties to the present Covenant recognize the right of everyone:

(a) To take part in cultural life;

(b) To enjoy the benefits of scientific progress and its applications;

(c) To benefit from the protection of the moral and material interests resulting from any scientific, literary or artistic production of which he is the author.

2. The steps to be taken by the States Parties to the present Covenant to achieve the full realization of this right shall include those necessary for the conservation, the development and the diffusion of science and culture.

3. The States Parties to the present Covenant undertake to respect the freedom indispensable for scientific research and creative activity.

4. The States Parties to the present Covenant recognize the benefits to be derived from the encouragement and development of international contacts and co-operation in the scientific and cultural fields.

Part 4

Article 16

1. The States Parties to the present Covenant undertake to submit in conformity with this part of the Covenant reports on the measures which they have adopted and the progress made in achieving the observance of the rights recognized herein.

. . .

Article 22

The Economic and Social Council may bring to the attention of other organs of the United Nations, their subsidiary organs and specialized agencies concerned with furnishing technical assistance any matters arising out of the reports referred to in this part of the present Covenant which may assist such bodies in deciding, each within its field of competence, on the advisability of international measures likely to contribute to the effective progressive implementation of the present Covenant.

Article 23

The States Parties to the present Covenant agree that international action for the achievement of the rights recognized in the present Covenant includes such methods as the conclusion of conventions, the adoption of recommendations, the furnishing of technical assistance and the holding of regional meetings and technical meetings for the purpose of consultation and study organized in conjunction with the Governments concerned.

Article 24

Nothing in the present Covenant shall be interpreted as impairing the provisions of the Charter of the United Nations and of the constitutions of the specialized agencies which define the respective responsibilities of the various organs of the United Nations and of the specialized agencies in regard to the matters dealt with in the present Covenant.

Article 25

Nothing in the present Covenant shall be interpreted as impairing the inherent right of all peoples to enjoy and utilize fully and freely their natural wealth and resources.

. . .

Article 28

The provisions of the present Covenant shall extend to all parts of federal States without any limitations or exceptions. . . .

. . .

Optional Protocol to the International Covenant on Economic, Social, and Cultural Rights

Preamble

The States Parties to the present Protocol,

Considering that, in accordance with the principles proclaimed in the Charter of the United Nations, recognition of the inherent dignity and of the equal and inalienable rights of all members of the human family is the foundation of freedom, justice and peace in the world,

Noting that the Universal Declaration of Human Rights 1 proclaims that all human beings are born free and equal in dignity and rights and that everyone is entitled to all the rights and freedoms set forth therein, without distinction of any kind, such as race, colour, sex, language, religion, political or other opinion, national or social origin, property, birth or other status,

Recalling that the Universal Declaration of Human Rights and the International Covenants on Human Rights 2 recognize that the ideal of free human beings enjoying freedom from fear and want can only be achieved if conditions are created whereby everyone may enjoy civil, cultural, economic, political and social rights,

Reaffirming the universality, indivisibility, interdependence and interrelatedness of all human rights and fundamental freedoms,

Recalling that each State Party to the International Covenant on Economic, Social and Cultural Rights (hereinafter referred to as the Covenant) undertakes to take steps, individually and through international assistance and cooperation, especially economic and technical, to the maximum of its available resources, with a view to achieving progressively the full realization of the rights recognized in the Covenant by all appropriate means, including particularly the adoption of legislative measures,

Considering that, in order further to achieve the purposes of the Covenant and the implementation of its provisions, it would be appropriate to enable the Committee on Economic, Social and Cultural Rights (hereinafter referred to as the Committee) to carry out the functions provided for in the present Protocol,

Have agreed as follows:

Article 1

Competence of the Committee to receive and consider communications

1. A State Party to the Covenant that becomes a Party to the present Protocol recognizes the competence of the Committee to receive and consider communications as provided for by the provisions of the present Protocol.

2. No communication shall be received by the Committee if it concerns a State Party to the Covenant which is not a Party to the present Protocol.

Article 2
Communications

Communications may be submitted by or on behalf of individuals or groups of individuals, under the jurisdiction of a State Party, claiming to be victims of a violation of any of the economic, social and cultural rights set forth in the Covenant by that State Party. Where a communication is submitted on behalf of individuals or groups of individuals, this shall be with their consent unless the author can justify acting on their behalf without such consent.

Article 3
Admissibility

1. The Committee shall not consider a communication unless it has ascertained that all available domestic remedies have been exhausted. This shall not be the rule where the application of such remedies is unreasonably prolonged.

2. The Committee shall declare a communication inadmissible when:

(a) It is not submitted within one year after the exhaustion of domestic remedies, except in cases where the author can demonstrate that it had not been possible to submit the communication within that time limit;

(b) The facts that are the subject of the communication occurred prior to the entry into force of the present Protocol for the State Party concerned unless those facts continued after that date;

(c) The same matter has already been examined by the Committee or has been or is being examined under another procedure of international investigation or settlement;

(d) It is incompatible with the provisions of the Covenant;

(e) It is manifestly ill-founded, not sufficiently substantiated or exclusively based on reports disseminated by mass media;

(f) It is an abuse of the right to submit a communication; or when

(g) It is anonymous or not in writing.

Article 4
Communications not revealing a clear disadvantage

The Committee may, if necessary, decline to consider a communication where it does not reveal that the author has suffered a clear disadvantage, unless the Committee considers that the communication raises a serious issue of general importance.

Article 5
Interim measures

1. At any time after the receipt of a communication and before a determination on the merits has been reached, the Committee may transmit to the State Party concerned for its urgent consideration a request that the State Party take such interim measures as may be necessary in exceptional circumstances to avoid possible irreparable damage to the victim or victims of the alleged violations.

2. Where the Committee exercises its discretion under paragraph 1 of the present article, this does not imply a determination on admissibility or on the merits of the communication.

Article 6
Transmission of the communication

1. Unless the Committee considers a communication inadmissible without reference to the State Party concerned, the Committee shall bring any communication submitted to it under the present Protocol confidentially to the attention of the State Party concerned.

2. Within six months, the receiving State Party shall submit to the Committee written explanations or statements clarifying the matter and the remedy, if any, that may have been provided by that State Party.

Article 7
Friendly settlement

1. The Committee shall make available its good offices to the parties concerned with a view to reaching a friendly settlement of the matter on the basis of the respect for the obligations set forth in the Covenant.

2. An agreement on a friendly settlement closes consideration of the communication under the present Protocol.

Article 8
Examination of communications

1. The Committee shall examine communications received under article 2 of the present Protocol in the light of all documentation submitted to it, provided that this documentation is transmitted to the parties concerned.

2. The Committee shall hold closed meetings when examining communications under the present Protocol.

3. When examining a communication under the present Protocol, the Committee may consult, as appropriate, relevant documentation emanating from other United Nations

bodies, specialized agencies, funds, programmes and mechanisms, and other international organizations, including from regional human rights systems, and any observations or comments by the State Party concerned.

4. When examining communications under the present Protocol, the Committee shall consider the reasonableness of the steps taken by the State Party in accordance with part II of the Covenant. In doing so, the Committee shall bear in mind that the State Party may adopt a range of possible policy measures for the implementation of the rights set forth in the Covenant.

Article 9
Follow-up to the views of the Committee

1. After examining a communication, the Committee shall transmit its views on the communication, together with its recommendations, if any, to the parties concerned.

2. The State Party shall give due consideration to the views of the Committee, together with its recommendations, if any, and shall submit to the Committee, within six months, a written response, including information on any action taken in the light of the views and recommendations of the Committee.

3. The Committee may invite the State Party to submit further information about any measures the State Party has taken in response to its views or recommendations, if any, including as deemed appropriate by the Committee, in the State Party's subsequent reports under articles 16 and 17 of the Covenant.

Article 10
Inter-State communications

1. A State Party to the present Protocol may at any time declare under the present article that it recognizes the competence of the Committee to receive and consider communications to the effect that a State Party claims that another State Party is not fulfilling its obligations under the Covenant. Communications under the present article may be received and considered only if submitted by a State Party that has made a declaration recognizing in regard to itself the competence of the Committee. No communication shall be received by the Committee if it concerns a State Party which has not made such a declaration. Communications received under the present article shall be dealt with in accordance with the following procedure:

(a) If a State Party to the present Protocol considers that another State Party is not fulfilling its obligations under the Covenant, it may, by written communication, bring the matter to the attention of that State Party. The State Party may also inform the Committee of the matter. Within three months after the receipt of the communication the receiving State shall afford the State that sent the communication an explanation, or any other statement in writing clarifying the matter, which should include, to the extent possible and pertinent, reference to domestic procedures and remedies taken, pending or available in the matter;

(b) If the matter is not settled to the satisfaction of both States Parties concerned within six months after the receipt by the receiving State of the initial communication, either State shall have the right to refer the matter to the Committee, by notice given to the Committee and to the other State;

(c) The Committee shall deal with a matter referred to it only after it has ascertained that all available domestic remedies have been invoked and exhausted in the matter. This shall not be the rule where the application of the remedies is unreasonably prolonged;

(d) Subject to the provisions of subparagraph (c) of the present paragraph the Committee shall make available its good offices to the States Parties concerned with a view to a friendly solution of the matter on the basis of the respect for the obligations set forth in the Covenant;

(e) The Committee shall hold closed meetings when examining communications under the present article;

(f) In any matter referred to it in accordance with subparagraph (b) of the present paragraph, the Committee may call upon the States Parties concerned, referred to in subparagraph (b), to supply any relevant information;

(g) The States Parties concerned, referred to in subparagraph (b) of the present paragraph, shall have the right to be represented when the matter is being considered by the Committee and to make submissions orally and/or in writing;

(h) The Committee shall, with all due expediency after the date of receipt of notice under subparagraph (b) of the present paragraph, submit a report, as follows:

(i) If a solution within the terms of subparagraph (d) of the present paragraph is reached, the Committee shall confine its report to a brief statement of the facts and of the solution reached;

(ii) If a solution within the terms of subparagraph (d) is not reached, the Committee shall, in its report, set forth the relevant facts concerning the issue between the States Parties concerned. The written submissions and record of the oral submissions made by the States Parties concerned shall be attached to the report. The Committee may also communicate only to the States Parties concerned any views that it may consider relevant to the issue between them. In every matter, the report shall be communicated to the States Parties concerned.

2. A declaration under paragraph 1 of the present article shall be deposited by the States Parties with the Secretary-General of the United Nations, who shall transmit copies thereof to the other States Parties. A declaration may be withdrawn at any time by notification to the Secretary-General. Such a withdrawal shall not prejudice the consideration of any matter that is the subject of a communication already transmitted under the present article; no further communication by any State Party shall be received under the present article after the notification of withdrawal of the declaration has been received by the Secretary-General, unless the State Party concerned has made a new declaration.

Article 11
Inquiry procedure

1. A State Party to the present Protocol may at any time declare that it recognizes the competence of the Committee provided for under the present article.

2. If the Committee receives reliable information indicating grave or systematic violations by a State Party of any of the economic, social and cultural rights set forth in the Covenant, the Committee shall invite that State Party to cooperate in the examination of the information and to this end to submit observations with regard to the information concerned.

3. Taking into account any observations that may have been submitted by the State Party concerned as well as any other reliable information available to it, the Committee may designate one or more of its members to conduct an inquiry and to report urgently to the Committee. Where warranted and with the consent of the State Party, the inquiry may include a visit to its territory.

4. Such an inquiry shall be conducted confidentially and the cooperation of the State Party shall be sought at all stages of the proceedings.

5. After examining the findings of such an inquiry, the Committee shall transmit these findings to the State Party concerned together with any comments and recommendations.

6. The State Party concerned shall, within six months of receiving the findings, comments and recommendations transmitted by the Committee, submit its observations to the Committee.

7. After such proceedings have been completed with regard to an inquiry made in accordance with paragraph 2 of the present article, the Committee may, after consultations with the State Party concerned, decide to include a summary account of the results of the proceedings in its annual report provided for in article 15 of the present Protocol.

8. Any State Party having made a declaration in accordance with paragraph 1 of the present article may, at any time, withdraw this declaration by notification to the Secretary-General.

Article 12
Follow-up to the inquiry procedure

1. The Committee may invite the State Party concerned to include in its report under articles 16 and 17 of the Covenant details of any measures taken in response to an inquiry conducted under article 11 of the present Protocol.

2. The Committee may, if necessary, after the end of the period of six months referred to in article 11, paragraph 6, invite the State Party concerned to inform it of the measures taken in response to such an inquiry.

Article 13
Protection measures

A State Party shall take all appropriate measures to ensure that individuals under its jurisdiction are not subjected to any form of ill-treatment or intimidation as a consequence of communicating with the Committee pursuant to the present Protocol.

Article 14
International assistance and cooperation

1. The Committee shall transmit, as it may consider appropriate, and with the consent of the State Party concerned, to United Nations specialized agencies, funds and programmes and other competent bodies, its views or recommendations concerning communications and inquiries that indicate a need for technical advice or assistance, along with the State Party's observations and suggestions, if any, on these views or recommendations.

2. The Committee may also bring to the attention of such bodies, with the consent of the State Party concerned, any matter arising out of communications considered under the present Protocol which may assist them in deciding, each within its field of competence, on the advisability of international measures likely to contribute to assisting States Parties in achieving progress in implementation of the rights recognized in the Covenant.

3. A trust fund shall be established in accordance with the relevant procedures of the General Assembly, to be administered in accordance with the financial regulations and rules of the United Nations, with a view to providing expert and technical assistance to States Parties, with the consent of the State Party concerned, for the enhanced implementation of the rights contained in the Covenant, thus contributing to building national capacities in the area of economic, social and cultural rights in the context of the present Protocol.

4. The provisions of the present article are without prejudice to the obligations of each State Party to fulfil its obligations under the Covenant.

Article 15
Annual report

The Committee shall include in its annual report a summary of its activities under the present Protocol.

Article 16
Dissemination and information

Each State Party undertakes to make widely known and to disseminate the Covenant and the present Protocol and to facilitate access to information about the views and recommendations of the Committee, in particular, on matters involving that State Party, and to do so in accessible formats for persons with disabilities.

Article 17
Signature, ratification and accession

1. The present Protocol is open for signature by any State that has signed, ratified or acceded to the Covenant.

2. The present Protocol is subject to ratification by any State that has ratified or acceded to the Covenant. Instruments of ratification shall be deposited with the Secretary-General of the United Nations.

3. The present Protocol shall be open to accession by any State that has ratified or acceded to the Covenant.

4. Accession shall be effected by the deposit of an instrument of accession with the Secretary-General of the United Nations....

Convention on the Elimination of All Forms of Discrimination against Women

The States Parties to the present Convention,

Noting that the Charter of the United Nations reaffirms faith in fundamental human rights, in the dignity and worth of the human person and in the equal rights of men and women,

Noting that the Universal Declaration of Human Rights affirms the principle of the inadmissibility of discrimination and proclaims that all human beings are born free and equal in dignity and rights and that everyone is entitled to all the rights and freedoms set forth therein, without distinction of any kind, including distinction based on sex,

Noting that the States Parties to the International Covenants on Human Rights have the obligation to ensure the equal rights of men and women to enjoy all economic, social, cultural, civil and political rights,

. . .

Concerned, however, that despite these various instruments extensive discrimination against women continues to exist,

Recalling that discrimination against women violates the principles of equality of rights and respect for human dignity, is an obstacle to the participation of women, on equal terms with men, in the political, social, economic and cultural life of their countries, hampers the growth of the prosperity of society and the family and makes more difficult the full development of the potentialities of women in the service of their countries and of humanity,

...

Convinced that the full and complete development of a country, the welfare of the world and the cause of peace require the maximum participation of women on equal terms with men in all fields,

Bearing in mind the great contribution of women to the welfare of the family and to the development of society, so far not fully recognized, the social significance of maternity and the role of both parents in the family and in the upbringing of children, and aware that the role of women in procreation should not be a basis for discrimination but that the upbringing of children requires a sharing of responsibility between men and women and society as a whole,

Aware that a change in the traditional role of men as well as the role of women in society and in the family is needed to achieve full equality between men and women,

...

Have agreed on the following:

Part 1

Article 1

For the purposes of the present Convention, the term "discrimination against women" shall mean any distinction, exclusion or restriction made on the basis of sex which has the effect or purpose of impairing or nullifying the recognition, enjoyment or exercise by women, irrespective of their marital status, on a basis of equality of men and women, of human rights and fundamental freedoms in the political, economic, social, cultural, civil or any other field.

Article 2

States Parties condemn discrimination against women in all its forms, agree to pursue by all appropriate means and without delay a policy of eliminating discrimination against women and, to this end, undertake:

(a) To embody the principle of the equality of men and women in their national constitutions or other appropriate legislation if not yet incorporated therein and to ensure, through law and other appropriate means, the practical realization of this principle;

(b) To adopt appropriate legislative and other measures, including sanctions where appropriate, prohibiting all discrimination against women;

(c) To establish legal protection of the rights of women on an equal basis with men and to ensure through competent national tribunals and other public institutions the effective protection of women against any act of discrimination;

(d) To refrain from engaging in any act or practice of discrimination against women and to ensure that public authorities and institutions shall act in conformity with this obligation;

(e) To take all appropriate measures to eliminate discrimination against women by any person, organization or enterprise;

(f) To take all appropriate measures, including legislation, to modify or abolish existing laws, regulations, customs and practices which constitute discrimination against women;

(g) To repeal all national penal provisions which constitute discrimination against women.

Article 3

States Parties shall take in all fields, in particular in the political, social, economic and cultural fields, all appropriate measures, including legislation, to ensure the full development and advancement of women, for the purpose of guaranteeing them the exercise and enjoyment of human rights and fundamental freedoms on a basis of equality with men.

Article 4

1. Adoption by States Parties of temporary special measures aimed at accelerating de facto equality between men and women shall not be considered discrimination as defined in the present Convention, but shall in no way entail as a consequence the maintenance of unequal or separate standards; these measures shall be discontinued when the objectives of equality of opportunity and treatment have been achieved.

2. Adoption by States Parties of special measures, including those measures contained in the present Convention, aimed at protecting maternity shall not be considered discriminatory.

Article 5

States Parties shall take all appropriate measures:

(a) To modify the social and cultural patterns of conduct of men and women, with a view to achieving the elimination of prejudices and customary and all other practices which are based on the idea of the inferiority or the superiority of either of the sexes or on stereotyped roles for men and women;

(b) To ensure that family education includes a proper understanding of maternity as a social function and the recognition of the common responsibility of men and women in the upbringing and development of their children, it being understood that the interest of the children is the primordial consideration in all cases.

Article 6

States Parties shall take all appropriate measures, including legislation, to suppress all forms of traffic in women and exploitation of prostitution of women.

Part 2

Article 7

States Parties shall take all appropriate measures to eliminate discrimination against women in the political and public life of the country and, in particular, shall ensure to women, on equal terms with men, the right:

(a) To vote in all elections and public referenda and to be eligible for election to all publicly elected bodies;

(b) To participate in the formulation of government policy and the implementation thereof and to hold public office and perform all public functions at all levels of government;

(c) To participate in non-governmental organizations and associations concerned with the public and political life of the country.

Article 8

States Parties shall take all appropriate measures to ensure to women, on equal terms with men and without any discrimination, the opportunity to represent their Governments at the international level and to participate in the work of international organizations.

Article 9

1. States Parties shall grant women equal rights with men to acquire, change or retain their nationality. They shall ensure in particular that neither marriage to an alien nor change of nationality by the husband during marriage shall automatically change the nationality of the wife, render her stateless or force upon her the nationality of the husband.

2. States Parties shall grant women equal rights with men with respect to the nationality of their children.

Part 3

Article 10

States Parties shall take all appropriate measures to eliminate discrimination against women in order to ensure to them equal rights with men in the field of education and in particular to ensure, on a basis of equality of men and women:

(a) The same conditions for career and vocational guidance, for access to studies and for the achievement of diplomas in educational establishments of all categories in rural as well as in urban areas; this equality shall be ensured in pre-school, general, technical, professional and higher technical education, as well as in all types of vocational training;

(b) Access to the same curricula, the same examinations, teaching staff with qualifications of the same standard and school premises and equipment of the same quality;

(c) The elimination of any stereotyped concept of the roles of men and women at all levels and in all forms of education by encouraging coeducation and other types of education which will help to achieve this aim and, in particular, by the revision of textbooks and school programmes and the adaptation of teaching methods;

(d) The same opportunities to benefit from scholarships and other study grants;

(e) The same opportunities for access to programmes of continuing education, including adult and functional literacy programmes, particularly those aimed at reducing, at the earliest possible time, any gap in education existing between men and women;

(f) The reduction of female student drop-out rates and the organization of programmes for girls and women who have left school prematurely;

(g) The same Opportunities to participate actively in sports and physical education;

(h) Access to specific educational information to help to ensure the health and well-being of families, including information and advice on family planning.

Article 11

1. States Parties shall take all appropriate measures to eliminate discrimination against women in the field of employment in order to ensure, on a basis of equality of men and women, the same rights, in particular:

(a) The right to work as an inalienable right of all human beings;

(b) The right to the same employment opportunities, including the application of the same criteria for selection in matters of employment;

(c) The right to free choice of profession and employment, the right to promotion, job security and all benefits and conditions of service and the right to receive vocational training and retraining, including apprenticeships, advanced vocational training and recurrent training;

(d) The right to equal remuneration, including benefits, and to equal treatment in respect of work of equal value, as well as equality of treatment in the evaluation of the quality of work;

(e) The right to social security, particularly in cases of retirement, unemployment, sickness, invalidity and old age and other incapacity to work, as well as the right to paid leave;

(f) The right to protection of health and to safety in working conditions, including the safeguarding of the function of reproduction.

2. In order to prevent discrimination against women on the grounds of marriage or maternity and to ensure their effective right to work, States Parties shall take appropriate measures:

(a) To prohibit, subject to the imposition of sanctions, dismissal on the grounds of pregnancy or of maternity leave and discrimination in dismissals on the basis of marital status;

(b) To introduce maternity leave with pay or with comparable social benefits without loss of former employment, seniority or social allowances;

(c) To encourage the provision of the necessary supporting social services to enable parents to combine family obligations with work responsibilities and participation in public life, in particular through promoting the establishment and development of a network of child-care facilities;

(d) To provide special protection to women during pregnancy in types of work proved to be harmful to them.

3. Protective legislation relating to matters covered in this article shall be reviewed periodically in the light of scientific and technological knowledge and shall be revised, repealed or extended as necessary.

Article 12

1. States Parties shall take all appropriate measures to eliminate discrimination against women in the field of health care in order to ensure, on a basis of equality of men and women, access to health care services, including those related to family planning.

2. Notwithstanding the provisions of paragraph I of this article, States Parties shall ensure to women appropriate services in connection with pregnancy, confinement and the post-natal period, granting free services where necessary, as well as adequate nutrition during pregnancy and lactation.

Article 13

States Parties shall take all appropriate measures to eliminate discrimination against women in other areas of economic and social life in order to ensure, on a basis of equality of men and women, the same rights, in particular:

(a) The right to family benefits;

(b) The right to bank loans, mortgages and other forms of financial credit;

(c) The right to participate in recreational activities, sports and all aspects of cultural life.

Article 14

1. States Parties shall take into account the particular problems faced by rural women and the significant roles which rural women play in the economic survival of their families, including their work in the non-monetized sectors of the economy, and shall take all appropriate measures to ensure the application of the provisions of the present Convention to women in rural areas.

2. States Parties shall take all appropriate measures to eliminate discrimination against women in rural areas in order to ensure, on a basis of equality of men and women, that they participate in and benefit from rural development and, in particular, shall ensure to such women the right:

(a) To participate in the elaboration and implementation of development planning at all levels;

(b) To have access to adequate health care facilities, including information, counselling and services in family planning;

(c) To benefit directly from social security programmes;

(d) To obtain all types of training and education, formal and non-formal, including that relating to functional literacy, as well as, *inter alia*, the benefit of all community and extension services, in order to increase their technical proficiency;

(e) To organize self-help groups and co-operatives in order to obtain equal access to economic opportunities through employment or self employment;

(f) To participate in all community activities;

(g) To have access to agricultural credit and loans, marketing facilities, appropriate technology and equal treatment in land and agrarian reform as well as in land resettlement schemes;

(h) To enjoy adequate living conditions, particularly in relation to housing, sanitation, electricity and water supply, transport and communications.

Part 4

Article 15

1. States Parties shall accord to women equality with men before the law.

2. States Parties shall accord to women, in civil matters, a legal capacity identical to that of men and the same opportunities to exercise that capacity. In particular, they shall give women equal rights to conclude contracts and to administer property and shall treat them equally in all stages of procedure in courts and tribunals.

3. States Parties agree that all contracts and all other private instruments of any kind with a legal effect which is directed at restricting the legal capacity of women shall be deemed null and void.

4. States Parties shall accord to men and women the same rights with regard to the law relating to the movement of persons and the freedom to choose their residence and domicile.

Article 16

1. States Parties shall take all appropriate measures to eliminate discrimination against women in all matters relating to marriage and family relations and in particular shall ensure, on a basis of equality of men and women:

(a) The same right to enter into marriage;

(b) The same right freely to choose a spouse and to enter into marriage only with their free and full consent;

(c) The same rights and responsibilities during marriage and at its dissolution;

(d) The same rights and responsibilities as parents, irrespective of their marital status, in matters relating to their children; in all cases the interests of the children shall be paramount;

(e) The same rights to decide freely and responsibly on the number and spacing of their children and to have access to the information, education and means to enable them to exercise these rights;

(f) The same rights and responsibilities with regard to guardianship, wardship, trusteeship and adoption of children, or similar institutions where these concepts exist in national legislation; in all cases the interests of the children shall be paramount;

(g) The same personal rights as husband and wife, including the right to choose a family name, a profession and an occupation;

(h) The same rights for both spouses in respect of the ownership, acquisition, management, administration, enjoyment and disposition of property, whether free of charge or for a valuable consideration.

2. The betrothal and the marriage of a child shall have no legal effect, and all necessary action, including legislation, shall be taken to specify a minimum age for marriage and to make the registration of marriages in an official registry compulsory.

Part 5

Article 17

1. For the purpose of considering the progress made in the implementation of the present Convention, there shall be established a Committee on the Elimination of Discrimination against Women (hereinafter referred to as the Committee) consisting, at the time of entry into force of the Convention, of eighteen and, after ratification of or accession to the Convention by the thirty-fifth State Party, of twenty-three experts of high moral standing and competence in the field covered by the Convention. The experts shall be elected by States Parties from among their nationals and shall serve in their personal capacity, consideration being given to equitable geographical distribution and to the representation of the different forms of civilization as well as the principal legal systems.

. . .

Article 18

1. States Parties undertake to submit to the Secretary-General of the United Nations, for consideration by the Committee, a report on the legislative, judicial, administrative or other measures which they have adopted to give effect to the provisions of the present Convention and on the progress made in this respect:

(a) Within one year after the entry into force for the State concerned;

(b) Thereafter at least every four years and further whenever the Committee so requests.

2. Reports may indicate factors and difficulties affecting the degree of fulfilment of obligations under the present Convention.

...

Article 21

1. The Committee shall, through the Economic and Social Council, report annually to the General Assembly of the United Nations on its activities and may make suggestions and general recommendations based on the examination of reports and information received from the States Parties. Such suggestions and general recommendations shall be included in the report of the Committee together with comments, if any, from States Parties.

...

Part 6

Article 23

Nothing in the present Convention shall affect any provisions that are more conducive to the achievement of equality between men and women which may be contained:

(a) In the legislation of a State Party; or

(b) In any other international convention, treaty or agreement in force for that State.

Article 24

States Parties undertake to adopt all necessary measures at the national level aimed at achieving the full realization of the rights recognized in the present Convention.

...

Article 28

1. The Secretary-General of the United Nations shall receive and circulate to all States the text of reservations made by States at the time of ratification or accession.

2. A reservation incompatible with the object and purpose of the present Convention shall not be permitted ...

Article 29

1. Any dispute between two or more States Parties concerning the interpretation or application of the present Convention which is not settled by negotiation shall, at the request of one of them, be submitted to arbitration. If within six months from the date of the request for arbitration the parties are unable to agree on the organization of the arbitration, any one of those parties may refer the dispute to the International Court of Justice by request in conformity with the Statute of the Court.

...

Optional Protocol to the Convention on the Elimination of All Forms of Discrimination against Women

The General Assembly,

Reaffirming the Vienna Declaration and Programme of Action and the Beijing Declaration and Platform for Action,

Recalling that the Beijing Platform for Action, pursuant to the Vienna Declaration and Programme of Action, supported the process initiated by the Commission on the Status of Women with a view to elaborating a draft optional protocol to the Convention on the Elimination of All Forms of Discrimination against Women that could enter into force as soon as possible on a right-to-petition procedure,

Noting that the Beijing Platform for Action also called on all States that have not yet ratified or acceded to the Convention to do so as soon as possible so that universal ratification of the Convention can be achieved by the year 2000,

Adopts and opens for signature, ratification and accession the Optional Protocol to the Convention, the text of which is annexed to the present resolution;

Calls upon all States that have signed, ratified or acceded to the Convention to sign and ratify or to accede to the Protocol as soon as possible;

Stresses that States parties to the Protocol should undertake to respect the rights and procedures provided by the Protocol and cooperate with the Committee on the Elimination of Discrimination against Women at all stages of its proceedings under the Protocol;

Stresses also that in the fulfillment of its mandate as well as its functions under the Protocol, the Committee should continue to be guided by the principles of non-selectivity, impartiality and objectivity;

Requests the Committee to hold meetings to exercise its functions under the Protocol after its entry into force, in addition to its meetings held under article 20 of the Convention; the duration of such meetings shall be determined and, if necessary, reviewed by a meeting of the States parties to the Protocol, subject to the approval of the General Assembly;

Requests the Secretary-General to provide the staff and facilities necessary for the effective performance of the functions of the Committee under the Protocol after its entry into force;

Also requests the Secretary-General to include information on the status of the Protocol in her or his regular reports submitted to the General Assembly on the status of the Convention.

Annex

Article 1

A State Party to the present Protocol ("State Party") recognizes the competence of the Committee on the Elimination of Discrimination against Women ("the Committee") to receive and consider communications submitted in accordance with article 2.

Article 2

Communications may be submitted by or on behalf of individuals or groups of individuals, under the jurisdiction of a State Party, claiming to be victims of a violation of any of the rights set forth in the Convention by that State Party. Where a communication is submitted on behalf of individuals or groups of individuals, this shall be with their consent unless the author can justify acting on their behalf without such consent.

Article 3

Communications shall be in writing and shall not be anonymous. No communication shall be received by the Committee if it concerns a State Party to the Convention that is not a party to the present Protocol.

Article 4

1. The Committee shall not consider a communication unless it has ascertained that all available domestic remedies have been exhausted unless the application of such remedies is unreasonably prolonged or unlikely to bring effective relief.

2. The Committee shall declare a communication inadmissible where:

(*a*) The same matter has already been examined by the Committee or has been or is being examined under another procedure of international investigation or settlement;

(*b*) It is incompatible with the provisions of the Convention;

(*c*) It is manifestly ill-founded or not sufficiently substantiated;

(*d*) It is an abuse of the right to submit a communication;

(*e*) The facts that are the subject of the communication occurred prior to the entry into force of the present Protocol for the State Party concerned unless those facts continued after that date.

Article 5

1. At any time after the receipt of a communication and before a determination on the merits has been reached, the Committee may transmit to the State Party concerned for its urgent consideration a request that the State Party take such interim measures as may be necessary to avoid possible irreparable damage to the victim or victims of the alleged violation.

2. Where the Committee exercises its discretion under paragraph 1 of the present article, this does not imply a determination on admissibility or on the merits of the communication.

Article 6

1. Unless the Committee considers a communication inadmissible without reference to the State Party concerned, and provided that the individual or individuals consent to the disclosure of their identity to that State Party, the Committee shall bring any communication submitted to it under the present Protocol confidentially to the attention of the State Party concerned.

2. Within six months, the receiving State Party shall submit to the Committee written explanations or statements clarifying the matter and the remedy, if any, that may have been provided by that State Party.

Article 7

1. The Committee shall consider communications received under the present Protocol in the light of all information made available to it by or on behalf of individuals or groups of individuals and by the State Party concerned, provided that this information is transmitted to the parties concerned.

2. The Committee shall hold closed meetings when examining communications under the present Protocol.

3. After examining a communication, the Committee shall transmit its views on the communication, together with its recommendations, if any, to the parties concerned.

4. The State Party shall give due consideration to the views of the Committee, together with its recommendations, if any, and shall submit to the Committee, within six months, a written response, including information on any action taken in the light of the views and recommendations of the Committee.

5. The Committee may invite the State Party to submit further information about any measures the State Party has taken in response to its views or recommendations, if any, including as deemed appropriate by the Committee, in the State Party's subsequent reports under article 18 of the Convention.

Article 8

1. If the Committee receives reliable information indicating grave or systematic violations by a State Party of rights set forth in the Convention, the Committee shall invite that State Party to cooperate in the examination of the information and to this end to submit observations with regard to the information concerned.

2. Taking into account any observations that may have been submitted by the State Party concerned as well as any other reliable information available to it, the Committee may designate one or more of its members to conduct an inquiry and to report urgently to the Committee. Where warranted and with the consent of the State Party, the inquiry may include a visit to its territory.

3. After examining the findings of such an inquiry, the Committee shall transmit these findings to the State Party concerned together with any comments and recommendations.

4. The State Party concerned shall, within six months of receiving the findings, comments and recommendations transmitted by the Committee, submit its observations to the Committee.

5. Such an inquiry shall be conducted confidentially and the cooperation of the State Party shall be sought at all stages of the proceedings.

Article 9

1. The Committee may invite the State Party concerned to include in its report under article 18 of the Convention details of any measures taken in response to an inquiry conducted under article 8 of the present Protocol.

2. The Committee may, if necessary, after the end of the period of six months referred to in article 8.4, invite the State Party concerned to inform it of the measures taken in response to such an inquiry.

Article 10

1. Each State Party may, at the time of signature or ratification of the present Protocol or accession thereto, declare that it does not recognize the competence of the Committee provided for in articles 8 and 9.

2. Any State Party having made a declaration in accordance with paragraph 1 of the present article may, at any time, withdraw this declaration by notification to the Secretary-General.

Article 11

A State Party shall take all appropriate steps to ensure that individuals under its jurisdiction are not subjected to ill treatment or intimidation as a consequence of communicating with the Committee pursuant to the present Protocol.

Article 12

The Committee shall include in its annual report under article 21 of the Convention a summary of its activities under the present Protocol.

Article 13

Each State Party undertakes to make widely known and to give publicity to the Convention and the present Protocol and to facilitate access to information about the views and recommendations of the Committee, in particular, on matters involving that State Party.

Article 14

The Committee shall develop its own rules of procedure to be followed when exercising the functions conferred on it by the present Protocol.

Article 15

1. The present Protocol shall be open for signature by any State that has signed, ratified or acceded to the Convention.

2. The present Protocol shall be subject to ratification by any State that has ratified or acceded to the Convention. Instruments of ratification shall be deposited with the Secretary-General of the United Nations.

3. The present Protocol shall be open to accession by any State that has ratified or acceded to the Convention.

4. Accession shall be effected by the deposit of an instrument of accession with the Secretary-General of the United Nations.

Article 16

1. The present Protocol shall enter into force three months after the date of the deposit with the Secretary-General of the United Nations of the tenth instrument of ratification or accession.

2. For each State ratifying the present Protocol or acceding to it after its entry into force, the present Protocol shall enter into force three months after the date of the deposit of its own instrument of ratification or accession.

Article 17

No reservations to the present Protocol shall be permitted.

Article 18

1. Any State Party may propose an amendment to the present Protocol and file it with the Secretary-General of the United Nations. The Secretary-General shall thereupon communicate any proposed amendments to the States Parties with a request that they notify her or him whether they favour a conference of States Parties for the purpose of considering and voting on the proposal. In the event that at least one third of the States Parties favour such a conference, the Secretary-General shall convene the conference under the auspices of the United Nations. Any amendment adopted by a majority of the States Parties present and voting at the conference shall be submitted to the General Assembly of the United Nations for approval.

2. Amendments shall come into force when they have been approved by the General Assembly of the United Nations and accepted by a two-thirds majority of the States Parties to the present Protocol in accordance with their respective constitutional processes.

3. When amendments come into force, they shall be binding on those States Parties that have accepted them, other States Parties still being bound by the provisions of the present Protocol and any earlier amendments that they have accepted.

Article 19

1. Any State Party may denounce the present Protocol at any time by written notification addressed to the Secretary-General of the United Nations. Denunciation shall take effect six months after the date of receipt of the notification by the Secretary-General.

2. Denunciation shall be without prejudice to the continued application of the provisions of the present Protocol to any communication submitted under article 2 or any inquiry initiated under article 8 before the effective date of denunciation.

Article 20

The Secretary-General of the United Nations shall inform all States of:

(*a*) Signatures, ratifications and accessions under the present Protocol;

(*b*) The date of entry into force of the present Protocol and of any amendment under article 18;

(*c*) Any denunciation under article 19.

Article 21

1. The present Protocol, of which the Arabic, Chinese, English, French, Russian and Spanish texts are equally authentic, shall be deposited in the archives of the United Nations.

2. The Secretary-General of the United Nations shall transmit certified copies of the present Protocol to all States referred to in article 25 of the Convention.

...

Convention against Torture and Other Cruel, Inhuman or Degrading Treatment or Punishment

The States Parties to this Convention,

Considering that, in accordance with the principles proclaimed in the Charter of the United Nations, recognition of the equal and inalienable rights of all members of the human family is the foundation of freedom, justice and peace in the world,

Recognizing that those rights derive from the inherent dignity of the human person,

Considering the obligation of States under the Charter, in particular Article 55, to promote universal respect for, and observance of, human rights and fundamental freedoms,

Having regard to article 5 of the Universal Declaration of Human Rights and article 7 of the International Covenant on Civil and Political Rights, both of which provide that no one shall be subjected to torture or to cruel, inhuman or degrading treatment or punishment,

Having regard also to the Declaration on the Protection of All Persons from Being Subjected to Torture and Other Cruel, Inhuman or Degrading Treatment or Punishment, adopted by the General Assembly on 9 December 1975,

Desiring to make more effective the struggle against torture and other cruel, inhuman or degrading treatment or punishment throughout the world,

Have agreed as follows:

Part 1

Article 1

1. For the purposes of this Convention, the term "torture" means any act by which severe pain or suffering, whether physical or mental, is intentionally inflicted on a person for such purposes as obtaining from him or a third person information or a confession, punishing him for an act he or a third person has committed or is suspected of having committed, or intimidating or coercing him or a third person, or for any reason based on discrimination of any kind, when such pain or suffering is inflicted by or at the instigation of or with the consent or acquiescence of a public official or other person acting in an official capacity. It does not include pain or suffering arising only from, inherent in or incidental to lawful sanctions.

2. This article is without prejudice to any international instrument or national legislation which does or may contain provisions of wider application.

Article 2

1. Each State Party shall take effective legislative, administrative, judicial or other measures to prevent acts of torture in any territory under its jurisdiction.

2. No exceptional circumstances whatsoever, whether a state of war or a threat of war, internal political instability or any other public emergency, may be invoked as a justification of torture.

3. An order from a superior officer or a public authority may not be invoked as a justification of torture.

Article 3

1. No State Party shall expel, return (*"refouler"*) or extradite a person to another State where there are substantial grounds for believing that he would be in danger of being subjected to torture.

2. For the purpose of determining whether there are such grounds, the competent authorities shall take into account all relevant considerations including, where applicable, the existence in the State concerned of a consistent pattern of gross, flagrant or mass violations of human rights.

Article 4

1. Each State Party shall ensure that all acts of torture are offences under its criminal law. The same shall apply to an attempt to commit torture and to an act by any person which constitutes complicity or participation in torture.

2. Each State Party shall make these offences punishable by appropriate penalties which take into account their grave nature.

Article 5

1. Each State Party shall take such measures as may be necessary to establish its jurisdiction over the offences referred to in article 4 in the following cases:

(a) When the offences are committed in any territory under its jurisdiction or on board a ship or aircraft registered in that State;

(b) When the alleged offender is a national of that State;

(c) When the victim is a national of that State if that State considers it appropriate.

2. Each State Party shall likewise take such measures as may be necessary to establish its jurisdiction over such offences in cases where the alleged offender is present in any

territory under its jurisdiction and it does not extradite him pursuant to article 8 to any of the States mentioned in paragraph 1 of this article.

3. This Convention does not exclude any criminal jurisdiction exercised in accordance with internal law.

Article 6

1. Upon being satisfied, after an examination of information available to it, that the circumstances so warrant, any State Party in whose territory a person alleged to have committed any offence referred to in article 4 is present shall take him into custody or take other legal measures to ensure his presence. The custody and other legal measures shall be as provided in the law of that State but may be continued only for such time as is necessary to enable any criminal or extradition proceedings to be instituted.

2. Such State shall immediately make a preliminary inquiry into the facts.

3. Any person in custody pursuant to paragraph 1 of this article shall be assisted in communicating immediately with the nearest appropriate representative of the State of which he is a national, or, if he is a stateless person, with the representative of the State where he usually resides.

4. When a State, pursuant to this article, has taken a person into custody, it shall immediately notify the States referred to in article 5, paragraph 1, of the fact that such person is in custody and of the circumstances which warrant his detention. The State which makes the preliminary inquiry contemplated in paragraph 2 of this article shall promptly report its findings to the said States and shall indicate whether it intends to exercise jurisdiction.

Article 7

1. The State Party in the territory under whose jurisdiction a person alleged to have committed any offence referred to in article 4 is found shall in the cases contemplated in article 5, if it does not extradite him, submit the case to its competent authorities for the purpose of prosecution.

2. These authorities shall take their decision in the same manner as in the case of any ordinary offence of a serious nature under the law of that State. In the cases referred to in article 5, paragraph 2, the standards of evidence required for prosecution and conviction shall in no way be less stringent than those which apply in the cases referred to in article 5, paragraph 1.

3. Any person regarding whom proceedings are brought in connection with any of the offences referred to in article 4 shall be guaranteed fair treatment at all stages of the proceedings.

Article 8

1. The offences referred to in article 4 shall be deemed to be included as extraditable offences in any extradition treaty existing between States Parties. States Parties undertake to include such offences as extraditable offences in every extradition treaty to be concluded between them.

2. If a State Party which makes extradition conditional on the existence of a treaty receives a request for extradition from another State Party with which it has no extradition treaty, it may consider this Convention as the legal basis for extradition in respect of such offences. Extradition shall be subject to the other conditions provided by the law of the requested State.

3. States Parties which do not make extradition conditional on the existence of a treaty shall recognize such offences as extraditable offences between themselves subject to the conditions provided by the law of the requested State.

4. Such offences shall be treated, for the purpose of extradition between States Parties, as if they had been committed not only in the place in which they occurred but also in the territories of the States required to establish their jurisdiction in accordance with article 5, paragraph 1.

Article 9

1. States Parties shall afford one another the greatest measure of assistance in connection with criminal proceedings brought in respect of any of the offences referred to in article 4, including the supply of all evidence at their disposal necessary for the proceedings.

2. States Parties shall carry out their obligations under paragraph I of this article in conformity with any treaties on mutual judicial assistance that may exist between them.

Article 10

1. Each State Party shall ensure that education and information regarding the prohibition against torture are fully included in the training of law enforcement personnel, civil or military, medical personnel, public officials and other persons who may be involved in the custody, interrogation or treatment of any individual subjected to any form of arrest, detention or imprisonment.

2. Each State Party shall include this prohibition in the rules or instructions issued in regard to the duties and functions of any such person.

Article 11

Each State Party shall keep under systematic review interrogation rules, instructions, methods and practices as well as arrangements for the custody and treatment of persons subjected to any form of arrest, detention or imprisonment in any territory under its jurisdiction, with a view to preventing any cases of torture.

Article 12

Each State Party shall ensure that its competent authorities proceed to a prompt and impartial investigation, wherever there is reasonable ground to believe that an act of torture has been committed in any territory under its jurisdiction.

Article 13

Each State Party shall ensure that any individual who alleges he has been subjected to torture in any territory under its jurisdiction has the right to complain to, and to have his case promptly and impartially examined by, its competent authorities. Steps shall be taken to ensure that the complainant and witnesses are protected against all ill-treatment or intimidation as a consequence of his complaint or any evidence given.

Article 14

1. Each State Party shall ensure in its legal system that the victim of an act of torture obtains redress and has an enforceable right to fair and adequate compensation, including the means for as full rehabilitation as possible. In the event of the death of the victim as a result of an act of torture, his dependants shall be entitled to compensation.

2. Nothing in this article shall affect any right of the victim or other persons to compensation which may exist under national law.

Article 15

Each State Party shall ensure that any statement which is established to have been made as a result of torture shall not be invoked as evidence in any proceedings, except against a person accused of torture as evidence that the statement was made.

Article 16

1. Each State Party shall undertake to prevent in any territory under its jurisdiction other acts of cruel, inhuman or degrading treatment or punishment which do not amount to torture as defined in article 1, when such acts are committed by or at the instigation of or with the consent or acquiescence of a public official or other person acting in an official capacity. In particular, the obligations contained in articles 10, 11, 12 and 13 shall apply with the substitution for references to torture of references to other forms of cruel, inhuman or degrading treatment or punishment.

2. The provisions of this Convention are without prejudice to the provisions of any other international instrument or national law which prohibits cruel, inhuman or degrading treatment or punishment or which relates to extradition or expulsion.

Part 2

Article 17

1. There shall be established a Committee against Torture (hereinafter referred to as the Committee) which shall carry out the functions hereinafter provided. The Committee shall consist of ten experts of high moral standing and recognized competence in the field of human rights, who shall serve in their personal capacity. The experts shall be elected by the States Parties, consideration being given to equitable geographical distribution and to the usefulness of the participation of some persons having legal experience.

2. The members of the Committee shall be elected by secret ballot from a list of persons nominated by States Parties. Each State Party may nominate one person from among its own nationals. States Parties shall bear in mind the usefulness of nominating persons who are also members of the Human Rights Committee established under the International Covenant on Civil and Political Rights and who are willing to serve on the Committee against Torture.

3. Elections of the members of the Committee shall be held at biennial meetings of States Parties convened by the Secretary-General of the United Nations. At those meetings, for which two thirds of the States Parties shall constitute a quorum, the persons elected to the Committee shall be those who obtain the largest number of votes and an absolute majority of the votes of the representatives of States Parties present and voting.

4. The initial election shall be held no later than six months after the date of the entry into force of this Convention. At least four months before the date of each election, the Secretary-General of the United Nations shall address a letter to the States Parties inviting them to submit their nominations within three months. The Secretary-General shall prepare a list in alphabetical order of all persons thus nominated, indicating the States Parties which have nominated them, and shall submit it to the States Parties.

5. The members of the Committee shall be elected for a term of four years. They shall be eligible for re-election if renominated. However, the term of five of the members elected at the first election shall expire at the end of two years; immediately after the first election the names of these five members shall be chosen by lot by the chairman of the meeting referred to in paragraph 3 of this article.

6. If a member of the Committee dies or resigns or for any other cause can no longer perform his Committee duties, the State Party which nominated him shall appoint another expert from among its nationals to serve for the remainder of his term, subject to the approval of the majority of the States Parties. The approval shall be considered given unless half or more of the States Parties respond negatively within six weeks after having been informed by the Secretary-General of the United Nations of the proposed appointment.

7. States Parties shall be responsible for the expenses of the members of the Committee while they are in performance of Committee duties.

Article 18

1. The Committee shall elect its officers for a term of two years. They may be re-elected.

2. The Committee shall establish its own rules of procedure, but these rules shall provide, *inter alia*, that:

(a) Six members shall constitute a quorum;

(b) Decisions of the Committee shall be made by a majority vote of the members present.

3. The Secretary-General of the United Nations shall provide the necessary staff and facilities for the effective performance of the functions of the Committee under this Convention.

4. The Secretary-General of the United Nations shall convene the initial meeting of the Committee. After its initial meeting, the Committee shall meet at such times as shall be provided in its rules of procedure.

5. The States Parties shall be responsible for expenses incurred in connection with the holding of meetings of the States Parties and of the Committee, including reimbursement to the United Nations for any expenses, such as the cost of staff and facilities, incurred by the United Nations pursuant to paragraph 3 of this article.

Article 19

1. The States Parties shall submit to the Committee, through the Secretary-General of the United Nations, reports on the measures they have taken to give effect to their undertakings under this Convention, within one year after the entry into force of the Convention for the State Party concerned. Thereafter the States Parties shall submit supplementary reports every four years on any new measures taken and such other reports as the Committee may request.

2. The Secretary-General of the United Nations shall transmit the reports to all States Parties.

3. Each report shall be considered by the Committee which may make such general comments on the report as it may consider appropriate and shall forward these to the State Party concerned. That State Party may respond with any observations it chooses to the Committee.

4. The Committee may, at its discretion, decide to include any comments made by it in accordance with paragraph 3 of this article, together with the observations thereon received from the State Party concerned, in its annual report made in accordance with article 24. If so requested by the State Party concerned, the Committee may also include a copy of the report submitted under paragraph 1 of this article.

Article 20

1. If the Committee receives reliable information which appears to it to contain well-founded indications that torture is being systematically practiced in the territory of a

State Party, the Committee shall invite that State Party to co-operate in the examination of the information and to this end to submit observations with regard to the information concerned.

2. Taking into account any observations which may have been submitted by the State Party concerned, as well as any other relevant information available to it, the Committee may, if it decides that this is warranted, designate one or more of its members to make a confidential inquiry and to report to the Committee urgently.

3. If an inquiry is made in accordance with paragraph 2 of this article, the Committee shall seek the co-operation of the State Party concerned. In agreement with that State Party, such an inquiry may include a visit to its territory.

4. After examining the findings of its member or members submitted in accordance with paragraph 2 of this article, the Commission shall transmit these findings to the State Party concerned together with any comments or suggestions which seem appropriate in view of the situation.

5. All the proceedings of the Committee referred to in paragraphs 1 to 4 of this article shall be confidential, and at all stages of the proceedings the co-operation of the State Party shall be sought. After such proceedings have been completed with regard to an inquiry made in accordance with paragraph 2, the Committee may, after consultations with the State Party concerned, decide to include a summary account of the results of the proceedings in its annual report made in accordance with article 24.

Article 21

1. A State Party to this Convention may at any time declare under this article that it recognizes the competence of the Committee to receive and consider communications to the effect that a State Party claims that another State Party is not fulfilling its obligations under this Convention. Such communications may be received and considered according to the procedures laid down in this article only if submitted by a State Party which has made a declaration recognizing in regard to itself the competence of the Committee. No communication shall be dealt with by the Committee under this article if it concerns a State Party which has not made such a declaration. Communications received under this article shall be dealt with in accordance with the following procedure;

(a) If a State Party considers that another State Party is not giving effect to the provisions of this Convention, it may, by written communication, bring the matter to the attention of that State Party. Within three months after the receipt of the communication the receiving State shall afford the State which sent the communication an explanation or any other statement in writing clarifying the matter, which should include, to the extent possible and pertinent, reference to domestic procedures and remedies taken, pending or available in the matter;

(b) If the matter is not adjusted to the satisfaction of both States Parties concerned within six months after the receipt by the receiving State of the initial communication, either State shall have the right to refer the matter to the Committee, by notice given to the Committee and to the other State;

(c) The Committee shall deal with a matter referred to it under this article only after it has ascertained that all domestic remedies have been invoked and exhausted in the matter, in conformity with the generally recognized principles of international law. This shall not be the rule where the application of the remedies is unreasonably prolonged or is unlikely to bring effective relief to the person who is the victim of the violation of this Convention;

(d) The Committee shall hold closed meetings when examining communications under this article;

(e) Subject to the provisions of subparagraph;

(f) ... the Committee shall make available its good offices to the States Parties concerned with a view to a friendly solution of the matter on the basis of respect for the obligations provided for in this Convention. For this purpose, the Committee may, when appropriate, set up an *ad hoc* conciliation commission;

(g) In any matter referred to it under this article, the Committee may call upon the States Parties concerned, referred to in subparagraph (b), to supply any relevant information;

(h) The States Parties concerned, referred to in subparagraph (b), shall have the right to be represented when the matter is being considered by the Committee and to make submissions orally and/or in writing;

(i) The Committee shall, within twelve months after the date of receipt of notice under subparagraph (b), submit a report:

> (i) If a solution within the terms of subparagraph (e) is reached, the Committee shall confine its report to a brief statement of the facts and of the solution reached;

> (ii) If a solution within the terms of subparagraph (e) is not reached, the Committee shall confine its report to a brief statement of the facts; the written submissions and record of the oral submissions made by the States Parties concerned shall be attached to the report.

In every matter, the report shall be communicated to the States Parties concerned.

2. The provisions of this article shall come into force when five States Parties to this Convention have made declarations under paragraph 1 of this article. Such declarations shall be deposited by the States Parties with the Secretary-General of the United Nations, who shall transmit copies thereof to the other States Parties. A declaration may be withdrawn at any time by notification to the Secretary-General. Such a withdrawal shall not prejudice the consideration of any matter which is the subject of a communication already transmitted under this article; no further communication by any State Party shall be received under this article after the notification of withdrawal of the declaration has been received by the Secretary-General, unless the State Party concerned has made a new declaration.

Article 22

1. A State Party to this Convention may at any time declare under this article that it recognizes the competence of the Committee to receive and consider communications from or on behalf of individuals subject to its jurisdiction who claim to be victims of a violation by a State Party of the provisions of the Convention. No communication shall be received by the Committee if it concerns a State Party which has not made such a declaration.

2. The Committee shall consider inadmissible any communication under this article which is anonymous or which it considers to be an abuse of the right of submission of such communications or to be incompatible with the provisions of this Convention.

3. Subject to the provisions of paragraph 2, the Committee shall bring any communications submitted to it under this article to the attention of the State Party to this Convention which has made a declaration under paragraph 1 and is alleged to be violating any provisions of the Convention. Within six months, the receiving State shall submit to the

Committee written explanations or statements clarifying the matter and the remedy, if any, that may have been taken by that State.

4. The Committee shall consider communications received under this article in the light of all information made available to it by or on behalf of the individual and by the State Party concerned.

5. The Committee shall not consider any communications from an individual under this article unless it has ascertained that:

(a) The same matter has not been, and is not being, examined under another procedure of international investigation or settlement;

(b) The individual has exhausted all available domestic remedies; this shall not be the rule where the application of the remedies is unreasonably prolonged or is unlikely to bring effective relief to the person who is the victim of the violation of this Convention.

6. The Committee shall hold closed meetings when examining communications under this article.

7. The Committee shall forward its views to the State Party concerned and to the individual.

8. The provisions of this article shall come into force when five States Parties to this Convention have made declarations under paragraph 1 of this article. Such declarations shall be deposited by the States Parties with the Secretary-General of the United Nations, who shall transmit copies thereof to the other States Parties. A declaration may be withdrawn at any time by notification to the Secretary-General. Such a withdrawal shall not prejudice the consideration of any matter which is the subject of a communication already transmitted under this article; no further communication by or on behalf of an individual shall be received under this article after the notification of withdrawal of the declaration has been received by the Secretary-General, unless the State Party has made a new declaration.

Article 23

The members of the Committee and of the *ad hoc* conciliation commissions which may be appointed under article 21, paragraph 1 (e), shall be entitled to the facilities, privileges and immunities of experts on mission for the United Nations as laid down in the relevant sections of the Convention on the Privileges and Immunities of the United Nations.

Article 24

The Committee shall submit an annual report on its activities under this Convention to the States Parties and to the General Assembly of the United Nations ...

...

Optional Protocol to the Convention against Torture and Other Cruel, Inhuman or Degrading Treatment or Punishment

The States Parties to the present Protocol,

Reaffirming that torture and other cruel, inhuman or degrading treatment or punishment are prohibited and constitute serious violations of human rights,

Convinced that further measures are necessary to achieve the purposes of the Convention against Torture and Other Cruel, Inhuman or Degrading Treatment or Punishment (hereinafter referred to as the Convention) and to strengthen the protection of persons deprived of their liberty against torture and other cruel, inhuman or degrading treatment or punishment,

Recalling that articles 2 and 16 of the Convention oblige each State Party to take effective measures to prevent acts of torture and other cruel, inhuman or degrading treatment or punishment in any territory under its jurisdiction,

Recognizing that States have the primary responsibility for implementing those articles, that strengthening the protection of people deprived of their liberty and the full respect for their human rights is a common responsibility shared by all and that international implementing bodies complement and strengthen national measures,

Recalling that the effective prevention of torture and other cruel, inhuman or degrading treatment or punishment requires education and a combination of various legislative, administrative, judicial and other measures,

Recalling also that the World Conference on Human Rights firmly declared that efforts to eradicate torture should first and foremost be concentrated on prevention and called for the adoption of an optional protocol to the Convention, intended to establish a preventive system of regular visits to places of detention,

Convinced that the protection of persons deprived of their liberty against torture and other cruel, inhuman or degrading treatment or punishment can be strengthened by non-judicial means of a preventive nature, based on regular visits to places of detention, Have agreed as follows:

Part 1: General Principles

Article 1

The objective of the present Protocol is to establish a system of regular visits undertaken by independent international and national bodies to places where people are deprived of their liberty, in order to prevent torture and other cruel, inhuman or degrading treatment or punishment.

Article 2

1. A Subcommittee on Prevention of Torture and Other Cruel, Inhuman or Degrading Treatment or Punishment of the Committee against Torture (hereinafter referred to as the Subcommittee on Prevention) shall be established and shall carry out the functions laid down in the present Protocol.

2. The Subcommittee on Prevention shall carry out its work within the framework of the Charter of the United Nations and shall be guided by the purposes and principles thereof, as well as the norms of the United Nations concerning the treatment of people deprived of their liberty.

3. Equally, the Subcommittee on Prevention shall be guided by the principles of confidentiality, impartiality, non-selectivity, universality and objectivity.

4. The Subcommittee on Prevention and the States Parties shall cooperate in the implementation of the present Protocol.

Article 3

Each State Party shall set up, designate or maintain at the domestic level one or several visiting bodies for the prevention of torture and other cruel, inhuman or degrading treatment or punishment (hereinafter referred to as the national preventive mechanism).

Article 4

1. Each State Party shall allow visits, in accordance with the present Protocol, by the mechanisms referred to in articles 2 and 3 to any place under its jurisdiction and control where persons are or may be deprived of their liberty, either by virtue of an order given by a public authority or at its instigation or with its consent or acquiescence (hereinafter referred to as places of detention). These visits shall be undertaken with a view to strengthening, if necessary, the protection of these persons against torture and other cruel, inhuman or degrading treatment or punishment.

2. For the purposes of the present Protocol, deprivation of liberty means any form of detention or imprisonment or the placement of a person in a public or private custodial setting which that person is not permitted to leave at will by order of any judicial, administrative or other authority.

Part 2: Subcommittee on Prevention

Article 5

1. The Subcommittee on Prevention shall consist of ten members. After the fiftieth ratification of or accession to the present Protocol, the number of the members of the Subcommittee on Prevention shall increase to twenty-five.

2. The members of the Subcommittee on Prevention shall be chosen from among persons of high moral character, having proven professional experience in the field of the administration of justice, in particular criminal law, prison or police administration, or in the various fields relevant to the treatment of persons deprived of their liberty.

3. In the composition of the Subcommittee on Prevention due consideration shall be given to equitable geographic distribution and to the representation of different forms of civilization and legal systems of the States Parties.

4. In this composition consideration shall also be given to balanced gender representation on the basis of the principles of equality and non-discrimination.

5. No two members of the Subcommittee on Prevention may be nationals of the same State.

6. The members of the Subcommittee on Prevention shall serve in their individual capacity, shall be independent and impartial and shall be available to serve the Subcommittee on Prevention efficiently.

Article 6

1. Each State Party may nominate, in accordance with paragraph 2 of the present article, up to two candidates possessing the qualifications and meeting the requirements set out in article 5, and in doing so shall provide detailed information on the qualifications of the nominees.

2. (a) The nominees shall have the nationality of a State Party to the present Protocol;

(b) At least one of the two candidates shall have the nationality of the nominating State Party;

(c) No more than two nationals of a State Party shall be nominated;

(d) Before a State Party nominates a national of another State Party, it shall seek and obtain the consent of that State Party.

3. At least five months before the date of the meeting of the States Parties during which the elections will be held, the Secretary-General of the United Nations shall address a letter to the States Parties inviting them to submit their nominations within three months.

The Secretary-General shall submit a list, in alphabetical order, of all persons thus nominated, indicating the States Parties that have nominated them.

...

Part 3: Mandate of the Subcommittee on Prevention

Article 11

1. The Subcommittee on Prevention shall:

(a) Visit the places referred to in article 4 and make recommendations to States Parties concerning the protection of persons deprived of their liberty against torture and other cruel, inhuman or degrading treatment or punishment;

(b) In regard to the national preventive mechanisms:

(i) Advise and assist States Parties, when necessary, in their establishment;

(ii) Maintain direct, and if necessary confidential, contact with the national preventive mechanisms and offer them training and technical assistance with a view to strengthening their capacities;

(iii) Advise and assist them in the evaluation of the needs and the means necessary to strengthen the protection of persons deprived of their liberty against torture and other cruel, inhuman or degrading treatment or punishment;

(iv) Make recommendations and observations to the States Parties with a view to strengthening the capacity and the mandate of the national preventive mechanisms for the prevention of torture and other cruel, inhuman or degrading treatment or punishment;

(c) Cooperate, for the prevention of torture in general, with the relevant United Nations organs and mechanisms as well as with the international, regional and national institutions or organizations working towards the strengthening of the protection of all persons against torture and other cruel, inhuman or degrading treatment or punishment.

Article 12

In order to enable the Subcommittee on Prevention to comply with its mandate as laid down in article 11, the States Parties undertake:

(a) To receive the Subcommittee on Prevention in their territory and grant it access to the places of detention as defined in article 4 of the present Protocol;

(b) To provide all relevant information the Subcommittee on Prevention may request to evaluate the needs and measures that should be adopted to strengthen the protection of persons deprived of their liberty against torture and other cruel, inhuman or degrading treatment or punishment;

(c) To encourage and facilitate contacts between the Subcommittee on Prevention and the national preventive mechanisms;

(d) To examine the recommendations of the Subcommittee on Prevention and enter into dialogue with it on possible implementation measures.

...

Article 14

1. In order to enable the Subcommittee on Prevention to fulfil its mandate, the States Parties to the present Protocol undertake to grant it:

(a) Unrestricted access to all information concerning the number of persons deprived of their liberty in places of detention as defined in article 4, as well as the number of places and their location;

(b) Unrestricted access to all information referring to the treatment of those persons as well as their conditions of detention;

(c) Subject to paragraph 2 below, unrestricted access to all places of detention and their installations and facilities;

(d) The opportunity to have private interviews with the persons deprived of their liberty without witnesses, either personally or with a translator if deemed necessary, as well as with any other person who the Subcommittee on Prevention believes may supply relevant information;

(e) The liberty to choose the places it wants to visit and the persons it wants to interview.

2. Objection to a visit to a particular place of detention may be made only on urgent and compelling grounds of national defense, public safety, natural disaster or serious disorder in the place to be visited that temporarily prevent the carrying out of such a visit. The existence of a declared state of emergency as such shall not be invoked by a State Party as a reason to object to a visit.

Article 15

No authority or official shall order, apply, permit or tolerate any sanction against any person or organization for having communicated to the Subcommittee on Prevention or to its delegates any information, whether true or false, and no such person or organization shall be otherwise prejudiced in any way.

Article 16

1. The Subcommittee on Prevention shall communicate its recommendations and observations confidentially to the State Party and, if relevant, to the national preventive mechanism.

2. The Subcommittee on Prevention shall publish its report, together with any comments of the State Party concerned, whenever requested to do so by that State Party. If the State Party makes part of the report public, the Subcommittee on Prevention may publish the report in whole or in part. However, no personal data shall be published without the express consent of the person concerned.

3. The Subcommittee on Prevention shall present a public annual report on its activities to the Committee against Torture.

4. If the State Party refuses to cooperate with the Subcommittee on Prevention according to articles 12 and 14, or to take steps to improve the situation in the light of the recommendations of the Subcommittee on Prevention, the Committee against Torture may, at the request of the Subcommittee on Prevention, decide, by a majority of its members, after the State Party has had an opportunity to make its views known, to make a public statement on the matter or to publish the report of the Subcommittee on Prevention.

Part 4: National Preventive Mechanisms

Article 17

Each State Party shall maintain, designate or establish, at the latest one year after the entry into force of the present Protocol or of its ratification or accession, one or several independent national preventive mechanisms for the prevention of torture at the domestic level. Mechanisms established by decentralized units may be designated as national preventive mechanisms for the purposes of the present Protocol if they are in conformity with its provisions.

...

Article 30

No reservations shall be made to the present Protocol.

...

Convention on the Rights of the Child

The States Parties to the present Convention,

...

Bearing in mind that, as indicated in the Declaration of the Rights of the Child, "the child, by reason of his physical and mental immaturity, needs special safeguards and care, including appropriate legal protection, before as well as after birth,"

...

Taking due account of the importance of the traditions and cultural values of each people for the protection and harmonious development of the child,

...

Have agreed as follows:

Part 1

Article 1

For the purposes of the present Convention, a child means every human being below the age of eighteen years unless under the law applicable to the child, majority is attained earlier.

Article 2

1. States Parties shall respect and ensure the rights set forth in the present Convention to each child within their jurisdiction without discrimination of any kind, irrespective of the child's or his or her parent's or legal guardian's race, colour, sex, language, religion, political or other opinion, national, ethnic or social origin, property, disability, birth or other status.

2. States Parties shall take all appropriate measures to ensure that the child is protected against all forms of discrimination or punishment on the basis of the status, activities, expressed opinions, or beliefs of the child's parents, legal guardians, or family members.

Article 3

1. In all actions concerning children, whether undertaken by public or private social welfare institutions, courts of law, administrative authorities or legislative bodies, the best interests of the child shall be a primary consideration.

2. States Parties undertake to ensure the child such protection and care as is necessary for his or her well-being, taking into account the rights and duties of his or her parents,

legal guardians, or other individuals legally responsible for him or her, and, to this end, shall take all appropriate legislative and administrative measures.

...

Article 4

States Parties shall undertake all appropriate legislative, administrative, and other measures for the implementation of the rights recognized in the present Convention. With regard to economic, social and cultural rights, States Parties shall undertake such measures to the maximum extent of their available resources and, where needed, within the framework of international co-operation.

Article 5

States Parties shall respect the responsibilities, rights and duties of parents or, where applicable, the members of the extended family or community as provided for by local custom, legal guardians or other persons legally responsible for the child, to provide, in a manner consistent with the evolving capacities of the child, appropriate direction and guidance in the exercise by the child of the rights recognized in the present Convention.

Article 6

1. States Parties recognize that every child has the inherent right to life.

2. States Parties shall ensure to the maximum extent possible the survival and development of the child.

Article 7

1. The child shall be registered immediately after birth and shall have the right from birth to a name, the right to acquire a nationality and. as far as possible, the right to know and be cared for by his or her parents.

...

Article 9

1. States Parties shall ensure that a child shall not be separated from his or her parents against their will, except when competent authorities subject to judicial review determine, in accordance with applicable law and procedures, that such separation is necessary for the best interests of the child ...

...

Article 10

1. In accordance with the obligation of States Parties under article 9, paragraph 1, applications by a child or his or her parents to enter or leave a State Party for the purpose of family reunification shall be dealt with by States Parties in a positive, humane and expeditious manner. States Parties shall further ensure that the submission of such a request shall entail no adverse consequences for the applicants and for the members of their family.

2. A child whose parents reside in different States shall have the right to maintain on a regular basis, save in exceptional circumstances, personal relations and direct contacts with both parents.

...

Article 11

1. States Parties shall take measures to combat the illicit transfer and non-return of children abroad.

2. To this end, States Parties shall promote the conclusion of bilateral or multilateral agreements or accession to existing agreements.

Article 12

1. States Parties shall assure to the child who is capable of forming his or her own views the right to express those views freely in all matters affecting the child, the views of the child being given due weight in accordance with the age and maturity of the child.

2. For this purpose, the child shall in particular be provided the opportunity to be heard in any judicial and administrative proceedings affecting the child, either directly, or through a representative or an appropriate body, in a manner consistent with the procedural rules of national law.

Article 13

1. The child shall have the right to freedom of expression; this right shall include freedom to seek, receive and impart information and ideas of all kinds, regardless of frontiers, either orally, in writing or in print, in the form of art, or through any other media of the child's choice.

2. The exercise of this right may be subject to certain restrictions, but these shall only be such as are provided by law and are necessary:

(a) For respect of the rights or reputations of others; or

(b) For the protection of national security or of public order (ordre public), or of public health or morals.

Article 14

1. States Parties shall respect the right of the child to freedom of thought, conscience and religion.

2. States Parties shall respect the rights and duties of the parents and, when applicable, legal guardians, to provide direction to the child in the exercise of his or her right in a manner consistent with the evolving capacities of the child.

...

Article 15

1. States Parties recognize the rights of the child to freedom of association and to freedom of peaceful assembly ...

Article 16

1. No child shall be subjected to arbitrary or unlawful interference with his or her privacy, family, home or correspondence, nor to unlawful attacks on his or her honour and reputation.

2. The child has the right to the protection of the law against such interference or attacks.

Article 17

States Parties recognize the important function performed by the mass media and shall ensure that the child has access to information and material from a diversity of national and international sources ...

...

Article 18

1. States Parties shall use their best efforts to ensure recognition of the principle that both parents have common responsibilities for the upbringing and development of the child. Parents or, as the case may be, legal guardians, have the primary responsibility for the upbringing and development of the child. The best interests of the child will be their basic concern.

2. For the purpose of guaranteeing and promoting the rights set forth in the present Convention, States Parties shall render appropriate assistance to parents and legal guardians in the performance of their child-rearing responsibilities and shall ensure the development of institutions, facilities and services for the care of children.

3. States Parties shall take all appropriate measures to ensure that children of working parents have the right to benefit from child-care services and facilities for which they are eligible.

Article 19

1. States Parties shall take all appropriate legislative, administrative, social and educational measures to protect the child from all forms of physical or mental violence, injury or abuse, neglect or negligent treatment, maltreatment or exploitation, including sexual abuse, while in the care of parent(s), legal guardian(s) or any other person who has the care of the child.

…

Article 20

1. A child temporarily or permanently deprived of his or her family environment, or in whose own best interests cannot be allowed to remain in that environment, shall be entitled to special protection and assistance provided by the State.

2. States Parties shall in accordance with their national laws ensure alternative care for such a child.

3. Such care could include, *inter alia*, foster placement, *kafalah* of Islamic law, adoption or if necessary placement in suitable institutions for the care of children. When considering solutions, due regard shall be paid to the desirability of continuity in a child's upbringing and to the child's ethnic, religious, cultural and linguistic background.

Article 21

States Parties that recognize and/or permit the system of adoption shall ensure that the best interests of the child shall be the paramount consideration …

…

Article 23

1. States Parties recognize that a mentally or physically disabled child should enjoy a full and decent life, in conditions which ensure dignity, promote self-reliance and facilitate the child's active participation in the community.

…

Article 24

1. States Parties recognize the right of the child to the enjoyment of the highest attainable standard of health and to facilities for the treatment of illness and rehabilitation of health. States Parties shall strive to ensure that no child is deprived of his or her right of access to such health care services.

...

3. States Parties shall take all effective and appropriate measures with a view to abolishing traditional practices prejudicial to the health of children.

4. States Parties undertake to promote and encourage international co-operation with a view to achieving progressively the full realization of the right recognized in the present article. In this regard, particular account shall be taken of the needs of developing countries.

Article 25

States Parties recognize the right of a child who has been placed by the competent authorities for the purposes of care, protection or treatment of his or her physical or mental health, to a periodic review of the treatment provided to the child and all other circumstances relevant to his or her placement.

...

Article 27

1. States Parties recognize the right of every child to a standard of living adequate for the child's physical, mental, spiritual, moral and social development.

2. The parent(s) or others responsible for the child have the primary responsibility to secure, within their abilities and financial capacities, the conditions of living necessary for the child's development.

3. States Parties, in accordance with national conditions and within their means, shall take appropriate measures to assist parents and others responsible for the child to implement this right and shall in case of need provide material assistance and support programmes, particularly with regard to nutrition, clothing and housing.

...

Article 28

1. States Parties recognize the right of the child to education, and with a view to achieving this right progressively and on the basis of equal opportunity, they shall, in particular:

(a) Make primary education compulsory and available free to all;

(b) Encourage the development of different forms of secondary education, including general and vocational education, make them available and accessible to every child, and take appropriate measures such as the introduction of free education and offering financial assistance in case of need;

(c) Make higher education accessible to all on the basis of capacity by every appropriate means;

(d) Make educational and vocational information and guidance available and accessible to all children;

(e) Take measures to encourage regular attendance at schools and the reduction of drop-out rates.

2. States Parties shall take all appropriate measures to ensure that school discipline is administered in a manner consistent with the child's human dignity and in conformity with the present Convention.

3. States Parties shall promote and encourage international cooperation in matters relating to education, in particular with a view to contributing to the elimination of igno-

rance and illiteracy throughout the world and facilitating access to scientific and technical knowledge and modern teaching methods. In this regard, particular account shall be taken of the needs of developing countries.

Article 29

1. States Parties agree that the education of the child shall be directed to:

(a) The development of the child's personality, talents and mental and physical abilities to their fullest potential;

(b) The development of respect for human rights and fundamental freedoms, and for the principles enshrined in the Charter of the United Nations;

(c) The development of respect for the child's parents, his or her own cultural identity, language and values, for the national values of the country in which the child is living, the country from which he or she may originate, and for civilizations different from his or her own;

(d) The preparation of the child for responsible life in a free society, in the spirit of understanding, peace, tolerance, equality of sexes, and friendship among all peoples, ethnic, national and religious groups and persons of indigenous origin;

(e) The development of respect for the natural environment.

2. No part of the present article or article 28 shall be construed so as to interfere with the liberty of individuals and bodies to establish and direct educational institutions ...

Article 30

In those States in which ethnic, religious or linguistic minorities or persons of indigenous origin exist, a child belonging to such a minority or who is indigenous shall not be denied the right, in community with other members of his or her group, to enjoy his or her own culture, to profess and practice his or her own religion, or to use his or her own language.

...

Article 32

1. States Parties recognize the right of the child to be protected from economic exploitation and from performing any work that is likely to be hazardous or to interfere with the child's education, or to be harmful to the child's health or physical, mental, spiritual, moral or social development.

2. States Parties shall take legislative, administrative, social and educational measures to ensure the implementation of the present article. To this end, and having regard to the relevant provisions of other international instruments, States Parties shall in particular:

(a) Provide for a minimum age or minimum ages for admission to employment;

(b) Provide for appropriate regulation of the hours and conditions of employment;

(c) Provide for appropriate penalties or other sanctions to ensure the effective enforcement of the present article.

Article 33

States Parties shall take all appropriate measures, including legislative, administrative, social and educational measures, to protect children from the illicit use of narcotic drugs and psychotropic substances as defined in the relevant international treaties, and to prevent the use of children in the illicit production and trafficking of such substances.

Article 34

States Parties undertake to protect the child from all forms of sexual exploitation and sexual abuse. For these purposes, States Parties shall in particular take all appropriate national, bilateral and multilateral measures to prevent:

> (a) The inducement or coercion of a child to engage in any unlawful sexual activity;

> (b) The exploitative use of children in prostitution or other unlawful sexual practices;

> (c) The exploitative use of children in pornographic performances and materials.

Article 35

States Parties shall take all appropriate national, bilateral and multilateral measures to prevent the abduction of, the sale of or traffic in children for any purpose or in any form.

...

Article 37

States Parties shall ensure that:

> (a) No child shall be subjected to torture or other cruel, inhuman or degrading treatment or punishment. Neither capital punishment nor life imprisonment without possibility of release shall be imposed for offences committed by persons below eighteen years of age;

> (b) No child shall be deprived of his or her liberty unlawfully or arbitrarily. The arrest, detention or imprisonment of a child shall be in conformity with the law and shall be used only as a measure of last resort and for the shortest appropriate period of time;

> (c) Every child deprived of liberty shall be treated with humanity and respect for the inherent dignity of the human person, and in a manner which takes into account the needs of persons of his or her age.

In particular, every child deprived of liberty shall be separated from adults unless it is considered in the child's best interest not to do so and shall have the right to maintain contact with his or her family through correspondence and visits, save in exceptional circumstances;

> (d) Every child deprived of his or her liberty shall have the right to prompt access to legal and other appropriate assistance, as well as the right to challenge the legality of the deprivation of his or her liberty before a court or other competent, independent and impartial authority, and to a prompt decision on any such action.

Article 38

1. States Parties undertake to respect and to ensure respect for rules of international humanitarian law applicable to them in armed conflicts which are relevant to the child.

2. States Parties shall take all feasible measures to ensure that persons who have not attained the age of fifteen years do not take a direct part in hostilities.

3. States Parties shall refrain from recruiting any person who has not attained the age of fifteen years into their armed forces. In recruiting among those persons who have attained the age of fifteen years but who have not attained the age of eighteen years, States Parties shall endeavour to give priority to those who are oldest.

4. In accordance with their obligations under international humanitarian law to protect the civilian population in armed conflicts, States Parties shall take all feasible measures to ensure protection and care of children who are affected by an armed conflict.

Article 39

States Parties shall take all appropriate measures to promote physical and psychological recovery and social reintegration of a child victim of: any form of neglect, exploitation, or abuse; torture or any other form of cruel, inhuman or degrading treatment or punishment; or armed conflicts. Such recovery and reintegration shall take place in an environment which fosters the health, self-respect and dignity of the child.

Article 40

1. States Parties recognize the right of every child alleged as, accused of, or recognized as having infringed the penal law to be treated in a manner consistent with the promotion of the child's sense of dignity and worth, which reinforces the child's respect for the human rights and fundamental freedoms of others and which takes into account the child's age and the desirability of promoting the child's reintegration and the child's assuming a constructive role in society.

. . .

3. States Parties shall seek to promote the establishment of laws, procedures, authorities and institutions specifically applicable to children alleged as, accused of, or recognized as having infringed the penal law, and, in particular:

(a) The establishment of a minimum age below which children shall be presumed not to have the capacity to infringe the penal law;

(b) Whenever appropriate and desirable, measures for dealing with such children without resorting to judicial proceedings, providing that human rights and legal safeguards are fully respected.

4. A variety of dispositions, such as care, guidance and supervision orders; counseling; probation; foster care; education and vocational training programmes and other alternatives to institutional care shall be available to ensure that children are dealt with in a manner appropriate to their well-being and proportionate both to their circumstances and the offence.

. . .

Part 2

Article 42

States Parties undertake to make the principles and provisions of the Convention widely known, by appropriate and active means, to adults and children alike.

Article 43

1. For the purpose of examining the progress made by States Parties in achieving the realization of the obligations undertaken in the present Convention, there shall be established a Committee on the Rights of the Child, which shall carry out the functions hereinafter provided.

2. The Committee shall consist of ten experts of high moral standing and recognized competence in the field covered by this Convention. The members of the Committee shall be elected by States Parties from among their nationals and shall serve in their personal capacity, consideration being given to equitable geographical distribution, as well as to the principal legal systems.

. . .

Article 44

1. States Parties undertake to submit to the Committee, through the Secretary-General of the United Nations, reports on the measures they have adopted which give effect to the rights recognized herein and on the progress made on the enjoyment of those rights

(a) Within two years of the entry into force of the Convention for the State Party concerned;

(b) Thereafter every five years.

2. Reports made under the present article shall indicate factors and difficulties, if any, affecting the degree of fulfillment of the obligations under the present Convention. Reports shall also contain sufficient information to provide the Committee with a comprehensive understanding of the implementation of the Convention in the country concerned.

...

6. States Parties shall make their reports widely available to the public in their own countries.

Article 45

In order to foster the effective implementation of the Convention and to encourage international co-operation in the field covered by the Convention:

(a) The specialized agencies, the United Nations Children's Fund, and other United Nations organs shall be entitled to be represented at the consideration of the implementation of such provisions of the present Convention as fall within the scope of their mandate. The Committee may invite the specialized agencies, the United Nations Children's Fund and other competent bodies as it may consider appropriate to provide expert advice on the implementation of the Convention in areas falling within the scope of their respective mandates. The Committee may invite the specialized agencies, the United Nations Children's Fund, and other United Nations organs to submit reports on the implementation of the Convention in areas falling within the scope of their activities;

...

Part 3

...

Article 51

...

2. A reservation incompatible with the object and purpose of the present Convention shall not be permitted.

...

First Optional Protocol to the Convention on the Rights of the Child on the Sale of Children, Child Prostitution, and Child Pornography

The States Parties to the present Protocol,

Considering that, in order further to achieve the purposes of the Convention on the Rights of the Child and the implementation of its provisions, especially articles 1, 11, 21, 32,

33, 34, 35 and 36, it would be appropriate to extend the measures that States Parties should undertake in order to guarantee the protection of the child from the sale of children, child prostitution and child pornography,

Considering also that the Convention on the Rights of the Child recognizes the right of the child to be protected from economic exploitation and from performing any work that is likely to be hazardous or to interfere with the child's education, or to be harmful to the child's health or physical, mental, spiritual, moral or social development,

Gravely concerned at the significant and increasing international traffic in children for the purpose of the sale of children, child prostitution and child pornography,

Deeply concerned at the widespread and continuing practice of sex tourism, to which children are especially vulnerable, as it directly promotes the sale of children, child prostitution and child pornography,

Recognizing that a number of particularly vulnerable groups, including girl children, are at greater risk of sexual exploitation and that girl children are disproportionately represented among the sexually exploited,

Concerned about the growing availability of child pornography on the Internet and other evolving technologies, and recalling the International Conference on Combating Child Pornography on the Internet, held in Vienna in 1999, in particular its conclusion calling for the worldwide criminalization of the production, distribution, exportation, transmission, importation, intentional possession and advertising of child pornography, and stressing the importance of closer cooperation and partnership between Governments and the Internet industry,

Believing that the elimination of the sale of children, child prostitution and child pornography will be facilitated by adopting a holistic approach, addressing the contributing factors, including underdevelopment, poverty, economic disparities, inequitable socio-economic structure, dysfunctioning families, lack of education, urban-rural migration, gender discrimination, irresponsible adult sexual behaviour, harmful traditional practices, armed conflicts and trafficking in children,

Believing also that efforts to raise public awareness are needed to reduce consumer demand for the sale of children, child prostitution and child pornography, and believing further in the importance of strengthening global partnership among all actors and of improving law enforcement at the national level,

Noting the provisions of international legal instruments relevant to the protection of children, including the Hague Convention on Protection of Children and Cooperation in Respect of Intercountry Adoption, the Hague Convention on the Civil Aspects of International Child Abduction, the Hague Convention on Jurisdiction, Applicable Law, Recognition, Enforcement and Cooperation in Respect of Parental Responsibility and Measures for the Protection of Children, and International Labour Organization Convention No. 182 on the Prohibition and Immediate Action for the Elimination of the Worst Forms of Child Labour,

Encouraged by the overwhelming support for the Convention on the Rights of the Child, demonstrating the widespread commitment that exists for the promotion and protection of the rights of the child,

Recognizing the importance of the implementation of the provisions of the Programme of Action for the Prevention of the Sale of Children, Child Prostitution and Child Pornography and the Declaration and Agenda for Action adopted at the World Congress against Commercial Sexual Exploitation of Children, held in Stockholm from 27 to 31 August 1996, and the other relevant decisions and recommendations of pertinent international bodies,

Taking due account of the importance of the traditions and cultural values of each people for the protection and harmonious development of the child,

Have agreed as follows:

Article 1

States Parties shall prohibit the sale of children, child prostitution and child pornography as provided for by the present Protocol.

Article 2

For the purpose of the present Protocol:

(a) Sale of children means any act or transaction whereby a child is transferred by any person or group of persons to another for remuneration or any other consideration;

(b) Child prostitution means the use of a child in sexual activities for remuneration or any other form of consideration;

(c) Child pornography means any representation, by whatever means, of a child engaged in real or simulated explicit sexual activities or any representation of the sexual parts of a child for primarily sexual purposes.

Article 3

1. Each State Party shall ensure that, as a minimum, the following acts and activities are fully covered under its criminal or penal law, whether these offences are committed domestically or transnationally or on an individual or organized basis:

(a) In the context of sale of children as defined in Article 2:

(i) The offering, delivering or accepting, by whatever means, a child for the purpose of:

a. Sexual exploitation of the child;

b. Transfer of organs of the child for profit;

c. Engagement of the child in forced labour.

(ii) Improperly inducing consent, as an intermediary, for the adoption of a child in violation of applicable international legal instruments on adoption;

(b) Offering, obtaining, procuring or providing a child for child prostitution, as defined in Article 2;

(c) Producing, distributing, disseminating, importing, exporting, offering, selling or possessing for the above purposes child pornography as defined in Article 2.

2. Subject to the provisions of a State Party's national law, the same shall apply to an attempt to commit any of these acts and to complicity or participation in any of these acts.

3. Each State Party shall make these offences punishable by appropriate penalties that take into account their grave nature.

4. Subject to the provisions of its national law, each State Party shall take measures, where appropriate, to establish the liability of legal persons for offences established in paragraph 1 of the present Article. Subject to the legal principles of the State Party, this liability of legal persons may be criminal, civil or administrative.

5. States Parties shall take all appropriate legal and administrative measures to ensure that all persons involved in the adoption of a child act in conformity with applicable international legal instruments.

Article 4

1. Each State Party shall take such measures as may be necessary to establish its jurisdiction over the offences referred to in Article 3, paragraph 1, when the offences are committed in its territory or on board a ship or aircraft registered in that State.

2. Each State Party may take such measures as may be necessary to establish its jurisdiction over the offences referred to in Article 3, paragraph 1, in the following cases:

(a) When the alleged offender is a national of that State or a person who has his habitual residence in its territory;

(b) When the victim is a national of that State.

3. Each State Party shall also take such measures as may be necessary to establish its jurisdiction over the above-mentioned offences when the alleged offender is present in its territory and it does not extradite him or her to another State Party on the ground that the offence has been committed by one of its nationals.

4. This Protocol does not exclude any criminal jurisdiction exercised in accordance with internal law.

Article 5

1. The offences referred to in Article 3, paragraph 1, shall be deemed to be included as extraditable offences in any extradition treaty existing between States Parties and shall be included as extraditable offences in every extradition treaty subsequently concluded between them, in accordance with the conditions set forth in those treaties.

2. If a State Party that makes extradition conditional on the existence of a treaty receives a request for extradition from another State Party with which it has no extradition treaty, it may consider this Protocol as a legal basis for extradition in respect of such offences. Extradition shall be subject to the conditions provided by the law of the requested State.

3. States Parties that do not make extradition conditional on the existence of a treaty shall recognize such offences as extraditable offences between themselves subject to the conditions provided by the law of the requested State.

4. Such offences shall be treated, for the purpose of extradition between States Parties, as if they had been committed not only in the place in which they occurred but also in the territories of the States required to establish their jurisdiction in accordance with Article 4.

5. If an extradition request is made with respect to an offence described in Article 3, paragraph 1, and if the requested State Party does not or will not extradite on the basis of the nationality of the offender, that State shall take suitable measures to submit the case to its competent authorities for the purpose of prosecution.

Article 6

1. States Parties shall afford one another the greatest measure of assistance in connection with investigations or criminal or extradition proceedings brought in respect of the offences set forth in Article 3, paragraph 1, including assistance in obtaining evidence at their disposal necessary for the proceedings.

2. States Parties shall carry out their obligations under paragraph 1 of the present Article in conformity with any treaties or other arrangements on mutual legal assistance that may exist between them. In the absence of such treaties or arrangements, States Parties shall afford one another assistance in accordance with their domestic law.

Article 7

States Parties shall, subject to the provisions of their national law:

(a) Take measures to provide for the seizure and confiscation, as appropriate, of:

(i) Goods such as materials, assets and other instrumentalities used to commit or facilitate offences under the present Protocol;

(ii) Proceeds derived from such offences;

(b) Execute requests from another State Party for seizure or confiscation of goods or proceeds referred to in subparagraph (a)(i);

(c) Take measures aimed at closing, on a temporary or definitive basis, premises used to commit such offences.

Article 8

1. States Parties shall adopt appropriate measures to protect the rights and interests of child victims of the practices prohibited under the present Protocol at all stages of the criminal justice process, in particular by:

(a) Recognizing the vulnerability of child victims and adapting procedures to recognize their special needs, including their special needs as witnesses;

(b) Informing child victims of their rights, their role and the scope, timing and progress of the proceedings and of the disposition of their cases;

(c) Allowing the views, needs and concerns of child victims to be presented and considered in proceedings where their personal interests are affected, in a mariner consistent with the procedural rules of national law;

(d) Providing appropriate support services to child victims throughout the legal process;

(e) Protecting, as appropriate, the privacy and identity of child victims and taking measures in accordance with national law to avoid the inappropriate dissemination of information that could lead to the identification of child victims;

(f) Providing, in appropriate cases, for the safety of child victims, as well as that of their families and witnesses on their behalf, from intimidation and retaliation;

(g) Avoiding unnecessary delay in the disposition of cases and the execution of orders or decrees granting compensation to child victims.

2. States Parties shall ensure that uncertainty as to the actual age of the victim shall not prevent the initiation of criminal investigations, including investigations aimed at establishing the age of the victim.

3. States Parties shall ensure that, in the treatment by the criminal justice system of children who are victims of the offences described in the present Protocol, the best interest of the child shall be a primary consideration.

4. States Parties shall take measures to ensure appropriate training, in particular legal and psychological training, for the persons who work with victims of the offences prohibited under the present Protocol.

5. States Parties shall, in appropriate cases, adopt measures in order to protect the safety and integrity of those persons and/or organizations involved in the prevention and/or protection and rehabilitation of victims of such offences.

6. Nothing in the present Article shall be construed as prejudicial to or inconsistent with the rights of the accused to a fair and impartial trial.

Article 9

1. States Parties shall adopt or strengthen, implement and disseminate laws, administrative measures, social policies and programmes to prevent the offences referred to in the present Protocol. Particular attention shall be given to protect children who are especially vulnerable to these practices.

2. States Parties shall promote awareness in the public at large, including children, through information by all appropriate means, education and training, about the preventive measures and harmful effects of the offences referred to in the present Protocol. In fulfilling their obligations under this Article, States Parties shall encourage the participation of the community and, in particular, children and child victims, in such information and education and training programmes, including at the international level.

3. States Parties shall take all feasible measures with the aim of ensuring all appropriate assistance to victims of such offences, including their full social reintegration and their full physical and psychological recovery.

4. States Parties shall ensure that all child victims of the offences described in the present Protocol have access to adequate procedures to seek, without discrimination, compensation for damages from those legally responsible.

5. States Parties shall take appropriate measures aimed at effectively prohibiting the production and dissemination of material advertising the offences described in the present Protocol.

Article 10

1. States Parties shall take all necessary steps to strengthen international cooperation by multilateral, regional and bilateral arrangements for the prevention, detection, investigation, prosecution and punishment of those responsible for acts involving the sale of children, child prostitution, child pornography and child sex tourism. States Parties shall also promote international cooperation and coordination between their authorities, national and international non-governmental organizations and international organizations.

2. States Parties shall promote international cooperation to assist child victims in their physical and psychological recovery, social reintegration and repatriation.

3. States Parties shall promote the strengthening of international cooperation in order to address the root causes, such as poverty and underdevelopment, contributing to the vulnerability of children to the sale of children, child prostitution, child pornography and child sex tourism.

4. States Parties in a position to do so shall provide financial, technical or other assistance through existing multilateral, regional, bilateral or other programmes.

Article 11

Nothing in the present Protocol shall affect any provisions that are more conducive to the realization of the rights of the child and that may be contained in:

(a) The law of a State Party;

(b) International law in force for that State.

Article 12

1. Each State Party shall submit, within two years following the entry into force of the Protocol for that State Party, a report to the Committee on the Rights of the Child pro-

viding comprehensive information on the measures it has taken to implement the provisions of the Protocol.

2. Following the submission of the comprehensive report, each State Party shall include in the reports they submit to the Committee on the Rights of the Child, in accordance with Article 44 of the Convention, any further information with respect to the implementation of the Protocol. Other States Parties to the Protocol shall submit a report every five years.

3. The Committee on the Rights of the Child may request from States Parties further information relevant to the implementation of this Protocol....

Second Optional Protocol to the Convention on the Rights of the Child on the Involvement of Children in Armed Conflict

The States Parties to the present Protocol,

Encouraged by the overwhelming support for the Convention on the Rights of the Child, demonstrating the widespread commitment that exists to strive for the promotion and protection of the rights of the child,

Reaffirming that the rights of children require special protection, and calling for continuous improvement of the situation of children without distinction, as well as for their development and education in conditions of peace and security,

Disturbed by the harmful and widespread impact of armed conflict on children and the long-term consequences this has for durable peace, security and development,

Condemning the targeting of children in situations of armed conflict and direct attacks on objects protected under international law, including places generally having a significant presence of children, such as schools and hospitals,

Noting the adoption of the Statute of the International Criminal Court and, in particular, its inclusion as a war crime of conscripting or enlisting children under the age of 15 years or using them to participate actively in hostilities in both international and non-international armed conflicts,

Considering, therefore, that to strengthen further the implementation of rights recognized in the Convention on the Rights of the Child there is a need to increase the protection of children from involvement in armed conflict,

Noting that article 1 of the Convention on the Rights of the Child specifies that, for the purposes of that Convention, a child means every human being below the age of 18 years unless, under the law applicable to the child, majority is attained earlier,

Convinced that an optional protocol to the Convention raising the age of possible recruitment of persons into armed forces and their participation in hostilities will contribute effectively to the implementation of the principle that the best interests of the child are to be a primary consideration in all actions concerning children,

Noting that the twenty-sixth international Conference of the Red Cross and Red Crescent in December 1995 recommended, *inter alia*, that parties to conflict take every feasible step to ensure that children under the age of 18 years do not take part in hostilities,

Welcoming the unanimous adoption, in June 1999, of International Labour Organization Convention No. 182 on the Prohibition and Immediate Action for the Elimination of the

Worst Forms of Child Labour, which prohibits, *inter alia*, forced or compulsory recruitment of children for use in armed conflict,

Condemning with the gravest concern the recruitment, training and use within and across national borders of children in hostilities by armed groups distinct from the armed forces of a State, and recognizing the responsibility of those who recruit, train and use children in this regard,

Recalling the obligation of each party to an armed conflict to abide by the provisions of international humanitarian law,

Stressing that this Protocol is without prejudice to the purposes and principles contained in the Charter of the United Nations, including Article 51, and relevant norms of humanitarian law,

Bearing in mind that conditions of peace and security based on full respect of the purposes and principles contained in the Charter and observance of applicable human rights instruments are indispensable for the full protection of children, in particular during armed conflicts and foreign occupation,

Recognizing the special needs of those children who are particularly vulnerable to recruitment or use in hostilities contrary to this Protocol owing to their economic or social status or gender,

Mindful of the necessity of taking into consideration the economic, social and political root causes of the involvement of children in armed conflicts,

Convinced of the need to strengthen international cooperation in the implementation of this Protocol, as well as the physical and psychosocial rehabilitation and social reintegration of children who are victims of armed conflict,

Encouraging the participation of the community and, in particular, children and child victims in the dissemination of informational and educational programmes concerning the implementation of the Protocol,

Have agreed as follows:

Article 1

States Parties shall take all feasible measures to ensure that members of their armed forces who have not attained the age of 18 years do not take a direct part in hostilities.

Article 2

States Parties shall ensure that persons who have not attained the age of 18 years are not compulsorily recruited into their armed forces.

Article 3

1. States Parties shall raise the minimum age for the voluntary recruitment of persons into their national armed forces from that set out in article 38, paragraph 3, of the Convention on the Rights of the Child, taking account of the principles contained in that article and recognizing that under the Convention persons under 18 are entitled to special protection.

2. Each State Party shall deposit a binding declaration upon ratification of or accession to this Protocol that sets forth the minimum age at which it will permit voluntary recruitment into its national armed forces and a description of the safeguards that it has adopted to ensure that such recruitment is not forced or coerced.

3. States Parties that permit voluntary recruitment into their national armed forces under the age of 18 shall maintain safeguards to ensure, as a minimum, that:

(a) Such recruitment is genuinely voluntary;

(b) Such recruitment is done with the informed consent of the person's parents or legal guardians;

(c) Such persons are fully informed of the duties involved in such military service;

(d) Such persons provide reliable proof of age prior to acceptance into national military service.

4. Each State Party may strengthen its declaration at any time by notification to that effect addressed to the Secretary-General of the United Nations, who shall inform all States Parties. Such notification shall take effect on the date on which it is received by the Secretary-General.

5. The requirement to raise the age in paragraph 1 of the present article does not apply to schools operated by or under the control of the armed forces of the States Parties, in keeping with articles 28 and 29 of the Convention on the Rights of the Child.

Article 4

1. Armed groups that are distinct from the armed forces of a State should not, under any circumstances, recruit or use in hostilities persons under the age of 18 years.

2. States Parties shall take all feasible measures to prevent such recruitment and use, including the adoption of legal measures necessary to prohibit and criminalize such practices.

3. The application of the present article under this Protocol shall not affect the legal status of any party to an armed conflict.

Article 5

Nothing in the present Protocol shall be construed as precluding provisions in the law of a State Party or in international instruments and international humanitarian law that are more conducive to the realization of the rights of the child.

Article 6

1. Each State Party shall take all necessary legal, administrative and other measures to ensure the effective implementation and enforcement of the provisions of this Protocol within its jurisdiction.

2. States Parties undertake to make the principles and provisions of the present Protocol widely known and promoted by appropriate means, to adults and children alike.

3. States Parties shall take all feasible measures to ensure that persons within their jurisdiction recruited or used in hostilities contrary to this Protocol are demobilized or otherwise released from service. States Parties shall, when necessary, accord to these persons all appropriate assistance for their physical and psychological recovery and their social reintegration.

Article 7

1. States Parties shall cooperate in the implementation of the present Protocol, including in the prevention of any activity contrary to the Protocol and in the rehabilitation and social reintegration of persons who are victims of acts contrary to this Protocol, including through technical cooperation and financial assistance. Such assistance and cooperation will be undertaken in consultation with concerned States Parties and relevant international organizations.

2. States Parties in a position to do so shall provide such assistance through existing multilateral, bilateral or other programmes, or, *inter alia*, through a voluntary fund established in accordance with the rules of the General Assembly.

Article 8

1. Each State Party shall submit, within two years following the entry into force of the Protocol for that State Party, a report to the Committee on the Rights of the Child providing comprehensive information on the measures it has taken to implement the provisions of the Protocol, including the measures taken to implement the provisions on participation and recruitment.

2. Following the submission of the comprehensive report, each State Party shall include in the reports they submit to the Committee on the Rights of the Child, in accordance with article 44 of the Convention, any further information with respect to the implementation of the Protocol. Other States Parties to the Protocol shall submit a report every five years.

3. The Committee on the Rights of the Child may request from States Parties further information relevant to the implementation of this Protocol.

Article 9

1. The present Protocol is open for signature by any State that is a party to the Convention or has signed it.

2. The present Protocol is subject to ratification and is open to accession by any State. Instruments of ratification or accession shall be deposited with the Secretary-General of the United Nations.

3. The Secretary-General, in his capacity as depositary of the Convention and the Protocol, shall inform all States Parties to the Convention and all States that have signed the Convention of each instrument of declaration pursuant to article 13.

Convention on the Rights of Persons with Disabilities

Preamble

The States Parties to the present Convention,

(*a*) *Recalling* the principles proclaimed in the Charter of the United Nations which recognize the inherent dignity and worth and the equal and inalienable rights of all members of the human family as the foundation of freedom, justice and peace in the world,

(*b*) *Recognizing* that the United Nations, in the Universal Declaration of Human Rights and in the International Covenants on Human Rights, has proclaimed and agreed that everyone is entitled to all the rights and freedoms set forth therein, without distinction of any kind,

(*c*) *Reaffirming* the universality, indivisibility, interdependence and interrelatedness of all human rights and fundamental freedoms and the need for persons with disabilities to be guaranteed their full enjoyment without discrimination,

(*d*) *Recalling* the International Covenant on Economic, Social, and Cultural Rights, the International Covenant on Civil and Political Rights, the International Convention on the Elimination of All Forms of Racial Discrimination, the Convention on the Elimination of All Forms of Discrimination against Women, the Convention against Torture and Other Cruel, Inhuman or Degrading Treatment or Punishment, the Convention on the Rights of the Child, and the International Convention on the Protection of the Rights of All Migrant Workers and Members of Their Families,

(e) *Recognizing* that disability is an evolving concept and that disability results from the interaction between persons with impairments and attitudinal and environmental barriers that hinders their full and effective participation in society on an equal basis with others,

(f) *Recognizing* the importance of the principles and policy guidelines contained in the World Programme of Action concerning Disabled Persons and in the Standard Rules on the Equalization of Opportunities for Persons with Disabilities in influencing the promotion, formulation and evaluation of the policies, plans, programmes and actions at the national, regional and international levels to further equalize opportunities for persons with disabilities,

(g) *Emphasizing* the importance of mainstreaming disability issues as an integral part of relevant strategies of sustainable development,

(h) *Recognizing also* that discrimination against any person on the basis of disability is a violation of the inherent dignity and worth of the human person,

(i) *Recognizing further* the diversity of persons with disabilities,

(j) *Recognizing* the need to promote and protect the human rights of all persons with disabilities, including those who require more intensive support,

(k) *Concerned* that, despite these various instruments and undertakings, persons with disabilities continue to face barriers in their participation as equal members of society and violations of their human rights in all parts of the world,

(l) *Recognizing* the importance of international cooperation for improving the living conditions of persons with disabilities in every country, particularly in developing countries,

(m) *Recognizing* the valued existing and potential contributions made by persons with disabilities to the overall well-being and diversity of their communities, and that the promotion of the full enjoyment by persons with disabilities of their human rights and fundamental freedoms and of full participation by persons with disabilities will result in their enhanced sense of belonging and in significant advances in the human, social and economic development of society and the eradication of poverty,

(n) *Recognizing* the importance for persons with disabilities of their individual autonomy and independence, including the freedom to make their own choices,

(o) *Considering* that persons with disabilities should have the opportunity to be actively involved in decision-making processes about policies and programmes, including those directly concerning them,

(p) *Concerned* about the difficult conditions faced by persons with disabilities who are subject to multiple or aggravated forms of discrimination on the basis of race, colour, sex, language, religion, political or other opinion, national, ethnic, indigenous or social origin, property, birth, age or other status,

(q) *Recognizing* that women and girls with disabilities are often at greater risk, both within and outside the home, of violence, injury or abuse, neglect or negligent treatment, maltreatment or exploitation, (*r*) *Recognizing* that children with disabilities should have full enjoyment of all human rights and fundamental freedoms on an equal basis with other children, and recalling obligations to that end undertaken by States Parties to the Convention on the Rights of the Child,

(*s*) *Emphasizing* the need to incorporate a gender perspective in all efforts to promote the full enjoyment of human rights and fundamental freedoms by persons with disabilities,

(*t*) *Highlighting* the fact that the majority of persons with disabilities live in conditions of poverty, and in this regard recognizing the critical need to address the negative impact of poverty on persons with disabilities,

(*u*) *Bearing in mind* that conditions of peace and security based on full respect for the purposes and principles contained in the Charter of the United Nations and observance of applicable human rights instruments are indispensable for the full protection of persons with disabilities, in particular during armed conflicts and foreign occupation,

(*v*) *Recognizing* the importance of accessibility to the physical, social, economic and cultural environment, to health and education and to information and communication, in enabling persons with disabilities to fully enjoy all human rights and fundamental freedoms,

(*w*) *Realizing* that the individual, having duties to other individuals and to the community to which he or she belongs, is under a responsibility to strive for the promotion and observance of the rights recognized in the International Bill of Human Rights,

(*x*) *Convinced* that the family is the natural and fundamental group unit of society and is entitled to protection by society and the State, and that persons with disabilities and their family members should receive the necessary protection and assistance to enable families to contribute towards the full and equal enjoyment of the rights of persons with disabilities,

(*y*) *Convinced* that a comprehensive and integral international convention to promote and protect the rights and dignity of persons with disabilities will make a significant contribution to redressing the profound social disadvantage of persons with disabilities and promote their participation in the civil, political, economic, social and cultural spheres with equal opportunities, in both developing and developed countries,

Have agreed as follows:

Article 1
Purpose

The purpose of the present Convention is to promote, protect and ensure the full and equal enjoyment of all human rights and fundamental freedoms by all persons with disabilities, and to promote respect for their inherent dignity.

Persons with disabilities include those who have long-term physical, mental, intellectual or sensory impairments which in interaction with various barriers may hinder their full and effective participation in society on an equal basis with others.

Article 2
Definitions

For the purposes of the present Convention:

"Communication" includes languages, display of text, Braille, tactile communication, large print, accessible multimedia as well as written, audio, plain-language, human-reader and augmentative and alternative modes, means and formats of communication, including accessible information and communication technology;

"Language" includes spoken and signed languages and other forms of non spoken languages;

"Discrimination on the basis of disability" means any distinction, exclusion or restriction on the basis of disability which has the purpose or effect of impairing or nullifying the recognition, enjoyment or exercise, on an equal basis with others, of all human rights and fundamental freedoms in the political, economic, social, cultural, civil or any other field. It includes all forms of discrimination, including denial of reasonable accommodation;

"Reasonable accommodation" means necessary and appropriate modification and adjustments not imposing a disproportionate or undue burden, where needed in a particular case, to ensure to persons with disabilities the enjoyment or exercise on an equal basis with others of all human rights and fundamental freedoms;

"Universal design" means the design of products, environments, programmes and services to be usable by all people, to the greatest extent possible, without the need for adaptation or specialized design. "Universal design" shall not exclude assistive devices for particular groups of persons with disabilities where this is needed.

Article 3
General principles

The principles of the present Convention shall be:

(*a*) Respect for inherent dignity, individual autonomy including the freedom to make one's own choices, and independence of persons;

(*b*) Non-discrimination;

(*c*) Full and effective participation and inclusion in society;

(*d*) Respect for difference and acceptance of persons with disabilities as part of human diversity and humanity;

(*e*) Equality of opportunity;

(*f*) Accessibility;

(*g*) Equality between men and women;

(*h*) Respect for the evolving capacities of children with disabilities and respect for the right of children with disabilities to preserve their identities.

Article 4
General obligations

1. States Parties undertake to ensure and promote the full realization of all human rights and fundamental freedoms for all persons with disabilities without discrimination of any kind on the basis of disability. To this end, States Parties undertake:

(*a*) To adopt all appropriate legislative, administrative and other measures for the implementation of the rights recognized in the present Convention;

(*b*) To take all appropriate measures, including legislation, to modify or abolish existing laws, regulations, customs and practices that constitute discrimination against persons with disabilities;

(*c*) To take into account the protection and promotion of the human rights of persons with disabilities in all policies and programmes;

(*d*) To refrain from engaging in any act or practice that is inconsistent with the present Convention and to ensure that public authorities and institutions act in conformity with the present Convention;

(*e*) To take all appropriate measures to eliminate discrimination on the basis of disability by any person, organization or private enterprise;

(*f*) To undertake or promote research and development of universally designed goods, services, equipment and facilities, as defined in article 2 of the present Convention, which should require the minimum possible adaptation and the least cost to meet the specific needs of a person with disabilities, to promote their availability and use, and to promote universal design in the development of standards and guidelines;

(*g*) To undertake or promote research and development of, and to promote the availability and use of new technologies, including information and communications technologies, mobility aids, devices and assistive technologies, suitable for persons with disabilities, giving priority to technologies at an affordable cost;

(*h*) To provide accessible information to persons with disabilities about mobility aids, devices and assistive technologies, including new technologies, as well as other forms of assistance, support services and facilities;

(*i*) To promote the training of professionals and staff working with persons with disabilities in the rights recognized in the present Convention so as to better provide the assistance and services guaranteed by those rights.

2. With regard to economic, social and cultural rights, each State Party undertakes to take measures to the maximum of its available resources and, where needed, within the framework of international cooperation, with a view to achieving progressively the full realization of these rights, without prejudice to those obligations contained in the present Convention that are immediately applicable according to international law.

3. In the development and implementation of legislation and policies to implement the present Convention, and in other decision-making processes concerning issues relating to persons with disabilities, States Parties shall closely consult with and actively involve persons with disabilities, including children with disabilities, through their representative organizations.

4. Nothing in the present Convention shall affect any provisions which are more conducive to the realization of the rights of persons with disabilities and which may be contained in the law of a State Party or international law in force for that State. There shall be no restriction upon or derogation from any of the human rights and fundamental freedoms recognized or existing in any State Party to the present Convention pursuant to law, conventions, regulation or custom on the pretext that the present Convention does not recognize such rights or freedoms or that it recognizes them to a lesser extent.

5. The provisions of the present Convention shall extend to all parts of federal States without any limitations or exceptions.

Article 5
Equality and non-discrimination

1. States Parties recognize that all persons are equal before and under the law and are entitled without any discrimination to the equal protection and equal benefit of the law.

2. States Parties shall prohibit all discrimination on the basis of disability and guarantee to persons with disabilities equal and effective legal protection against discrimination on all grounds.

3. In order to promote equality and eliminate discrimination, States Parties shall take all appropriate steps to ensure that reasonable accommodation is provided.

4. Specific measures which are necessary to accelerate or achieve de facto equality of persons with disabilities shall not be considered discrimination under the terms of the present Convention.

Article 6
Women with disabilities

1. States Parties recognize that women and girls with disabilities are subject to multiple discrimination, and in this regard shall take measures to ensure the full and equal enjoyment by them of all human rights and fundamental freedoms.

2. States Parties shall take all appropriate measures to ensure the full development, advancement and empowerment of women, for the purpose of guaranteeing them the exercise and enjoyment of the human rights and fundamental freedoms set out in the present Convention.

Article 7
Children with disabilities

1. States Parties shall take all necessary measures to ensure the full enjoyment by children with disabilities of all human rights and fundamental freedoms on an equal basis with other children.

2. In all actions concerning children with disabilities, the best interests of the child shall be a primary consideration.

3. States Parties shall ensure that children with disabilities have the right to express their views freely on all matters affecting them, their views being given due weight in accordance with their age and maturity, on an equal basis with other children, and to be provided with disability and age-appropriate assistance to realize that right.

Article 8
Awareness-raising

1. States Parties undertake to adopt immediate, effective and appropriate measures:

(*a*) To raise awareness throughout society, including at the family level, regarding persons with disabilities, and to foster respect for the rights and dignity of persons with disabilities;

(*b*) To combat stereotypes, prejudices and harmful practices relating to persons with disabilities, including those based on sex and age, in all areas of life;

(*c*) To promote awareness of the capabilities and contributions of persons with disabilities.

2. Measures to this end include:

(*a*) Initiating and maintaining effective public awareness campaigns designed:

(i) To nurture receptiveness to the rights of persons with disabilities;

(ii) To promote positive perceptions and greater social awareness towards persons with disabilities;

(iii) To promote recognition of the skills, merits and abilities of persons with disabilities, and of their contributions to the workplace and the labour market.

(*b*) Fostering at all levels of the education system, including in all children from an early age, an attitude of respect for the rights of persons with disabilities;

(*c*) Encouraging all organs of the media to portray persons with disabilities in a manner consistent with the purpose of the present Convention;

(*d*) Promoting awareness-training programmes regarding persons with disabilities and the rights of persons with disabilities.

Article 9
Accessibility

1. To enable persons with disabilities to live independently and participate fully in all aspects of life, States Parties shall take appropriate measures to ensure to persons with disabilities access, on an equal basis with others, to the physical environment, to transportation, to information and communications, including information and communications technologies and systems, and to other facilities and services open or provided to the public, both in urban and in rural areas. These measures, which shall include the identification and elimination of obstacles and barriers to accessibility, shall apply to, *inter alia*:

(*a*) Buildings, roads, transportation and other indoor and outdoor facilities, including schools, housing, medical facilities and workplaces;

(*b*) Information, communications and other services, including electronic services and emergency services.

2. States Parties shall also take appropriate measures:

(*a*) To develop, promulgate and monitor the implementation of minimum standards and guidelines for the accessibility of facilities and services open or provided to the public;

(*b*) To ensure that private entities that offer facilities and services which are open or provided to the public take into account all aspects of accessibility for persons with disabilities;

(*c*) To provide training for stakeholders on accessibility issues facing persons with disabilities;

(*d*) To provide in buildings and other facilities open to the public signage in Braille and in easy to read and understand forms;

(*e*) To provide forms of live assistance and intermediaries, including guides, readers and professional sign language interpreters, to facilitate accessibility to buildings and other facilities open to the public;

(*f*) To promote other appropriate forms of assistance and support to persons with disabilities to ensure their access to information;

(*g*) To promote access for persons with disabilities to new information and communications technologies and systems, including the Internet;

(*h*) To promote the design, development, production and distribution of accessible information and communications technologies and systems at an early stage, so that these technologies and systems become accessible at minimum cost.

Article 10
Right to life

States Parties reaffirm that every human being has the inherent right to life and shall take all necessary measures to ensure its effective enjoyment by persons with disabilities on an equal basis with others.

Article 11
Situations of risk and humanitarian emergencies

States Parties shall take, in accordance with their obligations under international law, including international humanitarian law and international human rights law, all necessary measures to ensure the protection and safety of persons with disabilities in situations of risk, including situations of armed conflict, humanitarian emergencies and the occurrence of natural disasters.

Article 12
Equal recognition before the law

1. States Parties reaffirm that persons with disabilities have the right to recognition everywhere as persons before the law.

2. States Parties shall recognize that persons with disabilities enjoy legal capacity on an equal basis with others in all aspects of life.

3. States Parties shall take appropriate measures to provide access by persons with disabilities to the support they may require in exercising their legal capacity.

4. States Parties shall ensure that all measures that relate to the exercise of legal capacity provide for appropriate and effective safeguards to prevent abuse in accordance with international human rights law. Such safeguards shall ensure that measures relating to the exercise of legal capacity respect the rights, will and preferences of the person, are free of conflict of interest and undue influence, are proportional and tailored to the person's circumstances, apply for the shortest time possible and are subject to regular review by a competent, independent and impartial authority or judicial body. The safeguards shall be proportional to the degree to which such measures affect the person's rights and interests.

5. Subject to the provisions of this article, States Parties shall take all appropriate and effective measures to ensure the equal right of persons with disabilities to own or inherit property, to control their own financial affairs and to have equal access to bank loans, mortgages and other forms of financial credit, and shall ensure that persons with disabilities are not arbitrarily deprived of their property.

Article 13
Access to justice

1. States Parties shall ensure effective access to justice for persons with disabilities on an equal basis with others, including through the provision of procedural and age-appropriate accommodations, in order to facilitate their effective role as direct and indirect participants, including as witnesses, in all legal proceedings, including at investigative and other preliminary stages.

2. In order to help to ensure effective access to justice for persons with disabilities, States Parties shall promote appropriate training for those working in the field of administration of justice, including police and prison staff.

Article 14
Liberty and security of person

1. States Parties shall ensure that persons with disabilities, on an equal basis with others:

(a) Enjoy the right to liberty and security of person;

(*b*) Are not deprived of their liberty unlawfully or arbitrarily, and that any deprivation of liberty is in conformity with the law, and that the existence of a disability shall in no case justify a deprivation of liberty.

2. States Parties shall ensure that if persons with disabilities are deprived of their liberty through any process, they are, on an equal basis with others, entitled to guarantees in accordance with international human rights law and shall be treated in compliance with the objectives and principles of the present Convention, including by provision of reasonable accommodation.

Article 15
Freedom from torture or cruel, inhuman or degrading treatment or punishment

1. No one shall be subjected to torture or to cruel, inhuman or degrading treatment or punishment. In particular, no one shall be subjected without his or her free consent to medical or scientific experimentation.

2. States Parties shall take all effective legislative, administrative, judicial or other measures to prevent persons with disabilities, on an equal basis with others, from being subjected to torture or cruel, inhuman or degrading treatment or punishment.

Article 16
Freedom from exploitation, violence and abuse

1. States Parties shall take all appropriate legislative, administrative, social, educational and other measures to protect persons with disabilities, both within and outside the home, from all forms of exploitation, violence and abuse, including their gender-based aspects.

2. States Parties shall also take all appropriate measures to prevent all forms of exploitation, violence and abuse by ensuring, *inter alia*, appropriate forms of gender- and age-sensitive assistance and support for persons with disabilities and their families and caregivers, including through the provision of information and education on how to avoid, recognize and report instances of exploitation, violence and abuse. States Parties shall ensure that protection services are age-, gender- and disability-sensitive.

3. In order to prevent the occurrence of all forms of exploitation, violence and abuse, States Parties shall ensure that all facilities and programmes designed to serve persons with disabilities are effectively monitored by independent authorities.

4. States Parties shall take all appropriate measures to promote the physical, cognitive and psychological recovery, rehabilitation and social reintegration of persons with disabilities who become victims of any form of exploitation, violence or abuse, including through the provision of protection services. Such recovery and reintegration shall take place in an environment that fosters the health, welfare, self-respect, dignity and autonomy of the person and takes into account gender- and age-specific needs.

5. States Parties shall put in place effective legislation and policies, including women- and child-focused legislation and policies, to ensure that instances of exploitation, violence and abuse against persons with disabilities are identified, investigated and, where appropriate, prosecuted.

Article 17
Protecting the integrity of the person

Every person with disabilities has a right to respect for his or her physical and mental integrity on an equal basis with others.

Article 18
Liberty of movement and nationality

1. States Parties shall recognize the rights of persons with disabilities to liberty of movement, to freedom to choose their residence and to a nationality, on an equal basis with others, including by ensuring that persons with disabilities:

(*a*) Have the right to acquire and change a nationality and are not deprived of their nationality arbitrarily or on the basis of disability;

(*b*) Are not deprived, on the basis of disability, of their ability to obtain, possess and utilize documentation of their nationality or other documentation of identification, or to utilize relevant processes such as immigration proceedings, that may be needed to facilitate exercise of the right to liberty of movement;

(*c*) Are free to leave any country, including their own;

(*d*) Are not deprived, arbitrarily or on the basis of disability, of the right to enter their own country.

2. Children with disabilities shall be registered immediately after birth and shall have the right from birth to a name, the right to acquire a nationality and, as far as possible, the right to know and be cared for by their parents.

Article 19
Living independently and being included in the community

States Parties to the present Convention recognize the equal right of all persons with disabilities to live in the community, with choices equal to others, and shall take effective and appropriate measures to facilitate full enjoyment by persons with disabilities of this right and their full inclusion and participation in the community, including by ensuring that:

(*a*) Persons with disabilities have the opportunity to choose their place of residence and where and with whom they live on an equal basis with others and are not obliged to live in a particular living arrangement;

(*b*) Persons with disabilities have access to a range of in-home, residential and other community support services, including personal assistance necessary to support living and inclusion in the community, and to prevent isolation or segregation from the community;

(*c*) Community services and facilities for the general population are available on an equal basis to persons with disabilities and are responsive to their needs.

Article 20
Personal mobility

States Parties shall take effective measures to ensure personal mobility with the greatest possible independence for persons with disabilities, including by:

(*a*) Facilitating the personal mobility of persons with disabilities in the manner and at the time of their choice, and at affordable cost;

(*b*) Facilitating access by persons with disabilities to quality mobility aids, devices, assistive technologies and forms of live assistance and intermediaries, including by making them available at affordable cost;

(*c*) Providing training in mobility skills to persons with disabilities and to specialist staff working with persons with disabilities;

(*d*) Encouraging entities that produce mobility aids, devices and assistive technologies to take into account all aspects of mobility for persons with disabilities.

Article 21
Freedom of expression and opinion, and access to information

States Parties shall take all appropriate measures to ensure that persons with disabilities can exercise the right to freedom of expression and opinion, including the freedom to seek, receive and impart information and ideas on an equal basis with others and through all forms of communication of their choice, as defined in article 2 of the present Convention, including by:

(*a*) Providing information intended for the general public to persons with disabilities in accessible formats and technologies appropriate to different kinds of disabilities in a timely manner and without additional cost;

(*b*) Accepting and facilitating the use of sign languages, Braille, augmentative and alternative communication, and all other accessible means, modes and formats of communication of their choice by persons with disabilities in official interactions;

(*c*) Urging private entities that provide services to the general public, including through the Internet, to provide information and services in accessible and usable formats for persons with disabilities;

(*d*) Encouraging the mass media, including providers of information through the Internet, to make their services accessible to persons with disabilities;

(*e*) Recognizing and promoting the use of sign languages.

Article 22
Respect for privacy

1. No person with disabilities, regardless of place of residence or living arrangements, shall be subjected to arbitrary or unlawful interference with his or her privacy, family, home or correspondence or other types of communication or to unlawful attacks on his or her honour and reputation. Persons with disabilities have the right to the protection of the law against such interference or attacks.

2. States Parties shall protect the privacy of personal, health and rehabilitation information of persons with disabilities on an equal basis with others.

Article 23
Respect for home and the family

1. States Parties shall take effective and appropriate measures to eliminate discrimination against persons with disabilities in all matters relating to marriage, family, parenthood and relationships, on an equal basis with others, so as to ensure that:

(*a*) The right of all persons with disabilities who are of marriageable age to marry and to found a family on the basis of free and full consent of the intending spouses is recognized;

(*b*) The rights of persons with disabilities to decide freely and responsibly on the number and spacing of their children and to have access to age-appropriate information, reproductive and family planning education are recognized, and the means necessary to enable them to exercise these rights are provided;

(*c*) Persons with disabilities, including children, retain their fertility on an equal basis with others.

2. States Parties shall ensure the rights and responsibilities of persons with disabilities, with regard to guardianship, wardship, trusteeship, adoption of children or similar institutions, where these concepts exist in national legislation; in all cases the best interests of the child shall be paramount. States Parties shall render appropriate assistance to persons with disabilities in the performance of their child-rearing responsibilities.

3. States Parties shall ensure that children with disabilities have equal rights with respect to family life. With a view to realizing these rights, and to prevent concealment, abandonment, neglect and segregation of children with disabilities, States Parties shall undertake to provide early and comprehensive information, services and support to children with disabilities and their families.

4. States Parties shall ensure that a child shall not be separated from his or her parents against their will, except when competent authorities subject to judicial review determine, in accordance with applicable law and procedures, that such separation is necessary for the best interests of the child. In no case shall a child be separated from parents on the basis of a disability of either the child or one or both of the parents.

5. States Parties shall, where the immediate family is unable to care for a child with disabilities, undertake every effort to provide alternative care within the wider family, and failing that, within the community in a family setting.

Article 24
Education

1. States Parties recognize the right of persons with disabilities to education. With a view to realizing this right without discrimination and on the basis of equal opportunity, States Parties shall ensure an inclusive education system at all levels and lifelong learning directed to:

(*a*) The full development of human potential and sense of dignity and self-worth, and the strengthening of respect for human rights, fundamental freedoms and human diversity;

(*b*) The development by persons with disabilities of their personality, talents and creativity, as well as their mental and physical abilities, to their fullest potential;

(*c*) Enabling persons with disabilities to participate effectively in a free society.

2. In realizing this right, States Parties shall ensure that:

(*a*) Persons with disabilities are not excluded from the general education system on the basis of disability, and that children with disabilities are not excluded from free and compulsory primary education, or from secondary education, on the basis of disability;

(*b*) Persons with disabilities can access an inclusive, quality and free primary education and secondary education on an equal basis with others in the communities in which they live;

(*c*) Reasonable accommodation of the individual's requirements is provided;

(*d*) Persons with disabilities receive the support required, within the general education system, to facilitate their effective education;

(*e*) Effective individualized support measures are provided in environments that maximize academic and social development, consistent with the goal of full inclusion.

3. States Parties shall enable persons with disabilities to learn life and social development skills to facilitate their full and equal participation in education and as members of the community. To this end, States Parties shall take appropriate measures, including:

(*a*) Facilitating the learning of Braille, alternative script, augmentative and alternative modes, means and formats of communication and orientation and mobility skills, and facilitating peer support and mentoring;

(*b*) Facilitating the learning of sign language and the promotion of the linguistic identity of the deaf community;

(*c*) Ensuring that the education of persons, and in particular children, who are blind, deaf or deafblind, is delivered in the most appropriate languages and modes and means of communication for the individual, and in environments which maximize academic and social development.

4. In order to help ensure the realization of this right, States Parties shall take appropriate measures to employ teachers, including teachers with disabilities, who are qualified in sign language and/or Braille, and to train professionals and staff who work at all levels of education. Such training shall incorporate disability awareness and the use of appropriate augmentative and alternative modes, means and formats of communication, educational techniques and materials to support persons with disabilities.

5. States Parties shall ensure that persons with disabilities are able to access general tertiary education, vocational training, adult education and lifelong learning without discrimination and on an equal basis with others. To this end, States Parties shall ensure that reasonable accommodation is provided to persons with disabilities.

Article 25
Health

States Parties recognize that persons with disabilities have the right to the enjoyment of the highest attainable standard of health without discrimination on the basis of disability. States Parties shall take all appropriate measures to ensure access for persons with disabilities to health services that are gender-sensitive, including health-related rehabilitation. In particular, States Parties shall:

(*a*) Provide persons with disabilities with the same range, quality and standard of free or affordable health care and programmes as provided to other persons, including in the area of sexual and reproductive health and population-based public health programmes;

(*b*) Provide those health services needed by persons with disabilities specifically because of their disabilities, including early identification and intervention as appropriate, and services designed to minimize and prevent further disabilities, including among children and older persons;

(*c*) Provide these health services as close as possible to people's own communities, including in rural areas;

(*d*) Require health professionals to provide care of the same quality to persons with disabilities as to others, including on the basis of free and informed consent by, *inter alia*, raising awareness of the human rights, dignity, autonomy and needs of persons with disabilities through training and the promulgation of ethical standards for public and private health care;

(*e*) Prohibit discrimination against persons with disabilities in the provision of health insurance, and life insurance where such insurance is permitted by national law, which shall be provided in a fair and reasonable manner;

(*f*) Prevent discriminatory denial of health care or health services or food and fluids on the basis of disability.

Article 26
Habilitation and rehabilitation

1. States Parties shall take effective and appropriate measures, including through peer support, to enable persons with disabilities to attain and maintain maximum independence, full physical, mental, social and vocational ability, and full inclusion and participation in all aspects of life. To that end, States Parties shall organize, strengthen and extend comprehensive habilitation and rehabilitation services and programmes, particularly in the areas of health, employment, education and social services, in such a way that these services and programmes:

(*a*) Begin at the earliest possible stage, and are based on the multidisciplinary assessment of individual needs and strengths;

(*b*) Support participation and inclusion in the community and all aspects of society, are voluntary, and are available to persons with disabilities as close as possible to their own communities, including in rural areas.

2. States Parties shall promote the development of initial and continuing training for professionals and staff working in habilitation and rehabilitation services.

3. States Parties shall promote the availability, knowledge and use of assistive devices and technologies, designed for persons with disabilities, as they relate to habilitation and rehabilitation.

Article 27
Work and employment

1. States Parties recognize the right of persons with disabilities to work, on an equal basis with others; this includes the right to the opportunity to gain a living by work freely chosen or accepted in a labour market and work environment that is open, inclusive and accessible to persons with disabilities. States Parties shall safeguard and promote the realization of the right to work, including for those who acquire a disability during the course of employment, by taking appropriate steps, including through legislation, to, *inter alia*:

(*a*) Prohibit discrimination on the basis of disability with regard to all matters concerning all forms of employment, including conditions of recruitment, hiring and employment, continuance of employment, career advancement and safe and healthy working conditions;

(*b*) Protect the rights of persons with disabilities, on an equal basis with others, to just and favourable conditions of work, including equal opportunities and equal remuneration for work of equal value, safe and healthy working conditions, including protection from harassment, and the redress of grievances;

(*c*) Ensure that persons with disabilities are able to exercise their labour and trade union rights on an equal basis with others;

(*d*) Enable persons with disabilities to have effective access to general technical and vocational guidance programmes, placement services and vocational and continuing training;

(*e*) Promote employment opportunities and career advancement for persons with disabilities in the labour market, as well as assistance in finding, obtaining, maintaining and returning to employment;

(*f*) Promote opportunities for self-employment, entrepreneurship, the development of cooperatives and starting one's own business;

(*g*) Employ persons with disabilities in the public sector;

(*h*) Promote the employment of persons with disabilities in the private sector through appropriate policies and measures, which may include affirmative action programmes, incentives and other measures;

(*i*) Ensure that reasonable accommodation is provided to persons with disabilities in the workplace;

(*j*) Promote the acquisition by persons with disabilities of work experience in the open labour market;

(*k*) Promote vocational and professional rehabilitation, job retention and return-to-work programmes for persons with disabilities.

2. States Parties shall ensure that persons with disabilities are not held in slavery or in servitude, and are protected, on an equal basis with others, from forced or compulsory labour.

Article 28
Adequate standard of living and social protection

1. States Parties recognize the right of persons with disabilities to an adequate standard of living for themselves and their families, including adequate food, clothing and housing, and to the continuous improvement of living conditions, and shall take appropriate steps to safeguard and promote the realization of this right without discrimination on the basis of disability.

2. States Parties recognize the right of persons with disabilities to social protection and to the enjoyment of that right without discrimination on the basis of disability, and shall take appropriate steps to safeguard and promote the realization of this right, including measures:

(*a*) To ensure equal access by persons with disabilities to clean water services, and to ensure access to appropriate and affordable services, devices and other assistance for disability-related needs;

(*b*) To ensure access by persons with disabilities, in particular women and girls with disabilities and older persons with disabilities, to social protection programmes and poverty reduction programmes;

(*c*) To ensure access by persons with disabilities and their families living in situations of poverty to assistance from the State with disability-related expenses, including adequate training, counseling, financial assistance and respite care;

(*d*) To ensure access by persons with disabilities to public housing programmes;

(*e*) To ensure equal access by persons with disabilities to retirement benefits and programmes.

Article 29
Participation in political and public life

States Parties shall guarantee to persons with disabilities political rights and the opportunity to enjoy them on an equal basis with others, and shall undertake:

(*a*) To ensure that persons with disabilities can effectively and fully participate in political and public life on an equal basis with others, directly or through freely chosen representatives, including the right and opportunity for persons with disabilities to vote and be elected, *inter alia*, by:

(i) Ensuring that voting procedures, facilities and materials are appropriate, accessible and easy to understand and use;

(ii) Protecting the right of persons with disabilities to vote by secret ballot in elections and public referendums without intimidation, and to stand for elections, to effectively hold office and perform all public functions at all levels of government, facilitating the use of assistive and new technologies where appropriate;

(iii) Guaranteeing the free expression of the will of persons with disabilities as electors and to this end, where necessary, at their request, allowing assistance in voting by a person of their own choice;

(*b*) To promote actively an environment in which persons with disabilities can effectively and fully participate in the conduct of public affairs, without discrimination and on an equal basis with others, and encourage their participation in public affairs, including:

(i) Participation in non-governmental organization and associations concerned with the public and political life of the country, and in the activities and administration of political parties;

(ii) Forming and joining organizations of persons with disabilities to represent persons with disabilities at international, national, regional and local levels.

Article 30
Participation in cultural life, recreation, leisure and sport

1. States Parties recognize the right of persons with disabilities to take part on an equal basis with others in cultural life, and shall take all appropriate measures to ensure that persons with disabilities:

(*a*) Enjoy access to cultural materials in accessible formats;

(*b*) Enjoy access to television programmes, films, theatre and other cultural activities, in accessible formats;

(*c*) Enjoy access to places for cultural performances or services, such as theatres, museums, cinemas, libraries and tourism services, and, as far as possible, enjoy access to monuments and sites of national cultural importance.

2. States Parties shall take appropriate measures to enable persons with disabilities to have the opportunity to develop and utilize their creative, artistic and intellectual potential, not only for their own benefit, but also for the enrichment of society.

3. States Parties shall take all appropriate steps, in accordance with international law, to ensure that laws protecting intellectual property rights do not constitute an unreasonable or discriminatory barrier to access by persons with disabilities to cultural materials.

4. Persons with disabilities shall be entitled, on an equal basis with others, to recognition and support of their specific cultural and linguistic identity, including sign languages and deaf culture.

5. With a view to enabling persons with disabilities to participate on an equal basis with others in recreational, leisure and sporting activities, States Parties shall take appropriate measures:

(*a*) To encourage and promote the participation, to the fullest extent possible, of persons with disabilities in mainstream sporting activities at all levels;

(*b*) To ensure that persons with disabilities have an opportunity to organize, develop and participate in disability-specific sporting and recreational activities and, to this end, encourage the provision, on an equal basis with others, of appropriate instruction, training and resources;

(c) To ensure that persons with disabilities have access to sporting, recreational and tourism venues;

(d) To ensure that children with disabilities have equal access with other children to participation in play, recreation and leisure and sporting activities, including those activities in the school system;

(e) To ensure that persons with disabilities have access to services from those involved in the organization of recreational, tourism, leisure and sporting activities.

Article 31
Statistics and data collection

1. States Parties undertake to collect appropriate information, including statistical and research data, to enable them to formulate and implement policies to give effect to the present Convention. The process of collecting and maintaining this information shall:

(a) Comply with legally established safeguards, including legislation on data protection, to ensure confidentiality and respect for the privacy of persons with disabilities;

(b) Comply with internationally accepted norms to protect human rights and fundamental freedoms and ethical principles in the collection and use of statistics.

2. The information collected in accordance with this article shall be disaggregated, as appropriate, and used to help assess the implementation of States Parties' obligations under the present Convention and to identify and address the barriers faced by persons with disabilities in exercising their rights.

3. States Parties shall assume responsibility for the dissemination of these statistics and ensure their accessibility to persons with disabilities and others.

Article 32
International cooperation

1. States Parties recognize the importance of international cooperation and its promotion, in support of national efforts for the realization of the purpose and objectives of the present Convention, and will undertake appropriate and effective measures in this regard, between and among States and, as appropriate, in partnership with relevant international and regional organizations and civil society, in particular organizations of persons with disabilities. Such measures could include, *inter alia*:

(a) Ensuring that international cooperation, including international development programmes, is inclusive of and accessible to persons with disabilities;

(b) Facilitating and supporting capacity-building, including through the exchange and sharing of information, experiences, training programmes and best practices;

(c) Facilitating cooperation in research and access to scientific and technical knowledge;

(d) Providing, as appropriate, technical and economic assistance, including by facilitating access to and sharing of accessible and assistive technologies, and through the transfer of technologies.

2. The provisions of this article are without prejudice to the obligations of each State Party to fulfill its obligations under the present Convention.

Article 33
National implementation and monitoring

1. States Parties, in accordance with their system of organization, shall designate one or more focal points within government for matters relating to the implementation of

the present Convention, and shall give due consideration to the establishment or designation of a coordination mechanism within government to facilitate related action in different sectors and at different levels.

2. States Parties shall, in accordance with their legal and administrative systems, maintain, strengthen, designate or establish within the State Party, a framework, including one or more independent mechanisms, as appropriate, to promote, protect and monitor implementation of the present Convention. When designating or establishing such a mechanism, States Parties shall take into account the principles relating to the status and functioning of national institutions for protection and promotion of human rights.

3. Civil society, in particular persons with disabilities and their representative organizations, shall be involved and participate fully in the monitoring process.

Article 34
Committee on the Rights of Persons with Disabilities

1. There shall be established a Committee on the Rights of Persons with Disabilities (hereafter referred to as "the Committee"), which shall carry out the functions hereinafter provided.

2. The Committee shall consist, at the time of entry into force of the present Convention, of twelve experts. After an additional sixty ratifications or accessions to the Convention, the membership of the Committee shall increase by six members, attaining a maximum number of eighteen members.

3. The members of the Committee shall serve in their personal capacity and shall be of high moral standing and recognized competence and experience in the field covered by the present Convention. When nominating their candidates, States Parties are invited to give due consideration to the provision set out in article 4, paragraph 3, of the present Convention.

4. The members of the Committee shall be elected by States Parties, consideration being given to equitable geographical distribution, representation of the different forms of civilization and of the principal legal systems, balanced gender representation and participation of experts with disabilities.

5. The members of the Committee shall be elected by secret ballot from a list of persons nominated by the States Parties from among their nationals at meetings of the Conference of States Parties. At those meetings, for which two thirds of States Parties shall constitute a quorum, the persons elected to the Committee shall be those who obtain the largest number of votes and an absolute majority of the votes of the representatives of States Parties present and voting.

6. The initial election shall be held no later than six months after the date of entry into force of the present Convention. At least four months before the date of each election, the Secretary-General of the United Nations shall address a letter to the States Parties inviting them to submit the nominations within two months. The Secretary-General shall subsequently prepare a list in alphabetical order of all persons thus nominated, indicating the State Parties which have nominated them, and shall submit it to the States Parties to the present Convention.

7. The members of the Committee shall be elected for a term of four years. They shall be eligible for re-election once. However, the term of six of the members elected at the first election shall expire at the end of two years; immediately after the first election, the names of these six members shall be chosen by lot by the chairperson of the meeting referred to in paragraph 5 of this article.

8. The election of the six additional members of the Committee shall be held on the occasion of regular elections, in accordance with the relevant provisions of this article.

9. If a member of the Committee dies or resigns or declares that for any other cause she or he can no longer perform her or his duties, the State Party which nominated the member shall appoint another expert possessing the qualifications and meeting the requirements set out in the relevant provisions of this article, to serve for the remainder of the term.

10. The Committee shall establish its own rules of procedure.

11. The Secretary-General of the United Nations shall provide the necessary staff and facilities for the effective performance of the functions of the Committee under the present Convention, and shall convene its initial meeting.

12. With the approval of the General Assembly of the United Nations, the members of the Committee established under the present Convention shall receive emoluments from United Nations resources on such terms and conditions as the Assembly may decide, having regard to the importance of the Committee's responsibilities.

13. The members of the Committee shall be entitled to the facilities, privileges and immunities of experts on mission for the United Nations as laid down in the relevant sections of the Convention on the Privileges and Immunities of the United Nations.

Article 35
Reports by States Parties

1. Each State Party shall submit to the Committee, through the Secretary-General of the United Nations, a comprehensive report on measures taken to give effect to its obligations under the present Convention and on the progress made in that regard, within two years after the entry into force of the present Convention for the State Party concerned.

2. Thereafter, States Parties shall submit subsequent reports at least every four years and further whenever the Committee so requests.

3. The Committee shall decide any guidelines applicable to the content of the reports.

4. A State Party which has submitted a comprehensive initial report to the Committee need not, in its subsequent reports, repeat information previously provided. When preparing reports to the Committee, States Parties are invited to consider doing so in an open and transparent process and to give due consideration to the provision set out in article 4, paragraph 3, of the present Convention.

5. Reports may indicate factors and difficulties affecting the degree of fulfillment of obligations under the present Convention.

Article 36
Consideration of reports

1. Each report shall be considered by the Committee, which shall make such suggestions and general recommendations on the report as it may consider appropriate and shall forward these to the State Party concerned. The State Party may respond with any information it chooses to the Committee. The Committee may request further information from States Parties relevant to the implementation of the present Convention.

2. If a State Party is significantly overdue in the submission of a report, the Committee may notify the State Party concerned of the need to examine the implementation of the present Convention in that State Party, on the basis of reliable information available

to the Committee, if the relevant report is not submitted within three months following the notification. The Committee shall invite the State Party concerned to participate in such examination. Should the State Party respond by submitting the relevant report, the provisions of paragraph 1 of this article will apply.

3. The Secretary-General of the United Nations shall make available the reports to all States Parties.

4. States Parties shall make their reports widely available to the public in their own countries and facilitate access to the suggestions and general recommendations relating to these reports.

5. The Committee shall transmit, as it may consider appropriate, to the specialized agencies, funds and programmes of the United Nations, and other competent bodies, reports from States Parties in order to address a request or indication of a need for technical advice or assistance contained therein, along with the Committee's observations and recommendations, if any, on these requests or indications.

Article 37
Cooperation between States Parties and the Committee

1. Each State Party shall cooperate with the Committee and assist its members in the fulfillment of their mandate.

2. In its relationship with States Parties, the Committee shall give due consideration to ways and means of enhancing national capacities for the implementation of the present Convention, including through international cooperation.

Article 38
Relationship of the Committee with other bodies

In order to foster the effective implementation of the present Convention and to encourage international cooperation in the field covered by the present Convention:

(a) The specialized agencies and other United Nations organs shall be entitled to be represented at the consideration of the implementation of such provisions of the present Convention as fall within the scope of their mandate. The Committee may invite the specialized agencies and other competent bodies as it may consider appropriate to provide expert advice on the implementation of the Convention in areas falling within the scope of their respective mandates. The Committee may invite specialized agencies and other United Nations organs to submit reports on the implementation of the Convention in areas falling within the scope of their activities;

(b) The Committee, as it discharges its mandate, shall consult, as appropriate, other relevant bodies instituted by international human rights treaties, with a view to ensuring the consistency of their respective reporting guidelines, suggestions and general recommendations, and avoiding duplication and overlap in the performance of their functions.

Article 39
Report of the Committee

The Committee shall report every two years to the General Assembly and to the Economic and Social Council on its activities, and may make suggestions and general recommendations based on the examination of reports and information received from the States Parties. Such suggestions and general recommendations shall be included in the report of the Committee together with comments, if any, from States Parties.

Article 40
Conference of States Parties

1. The States Parties shall meet regularly in a Conference of States Parties in order to consider any matter with regard to the implementation of the present Convention.

2. No later than six months after the entry into force of the present Convention, the Conference of States Parties shall be convened by the Secretary-General of the United Nations. The subsequent meetings shall be convened by the Secretary-General biennially or upon the decision of the Conference of States Parties.

Article 41
Depositary

The Secretary-General of the United Nations shall be the depositary of the present Convention.

Article 42
Signature

The present Convention shall be open for signature by all States and by regional integration organizations at United Nations Headquarters in New York as of 30 March 2007.

Article 43
Consent to be bound

The present Convention shall be subject to ratification by signatory States and to formal confirmation by signatory regional integration organizations. It shall be open for accession by any State or regional integration organization which has not signed the Convention.

Article 44
Regional integration organizations

1. "Regional integration organization" shall mean an organization constituted by sovereign States of a given region, to which its member States have transferred competence in respect of matters governed by the present Convention. Such organizations shall declare, in their instruments of formal confirmation or accession, the extent of their competence with respect to matters governed by the present Convention. Subsequently, they shall inform the depositary of any substantial modification in the extent of their competence.

2. References to "States Parties" in the present Convention shall apply to such organizations within the limits of their competence.

3. For the purposes of article 45, paragraph 1, and article 47, paragraphs 2 and 3, of the present Convention, any instrument deposited by a regional integration organization shall not be counted.

4. Regional integration organizations, in matters within their competence, may exercise their right to vote in the Conference of States Parties, with a number of votes equal to the number of their member States that are Parties to the present Convention. Such an organization shall not exercise its right to vote if any of its member States exercises its right, and vice versa.

Article 45
Entry into force

1. The present Convention shall enter into force on the thirtieth day after the deposit of the twentieth instrument of ratification or accession.

2. For each State or regional integration organization ratifying, formally confirming or acceding to the present Convention after the deposit of the twentieth such instrument, the Convention shall enter into force on the thirtieth day after the deposit of its own such instrument.

Article 46
Reservations

1. Reservations incompatible with the object and purpose of the present Convention shall not be permitted.

2. Reservations may be withdrawn at any time.

Article 47
Amendments

1. Any State Party may propose an amendment to the present Convention and submit it to the Secretary-General of the United Nations. The Secretary-General shall communicate any proposed amendments to States Parties, with a request to be notified whether they favour a conference of States Parties for the purpose of considering and deciding upon the proposals. In the event that, within four months from the date of such communication, at least one third of the States Parties favour such a conference, the Secretary-General shall convene the conference under the auspices of the United Nations. Any amendment adopted by a majority of two thirds of the States Parties present and voting shall be submitted by the Secretary-General to the General Assembly of the United Nations for approval and thereafter to all States Parties for acceptance.

2. An amendment adopted and approved in accordance with paragraph 1 of this article shall enter into force on the thirtieth day after the number of instruments of acceptance deposited reaches two thirds of the number of States Parties at the date of adoption of the amendment. Thereafter, the amendment shall enter into force for any State Party on the thirtieth day following the deposit of its own instrument of acceptance. An amendment shall be binding only on those States Parties which have accepted it.

3. If so decided by the Conference of States Parties by consensus, an amendment adopted and approved in accordance with paragraph 1 of this article which relates exclusively to articles 34, 38, 39 and 40 shall enter into force for all States Parties on the thirtieth day after the number of instruments of acceptance deposited reaches two thirds of the number of States Parties at the date of adoption of the amendment.

Article 48
Denunciation

A State Party may denounce the present Convention by written notification to the Secretary-General of the United Nations. The denunciation shall become effective one year after the date of receipt of the notification by the Secretary-General.

Article 49
Accessible format

The text of the present Convention shall be made available in accessible formats.

Article 50
Authentic texts

The Arabic, Chinese, English, French, Russian and Spanish texts of the present Convention shall be equally authentic.

IN WITNESS THEREOF the undersigned plenipotentiaries, being duly authorized thereto by their respective Governments, have signed the present Convention.

European Convention for the Protection of Human Rights and Fundamental Freedoms

[This text is a consolidation of the Convention pursuant to Protocol No. 11 & 14.]

The governments signatory hereto, being members of the Council of Europe,

Considering the Universal Declaration of Human Rights proclaimed by the General Assembly of the United Nations on 10th December 1948;

Considering that this Declaration aims at securing the universal and effective recognition and observance of the Rights therein declared;

Considering that the aim of the Council of Europe is the achievement of greater unity between its members and that one of the methods by which that aim is to be pursued is the maintenance and further realisation of human rights and fundamental freedoms;

Reaffirming their profound belief in those fundamental freedoms which are the foundation of justice and peace in the world and are best maintained on the one hand by an effective political democracy and on the other by a common understanding and observance of the human rights upon which they depend;

Being resolved, as the governments of European countries which are like-minded and have a common heritage of political traditions, ideals, freedom and the rule of law, to take the first steps for the collective enforcement of certain of the rights stated in the Universal Declaration,

Have agreed as follows:

Article 1

The High Contracting Parties shall secure to everyone within their jurisdiction the rights and freedoms defined in Section 1 of this Convention.

Section 1 — Rights and Freedoms

Article 2

1. Everyone's right to life shall be protected by law. No one shall be deprived of his life intentionally save in the execution of a sentence of a court following his conviction of a crime for which this penalty is provided by law.

2. Deprivation of life shall not be regarded as inflicted in contravention of this article when it results from the use of force which is no more than absolutely necessary:

   a. in defence of any person from unlawful violence;

   b. in order to effect a lawful arrest or to prevent the escape of a person lawfully detained;

   c. in action lawfully taken for the purpose of quelling a riot or insurrection.

Article 3

No one shall be subjected to torture or to inhuman or degrading treatment or punishment.

Article 4

1. No one shall be held in slavery or servitude.

2. No one shall be required to perform forced or compulsory labour.

...

Article 5

1. Everyone has the right to liberty and security of person. No one shall be deprived of his liberty save in the following cases and in accordance with a procedure prescribed by law:

a. the lawful detention of a person after conviction by a competent court;

b. the lawful arrest or detention of a person for non-compliance with the lawful order of a court or in order to secure the fulfilment of any obligation prescribed by law;

c. the lawful arrest or detention of a person effected for the purpose of bringing him before the competent legal authority on reasonable suspicion of having committed an offence or when it is reasonably considered necessary to prevent his committing an offence or fleeing after having done so;

...

2. Everyone who is arrested shall be informed promptly, in a language which he understands, of the reasons for his arrest and of any charge against him.

3. Everyone arrested or detained in accordance with the provisions of paragraph 1(c) of this article shall be brought promptly before a judge or other officer authorised by law to exercise judicial power and shall be entitled to trial within a reasonable time or to release pending trial. Release may be conditioned by guarantees to appear for trial.

4. Everyone who is deprived of his liberty by arrest or detention shall be entitled to take proceedings by which the lawfulness of his detention shall be decided speedily by a court and his release ordered if the detention is not lawful.

5. Everyone who has been the victim of arrest or detention in contravention of the provisions of this article shall have an enforceable right to compensation.

Article 6

1. In the determination of his civil rights and obligations or of any criminal charge against him, everyone is entitled to a fair and public hearing within a reasonable time by an independent and impartial tribunal established by law. Judgment shall be pronounced publicly but the press and public may be excluded from all or part of the trial in the interests of morals, public order or national security in a democratic society, where the interests of juveniles or the protection of the private life of the parties so require, or to the extent strictly necessary in the opinion of the court in special circumstances where publicity would prejudice the interests of justice.

2. Everyone charged with a criminal offence shall be presumed innocent until proved guilty according to law.

3. Everyone charged with a criminal offence has the following minimum rights:

a. to be informed promptly, in a language which he understands and in detail, of the nature and cause of the accusation against him;

b. to have adequate time and facilities for the preparation of his defence;

c. to defend himself in person or through legal assistance of his own choosing or, if he has not sufficient means to pay for legal assistance, to be given it free when the interests of justice so require;

d. to examine or have examined witnesses against him and to obtain the attendance and examination of witnesses on his behalf under the same conditions as witnesses against him;

e. to have the free assistance of an interpreter if he cannot understand or speak the language used in court.

Article 7

1. No one shall be held guilty of any criminal offence on account of any act or omission which did not constitute a criminal offence under national or international law at the time when it was committed. Nor shall a heavier penalty be imposed than the one that was applicable at the time the criminal offence was committed.

2. This article shall not prejudice the trial and punishment of any person for any act or omission which, at the time when it was committed, was criminal according to the general principles of law recognised by civilised nations.

Article 8

1. Everyone has the right to respect for his private and family life, his home and his correspondence.

2. There shall be no interference by a public authority with the exercise of this right except such as is in accordance with the law and is necessary in a democratic society in the interests of national security, public safety or the economic well-being of the country, for the prevention of disorder or crime, for the protection of health or morals, or for the protection of the rights and freedoms of others.

Article 9

1. Everyone has the right to freedom of thought, conscience and religion; this right includes freedom to change his religion or belief and freedom, either alone or in community with others and in public or private, to manifest his religion or belief, in worship, teaching, practice and observance.

2. Freedom to manifest one's religion or beliefs shall be subject only to such limitations as are prescribed by law and are necessary in a democratic society in the interests of public safety, for the protection of public order, health or morals, or for the protection of the rights and freedoms of others.

Article 10

1. Everyone has the right to freedom of expression. This right shall include freedom to hold opinions and to receive and impart information and ideas without interference by public authority and regardless of frontiers. This article shall not prevent States from requiring the licensing of broadcasting, television or cinema enterprises.

2. The exercise of these freedoms, since it carries with it duties and responsibilities, may be subject to such formalities, conditions, restrictions or penalties as are prescribed by law and are necessary in a democratic society, in the interests of national security, territorial integrity or public safety, for the prevention of disorder or crime, for the protection of health or morals, for the protection of the reputation or rights of others, for preventing the disclosure of information received in confidence, or for maintaining the authority and impartiality of the judiciary.

Article 11

1. Everyone has the right to freedom of peaceful assembly and to freedom of association with others, including the right to form and to join trade unions for the protection of his interests.

2. No restrictions shall be placed on the exercise of these rights other than such as are prescribed by law and are necessary in a democratic society in the interests of national se-

curity or public safety, for the prevention of disorder or crime, for the protection of health or morals or for the protection of the rights and freedoms of others. This article shall not prevent the imposition of lawful restrictions on the exercise of these rights by members of the armed forces, of the police or of the administration of the State.

Article 12

Men and women of marriageable age have the right to marry and to found a family, according to the national laws governing the exercise of this right.

Article 13

Everyone whose rights and freedoms as set forth in this Convention are violated shall have an effective remedy before a national authority notwithstanding that the violation has been committed by persons acting in an official capacity.

Article 14

The enjoyment of the rights and freedoms set forth in this Convention shall be secured without discrimination on any ground such as sex, race, colour, language, religion, political or other opinion, national or social origin, association with a national minority, property, birth or other status.

Article 15

1. In time of war or other public emergency threatening the life of the nation any High Contracting Party may take measures derogating from its obligations under this Convention to the extent strictly required by the exigencies of the situation, provided that such measures are not inconsistent with its other obligations under international law.

2. No derogation from Article 2, except in respect of deaths resulting from lawful acts of war, or from Articles 3, 4 (paragraph 1) and 7 shall be made under this provision.

3. Any High Contracting Party availing itself of this right of derogation shall keep the Secretary General of the Council of Europe fully informed of the measures which it has taken and the reasons therefor. It shall also inform the Secretary General of the Council of Europe when such measures have ceased to operate and the provisions of the Convention are again being fully executed.

Article 16

Nothing in Articles 10, 11 and 14 shall be regarded as preventing the High Contracting Parties from imposing restrictions on the political activity of aliens.

Article 17

Nothing in this Convention may be interpreted as implying for any State, group or person any right to engage in any activity or perform any act aimed at the destruction of any of the rights and freedoms set forth herein or at their limitation to a greater extent than is provided for in the Convention.

Article 18

The restrictions permitted under this Convention to the said rights and freedoms shall not be applied for any purpose other than those for which they have been prescribed.

Section 2 — European Court Of Human Rights

Article 19

To ensure the observance of the engagements undertaken by the High Contracting Parties in the Convention and the Protocols thereto, there shall be set up a European

Court of Human Rights, hereinafter referred to as "the Court." It shall function on a permanent basis.

Article 20

The Court shall consist of a number of judges equal to that of the High Contracting Parties.

Article 21

1. The judges shall be of high moral character and must either possess the qualifications required for appointment to high judicial office or be jurisconsults of recognised competence.

2. The judges shall sit on the Court in their individual capacity.

3. During their term of office the judges shall not engage in any activity which is incompatible with their independence, impartiality or with the demands of a full-time office; all questions arising from the application of this paragraph shall be decided by the Court.

Article 22

The judges shall be elected by the Parliamentary Assembly with respect to each High Contracting Party by a majority of votes cast from a list of three candidates nominated by the High Contracting Party.

...

Article 23

1. The judges shall be elected for a period of nine years. They may not be re-elected ...

2. The terms of office of judges shall expire when they reach the age of 70.

...

4. No judge may be dismissed from office unless the other judges decide by a majority of two-thirds that that judge has ceased to fulfill the required conditions.

...

Article 26

1. To consider cases brought before it, the Court shall sit in a single-judge formation, in committees of three judges, in Chambers of seven judges and in a Grand Chamber of seventeen judges. The Court's Chambers shall set up committees for a fixed period of time.

2. At the request of the plenary Court, the Committee of Ministers may, by a unanimous decision and for a fixed period, reduce to five the number of judges of the Chambers.

...

Article 27

1. A single judge may declare inadmissible or strike out of the Court's list of cases an application submitted under Article 34, where such a decision can be taken without further examination.

2. The decision shall be final.

3. If the single judge does not declare an application inadmissible or strike it out, that judge shall forward it to a committee or to a Chamber for further examination.

Article 29

1. If no decision is taken under Article 27 or 28, or no judgment rendered under Article 28, a Chamber shall decide on the admissibility and merits of individual applications submitted under Article 34. The decision on admissibility may be taken separately.

2. A Chamber shall decide on the admissibility and merits of inter-State applications submitted under Article 33. The decision on admissibility shall be taken separately unless the Court, in exceptional cases, decides otherwise.

Article 30

Where a case pending before a Chamber raises a serious question affecting the interpretation of the Convention or the protocols thereto, or where the resolution of a question before the Chamber might have a result inconsistent with a judgment previously delivered by the Court, the Chamber may, at any time before it has rendered its judgment, relinquish jurisdiction in favour of the Grand Chamber, unless one of the parties to the case objects.

Article 31

The Grand Chamber shall:

a. determine applications submitted either under Article 33 or Article 34 when a Chamber has relinquished jurisdiction under Article 30 or when the case has been referred to it under Article 43;

b. decide on issues referred to the Court by the Committee of Ministers in accordance with Article 46, paragraph 4; and

c. consider requests for advisory opinions submitted under Article 47.

Article 32

1. The jurisdiction of the Court shall extend to all matters concerning the interpretation and application of the Convention and the protocols thereto which are referred to it as provided in Articles 33, 34, 46 and 47.

2. In the event of dispute as to whether the Court has jurisdiction, the Court shall decide.

Article 33

Any High Contracting Party may refer to the Court any alleged breach of the provisions of the Convention and the protocols thereto by another High Contracting Party.

Article 34

The Court may receive applications from any person, non-governmental organisation or group of individuals claiming to be the victim of a violation by one of the High Contracting Parties of the rights set forth in the Convention or the protocols thereto. The High Contracting Parties undertake not to hinder in any way the effective exercise of this right.

Article 35

1. The Court may only deal with the matter after all domestic remedies have been exhausted, according to the generally recognised rules of international law, and within a period of six months from the date on which the final decision was taken.

2. The Court shall not deal with any application submitted under Article 34 that

a. is anonymous; or

b. is substantially the same as a matter that has already been examined by the Court or has already been submitted to another procedure of international investigation or settlement and contains no relevant new information.

3. The Court shall declare inadmissible any individual application submitted under Article 34 if it considers that:

a. the application is incompatible with the provisions of the Convention or the Protocols thereto, manifestly ill-founded, or an abuse of the right of individual application; or

b. the applicant has not suffered a significant disadvantage, unless respect for human rights as defined in the Convention and the Protocols thereto requires an examination of the application on the merits and provided that no case may be rejected on this ground which has not been duly considered by a domestic tribunal.

4. The Court shall reject any application which it considers inadmissible under this Article. It may do so at any stage of the proceedings.

Article 36

1. In all cases before a Chamber or the Grand Chamber, a High Contracting Party one of whose nationals is an applicant shall have the right to submit written comments and to take part in hearings.

2. The President of the Court may, in the interest of the proper administration of justice, invite any High Contracting Party which is not a party to the proceedings or any person concerned who is not the applicant to submit written comments or take part in hearings.

3. In all cases before a Chamber or the Grand Chamber, the Council of Europe Commissioner for Human Rights may submit written comments and take part in hearings.

. . .

Article 38

The Court shall examine the case together with the representatives of the parties and, if need be, undertake an investigation, for the effective conduct of which the High Contracting Parties concerned shall furnish all necessary facilities.

Article 39

1. At any stage of the proceedings, the Court may place itself at the disposal of the parties concerned with a view to securing a friendly settlement of the matter on the basis of respect for human rights as defined in the Convention and the Protocols thereto.

2. Proceedings conducted under paragraph 1 shall be confidential.

3. If a friendly settlement is effected, the Court shall strike the case out of its list by means of a decision which shall be confined to a brief statement of the facts and of the solution reached.

4. This decision shall be transmitted to the Committee of Ministers, which shall supervise the execution of the terms of the friendly settlement as set out in the decision.

Article 40

1. Hearings shall be in public unless the Court in exceptional circumstances decides otherwise.

2. Documents deposited with the Registrar shall be accessible to the public unless the President of the Court decides otherwise.

Article 41

If the Court finds that there has been a violation of the Convention or the protocols thereto, and if the internal law of the High Contracting Party concerned allows only partial reparation to be made, the Court shall, if necessary, afford just satisfaction to the injured party.

...

Article 43

1. Within a period of three months from the date of the judgment of the Chamber, any party to the case may, in exceptional cases, request that the case be referred to the Grand Chamber.

2. A panel of five judges of the Grand Chamber shall accept the request if the case raises a serious question affecting the interpretation or application of the Convention or the protocols thereto, or a serious issue of general importance.

...

Article 44

1. The judgment of the Grand Chamber shall be final.

2. The judgment of a Chamber shall become final

a. when the parties declare that they will not request that the case be referred to the Grand Chamber; or

b. three months after the date of the judgment, if reference of the case to the Grand Chamber has not been requested; or

c. when the panel of the Grand Chamber rejects the request to refer under Article 43.

3. The final judgment shall be published.

Article 45

1. Reasons shall be given for judgments as well as for decisions declaring applications admissible or inadmissible.

2. If a judgment does not represent, in whole or in part, the unanimous opinion of the judges, any judge shall be entitled to deliver a separate opinion.

Article 46

1. The High Contracting Parties undertake to abide by the final judgment of the Court in any case to which they are parties.

2. The final judgment of the Court shall be transmitted to the Committee of Ministers, which shall supervise its execution....

...

Article 47

1. The Court may, at the request of the Committee of Ministers, give advisory opinions on legal questions concerning the interpretation of the Convention and the protocols thereto.

2. Such opinions shall not deal with any question relating to the content or scope of the rights or freedoms defined in Section 1 of the Convention and the protocols thereto, or with any other question which the Court or the Committee of Ministers might have

to consider in consequence of any such proceedings as could be instituted in accordance with the Convention.

...

Article 49

1. Reasons shall be given for advisory opinions of the Court.

2. If the advisory opinion does not represent, in whole or in part, the unanimous opinion of the judges, any judge shall be entitled to deliver a separate opinion....

...

Section 3—Miscellaneous Provisions

Article 52

On receipt of a request from the Secretary General of the Council of Europe any High Contracting Party shall furnish an explanation of the manner in which its internal law ensures the effective implementation of any of the provisions of the Convention.

...

Article 57

1. Any State may, when signing this Convention or when depositing its instrument of ratification, make a reservation in respect of any particular provision of the Convention to the extent that any law then in force in its territory is not in conformity with the provision. Reservations of a general character shall not be permitted under this article.

2. Any reservation made under this article shall contain a brief statement of the law concerned.

Article 58

1. A High Contracting Party may denounce the present Convention only after the expiry of five years from the date on which it became a party to it and after six months' notice ...

...

Protocols to the European Convention for the Protection of Human Rights and Fundamental Freedoms

Protocol No. One

...

Article 1

Every natural or legal person is entitled to the peaceful enjoyment of his possessions. No one shall be deprived of his possessions except in the public interest and subject to the conditions provided for by law and by the general principles of international law. The preceding provisions shall not, however, in any way impair the right of a State to enforce such laws as it deems necessary to control the use of property in accordance with the general interest or to secure the payment of taxes or other contributions or penalties.

Article 2

No person shall be denied the right to education. In the exercise of any functions which it assumes in relation to education and to teaching, the State shall respect the right of parents to ensure such education and teaching in conformity with their own religions and philosophical convictions.

Article 3

The High Contracting Parties undertake to hold free elections at reasonable intervals by secret ballot, under conditions which will ensure the free expression of the opinion of the people in the choice of the legislature.

. . .

Protocol No. Four

. . .

Article 2

1. Everyone lawfully within the territory of a State shall, within that territory, have the right to liberty of movement and freedom to choose his residence.

2. Everyone shall be free to leave any country, including his own.

3. No restrictions shall be placed on the exercise of these rights other than such as are in accordance with law and are necessary in a democratic society in the interests of national security or public safety for the maintenance of 'ordre public', for the prevention of crime, for the protection of rights and freedoms of others.

4. The rights set forth in paragraph 1 may also be subject, in particular areas, to restrictions imposed in accordance with law and justified by the public interest in a democratic society.

Article 3

1. No one shall be expelled, by means either of an individual or of a collective measure, from the territory of the State of which he is a national.

2. No one shall be deprived of the right to enter the territory of the State of which he is a national.

Article 4

Collective expulsion of aliens is prohibited.

. . .

Protocol No. Six

Article 1

The death penalty shall be abolished. No-one shall be condemned to such penalty or executed.

Article 2

A State may make provision in its law for the death penalty in respect of acts committed in time of war or of imminent threat of war; such penalty shall be applied only in the instances laid down in the law and in accordance with its provisions. The State shall communicate to the Secretary General of the Council of Europe the relevant provisions of that law.

Article 3

No derogation from the provisions of this Protocol shall be made under Article 15 of the Convention.

. . .

Protocol No. Seven

Article 1

1. An alien lawfully resident in the territory of a State shall not be expelled therefrom except in pursuance of a decision reached in accordance with law and shall be allowed:

    a. to submit reasons against his expulsion,

    b. to have his case reviewed, and

    c. to be represented for these purposes before the competent authority or a person or persons designated by that authority.

2. An alien may be expelled before the exercise of his rights under paragraph 1(a), (b) and (c) of this Article, when such expulsion is necessary in the interests of public order or is grounded on reasons of national security.

Article 2

1. Everyone convicted of a criminal offence by a tribunal shall have the right to have his conviction or sentence reviewed by a higher tribunal. The exercise of this right, including the grounds on which it may be exercised, shall be governed by law.

2. This right may be subject to exceptions in regard to offences of a minor character, as prescribed by law, or in cases in which the person concerned was tried in the first instance by the highest tribunal or was convicted following an appeal against acquittal.

Article 3

When a person has by a final decision been convicted of a criminal offence and when subsequently his conviction has been reversed, or he has been pardoned, on the ground that a new or newly discovered fact shows conclusively that there has been a miscarriage of justice, the person who has suffered punishment as a result of such conviction shall be compensated according to the law or the practice of the State concerned, unless it is proved that the non-disclosure of the unknown fact in time is wholly or partly attributable to him.

Article 4

1. No one shall be liable to be tried or punished again in criminal proceedings under the jurisdiction of the same State for an offence for which he has already been finally acquitted or convicted in accordance with the law and penal procedure of that State.

2. The provisions of the preceding paragraph shall not prevent the reopening of the case in accordance with the law and penal procedure of the State concerned, if there is evidence of new or newly discovered facts, or if there has been a fundamental defect in the previous proceedings, which could affect the outcome of the case.

3. No derogation from this Article shall be made under Article 15 of the Convention.

Article 5

Spouses shall enjoy equality of rights and responsibilities of a private law character between them, and in their relations with their children, as to marriage, during marriage and in the event of its dissolution. This Article shall not prevent States from taking such measures as are necessary in the interests of the children.

American Convention on Human Rights

Preamble

The American states signatory to the present Convention,

Reaffirming their intention to consolidate in this hemisphere, within the framework of democratic institutions, a system of personal liberty and social justice based on respect for the essential rights of man;

Recognizing that the essential rights of man are not derived from one's being a national of a certain state, but are based upon attributes of the human personality, and that they therefore justify international protection in the form of a convention reinforcing or complementing the protection provided by the domestic law of the American states;

Considering that these principles have been set forth in the Charter of the Organization of American States, in the American Declaration of the Rights and Duties of Man, and in the Universal Declaration of Human Rights, and that they have been reaffirmed and refined in other international instruments, worldwide as well as regional in scope;

. . .

Have agreed upon the following:

Part 1 — State Obligations And Rights Protected

Chapter 1 — General Obligations

Article 1

1. The States Parties to this Convention undertake to respect the rights and freedoms recognized herein and to ensure to all persons subject to their jurisdiction the free and full exercise of those rights and freedoms, without any discrimination for reasons of race, color, sex, language, religion, political or other opinion, national or social origin, economic status, birth, or any other social condition.

2. For the purposes of this Convention, "person" means every human being.

Article 2

Where the exercise of any of the rights or freedoms referred to in Article 1 is not already ensured by legislative or other provisions, the States Parties undertake to adopt, in accordance with their constitutional processes and the provisions of this Convention, such legislative or other measures as may be necessary to give effect to those rights or freedoms.

Chapter 2 — Civil And Political Rights

Article 3

Every person has the right to recognition as a person before the law.

Article 4

1. Every person has the right to have his life respected. This right shall be protected by law and, in general, from the moment of conception. No one shall be arbitrarily deprived of his life.

2. In countries that have not abolished the death penalty, it may be imposed only for the most serious crimes and pursuant to a final judgment rendered by a competent court and in accordance with a law establishing such punishment, enacted prior to the commission

of the crime. The application of such punishment shall not be extended to crimes to which it does not presently apply.

3. The death penalty shall not be reestablished in states that have abolished it.

4. In no case shall capital punishment be inflicted for political offenses or related common crimes.

5. Capital punishment shall not be imposed upon persons who, at the time the crime was committed, were under 18 years of age or over 70 years of age; nor shall it be applied to pregnant women.

6. Every person condemned to death shall have the right to apply for amnesty, pardon, or commutation of sentence, which may be granted in all cases. Capital punishment shall not be imposed while such a petition is pending decision by the competent authority.

Article 5

1. Every person has the right to have his physical, mental, and moral integrity respected.

2. No one shall be subjected to torture or to cruel, inhuman, or degrading punishment or treatment. All persons deprived of their liberty shall be treated with respect for the inherent dignity of the human person.

3. Punishment shall not be extended to any person other than the criminal.

4. Accused persons shall, save in exceptional circumstances, be segregated from convicted persons, and shall be subject to separate treatment appropriate to their status as unconvicted persons.

5. Minors while subject to criminal proceedings shall be separated from adults and brought before specialized tribunals, as speedily as possible, so that they may be treated in accordance with their status as minors.

6. Punishments consisting of deprivation of liberty shall have as an essential aim the reform and social readaptation of the prisoners.

Article 6

1. No one shall be subject to slavery or to involuntary servitude, which are prohibited in all their forms, as are the slave trade and traffic in women.

...

Article 7

1. Every person has the right to personal liberty and security.

2. No one shall be deprived of his physical liberty except for the reasons and under the conditions established beforehand by the constitution of the State Party concerned or by a law established pursuant thereto.

3. No one shall be subject to arbitrary arrest or imprisonment.

4. Anyone who is detained shall be informed of the reasons for his detention and shall be promptly notified of the charge or charges against him.

5. Any person detained shall be brought promptly before a judge or other officer authorized by law to exercise judicial power and shall be entitled to trial within a reasonable time or to be released without prejudice to the continuation of the proceedings. His release may be subject to guarantees to assure his appearance for trial.

6. Anyone who is deprived of his liberty shall be entitled to recourse to a competent court, in order that the court may decide without delay on the lawfulness of his arrest or detention and order his release if the arrest or detention is unlawful. In States Parties whose laws provide that anyone who believes himself to be threatened with deprivation of his liberty is entitled to recourse to a competent court in order that it may decide on the lawfulness of such threat, this remedy may not be restricted or abolished. The interested party or another person in his behalf is entitled to seek these remedies.

7. No one shall be detained for debt. This principle shall not limit the orders of a competent judicial authority issued for nonfulfillment of duties of support.

Article 8

1. Every person has the right to a hearing, with due guarantees and within a reasonable time, by a competent, independent, and impartial tribunal, previously established by law, in the substantiation of any accusation of a criminal nature made against him or for the determination of his rights and obligations of a civil, labor, fiscal, or any other nature.

2. Every person accused of a criminal offense has the right to be presumed innocent so long as his guilt has not been proven according to law. During the proceedings, every person is entitled, with full equality, to the following minimum guarantees:

   a. the right of the accused to be assisted without charge by a translator or interpreter, if he does not understand or does not speak the language of the tribunal or court;

   b. prior notification in detail to the accused of the charges against him;

   c. adequate time and means for the preparation of his defense;

   d. the right of the accused to defend himself personally or to be assisted by legal counsel of his own choosing, and to communicate freely and privately with his counsel;

   e. the inalienable right to be assisted by counsel provided by the state, paid or not as the domestic law provides, if the accused does not defend himself personally or engage his own counsel within the time period established by law;

   f. the right of the defense to examine witnesses present in the court and to obtain the appearance, as witnesses, of experts or other persons who may throw light on the facts;

   g. the right not to be compelled to be a witness against himself or to plead guilty; and

   h. the right to appeal the judgment to a higher court.

3. A confession of guilt by the accused shall be valid only if it is made without coercion of any kind.

4. An accused person acquitted by a nonappealable judgment shall not be subjected to a new trial for the same cause.

5. Criminal proceedings shall be public, except insofar as may be necessary to protect the interests of justice.

Article 9

No one shall be convicted of any act or omission that did not constitute a criminal offense, under the applicable law, at the time it was committed. A heavier penalty shall not be imposed than the one that was applicable at the time the criminal offense was committed. If subsequent to the commission of the offense the law provides for the imposition of a lighter punishment, the guilty person shall benefit therefrom.

Article 10

Every person has the right to be compensated in accordance with the law in the event he has been sentenced by a final judgment through a miscarriage of justice.

Article 11

1. Everyone has the right to have his honor respected and his dignity recognized.

2. No one may be the object of arbitrary or abusive interference with his private life, his family, his home, or his correspondence, or of unlawful attacks on his honor or reputation.

3. Everyone has the right to the protection of the law against such interference or attacks.

Article 12

1. Everyone has the right to freedom of conscience and of religion. This right includes freedom to maintain or to change one's religion or beliefs, and freedom to profess or disseminate one's religion or beliefs, either individually or together with others, in public or in private.

2. No one shall be subject to restrictions that might impair his freedom to maintain or to change his religion or beliefs.

3. Freedom to manifest one's religion and beliefs may be subject only to the limitations prescribed by law that are necessary to protect public safety, order, health, or morals, or the rights or freedoms of others.

4. Parents or guardians, as the case may be, have the right to provide for the religious and moral education of their children or wards that is in accord with their own convictions.

Article 13

1. Everyone has the right to freedom of thought and expression. This right includes freedom to seek, receive, and impart information and ideas of all kinds, regardless of frontiers, either orally, in writing, in print, in the form of art, or through any other medium of one's choice.

2. The exercise of the right provided for in the foregoing paragraph shall not be subject to prior censorship but shall be subject to subsequent imposition of liability, which shall be expressly established by law to the extent necessary to ensure:

 a. respect for the rights or reputations of others; or

 b. the protection of national security, public order, or public health or morals.

3. The right of expression may not be restricted by indirect methods or means, such as the abuse of government or private controls over newsprint, radio broadcasting frequencies, or equipment used in the dissemination of information, or by any other means tending to impede the communication and circulation of ideas and opinions.

4. Notwithstanding the provisions of paragraph 2 above, public entertainments may be subject by law to prior censorship for the sole purpose of regulating access to them for the moral protection of childhood and adolescence.

5. Any propaganda for war and any advocacy of national, racial, or religious hatred that constitute incitements to lawless violence or to any other similar action against any per-

son or group of persons on any grounds including those of race, color, religion, language, or national origin shall be considered as offenses punishable by law.

. . .

Article 15

The right of peaceful assembly, without arms, is recognized. No restrictions may be placed on the exercise of this right other than those imposed in conformity with the law and necessary in a democratic society in the interest of national security, public safety or public order, or to protect public health or morals or the rights or freedom of others.

Article 16

1. Everyone has the right to associate freely for ideological, religious, political, economic, labor, social, cultural, sports, or other purposes.

2. The exercise of this right shall be subject only to such restrictions established by law as may be necessary in a democratic society, in the interest of national security, public safety or public order, or to protect public health or morals or the rights and freedoms of others.

3. The provisions of this article do not bar the imposition of legal restrictions, including even deprivation of the exercise of the right of association, on members of the armed forces and the police.

Article 17

1. The family is the natural and fundamental group unit of society and is entitled to protection by society and the state.

2. The right of men and women of marriageable age to marry and to raise a family shall be recognized, if they meet the conditions required by domestic laws, insofar as such conditions do not affect the principle of nondiscrimination established in this Convention.

3. No marriage shall be entered into without the free and full consent of the intending spouses.

4. The States Parties shall take appropriate steps to ensure the equality of rights and the adequate balancing of responsibilities of the spouses as to marriage, during marriage, and in the event of its dissolution. In case of dissolution, provision shall be made for the necessary protection of any children solely on the basis of their own best interests.

5. The law shall recognize equal rights for children born out of wedlock and those born in wedlock.

. . .

Article 19

Every minor child has the right to the measures of protection required by his condition as a minor on the part of his family, society, and the state.

Article 20

1. Every person has the right to a nationality.

2. Every person has the right to the nationality of the state in whose territory he was born if he does not have the right to any other nationality.

3. No one shall be arbitrarily deprived of his nationality or of the right to change it.

Article 21

1. Everyone has the right to the use and enjoyment of his property. The law may subordinate such use and enjoyment to the interest of society.

2. No one shall be deprived of his property except upon payment of just compensation, for reasons of public utility or social interest, and in the cases and according to the forms established by law.

3. Usury and any other form of exploitation of man by man shall be prohibited by law.

Article 22

1. Every person lawfully in the territory of a State Party has the right to move about in it, and to reside in it subject to the provisions of the law.

2. Every person has the right to leave any country freely, including his own.

3. The exercise of the foregoing rights may be restricted only pursuant to a law to the extent necessary in a democratic society to prevent crime or to protect national security, public safety, public order, public morals, public health, or the rights or freedoms of others.

4. The exercise of the rights recognized in paragraph 1 may also be restricted by law in designated zones for reasons of public interest.

5. No one can be expelled from the territory of the state of which he is a national or be deprived of the right to enter it.

6. An alien lawfully in the territory of a State Party to this Convention may be expelled from it only pursuant to a decision reached in accordance with law.

7. Every person has the right to seek and be granted asylum in a foreign territory, in accordance with the legislation of the state and international conventions, in the event he is being pursued for political offenses or related common crimes.

8. In no case may an alien be deported or returned to a country, regardless of whether or not it is his country of origin, if in that country his right to life or personal freedom is in danger of being violated because of his race, nationality, religion, social status, or political opinions.

9. The collective expulsion of aliens is prohibited.

Article 23

1. Every citizen shall enjoy the following rights and opportunities:

   a. to take part in the conduct of public affairs, directly or through freely chosen representatives;

   b. to vote and to be elected in genuine periodic elections, which shall be by universal and equal suffrage and by secret ballot that guarantees the free expression of the will of the voters; and

   c. to have access, under general conditions of equality, to the public service of his country.

2. The law may regulate the exercise of the rights and opportunities referred to in the preceding paragraph only on the basis of age, nationality, residence, language, education, civil and mental capacity, or sentencing by a competent court in criminal proceedings.

Article 24

All persons are equal before the law. Consequently, they are entitled, without discrimination, to equal protection of the law.

Article 25

1. Everyone has the right to simple and prompt recourse, or any other effective recourse, to a competent court or tribunal for protection against acts that violate his fundamental rights recognized by the constitution or laws of the state concerned or by this Convention, even though such violation may have been committed by persons acting in the course of their official duties.

2. The States Parties undertake:

a. to ensure that any person claiming such remedy shall have his rights determined by the competent authority provided for by the legal system of the state;

b. to develop the possibilities of judicial remedy; and

c. to ensure that the competent authorities shall enforce such remedies when granted.

Chapter 3 — Economic, Social, And Cultural Rights

Article 26

The States Parties undertake to adopt measures, both internally and through international cooperation, especially those of an economic and technical nature, with a view to achieving progressively, by legislation or other appropriate means, the full realization of the rights implicit in the economic, social, educational, scientific, and cultural standards set forth in the Charter of the Organization of American States as amended by the Protocol of Buenos Aires.

Chapter 4 — Suspension Of Guarantees, Interpretation, And Application

Article 27

1. In time of war, public danger, or other emergency that threatens the independence or security of a State Party, it may take measures derogating from its obligations under the present Convention to the extent and for the period of time strictly required by the exigencies of the situation, provided that such measures are not inconsistent with its other obligations under international law and do not involve discrimination on the ground of race, color, sex, language, religion, or social origin.

2. The foregoing provision does not authorize any suspension of the following articles: Article 3 (Right to Juridical Personality), Article 4 (Right to Life), Article 5 (Right to Humane Treatment), Article 6 (Freedom from Slavery), Article 9 (Freedom from *Ex Post Facto* Laws), Article 12 (Freedom of Conscience and Religion), Article 17 (Rights of the Family), Article 18 (Right to a Name), Article 19 (Rights of the Child), Article 20 (Right to Nationality), and Article 23 (Right to Participate in Government), or of the judicial guarantees essential for the protection of such rights.

3. Any State Party availing itself of the right of suspension shall immediately inform the other States Parties, through the Secretary General of the Organization of American States, of the provisions the application of which it has suspended, the reasons that gave rise to the suspension, and the date set for the termination of such suspension.

. . .

Chapter 5 — Personal Responsibilities

Article 32

1. Every person has responsibilities to his family, his community, and mankind.

2. The rights of each person are limited by the rights of others, by the security of all, and by the just demands of the general welfare, in a democratic society.

Part 2 — Means of Protection

Chapter 6 — Competent Organs

Article 33

The following organs shall have competence with respect to matters relating to the fulfillment of the commitments made by the States Parties to this Convention:

a. the Inter-American Commission on Human Rights, referred to as "The Commission"; and

b. the Inter-American Court of Human Rights, referred to as "The Court."

Chapter 7 — Inter-American Commission On Human Rights

Section 1. Organization

Article 34

The Inter-American Commission on Human Rights shall be composed of seven members, who shall be persons of high moral character and recognized competence in the field of human rights.

Article 35

The Commission shall represent all the member countries of the Organization of American States.

Article 36

1. The members of the Commission shall be elected in a personal capacity by the General Assembly of the Organization from a list of candidates proposed by the governments of the member states.

...

Section 3. Competence

Article 44

Any person or group of persons, or any nongovernmental entity legally recognized in one or more member states of the Organization, may lodge petitions with the Commission containing denunciations or complaints of violation of this Convention by a State Party.

...

[Article 48 sets forth procedures for the Commission after it receives a petition or communication alleging violation of any protected rights. The Commission is to 'place itself at the disposal of the parties concerned with a view to reaching a friendly settlement of the matter on the basis of respect for the human rights recognized in this Convention.' Article 49 concerns situations where such a settlement has been reached.]

Chapter 8 — Inter-American Court Of Human Rights

Section 1. Organization

Article 52

1. The Court shall consist of seven judges, nationals of the member states of the Organization, elected in an individual capacity from among jurists of the highest moral authority and of recognized competence in the field of human rights, who possess the qualifications required for the exercise of the highest judicial functions in conformity with the law of the state of which they are nationals or of the state that proposes them as candidates.

2. No two judges may be nationals of the same state.

...

Section 2. Jurisdiction and Functions

Article 61

1. Only the States Parties and the Commission shall have the right to submit a case to the Court.

2. In order for the Court to hear a case, it is necessary that the procedures set forth in Articles 48 and 50 shall have been completed.

...

African Charter on Human and People's Rights

[Preamble]

The African States members of the Organization of African Unity, parties to the present convention entitled "African Charter on Human and Peoples' Rights,"

Considering the Charter of the Organization of African Unity, which stipulates that "freedom, equality, justice and dignity are essential objectives for the achievement of the legitimate aspirations of the African peoples";

Reaffirming the pledge they solemnly made in Article 2 of the said Charter to eradicate all forms of colonialism from Africa, to coordinate and intensify their cooperation and efforts to achieve a better life for the peoples of Africa and to promote international cooperation having due regard to the Charter of the United Nations. and the Universal Declaration of Human Rights;

Taking into consideration the virtues of their historical tradition and the values of African civilization which should inspire and characterize their reflection on the concept of human and peoples' rights;

...

Considering that the enjoyment of rights and freedoms also implies the performance of duties on the part of everyone;

Convinced that it is henceforth essential to pay a particular attention to the right to development and that civil and political rights cannot be dissociated from economic, social and cultural rights in their conception as well as universality and that the satisfaction of economic, social and cultural rights is a guarantee for the enjoyment of civil and political rights;

Conscious of their duty to achieve the total liberation of Africa, the peoples of which are still struggling for their dignity and genuine independence, and undertaking to eliminate colonialism, neo-colonialism, apartheid, zionism and to dismantle aggressive foreign military bases and all forms of discrimination, particularly those based on race, ethnic group, color, sex, language, religion or political opinions;

. . .

Firmly convinced of their duty to promote and protect human and people' rights and freedoms taking into account the importance traditionally attached to these rights and freedoms in Africa;

Have agreed as follows

Part 1: Rights And Duties

Chapter 2: Human And People's Rights

Article 1

The Member States of the Organization of African Unity parties to the present Charter shall recognize the rights, duties and freedoms enshrined in this Chapter and shall undertake to adopt legislative or other measures to give effect to them.

Article 2

Every individual shall be entitled to the enjoyment of the rights and freedoms recognized and guaranteed in the present Charter without distinction of any kind such as race, ethnic group, color, sex, language, religion, political or any other opinion, national and social origin, fortune, birth or other status.

Article 3

1. Every individual shall be equal before the law.

2. Every individual shall be entitled to equal protection of the law.

Article 4

Human beings are inviolable. Every human being shall be entitled to respect for his life and the integrity of his person. No one may be arbitrarily deprived of this right.

Article 5

Every individual shall have the right to the respect of the dignity inherent in a human being and to the recognition of his legal status. All forms of exploitation and degradation of man particularly slavery, slave trade, torture, cruel, inhuman or degrading punishment and treatment shall be prohibited.

Article 6

Every individual shall have the right to liberty and to the security of his person. No one may be deprived of his freedom except for reasons and conditions previously laid down by law. In particular, no one may be arbitrarily arrested or detained.

Article 7

1. Every individual shall have the right to have his cause heard. This comprises: (a) the right to an appeal to competent national organs against acts of violating his fundamental rights as recognized and guaranteed by conventions, laws, regulations and customs

in force; (b) the right to be presumed innocent until proved guilty by a competent court or tribunal; (c) the right to defense, including the right to be defended by counsel of his choice; (d) the right to be tried within a reasonable time by an impartial court or tribunal.

2. No one may be condemned for an act or omission which did not constitute a legally punishable offence at the time it was committed. No penalty may be inflicted for an offence for which no provision was made at the time it was committed. Punishment is personal and can be imposed only on the offender.

Article 8

Freedom of conscience, the profession and free practice of religion shall be guaranteed. No one may, subject to law and order, be submitted to measures restricting the exercise of these freedoms.

Article 9

1. Every individual shall have the right to receive information.

2. Every individual shall have the right to express and disseminate his opinions within the law.

Article 10

1. Every individual shall have the right to free association provided that he abides by the law.

2. Subject to the obligation of solidarity provided for in 29, no one may be compelled to join an association.

Article 11

Every individual shall have the right to assemble freely with others. The exercise of this right shall be subject only to necessary restrictions provided for by law in particular those enacted in the interest of national security, the safety, health, ethics and rights and freedoms of others.

Article 12

1. Every individual shall have the right to freedom of movement and residence within the borders of a State provided he abides by the law.

2. Every individual shall have the right to leave any country including his own, and to return to his country. This right may only be subject to restrictions, provided for by law for the protection of national security, law and order, public health or morality.

3. Every individual shall have the right, when persecuted, to seek and obtain asylum in other countries in accordance with laws of those countries and international conventions.

4. A non-national legally admitted in a territory of a State Party to the present Charter, may only be expelled from it by virtue of a decision taken in accordance with the law.

5. The mass expulsion of non-nationals shall be prohibited. Mass expulsion shall be that which is aimed at national, racial, ethnic or religious groups.

Article 13

1. Every citizen shall have the right to participate freely in the government of his country, either directly or through freely chosen representatives in accordance with the provisions of the law.

2. Every citizen shall have the right of equal access to the public service of his country.

3. Every individual shall have the right of access to public property and services in strict equality of all persons before the law.

Article 14

The right to property shall be guaranteed. It may only be encroached upon in the interest of public need or in the general interest of the community and in accordance with the provisions of appropriate laws.

Article 15

Every individual shall have the right to work under equitable and satisfactory conditions, and shall receive equal pay for equal work.

Article 16

1. Every individual shall have the right to enjoy the best attainable state of physical and mental health.

2. States parties to the present Charter shall take the necessary measures to protect the health of their people and to ensure that they receive medical attention when they are sick.

Article 17

1. Every individual shall have the right to education.

2. Every individual may freely, take part in the cultural life of his community.

3. The promotion and protection of morals and traditional values recognized by the community shall be the duty of the State.

Article 18

1. The family shall be the natural unit and basis of society. It shall be protected by the State which shall take care of its physical health and moral.

2. The State shall have the duty to assist the family which is the custodian or morals and traditional values recognized by the community.

3. The State shall ensure the elimination of every discrimination against women and also ensure the protection of the rights of the woman and the child as stipulated in international declarations and conventions.

4. The aged and the disabled shall also have the right to special measures of protection in keeping with their physical or moral needs.

Article 19

All peoples shall be equal; they shall enjoy the same respect and shall have the same rights. Nothing shall justify the domination of a people by another.

Article 20

1. All peoples shall have the right to existence. They shall have the unquestionable and inalienable right to self-determination. They shall freely determine their political status and shall pursue their economic and social development according to the policy they have freely chosen.

2. Colonized or oppressed peoples shall have the right to free themselves from the bonds of domination by resorting to any means recognized by the international community.

3. All peoples shall have the right to the assistance of the States parties to the present Charter in their liberation struggle against foreign domination, be it political, economic or cultural.

Article 21

1. All peoples shall freely dispose of their wealth and natural resources. This right shall be exercised in the exclusive interest of the people. In no case shall a people be deprived of it.

2. In case of spoliation the dispossessed people shall have the right to the lawful recovery of its property as well as to an adequate compensation.

3. The free disposal of wealth and natural resources shall be exercised without prejudice to the obligation of promoting international economic cooperation based on mutual respect, equitable exchange and the principles of international law.

4. States parties to the present Charter shall individually and collectively exercise the right to free disposal of their wealth and natural resources with a view to strengthening African unity and solidarity.

5. States parties to the present Charter shall undertake to eliminate all forms of foreign economic exploitation particularly that practiced by international monopolies so as to enable their peoples to fully benefit from the advantages derived from their national resources.

Article 22

1. All peoples shall have the right to their economic, social and cultural development with due regard to their freedom and identity and in the equal enjoyment of the common heritage of mankind.

2. States shall have the duty, individually or collectively, to ensure the exercise of the right to development.

Article 23

1. All peoples shall have the right to national and international peace and security. The principles of solidarity and friendly relations implicitly affirmed by the Charter of the United Nations and reaffirmed by that of the Organization of African Unity shall govern relations between States.

2. For the purpose of strengthening peace, solidarity and friendly relations, States parties to the present Charter shall ensure that: (a) any individual enjoying the right of asylum under 12 of the present Charter shall not engage in subversive activities against his country of origin or any other State party to the present Charter; (b) their territories shall not be used as bases for subversive or terrorist activities against the people of any other State party to the present Charter.

Article 24

All peoples shall have the right to a general satisfactory environment favorable to their development.

Article 25

States parties to the present Charter shall have the duty to promote and ensure through teaching, education and publication, the respect of the rights and freedoms contained in the present Charter and to see to it that these freedoms and rights as well as corresponding obligations and duties are understood.

Article 26

States parties to the present Charter shall have the duty to guarantee the independence of the Courts and shall allow the establishment and improvement of appropriate national institutions entrusted with the promotion and protection of the rights and freedoms guaranteed by the present Charter.

Chapter 2: Duties

Article 27

1. Every individual shall have duties towards his family and society, the State and other legally recognized communities and the international community.

2. The rights and freedoms of each individual shall be exercised with due regard to the rights of others, collective security, morality and common interest.

Article 28

Every individual shall have the duty to respect and consider his fellow beings without discrimination, and to maintain relations aimed at promoting, safeguarding and reinforcing mutual respect and tolerance.

Article 29

The individual shall also have the duty:

1. To preserve the harmonious development of the family and to work for the cohesion and respect of the family; to respect his parents at all times, to maintain them in case of need;

2. To serve his national community by placing his physical and intellectual abilities at its service;

3. Not to compromise the security of the State whose national or resident he is;

4. To preserve and strengthen social and national solidarity, particularly when the latter is threatened;

5. To preserve and strengthen the national independence and the territorial integrity of his country and to contribute to its defense in accordance with the law;

6. To work to the best of his abilities and competence, and to pay taxes imposed by law in the interest of the society;

7. To preserve and strengthen positive African cultural values in his relations with other members of the society, in the spirit of tolerance, dialogue and consultation and, in general, to contribute to the promotion of the moral well being of society;

8. To contribute to the best of his abilities, at all times and at all levels, to the promotion and achievement of African unity.

Part 2: Measures of Safeguard

Chapter 1: Establishment and Organization of the African Commission on Human and Peoples' Rights

Article 30

An African Commission on Human and Peoples' Rights, hereinafter called "the Commission," shall be established within the Organization of African Unity to promote human and peoples' rights and ensure their protection in Africa.

Article 31

1. The Commission shall consist of eleven members chosen from amongst African personalities of the highest reputation, known for their high morality, integrity, impartiality and competence in matters of human and peoples' rights; particular consideration being given to persons having legal experience.

2. The members of the Commission shall serve in their personal capacity.

...

Chapter 2: Mandate of the Commission

Article 45

The functions of the Commission shall be:

1. To promote Human and Peoples' Rights and in particular:

(a) To collect documents, undertake studies and researches on African problems in the field of human and peoples' rights, organize seminars, symposia and conferences, disseminate information, encourage national and local institutions concerned with human and peoples' rights, and should the case arise, give its views or make recommendations to Governments.

(b) To formulate and lay down, principles and rules aimed at solving legal problems relating to human and peoples' rights and fundamental freedoms upon which African Governments may base their legislations.

(c) Co-operate with other African and international institutions concerned with the promotion and protection of human and peoples' rights.

2. Ensure the protection of human and peoples' rights under conditions laid down by the present Charter.

3. Interpret all the provisions of the present Charter at the request of a State party, an institution of the OAU or an African Organization recognized by the OAU.

4. Perform any other tasks which may be entrusted to it by the Assembly of Heads of State and Government.

...

Chapter 4: Applicable Principles

Article 60

The Commission shall draw inspiration from international law on human and peoples' rights, particularly from the provisions of various African instruments on human and peoples' rights, the Charter of the United Nations, the Charter of the Organization of African Unity, the Universal Declaration of Human Rights, other instruments adopted by the United Nations and by African countries in the field of human and peoples' rights as well as from the provisions of various instruments adopted within the Specialized Agencies of the United Nations of which the parties to the present Charter are members.

Article 61

The Commission shall also take into consideration, as subsidiary measures to determine the principles of law, other general or special international conventions, laying down rules expressly recognized by member states of the Organization of African Unity, African practices consistent with international norms on human and people's rights, customs generally accepted as law, general principles of law recognized by African states as well as legal precedents and doctrine.

...

Vienna Conventions on the Law of Treaties

...

Article 2

1. For the purposes of the present Convention:

(*a*) "treaty" means an international agreement concluded between States in written form and governed by international law, whether embodied in a single instrument or in two or more related instruments and whatever its particular designation;

(*b*) "ratification," "acceptance," "approval" and "accession" mean in each case the international act so named whereby a State establishes on the international plane its consent to be bound by a treaty;

...

(*d*) "reservation" means a unilateral statement, however phrased or named, made by a State, when signing, ratifying, accepting, approving or acceding to a treaty, whereby it purports to exclude or to modify the legal effect of certain provisions of the treaty in their application to that State;

...

Article 18

A State is obliged to refrain from acts which would defeat the object and purpose of a treaty when:

(*a*) it has signed the treaty or has exchanged instruments constituting the treaty subject to ratification, acceptance or approval, until it shall have made its intention clear not to become a party to the treaty; or

(*b*) it has expressed its consent to be bound by the treaty, pending the entry into force of the treaty and provided that such entry into force is not unduly delayed.

Article 19

A State may, when signing, ratifying, accepting, approving or acceding to a treaty, formulate a reservation unless:

(*a*) the reservation is prohibited by the treaty;

(*b*) the treaty provides that only specified reservations, which do not include the reservation in question, may be made; or

(*c*) in cases not failing under subparagraphs (*a*) and (*b*), the reservation is incompatible with the object and purpose of the treaty.

Article 20

1. A reservation expressly authorized by a treaty does not require any subsequent acceptance by the other contracting States unless the treaty so provides.

2. When it appears from the limited number of the negotiating States and the object and purpose of a treaty that the application of the treaty in its entirety between all the parties is an essential condition of the consent of each one to be bound by the treaty, a reservation requires acceptance by all the parties;

...

4. In cases not falling under the preceding paragraphs and unless the treaty otherwise provides:

(*a*) acceptance by another contracting State of a reservation constitutes the reserving State a party to the treaty in relation to that other State if or when the treaty is in force for those States;

(*b*) an objection by another contracting State to a reservation does not preclude the entry into force of the treaty as between the objecting and reserving States unless a contrary intention is definitely expressed by the objecting State;

...

Article 21

1. A reservation established with regard to another party in accordance with articles 19, 20 and 23:

(*a*) modifies for the reserving State in its relations with that other party the provisions of the treaty to which the reservation relates to the extent of the reservation; and

(*b*) modifies those provisions to the same extent for that other party in its relations with the reserving State.

2. The reservation does not modify the provisions of the treaty for the other parties to the treaty *inter se*.

3. When a State objecting to a reservation has not opposed the entry into force of the treaty between itself and the reserving State, the provisions to which the reservation relates do not apply as between the two States to the extent of the reservation.

...

Article 26
'*Pacta Sunt Servanda*'

Every treaty in force is binding upon the parties to it and must be performed by them in good faith.

Article 27

A party may not invoke the provisions of its internal law as justification for its failure to perform a treaty ...

...

Article 31

1. A treaty shall be interpreted in good faith in accordance with the ordinary meaning to be given to the terms of the treaty in their context and in the light of its object and purpose.

...

3. There shall be taken into account, together with the context:

(*a*) any subsequent agreement between the parties regarding the interpretation of the treaty or the application of its provisions;

(*b*) any subsequent practice in the application of the treaty which establishes the agreement of the parties regarding its interpretation;

(*c*) any relevant rules of international law applicable in the relations between the parties.

4. A special meaning shall be given to a term if it is established that the parties so intended.

Article 32

Recourse may be had to supplementary means of interpretation, including the preparatory work of the treaty and the circumstances of its conclusion, in order to confirm the meaning resulting from the application of article 31, or to determine the meaning when the interpretation according to article 31:

(*a*) leaves the meaning ambiguous or obscure; or

(*b*) leads to a result which is manifestly absurd or unreasonable.

. . .

Article 35

An obligation arises for a third State from a provision of a treaty if the parties to the treaty intend the provision to be the means of establishing the obligation and the third State expressly accepts that obligation in writing.

Article 38

Nothing in articles 34 to 37 precludes a rule set forth in a treaty from becoming binding upon a third State as a customary rule of international law, recognized as such.

. . .

Article 40

1. Unless the treaty otherwise provides, the amendment of multilateral treaties shall be governed by the following paragraphs.

. . .

4. The amending agreement does not bind any State already a party to the treaty which does not become a party to the amending agreement..

. . .

Article 43

The invalidity, termination or denunciation of a treaty, the withdrawal of a party from it, or the suspension of its operation, as a result of the application of the present Convention or of the provisions of the treaty, shall not in any way impair the duty of any State to fulfil any obligation embodied in the treaty to which it would be subject under international law independently of the treaty.

. . .

Article 46

1. A State may not invoke the fact that its consent to be bound by a treaty has been expressed in violation of a provision of its internal law regarding competence to conclude treaties as invalidating its consent unless that violation was manifest and concerned a rule of its internal law of fundamental importance.

2. A violation is manifest if it would be objectively evident to any State conducting itself in the matter in accordance with normal practice and in good faith.

...

Article 53

A treaty is void if, at the time of its conclusion, it conflicts with a peremptory norm of general international law. For the purposes of the present Convention, a peremptory norm of general international law is a norm accepted and recognized by the international community of States as a whole as a norm from which no derogation is permitted and which can be modified only by a subsequent norm of general international law having the same character.

...

Article 62

1. A fundamental change of circumstances which has occurred with regard to those existing at the time of the conclusion of a treaty, and which was not foreseen by the parties, may not be invoked as a ground for terminating or withdrawing from the treaty unless:

(*a*) the existence of those circumstances constituted an essential basis of the consent of the parties to be bound by the treaty; and

(*b*) the effect of the change is radically to transform the extent of obligations still to be performed under the treaty.

...

Article 64

If a new peremptory norm of general international law emerges, any existing treaty which is in conflict with that norm becomes void and terminates.

...

Constitution of the United States

We the People of the United States, in Order to form a more perfect Union, establish Justice, insure domestic Tranquility, provide for the common defence, promote the general Welfare, and secure the Blessings of Liberty to ourselves and our Posterity, do ordain and establish this Constitution for the United States of America.

Article 1

Section 1. All legislative Powers herein granted shall be vested in a Congress of the United States, which shall consist of a Senate and House of Representatives.

...

Section 7. ... Every Bill which shall have passed the House of Representatives and the Senate, shall, before it become a Law, be presented to the President of the United States; If he approve he shall sign it, but if not he shall return it, with his Objections to that House in which it shall have originated, who shall enter the Objections at large on their Journal, and proceed to reconsider it. If after such Reconsideration two thirds of that House shall agree to pass the Bill, it shall be sent, together with the Objections, to the other House, by which it shall likewise be reconsidered, and if approved by two thirds of that House, it shall become a Law....

...

Section 8. The Congress shall have Power To lay and collect Taxes, Duties, Imposts and Excises, to pay the Debts and provide for the common Defence and general Welfare of the United States....

To regulate Commerce with foreign Nations, and among the several States, and with the Indian Tribes;

To define and punish Piracies and Felonies committed on the high Seas, and Offenses against the Law of Nations;

To declare War, grant Letters of Marque and Reprisal, and make Rules concerning Captures on Land and Water;

...

To make all Laws which shall be necessary and proper for carrying into Execution the foregoing Powers, and all other Powers vested by this Constitution in the Government of the United States, or in any Department or Officer thereof.

Section 9. ...

The privilege of the Writ of Habeas Corpus shall not be suspended, unless when in Cases of Rebellion or Invasion the public Safety may require it.

No Bill of Attainder or ex post facto Law shall be passed.

...

No Money shall be drawn from the Treasury, but in Consequence of Appropriations made by Law....

...

Section 10.

No State shall enter into any Treaty, Alliance, or Confederation....

...

No State shall, without the Consent of the Congress, ... enter into any Agreement or Compact with another State, or with a foreign Power....

Article 2

Section 1. The executive Power shall be vested in a President of the United States of America....

Section 2. The President shall be Commander in Chief of the Army and Navy of the United States, and of the Militia of the several States, when called into the actual Service of the United States....

He shall have Power, by and with the Advice and Consent of the Senate, to make Treaties, provided two thirds of the Senators present concur; and he shall nominate, and by and with the Advice and Consent of the Senate, shall appoint Ambassadors, other public Ministers and Consuls, Judges of the supreme Court, and all other Officers of the United States, whose Appointments are not herein otherwise provided for, and which shall be established by Law....

...

Section 3. ... [H]e shall receive Ambassadors and other public Ministers; he shall take Care that the Laws be faithfully executed, and shall Commission all the Officers of the United States.

...

Article 3

Section 1. The judicial Power of the United States, shall be vested in one supreme Court, and in such inferior Courts as the Congress may from time to time ordain and establish....

Section 2. The judicial Power shall extend to all Cases, in Law and Equity, arising under this Constitution, the Laws of the United States, and Treaties made, or which shall be made, under their Authority; to all Cases affecting Ambassadors, other public Ministers and Consuls; to all Cases of admiralty and maritime Jurisdiction; to Controversies to which the United States shall be a Party; to Controversies between two or more States; between a State and Citizens of another State; between Citizens of different States; between Citizens of the same State claiming Lands under Grants of different States, and between a State, or the Citizens thereof, and foreign States, Citizens or Subjects.

...

The Trial of all Crimes, except in Cases of Impeachment, shall be by Jury; and such Trial shall be held in the State where the said Crimes shall have been committed; but when not committed within any State, the Trial shall be at such Place or Places as the Congress may by Law have directed.

...

Article 5

...

The Congress, whenever two thirds of both Houses shall deem it necessary, shall propose Amendments to this Constitution, or, on the Application of the Legislatures of two thirds of the several States, shall call a Convention for proposing Amendments, which, in either Case, shall be valid to all Intents and Purposes, as part of this Constitution, when ratified by the Legislatures of three fourths of the several States, or by Conventions in three fourths thereof, as the one or the other Mode of Ratification may be proposed by the Congress....

Article 6

This Constitution, and the Laws of the United States which shall be made in Pursuance thereof; and all Treaties made, or which shall be made, under the Authority of the United States, shall be the supreme Law of the Land; and the Judges in every State shall be bound thereby, any Thing in the Constitution or Laws of any State to the Contrary notwithstanding.

...

Articles in Addition to, and Amendment of, the Constitution of the United States of America, Proposed by Congress and Ratified by the Several States, Pursuant to the Fifth Article of the Original Constitution.

[The first ten amendments constitute the Bill of Rights.]

Amendment 1

Congress shall make no law respecting an establishment of religion, or prohibiting the free exercise thereof; or abridging the freedom of speech, or of the press; or the right of the people peaceably to assemble, and to petition the Government for a redress of grievances.

...

Amendment 4

The right of the people to be secure in their persons, houses, papers, and effects, against unreasonable searches and seizures, shall not be violated, and no Warrants shall issue, but upon probable cause, supported by Oath or affirmation, and particularly describing the place to be searched, and the persons or things to be seized.

Amendment 5

No person shall be held to answer for a capital, or otherwise infamous crime, unless on a presentment or indictment of a Grand Jury, except in cases arising in the land or naval forces, or in the Militia, when in actual service in time of War or public danger; nor shall any person be subject for the same offense to be twice put in jeopardy of life or limb; nor shall be compelled in any criminal case to be a witness against himself, nor be deprived of life, liberty, or property, without due process of law; nor shall private property be taken for public use, without just compensation.

Amendment 6

In all criminal prosecutions, the accused shall enjoy the right to a speedy and public trial, by an impartial jury of the State and district wherein the crime shall have been committed, which district shall have been previously ascertained by law, and to be informed of the nature and cause of the accusation; to be confronted with the witnesses against him; to have compulsory process for obtaining witnesses in his favor, and to have the Assistance of Counsel for his defence.

Amendment 7

In Suits at common law, where the value in controversy shall exceed twenty dollars, the right of trial by jury shall be preserved, and no fact tried by a jury, shall be otherwise re-examined in any Court of the United States, than according to the rules of the common law.

Amendment 8

Excessive bail shall not be required, nor excessive fines imposed, nor cruel and unusual punishments inflicted.

Amendment 9

The enumeration in the Constitution, of certain rights, shall not be construed to deny or disparage others retained by the people.

Amendment 10

The powers not delegated to the United States by the Constitution, nor prohibited by it to the States, are reserved to the States respectively, or to the people.

...

Amendment 13

Section 1. Neither slavery nor involuntary servitude, except as a punishment for crime whereof the party shall have been duly convicted, shall exist within the United States, or any place subject to their jurisdiction.

...

Amendment 14

Section 1. All persons born or naturalized in the United States, and subject to the jurisdiction thereof, are citizens of the United States and of the State wherein they reside. No State shall make or enforce any law which shall abridge the privileges or immunities of citizens of the United States; nor shall any State deprive any person of life, liberty, or property, without due process of law; nor deny to any person within its jurisdiction the equal protection of the laws.

...

Section 5. The Congress shall have power to enforce, by appropriate legislation, the provisions of this article.

Amendment 15

Section 1. The right of citizens of the United States to vote shall not be denied or abridged by the United States or by any State on account of race, color, or previous condition of servitude.

Section 2. The Congress shall have power to enforce this article by appropriate legislation.

...

Amendment 19

The right of citizens of the United States to vote shall not be denied or abridged by the United States or by any State on account of sex.

Congress shall have power to enforce this article by appropriate legislation.

...

Amendment 24

1. The right of citizens of the United States to vote in any primary or other election for President or Vice President, for electors for President or Vice President, or for Senator or Representative in Congress, shall not be denied or abridged by the United States or any State by reason of failure to pay any poll tax or other tax.

...

Amendment 26

Section 1. The right of citizens of the United States, who are eighteen years of age or older, to vote shall not be denied or abridged by the United States or by any State on account of age.

...

Rome Statute of the International Criminal Court

The States Parties to this Statute,

Conscious that all peoples are united by common bonds, their cultures pieced together in a shared heritage, and concerned that this delicate mosaic may be shattered at any time,

Mindful that during this century millions of children, women and men have been victims of unimaginable atrocities that deeply shock the conscience of humanity,

Recognizing that such grave crimes threaten the peace, security and well-being of the world,

Affirming that the most serious crimes of concern to the international community as a whole must not go unpunished and that their effective prosecution must be ensured by taking measures at the national level and by enhancing international cooperation,

Determined to put an end to impunity for the perpetrators of these crimes and thus to contribute to the prevention of such crimes,

Recalling that it is the duty of every State to exercise its criminal jurisdiction over those responsible for international crimes,

Reaffirming the Purposes and Principles of the Charter of the United Nations, and in particular that all States shall refrain from the threat or use of force against the territorial integrity or political independence of any State, or in any other manner inconsistent with the Purposes of the United Nations,

Emphasizing in this connection that nothing in this Statute shall be taken as authorizing any State Party to intervene in an armed conflict or in the internal affairs of any State,

Determined to these ends and for the sake of present and future generations, to establish an independent permanent International Criminal Court in relationship with the United Nations system, with jurisdiction over the most serious crimes of concern to the international community as a whole,

Emphasizing that the International Criminal Court established under this Statute shall be complementary to national criminal jurisdictions,

Resolved to guarantee lasting respect for and the enforcement of international justice,

Have agreed as follows:

Part 1. Establishment of the Court

Article 1
The Court

An International Criminal Court ("the Court") is hereby established. It shall be a permanent institution and shall have the power to exercise its jurisdiction over persons for the most serious crimes of international concern, as referred to in this Statute, and shall be complementary to national criminal jurisdictions. The jurisdiction and functioning of the Court shall be governed by the provisions of this Statute.

Article 2
Relationship of the Court with the United Nations

The Court shall be brought into relationship with the United Nations through an agreement to be approved by the Assembly of States Parties to this Statute and thereafter concluded by the President of the Court on its behalf.

Article 3
Seat of the Court

1. The seat of the Court shall be established at The Hague in the Netherlands ("the host State").

2. The Court shall enter into a headquarters agreement with the host State, to be approved by the Assembly of States Parties and thereafter concluded by the President of the Court on its behalf.

3. The Court may sit elsewhere, whenever it considers it desirable, as provided in this Statute.

Article 4
Legal status and powers of the Court

1. The Court shall have international legal personality. It shall also have such legal capacity as may be necessary for the exercise of its functions and the fulfillment of its purposes.

2. The Court may exercise its functions and powers, as provided in this Statute, on the territory of any State Party and, by special agreement, on the territory of any other State.

Part 2. Jurisdiction, Admissibility And Applicable Law

Article 5
Crimes within the jurisdiction of the Court

1. The jurisdiction of the Court shall be limited to the most serious crimes of concern to the international community as a whole. The Court has jurisdiction in accordance with this Statute with respect to the following crimes:

(a) The crime of genocide;

(b) Crimes against humanity;

(c) War crimes;

(d) The crime of aggression.

2. The Court shall exercise jurisdiction over the crime of aggression once a provision is adopted in accordance with articles 121 and 123 defining the crime and setting out the conditions under which the Court shall exercise jurisdiction with respect to this crime. Such a provision shall be consistent with the relevant provisions of the Charter of the United Nations.

Article 6
Genocide

For the purpose of this Statute, "genocide" means any of the following acts committed with intent to destroy, in whole or in part, a national, ethnical, racial or religious group, as such:

(a) Killing members of the group;

(b) Causing serious bodily or mental harm to members of the group;

(c) Deliberately inflicting on the group conditions of life calculated to bring about its physical destruction in whole or in part;

(d) Imposing measures intended to prevent births within the group;

(e) Forcibly transferring children of the group to another group.

Article 7
Crimes against humanity

1. For the purpose of this Statute, "crime against humanity" means any of the following acts when committed as part of a widespread or systematic attack directed against any civilian population, with knowledge of the attack:

(a) Murder;

(b) Extermination;

(c) Enslavement;

(d) Deportation or forcible transfer of population;

(e) Imprisonment or other severe deprivation of physical liberty in violation of fundamental rules of international law;

(f) Torture;

(g) Rape, sexual slavery, enforced prostitution, forced pregnancy, enforced sterilization, or any other form of sexual violence of comparable gravity;

(h) Persecution against any identifiable group or collectivity on political, racial, national, ethnic, cultural, religious, gender as defined in paragraph 3, or other grounds that are universally recognized as impermissible under international law, in connection with any act referred to in this paragraph or any crime within the jurisdiction of the Court;

(i) Enforced disappearance of persons;

(j) The crime of apartheid;

(k) Other inhumane acts of a similar character intentionally causing great suffering, or serious injury to body or to mental or physical health.

2. For the purpose of paragraph 1:

(a) "Attack directed against any civilian population" means a course of conduct involving the multiple commission of acts referred to in paragraph 1 against any civilian population, pursuant to or in furtherance of a State or organizational policy to commit such attack;

(b) "Extermination" includes the intentional infliction of conditions of life, *inter alia* the deprivation of access to food and medicine, calculated to bring about the destruction of part of a population;

(c) "Enslavement" means the exercise of any or all of the powers attaching to the right of ownership over a person and includes the exercise of such power in the course of trafficking in persons, in particular women and children;

(d) "Deportation or forcible transfer of population" means forced displacement of the persons concerned by expulsion or other coercive acts from the area in which they are lawfully present, without grounds permitted under international law;

(e) "Torture" means the intentional infliction of severe pain or suffering, whether physical or mental, upon a person in the custody or under the control of the accused; except that torture shall not include pain or suffering arising only from, inherent in or incidental to, lawful sanctions;

(f) "Forced pregnancy" means the unlawful confinement of a woman forcibly made pregnant, with the intent of affecting the ethnic composition of any population or carrying out other grave violations of international law. This definition shall not in any way be interpreted as affecting national laws relating to pregnancy;

(g) "Persecution" means the intentional and severe deprivation of fundamental rights contrary to international law by reason of the identity of the group or collectivity;

(h) "The crime of apartheid" means inhumane acts of a character similar to those referred to in paragraph 1, committed in the context of an institutionalized regime of systematic oppression and domination by one racial group over any other racial group or groups and committed with the intention of maintaining that regime;

(i) "Enforced disappearance of persons" means the arrest, detention or abduction of persons by, or with the authorization, support or acquiescence of, a State or a political organization, followed by a refusal to acknowledge that deprivation of freedom or to give information on the fate or whereabouts of those persons, with the intention of removing them from the protection of the law for a prolonged period of time.

3. For the purpose of this Statute, it is understood that the term "gender" refers to the two sexes, male and female, within the context of society. The term "gender" does not indicate any meaning different from the above.

Article 8
War crimes

1. The Court shall have jurisdiction in respect of war crimes in particular when committed as part of a plan or policy or as part of a large-scale commission of such crimes.

2. For the purpose of this Statute, "war crimes" means:

(a) Grave breaches of the Geneva Conventions of 12 August 1949, namely, any of the following acts against persons or property protected under the provisions of the relevant Geneva Convention:

(i) Wilful killing;

(ii) Torture or inhuman treatment, including biological experiments;

(iii) Wilfully causing great suffering, or serious injury to body or health;

(iv) Extensive destruction and appropriation of property, not justified by military necessity and carried out unlawfully and wantonly;

(v) Compelling a prisoner of war or other protected person to serve in the forces of a hostile Power;

(vi) Wilfully depriving a prisoner of war or other protected person of the rights of fair and regular trial;

(vii) Unlawful deportation or transfer or unlawful confinement;

(viii) Taking of hostages.

(b) Other serious violations of the laws and customs applicable in international armed conflict, within the established framework of international law, namely, any of the following acts:

(i) Intentionally directing attacks against the civilian population as such or against individual civilians not taking direct part in hostilities;

(ii) Intentionally directing attacks against civilian objects, that is, objects which are not military objectives;

(iii) Intentionally directing attacks against personnel, installations, material, units or vehicles involved in a humanitarian assistance or peacekeeping mission in accordance with the Charter of the United Nations, as long as they are entitled to the protection given to civilians or civilian objects under the international law of armed conflict;

(iv) Intentionally launching an attack in the knowledge that such attack will cause incidental loss of life or injury to civilians or damage to civilian objects or widespread, long-term and severe damage to the natural environment which would be clearly excessive in relation to the concrete and direct overall military advantage anticipated;

(v) Attacking or bombarding, by whatever means, towns, villages, dwellings or buildings which are undefended and which are not military objectives;

(vi) Killing or wounding a combatant who, having laid down his arms or having no longer means of defence, has surrendered at discretion;

(vii) Making improper use of a flag of truce, of the flag or of the military insignia and uniform of the enemy or of the United Nations, as well as of the distinctive emblems of the Geneva Conventions, resulting in death or serious personal injury;

(viii) The transfer, directly or indirectly, by the Occupying Power of parts of its own civilian population into the territory it occupies, or the deportation or transfer of all or parts of the population of the occupied territory within or outside this territory;

(ix) Intentionally directing attacks against buildings dedicated to religion, education, art, science or charitable purposes, historic monuments, hospitals and places where the sick and wounded are collected, provided they are not military objectives;

(x) Subjecting persons who are in the power of an adverse party to physical mutilation or to medical or scientific experiments of any kind which are neither justified by the medical, dental or hospital treatment of the person concerned nor carried out in his or her interest, and which cause death to or seriously endanger the health of such person or persons;

(xi) Killing or wounding treacherously individuals belonging to the hostile nation or army;

(xii) Declaring that no quarter will be given;

(xiii) Destroying or seizing the enemy's property unless such destruction or seizure be imperatively demanded by the necessities of war;

(xiv) Declaring abolished, suspended or inadmissible in a court of law the rights and actions of the nationals of the hostile party;

(xv) Compelling the nationals of the hostile party to take part in the operations of war directed against their own country, even if they were in the belligerent's service before the commencement of the war;

(xvi) Pillaging a town or place, even when taken by assault;

(xvii) Employing poison or poisoned weapons;

(xviii) Employing asphyxiating, poisonous or other gases, and all analogous liquids, materials or devices;

(xix) Employing bullets which expand or flatten easily in the human body, such as bullets with a hard envelope which does not entirely cover the core or is pierced with incisions;

(xx) Employing weapons, projectiles and material and methods of warfare which are of a nature to cause superfluous injury or unnecessary suffering or which are inherently indiscriminate in violation of the international law of armed conflict, provided that such weapons, projectiles and material and methods of warfare are the subject of a comprehensive prohibition and are included in an annex to this Statute, by an amendment in accordance with the relevant provisions set forth in articles 121 and 123;

(xxi) Committing outrages upon personal dignity, in particular humiliating and degrading treatment;

(xxii) Committing rape, sexual slavery, enforced prostitution, forced pregnancy, as defined in article 7, paragraph 2 (f), enforced sterilization, or any other form of sexual violence also constituting a grave breach of the Geneva Conventions;

(xxiii) Utilizing the presence of a civilian or other protected person to render certain points, areas or military forces immune from military operations;

(xxiv) Intentionally directing attacks against buildings, material, medical units and transport, and personnel using the distinctive emblems of the Geneva Conventions in conformity with international law;

(xxv) Intentionally using starvation of civilians as a method of warfare by depriving them of objects indispensable to their survival, including wilfully impeding relief supplies as provided for under the Geneva Conventions;

(xxvi) Conscripting or enlisting children under the age of fifteen years into the national armed forces or using them to participate actively in hostilities.

(c) In the case of an armed conflict not of an international character, serious violations of article 3 common to the four Geneva Conventions of 12 August 1949, namely, any of the following acts committed against persons taking no active part in the hostilities, including members of armed forces who have laid down their arms and those placed *hors de combat* by sickness, wounds, detention or any other cause:

(i) Violence to life and person, in particular murder of all kinds, mutilation, cruel treatment and torture;

(ii) Committing outrages upon personal dignity, in particular humiliating and degrading treatment;

(iii) Taking of hostages;

(iv) The passing of sentences and the carrying out of executions without previous judgement pronounced by a regularly constituted court, affording all judicial guarantees which are generally recognized as indispensable.

(d) Paragraph 2 (c) applies to armed conflicts not of an international character and thus does not apply to situations of internal disturbances and tensions, such as riots, isolated and sporadic acts of violence or other acts of a similar nature.

(e) Other serious violations of the laws and customs applicable in armed conflicts not of an international character, within the established framework of international law, namely, any of the following acts:

(i) Intentionally directing attacks against the civilian population as such or against individual civilians not taking direct part in hostilities;

(ii) Intentionally directing attacks against buildings, material, medical units and transport, and personnel using the distinctive emblems of the Geneva Conventions in conformity with international law;

(iii) Intentionally directing attacks against personnel, installations, material, units or vehicles involved in a humanitarian assistance or peacekeeping mission in accordance with the Charter of the United Nations, as long as they are entitled to the protection given to civilians or civilian objects under the international law of armed conflict;

(iv) Intentionally directing attacks against buildings dedicated to religion, education, art, science or charitable purposes, historic monuments, hospitals and places where the sick and wounded are collected, provided they are not military objectives;

(v) Pillaging a town or place, even when taken by assault;

(vi) Committing rape, sexual slavery, enforced prostitution, forced pregnancy, as defined in article 7, paragraph 2 (f), enforced sterilization, and any other form of sexual violence also constituting a serious violation of article 3 common to the four Geneva Conventions;

(vii) Conscripting or enlisting children under the age of fifteen years into armed forces or groups or using them to participate actively in hostilities;

(viii) Ordering the displacement of the civilian population for reasons related to the conflict, unless the security of the civilians involved or imperative military reasons so demand;

(ix) Killing or wounding treacherously a combatant adversary;

(x) Declaring that no quarter will be given;

(xi) Subjecting persons who are in the power of another party to the conflict to physical mutilation or to medical or scientific experiments of any kind which are neither justified by the medical, dental or hospital treatment of the person concerned nor carried out in his or her interest, and which cause death to or seriously endanger the health of such person or persons;

(xii) Destroying or seizing the property of an adversary unless such destruction or seizure be imperatively demanded by the necessities of the conflict;

(f) Paragraph 2 (e) applies to armed conflicts not of an international character and thus does not apply to situations of internal disturbances and tensions, such as riots, isolated and sporadic acts of violence or other acts of a similar nature. It applies to armed conflicts that take place in the territory of a State when there is protracted armed conflict between governmental authorities and organized armed groups or between such groups.

3. Nothing in paragraph 2 (c) and (e) shall affect the responsibility of a Government to maintain or re-establish law and order in the State or to defend the unity and territorial integrity of the State, by all legitimate means.

Article 9
Elements of Crimes

1. Elements of Crimes shall assist the Court in the interpretation and application of articles 6, 7 and 8. They shall be adopted by a two-thirds majority of the members of the Assembly of States Parties.

2. Amendments to the Elements of Crimes may be proposed by:

(a) Any State Party;

(b) The judges acting by an absolute majority;

(c) The Prosecutor.

Such amendments shall be adopted by a two-thirds majority of the members of the Assembly of States Parties.

3. The Elements of Crimes and amendments thereto shall be consistent with this Statute.

Article 10

Nothing in this Part shall be interpreted as limiting or prejudicing in any way existing or developing rules of international law for purposes other than this Statute.

Article 11
Jurisdiction *ratione temporis*

1. The Court has jurisdiction only with respect to crimes committed after the entry into force of this Statute.

2. If a State becomes a Party to this Statute after its entry into force, the Court may exercise its jurisdiction only with respect to crimes committed after the entry into force of this Statute for that State, unless that State has made a declaration under article 12, paragraph 3.

Article 12
Preconditions to the exercise of jurisdiction

1. A State which becomes a Party to this Statute thereby accepts the jurisdiction of the Court with respect to the crimes referred to in article 5.

2. In the case of article 13, paragraph (a) or (c), the Court may exercise its jurisdiction if one or more of the following States are Parties to this Statute or have accepted the jurisdiction of the Court in accordance with paragraph 3:

> (a) The State on the territory of which the conduct in question occurred or, if the crime was committed on board a vessel or aircraft, the State of registration of that vessel or aircraft;

> (b) The State of which the person accused of the crime is a national.

3. If the acceptance of a State which is not a Party to this Statute is required under paragraph 2, that State may, by declaration lodged with the Registrar, accept the exercise of jurisdiction by the Court with respect to the crime in question. The accepting State shall cooperate with the Court without any delay or exception in accordance with Part 9.

Article 13
Exercise of jurisdiction

The Court may exercise its jurisdiction with respect to a crime referred to in article 5 in accordance with the provisions of this Statute if:

> (a) A situation in which one or more of such crimes appears to have been committed is referred to the Prosecutor by a State Party in accordance with article 14;

> (b) A situation in which one or more of such crimes appears to have been committed is referred to the Prosecutor by the Security Council acting under Chapter VII of the Charter of the United Nations; or

> (c) The Prosecutor has initiated an investigation in respect of such a crime in accordance with article 15.

Article 14
Referral of a situation by a State Party

1. A State Party may refer to the Prosecutor a situation in which one or more crimes within the jurisdiction of the Court appear to have been committed requesting the Prosecutor to investigate the situation for the purpose of determining whether one or more specific persons should be charged with the commission of such crimes.

2. As far as possible, a referral shall specify the relevant circumstances and be accompanied by such supporting documentation as is available to the State referring the situation.

Article 15
Prosecutor

1. The Prosecutor may initiate investigations *proprio motu* on the basis of information on crimes within the jurisdiction of the Court.

2. The Prosecutor shall analyse the seriousness of the information received. For this purpose, he or she may seek additional information from States, organs of the United Nations, intergovernmental or non-governmental organizations, or other reliable sources that he or she deems appropriate, and may receive written or oral testimony at the seat of the Court.

3. If the Prosecutor concludes that there is a reasonable basis to proceed with an investigation, he or she shall submit to the Pre-Trial Chamber a request for authorization of an investigation, together with any supporting material collected. Victims may make representations to the Pre-Trial Chamber, in accordance with the Rules of Procedure and Evidence.

4. If the Pre-Trial Chamber, upon examination of the request and the supporting material, considers that there is a reasonable basis to proceed with an investigation, and that the case appears to fall within the jurisdiction of the Court, it shall authorize the commencement of the investigation, without prejudice to subsequent determinations by the Court with regard to the jurisdiction and admissibility of a case.

5. The refusal of the Pre-Trial Chamber to authorize the investigation shall not preclude the presentation of a subsequent request by the Prosecutor based on new facts or evidence regarding the same situation.

6. If, after the preliminary examination referred to in paragraphs 1 and 2, the Prosecutor concludes that the information provided does not constitute a reasonable basis for an investigation, he or she shall inform those who provided the information. This shall not preclude the Prosecutor from considering further information submitted to him or her regarding the same situation in the light of new facts or evidence.

Article 16
Deferral of investigation or prosecution

No investigation or prosecution may be commenced or proceeded with under this Statute for a period of 12 months after the Security Council, in a resolution adopted under Chapter VII of the Charter of the United Nations, has requested the Court to that effect; that request may be renewed by the Council under the same conditions.

Article 17
Issues of admissibility

1. Having regard to paragraph 10 of the Preamble and article 1, the Court shall determine that a case is inadmissible where:

(a) The case is being investigated or prosecuted by a State which has jurisdiction over it, unless the State is unwilling or unable genuinely to carry out the investigation or prosecution;

(b) The case has been investigated by a State which has jurisdiction over it and the State has decided not to prosecute the person concerned, unless the decision resulted from the unwillingness or inability of the State genuinely to prosecute;

(c) The person concerned has already been tried for conduct which is the subject of the complaint, and a trial by the Court is not permitted under article 20, paragraph 3;

(d) The case is not of sufficient gravity to justify further action by the Court.

2. In order to determine unwillingness in a particular case, the Court shall consider, having regard to the principles of due process recognized by international law, whether one or more of the following exist, as applicable:

(a) The proceedings were or are being undertaken or the national decision was made for the purpose of shielding the person concerned from criminal responsibility for crimes within the jurisdiction of the Court referred to in article 5;

(b) There has been an unjustified delay in the proceedings which in the circumstances is inconsistent with an intent to bring the person concerned to justice;

(c) The proceedings were not or are not being conducted independently or impartially, and they were or are being conducted in a manner which, in the circumstances, is inconsistent with an intent to bring the person concerned to justice.

3. In order to determine inability in a particular case, the Court shall consider whether, due to a total or substantial collapse or unavailability of its national judicial system, the State is unable to obtain the accused or the necessary evidence and testimony or otherwise unable to carry out its proceedings.

Article 18
Preliminary rulings regarding admissibility

1. When a situation has been referred to the Court pursuant to article 13 (a) and the Prosecutor has determined that there would be a reasonable basis to commence an investigation, or the Prosecutor initiates an investigation pursuant to articles 13 (c) and 15, the Prosecutor shall notify all States Parties and those States which, taking into account the information available, would normally exercise jurisdiction over the crimes concerned. The Prosecutor may notify such States on a confidential basis and, where the Prosecutor believes it necessary to protect persons, prevent destruction of evidence or prevent the absconding of persons, may limit the scope of the information provided to States.

2. Within one month of receipt of that notification, a State may inform the Court that it is investigating or has investigated its nationals or others within its jurisdiction with respect to criminal acts which may constitute crimes referred to in article 5 and which relate to the information provided in the notification to States. At the request of that State, the Prosecutor shall defer to the State's investigation of those persons unless the Pre-Trial Chamber, on the application of the Prosecutor, decides to authorize the investigation.

3. The Prosecutor's deferral to a State's investigation shall be open to review by the Prosecutor six months after the date of deferral or at any time when there has been a significant change of circumstances based on the State's unwillingness or inability genuinely to carry out the investigation.

4. The State concerned or the Prosecutor may appeal to the Appeals Chamber against a ruling of the Pre-Trial Chamber, in accordance with article 82. The appeal may be heard on an expedited basis.

5. When the Prosecutor has deferred an investigation in accordance with paragraph 2, the Prosecutor may request that the State concerned periodically inform the Prosecutor of the progress of its investigations and any subsequent prosecutions. States Parties shall respond to such requests without undue delay.

6. Pending a ruling by the Pre-Trial Chamber, or at any time when the Prosecutor has deferred an investigation under this article, the Prosecutor may, on an exceptional basis, seek authority from the Pre-Trial Chamber to pursue necessary investigative steps for the purpose of preserving evidence where there is a unique opportunity to obtain important evidence or there is a significant risk that such evidence may not be subsequently available.

7. A State which has challenged a ruling of the Pre-Trial Chamber under this article may challenge the admissibility of a case under article 19 on the grounds of additional significant facts or significant change of circumstances.

Article 19
Challenges to the jurisdiction of the Court or the admissibility of a case

1. The Court shall satisfy itself that it has jurisdiction in any case brought before it. The Court may, on its own motion, determine the admissibility of a case in accordance with article 17.

2. Challenges to the admissibility of a case on the grounds referred to in article 17 or challenges to the jurisdiction of the Court may be made by:

(a) An accused or a person for whom a warrant of arrest or a summons to appear has been issued under article 58;

(b) A State which has jurisdiction over a case, on the ground that it is investigating or prosecuting the case or has investigated or prosecuted; or

(c) A State from which acceptance of jurisdiction is required under article 12.

3. The Prosecutor may seek a ruling from the Court regarding a question of jurisdiction or admissibility. In proceedings with respect to jurisdiction or admissibility, those who have referred the situation under article 13, as well as victims, may also submit observations to the Court.

4. The admissibility of a case or the jurisdiction of the Court may be challenged only once by any person or State referred to in paragraph 2. The challenge shall take place prior to or at the commencement of the trial. In exceptional circumstances, the Court may grant leave for a challenge to be brought more than once or at a time later than the commencement of the trial. Challenges to the admissibility of a case, at the commencement of a trial, or subsequently with the leave of the Court, may be based only on article 17, paragraph 1 (c).

5. A State referred to in paragraph 2 (b) and (c) shall make a challenge at the earliest opportunity.

6. Prior to the confirmation of the charges, challenges to the admissibility of a case or challenges to the jurisdiction of the Court shall be referred to the Pre-Trial Chamber. After confirmation of the charges, they shall be referred to the Trial Chamber. Decisions with respect to jurisdiction or admissibility may be appealed to the Appeals Chamber in accordance with article 82.

7. If a challenge is made by a State referred to in paragraph 2 (b) or (c), the Prosecutor shall suspend the investigation until such time as the Court makes a determination in accordance with article 17.

8. Pending a ruling by the Court, the Prosecutor may seek authority from the Court:

(a) To pursue necessary investigative steps of the kind referred to in article 18, paragraph 6;

(b) To take a statement or testimony from a witness or complete the collection and examination of evidence which had begun prior to the making of the challenge; and

(c) In cooperation with the relevant States, to prevent the absconding of persons in respect of whom the Prosecutor has already requested a warrant of arrest under article 58.

9. The making of a challenge shall not affect the validity of any act performed by the Prosecutor or any order or warrant issued by the Court prior to the making of the challenge.

10. If the Court has decided that a case is inadmissible under article 17, the Prosecutor may submit a request for a review of the decision when he or she is fully satisfied that new facts have arisen which negate the basis on which the case had previously been found inadmissible under article 17.

11. If the Prosecutor, having regard to the matters referred to in article 17, defers an investigation, the Prosecutor may request that the relevant State make available to the Prosecutor information on the proceedings. That information shall, at the request of the State concerned, be confidential. If the Prosecutor thereafter decides to proceed with an investigation, he or she shall notify the State to which deferral of the proceedings has taken place.

Article 20
Ne bis in idem

1. Except as provided in this Statute, no person shall be tried before the Court with respect to conduct which formed the basis of crimes for which the person has been convicted or acquitted by the Court.

2. No person shall be tried by another court for a crime referred to in article 5 for which that person has already been convicted or acquitted by the Court.

3. No person who has been tried by another court for conduct also proscribed under article 6, 7 or 8 shall be tried by the Court with respect to the same conduct unless the proceedings in the other court:

(a) Were for the purpose of shielding the person concerned from criminal responsibility for crimes within the jurisdiction of the Court; or

(b) Otherwise were not conducted independently or impartially in accordance with the norms of due process recognized by international law and were conducted in a manner which, in the circumstances, was inconsistent with an intent to bring the person concerned to justice.

Article 21
Applicable law

1. The Court shall apply:

(a) In the first place, this Statute, Elements of Crimes and its Rules of Procedure and Evidence;

(b) In the second place, where appropriate, applicable treaties and the principles and rules of international law, including the established principles of the international law of armed conflict;

(c) Failing that, general principles of law derived by the Court from national laws of legal systems of the world including, as appropriate, the national laws of States that would normally exercise jurisdiction over the crime, provided that those principles are not inconsistent with this Statute and with international law and internationally recognized norms and standards.

2. The Court may apply principles and rules of law as interpreted in its previous decisions.

3. The application and interpretation of law pursuant to this article must be consistent with internationally recognized human rights, and be without any adverse distinction founded on grounds such as gender as defined in article 7, paragraph 3, age, race, colour, language, religion or belief, political or other opinion, national, ethnic or social origin, wealth, birth or other status.

Part 3. General Principles Of Criminal Law

Article 22
Nullum crimen sine lege

1. A person shall not be criminally responsible under this Statute unless the conduct in question constitutes, at the time it takes place, a crime within the jurisdiction of the Court.

2. The definition of a crime shall be strictly construed and shall not be extended by analogy. In case of ambiguity, the definition shall be interpreted in favour of the person being investigated, prosecuted or convicted.

3. This article shall not affect the characterization of any conduct as criminal under international law independently of this Statute.

Article 23
Nulla poena sine lege

A person convicted by the Court may be punished only in accordance with this Statute.

Article 24
Non-retroactivity *ratione personae*

1. No person shall be criminally responsible under this Statute for conduct prior to the entry into force of the Statute.

2. In the event of a change in the law applicable to a given case prior to a final judgement, the law more favourable to the person being investigated, prosecuted or convicted shall apply.

Article 25
Individual criminal responsibility

1. The Court shall have jurisdiction over natural persons pursuant to this Statute.

2. A person who commits a crime within the jurisdiction of the Court shall be individually responsible and liable for punishment in accordance with this Statute.

3. In accordance with this Statute, a person shall be criminally responsible and liable for punishment for a crime within the jurisdiction of the Court if that person:

(a) Commits such a crime, whether as an individual, jointly with another or through another person, regardless of whether that other person is criminally responsible;

(b) Orders, solicits or induces the commission of such a crime which in fact occurs or is attempted;

(c) For the purpose of facilitating the commission of such a crime, aids, abets or otherwise assists in its commission or its attempted commission, including providing the means for its commission;

(d) In any other way contributes to the commission or attempted commission of such a crime by a group of persons acting with a common purpose. Such contribution shall be intentional and shall either:

(i) Be made with the aim of furthering the criminal activity or criminal purpose of the group, where such activity or purpose involves the commission of a crime within the jurisdiction of the Court; or

(ii) Be made in the knowledge of the intention of the group to commit the crime;

(e) In respect of the crime of genocide, directly and publicly incites others to commit genocide;

(f) Attempts to commit such a crime by taking action that commences its execution by means of a substantial step, but the crime does not occur because of circumstances independent of the person's intentions. However, a person who abandons the effort to commit the crime or otherwise prevents the completion of the crime shall not be liable for punishment under this Statute for the attempt to commit that crime if that person completely and voluntarily gave up the criminal purpose.

4. No provision in this Statute relating to individual criminal responsibility shall affect the responsibility of States under international law.

Article 26
Exclusion of jurisdiction over persons under eighteen

The Court shall have no jurisdiction over any person who was under the age of 18 at the time of the alleged commission of a crime.

Article 27
Irrelevance of official capacity

1. This Statute shall apply equally to all persons without any distinction based on official capacity. In particular, official capacity as a Head of State or Government, a member of a Government or parliament, an elected representative or a government official shall in no case exempt a person from criminal responsibility under this Statute, nor shall it, in and of itself, constitute a ground for reduction of sentence.

2. Immunities or special procedural rules which may attach to the official capacity of a person, whether under national or international law, shall not bar the Court from exercising its jurisdiction over such a person.

Article 28
Responsibility of commanders and other superiors

In addition to other grounds of criminal responsibility under this Statute for crimes within the jurisdiction of the Court:

(a) A military commander or person effectively acting as a military commander shall be criminally responsible for crimes within the jurisdiction of the Court committed by forces under his or her effective command and control, or effective authority and control as the case may be, as a result of his or her failure to exercise control properly over such forces, where:

(i) That military commander or person either knew or, owing to the circumstances at the time, should have known that the forces were committing or about to commit such crimes; and

(ii) That military commander or person failed to take all necessary and reasonable measures within his or her power to prevent or repress their commission or to submit the matter to the competent authorities for investigation and prosecution.

(b) With respect to superior and subordinate relationships not described in paragraph

(a) ... a superior shall be criminally responsible for crimes within the jurisdiction of the Court committed by subordinates under his or her effective authority and control, as a result of his or her failure to exercise control properly over such subordinates, where:

(i) The superior either knew, or consciously disregarded information which clearly indicated, that the subordinates were committing or about to commit such crimes;

(ii) The crimes concerned activities that were within the effective responsibility and control of the superior; and

(iii) The superior failed to take all necessary and reasonable measures within his or her power to prevent or repress their commission or to submit the matter to the competent authorities for investigation and prosecution.

Article 29
Non-applicability of statute of limitations

The crimes within the jurisdiction of the Court shall not be subject to any statute of limitations.

Article 30
Mental element

1. Unless otherwise provided, a person shall be criminally responsible and liable for punishment for a crime within the jurisdiction of the Court only if the material elements are committed with intent and knowledge.

2. For the purposes of this article, a person has intent where:

(a) In relation to conduct, that person means to engage in the conduct;

(b) In relation to a consequence, that person means to cause that consequence or is aware that it will occur in the ordinary course of events.

3. For the purposes of this article, "knowledge" means awareness that a circumstance exists or a consequence will occur in the ordinary course of events. "Know" and "knowingly" shall be construed accordingly.

Article 31
Grounds for excluding criminal responsibility

1. In addition to other grounds for excluding criminal responsibility provided for in this Statute, a person shall not be criminally responsible if, at the time of that person's conduct:

(a) The person suffers from a mental disease or defect that destroys that person's capacity to appreciate the unlawfulness or nature of his or her conduct, or capacity to control his or her conduct to conform to the requirements of law;

(b) The person is in a state of intoxication that destroys that person's capacity to appreciate the unlawfulness or nature of his or her conduct, or capacity to control his or her conduct to conform to the requirements of law, unless the person has become voluntarily intoxicated under such circumstances that the person knew, or disregarded the risk, that, as a result of the intoxication, he or she was likely to engage in conduct constituting a crime within the jurisdiction of the Court;

(c) The person acts reasonably to defend himself or herself or another person or, in the case of war crimes, property which is essential for the survival of the person or another person or property which is essential for accomplishing a military mission, against an imminent and unlawful use of force in a manner proportionate to the degree of danger to the person or the other person or property protected. The fact that the person was involved in a defensive operation conducted by forces shall not in itself constitute a ground for excluding criminal responsibility under this subparagraph;

(d) The conduct which is alleged to constitute a crime within the jurisdiction of the Court has been caused by duress resulting from a threat of imminent death or of continuing or imminent serious bodily harm against that person or another person, and the person acts necessarily and reasonably to avoid this threat, provided that the person does not intend to cause a greater harm than the one sought to be avoided. Such a threat may either be:

(i) Made by other persons; or

(ii) Constituted by other circumstances beyond that person's control.

2. The Court shall determine the applicability of the grounds for excluding criminal responsibility provided for in this Statute to the case before it.

3. At trial, the Court may consider a ground for excluding criminal responsibility other than those referred to in paragraph 1 where such a ground is derived from applicable law as set forth in article 21. The procedures relating to the consideration of such a ground shall be provided for in the Rules of Procedure and Evidence.

Article 32
Mistake of fact or mistake of law

1. A mistake of fact shall be a ground for excluding criminal responsibility only if it negates the mental element required by the crime.

2. A mistake of law as to whether a particular type of conduct is a crime within the jurisdiction of the Court shall not be a ground for excluding criminal responsibility. A mistake of law may, however, be a ground for excluding criminal responsibility if it negates the mental element required by such a crime, or as provided for in article 33.

Article 33
Superior orders and prescription of law

1. The fact that a crime within the jurisdiction of the Court has been committed by a person pursuant to an order of a Government or of a superior, whether military or civilian, shall not relieve that person of criminal responsibility unless:

(a) The person was under a legal obligation to obey orders of the Government or the superior in question;

(b) The person did not know that the order was unlawful; and

(c) The order was not manifestly unlawful.

2. For the purposes of this article, orders to commit genocide or crimes against humanity are manifestly unlawful.

Part 4. Composition and Administration of the Court

Article 34
Organs of the Court

The Court shall be composed of the following organs:

(a) The Presidency;

(b) An Appeals Division, a Trial Division and a Pre-Trial Division;

(c) The Office of the Prosecutor;

(d) The Registry.

Article 35
Service of judges

1. All judges shall be elected as full-time members of the Court and shall be available to serve on that basis from the commencement of their terms of office.

2. The judges composing the Presidency shall serve on a full-time basis as soon as they are elected.

3. The Presidency may, on the basis of the workload of the Court and in consultation with its members, decide from time to time to what extent the remaining judges shall be required to serve on a full-time basis. Any such arrangement shall be without prejudice to the provisions of article 40.

4. The financial arrangements for judges not required to serve on a full-time basis shall be made in accordance with article 49.

Article 36
Qualifications, nomination and election of judges

1. Subject to the provisions of paragraph 2, there shall be 18 judges of the Court.

2: (a) The Presidency, acting on behalf of the Court, may propose an increase in the number of judges specified in paragraph 1, indicating the reasons why this is considered necessary and appropriate. The Registrar shall promptly circulate any such proposal to all States Parties.

(b) Any such proposal shall then be considered at a meeting of the Assembly of States Parties to be convened in accordance with article 112. The proposal shall be considered adopted if approved at the meeting by a vote of two thirds of the members of the Assembly of States Parties and shall enter into force at such time as decided by the Assembly of States Parties.

(c) (i) Once a proposal for an increase in the number of judges has been adopted under subparagraph (b), the election of the additional judges shall take place at the next session of the Assembly of States Parties in accordance with paragraphs 3 to 8, and article 37, paragraph 2;

(ii) Once a proposal for an increase in the number of judges has been adopted and brought into effect under subparagraphs (b) and (c)(i), it shall be open to the Presidency at any time thereafter, if the workload of the Court justifies it, to propose a reduction in the number of judges, provided that the number of judges shall not be reduced below that specified in paragraph 1. The proposal shall be dealt with in accordance with the procedure laid down in subparagraphs (a) and (b). In the event that the proposal is adopted, the number of judges shall be progressively decreased as the terms of office of serving judges expire, until the necessary number has been reached. The judges shall be chosen from among persons of high moral character, impartiality and integrity who possess the qualifications required in their respective States for appointment to the highest judicial offices.

3. Every candidate for election to the Court shall:

(a) Have established competence in criminal law and procedure, and the necessary relevant experience, whether as judge, prosecutor, advocate or in other similar capacity, in criminal proceedings; or

(b) Have established competence in relevant areas of international law such as international humanitarian law and the law of human rights, and extensive experience in a professional legal capacity which is of relevance to the judicial work of the Court;

4. (a) Nominations of candidates for election to the Court may be made by any State Party to this Statute, and shall be made either:

(i) By the procedure for the nomination of candidates for appointment to the highest judicial offices in the State in question; or

(ii) By the procedure provided for the nomination of candidates for the International Court of Justice in the Statute of that Court.

Nominations shall be accompanied by a statement in the necessary detail specifying how the candidate fulfils the requirements of paragraph 3.

(b) Each State Party may put forward one candidate for any given election who need not necessarily be a national of that State Party but shall in any case be a national of a State Party.

(c) The Assembly of States Parties may decide to establish, if appropriate, an Advisory Committee on nominations. In that event, the Committee's composition and mandate shall be established by the Assembly of States Parties.

5. For the purposes of the election, there shall be two lists of candidates:

List A containing the names of candidates with the qualifications specified in paragraph 3 (b)(i); and

List B containing the names of candidates with the qualifications specified in paragraph 3 (b)(ii).

A candidate with sufficient qualifications for both lists may choose on which list to appear. At the first election to the Court, at least nine judges shall be elected from list A and at least five judges from list B. Subsequent elections shall be so organized as to maintain the equivalent proportion on the Court of judges qualified on the two lists.

6. (a) The judges shall be elected by secret ballot at a meeting of the Assembly of States Parties convened for that purpose under article 112. Subject to paragraph 7, the persons elected to the Court shall be the 18 candidates who obtain the highest number of votes and a two-thirds majority of the States Parties present and voting.

(b) In the event that a sufficient number of judges is not elected on the first ballot, successive ballots shall be held in accordance with the procedures laid down in subparagraph (a) until the remaining places have been filled.

7. No two judges may be nationals of the same State. A person who, for the purposes of membership of the Court, could be regarded as a national of more than one State shall

be deemed to be a national of the State in which that person ordinarily exercises civil and political rights.

8. (a) The States Parties shall, in the selection of judges, take into account the need, within the membership of the Court, for:

(i) The representation of the principal legal systems of the world; (ii) Equitable geographical representation; and

(iii) A fair representation of female and male judges.

(b) States Parties shall also take into account the need to include judges with legal expertise on specific issues, including, but not limited to, violence against women or children.

9. (a) Subject to subparagraph (b), judges shall hold office for a term of nine years and, subject to subparagraph (c) and to article 37, paragraph 2, shall not be eligible for re-election.

(b) At the first election, one third of the judges elected shall be selected by lot to serve for a term of three years; one third of the judges elected shall be selected by lot to serve for a term of six years; and the remainder shall serve for a term of nine years.

(c) A judge who is selected to serve for a term of three years under subparagraph (b) shall be eligible for re-election for a full term.

10. Notwithstanding paragraph 9, a judge assigned to a Trial or Appeals Chamber in accordance with article 39 shall continue in office to complete any trial or appeal the hearing of which has already commenced before that Chamber.

Article 37
Judicial vacancies

1. In the event of a vacancy, an election shall be held in accordance with article 36 to fill the vacancy.

2. A judge elected to fill a vacancy shall serve for the remainder of the predecessor's term and, if that period is three years or less, shall be eligible for re-election for a full term under article 36.

Article 38
The Presidency

1. The President and the First and Second Vice-Presidents shall be elected by an absolute majority of the judges. They shall each serve for a term of three years or until the end of their respective terms of office as judges, whichever expires earlier. They shall be eligible for re-election once.

2. The First Vice-President shall act in place of the President in the event that the President is unavailable or disqualified. The Second Vice-President shall act in place of the President in the event that both the President and the First Vice-President are unavailable or disqualified.

3. The President, together with the First and Second Vice-Presidents, shall constitute the Presidency, which shall be responsible for:

(a) The proper administration of the Court, with the exception of the Office of the Prosecutor; and

(b) The other functions conferred upon it in accordance with this Statute.

4. In discharging its responsibility under paragraph 3(a), the Presidency shall coordinate with and seek the concurrence of the Prosecutor on all matters of mutual concern.

Article 39
Chambers

1. As soon as possible after the election of the judges, the Court shall organize itself into the divisions specified in article 34, paragraph (b). The Appeals Division shall be composed of the President and four other judges, the Trial Division of not less than six judges and the Pre-Trial Division of not less than six judges. The assignment of judges to divisions shall be based on the nature of the functions to be performed by each division and the qualifications and experience of the judges elected to the Court, in such a way that each division shall contain an appropriate combination of expertise in criminal law and procedure and in international law. The Trial and Pre-Trial Divisions shall be composed predominantly of judges with criminal trial experience.

2. (a) The judicial functions of the Court shall be carried out in each division by Chambers.

(b)   (i) The Appeals Chamber shall be composed of all the judges of the Appeals Division;

(ii) The functions of the Trial Chamber shall be carried out by three judges of the Trial Division;

(iii) The functions of the Pre-Trial Chamber shall be carried out either by three judges of the Pre-Trial Division or by a single judge of that division in accordance with this Statute and the Rules of Procedure and Evidence;

(c) Nothing in this paragraph shall preclude the simultaneous constitution of more than one Trial Chamber or Pre-Trial Chamber when the efficient management of the Court's workload so requires.

3. (a) Judges assigned to the Trial and Pre-Trial Divisions shall serve in those divisions for a period of three years, and thereafter until the completion of any case the hearing of which has already commenced in the division concerned.

(b) Judges assigned to the Appeals Division shall serve in that division for their entire term of office.

4. Judges assigned to the Appeals Division shall serve only in that division. Nothing in this article shall, however, preclude the temporary attachment of judges from the Trial Division to the Pre-Trial Division or vice versa, if the Presidency considers that the efficient management of the Court's workload so requires, provided that under no circumstances shall a judge who has participated in the pre-trial phase of a case be eligible to sit on the Trial Chamber hearing that case.

Article 40
Independence of the judges

1. The judges shall be independent in the performance of their functions.

2. Judges shall not engage in any activity which is likely to interfere with their judicial functions or to affect confidence in their independence.

3. Judges required to serve on a full-time basis at the seat of the Court shall not engage in any other occupation of a professional nature.

4. Any question regarding the application of paragraphs 2 and 3 shall be decided by an absolute majority of the judges. Where any such question concerns an individual judge, that judge shall not take part in the decision.

Article 41
Excusing and disqualification of judges

1. The Presidency may, at the request of a judge, excuse that judge from the exercise of a function under this Statute, in accordance with the Rules of Procedure and Evidence.

2. (a) A judge shall not participate in any case in which his or her impartiality might reasonably be doubted on any ground. A judge shall be disqualified from a case in accordance with this paragraph if, *inter alia*, that judge has previously been involved in any capacity in that case before the Court or in a related criminal case at the national level involving the person being investigated or prosecuted. A judge shall also be disqualified on such other grounds as may be provided for in the Rules of Procedure and Evidence.

(b) The Prosecutor or the person being investigated or prosecuted may request the disqualification of a judge under this paragraph.

(c) Any question as to the disqualification of a judge shall be decided by an absolute majority of the judges. The challenged judge shall be entitled to present his or her comments on the matter, but shall not take part in the decision.

Article 42
The Office of the Prosecutor

1. The Office of the Prosecutor shall act independently as a separate organ of the Court. It shall be responsible for receiving referrals and any substantiated information on crimes within the jurisdiction of the Court, for examining them and for conducting investigations and prosecutions before the Court. A member of the Office shall not seek or act on instructions from any external source.

2. The Office shall be headed by the Prosecutor. The Prosecutor shall have full authority over the management and administration of the Office, including the staff, facilities and other resources thereof. The Prosecutor shall be assisted by one or more Deputy Prosecutors, who shall be entitled to carry out any of the acts required of the Prosecutor under this Statute. The Prosecutor and the Deputy Prosecutors shall be of different nationalities. They shall serve on a full-time basis.

3. The Prosecutor and the Deputy Prosecutors shall be persons of high moral character, be highly competent in and have extensive practical experience in the prosecution or trial of criminal cases. They shall have an excellent knowledge of and be fluent in at least one of the working languages of the Court.

4. The Prosecutor shall be elected by secret ballot by an absolute majority of the members of the Assembly of States Parties. The Deputy Prosecutors shall be elected in the same way from a list of candidates provided by the Prosecutor. The Prosecutor shall nominate three candidates for each position of Deputy Prosecutor to be filled. Unless a shorter term is decided upon at the time of their election, the Prosecutor and the Deputy Prosecutors shall hold office for a term of nine years and shall not be eligible for re-election.

5. Neither the Prosecutor nor a Deputy Prosecutor shall engage in any activity which is likely to interfere with his or her prosecutorial functions or to affect confidence in his or her independence. They shall not engage in any other occupation of a professional nature.

6. The Presidency may excuse the Prosecutor or a Deputy Prosecutor, at his or her request, from acting in a particular case.

7. Neither the Prosecutor nor a Deputy Prosecutor shall participate in any matter in which their impartiality might reasonably be doubted on any ground. They shall be dis-

qualified from a case in accordance with this paragraph if, *inter alia*, they have previously been involved in any capacity in that case before the Court or in a related criminal case at the national level involving the person being investigated or prosecuted.

8. Any question as to the disqualification of the Prosecutor or a Deputy Prosecutor shall be decided by the Appeals Chamber.

(a) The person being investigated or prosecuted may at any time request the disqualification of the Prosecutor or a Deputy Prosecutor on the grounds set out in this article;

(b) The Prosecutor or the Deputy Prosecutor, as appropriate, shall be entitled to present his or her comments on the matter;

9. The Prosecutor shall appoint advisers with legal expertise on specific issues, including, but not limited to, sexual and gender violence and violence against children.

Article 43
The Registry

1. The Registry shall be responsible for the non-judicial aspects of the administration and servicing of the Court, without prejudice to the functions and powers of the Prosecutor in accordance with article 42.

2. The Registry shall be headed by the Registrar, who shall be the principal administrative officer of the Court. The Registrar shall exercise his or her functions under the authority of the President of the Court.

3. The Registrar and the Deputy Registrar shall be persons of high moral character, be highly competent and have an excellent knowledge of and be fluent in at least one of the working languages of the Court.

4. The judges shall elect the Registrar by an absolute majority by secret ballot, taking into account any recommendation by the Assembly of States Parties. If the need arises and upon the recommendation of the Registrar, the judges shall elect, in the same manner, a Deputy Registrar.

5. The Registrar shall hold office for a term of five years, shall be eligible for re-election once and shall serve on a full-time basis. The Deputy Registrar shall hold office for a term of five years or such shorter term as may be decided upon by an absolute majority of the judges, and may be elected on the basis that the Deputy Registrar shall be called upon to serve as required.

6. The Registrar shall set up a Victims and Witnesses Unit within the Registry. This Unit shall provide, in consultation with the Office of the Prosecutor, protective measures and security arrangements, counseling and other appropriate assistance for witnesses, victims who appear before the Court, and others who are at risk on account of testimony given by such witnesses. The Unit shall include staff with expertise in trauma, including trauma related to crimes of sexual violence.

Article 44
Staff

1. The Prosecutor and the Registrar shall appoint such qualified staff as may be required to their respective offices. In the case of the Prosecutor, this shall include the appointment of investigators.

2. In the employment of staff, the Prosecutor and the Registrar shall ensure the highest standards of efficiency, competency and integrity, and shall have regard, *mutatis mutandis*, to the criteria set forth in article 36, paragraph 8.

3. The Registrar, with the agreement of the Presidency and the Prosecutor, shall propose Staff Regulations which include the terms and conditions upon which the staff of the Court shall be appointed, remunerated and dismissed. The Staff Regulations shall be approved by the Assembly of States Parties.

4. The Court may, in exceptional circumstances, employ the expertise of gratis personnel offered by States Parties, intergovernmental organizations or non-governmental organizations to assist with the work of any of the organs of the Court. The Prosecutor may accept any such offer on behalf of the Office of the Prosecutor. Such gratis personnel shall be employed in accordance with guidelines to be established by the Assembly of States Parties.

Article 45
Solemn undertaking

Before taking up their respective duties under this Statute, the judges, the Prosecutor, the Deputy Prosecutors, the Registrar and the Deputy Registrar shall each make a solemn undertaking in open court to exercise his or her respective functions impartially and conscientiously.

Article 46
Removal from office

1. A judge, the Prosecutor, a Deputy Prosecutor, the Registrar or the Deputy Registrar shall be removed from office if a decision to this effect is made in accordance with paragraph 2, in cases where that person:

(a) Is found to have committed serious misconduct or a serious breach of his or her duties under this Statute, as provided for in the Rules of Procedure and Evidence; or

(b) Is unable to exercise the functions required by this Statute.

2. A decision as to the removal from office of a judge, the Prosecutor or a Deputy Prosecutor under paragraph 1 shall be made by the Assembly of States Parties, by secret ballot:

(a) In the case of a judge, by a two-thirds majority of the States Parties upon a recommendation adopted by a two-thirds majority of the other judges;

(b) In the case of the Prosecutor, by an absolute majority of the States Parties;

(c) In the case of a Deputy Prosecutor, by an absolute majority of the States Parties upon the recommendation of the Prosecutor.

3. A decision as to the removal from office of the Registrar or Deputy Registrar shall be made by an absolute majority of the judges.

4. A judge, Prosecutor, Deputy Prosecutor, Registrar or Deputy Registrar whose conduct or ability to exercise the functions of the office as required by this Statute is challenged under this article shall have full opportunity to present and receive evidence and to make submissions in accordance with the Rules of Procedure and Evidence. The person in question shall not otherwise participate in the consideration of the matter.

Article 47
Disciplinary measures

A judge, Prosecutor, Deputy Prosecutor, Registrar or Deputy Registrar who has committed misconduct of a less serious nature than that set out in article 46, paragraph 1, shall be subject to disciplinary measures, in accordance with the Rules of Procedure and Evidence.

Article 48
Privileges and immunities

1. The Court shall enjoy in the territory of each State Party such privileges and immunities as are necessary for the fulfillment of its purposes.

2. The judges, the Prosecutor, the Deputy Prosecutors and the Registrar shall, when engaged on or with respect to the business of the Court, enjoy the same privileges and immunities as are accorded to heads of diplomatic missions and shall, after the expiry of their terms of office, continue to be accorded immunity from legal process of every kind in respect of words spoken or written and acts performed by them in their official capacity.

3. The Deputy Registrar, the staff of the Office of the Prosecutor and the staff of the Registry shall enjoy the privileges and immunities and facilities necessary for the performance of their functions, in accordance with the agreement on the privileges and immunities of the Court.

4. Counsel, experts, witnesses or any other person required to be present at the seat of the Court shall be accorded such treatment as is necessary for the proper functioning of the Court, in accordance with the agreement on the privileges and immunities of the Court.

5. The privileges and immunities of:

(a) A judge or the Prosecutor may be waived by an absolute majority of the judges;

(b) The Registrar may be waived by the Presidency;

(c) The Deputy Prosecutors and staff of the Office of the Prosecutor may be waived by the Prosecutor;

(d) The Deputy Registrar and staff of the Registry may be waived by the Registrar.

Article 49
Salaries, allowances and expenses

The judges, the Prosecutor, the Deputy Prosecutors, the Registrar and the Deputy Registrar shall receive such salaries, allowances and expenses as may be decided upon by the Assembly of States Parties. These salaries and allowances shall not be reduced during their terms of office.

Article 50
Official and working languages

1. The official languages of the Court shall be Arabic, Chinese, English, French, Russian and Spanish. The judgements of the Court, as well as other decisions resolving fundamental issues before the Court, shall be published in the official languages. The Presidency shall, in accordance with the criteria established by the Rules of Procedure and Evidence, determine which decisions may be considered as resolving fundamental issues for the purposes of this paragraph.

2. The working languages of the Court shall be English and French. The Rules of Procedure and Evidence shall determine the cases in which other official languages may be used as working languages.

3. At the request of any party to a proceeding or a State allowed to intervene in a proceeding, the Court shall authorize a language other than English or French to be used by such a party or State, provided that the Court considers such authorization to be adequately justified.

Article 51
Rules of Procedure and Evidence

1. The Rules of Procedure and Evidence shall enter into force upon adoption by a two-thirds majority of the members of the Assembly of States Parties.

2. Amendments to the Rules of Procedure and Evidence may be proposed by:

(a) Any State Party;

(b) The judges acting by an absolute majority; or

(c) The Prosecutor.

Such amendments shall enter into force upon adoption by a two-thirds majority of the members of the Assembly of States Parties.

3. After the adoption of the Rules of Procedure and Evidence, in urgent cases where the Rules do not provide for a specific situation before the Court, the judges may, by a two-thirds majority, draw up provisional Rules to be applied until adopted, amended or rejected at the next ordinary or special session of the Assembly of States Parties.

4. The Rules of Procedure and Evidence, amendments thereto and any provisional Rule shall be consistent with this Statute. Amendments to the Rules of Procedure and Evidence as well as provisional Rules shall not be applied retroactively to the detriment of the person who is being investigated or prosecuted or who has been convicted.

5. In the event of conflict between the Statute and the Rules of Procedure and Evidence, the Statute shall prevail.

Article 52
Regulations of the Court

1. The judges shall, in accordance with this Statute and the Rules of Procedure and Evidence, adopt, by an absolute majority, the Regulations of the Court necessary for its routine functioning.

2. The Prosecutor and the Registrar shall be consulted in the elaboration of the Regulations and any amendments thereto.

3. The Regulations and any amendments thereto shall take effect upon adoption unless otherwise decided by the judges. Immediately upon adoption, they shall be circulated to States Parties for comments. If within six months there are no objections from a majority of States Parties, they shall remain in force.

Part 5. Investigation and Prosecution

Article 53
Initiation of an investigation

1. The Prosecutor shall, having evaluated the information made available to him or her, initiate an investigation unless he or she determines that there is no reasonable basis to proceed under this Statute. In deciding whether to initiate an investigation, the Prosecutor shall consider whether:

(a) The information available to the Prosecutor provides a reasonable basis to believe that a crime within the jurisdiction of the Court has been or is being committed;

(b) The case is or would be admissible under article 17; and

(c) Taking into account the gravity of the crime and the interests of victims, there are nonetheless substantial reasons to believe that an investigation would not serve the interests of justice.

If the Prosecutor determines that there is no reasonable basis to proceed and his or her determination is based solely on subparagraph (c) above, he or she shall inform the Pre-Trial Chamber.

2. If, upon investigation, the Prosecutor concludes that there is not a sufficient basis for a prosecution because:

(a) There is not a sufficient legal or factual basis to seek a warrant or summons under article 58;

(b) The case is inadmissible under article 17; or

(c) A prosecution is not in the interests of justice, taking into account all the circumstances, including the gravity of the crime, the interests of victims and the age or infirmity of the alleged perpetrator, and his or her role in the alleged crime; the Prosecutor shall inform the Pre-Trial Chamber and the State making a referral under article 14 or the Security Council in a case under article 13, paragraph (b), of his or her conclusion and the reasons for the conclusion.

3. (a) At the request of the State making a referral under article 14 or the Security Council under article 13, paragraph (b), the Pre-Trial Chamber may review a decision of the Prosecutor under paragraph 1 or 2 not to proceed and may request the Prosecutor to reconsider that decision.

(b) In addition, the Pre-Trial Chamber may, on its own initiative, review a decision of the Prosecutor not to proceed if it is based solely on paragraph 1(c) or 2(c). In such a case, the decision of the Prosecutor shall be effective only if confirmed by the Pre-Trial Chamber.

4. The Prosecutor may, at any time, reconsider a decision whether to initiate an investigation or prosecution based on new facts or information.

Article 54
Duties and powers of the Prosecutor with respect to investigations

1. The Prosecutor shall:

(a) In order to establish the truth, extend the investigation to cover all facts and evidence relevant to an assessment of whether there is criminal responsibility under this Statute, and, in doing so, investigate incriminating and exonerating circumstances equally;

(b) Take appropriate measures to ensure the effective investigation and prosecution of crimes within the jurisdiction of the Court, and in doing so, respect the interests and personal circumstances of victims and witnesses, including age, gender as defined in article 7, paragraph 3, and health, and take into account the nature of the crime, in particular where it involves sexual violence, gender violence or violence against children; and

(c) Fully respect the rights of persons arising under this Statute.

2. The Prosecutor may conduct investigations on the territory of a State:

(a) In accordance with the provisions of Part 9; or

(b) As authorized by the Pre-Trial Chamber under article 57, paragraph 3(d).

3. The Prosecutor may:

(a) Collect and examine evidence;

(b) Request the presence of and question persons being investigated, victims and witnesses;

(c) Seek the cooperation of any State or intergovernmental organization or arrangement in accordance with its respective competence and/or mandate;

(d) Enter into such arrangements or agreements, not inconsistent with this Statute, as may be necessary to facilitate the cooperation of a State, intergovernmental organization or person;

(e) Agree not to disclose, at any stage of the proceedings, documents or information that the Prosecutor obtains on the condition of confidentiality and solely for the purpose of generating new evidence, unless the provider of the information consents; and

(f) Take necessary measures, or request that necessary measures be taken, to ensure the confidentiality of information, the protection of any person or the preservation of evidence.

Article 55
Rights of persons during an investigation

1. In respect of an investigation under this Statute, a person:

(a) Shall not be compelled to incriminate himself or herself or to confess guilt;

(b) Shall not be subjected to any form of coercion, duress or threat, to torture or to any other form of cruel, inhuman or degrading treatment or punishment;

(c) Shall, if questioned in a language other than a language the person fully understands and speaks, have, free of any cost, the assistance of a competent interpreter and such translations as are necessary to meet the requirements of fairness; and

(d) Shall not be subjected to arbitrary arrest or detention, and shall not be deprived of his or her liberty except on such grounds and in accordance with such procedures as are established in this Statute.

2. Where there are grounds to believe that a person has committed a crime within the jurisdiction of the Court and that person is about to be questioned either by the Prosecutor, or by national authorities pursuant to a request made under Part 9, that person shall also have the following rights of which he or she shall be informed prior to being questioned:

(a) To be informed, prior to being questioned, that there are grounds to believe that he or she has committed a crime within the jurisdiction of the Court;

(b) To remain silent, without such silence being a consideration in the determination of guilt or innocence;

(c) To have legal assistance of the person's choosing, or, if the person does not have legal assistance, to have legal assistance assigned to him or her, in any case where the interests of justice so require, and without payment by the person in any such case if the person does not have sufficient means to pay for it; and

(d) To be questioned in the presence of counsel unless the person has voluntarily waived his or her right to counsel.

Article 56
Role of the Pre-Trial Chamber in relation to a unique investigative opportunity

1. (a) Where the Prosecutor considers an investigation to present a unique opportunity to take testimony or a statement from a witness or to examine, collect or test

evidence, which may not be available subsequently for the purposes of a trial, the Prosecutor shall so inform the Pre-Trial Chamber.

(b) In that case, the Pre-Trial Chamber may, upon request of the Prosecutor, take such measures as may be necessary to ensure the efficiency and integrity of the proceedings and, in particular, to protect the rights of the defence.

(c) Unless the Pre-Trial Chamber orders otherwise, the Prosecutor shall provide the relevant information to the person who has been arrested or appeared in response to a summons in connection with the investigation referred to in subparagraph (a), in order that he or she may be heard on the matter.

2. The measures referred to in paragraph 1(b) may include:

(a) Making recommendations or orders regarding procedures to be followed;

(b) Directing that a record be made of the proceedings;

(c) Appointing an expert to assist;

(d) Authorizing counsel for a person who has been arrested, or appeared before the Court in response to a summons, to participate, or where there has not yet been such an arrest or appearance or counsel has not been designated, appointing another counsel to attend and represent the interests of the defence;

(e) Naming one of its members or, if necessary, another available judge of the Pre-Trial or Trial Division to observe and make recommendations or orders regarding the collection and preservation of evidence and the questioning of persons;

(f) Taking such other action as may be necessary to collect or preserve evidence.

3. (a) Where the Prosecutor has not sought measures pursuant to this article but the Pre-Trial Chamber considers that such measures are required to preserve evidence that it deems would be essential for the defence at trial, it shall consult with the Prosecutor as to whether there is good reason for the Prosecutor's failure to request the measures. If upon consultation, the Pre-Trial Chamber concludes that the Prosecutor's failure to request such measures is unjustified, the Pre-Trial Chamber may take such measures on its own initiative.

(b) A decision of the Pre-Trial Chamber to act on its own initiative under this paragraph may be appealed by the Prosecutor. The appeal shall be heard on an expedited basis.

4. The admissibility of evidence preserved or collected for trial pursuant to this article, or the record thereof, shall be governed at trial by article 69, and given such weight as determined by the Trial Chamber.

Article 57
Functions and powers of the Pre-Trial Chamber

1. Unless otherwise provided in this Statute, the Pre-Trial Chamber shall exercise its functions in accordance with the provisions of this article.

2. (a) Orders or rulings of the Pre-Trial Chamber issued under articles 15, 18, 19, 54, paragraph 2, 61, paragraph 7, and 72 must be concurred in by a majority of its judges.

(b) In all other cases, a single judge of the Pre-Trial Chamber may exercise the functions provided for in this Statute, unless otherwise provided for in the Rules of Procedure and Evidence or by a majority of the Pre-Trial Chamber.

3. In addition to its other functions under this Statute, the Pre-Trial Chamber may:

(a) At the request of the Prosecutor, issue such orders and warrants as may be required for the purposes of an investigation;

(b) Upon the request of a person who has been arrested or has appeared pursuant to a summons under article 58, issue such orders, including measures such as those described in article 56, or seek such cooperation pursuant to Part 9 as may be necessary to assist the person in the preparation of his or her defence;

(c) Where necessary, provide for the protection and privacy of victims and witnesses, the preservation of evidence, the protection of persons who have been arrested or appeared in response to a summons, and the protection of national security information;

(d) Authorize the Prosecutor to take specific investigative steps within the territory of a State Party without having secured the cooperation of that State under Part 9 if, whenever possible having regard to the views of the State concerned, the Pre-Trial Chamber has determined in that case that the State is clearly unable to execute a request for cooperation due to the unavailability of any authority or any component of its judicial system competent to execute the request for cooperation under Part 9.

(e) Where a warrant of arrest or a summons has been issued under article 58, and having due regard to the strength of the evidence and the rights of the parties concerned, as provided for in this Statute and the Rules of Procedure and Evidence, seek the cooperation of States pursuant to article 93, paragraph 1(k), to take protective measures for the purpose of forfeiture, in particular for the ultimate benefit of victims.

Article 58
Issuance by the Pre-Trial Chamber of a warrant of arrest or a summons to appear

1. At any time after the initiation of an investigation, the Pre-Trial Chamber shall, on the application of the Prosecutor, issue a warrant of arrest of a person if, having examined the application and the evidence or other information submitted by the Prosecutor, it is satisfied that:

(a) There are reasonable grounds to believe that the person has committed a crime within the jurisdiction of the Court; and

(b) The arrest of the person appears necessary:

(i) To ensure the person's appearance at trial,

(ii) To ensure that the person does not obstruct or endanger the investigation or the court proceedings, or

(iii) Where applicable, to prevent the person from continuing with the commission of that crime or a related crime which is within the jurisdiction of the Court and which arises out of the same circumstances.

2. The application of the Prosecutor shall contain:

(a) The name of the person and any other relevant identifying information;

(b) A specific reference to the crimes within the jurisdiction of the Court which the person is alleged to have committed;

(c) A concise statement of the facts which are alleged to constitute those crimes;

(d) A summary of the evidence and any other information which establish reasonable grounds to believe that the person committed those crimes; and

(e) The reason why the Prosecutor believes that the arrest of the person is necessary.

3. The warrant of arrest shall contain:

(a) The name of the person and any other relevant identifying information;

(b) A specific reference to the crimes within the jurisdiction of the Court for which the person's arrest is sought; and

(c) A concise statement of the facts which are alleged to constitute those crimes.

4. The warrant of arrest shall remain in effect until otherwise ordered by the Court.

5. On the basis of the warrant of arrest, the Court may request the provisional arrest or the arrest and surrender of the person under Part 9.

6. The Prosecutor may request the Pre-Trial Chamber to amend the warrant of arrest by modifying or adding to the crimes specified therein. The Pre-Trial Chamber shall so amend the warrant if it is satisfied that there are reasonable grounds to believe that the person committed the modified or additional crimes.

7. As an alternative to seeking a warrant of arrest, the Prosecutor may submit an application requesting that the Pre-Trial Chamber issue a summons for the person to appear. If the Pre-Trial Chamber is satisfied that there are reasonable grounds to believe that the person committed the crime alleged and that a summons is sufficient to ensure the person's appearance, it shall issue the summons, with or without conditions restricting liberty (other than detention) if provided for by national law, for the person to appear. The summons shall contain:

(a) The name of the person and any other relevant identifying information;

(b) The specified date on which the person is to appear;

(c) A specific reference to the crimes within the jurisdiction of the Court which the person is alleged to have committed; and

(d) A concise statement of the facts which are alleged to constitute the crime. The summons shall be served on the person.

Article 59
Arrest proceedings in the custodial State

1. A State Party which has received a request for provisional arrest or for arrest and surrender shall immediately take steps to arrest the person in question in accordance with its laws and the provisions of Part 9.

2. A person arrested shall be brought promptly before the competent judicial authority in the custodial State which shall determine, in accordance with the law of that State, that:

(a) The warrant applies to that person;

(b) The person has been arrested in accordance with the proper process; and

(c) The person's rights have been respected.

3. The person arrested shall have the right to apply to the competent authority in the custodial State for interim release pending surrender.

4. In reaching a decision on any such application, the competent authority in the custodial State shall consider whether, given the gravity of the alleged crimes, there are urgent and exceptional circumstances to justify interim release and whether necessary safeguards exist to ensure that the custodial State can fulfill its duty to surrender the person to the Court. It shall not be open to the competent authority of the custodial State to consider whether the warrant of arrest was properly issued in accordance with article 58, paragraph 1(a) and (b).

5. The Pre-Trial Chamber shall be notified of any request for interim release and shall make recommendations to the competent authority in the custodial State. The competent authority in the custodial State shall give full consideration to such recommendations, including any recommendations on measures to prevent the escape of the person, before rendering its decision.

6. If the person is granted interim release, the Pre-Trial Chamber may request periodic reports on the status of the interim release.

7. Once ordered to be surrendered by the custodial State, the person shall be delivered to the Court as soon as possible.

Article 60
Initial proceedings before the Court

1. Upon the surrender of the person to the Court, or the person's appearance before the Court voluntarily or pursuant to a summons, the Pre-Trial Chamber shall satisfy itself that the person has been informed of the crimes which he or she is alleged to have committed, and of his or her rights under this Statute, including the right to apply for interim release pending trial.

2. A person subject to a warrant of arrest may apply for interim release pending trial. If the Pre-Trial Chamber is satisfied that the conditions set forth in article 58, paragraph 1, are met, the person shall continue to be detained. If it is not so satisfied, the Pre-Trial Chamber shall release the person, with or without conditions.

3. The Pre-Trial Chamber shall periodically review its ruling on the release or detention of the person, and may do so at any time on the request of the Prosecutor or the person. Upon such review, it may modify its ruling as to detention, release or conditions of release, if it is satisfied that changed circumstances so require.

4. The Pre-Trial Chamber shall ensure that a person is not detained for an unreasonable period prior to trial due to inexcusable delay by the Prosecutor. If such delay occurs, the Court shall consider releasing the person, with or without conditions.

5. If necessary, the Pre-Trial Chamber may issue a warrant of arrest to secure the presence of a person who has been released.

Article 61
Confirmation of the charges before trial

1. Subject to the provisions of paragraph 2, within a reasonable time after the person's surrender or voluntary appearance before the Court, the Pre-Trial Chamber shall hold a hearing to confirm the charges on which the Prosecutor intends to seek trial. The hearing shall be held in the presence of the Prosecutor and the person charged, as well as his or her counsel.

2. The Pre-Trial Chamber may, upon request of the Prosecutor or on its own motion, hold a hearing in the absence of the person charged to confirm the charges on which the Prosecutor intends to seek trial when the person has:

(a) Waived his or her right to be present; or

(b) Fled or cannot be found and all reasonable steps have been taken to secure his or her appearance before the Court and to inform the person of the charges and that a hearing to confirm those charges will be held.

In that case, the person shall be represented by counsel where the Pre-Trial Chamber determines that it is in the interests of justice.

3. Within a reasonable time before the hearing, the person shall:

(a) Be provided with a copy of the document containing the charges on which the Prosecutor intends to bring the person to trial; and

(b) Be informed of the evidence on which the Prosecutor intends to rely at the hearing. The Pre-Trial Chamber may issue orders regarding the disclosure of information for the purposes of the hearing.

4. Before the hearing, the Prosecutor may continue the investigation and may amend or withdraw any charges. The person shall be given reasonable notice before the hearing of any amendment to or withdrawal of charges. In case of a withdrawal of charges, the Prosecutor shall notify the Pre-Trial Chamber of the reasons for the withdrawal.

5. At the hearing, the Prosecutor shall support each charge with sufficient evidence to establish substantial grounds to believe that the person committed the crime charged. The Prosecutor may rely on documentary or summary evidence and need not call the witnesses expected to testify at the trial.

6. At the hearing, the person may:

(a) Object to the charges;

(b) Challenge the evidence presented by the Prosecutor; and

(c) Present evidence.

7. The Pre-Trial Chamber shall, on the basis of the hearing, determine whether there is sufficient evidence to establish substantial grounds to believe that the person committed each of the crimes charged. Based on its determination, the Pre-Trial Chamber shall:

(a) Confirm those charges in relation to which it has determined that there is sufficient evidence, and commit the person to a Trial Chamber for trial on the charges as confirmed;

(b) Decline to confirm those charges in relation to which it has determined that there is insufficient evidence;

(c) Adjourn the hearing and request the Prosecutor to consider:

(i) Providing further evidence or conducting further investigation with respect to a particular charge; or

(ii) Amending a charge because the evidence submitted appears to establish a different crime within the jurisdiction of the Court.

8. Where the Pre-Trial Chamber declines to confirm a charge, the Prosecutor shall not be precluded from subsequently requesting its confirmation if the request is supported by additional evidence.

9. After the charges are confirmed and before the trial has begun, the Prosecutor may, with the permission of the Pre-Trial Chamber and after notice to the accused, amend the charges. If the Prosecutor seeks to add additional charges or to substitute more serious charges, a hearing under this article to confirm those charges must be held. After commencement of the trial, the Prosecutor may, with the permission of the Trial Chamber, withdraw the charges.

10. Any warrant previously issued shall cease to have effect with respect to any charges which have not been confirmed by the Pre-Trial Chamber or which have been withdrawn by the Prosecutor.

11. Once the charges have been confirmed in accordance with this article, the Presidency shall constitute a Trial Chamber which, subject to paragraph 9 and to article 64, para-

graph 4, shall be responsible for the conduct of subsequent proceedings and may exercise any function of the Pre-Trial Chamber that is relevant and capable of application in those proceedings.

Part 6. The Trial

Article 62
Place of trial

Unless otherwise decided, the place of the trial shall be the seat of the Court.

Article 63
Trial in the presence of the accused

1. The accused shall be present during the trial.

2. If the accused, being present before the Court, continues to disrupt the trial, the Trial Chamber may remove the accused and shall make provision for him or her to observe the trial and instruct counsel from outside the courtroom, through the use of communications technology, if required. Such measures shall be taken only in exceptional circumstances after other reasonable alternatives have proved inadequate, and only for such duration as is strictly required.

Article 64
Functions and powers of the Trial Chamber

1. The functions and powers of the Trial Chamber set out in this article shall be exercised in accordance with this Statute and the Rules of Procedure and Evidence.

2. The Trial Chamber shall ensure that a trial is fair and expeditious and is conducted with full respect for the rights of the accused and due regard for the protection of victims and witnesses.

3. Upon assignment of a case for trial in accordance with this Statute, the Trial Chamber assigned to deal with the case shall:

(a) Confer with the parties and adopt such procedures as are necessary to facilitate the fair and expeditious conduct of the proceedings;

(b) Determine the language or languages to be used at trial; and

(c) Subject to any other relevant provisions of this Statute, provide for disclosure of documents or information not previously disclosed, sufficiently in advance of the commencement of the trial to enable adequate preparation for trial.

4. The Trial Chamber may, if necessary for its effective and fair functioning, refer preliminary issues to the Pre-Trial Chamber or, if necessary, to another available judge of the Pre-Trial Division.

5. Upon notice to the parties, the Trial Chamber may, as appropriate, direct that there be joinder or severance in respect of charges against more than one accused.

6. In performing its functions prior to trial or during the course of a trial, the Trial Chamber may, as necessary:

(a) Exercise any functions of the Pre-Trial Chamber referred to in article 61, paragraph 11;

(b) Require the attendance and testimony of witnesses and production of documents and other evidence by obtaining, if necessary, the assistance of States as provided in this Statute;

(c) Provide for the protection of confidential information;

(d) Order the production of evidence in addition to that already collected prior to the trial or presented during the trial by the parties;

(e) Provide for the protection of the accused, witnesses and victims; and

(f) Rule on any other relevant matters.

7. The trial shall be held in public. The Trial Chamber may, however, determine that special circumstances require that certain proceedings be in closed session for the purposes set forth in article 68, or to protect confidential or sensitive information to be given in evidence.

8. (a) At the commencement of the trial, the Trial Chamber shall have read to the accused the charges previously confirmed by the Pre-Trial Chamber. The Trial Chamber shall satisfy itself that the accused understands the nature of the charges. It shall afford him or her the opportunity to make an admission of guilt in accordance with article 65 or to plead not guilty.

(b) At the trial, the presiding judge may give directions for the conduct of proceedings, including to ensure that they are conducted in a fair and impartial manner. Subject to any directions of the presiding judge, the parties may submit evidence in accordance with the provisions of this Statute.

9. The Trial Chamber shall have, *inter alia,* the power on application of a party or on its own motion to:

(a) Rule on the admissibility or relevance of evidence; and

(b) Take all necessary steps to maintain order in the course of a hearing.

10. The Trial Chamber shall ensure that a complete record of the trial, which accurately reflects the proceedings, is made and that it is maintained and preserved by the Registrar.

Article 65
Proceedings on an admission of guilt

1. Where the accused makes an admission of guilt pursuant to article 64, paragraph 8 (a), the Trial Chamber shall determine whether:

(a) The accused understands the nature and consequences of the admission of guilt;

(b) The admission is voluntarily made by the accused after sufficient consultation with defence counsel; and

(c) The admission of guilt is supported by the facts of the case that are contained in:

(i) The charges brought by the Prosecutor and admitted by the accused;

(ii) Any materials presented by the Prosecutor which supplement the charges and which the accused accepts; and

(iii) Any other evidence, such as the testimony of witnesses, presented by the Prosecutor or the accused.

2. Where the Trial Chamber is satisfied that the matters referred to in paragraph 1 are established, it shall consider the admission of guilt, together with any additional evidence presented, as establishing all the essential facts that are required to prove the crime to which the admission of guilt relates, and may convict the accused of that crime.

3. Where the Trial Chamber is not satisfied that the matters referred to in paragraph 1 are established, it shall consider the admission of guilt as not having been made, in

which case it shall order that the trial be continued under the ordinary trial procedures provided by this Statute and may remit the case to another Trial Chamber.

4. Where the Trial Chamber is of the opinion that a more complete presentation of the facts of the case is required in the interests of justice, in particular the interests of the victims, the Trial Chamber may:

(a) Request the Prosecutor to present additional evidence, including the testimony of witnesses; or

(b) Order that the trial be continued under the ordinary trial procedures provided by this Statute, in which case it shall consider the admission of guilt as not having been made and may remit the case to another Trial Chamber.

5. Any discussions between the Prosecutor and the defence regarding modification of the charges, the admission of guilt or the penalty to be imposed shall not be binding on the Court.

Article 66
Presumption of innocence

1. Everyone shall be presumed innocent until proved guilty before the Court in accordance with the applicable law.

2. The onus is on the Prosecutor to prove the guilt of the accused.

3. In order to convict the accused, the Court must be convinced of the guilt of the accused beyond reasonable doubt.

Article 67
Rights of the accused

1. In the determination of any charge, the accused shall be entitled to a public hearing, having regard to the provisions of this Statute, to a fair hearing conducted impartially, and to the following minimum guarantees, in full equality:

(a) To be informed promptly and in detail of the nature, cause and content of the charge, in a language which the accused fully understands and speaks;

(b) To have adequate time and facilities for the preparation of the defence and to communicate freely with counsel of the accused's choosing in confidence;

(c) To be tried without undue delay;

(d) Subject to article 63, paragraph 2, to be present at the trial, to conduct the defence in person or through legal assistance of the accused's choosing, to be informed, if the accused does not have legal assistance, of this right and to have legal assistance assigned by the Court in any case where the interests of justice so require, and without payment if the accused lacks sufficient means to pay for it;

(e) To examine, or have examined, the witnesses against him or her and to obtain the attendance and examination of witnesses on his or her behalf under the same conditions as witnesses against him or her. The accused shall also be entitled to raise defences and to present other evidence admissible under this Statute;

(f) To have, free of any cost, the assistance of a competent interpreter and such translations as are necessary to meet the requirements of fairness, if any of the proceedings of or documents presented to the Court are not in a language which the accused fully understands and speaks;

(g) Not to be compelled to testify or to confess guilt and to remain silent, without such silence being a consideration in the determination of guilt or innocence;

(h) To make an unsworn oral or written statement in his or her defence; and

(i) Not to have imposed on him or her any reversal of the burden of proof or any onus of rebuttal.

2. In addition to any other disclosure provided for in this Statute, the Prosecutor shall, as soon as practicable, disclose to the defence evidence in the Prosecutor's possession or control which he or she believes shows or tends to show the innocence of the accused, or to mitigate the guilt of the accused, or which may affect the credibility of prosecution evidence. In case of doubt as to the application of this paragraph, the Court shall decide.

Article 68
Protection of the victims and witnesses and their participation in the proceedings

1. The Court shall take appropriate measures to protect the safety, physical and psychological well-being, dignity and privacy of victims and witnesses. In so doing, the Court shall have regard to all relevant factors, including age, gender as defined in article 7, paragraph 3, and health, and the nature of the crime, in particular, but not limited to, where the crime involves sexual or gender violence or violence against children. The Prosecutor shall take such measures particularly during the investigation and prosecution of such crimes. These measures shall not be prejudicial to or inconsistent with the rights of the accused and a fair and impartial trial.

2. As an exception to the principle of public hearings provided for in article 67, the Chambers of the Court may, to protect victims and witnesses or an accused, conduct any part of the proceedings in camera or allow the presentation of evidence by electronic or other special means. In particular, such measures shall be implemented in the case of a victim of sexual violence or a child who is a victim or a witness, unless otherwise ordered by the Court, having regard to all the circumstances, particularly the views of the victim or witness.

3. Where the personal interests of the victims are affected, the Court shall permit their views and concerns to be presented and considered at stages of the proceedings determined to be appropriate by the Court and in a manner which is not prejudicial to or inconsistent with the rights of the accused and a fair and impartial trial. Such views and concerns may be presented by the legal representatives of the victims where the Court considers it appropriate, in accordance with the Rules of Procedure and Evidence.

4. The Victims and Witnesses Unit may advise the Prosecutor and the Court on appropriate protective measures, security arrangements, counseling and assistance as referred to in article 43, paragraph 6.

5. Where the disclosure of evidence or information pursuant to this Statute may lead to the grave endangerment of the security of a witness or his or her family, the Prosecutor may, for the purposes of any proceedings conducted prior to the commencement of the trial, withhold such evidence or information and instead submit a summary thereof. Such measures shall be exercised in a manner which is not prejudicial to or inconsistent with the rights of the accused and a fair and impartial trial.

6. A State may make an application for necessary measures to be taken in respect of the protection of its servants or agents and the protection of confidential or sensitive information.

Article 69
Evidence

1. Before testifying, each witness shall, in accordance with the Rules of Procedure and Evidence, give an undertaking as to the truthfulness of the evidence to be given by that witness.

2. The testimony of a witness at trial shall be given in person, except to the extent provided by the measures set forth in article 68 or in the Rules of Procedure and Evidence. The Court may also permit the giving of *viva voce* (oral) or recorded testimony of a witness by means of video or audio technology, as well as the introduction of documents or written transcripts, subject to this Statute and in accordance with the Rules of Procedure and Evidence. These measures shall not be prejudicial to or inconsistent with the rights of the accused.

3. The parties may submit evidence relevant to the case, in accordance with article 64. The Court shall have the authority to request the submission of all evidence that it considers necessary for the determination of the truth.

4. The Court may rule on the relevance or admissibility of any evidence, taking into account, *inter alia*, the probative value of the evidence and any prejudice that such evidence may cause to a fair trial or to a fair evaluation of the testimony of a witness, in accordance with the Rules of Procedure and Evidence.

5. The Court shall respect and observe privileges on confidentiality as provided for in the Rules of Procedure and Evidence.

6. The Court shall not require proof of facts of common knowledge but may take judicial notice of them.

7. Evidence obtained by means of a violation of this Statute or internationally recognized human rights shall not be admissible if:

(a) The violation casts substantial doubt on the reliability of the evidence; or

(b) The admission of the evidence would be antithetical to and would seriously damage the integrity of the proceedings.

8. When deciding on the relevance or admissibility of evidence collected by a State, the Court shall not rule on the application of the State's national law.

Article 70
Offences against the administration of justice

1. The Court shall have jurisdiction over the following offences against its administration of justice when committed intentionally:

(a) Giving false testimony when under an obligation pursuant to article 69, paragraph 1, to tell the truth;

(b) Presenting evidence that the party knows is false or forged;

(c) Corruptly influencing a witness, obstructing or interfering with the attendance or testimony of a witness, retaliating against a witness for giving testimony or destroying, tampering with or interfering with the collection of evidence;

(d) Impeding, intimidating or corruptly influencing an official of the Court for the purpose of forcing or persuading the official not to perform, or to perform improperly, his or her duties;

(e) Retaliating against an official of the Court on account of duties performed by that or another official;

(f) Soliciting or accepting a bribe as an official of the Court in connection with his or her official duties.

2. The principles and procedures governing the Court's exercise of jurisdiction over offences under this article shall be those provided for in the Rules of Procedure and Evidence. The conditions for providing international cooperation to the Court with respect to its proceedings under this article shall be governed by the domestic laws of the requested State.

3. In the event of conviction, the Court may impose a term of imprisonment not exceeding five years, or a fine in accordance with the Rules of Procedure and Evidence, or both.

4. (a) Each State Party shall extend its criminal laws penalizing offences against the integrity of its own investigative or judicial process to offences against the administration of justice referred to in this article, committed on its territory, or by one of its nationals;

(b) Upon request by the Court, whenever it deems it proper, the State Party shall submit the case to its competent authorities for the purpose of prosecution. Those authorities shall treat such cases with diligence and devote sufficient resources to enable them to be conducted effectively.

Article 71
Sanctions for misconduct before the Court

1. The Court may sanction persons present before it who commit misconduct, including disruption of its proceedings or deliberate refusal to comply with its directions, by administrative measures other than imprisonment, such as temporary or permanent removal from the courtroom, a fine or other similar measures provided for in the Rules of Procedure and Evidence.

2. The procedures governing the imposition of the measures set forth in paragraph 1 shall be those provided for in the Rules of Procedure and Evidence.

Article 72
Protection of national security information

1. This article applies in any case where the disclosure of the information or documents of a State would, in the opinion of that State, prejudice its national security interests. Such cases include those falling within the scope of article 56, paragraphs 2 and 3, article 61, paragraph 3, article 64, paragraph 3, article 67, paragraph 2, article 68, paragraph 6, article 87, paragraph 6 and article 93, as well as cases arising at any other stage of the proceedings where such disclosure may be at issue.

2. This article shall also apply when a person who has been requested to give information or evidence has refused to do so or has referred the matter to the State on the ground that disclosure would prejudice the national security interests of a State and the State concerned confirms that it is of the opinion that disclosure would prejudice its national security interests.

3. Nothing in this article shall prejudice the requirements of confidentiality applicable under article 54, paragraph 3(e) and (f), or the application of article 73.

4. If a State learns that information or documents of the State are being, or are likely to be, disclosed at any stage of the proceedings, and it is of the opinion that disclosure would prejudice its national security interests, that State shall have the right to intervene in order to obtain resolution of the issue in accordance with this article.

5. If, in the opinion of a State, disclosure of information would prejudice its national security interests, all reasonable steps will be taken by the State, acting in conjunction with the Prosecutor, the defence or the Pre-Trial Chamber or Trial Chamber, as the case may be, to seek to resolve the matter by cooperative means. Such steps may include:

(a) Modification or clarification of the request;

(b) A determination by the Court regarding the relevance of the information or evidence sought, or a determination as to whether the evidence, though relevant, could be or has been obtained from a source other than the requested State;

(c) Obtaining the information or evidence from a different source or in a different form; or

(d) Agreement on conditions under which the assistance could be provided including, among other things, providing summaries or redactions, limitations on disclosure, use of *in camera* or *ex parte* proceedings, or other protective measures permissible under the Statute and the Rules of Procedure and Evidence.

6. Once all reasonable steps have been taken to resolve the matter through cooperative means, and if the State considers that there are no means or conditions under which the information or documents could be provided or disclosed without prejudice to its national security interests, it shall so notify the Prosecutor or the Court of the specific reasons for its decision, unless a specific description of the reasons would itself necessarily result in such prejudice to the State's national security interests.

7. Thereafter, if the Court determines that the evidence is relevant and necessary for the establishment of the guilt or innocence of the accused, the Court may undertake the following actions:

(a) Where disclosure of the information or document is sought pursuant to a request for cooperation under Part 9 or the circumstances described in paragraph 2, and the State has invoked the ground for refusal referred to in article 93, paragraph 4:

(i) The Court may, before making any conclusion referred to in subparagraph 7(a) (ii), request further consultations for the purpose of considering the State's representations, which may include, as appropriate, hearings *in camera* and *ex parte*;

(ii) If the Court concludes that, by invoking the ground for refusal under article 93, paragraph 4, in the circumstances of the case, the requested State is not acting in accordance with its obligations under this Statute, the Court may refer the matter in accordance with article 87, paragraph 7, specifying the reasons for its conclusion; and

(iii) The Court may make such inference in the trial of the accused as to the existence or non-existence of a fact, as may be appropriate in the circumstances; or

(b) In all other circumstances:

(i) Order disclosure; or

(ii) To the extent it does not order disclosure, make such inference in the trial of the accused as to the existence or non-existence of a fact, as may be appropriate in the circumstances.

Article 73
Third-party information or documents

If a State Party is requested by the Court to provide a document or information in its custody, possession or control, which was disclosed to it in confidence by a State, intergovernmental organization or international organization, it shall seek the consent of the originator to disclose that document or information. If the originator is a State Party, it shall either consent to disclosure of the information or document or undertake to resolve the issue of disclosure with the Court, subject to the provisions of article 72. If the originator is not a State Party and refuses to consent to disclosure, the requested State shall inform the Court that it is unable to provide the document or information because of a pre-existing obligation of confidentiality to the originator.

Article 74
Requirements for the decision

1. All the judges of the Trial Chamber shall be present at each stage of the trial and throughout their deliberations. The Presidency may, on a case-by-case basis, designate, as available, one or more alternate judges to be present at each stage of the trial and to replace a member of the Trial Chamber if that member is unable to continue attending.

2. The Trial Chamber's decision shall be based on its evaluation of the evidence and the entire proceedings. The decision shall not exceed the facts and circumstances described in the charges and any amendments to the charges. The Court may base its decision only on evidence submitted and discussed before it at the trial.

3. The judges shall attempt to achieve unanimity in their decision, failing which the decision shall be taken by a majority of the judges.

4. The deliberations of the Trial Chamber shall remain secret.

5. The decision shall be in writing and shall contain a full and reasoned statement of the Trial Chamber's findings on the evidence and conclusions. The Trial Chamber shall issue one decision. When there is no unanimity, the Trial Chamber's decision shall contain the views of the majority and the minority. The decision or a summary thereof shall be delivered in open court.

Article 75
Reparations to victims

1. The Court shall establish principles relating to reparations to, or in respect of, victims, including restitution, compensation and rehabilitation. On this basis, in its decision the Court may, either upon request or on its own motion in exceptional circumstances, determine the scope and extent of any damage, loss and injury to, or in respect of, victims and will state the principles on which it is acting.

2. The Court may make an order directly against a convicted person specifying appropriate reparations to, or in respect of, victims, including restitution, compensation and rehabilitation. Where appropriate, the Court may order that the award for reparations be made through the Trust Fund provided for in article 79.

3. Before making an order under this article, the Court may invite and shall take account of representations from or on behalf of the convicted person, victims, other interested persons or interested States.

4. In exercising its power under this article, the Court may, after a person is convicted of a crime within the jurisdiction of the Court, determine whether, in order to give effect to an order which it may make under this article, it is necessary to seek measures under article 93, paragraph 1.

5. A State Party shall give effect to a decision under this article as if the provisions of article 109 were applicable to this article.

6. Nothing in this article shall be interpreted as prejudicing the rights of victims under national or international law.

Article 76
Sentencing

1. In the event of a conviction, the Trial Chamber shall consider the appropriate sentence to be imposed and shall take into account the evidence presented and submissions made during the trial that are relevant to the sentence.

2. Except where article 65 applies and before the completion of the trial, the Trial Chamber may on its own motion and shall, at the request of the Prosecutor or the accused, hold a further hearing to hear any additional evidence or submissions relevant to the sentence, in accordance with the Rules of Procedure and Evidence.

3. Where paragraph 2 applies, any representations under article 75 shall be heard during the further hearing referred to in paragraph 2 and, if necessary, during any additional hearing.

4. The sentence shall be pronounced in public and, wherever possible, in the presence of the accused.

Part 7. Penalties

Article 77
Applicable penalties

1. Subject to article 110, the Court may impose one of the following penalties on a person convicted of a crime referred to in article 5 of this Statute:

   (a) Imprisonment for a specified number of years, which may not exceed a maximum of 30 years; or

   (b) A term of life imprisonment when justified by the extreme gravity of the crime and the individual circumstances of the convicted person.

2. In addition to imprisonment, the Court may order:

   (a) A fine under the criteria provided for in the Rules of Procedure and Evidence;

   (b) A forfeiture of proceeds, property and assets derived directly or indirectly from that crime, without prejudice to the rights of *bona fide* third parties.

Article 78
Determination of the sentence

1. In determining the sentence, the Court shall, in accordance with the Rules of Procedure and Evidence, take into account such factors as the gravity of the crime and the individual circumstances of the convicted person.

2. In imposing a sentence of imprisonment, the Court shall deduct the time, if any, previously spent in detention in accordance with an order of the Court. The Court may deduct any time otherwise spent in detention in connection with conduct underlying the crime.

3. When a person has been convicted of more than one crime, the Court shall pronounce a sentence for each crime and a joint sentence specifying the total period of imprisonment. This period shall be no less than the highest individual sentence pronounced and shall not exceed 30 years imprisonment or a sentence of life imprisonment in conformity with article 77, paragraph 1(b).

Article 79
Trust Fund

1. A Trust Fund shall be established by decision of the Assembly of States Parties for the benefit of victims of crimes within the jurisdiction of the Court, and of the families of such victims.

2. The Court may order money and other property collected through fines or forfeiture to be transferred, by order of the Court, to the Trust Fund.

3. The Trust Fund shall be managed according to criteria to be determined by the Assembly of States Parties.

Article 80
Non-prejudice to national application of penalties and national laws

Nothing in this Part affects the application by States of penalties prescribed by their national law, nor the law of States which do not provide for penalties prescribed in this Part.

Part 8. Appeal And Revision

Article 81
Appeal against decision of acquittal or conviction or against sentence

1. A decision under article 74 may be appealed in accordance with the Rules of Procedure and Evidence as follows:

   (a) The Prosecutor may make an appeal on any of the following grounds:

   (i) Procedural error,

   (ii) Error of fact, or

   (iii) Error of law;

   (b) The convicted person, or the Prosecutor on that person's behalf, may make an appeal on any of the following grounds:

   (i) Procedural error,

   (ii) Error of fact,

   (iii) Error of law, or

   (iv) Any other ground that affects the fairness or reliability of the proceedings or decision.

2. (a) A sentence may be appealed, in accordance with the Rules of Procedure and Evidence, by the Prosecutor or the convicted person on the ground of disproportion between the crime and the sentence;

   (b) If on an appeal against sentence the Court considers that there are grounds on which the conviction might be set aside, wholly or in part, it may invite the Prosecutor and the convicted person to submit grounds under article 81, paragraph 1(a) or (b), and may render a decision on conviction in accordance with article 83;

   (c) The same procedure applies when the Court, on an appeal against conviction only, considers that there are grounds to reduce the sentence under paragraph 2(a).

3. (a) Unless the Trial Chamber orders otherwise, a convicted person shall remain in custody pending an appeal;

(b) When a convicted person's time in custody exceeds the sentence of imprisonment imposed, that person shall be released, except that if the Prosecutor is also appealing, the release may be subject to the conditions under subparagraph (c) below;

(c) In case of an acquittal, the accused shall be released immediately, subject to the following:

(i) Under exceptional circumstances, and having regard, *inter alia*, to the concrete risk of flight, the seriousness of the offence charged and the probability of success on appeal, the Trial Chamber, at the request of the Prosecutor, may maintain the detention of the person pending appeal;

(ii) A decision by the Trial Chamber under subparagraph (c)(i) may be appealed in accordance with the Rules of Procedure and Evidence.

4. Subject to the provisions of paragraph 3(a) and (b), execution of the decision or sentence shall be suspended during the period allowed for appeal and for the duration of the appeal proceedings.

Article 82
Appeal against other decisions

1. Either party may appeal any of the following decisions in accordance with the Rules of Procedure and evidence:

(a) A decision with respect to jurisdiction or admissibility;

(b) A decision granting or denying release of the person being investigated or prosecuted;

(c) A decision of the Pre-Trial Chamber to act on its own initiative under article 56, paragraph 3;

(d) A decision that involves an issue that would significantly affect the fair and expeditious conduct of the proceedings or the outcome of the trial, and for which, in the opinion of the Pre-Trial or Trial Chamber, an immediate resolution by the Appeals Chamber may materially advance the proceedings.

2. A decision of the Pre-Trial Chamber under article 57, paragraph 3(d), may be appealed against by the State concerned or by the Prosecutor, with the leave of the Pre-Trial Chamber. The appeal shall be heard on an expedited basis.

3. An appeal shall not of itself have suspensive effect unless the Appeals Chamber so orders, upon request, in accordance with the Rules of Procedure and Evidence.

4. A legal representative of the victims, the convicted person or a *bona fide* owner of property adversely affected by an order under article 75 may appeal against the order for reparations, as provided in the Rules of Procedure and Evidence.

Article 83
Proceedings on appeal

1. For the purposes of proceedings under article 81 and this article, the Appeals Chamber shall have all the powers of the Trial Chamber.

2. If the Appeals Chamber finds that the proceedings appealed from were unfair in a way that affected the reliability of the decision or sentence, or that the decision or sentence appealed from was materially affected by error of fact or law or procedural error, it may:

(a) Reverse or amend the decision or sentence; or

(b) Order a new trial before a different Trial Chamber.

For these purposes, the Appeals Chamber may remand a factual issue to the original Trial Chamber for it to determine the issue and to report back accordingly, or may itself call evidence to determine the issue. When the decision or sentence has been appealed only by the person convicted, or the Prosecutor on that person's behalf, it cannot be amended to his or her detriment.

3. If in an appeal against sentence the Appeals Chamber finds that the sentence is disproportionate to the crime, it may vary the sentence in accordance with Part 7.

4. The judgment of the Appeals Chamber shall be taken by a majority of the judges and shall be delivered in open court. The judgment shall state the reasons on which it is based. When there is no unanimity, the judgment of the Appeals Chamber shall contain the views of the majority and the minority, but a judge may deliver a separate or dissenting opinion on a question of law.

5. The Appeals Chamber may deliver its judgment in the absence of the person acquitted or convicted.

Article 84
Revision of conviction or sentence

1. The convicted person or, after death, spouses, children, parents or one person alive at the time of the accused's death who has been given express written instructions from the accused to bring such a claim, or the Prosecutor on the person's behalf, may apply to the Appeals Chamber to revise the final judgment of conviction or sentence on the grounds that:

(a) New evidence has been discovered that:

(i) Was not available at the time of trial, and such unavailability was not wholly or partially attributable to the party making application; and

(ii) Is sufficiently important that had it been proved at trial it would have been likely to have resulted in a different verdict;

(b) It has been newly discovered that decisive evidence, taken into account at trial and upon which the conviction depends, was false, forged or falsified;

(c) One or more of the judges who participated in conviction or confirmation of the charges has committed, in that case, an act of serious misconduct or serious breach of duty of sufficient gravity to justify the removal of that judge or those judges from office under article 46.

2. The Appeals Chamber shall reject the application if it considers it to be unfounded. If it determines that the application is meritorious, it may, as appropriate:

(a) Reconvene the original Trial Chamber;

(b) Constitute a new Trial Chamber; or

(c) Retain jurisdiction over the matter,

Article 85
Compensation to an arrested or convicted person

1. Anyone who has been the victim of unlawful arrest or detention shall have an enforceable right to compensation.

2. When a person has by a final decision been convicted of a criminal offence, and when subsequently his or her conviction has been reversed on the ground that a new or

newly discovered fact shows conclusively that there has been a miscarriage of justice, the person who has suffered punishment as a result of such conviction shall be compensated according to law, unless it is proved that the non-disclosure of the unknown fact in time is wholly or partly attributable to him or her.

3. In exceptional circumstances, where the Court finds conclusive facts showing that there has been a grave and manifest miscarriage of justice, it may in its discretion award compensation, according to the criteria provided in the Rules of Procedure and Evidence, to a person who has been released from detention following a final decision of acquittal or a termination of the proceedings for that reason.

Part 9. International Cooperation And Judicial Assistance

Article 86
General obligation to cooperate

States Parties shall, in accordance with the provisions of this Statute, cooperate fully with the Court in its investigation and prosecution of crimes within the jurisdiction of the Court.

Article 87
Requests for cooperation: general provisions

1. (a) The Court shall have the authority to make requests to States Parties for cooperation. The requests shall be transmitted through the diplomatic channel or any other appropriate channel as may be designated by each State Party upon ratification, acceptance, approval or accession.

Subsequent changes to the designation shall be made by each State Party in accordance with the Rules of Procedure and Evidence.

(b) When appropriate, without prejudice to the provisions of subparagraph (a), requests may also be transmitted through the International Criminal Police Organization or any appropriate regional organization.

2. Requests for cooperation and any documents supporting the request shall either be in or be accompanied by a translation into an official language of the requested State or one of the working languages of the Court, in accordance with the choice made by that State upon ratification, acceptance, approval or accession.

Subsequent changes to this choice shall be made in accordance with the Rules of Procedure and Evidence.

3. The requested State shall keep confidential a request for cooperation and any documents supporting the request, except to the extent that the disclosure is necessary for execution of the request.

4. In relation to any request for assistance presented under this Part, the Court may take such measures, including measures related to the protection of information, as may be necessary to ensure the safety or physical or psychological well-being of any victims, potential witnesses and their families. The Court may request that any information that is made available under this Part shall be provided and handled in a manner that protects the safety and physical or psychological well-being of any victims, potential witnesses and their families.

5. (a) The Court may invite any State not party to this Statute to provide assistance under this Part on the basis of an *ad hoc* arrangement, an agreement with such State or any other appropriate basis.

(b) Where a State not party to this Statute, which has entered into an *ad hoc* arrangement or an agreement with the Court, fails to cooperate with requests pursuant to any such arrangement or agreement, the Court may so inform the Assembly of States Parties or, where the Security Council referred the matter to the Court, the Security Council.

6. The Court may ask any intergovernmental organization to provide information or documents. The Court may also ask for other forms of cooperation and assistance which may be agreed upon with such an organization and which are in accordance with its competence or mandate.

7. Where a State Party fails to comply with a request to cooperate by the Court contrary to the provisions of this Statute, thereby preventing the Court from exercising its functions and powers under this Statute, the Court may make a finding to that effect and refer the matter to the Assembly of States Parties or, where the Security Council referred the matter to the Court, to the Security Council.

Article 88
Availability of procedures under national law

States Parties shall ensure that there are procedures available under their national law for all of the forms of cooperation which are specified under this Part.

Article 89
Surrender of persons to the Court

1. The Court may transmit a request for the arrest and surrender of a person, together with the material supporting the request outlined in article 91, to any State on the territory of which that person may be found and shall request the cooperation of that State in the arrest and surrender of such a person. States Parties shall, in accordance with the provisions of this Part and the procedure under their national law, comply with requests for arrest and surrender.

2. Where the person sought for surrender brings a challenge before a national court on the basis of the principle of *ne bis in idem* as provided in article 20, the requested State shall immediately consult with the Court to determine if there has been a relevant ruling on admissibility. If the case is admissible, the requested State shall proceed with the execution of the request. If an admissibility ruling is pending, the requested State may postpone the execution of the request for surrender of the person until the Court makes a determination on admissibility.

3. (a) A State Party shall authorize, in accordance with its national procedural law, transportation through its territory of a person being surrendered to the Court by another State, except where transit through that State would impede or delay the surrender.

(b) A request by the Court for transit shall be transmitted in accordance with article 87. The request for transit shall contain:

(i) A description of the person being transported;

(ii) A brief statement of the facts of the case and their legal characterization; and

(iii) The warrant for arrest and surrender;

(c) A person being transported shall be detained in custody during the period of transit;

(d) No authorization is required if the person is transported by air and no landing is scheduled on the territory of the transit State;

(e) If an unscheduled landing occurs on the territory of the transit State, that State may require a request for transit from the Court as provided for in subparagraph (b). The transit State shall detain the person being transported until the request for transit is received and the transit is effected, provided that detention for purposes of this subparagraph may not be extended beyond 96 hours from the unscheduled landing unless the request is received within that time.

4. If the person sought is being proceeded against or is serving a sentence in the requested State for a crime different from that for which surrender to the Court is sought, the requested State, after making its decision to grant the request, shall consult with the Court.

Article 90
Competing requests

1. A State Party which receives a request from the Court for the surrender of a person under article 89 shall, if it also receives a request from any other State for the extradition of the same person for the same conduct which forms the basis of the crime for which the Court seeks the person's surrender, notify the Court and the requesting State of that fact.

2. Where the requesting State is a State Party, the requested State shall give priority to the request from the Court if:

(a) The Court has, pursuant to article 18 or 19, made a determination that the case in respect of which surrender is sought is admissible and that determination takes into account the investigation or prosecution conducted by the requesting State in respect of its request for extradition; or

(b) The Court makes the determination described in subparagraph (a) pursuant to the requested State's notification under paragraph 1.

3. Where a determination under paragraph 2(a) has not been made, the requested State may, at its discretion, pending the determination of the Court under paragraph 2(b), proceed to deal with the request for extradition from the requesting State but shall not extradite the person until the Court has determined that the case is inadmissible. The Court's determination shall be made on an expedited basis.

4. If the requesting State is a State not Party to this Statute the requested State, if it is not under an international obligation to extradite the person to the requesting State, shall give priority to the request for surrender from the Court, if the Court has determined that the case is admissible.

5. Where a case under paragraph 4 has not been determined to be admissible by the Court, the requested State may, at its discretion, proceed to deal with the request for extradition from the requesting State.

6. In cases where paragraph 4 applies except that the requested State is under an existing international obligation to extradite the person to the requesting State not Party to this Statute, the requested State shall determine whether to surrender the person to the Court or extradite the person to the requesting State. In making its decision, the requested State shall consider all the relevant factors, including but not limited to:

(a) The respective dates of the requests;

(b) The interests of the requesting State including, where relevant, whether the crime was committed in its territory and the nationality of the victims and of the person sought; and

(c) The possibility of subsequent surrender between the Court and the requesting State.

7. Where a State Party which receives a request from the Court for the surrender of a person also receives a request from any State for the extradition of the same person for conduct other than that which constitutes the crime for which the Court seeks the person's surrender:

(a) The requested State shall, if it is not under an existing international obligation to extradite the person to the requesting State, give priority to the request from the Court;

(b) The requested State shall, if it is under an existing international obligation to extradite the person to the requesting State, determine whether to surrender the person to the Court or to extradite the person to the requesting State. In making its decision, the requested State shall consider all the relevant factors, including but not limited to those set out in paragraph 6, but shall give special consideration to the relative nature and gravity of the conduct in question.

8. Where pursuant to a notification under this article, the Court has determined a case to be inadmissible, and subsequently extradition to the requesting State is refused, the requested State shall notify the Court of this decision.

Article 91
Contents of request for arrest and surrender

1. A request for arrest and surrender shall be made in writing. In urgent cases, a request may be made by any medium capable of delivering a written record, provided that the request shall be confirmed through the channel provided for in article 87, paragraph 1(a).

2. In the case of a request for the arrest and surrender of a person for whom a warrant of arrest has been issued by the Pre-Trial Chamber under article 58, the request shall contain or be supported by:

(a) Information describing the person sought, sufficient to identify the person, and information as to that person's probable location;

(b) A copy of the warrant of arrest; and

(c) Such documents, statements or information as may be necessary to meet the requirements for the surrender process in the requested State, except that those requirements should not be more burdensome than those applicable to requests for extradition pursuant to treaties or arrangements between the requested State and other States and should, if possible, be less burdensome, taking into account the distinct nature of the Court.

3. In the case of a request for the arrest and surrender of a person already convicted, the request shall contain or be supported by:

(a) A copy of any warrant of arrest for that person;

(b) A copy of the judgment of conviction;

(c) Information to demonstrate that the person sought is the one referred to in the judgment of conviction; and

(d) If the person sought has been sentenced, a copy of the sentence imposed and, in the case of a sentence for imprisonment, a statement of any time already served and the time remaining to be served.

4. Upon the request of the Court, a State Party shall consult with the Court, either generally or with respect to a specific matter, regarding any requirements under its na-

tional law that may apply under paragraph 2(c). During the consultations, the State Party shall advise the Court of the specific requirements of its national law.

Article 92
Provisional arrest

1. In urgent cases, the Court may request the provisional arrest of the person sought, pending presentation of the request for surrender and the documents supporting the request as specified in article 91.

2. The request for provisional arrest shall be made by any medium capable of delivering a written record and shall contain:

(a) Information describing the person sought, sufficient to identify the person, and information as to that person's probable location;

(b) A concise statement of the crimes for which the person's arrest is sought and of the facts which are alleged to constitute those crimes, including, where possible, the date and location of the crime;

(c) A statement of the existence of a warrant of arrest or a judgement of conviction against the person sought; and

(d) A statement that a request for surrender of the person sought will follow.

3. A person who is provisionally arrested may be released from custody if the requested State has not received the request for surrender and the documents supporting the request as specified in article 91 within the time limits specified in the Rules of Procedure and Evidence. However, the person may consent to surrender before the expiration of this period if permitted by the law of the requested State. In such a case, the requested State shall proceed to surrender the person to the Court as soon as possible.

4. The fact that the person sought has been released from custody pursuant to paragraph 3 shall not prejudice the subsequent arrest and surrender of that person if the request for surrender and the documents supporting the request are delivered at a later date.

Article 93
Other forms of cooperation

1. States Parties shall, in accordance with the provisions of this Part and under procedures of national law, comply with requests by the Court to provide the following assistance in relation to investigations or prosecutions:

(a) The identification and whereabouts of persons or the location of items;

(b) The taking of evidence, including testimony under oath, and the production of evidence, including expert opinions and reports necessary to the Court;

(c) The questioning of any person being investigated or prosecuted;

(d) The service of documents, including judicial documents;

(e) Facilitating the voluntary appearance of persons as witnesses or experts before the Court;

(f) The temporary transfer of persons as provided in paragraph 7;

(g) The examination of places or sites, including the exhumation and examination of grave sites;

(h) The execution of searches and seizures;

(i) The provision of records and documents, including official records and documents;

(j) The protection of victims and witnesses and the preservation of evidence;

(k) The identification, tracing and freezing or seizure of proceeds, property and assets and instrumentalities of crimes for the purpose of eventual forfeiture, without prejudice to the rights of *bona fide* third parties; and

(l) Any other type of assistance which is not prohibited by the law of the requested State, with a view to facilitating the investigation and prosecution of crimes within the jurisdiction of the Court.

2. The Court shall have the authority to provide an assurance to a witness or an expert appearing before the Court that he or she will not be prosecuted, detained or subjected to any restriction of personal freedom by the Court in respect of any act or omission that preceded the departure of that person from the requested State.

3. Where execution of a particular measure of assistance detailed in a request presented under paragraph 1, is prohibited in the requested State on the basis of an existing fundamental legal principle of general application, the requested State shall promptly consult with the Court to try to resolve the matter. In the consultations, consideration should be given to whether the assistance can be rendered in another manner or subject to conditions. If after consultations the matter cannot be resolved, the Court shall modify the request as necessary.

4. In accordance with article 72, a State Party may deny a request for assistance, in whole or in part, only if the request concerns the production of any documents or disclosure of evidence which relates to its national security.

5. Before denying a request for assistance under paragraph 1(l), the requested State shall consider whether the assistance can be provided subject to specified conditions, or whether the assistance can be provided at a later date or in an alternative manner, provided that if the Court or the Prosecutor accepts the assistance subject to conditions, the Court or the Prosecutor shall abide by them.

6. If a request for assistance is denied, the requested State Party shall promptly inform the Court or the Prosecutor of the reasons for such denial.

7. (a) The Court may request the temporary transfer of a person in custody for purposes of identification or for obtaining testimony or other assistance. The person may be transferred if the following conditions are fulfilled:

(i) The person freely gives his or her informed consent to the transfer; and

(ii) The requested State agrees to the transfer, subject to such conditions as that State and the Court may agree.

(b) The person being transferred shall remain in custody. When the purposes of the transfer have been fulfilled, the Court shall return the person without delay to the requested State.

8. (a) The Court shall ensure the confidentiality of documents and information, except as required for the investigation and proceedings described in the request.

(b) The requested State may, when necessary, transmit documents or information to the Prosecutor on a confidential basis. The Prosecutor may then use them solely for the purpose of generating new evidence.

(c) The requested State may, on its own motion or at the request of the Prosecutor, subsequently consent to the disclosure of such documents or information. They may then be used as evidence pursuant to the provisions of Parts 5 and 6 and in accordance with the Rules of Procedure and Evidence.

9. (a) (i) In the event that a State Party receives competing requests, other than for surrender or extradition, from the Court and from another State pursuant to an international obligation, the State Party shall endeavour, in consultation with the Court and the other State, to meet both requests, if necessary by postponing or attaching conditions to one or the other request.

(ii) Failing that, competing requests shall be resolved in accordance with the principles established in article 90.

(b) Where, however, the request from the Court concerns information, property or persons which are subject to the control of a third State or an international organization by virtue of an international agreement, the requested States shall so inform the Court, and the Court shall direct its request to the third State or international organization.

10. (a) The Court may, upon request, cooperate with and provide assistance to a State Party conducting an investigation into or trial in respect of conduct which constitutes a crime within the jurisdiction of the Court or which constitutes a serious crime under the national law of the requesting State.

(b) (i) The assistance provided under subparagraph (a) shall include, *inter alia*:

a. The transmission of statements, documents or other types of evidence obtained in the course of an investigation or a trial conducted by the Court; and

b. The questioning of any person detained by order of the Court;

(ii) In the case of assistance under subparagraph (b)(i) a:

a. If the documents or other types of evidence have been obtained with the assistance of a State, such transmission shall require the consent of that State;

b. If the statements, documents or other types of evidence have been provided by a witness or expert, such transmission shall be subject to the provisions of article 68.

(c) The Court may, under the conditions set out in this paragraph, grant a request for assistance under this paragraph from a State which is not a Party to this Statute.

Article 94
Postponement of execution of a request in respect of ongoing investigation or prosecution

1. If the immediate execution of a request would interfere with an ongoing investigation or prosecution of a case different from that to which the request relates, the requested State may postpone the execution of the request for a period of time agreed upon with the Court. However, the postponement shall be no longer than is necessary to complete the relevant investigation or prosecution in the requested State. Before making a decision to postpone, the requested State should consider whether the assistance may be immediately provided subject to certain conditions.

2. If a decision to postpone is taken pursuant to paragraph 1, the Prosecutor may, however, seek measures to preserve evidence, pursuant to article 93, paragraph 1(j).

Article 95
Postponement of execution of a request in respect of an admissibility challenge

Where there is an admissibility challenge under consideration by the Court pursuant to article 18 or 19, the requested State may postpone the execution of a request under this Part pending a determination by the Court, unless the Court has specifically ordered that the Prosecutor may pursue the collection of such evidence pursuant to article 18 or 19.

Article 96
Contents of request for other forms of assistance under article 93

1. A request for other forms of assistance referred to in article 93 shall be made in writing. In urgent cases, a request may be made by any medium capable of delivering a written record, provided that the request shall be confirmed through the channel provided for in article 87, paragraph 1(a).

2. The request shall, as applicable, contain or be supported by the following:

(a) A concise statement of the purpose of the request and the assistance sought, including the legal basis and the grounds for the request;

(b) As much detailed information as possible about the location or identification of any person or place that must be found or identified in order for the assistance sought to be provided;

(c) A concise statement of the essential facts underlying the request;

(d) The reasons for and details of any procedure or requirement to be followed;

(e) Such information as may be required under the law of the requested State in order to execute the request; and

(f) Any other information relevant in order for the assistance sought to be provided.

3. Upon the request of the Court, a State Party shall consult with the Court, either generally or with respect to a specific matter, regarding any requirements under its national law that may apply under paragraph 2(e). During the consultations, the State Party shall advise the Court of the specific requirements of its national law.

4. The provisions of this article shall, where applicable, also apply in respect of a request for assistance made to the Court.

Article 97
Consultations

Where a State Party receives a request under this Part in relation to which it identifies problems which may impede or prevent the execution of the request, that State shall consult with the Court without delay in order to resolve the matter. Such problems may include, *inter alia*:

(a) Insufficient information to execute the request;

(b) In the case of a request for surrender, the fact that despite best efforts, the person sought cannot be located or that the investigation conducted has determined that the person in the requested State is clearly not the person named in the warrant; or

(c) The fact that execution of the request in its current form would require the requested State to breach a pre-existing treaty obligation undertaken with respect to another State.

Article 98
Cooperation with respect to waiver of immunity and consent to surrender

1. The Court may not proceed with a request for surrender or assistance which would require the requested State to act inconsistently with its obligations under international law with respect to the State or diplomatic immunity of a person or property of a third

State, unless the Court can first obtain the cooperation of that third State for the waiver of the immunity.

2. The Court may not proceed with a request for surrender which would require the requested State to act inconsistently with its obligations under international agreements pursuant to which the consent of a sending State is required to surrender a person of that State to the Court, unless the Court can first obtain the cooperation of the sending State for the giving of consent for the surrender.

Article 99
Execution of requests under articles 93 and 96

1. Requests for assistance shall be executed in accordance with the relevant procedure under the law of the requested State and, unless prohibited by such law, in the manner specified in the request, including following any procedure outlined therein or permitting persons specified in the request to be present at and assist in the execution process.

2. In the case of an urgent request, the documents or evidence produced in response shall, at the request of the Court, be sent urgently.

3. Replies from the requested State shall be transmitted in their original language and form.

4. Without prejudice to other articles in this Part, where it is necessary for the successful execution of a request which can be executed without any compulsory measures, including specifically the interview of or taking evidence from a person on a voluntary basis, including doing so without the presence of the authorities of the requested State Party if it is essential for the request to be executed, and the examination without modification of a public site or other public place, the Prosecutor may execute such request directly on the territory of a State as follows:

(a) When the State Party requested is a State on the territory of which the crime is alleged to have been committed, and there has been a determination of admissibility pursuant to article 18 or 19, the Prosecutor may directly execute such request following all possible consultations with the requested State Party;

(b) In other cases, the Prosecutor may execute such request following consultations with the requested State Party and subject to any reasonable conditions or concerns raised by that State Party. Where the requested State Party identifies problems with the execution of a request pursuant to this subparagraph it shall, without delay, consult with the Court to resolve the matter.

5. Provisions allowing a person heard or examined by the Court under article 72 to invoke restrictions designed to prevent disclosure of confidential information connected with national security shall also apply to the execution of requests for assistance under this article.

Article 100
Costs

1. The ordinary costs for execution of requests in the territory of the requested State shall be borne by that State, except for the following, which shall be borne by the Court:

(a) Costs associated with the travel and security of witnesses and experts or the transfer under article 93 of persons in custody;

(b) Costs of translation, interpretation and transcription;

(c) Travel and subsistence costs of the judges, the Prosecutor, the Deputy Prosecutors, the Registrar, the Deputy Registrar and staff of any organ of the Court;

(d) Costs of any expert opinion or report requested by the Court;

(e) Costs associated with the transport of a person being surrendered to the Court by a custodial State; and

(f) Following consultations, any extraordinary costs that may result from the execution of a request.

2. The provisions of paragraph 1 shall, as appropriate, apply to requests from States Parties to the Court. In that case, the Court shall bear the ordinary costs of execution.

Article 101
Rule of Speciality

1. A person surrendered to the Court under this Statute shall not be proceeded against, punished or detained for any conduct committed prior to surrender, other than the conduct or course of conduct which forms the basis of the crimes for which that person has been surrendered.

2. The Court may request a waiver of the requirements of paragraph 1 from the State which surrendered the person to the Court and, if necessary, the Court shall provide additional information in accordance with article 91. States Parties shall have the authority to provide a waiver to the Court and should endeavour to do so.

Article 102
Use of terms

For the purposes of this Statute:

(a) "surrender" means the delivering up of a person by a State to the Court, pursuant to this Statute.

(b) "extradition" means the delivering up of a person by one State to another as provided by treaty, convention or national legislation.

Part 10. Enforcement

Article 103
Role of States in enforcement of sentences of imprisonment

1. (a) A sentence of imprisonment shall be served in a State designated by the Court from a list of States which have indicated to the Court their willingness to accept sentenced persons.

(b) At the time of declaring its willingness to accept sentenced persons, a State may attach conditions to its acceptance as agreed by the Court and in accordance with this Part.

(c) A State designated in a particular case shall promptly inform the Court whether it accepts the Court's designation.

2. (a) The State of enforcement shall notify the Court of any circumstances, including the exercise of any conditions agreed under paragraph 1, which could materially affect the terms or extent of the imprisonment. The Court shall be given at least 45 days' notice of any such known or foreseeable circumstances. During this period, the State of enforcement shall take no action that might prejudice its obligations under article 110.

(b) Where the Court cannot agree to the circumstances referred to in subparagraph (a), it shall notify the State of enforcement and proceed in accordance with article 104, paragraph 1.

3. In exercising its discretion to make a designation under paragraph 1, the Court shall take into account the following:

(a) The principle that States Parties should share the responsibility for enforcing sentences of imprisonment, in accordance with principles of equitable distribution, as provided in the Rules of Procedure and Evidence;

(b) The application of widely accepted international treaty standards governing the treatment of prisoners;

(c) The views of the sentenced person;

(d) The nationality of the sentenced person;

(e) Such other factors regarding the circumstances of the crime or the person sentenced, or the effective enforcement of the sentence, as may be appropriate in designating the State of enforcement.

4. If no State is designated under paragraph 1, the sentence of imprisonment shall be served in a prison facility made available by the host State, in accordance with the conditions set out in the headquarters agreement referred to in article 3, paragraph 2. In such a case, the costs arising out of the enforcement of a sentence of imprisonment shall be borne by the Court.

Article 104
Change in designation of State of enforcement

1. The Court may, at any time, decide to transfer a sentenced person to a prison of another State.

2. A sentenced person may, at any time, apply to the Court to be transferred from the State of enforcement.

Article 105
Enforcement of the sentence

1. Subject to conditions which a State may have specified in accordance with article 103, paragraph 1(b), the sentence of imprisonment shall be binding on the States Parties, which shall in no case modify it.

2. The Court alone shall have the right to decide any application for appeal and revision. The State of enforcement shall not impede the making of any such application by a sentenced person.

Article 106
Supervision of enforcement of sentences and conditions of imprisonment

1. The enforcement of a sentence of imprisonment shall be subject to the supervision of the Court and shall be consistent with widely accepted international treaty standards governing treatment of prisoners.

2. The conditions of imprisonment shall be governed by the law of the State of enforcement and shall be consistent with widely accepted international treaty standards governing treatment of prisoners; in no case shall such conditions be more or less favourable than those available to prisoners convicted of similar offences in the State of enforcement.

3. Communications between a sentenced person and the Court shall be unimpeded and confidential.

Article 107
Transfer of the person upon completion of sentence

1. Following completion of the sentence, a person who is not a national of the State of enforcement may, in accordance with the law of the State of enforcement, be transferred to a State which is obliged to receive him or her, or to another State which agrees to receive him or her, taking into account any wishes of the person to be transferred to that State, unless the State of enforcement authorizes the person to remain in its territory.

2. If no State bears the costs arising out of transferring the person to another State pursuant to paragraph 1, such costs shall be borne by the Court.

3. Subject to the provisions of article 108, the State of enforcement may also, in accordance with its national law, extradite or otherwise surrender the person to a State which has requested the extradition or surrender of the person for purposes of trial or enforcement of a sentence.

Article 108
Limitation on the prosecution or punishment of other offences

1. A sentenced person in the custody of the State of enforcement shall not be subject to prosecution or punishment or to extradition to a third State for any conduct engaged in prior to that person's delivery to the State of enforcement, unless such prosecution, punishment or extradition has been approved by the Court at the request of the State of enforcement.

2. The Court shall decide the matter after having heard the views of the sentenced person.

3. Paragraph 1 shall cease to apply if the sentenced person remains voluntarily for more than 30 days in the territory of the State of enforcement after having served the full sentence imposed by the Court, or returns to the territory of that State after having left it.

Article 109
Enforcement of fines and forfeiture measures

1. States Parties shall give effect to fines or forfeitures ordered by the Court under Part 7, without prejudice to the rights of *bona fide* third parties, and in accordance with the procedure of their national law.

2. If a State Party is unable to give effect to an order for forfeiture, it shall take measures to recover the value of the proceeds, property or assets ordered by the Court to be forfeited, without prejudice to the rights of *bona fide* third parties.

3. Property, or the proceeds of the sale of real property or, where appropriate, the sale of other property, which is obtained by a State Party as a result of its enforcement of a judgement of the Court shall be transferred to the Court.

Article 110
Review by the Court concerning reduction of sentence

1. The State of enforcement shall not release the person before expiry of the sentence pronounced by the Court.

2. The Court alone shall have the right to decide any reduction of sentence, and shall rule on the matter after having heard the person.

3. When the person has served two thirds of the sentence, or 25 years in the case of life imprisonment, the Court shall review the sentence to determine whether it should be reduced. Such a review shall not be conducted before that time.

4. In its review under paragraph 3, the Court may reduce the sentence if it finds that one or more of the following factors are present:

(a) The early and continuing willingness of the person to cooperate with the Court in its investigations and prosecutions;

(b) The voluntary assistance of the person in enabling the enforcement of the judgements and orders of the Court in other cases, and in particular providing assistance in locating assets subject to orders of fine, forfeiture or reparation which may be used for the benefit of victims; or

(c) Other factors establishing a clear and significant change of circumstances sufficient to justify the reduction of sentence, as provided in the Rules of Procedure and Evidence.

5. If the Court determines in its initial review under paragraph 3 that it is not appropriate to reduce the sentence, it shall thereafter review the question of reduction of sentence at such intervals and applying such criteria as provided for in the Rules of Procedure and Evidence.

Article 111
Escape

If a convicted person escapes from custody and flees the State of enforcement, that State may, after consultation with the Court, request the person's surrender from the State in which the person is located pursuant to existing bilateral or multilateral arrangements, or may request that the Court seek the person's surrender, in accordance with Part 9. It may direct that the person be delivered to the State in which he or she was serving the sentence or to another State designated by the Court.

Part 2. Assembly Of States Parties

Article 112
Assembly of States Parties

1. An Assembly of States Parties to this Statute is hereby established. Each State Party shall have one representative in the Assembly who may be accompanied by alternates and advisers. Other States which have signed this Statute or the Final Act may be observers in the Assembly.

2. The Assembly shall:

(a) Consider and adopt, as appropriate, recommendations of the Preparatory Commission;

(b) Provide management oversight to the Presidency, the Prosecutor and the Registrar regarding the administration of the Court;

(c) Consider the reports and activities of the Bureau established under paragraph 3 and take appropriate action in regard thereto;

(d) Consider and decide the budget for the Court;

(e) Decide whether to alter, in accordance with article 36, the number of judges;

(f) Consider pursuant to article 87, paragraphs 5 and 7, any question relating to non-cooperation;

(g) Perform any other function consistent with this Statute or the Rules of Procedure and Evidence.

3. (a) The Assembly shall have a Bureau consisting of a President, two Vice-Presidents and 18 members elected by the Assembly for three-year terms.

(b) The Bureau shall have a representative character, taking into account, in particular, equitable geographical distribution and the adequate representation of the principal legal systems of the world.

(c) The Bureau shall meet as often as necessary, but at least once a year. It shall assist the Assembly in the discharge of its responsibilities.

4. The Assembly may establish such subsidiary bodies as may be necessary, including an independent oversight mechanism for inspection, evaluation and investigation of the Court, in order to enhance its efficiency and economy.

5. The President of the Court, the Prosecutor and the Registrar or their representatives may participate, as appropriate, in meetings of the Assembly and of the Bureau.

6. The Assembly shall meet at the seat of the Court or at the Headquarters of the United Nations once a year and, when circumstances so require, hold special sessions. Except as otherwise specified in this Statute, special sessions shall be convened by the Bureau on its own initiative or at the request of one third of the States Parties.

7. Each State Party shall have one vote. Every effort shall be made to reach decisions by consensus in the Assembly and in the Bureau. If consensus cannot be reached, except as otherwise provided in the Statute:

(a) Decisions on matters of substance must be approved by a two-thirds majority of those present and voting provided that an absolute majority of States Parties constitutes the quorum for voting;

(b) Decisions on matters of procedure shall be taken by a simple majority of States Parties present and voting.

8. A State Party which is in arrears in the payment of its financial contributions towards the costs of the Court shall have no vote in the Assembly and in the Bureau if the amount of its arrears equals or exceeds the amount of the contributions due from it for the preceding two full years. The Assembly may, nevertheless, permit such a State Party to vote in the Assembly and in the Bureau if it is satisfied that the failure to pay is due to conditions beyond the control of the State Party.

9. The Assembly shall adopt its own rules of procedure.

10. The official and working languages of the Assembly shall be those of the General Assembly of the United Nations.

Part 12. Financing

Article 113
Financial Regulations

Except as otherwise specifically provided, all financial matters related to the Court and the meetings of the Assembly of States Parties, including its Bureau and subsidiary bodies, shall be governed by this Statute and the Financial Regulations and Rules adopted by the Assembly of States Parties.

Article 114
Payment of expenses

Expenses of the Court and the Assembly of States Parties, including its Bureau and subsidiary bodies, shall be paid from the funds of the Court.

Article 115
Funds of the Court and of the Assembly of States Parties

The expenses of the Court and the Assembly of States Parties, including its Bureau and subsidiary bodies, as provided for in the budget decided by the Assembly of States Parties, shall be provided by the following sources:

(a) Assessed contributions made by States Parties;

(b) Funds provided by the United Nations, subject to the approval of the General Assembly, in particular in relation to the expenses incurred due to referrals by the Security Council.

Article 116
Voluntary contributions

Without prejudice to article 115, the Court may receive and utilize, as additional funds, voluntary contributions from Governments, international organizations, individuals, corporations and other entities, in accordance with relevant criteria adopted by the Assembly of States Parties.

Article 117
Assessment of contributions

The contributions of States Parties shall be assessed in accordance with an agreed scale of assessment, based on the scale adopted by the United Nations for its regular budget and adjusted in accordance with the principles on which that scale is based.

Article 118
Annual audit

The records, books and accounts of the Court, including its annual financial statements, shall be audited annually by an independent auditor.

Part 13. Final Clauses

Article 119
Settlement of disputes

1. Any dispute concerning the judicial functions of the Court shall be settled by the decision of the Court.

2. Any other dispute between two or more States Parties relating to the interpretation or application of this Statute which is not settled through negotiations within three months of their commencement shall be referred to the Assembly of States Parties. The Assembly may itself seek to settle the dispute or may make recommendations on further means of settlement of the dispute, including referral to the International Court of Justice in conformity with the Statute of that Court.

Article 120
Reservations

No reservations may be made to this Statute.

Article 121
Amendments

1. After the expiry of seven years from the entry into force of this Statute, any State Party may propose amendments thereto. The text of any proposed amendment shall be submitted to the Secretary-General of the United Nations, who shall promptly circulate it to all States Parties.

2. No sooner than three months from the date of notification, the Assembly of States Parties, at its next meeting, shall, by a majority of those present and voting, decide whether to take up the proposal. The Assembly may deal with the proposal directly or convene a Review Conference if the issue involved so warrants.

3. The adoption of an amendment at a meeting of the Assembly of States Parties or at a Review Conference on which consensus cannot be reached shall require a two-thirds majority of States Parties.

4. Except as provided in paragraph 5, an amendment shall enter into force for all States Parties one year after instruments of ratification or acceptance have been deposited with the Secretary-General of the United Nations by seven-eighths of them.

5. Any amendment to articles 5, 6, 7 and 8 of this Statute shall enter into force for those States Parties which have accepted the amendment one year after the deposit of their instruments of ratification or acceptance. In respect of a State Party which has not accepted the amendment, the Court shall not exercise its jurisdiction regarding a crime covered by the amendment when committed by that State Party's nationals or on its territory.

6. If an amendment has been accepted by seven-eighths of States Parties in accordance with paragraph 4, any State Party which has not accepted the amendment may withdraw from this Statute with immediate effect, notwithstanding article 127, paragraph 1, but subject to article 127, paragraph 2, by giving notice no later than one year after the entry into force of such amendment.

7. The Secretary-General of the United Nations shall circulate to all States Parties any amendment adopted at a meeting of the Assembly of States Parties or at a Review Conference.

Article 122
Amendments to provisions of an institutional nature

1. Amendments to provisions of this Statute which are of an exclusively institutional nature, namely, article 35, article 36, paragraphs 8 and 9, article 37, article 38, article 39, paragraphs 1 (first two sentences), 2 and 4, article 42, paragraphs 4 to 9, article 43, paragraphs 2 and 3, and articles 44, 46, 47 and 49, may be proposed at any time, notwithstanding article 121, paragraph 1, by any State Party. The text of any proposed amendment shall be submitted to the Secretary-General of the United Nations or such other person designated by the Assembly of States Parties who shall promptly circulate it to all States Parties and to others participating in the Assembly.

2. Amendments under this article on which consensus cannot be reached shall be adopted by the Assembly of States Parties or by a Review Conference, by a two-thirds

majority of States Parties. Such amendments shall enter into force for all States Parties six months after their adoption by the Assembly or, as the case may be, by the Conference.

Article 123
Review of the Statute

1. Seven years after the entry into force of this Statute the Secretary-General of the United Nations shall convene a Review Conference to consider any amendments to this Statute. Such review may include, but is not limited to, the list of crimes contained in article 5. The Conference shall be open to those participating in the Assembly of States Parties and on the same conditions.

2. At any time thereafter, at the request of a State Party and for the purposes set out in paragraph 1, the Secretary-General of the United Nations shall, upon approval by a majority of States Parties, convene a Review Conference.

3. The provisions of article 121, paragraphs 3 to 7, shall apply to the adoption and entry into force of any amendment to the Statute considered at a Review Conference.

Article 124
Transitional Provision

Notwithstanding article 12, paragraphs 1 and 2, a State, on becoming a party to this Statute, may declare that, for a period of seven years after the entry into force of this Statute for the State concerned, it does not accept the jurisdiction of the Court with respect to the category of crimes referred to in article 8 when a crime is alleged to have been committed by its nationals or on its territory. A declaration under this article may be withdrawn at any time. The provisions of this article shall be reviewed at the Review Conference convened in accordance with article 123, paragraph 1.

Article 125
Signature, ratification, acceptance, approval or accession

1. This Statute shall be open for signature by all States in Rome, at the headquarters of the Food and Agriculture Organization of the United Nations, on 17 July 1998. Thereafter, it shall remain open for signature in Rome at the Ministry of Foreign Affairs of Italy until 17 October 1998. After that date, the Statute shall remain open for signature in New York, at United Nations Headquarters, until 31 December 2000.

2. This Statute is subject to ratification, acceptance or approval by signatory States. Instruments of ratification, acceptance or approval shall be deposited with the Secretary-General of the United Nations.

3. This Statute shall be open to accession by all States. Instruments of accession shall be deposited with the Secretary-General of the United Nations.

Article 126
Entry into force

1. This Statute shall enter into force on the first day of the month after the 60th day following the date of the deposit of the 60th instrument of ratification, acceptance, approval or accession with the Secretary-General of the United Nations.

2. For each State ratifying, accepting, approving or acceding to this Statute after the deposit of the 60th instrument of ratification, acceptance, approval or accession, the Statute shall enter into force on the first day of the month after the 60th day following the deposit by such State of its instrument of ratification, acceptance, approval or accession.

Article 127
Withdrawal

1. A State Party may, by written notification addressed to the Secretary-General of the United Nations, withdraw from this Statute. The withdrawal shall take effect one year after the date of receipt of the notification, unless the notification specifies a later date.

2. A State shall not be discharged, by reason of its withdrawal, from the obligations arising from this Statute while it was a Party to the Statute, including any financial obligations which may have accrued. Its withdrawal shall not affect any cooperation with the Court in connection with criminal investigations and proceedings in relation to which the withdrawing State had a duty to cooperate and which were commenced prior to the date on which the withdrawal became effective, nor shall it prejudice in any way the continued consideration of any matter which was already under consideration by the Court prior to the date on which the withdrawal became effective.

Article 128
Authentic texts

The original of this Statute, of which the Arabic, Chinese, English, French, Russian and Spanish texts are equally authentic, shall be deposited with the Secretary-General of the United Nations, who shall send certified copies thereof to all States.

IN WITNESS WHEREOF, the undersigned, being duly authorized thereto by their respective Governments, have signed this Statute.

DONE at Rome, this 17th day of July 1998.

About the Author

Professor Tiefenbrun has a J.D. degree from New York University School of Law, a Ph.D in French from Columbia University (summa cum laude), a Master of Science from Wisconsin University, and a Bachelor of Arts from Wisconsin University (Phi Beta Kappa as a junior) where she majored in French, Russian, and Education. Professor Tiefenbrun taught French language and literature for many years in Columbia University and Sarah Lawrence College. She now teaches international law in Thomas Jefferson School of Law where she is the Director of the Center for Global Legal Studies and the former Director of the LL.M. Program. She practiced law and worked on international business transactions at Coudert Brothers for many years. At Thomas Jefferson School of Law, she continues to direct and teach in the study abroad programs in France (which she founded nineteen years ago) and in China (which she founded six years ago). For her efforts at fostering educational and cultural cooperation between France and the United States, she was awarded the French Legion of Honor medal by President Jacques Chirac in 2003. Her special interests are international law, corporate law, securities law, international intellectual property, women and international human rights law, and law and literature. She is the President of the Law and Humanities Institute West Coast Branch. She has written extensively on human trafficking as a form of contemporary slavery. She speaks ten foreign languages including Mandarin Chinese. Among her numerous written works are a book length study of Chinese, Russian and Eastern European joint venture laws and numerous articles on international intellectual property, international law issues, and human trafficking. She has edited three books on law and the arts, war crimes, and legal ethics. Her most recent books are *Decoding International Law: Semiotics and the Humanities* (Oxford Press, 2010) and *Free-Trade Zones in the World and in the United States* (Elgar Press, 2012). To access Professor Tiefenbrun's publications, contact http://ssrn.com/author=113258.

Index